943.6
G95
v.1

DB96
G8
V.1

AUSTRIA

FROM HABSBURG TO HITLER

Volume I

LABOR'S WORKSHOP OF DEMOCRACY

By Charles A. Gulick

With a Foreword by Walther Federn

UNIVERSITY OF CALIFORNIA PRESS

Berkeley and Los Angeles · 1948

UNIVERSITY OF CALIFORNIA PRESS
BERKELEY AND LOS ANGELES
CALIFORNIA

◇

CAMBRIDGE UNIVERSITY PRESS
LONDON, ENGLAND

COPYRIGHT, 1948, BY
THE REGENTS OF THE UNIVERSITY OF CALIFORNIA

PRINTED IN THE UNITED STATES OF AMERICA
BY THE UNIVERSITY OF CALIFORNIA PRESS

To

MY WIFE

Jan 4 9

39603

Foreword

I AM DEEPLY *appreciative of the privilege of writing a foreword to this outstanding book. The more so because in former times I was rather well known in Central Europe as a specialist in politics and economics, but since my arrival in the United States I have rarely had the opportunity of publishing anything over my own signature. I had the pleasure of meeting Professor Charles A. Gulick in Vienna in 1936 and of reading his manuscript chapter by chapter here in the United States. Having lived in Austria during the fateful years covered by this book, I can appreciate the wise judgments and the rare thoroughness displayed in Professor Gulick's work.*

The author first became interested in the Austrian working-class movement during a short stay in Vienna in 1930. Soon after the defeat of that movement in the brief but bloody civil war of 1934 he began to study its origins, growth, and temporary eclipse. For a year, beginning in June, 1936, he was in Austria investigating the movement in its own setting. He spent the subsequent ten years in writing this comprehensive work which he calls Austria from Habsburg to Hitler *because it is a detailed history of the first Austrian republic.*

The early chapters tell of the growth of the working-class movement and the scanty beginnings of social legislation and reforms carried out during the Habsburg rule. Indeed, Professor Gulick finds little to tell about social legislation at that time. In this connection I recall the well-known statement of a Habsburg minister, "The social problem ends at Bodenbach"—an Austrian town on the old German-Austrian border. Under the monarchy the young working-class movement expended most of its energy in attaining the franchise and other civic rights for the masses. The workers' party stood in the forefront of this struggle and in the last two decades of Habsburg rule was able to boast of some success. Labor was almost helpless in striving to obtain better housing in Vienna and in other cities ruled by reactionaries who themselves were backed by landlords. The franchise was a prerequisite to further social achievements.

Succeeding chapters in this book give the story of the republic in astonishing minuteness of detail. The reader is told of the diffi-

culties which the republic encountered in the dismemberment of the centuries-old economic unit of the empire. The pygmy state suffered from a lack of markets and of materials, of fuel and food which the neighbor states that had emerged from the collapse of the empire were unwilling to supply, transferring their age-old hatred of the Habsburgs to the republic. Austria, with a population half starved by the privations of war, had to rebuild her economy from the foundation. The young republic was confronted with increasing unemployment, with crumbling industries, with a huge deficit in the national budget, with inflation of the currency, and with failing banks which formerly had their main assets and business dealings in areas of the empire now separated from Austria. The complete collapse of the Austrian currency was eventually avoided with the help of the League of Nations—help which came four years after the end of the war.

The emphasis in these early chapters is placed on the astounding performances of the workers' party which, from a small minority with limited rights and influence, emerged in February, 1919, with more seats in the Constituent Assembly than any other party. This party dominated the capital city of Vienna and the other industrial centers of the republic.

The party, backed by the trade unions, worked for higher wages, for the eight-hour working day, for social insurance, and for a long overdue school reform which would enable the children of the proletariat to attend high schools and even universities.

The Socialist administration of Vienna fostered health-improvement programs, combated the high infant-mortality rate, and worked to curb tuberculosis. The city built hospitals, maternity homes, kindergartens, day homes for children, public baths, playgrounds, and parks. The party promoted all kinds of sports—swimming, mountain climbing, hiking, and skiing—to acquaint the workers with the beauties which nature had bestowed so prodigally on their homeland. Intellectual and artistic activities were not neglected, for the people were provided with low-priced tickets for theaters, concerts, and museums.

In the forefront of Socialist endeavors to assist the workers was the housing and tenants protection program in cities where the dwellings of the poor classes had always been wretched. Limitations on rents and protection against eviction as temporary measures had been initiated from sheer necessity during the war. The Social Democratic party made them permanent. Conscious that protection alone could not help the masses of its citizens during a period of a scarcity of dwellings when economic misery prevented any private building, the city of Vienna soon set in motion a great building program which, within a few years, provided thousands of homes for the proletariat. These dwellings, available at very moderate rents, were far more hygienic in design and better equipped than anything the Viennese workers had known before. Many of the housing complexes were, in addition, architecturally beautiful.

All these intricate performances were linked together to form a unitary plan conceived and carried out by men of superior capacities and tireless zeal whose first motivation was a true love for the people. These achievements were most outstanding in a city whose finances in the beginning were as moribund as those of the republic. By means of a strong and honest administration and a rigid system of sharply progressive taxes, the financial administrator of Vienna, Hugo Breitner, succeeded in providing huge sums for this work without endangering the financial stability of the city. In contrast to almost all of the cities of Germany which suffered extreme financial difficulties in the crisis, particularly in 1931, the finances of Vienna remained stable until the moment when the reactionary government, after eliminating the parliament on a pretext, deprived the city of a large part of its revenues.

From the beginning, the Social Democratic party had to restrain a small, but, especially during the short period of Bolshevistic rule in Hungary and Bavaria, potentially dangerous Communistic group. It had to struggle too against the ever-growing opposition of the reactionary bourgeois parties, representing the big businessmen, the landowners, the Church, the army, and the Monarchists, who longed for the days when they had been all-powerful under the Habsburgs.

I do not want to say that everything in the party's social, economic, and political programs was good. In some instances they may have gone too far, for example, in overtaxing business then in the midst of its own difficulties. However, in general, the Socialists were moderate in their demands and showed an understanding of the problems which beset business and other fields of endeavor. I share

Professor Gulick's high appraisal of the Socialists' achievements in Austria.

Members of the Social Democratic party certainly merited a better answer from the bourgeoisie than they found in the abusive words bestowed on them—"Welfare inflationists" and "Austro-Marxists"—expressions which depict them as wild radicals lacking any sense of responsibility. In one of his most brilliant chapters Professor Gulick shows that these Austro-Marxists, though clinging to some orthodox Marxist doctrines, grew more Revisionist with their understanding of the needs of certain groups, for example, of the peasantry, and even restrained the expression of their traditional antireligious attitude.

It is true that very early they had formed an armed force, in agreement with the other Austrian parties, for the purpose of defending the country's borders against potentially aggressive neighboring states. The workers' party felt strongly that the Republikanische Schutzbund should never be used for any purpose except the defense of the democratic republic. Its members abjured any revolution by force. Perhaps the party relied too much on its supporters at the polls and expected, possibly too trustingly, to attain a majority of votes. Nevertheless the mere existence of the Schutzbund was used by the reactionary parties as a pretext for expanding their own armed forces. With the spread of Fascism in neighboring states, the reactionaries built up the Heimwehr and other armed groups to the status of private armies designed to destroy not only the hated workers' party and its social reforms but also democracy itself.

The story of the workers' party's achievements and its struggle against the reactionaries, whether in parliament or on the streets, is related by Professor Gulick in great detail. With the facts, he gives us too, by quotations of speeches and writings, by a recital of their deeds, sharply etched portraits of the leading personalities on the stage or in the wings during this, first rather peaceful and later turbulent, period in the history of Austria.

On the "left" are Viktor Adler, Otto Bauer, Karl Renner, Ferdinand Hanusch, Hugo Breitner, Robert Danneberg, Professor Julius Tandler, Otto Glöckel, and many others. On the other side stand Prince Ernst Rüdiger von Starhemberg, Emil Fey, Ernst von Streeruwitz, Johannes Schober, and the more democratic Leopold Kun-

schak. More important than these figures is the shrewd and truly ingenious Monsignor Ignaz Seipel who, precisely because of these characteristics, was the evil genius of the republic. It was Seipel who did more than any other man to bring the Heimwehr to surpassing power. He may have thought he could always control its quarrelsome leaders and perhaps he might have done so, but he officially withdrew and died. His successors, Chancellors Dollfuss and Schuschnigg, became increasingly the prisoners of the Heimwehr leaders.

Professor Gulick's history of the first republic is crammed with facts. Every fact is amply documented. The author's investigation of printed materials—books, documents, periodicals, and newspapers—was supplemented by interviews and conversations with government officials, party leaders, scholars, and plain people of all political orientations. This painstaking comprehensiveness makes special monographs of several of the chapters: those on trade unions, cooperatives, education, welfare work, and finance. The fullness of detail has added value for readers especially interested in social problems. Those chapters of more general interest on the political, social, and economic history of the republic are truly dramatic. The author's thoroughness in the exposition of facts and conflicting arguments, whether economic or political, provides the reader with all the evidence necessary to judge for himself whether the author is correct in his appraisal of the performances of the Socialists and of the aims and practices of their enemies.

The second volume of this study concerns the last fights between the enemies of democracy and the workers' party, the elimination of parliament, the rule by emergency decrees, the replacing of the republican constitution by a Fascist authoritarian one, the canceling of many of the social and educational achievements of the Social Democrats, and finally, Austria's temporary extinction by Hitler's Germany.

As a native-born Austrian, an economist and publisher, a believer in democracy, a politically minded man yet unattached to any political party, I give my thanks to Professor Gulick for his thorough history of the first republic. Only his deep love for Austria and her people could have induced him to give so many years to the research and writing that produced this unique and excellent book.

I, too, love Austria, her countryside, and her artistic and charming people, but I am not unaware of the flaws in the character of her people. As a Jew, compelled to leave my homeland, I have no reason to be predisposed toward Austrians in recent years. I have no desire to condemn or praise a people as distinct from a government, but I do want to understand the motives for their behavior. For that reason I take this opportunity to say a few words on the much discussed position of Austria in relation to Nazism.

There is no doubt that only too many Austrians, I am sure not the majority, went willingly into Hitler's camp. There are several reasons why they did so. It is clear that most of the guilt falls on Chancellors Dollfuss and Schuschnigg, who do not merit the halo bestowed on them in the United States because of their fate at the hands of the Nazis. They were the victims of their own deeds, of their own politics. I do not doubt that Dollfuss and Schuschnigg were sincere in striving to preserve their country from being engulfed in Hitler's plan for world conquest. I can also acknowledge that their position was very difficult, placed as they were in the midst of totalitarian governments and faced with growing adherence to Nazism in Austria herself. But their position need not have been half so hopeless had they not seen their first enemies in the Social Democratic party and had they not done their utmost, unwillingly to be sure, to press great numbers of Austrians into Hitler's ranks. By their own unprovoked bloody fight with the workers, by continued persecution of Socialists, leaders and rank and file, by destroying democracy and introducing a totalitarian constitution—far from the encyclical Quadragesimo Anno *which they contended was their model, instead formed on Mussolini's corporate-estate Fascism—they had alienated almost half of the population of Austria, that half which was precisely the most reliable and the bitterest enemy of Nazism.*

The longer Austrian totalitarianism lasted the more it grew to resemble the German model—though it was never half so brutal. It is an axiom that a doctrine can be combated by imposing a strictly contrary one, but it can never be defeated by emulation, even though it be in milder form. Chancellor Schuschnigg was ignorant of this elementary fact. Even the Jew-baiting in Austria followed the Nazi example. Anti-Semitism was always widespread, particularly among Austrian university youths, lower clergy, and peasantry. The Austro-Fascists, however, were the first to foster anti-Semitism from above.

Of course, those individuals who felt similarly inclined asked themselves, "Since Jew-baiting is all right, why don't I go all the way?" They flew to join the Nazi colors.

Others felt that Austro-Fascism was a failure. It had received no support from the masses, and its leaders, always quarreling among themselves, were united only in destroying democracy and labor. Austro-Fascism had succeeded in having a new constitution drafted, yet it lacked the capacity to put it to work. Up to the final hour the Corporate Estates existed only on paper. Therefore, Fascism's adherents and adversaries alike felt that if totalitarianism had to be, it would be better to choose a working instead of an impotent form.

For these and many other reasons—not the least of which was anschluss with Germany—great sections of the people were prepared to join the Nazis. Anschluss was always favored by a large part, if not most of Austria's population. They should not be blamed for this desire, for Austrians and Germans have the same language, the same culture, and the same centuries-long history as one people. What was wanted was a free union with a free Germany, not submergence under a brutal dictator. But at the decisive hour there was no choice.

The Austro-Fascists had managed so well that there was hardly a chance to fight. There was no help from outside. Mussolini had betrayed Austria. The Western powers too, showed a complacency toward Hitler—as G. E. R. Gedye has clearly demonstrated in his Betrayal in Central Europe. *It is not too much to ask that the Allied victors consider the prewar position of Austria in making their decision whether she should be dealt with as one of Hitler's satellites or as a Nazi conquest. Austria was conquered by Hitler, though had it not been for the disastrous politics of Dollfuss and Schuschnigg, the outcome might not have been such an ignominious surrender as actually took place.*

With the help of the United Nations Austria can rise again, as she did after the First World War. She has shown her capacity to form a modern democracy. If that democracy was destroyed, it was largely because of the influence of Fascist regimes in the neighboring states on which Austria depended. Let us hope that there is no danger of a repetition of Fascism in Central Europe.

Professor Gulick's book will find eager readers in Austria, but principally in the United States where the interest in the social prob-

lems with which it deals grows increasingly keener. Similar social problems, I need mention only tenants protection and housing difficulties, are becoming more acute in the United States. There is much to learn from Professor Gulick's investigations of these problems as they arose and were solved in republican Austria. But, above all, the democratically minded must be interested in the vivid story of the tragic struggle between progressive democrats and reactionary totalitarians in Austria.

WALTHER FEDERN
Founder and Publisher of the Oesterreichische Volkswirt, *1908–1934.*

January, 1947

Preface

FOR CENTURIES *the territory ruled from Vienna has been a stage upon which dramas of international importance have appeared. Among the most fateful of these dramas were those which took place in 1683, when the Turks were repulsed, and in 1914, when the First World War began. After the collapse of the Habsburg empire in 1918 the tiny country that had the name Austria forced upon her by the victorious Allies was pushed from the center of the stage, but during the intervening thirty years she has frequently returned to it, and now, in the spring of 1947, is again in the spotlight. As in 1683, the struggle over Austria is commonly thought of as one between East and West, or between two ways of life.*

In the segment of the history of Austria treated in this study, 1918 to 1938, there was a similar struggle over her, this time between her northern and southern neighbors, Germany and Italy. But the conflict upon which these volumes center was internal. As Mr. Federn notes in his Foreword, I became interested in this conflict in 1930, and after it reached one climax in 1934 I decided to examine it because of my general interest in the rise of international Fascism and because of my special interest in comparative labor history.

Although Mr. Federn kindly praises my documentation, it is necessary to point out that the seizure of Austria by Hitler and the outbreak of the Second World War prevented me from securing certain printed sources that would have been useful and compelled me to piece together other sources. For examples, I was never able to acquire a complete file of the Vienna newspaper, the Reichspost; *and I had to bridge the gap between the holdings of the labor daily, the* Arbeiter Zeitung, *in the Hoover Library at Stanford University and in the University of California Library by securing microfilms from the file in the New York Public Library. The acquisition by the University of California Library of a third Vienna paper, the* Neue Freie Presse, *for the years 1864–1938 partly, though not completely, compensated for the broken file of the* Reichspost.

In the course of almost thirteen years' intensive work on this study I have become indebted for help of various sorts to hundreds of individuals and dozens of organizations and institutions. I am extremely grateful to all of them and particularly regret that a few of the most important individuals can never see this acknowledgment because they died in exile or were murdered in Hitler's concentration camps. A few others must remain anonymous because even after the liberation of Austria it is unwise to name them in connection with the information they provided.

Of all my debts the greatest by far is to Dr. Alexander Gerschenkron, a former colleague in the Department of Economics at the University of California, Berkeley, and now Economist with the Board of Governors of the Federal Reserve System. Dr. Gerschenkron's intimate knowledge of the economic and political problems of the first Austrian republic, his analyses and interpretations of complex relationships, and his fruitful suggestions on innumerable points are integral parts of the book.

To three friends who read critically the entire manuscript I am also greatly indebted. Dr. Bruno Schonfeld, formerly a lawyer in Vienna, was an active participant in some of the most important events narrated and supplied facts and side lights available in no printed source.

Mr. Walther Federn gave me the benefit of his many years as editor of an important Austrian economic and political journal in addition to writing the Foreword.

Professor Ralph H. Lutz of the Department of History of Stanford University made numerous valuable suggestions for improvement of the manuscript, not only on strictly internal Austrian matters but also on international relations affecting Austria.

Of the major working-class leaders Dr. Karl Renner, now president of the second republic of Austria, was able to give me the most time. Dr. Otto Bauer, Dr. Robert Danneberg, Mr. Hugo Breitner, Dr. Max Adler, and his wife Dr. Jenny Adler were also very helpful during my fourteen months in Europe, 1936–1937. Subsequently, many other figures in the labor movement have coöperated by correspondence. Among these I would like to mention particularly Dr. Julius Deutsch and Mr. Heinrich Schneidmadl.

To scores of less prominent leaders and rank-and-file members of the Social Democratic organizations I am most grateful. Included in this group are Mr. Josef Afritsch, Mr. Anton Tesarek, Mr. Oliver Grover, Mr. Wilhelm Svatos, and Captain Rudolf Löw.

But it should be noted that some of the most interesting and enlightening information and comment came to me from streetcar- and railwayworkers, waiters, metalworkers, clerks, and various other representatives of manual and white-collar employees of different political orientations whom it is impossible to list.

Among the opponents of the Social Democratic working-class movement, and more or less enthusiastic supporters of the Dollfuss-Schuschnigg regime, I received the greatest assistance from Dr. Franz Hemala and Dr. Walther Peinsipp. Dr. Hemala was a prominent Catholic party leader and author of a history of trade unions. Dr. Peinsipp was the official in the Heimatdienst, the propaganda office of the Clerical-Fascist regime, to whom the head of that office, Colonel Walter Adam, referred most of my numerous questions.

Although he was able to see me only a few times, Mr. Leopold Kunschak, Catholic political and trade-union leader, gave me some of the most valuable information I secured during my last stay in Vienna. As is true of many other individuals named above, this information supplemented that contained in voluminous writings.

To Dr. Eugen Margarétha of the Austrian Association of Manufacturers I am grateful for giving me certain documents printed in limited quantities and reported as unavailable by Vienna bookdealers.

Dr. Ernst Karl Winter, appointed by Dollfuss as third vice-mayor of Vienna after February, 1934, was also generous with his time and in supplying me with publications otherwise unavailable.

From Professor Johannes Messner of the University of Vienna I received numerous valuable suggestions about the literature of the Catholic social reform and political movements.

Several functionaries of the Fatherland Front were helpful in interviews and in providing me with printed matter. Among them I am most indebted to Dr. Georg Blocher.

Of my colleagues in the University of California I am most grateful to Professors Hans Kelsen, Fletcher H. Swift, Malcolm M. Davisson, John B. Condliffe, Frank L. Kidner, and Carl Landauer. In various ways, and at times under trying circumstances, they gave assistance in the finest spirit of academic coöperation.

Special thanks are due to Dr. Erwin Reisner, my research associate for five years, for his painstaking and conscientious work and his numerous excellent suggestions. His help in the drafting of several chapters was particularly valuable.

Of other helpers I wish particularly to mention Mr. Ernst Winkler, Mr. Gordon Haskell, Mrs. Joan Livingston, Mrs. Rosa Jaeger, and Dr. Helen Rosenberg. On tasks ranging from verifying citations and translations to deciphering and typing untidy manuscript they worked faithfully, and, in emergencies, for unreasonably long hours.

Throughout the years since December of 1934, when intensive work on this book was begun, my chief support and source of encouragement has been my wife. To the collection of bibliography and notes, to the typing of manuscript, to the reading of proofs, to the discussion of numberless questions that came up during the writing, and to the execution of equally numberless tasks that should have fallen to me in a normal "division of labor" in our household she has given literally years. For the vacations and week-end trips she has not had, for the plays she has not seen, and for the symphony concerts she has not heard—all cheerfully sacrificed to further the completion of this work—no expression of appreciation can be adequate.

In the execution of a project of the nature of this one substantial financial assistance was necessary. For such assistance I wish to express most sincere thanks to the Social Science Research Council, to the Carnegie Corporation, and to three organizations of the University of California: the Institute of Social Sciences, the Bureau of Business and Economic Research, and the Committee on Research of the Academic Senate. Each of the five gave me a grant-in-aid on more than one occasion. Without their help I could never have completed the study.

It would likewise have been impossible to carry on my work without the cordial coöperation of the Library of the University of California and numerous members of its staff.

As indicated earlier, the Hoover Library at Stanford University has a unique collection of documents and other material on Austria. This collection and the cheerful and efficient services of the staff were always at my disposal. In particular I wish to voice my appreciation to Miss Nina Almond.

Other libraries in which I had access to excellent material are the New York Public Library and those of the Chamber of Labor in

Vienna and of the Chamber of Commerce in Vienna. The staffs in all of them were also very helpful; especially Dr. Anton Birti of the Chamber of Labor Library.

The same is true of the staff of the Chamber of Labor as a whole, particularly of Dr. Friedrich Kühr and Dr. Benedikt Kautsky.

A portion of my obligations to the University of California Press is obvious to the reader. In addition, I wish to express my warmest thanks to Mr. Samuel Farquhar, its manager, for his sympathetic understanding for and settlement of many problems.

To Miss Lucie E. N. Dobbie, who did the editorial work on both volumes, it is again impossible to express adequately my appreciation. The manuscript was, to say the least, of extraordinary length. Its composition had required more than nine years. Inconsistencies in style and method of citation as well as errors of various sorts remained. In clearing away these and similar difficulties for the reader and for me Miss Dobbie demonstrated skill, ingenuity, and—what was most important at times—remarkable patience.

For reasons explained in Chapter I, these volumes contain hundreds of quotations. Since the overwhelming majority of them are short, it seemed that the courtesy of precise citation was adequate. In other instances, where the quotations were longer or where there were a considerable number from one source, the permission of the publisher has been secured. In particular I wish to express my thanks to:

The Brookings Institution for permission to quote from The Housing Program of the City of Vienna *by C. O. Hardy.*

The editor of the California Law Review *for permission to reprint the greater part of my article, "Administrative and Judicial Processes As Instruments of Clerical Fascism In Austria," from the June, 1944, issue of the* Review.

Harper and Brothers for permission to quote from Between Hitler and Mussolini *by Ernst Rudiger Prince Starhemberg.*

Houghton, Mifflin Company for permission to quote from Plot and Counterplot in Central Europe *by M. W. Fodor.*

Alfred A. Knopf for permission to quote from My Austria *by Kurt Schuschnigg.*

Longmans, Green and Company for permission to quote from Die Wahrheit über Oesterreich *by Guido Zernatto.*

The Macmillan Company for permission to quote from:

Insuring the Essentials *by Barbara Nachtrieb Armstrong;*

American Government and Politics *by Charles A. Beard;*

Cambridge Modern History, *Vol. XI;*

Encyclopaedia of the Social Sciences;

The Government of the United States *by William Bennet Munro;*

A Theory of the Labor Movement *by Selig Perlman;*

Emperor Francis Joseph of Austria *by Joseph Redlich.*

The editor of the Political Science Quarterly *for permission to reproduce extracts from my article "Vienna Taxes since 1918" from the December, 1938, issue of the* Quarterly.

G. P. Putnam's Sons for permission to quote from:

Showdown in Vienna *by Martin Fuchs. This book was first published in France as* Un Pacte avec Hitler (*Paris, Plon* [*1938*]); *and in England as* A Pact with Hitler *(London, Gollancz, 1939).*

Austrian Requiem *by Kurt von Schuschnigg.*

Dr. Ralph Arthur Reynolds for permission to quote from Julius Tandler, a Biography *by the late Alfred Goetzl and Ralph Arthur Reynolds.*

I wish to thank Mr. G. E. R. Gedye for the suggestive value and the use I made of his Fallen Bastions (*London, Gollancz, 1938); and to thank Harper and Brothers who hold the United States copyright for the same book published here as* Betrayal in Central Europe. *My citations, however, are to the English edition.*

My thanks are due also to Mrs. Eugene Lennhoff for permission to quote from The Last Five Hours of Austria *by the late Eugene Lennhoff.*

Finally, I wish to thank Dr. May Hollis Siegl for the liberal use I made of her uncopyrighted thesis, Reform of Elementary Education in Austria.

It is customary in publications of this kind to note that the opinions and conclusions are exclusively those of the author. In this instance it is necessary to emphasize that fact because so many of the individuals who gave me information will dissent vigorously from my conclusions.

CHARLES A. GULICK

March, 1947

Contents

CHAPTER PAGE

I. Introduction 1

PART ONE: FROM AUTOCRACY TO DEMOCRACY

II. Labor under the Habsburgs 15

III. Foundation of the Republic 43

Nationalist Revolutions and the Breakup of the Empire—The Revolution in German-Austria

PART TWO: TOWARD POLITICAL AND ECONOMIC STABILIZATION

IV. Struggle Against Bolshevism 69

V. State Separatism 84

VI. Constitutional Settlement 95

VII. Foreign Policy and Fascist Preludes 112

VIII. Socialization 134

IX. Inflation and Other Economic Problems . . . 144

PART THREE: DEMOCRACY CULMINANT

X. Social and Labor Legislation 175

Social and Labor Legislation under the Habsburgs—Social and Labor Legislation in the Republic—First Period: Emergency Measures—Second Period: Radicalism in Social Legislation—Third Period: Consolidation—Fourth Period: Last Measures and Struggle against Social Burdens

XI. Trade Unions 256

Statistical Survey—Industrial Unionism—The Closed Union Shop—Unions and Party

CHAPTER PAGE

XII. Coöperatives 309

Workers' Coöperatives in the Empire—Workers' Coöperatives in the Republic—Workers' Coöperatives and the Social Democratic Party—Workers' Coöperatives and Trade Unions—The Labor Bank—Workers' Coöperatives and Municipal Activities—Educational and Propaganda Work of Coöperatives

XIII. Tax Reforms in Vienna 354

XIV. Municipal Housing and Tenants Protection . . . 407

Housing Conditions Prior to 1914—War and Housing Problems—Origins of Tenants Protection—Housing Problems in the First Years of the Republic—Consequences of War and Peace—Redistribution of Available Housing Supply—Public Building Activities to 1922—The Reform of 1922—Building Activities of Vienna, 1923–1933—The Problem of Housing Shortage and the Aims of the City Council's Policy—The City Houses—Struggle against Tenants Protection and City Building—First Phase: 1922–1923—Second Phase: Parliamentary Struggles—Pro and Contra of Tenants Protection and City Building—Last Phase: Fascist Pressure and the Reforms of 1929—Conclusion

XV. Welfare Work 505

Care of Children and Youth—Care of Indigent Adults—Care of Sick—Recreational Program—Evaluation of the Welfare Program

XVI. Education for Democracy 544

XVII. Children and Youth in the Labor Movement . 583

Origins in the Working-Class Movement—History and Analysis of Individual Organizations—The Kinderfreunde—The Free School—The Hort and Socialist Education—The Red Falcon Movement—Workers' Youth Organizations—The Association of Socialist Workers' Youth—Students' Youth Organizations—The Association of Socialist Students of Austria

CHAPTER PAGE

XVIII. Workers' Cultural Activities 644

Science for the People—Nonselective Activities—Selective Activities—Other Educational Activities—Art for the People—Sport for the People—For and Against Religion—Other Cultural Organizations

XIX. Struggle for Majority, 1923–1927 683

PART FOUR: THE TURNING POINT?

XX. July 15, 1927 717

The "Breach of Discipline"—The Aftermath

VOLUME II: FASCISM'S SUBVERSION OF DEMOCRACY

Part Five: The Counterrevolution

Part Six: Austro-Marxism

Part Seven: The Clerical-Fascist Police State

Index

ABBREVIATIONS

NOTE.—The titles of many of the serial publications of the government and of the Social Democratic party abbreviated in this list were changed during the course of Austria's history.

AfSS.=*Archiv für Sozialwissenschaft und Sozialpolitik*

BGBl.=*Bundesgesetzblatt für die Republik Oesterreich*

Geldentwertung und Stabilisierung.=*Geldentwertung und Stabilisierung in Ihren Einflüssen auf die soziale Entwicklung in Oesterreich* in *SVfS,* vol. 169 (1925)

Gerwerkschaftsbund, *Jahrbuch.*=*Jahrbuch* [*year*] *des Bundes der Freien Gewerkschaften Oesterreichs*

GöC, *Bericht.*=Grosseinkaufsgesellschaft österreichischer Consumvereine, *Bericht*

Informationsdienst.=*Informationsdienst der Revolutionären Sozialisten*

Jahrbuch.=[Abbreviated in Chapter XVIII only] *Jahrbuch der österreichischen Arbeiterbewegung*

Konstituierende Nationalversammlung, *Protokoll.*=*Stenographisches Protokoll* [*number*]. *Sitzung der Konstituierenden Nationalversammlung der Republik Deutschösterreich*

Konsumvereine, *Jahrbuch.*=Verband deutschösterreichischer Konsumvereine, *Jahrbuch*

LGBl. für Wien.=*Landesgesetzblatt für Wien*

LGuVBl. für Niederösterreich.=*Landesgesetz- und Verordnungsblatt für Niederösterreich*

Mitteilungen.=*Mitteilungen des Auslandsbüros österreichischer Sozialisten*

Nationalrat, *Protokoll.*=*Stenographisches Protokoll* [*number*]. *Sitzung des Nationalrates der Republik Oesterreich*

Parteitag.=*Verhandlungen des Parteitages der Oesterreichischen Sozialdemokratie*

Provisorische Nationalversammlung, *Protokoll.*=*Stenographische Protokolle über die Sitzungen der Provisorischen Nationalversammlung für Deutschösterreich*

RGBl.=*Reichsgesetzblatt für die im Reichsrathe vertretenen Königreiche und Länder*

Schutzbund Decision, 1935.=Landesgericht für Strafsachen Wien II als Schwurgericht, Geschäftszahl 2 Vr. 3553/34

SE.=*Die Sozialistische Erziehung*

SHfRO.=Bundesamt für Statistik, *Statistisches Handbuch für die Republik Oesterreich*

StGBl.=*Staatsgesetzblatt für den Staat Deutschösterreich*

SVfS.=*Schriften des Vereins für Sozialpolitik*

Tätigkeits-Bericht.=*Die Tätigkeit des Sozialdemokratischen Verbandes im Abgeordnetenhause*

Weissbuch.=*Ausschreitungen in Wien am 15. und 16. Juli 1927: Weissbuch* herausgegeben von der Polizeidirektion in Wien

CHAPTER I

Introduction

TO A DEGREE unique in the history of nations the story of Austria between the world wars, particularly between 1918 and 1934, was that of the fight for and against the aspirations and achievements of the working-class movement. Otherwise stated, this struggle was that between democracy on the one side and reaction and Fascism on the other in political, economic, and social fields. The decisive majority of the democratic element was composed of workers. As long as it was possible they and some middle-class and peasant allies fought by democratic means—on the floors of city councils, state diets, and parliament, in countless meetings, through the printed page, and over the radio—but when Chancellor Dollfuss succumbed to the temptations of authoritarian ideology and began the installation of a native form of Clerical Fascism, they continued the battle in the streets, in the courtyards, and on the staircases of the municipal apartments of Vienna, as well as in other localities, by means of machine guns, rifles, and kitchen knives against more machine guns and rifles supported by tanks and field artillery. The Austrian workers, leaders and rank and file, recognized the dangers of the international Fascist counterrevolution at least fifteen years before the statesmen of the Western democracies gave any tangible proof that they had. More than four years before Czechoslovakia was betrayed at Munich these Austrian workers had taken up arms in a vain endeavor to stop their own home-grown variety of authoritarianism. William Shirer was correct when he said that the first shots in the war against Fascism in Europe were fired in Austria on February 12, 1934.

Not the least important reason why the workers were willing to fight to try to save the democratic republic of Austria was that it was in large measure their creation. Traditionally, working-class movements have been described as composed of three elements: trade unions, political parties, and coöperatives. The political group was always predominant in Austria. Its untiring efforts finally helped to force the reluctant Franz Joseph to grant universal manhood suffrage. With the collapse of the Habsburg empire one of its leaders, Karl Renner, became the chancellor of the new state of German-Austria and retained that place in a cabinet dominated by the workers' or Social Democratic party for a little less than two years. In 1945 he resumed that position in the first government formed after his country had been liberated from the Nazis and subsequently was elected president. The party held around 40 per cent of the seats in the republican parliament and around 64 per cent of those in the city council of Vienna as long as those were democratic bodies. Keeping in mind the fact that the capital city included between 28 and 30 per cent of the population of the nation, it becomes even clearer that the strength of the workers' party there and in parliament gave it an important voice in political questions. And it was the current observation in republican Austria that all questions became political questions.

As in all countries, however, the working-class movement in the little Danubian republic fell short of attaining complete unity. As indicated, the great majority of the workers belonged to the Social Democrats, the dominant group in Central Europe. The unions associated with the political group of that name were designated as "free" unions.[1] The chief dissenters, who never attained 15 per cent of the total union membership, had split off on a religious basis. The party which called itself "Christian" never attracted more than a small percentage of the workers despite the fact that the overwhelming majority of the population was at least formally Roman Catholic. The Nationalist, Heimwehr, and Communist unions were

[1] The origin of the term "free" as applied only to Socialist unions is not completely clear in the literature or in the minds of many Germans and Austrians questioned on the point. There is some connection with the "freedom of association" granted by the industrial code of the North German Confederation in 1869 and by the associations act of Austria in 1867. There are also indications in the writings both of German and of Austrian labor historians that the word was used to distinguish the bodies formed under the legislation just mentioned from the earlier compulsory associations, particularly the industrial guilds set up by the Austrian industrial code of 1859. In these guilds the employers were members (*Mitglieder*) and the workers associates (*Angehörige*). The whole arrangement, and especially the distinction between bosses and men, was the object of bitter protest among the Austrian workers. Generally speaking, the purpose behind the use of the word in both countries seems to have been to emphasize the idea that the unions were "free" from employer domination. Cf. International Labor Office, *Freedom of Association* [Studies and Reports, Series A, No. 30] (Geneva, 1928), Vol. III, 7, 108, 114–116; Wilhelm Kulemann, *Die Berufsvereine* (Jena, 1908), Vol. I, 1; Julius Deutsch, *Geschichte der österreichischen Gewerkschaftsbewegung*, Vol. I (Wien, 1929), pp. 75, 78, 81, 82, 117; Richard Wagner, *Geschichte der Kleiderarbeiter in Oesterreich* (Wien, 1930), pp. 98, 99, 104, 116, 117, 120, 121, 125.

always insignificant numerically. Consequently, for most purposes, except disruptive ones, it is correct to consider the Social Democratic movement as *the* working-class movement of Austria.

To the three traditional components of a workers' movement the Austrians added a fourth that in the degree of its development put it in the first rank if not in a unique position. For want of a better term this element may be called "cultural activities." The variety and extent of these activities provide an interesting contrast to the narrow economism into which Samuel Gompers led the American movement and in which the greater part of it has remained.

In order to develop the ramifications of the fourfold character of the Austrian movement a large section of the study, especially Part Three, is a description and analysis of what it extended or created in the fields of political, economic, and social democracy. As the reader knows, the movement was not able to form a Socialist island in the heart of capitalist Europe; in fact, most persons competent to make distinctions would hold that very little of what it did was in any accurate sense Socialistic. Because of the legends, misrepresentations, and deliberate lies which its opponents have circulated so widely, and because of the common idea that a group that commits itself to a Socialist philosophy thereby limits itself to "destructive" criticism—more bluntly put, to "hell-raising" in general—it is important to record in some detail what this group accomplished. Not the least valuable aspect of such a record is its revelation of precisely what Dollfuss, Schuschnigg, and their associates prostituted, mutilated, or destroyed in the name of creating a "Christian" state. In the spring of 1944, as earlier, there was considerable agitation in England and the United States to secure the recognition of the remnants of Schuschnigg's last cabinet as a government-in-exile. The occupation of Vienna by the Russians was considered by many to have placed the tombstone over that plan. Events have proved them correct, but the idea behind the plan, that is, to restore to power the groups who ruled Austria from 1934 to 1938, is by no means dead. Moreover, the elections of November 25, 1945, gave a majority of the seats in parliament, though not of the popular vote, to the People's party—the renamed party of Seipel, Dollfuss, and Schuschnigg. After 1927 this political organization had continually demonstrated that its allegiance to democracy could not be relied upon.

For weeks prior to the elections of 1945 the People's party fought to secure voting rights for the so-called paper-Nazis. Its branch in Salzburg protested against the action of American occupation authorities classifying the former active members of Austrian Fascist armed formations along with the Nazis as "unfit for public office," and threatened to boycott the elections. Just two weeks before the polling took place Baron Raoul Bumballa resigned his position as vice-president of the renamed party. His stated reasons were that it was too much under clerical influence and that it had offered as candidates too many reactionary politicians from former times. Subsequently, various leaders of the party indicated their sympathy for the political line of Dollfuss and Schuschnigg. Chancellor Figl, its chief leader, openly declared himself to be Schuschnigg's successor.

As has been indicated above, Hitler did not bring Fascism to Austria. That fact must be underscored because of the tendency to forget it and because of the strenuous efforts made by many who know better to see to it that it is forgotten or obscured. The job preceding Hitler was done by a combination of indigenous Fascists with Roman Catholic political leaders who either betrayed their one-time democratic principles, or who never had any to betray. But before suggesting the nature of the evidence supporting the foregoing conclusions, developed at length in later chapters, it is in order to record certain generalizations concerning Fascism with the hope that they will clarify the criteria used in evaluating the Austrian variety.

At a time more than twenty years after Mussolini's miscalled "March on Rome" it is scarcely necessary to emphasize that there is no generally recognized definition of Fascism and that there is little probability that one will ever be formulated. To those trained in the democratic tradition the most outstanding characteristic of Fascism is its negativeness. It is a negation of liberalism, of parliamentarism, and of political, social, and economic democracy. It has a particular contempt for the democratic principle that leaders should be elected. It denies the right of existence to any political organization except that created by the Fascists themselves. It denies really significant autonomy to province and community by centralization of administration. In legislative matters it operates through arbitrary decree or a rubber-stamp body which it is insulting to designate as a parliament. It enforces its laws by means of a secret police and a more or less lickspittle judiciary. It denies the importance of the individual, except, in practice, for the elite. As has been well said, it takes the sovereignty of the state to a point where it is the duty of the individual "to elevate himself to the heights of the national consciousness and to lose completely his own identity in it." It denies to working people the right to organize freely in unions of their own choosing and substitutes for such bodies a "labor front" or a "unified trade union" which it dominates. With reference to the fields of industry, business, and commerce there is, in most of the original blueprints at least, less of a denial of the merits and advantages of individual initiative. The "corporations" or "occupational estates" are supposed to have a considerable degree of autonomy and self-administration. But the business leaders who subsidized Fascism in Europe were in some respects remarkably similar to a number of their American cousins who give such eloquent lip service to "rugged individualism" and "free enterprise" and prove by their predilection for gentlemen's agreements, trusts, and monopolistic trade associations that they believe in competition almost exclusively "for the other fellow." Perhaps it goes too far to generalize that "Fascism has come to be synonymous with Monopoly Capitalism," or that it is properly defined as "monopoly capitalism become conscious of its powers, the conditions of its survival, and mobilized to crush all opposition"; nevertheless, the facts to be presented will show that in Austria for years big business and big finance provided the main drive behind the Fascist forces. They will also show that the Austrian system did not include a pure example of the "total principle"; that is, an attempt "to control completely all activities and all thoughts, ideas, and values of the entire nation." The totalitarianism that existed was shared, by constitutional stipulation, with the Roman Catholic Church. On the other hand, the Austrians did emphasize the "leader principle" and the "authority principle." And, as has been pointed out so often with reference to all brands of Fascism, authority was from the top down, responsibility from the bottom up—a complete reversal of democracy in form and spirit.[2]

[2] Cf. E. von Beckerath's article on "Fascism," *The Encyclopaedia of the Social Sciences*, vol. 6, 133–138; L. T. Morgan, *Fascism* (Toronto, n.d.), esp. pp. 1, 10; R. A. Brady, *The Spirit and Structure of German Fascism* (New York, 1937).

The fight against the Nazis by the last two chancellors of Austria before Hitler was a strange mixture of a sham battle and a desperate struggle for survival. It was a sham battle because to be meaningful the fight against Fascism has to be against its ideology and spirit. But both Dollfuss and Schuschnigg adopted that ideology and spirit. It was a desperate struggle for survival because they wanted to preserve their own brand of authoritarianism. The claim that they fought also to preserve Austrian independence is a hollow one, for Dollfuss pawned his country to Mussolini and Schuschnigg left it with him until the development of the relations between the Duce and the Führer forced the disastrous Austro-German "agreement" of July 11, 1936. Thereafter, given the attitude of the Western democracies, it was only a question of the date on which Hitler would assert his mastery in the pawnshop and seize whatever he wanted. Because Dollfuss was murdered and Schuschnigg brutally mistreated by the Nazis they have become the beneficiaries of a series of legends which will be shown to have practically no relation to the facts. And this is true after all allowances are made for the undeniably difficult position in which they were placed. As just suggested, Austria was betrayed by the Western democracies as surely as was Czechoslovakia, but this does not excuse Dollfuss and Schuschnigg. After some wavering by the former they not only refused the help of the one solidly reliable democratic force of any real importance in Austria—the workers' movement—but smashed it, and kept the remnants under a vicious system of police terror and concentration camps until almost the day Hitler sent his troops across the border.

The Austrian brand of Fascism never acquired the character of a mass movement as did its counterparts in Italy and Germany. For this there were a number of reasons. The old German Nationalist group, precisely because it was that, was more attracted by Hitler's brand. Moreover, since this group was to a considerable degree Protestant, it was repelled in general by the clericalism that permeated the appeals of Dollfuss and Schuschnigg and in particular by the claim that they were basing their "New Order" on the papal encyclical, *Quadragesimo Anno,* of 1931.

Partly as a result of the tragic events of July 15, 1927, which cost the lives of almost one hundred persons, and partly because of the influence of Dollfuss, large numbers of peasants associated themselves with Fascist ideas and gave the Austrian movement its numerically strongest support. But a substantial number of them, avowedly staunch Roman Catholics, who might have been expected to follow wherever Dollfuss led, preferred the Nazis. The explanation for this development is, of course, a matter of dispute—as is so much in the history of Fascism. At least in Tirol and Salzburg, however, the motive seems to have been primarily economic, especially after Hitler throttled their tourist trade by requiring a 1,000-mark visa fee from noncommercial travelers in 1933. The most substantial peasantry in the country, that of Lower Austria, is generally and deservedly given credit for being basically democratic; nevertheless, its chief organization—the Peasants' Federation—lined up its 100,000 members with the Heimwehr in the late summer of 1929, only to withdraw them in June of the next year, and then to help Dollfuss smash the workers in 1934. As is generally known, the Heimwehr, Heimatschutz, Frontkämpfer, Sturmscharen, and so on were Fascist formations, Austrian counterparts of Hitler's S. A. With the urban middle class this movement for a long time had much less success than its Italian and German equivalents. For this the housing and tenants protection program of the workers' party was in great degree responsible. Some of the industrial workers were forced into fake Heimwehr trade unions, particularly by the big *Alpine* iron and steel company, but the overwhelming majority of them remained faithful to the traditions of the independent labor movement. Even the workers in the Roman Catholic trade unions, ostensibly loyal to Dollfuss and Schuschnigg, were more than a little unhappy over the developments after February, 1934.

The real impetus and support within Austria for Heimwehr-Clerical Fascism came primarily from the following groups: 1. Big business. 2. Big finance. 3. A few relatively big landowners such as Prince Starhemberg. 4. Many Roman Catholic political leaders of whom the most important were the priest, Ignaz Seipel (who was chancellor in several cabinets), Steidle, Dollfuss, and Schuschnigg. 5. Many Roman Catholic priests who, without identifying their Church with the movement, gave it substantial and important support. 6. Disgruntled army officers and aristocrats who had been declassed by the disintegration of the empire. 7. Political adventurers, not to say "thugs," of the type who flocked into Hitler's S. A. and S. S. formations. 8. Large groups of peasants. 9. Middle-class and "new" middle-class groups; that is, professional and small businessmen and the white-collar proletariat.

At first glance this list may seem rather formidable; in fact, to run counter to the statement that Fascism in Austria was not a mass movement. A second look will reveal that only the last two groups could have been numerically strong. As already mentioned, the peasants did join the Heimwehr in large numbers. Among the most important reasons for their action was the influence of their Roman Catholic political and spiritual leaders; in other words, groups 4 and 5. Group 9, composed of the middle classes, is that which many students consider the most important in the Fascist movements of Austria's northern and southern neighbors; in fact, they characterize Fascism in general as an international movement primarily of the middle classes. That appreciable numbers of these groups finally supported either the Nazi or the clerical brand of Fascism in Austria is true, but, as has also been brought out, they came in relatively late and were not so important in the clerical variety as they were generally in other countries.

With reference to "big business" and "big finance" it is essential to observe that their most important representative, the previously mentioned *Alpine* iron and steel concern, shifted into the Nazi camp in the early 'thirties and became a source of great trouble to the Schuschnigg regime. Its example was followed by a considerable number of other business leaders. But in the earlier years the major industrialists and bankers were putting their money on the Heimwehr horse. As will be documented hereafter from the published writings of one of the most prominent industrialists in Austria and from other sources, they were convinced that they could not secure for themselves "appropriate" representation and influence in parliament "under the existing electoral conditions," and so they organized and furthered "with the greatest vigor" and with "substantial sums of money" those "instruments of force" (i.e., the Fascist formations) which destroyed the independent labor movement and parliamentary democracy in Austria. Stated otherwise, the frequent criticism that an explanation of the rise of Fascism in terms of the determination of big business and big finance to crush labor and democracy is too facile, a piece of leftist propaganda to be dismissed out of hand, is invalid for Austria. Indeed, the stock exchange sheet of Vienna, the *Neue Freie Presse,* editorially chided the workers' daily of that city for trying to make a sensation of the contributions of business to the Heimwehr. As it pointed out, the annual reports of the Manufacturers' Association of Styria showed that industry was not even attempting to make a secret of such contributions. On the other hand, the foregoing list should make it clear that it is not claimed that the determination of business to crush labor and democracy was the only factor. The facts recorded in subsequent chapters will show, nevertheless, that this firm resolution and the willingness to put hard cash behind it were for years the mainspring of the Austrian Fascist groups. The resolution and the cash kept those groups alive in difficult years and pumped fresh blood into them after July 15, 1927, when the priest-chancellor Seipel decided to use them for his antilabor and antidemocratic purposes. Thus industry, finance, and Catholic politicians and priests planted and cultivated what Streeruwitz called the second root of the Heimwehr movement. The first root is indicated by the name; that is, Home Defense Corps, originally organized to repel the aggressions of the Yugoslavs and other neighbors. The second was an "instrument of force" against labor and democracy. If, as one friendly critic has suggested, the foregoing analysis indicates that Austrian industrialists and bankers were "particularly stupid," it may be said, first, that the evidence completely supports such a conclusion, and, second, that this was not the first instance in which an economic group acted contrary to its own best interests. As a matter of fact parts of this group became alarmed over some Heimwehr methods in the fall of 1928 and even more so a year later when the Fascists were bent on amending the federal constitution by unconstitutional means. Because the last stages of this conflict coincided with the beginnings of the world-wide economic disturbances that led into the Great Depression, some business interests had no more funds with which to subsidize the Heimwehr. Others, as said before, transferred their support to the Nazis. Thereupon one Heimwehr leader after another repaired to Italy to seek advice—and cash—from Mussolini. Their success is recorded in detail in numerous sources, for example, in Prince Starhemberg's memoirs.

And this brings me to the impetus toward and support for Austrian Fascism from without, a story that will fill many pages in the latter parts of this study. As is generally known, there was for years a battle between Mussolini and Hitler over Austria. The Duce supported the Heimwehr and Dollfuss in every way; the Führer backed the Austrian Nazis. Many competent observers believe that without Italian help the indigenous Fascists of Austria would never have defeated the democratic forces. Although there is always an element of speculation in such judgments, the evidence to be presented supports this one.

In presenting this and other evidence liberal use has been made of summaries and direct quotations from documents and contemporary accounts. They have added greatly to the length of the book. The quotations seemed particularly indispensable if at least two purposes were to be achieved. Dollfuss and Schuschnigg have been the beneficiaries of legends. Their conflicts with the Nazis have left the impression with all too many people that they were anti-Fascist. There is no better proof of the falsity of this impression than a precise translation of their public statements during the decisive years of the counterrevolution. A second purpose was to preserve as completely as possible the feel, the color, the emotion—at times it is scarcely too much to say the smell—of the numberless controversies that raged around the workers' movement and its struggle for democracy. For Americans, living in a country where the Socialist party has never amounted to anything and where there has never been a Roman Catholic party, it is naturally a bit difficult to visualize a situation in which these two were the main parties and in which, consequently, political issues were closely related to religious teachings. And it seems extraordinarily difficult for most Americans, in the light of what they have learned about Fascism in the past twenty-five years, to understand how Catholic political leaders, including a brilliant member of the clergy, could have fostered a "hard-boiled" Fascism that was little better, in its hypocrisy worse, than the varieties that ruled Austria's neighbors to the north and to the south. But the truth is that no substantial opposition of a steadfast character developed against the indigenous Fascist tendencies among the political representatives of Catholicism in Austria. The situation was very different from that in Italy where Don

Sturzo and his friends were found among the staunchest fighters against Mussolini, and perhaps still more different from that in the German republic before Hitler came to power. Although even in the Reich some prominent Catholic politicians turned against democracy, the overwhelming majority of both the leaders and the rank and file of the Catholic Center party helped the German Social Democrats to defend the free institutions of the republic and to promote social legislation. The attitude which German Centrists such as Matthias Erzberger, Joseph Wirth, and even the Monarchist Heinrich Brüning took toward the Socialist workers' movement was diametrically opposed to that of Seipel, Dollfuss, and Schuschnigg.

After what has preceded it is almost needless to add that I hold that whenever possible the social scientist has not only the right but the duty to draw conclusions from, and express value judgments on, the factual evidence available. In other words, I have no patience with the intellectual contortionist who apparently thinks he is "unscientific" unless he tries to get a part of each foot on each side of every question that is faintly controversial. Almost without exception the topics presented in the following pages have been the centers of bitter controversies; many still are; some will remain so as long as students are interested in the history of Austria.

To some readers the conclusions and judgments may, at times, seem to read more like a bill of indictment. As a matter of fact, they sum up to a bill of indictment. Moreover, no apology is required or offered for indicting Fascists, especially not for indicting those who, in paraphrase of the encyclical they claimed to be following, "even abuse religion itself, cloaking their own unjust impositions under its name, that they may protect themselves against the clearly just demands of their" fellow citizens for liberty and equality. On the other hand, nothing that has been or will be said is intended as a criticism of the honest and sincere Austrian Roman Catholics who believed implicitly that the principles of that encyclical could be translated into practical social action without the inclusion of Fascist political elements.

Although the nature of Austrian Social Democracy has been indicated, it may be helpful to summarize its outstanding aspects. Austrian Social Democratic *theory* embodied a political, economic, and social philosophy well to the left of that preferred, in spite of the British elections of 1945, by most Anglo-Saxons. The Social Democratic leaders used violent language all too frequently. Their purpose was to prevent the rise of a strong Communist group, as happened in Germany with disastrous results, and they were successful. The *practice* of the workers' movement was "revisionist" and social reformist. Its accomplishments in school reform, social welfare, and housing were recognized and acclaimed throughout the world. But the most important consideration, which should be kept in mind at all times, is the fact that particularly in the last years of the republic there were only two practical choices for the Austrian who took his citizenship seriously: some form of Fascism or this leftist type of democracy. However much of it may have deviated from our ideals, it was much nearer them than the system that boasted of destroying it.

PART ONE: FROM AUTOCRACY TO DEMOCRACY

CHAPTER II

Labor under the Habsburgs

CONTRARY TO the idea generally accepted among Anglo-Saxon students of labor that there is no connection between medieval guilds and modern trade unions, the chief historian of the Austrian unions, Julius Deutsch, contends that in his country and in Germany such a connection in certain trades can be clearly established. He does not claim that Sidney and Beatrice Webb, the most noted proponents of the usual view, are incorrect for England—only that the facts were different in the Habsburg and Hohenzollern empires. Among the examples he offers the most convincing is that of the tanners and leather workers. Indeed, the evidence indicates that the Vienna organization of these laborers did not shift from a guild to a trade-union form until about 1870, reverted to a guild in the middle of the 'eighties, and did not finally become a union until 1896. In 1899 a Marburg guild that had existed since the sixteenth century transformed itself into a "Christian" trade union.[1]

Although it is clear from the preceding chapter that the emphasis of this study is upon the period 1918–1938, it goes without saying that the events of those twenty years can be understood only in the light of previous happenings. Such earlier developments are particularly important for most of the economic, social, and cultural changes discussed in Part Three; consequently, the material in this chapter is intended to provide only an over-all view of a part of the background.

For over six hundred years the major conflicts of manual workers in what came to be called Austria were with the authorities—civil, military, and ecclesiastical. It is not without significance for later events that in 1278 the first Habsburg emperor dissolved all the existing artisans' guilds of Vienna. Despite this, and similar tactics by Rudolf's successors, guilds were well established in the cities by the fifteenth century. Among the workers in the coal and iron mines of Tirol, Salzburg, Carinthia, and Styria there developed

---

[1] Julius Deutsch, "Zunft und Gewerkschaft," *Der Kampf*, vol. 1 (Jan., 1908), 172–177. See also his *Geschichte der österreichischen Gewerkschaftsbewegung*, Vol. I (Wien, 1929), pp. 84 ff.

organizations similar to guilds which were also armed formations. As early as 1477 the archbishop of Salzburg attempted to put an end to these groups, but again with only temporary success. During the Peasants' War of 1525 the miners fought shoulder to shoulder with the farmers against the princes and the landed aristocracy. A hundred years later their fellows in Carinthia rose in armed rebellion at Hüttenberg, the first of a series of conflicts which lasted until 1755 when the miners were decisively defeated and the attempts to deprive them of the right to bear arms finally carried through.

Meanwhile the government had introduced in 1712 a "workslip" for apprentice shoemakers. This predecessor of the workbook was vigorously opposed by the artisans in a succession of strikes that were terminated only by the introduction of military law in Vienna, and the execution of two of the leaders in 1722. The other major controversy in the eighteenth century worth noting here was likewise precipitated by administrative action. For years the workers in the cloth industry had watched with apprehension the introduction by their employers of more and more female and child labor and the accompanying depression in wages, so that when Maria Theresia by decree of 1770 opened to women "certain unimportant sorts of silk cloth making which were not able to carry the burden of journeymen's wages," these journeymen determined to resist. Their effort was promptly squelched by imprisoning 146 workers on limited rations of bread and water.

In the foregoing paragraphs it has not been intended to leave the impression that workers' protests were directed exclusively against governmental or other authorities—conflicts with employers were not uncommon—but it remains true that the most outstanding ones were those in which the government, the Church, or both were involved.

The beginnings of the modern working-class movement in Austria are to be found in the "factory funds" established about 1800 in the textile and porcelain concerns of Bohemia. Although their original purposes were the provision of sickness and travel benefits, many soon added the support of unemployed members so that they assumed more of the characteristics of a trade union. Typographical workers in Linz, Innsbruck, and Vienna organized similar funds that were more or less successful in 1824, 1826, and 1842. By March

12, 1845, the date of the first official report[2] on such funds which I have found, the scope of activities in Bohemia had been still further broadened to include burial benefits and support for members no longer capable of working.

From this same report it is learned that the funds of the calico printers honored memberships established in other localities. Contrariwise, some of the funds refused admittance to workers coming from another locality and thus prevented them from securing jobs. Partly on the basis of this "misuse" of strength, the Bohemian authorities prohibited on the third day after the issuance of the report any further collection of money among factory employees unless it had previously been officially approved. Moreover, no new factory funds would be sanctioned. From other evidence it is clear that these organizations were looked upon as centers of "Socialist agitation," and it is probable that there was some connection between this decree and the machine-smashing in textile mills which had reached a high point only the year before. In the following year, 1846, there were even more serious disturbances in Prague, Pilsen, Komotau, and Eger and, a little later, in the outlying districts of Vienna. Increasing unemployment and need vented themselves not only in attacks on factories, but also in the plundering of bakeries and meat shops. Police and troops were called in; the stage was being set for the revolutionary days of 1848.

That Austrian workers would participate in the democratic uprisings of the late 'forties was inevitable. They believed that they, not the nobility and the landlords, had freed their country from the French armies. They knew that the promises made to them during the Napoleonic Wars had not been kept; they knew that Austria under Metternich was one of the most reactionary of all reactionary lands. Many of them traveled as journeymen to Germany and to Switzerland where they made contacts with such organizations as the League of the Outlawed and the League of the Just. Notwithstanding the best efforts of the police the radical and democratic propaganda of these and other groups was well distributed among Austrian intellectuals and to a considerable degree among workers. Students, particularly from the faculty of medicine, played the lead-

[2] The text of this document is reprinted in part in Deutsch, *Geschichte der österreichischen Gewerkschaftsbewegung,* Vol I, 19–22.

ing role in the dramatic events of March, 1848, but they received substantial assistance from proletarian groups that had greatly increased in number in the preceding decade. In addition the peasants supported the revolution at first in order to secure the abolition of feudal services.

On March 13 the first street fighting took place in Vienna. That evening Metternich fled to England. On the next day the censorship was abolished and an assembly of representatives from all provinces except Hungary and Venetia promised. Twenty-four hours later a constitution was also promised. To most of the citizens and students and many of the workers the fulfillment of these pledges would have been adequate; they were not attempting to establish a republic; a constitutional monarchy would have been sufficient. But the constitution promulgated on April 25 and the provisional election law of May 11 were by no means satisfactory. The students had already protested on May 5 against the upper chamber of the parliament as representative of the "most dangerous of all aristocracies the moneyed aristocracy,"[3] and the workers were furious because they were excluded from voting for members of the lower house. Together with the national guard and armed citizens they stormed into the Inner City and forced the ministry to accept their demands for a single chamber elected by universal suffrage. In addition the government approved the organization of a Committee of Safety composed of citizens, national guards, and students to which was entrusted entire responsibility for public order and peace as well as preservation of person and property.

Meanwhile the working class was raising economic and social demands. These took the traditional forms—increases in wages, decreases in hours, and better working conditions—but the equalitarian spirit of the times is reflected in the frequency with which the employees demanded that they be addressed by the formal *Sie* rather than the familiar *Du*. At the outset the requests were rather generally granted. The first formal collective agreement in Austrian history is reported as signed in April, 1848, by the printers and their employers. Unemployment, however, remained severe. The government set up public works projects and attempted to stimulate private employment through remission of taxes and other measures. In

[3] J. Goldmark, *Pilgrims of '48* (New Haven, 1930), pp. 53–54.

August the minister of labor reduced the wages of women and children in public employment. Rioting followed in which 22 persons were killed and about 350 wounded. Deplorable as this was, it had the perhaps more unfortunate effect of splitting the forces which had heretofore fought the Habsburg reaction, for the student and other liberal leaders strongly disapproved of the workers' moves. Only six days later, August 31, the Reichstag passed a bill freeing the peasants from forced labor on the lords' estates and from feudal dues in money and kind. From this time on the farmers were no longer interested in the revolution; they had received all they wanted.

To the further details there is no need for giving much space here. The opponents of democratic reforms were winning all along the line and the high hopes of March were actually destroyed when Windischgrätz captured Vienna on the last day of October. Only in passing it should be noted that the Kremsier Constitution, completed in the spring of 1849, might have prevented many of the misfortunes which were to overtake Austria. There is the word of one of her most illustrious historians that this constitution's "abundance of political ideas and its intellectual height were never afterward reached, not to speak of being exceeded, by any legislative achievement of the great national middle-class parties of Austria in her later constitutional period."[4] But ". . . the Schwarzenberg Government on March 4 perpetrated its *coup d'état*. On that day it published by imperial authority a Constitution of the one and indivisible Austrian Monarchy; the occupation of the Kremsier Diet, after its many months of labour, was gone, and on March 7 it was dissolved." Within a short space of time this imposed constitution "appeared to those who controlled the destinies of the State a piece of obsolete machinery"; Schwarzenberg openly called it "abortive."[5] For more than a decade the empire was plunged into one of the blackest reactions that has ever disgraced a self-styled Christian and civilized country.

Military defeat in 1859 brought some glimmerings of real constitutional concessions. In the light of current efforts to invest the Habsburgs with virtues they never possessed it is worth recalling that on June 29, 1860, Franz Josef expressed his firm determination

[4] Josef Redlich, *Das österreichische Staats- und Reichsproblem* (Leipzig, 1920), Vol. I, 322.

[5] *Cambridge Modern History* (New York, 1909), Vol. XI, 191, 216.

to permit "no limitation of the power of the monarchy by a constitution" and to combat all such efforts.[6] Despite this stiff-necked attitude the concessions mentioned were expanded in the *Oktober Diplom* of 1860 and the *Februar Patent* of 1861. Members of the working class, however, remained political serfs. Attempts to organize workingmen's associations were brusquely rejected in 1862, since the government held that their proponents were concealing "Socialist tendencies." Only the collapse of their armies at Königgrätz (1866) forced from the emperor, the feudal nobility, and the higher bureaucracy a constitution that more than halfway deserved the name. Under it and the legislation of 1867 and 1870 workers were at last able to form associations, but provincial authorities were given the power to prohibit organizations which were "dangerous to the state" with all the possibilities of arbitrary construction which that undefined and elastic phrase contains. No political rights were granted.

Now that associations were legally tolerated the already existing differences of opinion among working people about the most desirable form assumed real significance. Generally speaking the issue was "state-help" *versus* "self-help," or the ideas of Ferdinand Lassalle *versus* those of Hermann Schulze-Delitzsch. The former put the emphasis on a struggle for political power—universal suffrage once achieved, the resulting control of the state would be used to subsidize workers' producers' coöperatives by state credit and taxation. The latter opposed political activity by laborers, believing that voluntary savings associations and producers' and consumers' coöperatives without government assistance provided the road to salvation. Though the issue of political activity was won by the Lassallean group there was also a prompt development of craft unions which strict Lassallean principles would have rejected.

The first organization approved under the new legislation was the Workers' Educational Association of Vienna, November 23, 1867, but by the end of 1868 there were about a dozen full-fledged trade unions. The most advanced of these was the printers. Their convention of August, 1868, brought together representatives of unions in eighteen cities. This union and similar ones were not national bodies, however, for as yet only local organizations were permitted.

[6] *Ibid.*, p. 504.

Though officially designated as an "educational association" the Vienna group just mentioned considered itself to be a "labor party" and is so referred to in the literature generally. Both it and the trade unions were the objects of literal persecution by the authorities. Frequently this took the form of a rigid application to the activities of workers' organizations of the corporation law doctrine of *ultra vires*. Anything which could be construed as a deviation from the strict letter of the "charter"; that is, the constitution and by-laws as approved, brought dissolution.

The most famous of the conflicts in this period culminated in the high treason trial of 1870. On December 13, 1869, a workers' demonstration of 15,000 to 20,000 persons sent into the parliament a petition expressing their desires for unrestricted rights of association and assembly, absolute freedom of the press, introduction of equal and direct suffrage, and several less important matters. The final paragraph of this brief document read: "If the stated demands are not taken heed of in this session of the Reichsrat, it may be possible that the people will appear again and in greater masses in order to express their will." A few days later the members of the deputation which presented the petition and some other leaders were arrested. The prosecutor charged that the whole demonstration was practically a "dress rehearsal" for a planned revolution, that the final paragraph of the petition constituted a threatening of the government, and that the Eisenach conference of the German Social Democrats, with which the Austrian group had allied itself, had set up an organization and a program the realization of which, "indeed the simple agitation for and dissemination of which in Austria proved the crime of high treason." In reply it was urged that nothing had been established except that the defendants acknowledged themselves to be Socialists, made Socialist speeches, read Socialist newspapers, and corresponded with Socialists in other countries. The common opinion in working-class circles was that the whole prosecution was simply a pretext to deprive them of their most vigorous leaders and hamstring the movement, an opinion that became firm conviction when the government dissolved every trade union in Vienna, except that of the printers, two weeks after the defendants were held guilty. Similar, though not such comprehensive measures were taken in the provinces. Even the Lower Austrian chamber of commerce and industry registered a protest against the repressive activities of the government.[7]

For a time in 1871 it seemed that a change was in prospect since one of the first acts of the new Hohenwart ministry was to grant amnesty to the "traitors" of 1870. Economically, Austria appeared to be in excellent condition; unemployment practically disappeared. Before long, however, workers' organizations were again in trouble; dissolutions of the newly created unions became frequent. The economic depression, beginning in 1873 and lasting about five years, further weakened the movement. As if these difficulties were not enough, a serious rift developed between two of the outstanding leaders, Oberwinder and Scheu. Although it began over a matter of tactics, Oberwinder favoring coöperation with left-wing liberals and Scheu insisting on a purely proletarian course, it rapidly degenerated into personal bickering in which, unfortunately, most of the workers took sides. Unity was temporarily achieved in 1877 after both leaders had left Austria permanently, only to break out again in more extreme form in the conflict between Radicals and Moderates.

In 1878 Bismarck put through his anti-Socialist law in Germany. One result of this was the disappearance of the German labor papers which had been widely read in Austria. Johann Most, one of those convicted in the high treason trial of 1870 but amnestied on condition that he leave Austria, was now compelled to flee from Germany to London where he began publication of his famous paper, *Freiheit,* in January, 1879. Despite the police the sheet soon acquired considerable circulation and influence in Austria. The Radicals, who distributed the *Freiheit* and similar writings, believed that the time had come for the destruction of the whole system of private capitalism by revolution. Some of them favored individual terrorist acts. The Moderates stood for immediate political and social reforms such as universal suffrage and protective labor legislation. The repressive policy and acts of the government aided the Radicals. Among the dozens of cases contained in contemporary reports a few may be mentioned. In 1880 there were 635 instances in which newspapers were confiscated. In July, 1881, the *Metallarbeiter-*

[7] This protest appeared in the organization's report for 1869, published after the wholesale dissolutions of mid-1870. Cf. Deutsch, *op. cit.,* Vol. I, 93, 94, 102, 104–107.

Fachblatt was so treated because the word "exploitation" had been used in an article. The public prosecutor, Dr. Pelser, gravely informed the editor that "this terrible word could not be tolerated, either written or spoken."[8] In 1881 Leo Walecka was sentenced to four years' imprisonment for smuggling copies of *Freiheit* into Austria. In 1882 Johann Richter attempted to get 50,000 copies of a radical handbill printed. The printer reported him to the police and he was sentenced to twelve years' imprisonment. Also in 1882 the Vienna shoemakers' union was dissolved and its funds confiscated on the charge that it was distributing illegal literature. This lead to intermittent rioting over a period of nine days.

Although the government's stupidity and brutality do not excuse the terrorism indulged in by a few workers, they help to explain it. On the other hand, the influence of the Anarchist ideas widely disseminated throughout the western world in the 'eighties must not be underestimated. Several assaults and at least two murders in the fifteen months before February, 1884, were perpetrated by Radicals. And though few of them approved terrorism, there can be no doubt that the majority of the workers active in political or economic organizations of this day were in the Radical camp. To meet this situation the government proclaimed martial law for Vienna and vicinity on January 30, 1884, a situation which persisted until June 9, 1891.[9]

Again there were hundreds of arrests, long prison sentences, persecutions of all sorts. Many unions and political clubs dissolved, some became secret radical clubs, those remaining lost heavily in membership. Still the government was not satisfied since its obvious purpose was to destroy the working-class movement. In January, 1885, an anti-Socialist bill was introduced into parliament, but through the efforts of a few "left democrats" was sidetracked into committee. The next year the bill was altered into an anti-Anarchist form, passed, and approved by the emperor on June 25. But these measures had brought about one of the last results the government could have desired; great progress toward unity among Radicals and Moderates. Moreover, additional liberal and democratic

[8] Deutsch, *op. cit.*, Vol. I, 162.

[9] *Reichsgesetzblatt für die im Reichsrathe vertretenen Königreiche und Länder*, 1884, Nr. 15; 1891, Nr. 69. This collection of imperial statutes, in all its variant titles, is cited hereafter as *RGBl.*, followed by the year and the number of the law, decree, or order.

middle-class citizens were brought over to the point of view that reaction had gone too far. Not only had their political representatives objected to the anti-Socialist bill, but also, when permission was refused the workers to hold a mass meeting to protest the second draft, a manufacturer had joined with liberal and Socialist politicians in sponsoring the protest and securing a permit. The anti-Anarchist law expired under its own terms two years after its approval. When the Taaffe government made a last attempt in June, 1891, to pass an anti-Socialist law, it could get nowhere.

The individual who did most in reconciling conflict within the political movement was Dr. Viktor Adler. On December 11, 1886, he began publication of *Gleichheit;* in its columns he took middle ground on the remaining points of difference and hammered on the need for completing the unification process. In a short time he had secured the confidence of both sides and this, in turn, led to the achievement of his aims in the Hainfeld Congress of December 30, 1888–January 1, 1889. The demand of the Radicals had been for years that the struggle for changes in working-class status should be carried on "with all methods." This procedure they now gave up and agreed to a formula which stated that the proletarian fight should be waged "with all methods that were serviceable and that corresponded to the natural feeling for justice [*Rechtsbewusstsein*] of the people." A resolution declaring the differences at an end was adopted and the Social Democratic Workers' party of Austria came into existence under that name.[10] As already indicated the old Workers' Educational Associations had really been political organizations and as early as 1868 the expression "Social Democratic party" had been used.[11]

Unification in the political field cleared the way for renewed activities in the economic. As far back as 1881 the editor of the metal-workers' paper had expressed the sentiments of his group in terms remarkably similar to those current among twentieth-century American unionists: "And we repeat that we've got a belly-full of this business of making the trade-union movement the punching bag of political differences." Fortunately for the unions the early 'nineties

[10] *Verhandlungen des Parteitages der Oesterreichischen Sozialdemokratie, 1888/89* (Wien, 1889), pp. 3, 28, 29. These proceedings of the Socialist party congresses appeared under various titles over the years, but, following Austrian usage, will be cited as *Parteitag.*

[11] Deutsch, *op. cit.,* Vol. I, 66–67.

were a period of business upswing, but unfortunately some of them were not content with moderate progress. In spite of warnings from cooler heads a number of "wild" strikes were called which did more harm than good to the movement. Nevertheless some progress was being made in bringing the more radical workers to understand the value and the importance of those unspectacular but effective methods of bargaining and compromise that were necessary in view of the strength of the opposition—even if for no better reasons. Attempts at centralization were hampered by the knowledge of government disapproval. Gradually permission was secured for associations that would unite the local unions in a provincial body and finally, August 6, 1892, the metalworkers secured official sanction for the first nation-wide union in Austria. In October of the same year a general meeting of the unions of Vienna was held to protest the action of the British Trades-Union Congress in calling an international trade-union congress which the Austrian leaders believed would interfere with the Socialist assembly planned for Zurich in the same year. The protest meeting elected a committee authorized to bring the Vienna unions together whenever the need arose, and out of this committee developed the Provisional Commission which promptly took a place similar to that which the Junta had filled some thirty years earlier in England. In late December, 1893, the first general trade-union congress in Austrian history turned the Provisional Commission into the National Trade-Union Commission. Not until 1928 was this loosely constituted group reorganized as the Federation of the Free Trade Unions of Austria.

In thus summarizing the unification of the Socialist working-class movement in both political and trade-union fields I have passed over another development to which I must now return; namely, the rise of the Roman Catholic movement which was, after many changes, to find its culmination in the Clerical Fascism of Dollfuss and Schuschnigg. One of the leaders of the Catholic workers in Austria, Leopold Kunschak, has pointed with pride to the fact that a German priest, Adolph Kolping, founded a journeymen's association before the publication of the Communist Manifesto, that is, in 1847.[12] These *Vereine* were by no means trade unions, having as their main purpose in early years the regeneration of home life.

[12] *Das Volkswohl,* vol. 14 (Aug.–Sept., 1923), 246 ff.

Later they acquired broadly cultural and political aims. Since Austria was so strongly Catholic it is natural to expect that associations would be formed there, but, as Kunschak pointed out, there was really no place for the new factory workers in them because of the restrictions on membership to *journeymen.*[13] Again, ideas for the organization of the new group came from a dignitary of the Roman Catholic Church, Wilhelm E. Ketteler, bishop of Mainz. The first *Arbeiter-Verein* in Austria of which record has been found was formed in 1869. Meanwhile, in 1864, one of the greatest leaders of the Catholic conservative social-reform movement, Baron Karl von Vogelsang, had migrated to Austria from Prussia. His writings were largely instrumental in bringing to Catholics an understanding of the social problems of capitalism. His attacks on that system were vigorous, and, because he considered the liberals and the Jews as the main perpetrators and perpetuators of it, his attacks on them were equally vigorous. The stock exchange crash of 1873 and the crisis of the 'eighties shook the old liberal ideas severely. In October of 1882 the feudal aristocracy, through hate of the rising "big" bourgeoisie, threw open the gate to political power to the petty bourgeoisie by reducing to five gulden the tax payment prescribed as a qualification for voting in towns and cities. Karl Lueger, one of the most colorful figures in recent Austrian political history, immediately seized the opportunity to form a new party. A violent denouncer of Jews as a group, despite close personal friendships with some of them, and a demagogue par excellence, Lueger literally searched out the new electorate in the wine and beer rooms of the suburbs of Vienna and forged them into the Christian Social party. The program of the new leader was a hodgepodge, but the elements which held its adherents together were anti-Semitism and antiliberalism. In the light of subsequent developments, however, it should be observed that Lueger's anti-Semitism was more economic than "racial" in character. As early as 1885 his party achieved resounding electoral successes.

[13] It must always be kept in mind that even in the twentieth century Austria remained a country in which the small producer working with a minimum of capital and few or no machines continued to exist in relatively greater numbers than in most industrialized lands. The master leather worker or button maker or confectioner employed one to a half dozen or so journeymen and operated in a fashion differing little from that of his medieval predecessor. Such producers were frequently organized into an association which retained the medieval designation *Zunft,* or guild. In the last half of the nineteenth century this situation was even more prevalent.

The real impetus to a labor movement with a religious basis was derived in 1891 from Leo XIII's encyclical, *Rerum Novarum*. We have the word of the foremost historian of the Austrian part of that movement that until this time "the few Catholic workers' organizations led a more or less contemplative existence and did not make a fight for the working masses."[14] Among the leaders who felt impelled to action by the papal injunction to create workingmen's associations was the Jesuit, Father Heinrich Abel. He was supported by Baron Vittinghof-Schell and Baron Dallberg. To those unacquainted with the details of the struggles going on in Austria at this time and the attitudes in which men approached them the following extract from Father Abel's reminiscences may be illuminating.

> From the outset I placed myself on the side of Schönerer in tne accurate discernment that the misfortune of the Austrian people was their servitude to the Jews and to the Jewish spirit. [After some comments on his early associates in the movement who at that time were "Christ-deniers" and "only anti-Semites" he related a bit of family history.] My father, who was serving as chief inspector . . . in the Bavarian financial ministry, had an altercation with a Jew while on a trip, because the Jew slandered the king [Maximilian II]. My father made use of a handsome walking stick. The Jew brought charges of assault and battery against my father. At the trial my father was as a matter of fact fined five gulden because of the attack. Later my father brought a countercharge of high treason against him. Nevertheless the Jew understood how to extricate himself from the difficulty without consequences. After my father's death his stick was put up at public auction. Since the story concerning the stick was widely discussed and it went from mouth to mouth that that was the stick with which the Jew had been whipped, the stick became a sort of rarity which acquaintances of mine endeavored to acquire. I myself naturally knew nothing of the fate of the stick. Finally Baroness Tschovanelli acquired it. She turned the stick over to me. So after thirty years I got my father's stick back again. Then I gave this stick as a present to Dr. Psenner, [himself] a staunch anti-Semite.[15]

Father Abel's idea was to combine both laborers and petty manufacturers (in the literal sense) in the same organization. The attempt failed and has been sharply criticized by later leaders and commentators such as Kunschak, Hans Schmitz, and Hemala, the last going

[14] Franz Hemala, *Geschichte der Gewerkschaften* (Wien, 1930), p. 182.

[15] Hans Schmitz, "Aus P. Abels Erinnerungen an die christlichsoziale Frühzeit," *Das Volkswohl*, vol. 14 (Dec., 1923), 342–343.

so far as to say that the workers were treated like "Cinderellas." Kunschak contended vigorously for an association exclusively of laborers and though he was only twenty was largely instrumental in creating the Christian Social Workers' Association, December 4, 1892. During the preceding months there had been much trouble with the Social Democrats who had on more than one occasion violently broken up Catholic workers' meetings. In this connection it should also be noted that prominent Socialist leaders of this period were agnostics or atheists who never hesitated to make the most bitter attacks on the Roman Catholic Church and the new Christian Social movement.

Despite the election of Lueger as mayor of Vienna in 1897 the progress of the Catholic movement was slow. In fact many higher dignitaries of the Church were opposed to it. Father Abel relates that the cardinal of Prague and the bishop of Brünn made a special trip to Rome to secure a condemnation of the whole Christian Social movement from Pope Leo, but without success. On the contrary, His Holiness indicated his approval of Lueger in particular by keeping a photograph of him on his writing desk for a "long time."[16] After 1900 the movement became stronger politically among the peasants, but the trade-union group was always weak. The craft organizations which came into existence in the middle and late 'nineties were not organized into a national *Kommission* until 1906. The membership of the unions affiliated to that central body at its creation was only 18,164 but by 1910 it had reached 46,553, the high point before the First World War. In 1913 it had sunk to 37,237 and in 1915 to 13,666, the lowest recorded. The big jump in affiliated membership was made immediately after the war: 1919, 30,725; 1920, 64,478; 1921, 78,737. Affiliated membership remained practically constant at the last figure through 1927 and crossed the 100,000 mark in 1928, but, as explained in more detail in Chapter XI (below, pp. 266–267), the Catholic unions claimed an additional 70,000 unaffiliated members in both 1921 and 1922, 50,000 in 1925, and 15,000 in 1928. In various years the free unions also claimed from 20,000 to 40,000 unaffiliated members. Austrian practice, however, was to make comparisons only of the membership affiliated to the respective central bodies. On this basis the strength of the Catholic unions never quite

[16] *Ibid.*, p. 345.

reached 20 per cent of that of the Socialist groups and from 1918 through 1925 was less than 10 per cent. If a comparison is made including the unaffiliated members the percentage of Catholic to Socialist unionists was just under 15 in 1921 and 1922, a little more than 16 in 1925 and 13.6 in 1928. An analysis[17] of the data shows, moreover, that the Catholics did not have an industrial workers' movement. From a total of 112,000 in the year of largest affiliated membership there were 23,838 clerks and *Angestellte* in public and private employ; 17,154 soldiers; 10,802 teachers; 9,460 agricultural and dairy workers; 5,847 house caretakers and janitors; 5,831 domestics. These groups account for about 70 per cent of the total. Comparisons with Socialist unions in a few important occupations make the situation even clearer. The figures are likewise for 1930. On

Occupations	Catholic union membership	Socialist union membership
Wood and building trades . . .	5,786	67,742
Food industry	1,745	38,266
Metal trades	5,081	107,526

the basis of the facts presented it seems clear that viewed strictly as unions the Catholic organizations were unimportant; in fact, most of them were insignificant.[18] Viewed from another angle, however, they were important and had a most unhappy significance. As the Catholic sociologist and third vice-mayor of Vienna in the Dollfuss-Schuschnigg era, Dr. E. K. Winter, pointed out they provided a splitting and disruptive element. It is particularly noteworthy that this loyal and devout member of the Roman Catholic Church emphasized the idea that the development of a "dual" movement on a religious basis was one of the greatest misfortunes for Austrian labor.[19] As will be seen, the overwhelming majority of the leaders of that movement were all too willing to accept positions in the government-dominated "unified trade union" set up as a part of Austrian Fascism.

For the reasons just indicated, therefore, an account which seeks to focus attention on the relation of the working-class movement

[17] This has to be limited to affiliated members since no occupational details are available for the others.

[18] Hemala, *op. cit.*, pp. 267, 268; *Wirtschaftsstatistisches Jahrbuch, 1931/32*, pp. 164, 165, 166; Deutsch, *op. cit.*, Vol. I, 461.

[19] Conversation with Dr. Winter in July, 1939.

to the fight for democracy and against Fascism in Austria has to be almost exclusively a history of the Socialist groups. Despite the efforts of such men as Kunschak, the Catholic political organization was never successful in breaking the hold of the Social Democrats on the workers. Consequently, unless otherwise indicated, references to "the working-class movement" will be understood as designating the Social Democratic development.

As already brought out, it appeared in the early 'nineties that the working-class movement was at last on the highroad to success—and indeed it accomplished little short of miracles, in the light of the existing circumstances, before its destruction forty years later—but unity had scarcely been achieved before it was disrupted again. This time the issue was that of nationalities. As far back as 1878 the Czechs had attempted to found an independent Social Democratic political group. Destroyed by the police before it really began, the party established itself in 1887 with a somewhat peculiar declaration to the effect that though it considered itself an integral part of the Austrian party it would maintain an individual organization. Six years later further steps toward independence were made in the adoption of a separate constitution, a party levy, and so on. The general party congress of 1896 gave recognition to the Czech and other nationality groups by arranging that representatives of the German, Czech, Polish, Italian, and Slovenian organizations should constitute the central executive of the party. The congress of the next year carried through a reorganization providing for a "total party" made up of national parties representing the groups just named and the Ruthenians (Ukranians). Apparently the difficulties were being overcome by the creation of a party which was actually a federation of parties.

But in the same year, 1896, that the first step toward federalization in the political field was achieved, trouble in the economic area came to a head. At the trade-union congress a number of the Czech organizations demanded a secretary of their nationality in the *Kommission.* The demand was refused, the position of the German group being that authority would have been divided and the efficiency of the central body hamstrung. On the other hand, it must be remembered that the Czechs were with reason generally distrustful of the Germans, so that it was incumbent upon the latter group to be extremely conciliatory. If unity in the movement could have been maintained at the expense of some friction in the offices of the *Kommission* it seems that the price was cheap. Since it would not be paid, the Czechs withdrew and established their own Trade-Union Commission in January of 1897. Numerous attempts at reconciling the differences were made, but to no avail. The controversy extended into the political area and became the source of unseemly squabbles in the trade-union and Socialist international organizations. In September of 1906 the Czech party adopted a resolution favoring separatism in the trade-union field. Czech trade unionists who desired to remain attached to the Vienna *Kommission* were forced out of the Czech political organization. Thereupon they organized a separate party which stood for internationalism in the political field and centralism in that of the trade unions. The German Social Democratic party of Austria recognized the new Czech political group and, consequently, the old Czech party in 1912 severed all connections with the "total party" set up in 1897. The splitting up of the empire was being foreshadowed in the workers' movement.[20]

Meanwhile the fight for a parliament based on free and equal suffrage went on with renewed vigor. The Hainfeld program had stated that this would be done "without any false illusions on the value of parliamentarism—a form of modern class control." In 1891 the "iron ring" of the conservative parties was cracked by the election successes of the democratic Young Czechs. Prime Minister Taaffe wavered for two years; suddenly, in October, 1893, he introduced a reform bill which would have abolished two of the privileged *curia* and given the vote to every person of twenty-four years of age who could read and write and had maintained residence in one locality for six months. For various reasons opposition came from practically all sectors of the political compass, the government's position was impossible and Taaffe resigned without even bringing the matter to a vote. A part of the working class was exasperated by the facts that the *curia* of large landed proprietors and that of the chambers of commerce would have remained untouched by Taaffe's reform, as well as by the repeated delays; consequently,

[20] Deutsch, *Geschichte der deutschösterreichischen Arbeiterbewegung* (Wien, 1922), pp. 31–34; Hemala, *op. cit.*, pp. 152–158.

its leaders introduced a resolution in the first trade-union congress (December, 1893) demanding a general strike to force the adoption of complete and equal suffrage. This failed, but in the party congress three months later the executive was authorized to proclaim such a strike "as a last resource at an appropriate time." After the immediate successor of the Taaffe government, the so-called coalition cabinet of Windischgrätz, had been pitifully unsuccessful, July, 1895, brought still another ministry. Its chief, Count Badeni, carried a suffrage reform act which added a fifth general *curia* to the four privileged ones existing. The Social Democrats were by no means satisfied; nevertheless they put up candidates in the election of 1897 and obtained 14 seats. The parliamentary situation degenerated steadily. Filibustering and verbal attacks by one member on another grew into fist fights in which whole party groups were involved. Passing even the simplest legislation became almost impossible. Serving as president of the chamber was a test of physical courage. On one occasion the entire Social Democratic deputation replied to a crass violation of the rules of procedure by storming the platform, destroying papers, and pinning the president against the wall. Eighty police officers were required to restore order and expel the Socialists. The sources of these difficulties were, of course, in the conflicting national and class interests which had been so ruthlessly put down in 1848 and 1849 and had been seething for fifty years.

The parliament elected in 1901 contained only 11 Social Democrats and proved no more capable of meeting the situation than had its predecessors. For a time the masses lost interest in the attempt to secure votes which would apparently be wasted. Then the conflict between the Magyar nobles and the crown developed a new crisis over the control of the army. Franz Joseph had rejected demands that Hungarian be made the official "language of command" in the Hungarian regiments. Finally, August 10, 1905, the emperor decided to break the opposition by offering general, equal, and direct suffrage to that part of the population which was subject to him as king of Hungary. The Austrian workers were naturally encouraged to demand the same rights for themselves; when the October manifesto of the Russian czar promised constitutional parliamentary government on a basis of general suffrage, they were no longer to be denied. The railroad employees adopted a policy of "passive resistance," huge demonstrations paraded along the Ringstrasse and finally a three-day general strike was threatened. At the same time, however, Viktor Adler had been carrying on most involved and painstaking negotiations in the electoral reform committee of the parliament, jockeying for position, supporting now one, now another middle-class political group from which he could get concessions, but always coöperating with the emperor and his cabinet in the hope of circumventing the obstructive tactics used by opponents of the reform and destroying the privileged legislative body. Under this combination of pressures the resistance collapsed and in January, 1907,[21] universal suffrage was attained. It is extremely important to note, however, that this extension of voting rights was limited to elections for members of parliament. Members of provincial diets and of city councils were not elected by general suffrage until after Austria became a republic. Unfortunately, it must also be recorded that because of the continuance of conflict among the various nationalities in parliament the 87 representatives of the workers' party (from a total of 516) were not able to accomplish a great deal.

The remaining years before the outbreak of the First World War deserve no detailed comment in this summary account. Membership in the unions affiliated to the Vienna *Kommission* remained practically constant at a little above 400,000; that in the "German" Socialist party moved up from about 90,000 to about 145,000. Votes recorded for candidates of this party in the 1907 and 1911 parliamentary elections were 513,219 and 542,349, respectively. The total Social Democratic votes cast by all national groups was 1,040,662 in 1907 and 1,043,297 in 1911.[22] In 1909 and subsequent years the party began the process of developing financial independence from the unions, undertook some reorganization, and debated tactical issues vigorously. During this period there was a definite tendency toward industrial concentration and employers' organizations gath-

[21] The parliament passed the bill in December, 1906, but the law is dated January 26, 1907. *RGBl.*, 1907, Nr. 17.

[22] There are minor discrepancies in the totals given in various sources. Those used appear in *Die Tätigkeit des Sozialdemokratischen Verbandes im Abgeordnetenhause*, Heft 1, (Wien, 1909), p. 3; *Die Tätigkeit der deutschen sozialdemokratischen Abgeordneten im österreichischen Reichsrat*, Heft 5, (Wien, 1912), p. 5; Deutsch, *Geschichte der österreichischen Gewerkschaftsbewegung*, Vol. I, 436. Following Austrian practice, the reports on the activities of Socialist members of parliament are cited hereafter as *Tätigkeits-Bericht* despite numerous changes in the title. *Heft* numbers are those of the *Gesamtausgabe*.

ered strength. Though there is some evidence of increased class conflicts, such as the more extensive use of strike-breaking organizations, "yellow-dog contracts" and "company unions," and a united bourgeois front against the Social Democrats in parliament, the truth is that the succession of crises in the Balkans was receiving most of the nation's attention. In a budget debate of November 28, 1912, Viktor Adler protested against Austria-Hungary's further meddling in Balkan affairs in the name of the "entire united international cannon fodder."[23]

This attitude of opposition to war persisted until the actual outbreak of hostilities on July 28, 1914, but on August 5, the *Arbeiter Zeitung,* official organ of the party, carried a leading editorial praising the Social Democratic members of the German Reichstag who had voted for war credits the day before. There can be no doubt that an overwhelming majority of Austrian workers believed at this time that it was necessary to defend their country and to attempt to avoid the consequences of military defeat.[24]

On August 4 the Trade-Union Commission had issued a proclamation to all union deputies[25] pointing out the fact that a whole series of legal provisions upon which the entire activity of their organizations rested had been suspended. Nevertheless, the *Kommission* announced the intention of all the constituent unions to continue their work and urged all the deputies to see to it that such work was strictly confined to trade-union functions. Particular mention was made of the suspension of the constitution and of the laws guaranteeing the rights of association and assembly, of inviolability of letters, and of freedom of the press.

Serious as the matters just mentioned were to prove, they were overshadowed by two decrees issued on July 25, three days before

[23] Oesterreichischer Reichsrat, Haus der Abgeordneten, *Protokoll,* 1912, p. 5971.

[24] Cf. Otto Bauer, *Die österreichische Revolution,* p. 53; Deutsch, *Geschichte der österreichischen Gewerkschaftsbewegung,* Vol. II, 11–12. The editor of a collection of papers of F. Austerlitz, editor in chief of the *Arbeiter Zeitung,* explains the latter's statements of August 5 on the basis of a misleading if not absolutely false summary issued by the Austrian government of the declaration made by the German Socialists in the Reichstag at the time they voted for the war credits. Julius Braunthal, *Austerlitz spricht* (Wien, 1931), pp. 99–102.

[25] "Deputies" has been used here as a translation of *Vertrauensmänner.* This conforms to American terminology in some trade agreements. To a number of readers "stewards" or "representatives" may seem a better translation. It is perhaps unfortunate that the English language does not have a word that expresses so precisely the idea of confidence embodied in the German term.

the formal declaration of war on Serbia.[26] One of these authorized the minister of the interior to place undertakings that were particularly important for purposes of the nation or for public welfare under state protection. Within a few weeks this action had been taken for hundreds of concerns. Employees of such businesses who concertedly refused or abstained from carrying out their duties with the intent of interfering with personal service or operation, or carried on their work in such a way as to make the service or operation more difficult, were punishable by imprisonment for from six weeks to one year.

The other decree made effective on the following day was the war service law of December 26, 1912. As a matter of practice this statute obligated every male civilian between the ages of eighteen and fifty (after January, 1916, fifty-five) to perform any services of which he was capable. The only important exceptions were public officials, priests, and ministers. Some other groups could be held in service for a limited time only. Such persons were not, of course, soldiers, but if they were occupied in any undertaking which had been placed under military control they had to obey implicitly any and all orders given them. Failure to do so subjected them to trial in a military court and punishment for a breach of discipline. As Richard Riedl, "general commissar for war and reconstruction economy," put it, the chief advantage of the law to the owner of a concern was that "from the moment he was placed under war service, he was certain of his work force."[27] And as he also noted, not only was the owner under no pressure to concede wage increases for fear of losing his workers, but he was also insured against stoppages of work and insubordination. Employers soon recognized that despite one significant drawback of the war service law—the frequent assignment to their factories or mines of a military director who was incompetent as a business executive—the balance lay on the other side. Although some officers showed understanding for the workers' problems, Riedl points out that the opposite attitude was the more

[26] The parliament had been "sent home" in March on the ground that it was not capable of functioning and, contrary to the policy of other nations involved in the war, was not assembled in July or August of 1914. Until May 30, 1917, government was by fiat. *Tätigkeits-Bericht,* Heft 9, (Wien, 1917), pp. 3, 21.

[27] R. Riedl, *Die Industrie Oesterreichs während des Krieges* (Wien and New Haven, 1932), p. 10. This volume is one in the series *Economic and Social History of the World War,* edited by Professor James T. Shotwell.

frequent one. This position is substantiated by the reports of the factory inspectors during the war years; by an imposing collection of cases and documents presented to the workers' conference of November 5, 1916, at which a number of representatives of the government were present; and by the findings of the authors of a volume entirely on labor issues in the *Economic and Social History of the World War* series.[28] Among the hundreds of examples which might be cited a few are particularly worthy of note. In the weapon factory at Steyr a welfare association was organized. One of its major purposes was the purchase of food for the members—under the prevailing conditions a vital service. A condition of membership was renunciation of any connection with a trade union. This condition was approved by the government. An employee of the Hirtenberg cartridge factory lost two fingers and part of the palm of his hand in an accident in the plant. After the wound had healed he was ordered to do other work in which the hand was exposed to strong acids. He objected that the skin was too tender and requested discharge. This was refused; the lieutenant colonel in control of the plant again ordered him to do the work. On the man's refusal he was finally dismissed, but the officer wrote into his workbook the statement that he was shiftless and unreliable. On September 5, 1916, miners in a Styrian town were ordered by the military director to work Sunday shifts and not to visit coffeehouses or other public places after eight in the evening. Military patrols were to enforce the decree and imprisonment was the punishment for disobedience. Complaints against the ostentatious carrying of dog whips by managers were frequent. In the mines near Ostrau beatings were given systematically. "Impudent" workers were taken to the guardroom, stretched out on a bench, held by two soldiers and unmercifully thrashed. Protests and proofs submitted by the parliamentary deputy Cingr resulted in more beatings for the workers who had supplied Cingr with his information. A second protest finally secured results.[29]

But the "punishment" which caused the most bitter resentment was ordered in a decree of the war ministry of June 15, 1915. After

[28] Gewerkschaftskommission, *Bericht,* 1919, pp. 57–109; F. Hanusch *et al., Die Regelung der Arbeitsverhältnisse im Kriege* (Wien and New Haven, 1927), pp. 72–73, 113, *passim.* The Hanusch volume is also a part of the *Economic and Social History of the World War.*

[29] Cf. particularly, Gewerkschaftskommission, *Bericht,* 1919, pp. 62, 68, 75.

reference to the extraordinarily unsatisfactory attitude of the workers in numerous war undertakings—their insubordination, impudence, complaints, passive resistance, and deliberate sabotage—the edict provided that "ringleaders," after serving whatever sentences were prescribed, should not be returned to their jobs but sent into active service at the front as soon as possible. If the offenders were capable only of guard duty as distinguished from combat service, care was to be taken that they be placed close to the lines.[30] Protests from Social Democratic members secured the formal withdrawal of the decree, but the practice remained the same. Threats of being sent to the trenches were a matter of everyday occurrence, and hundreds were actually sent as a disciplinary measure. The impression left was still fresh in the minds of many workers with whom I spoke in 1936 and 1937: "A hero's death for the Fatherland? Hell, we faced that death because some military director of a factory thought we were 'impudent'!" However much the facts may have been exaggerated, the psychological results cannot be. They explain in appreciable measure the bitterness that prevailed among workers during the early postwar period toward war, the army, and individual officers.

Other causes of dissatisfaction were the failure of wages to keep up with rising costs of living, inadequate food, excessive hours of work, and the practice of mustering workers into the army, assigning them to their former jobs in some factory and paying them only the pittance given to soldiers in the field. A decree of November 14, 1914, interpreting the war service statute, required in all contracts between the military administration and the owners of concerns taken over, the stipulation by said owners that no changes in wages and conditions of employment would be undertaken without agreement with the workers. As a practical matter the principle thus set out was not observed; in fact, its clear purpose was perverted into an argument against *increases* in wages. Complaints accumulated, but since the majority of military directors refused to deal with union representatives and made full use of the powers already described, nothing could be effected. The metalworkers' union finally secured from the war ministry on June 20, 1915, recognition of the desirability of complaint offices, and one month later a decree from

---

[30] Text quoted in *ibid.*, p. 63.

this ministry provided for the creation of such offices. Not until August did the first one of them begin to operate in Vienna, but after thirteen months their activities were severely restricted by another decree requiring that all complaints must first go through the hands of the military director of the concern in which the trouble arose. Just a few weeks before, however (July 15, 1916), a decree of the war ministry had corrected one of the major sources of complaint: the payment to mustered-in soldiers working in factories of only their military pay instead of the "customary wages." The same decree provided that persons performing labor under the war service law must also receive "customary wages." The evidence indicates that this order was observed.[31]

Despite the gain just mentioned life in Austria was becoming more and more militarized, the economic situation was going from bad to worse, and large masses of the population were existing on half-starvation rations. Attempts to recall the parliament into activity were shattered by the obstinate refusal of Prime Minister Stürgkh. In October, 1916, a group of university professors attempted to hold a meeting at which the president of the lower house of parliament was to speak. The chief of the cabinet prohibited the assembly. On the same day that this action was publicly announced, October 21, Dr. Friedrich Adler, son of the founder of the Social Democratic party and leader of the left wing of that party, assassinated Stürgkh. With justice, the editor of the *Arbeiter Zeitung* wrote on the next day that this act was inexplicable and incomprehensible to all who knew Adler. It was not that his friends were any less clear than he on the implications of Stürgkh's last blow at what little freedom remained in Austria, but that they knew this desperate protest was contrary to every idea and principle of its perpetrator.

There can be no doubt that October 21 marked a turning point in the history of the Austrian working-class movement. To thousands of workers Adler became a hero who had avenged in part the physical and spiritual indignities which they had suffered for more than two years. Stürgkh's successor, Koerber, began the process of relaxing some of the war absolutism; hopes for the assembling of parliament grew. Although war restrictions made it impossible to hold regular party congresses until 1917, there were three so-called

[31] *Ibid.*, pp. 67, 69–70; Hanusch *et al.*, *op. cit.*, p. 235.

national party "conferences" which served much the same purpose. The last of these met November 2–4, 1916, soon after the assassination of Stürgkh. The delegates protested against the inefficiency of the government's efforts to supply adequate food to the population, urged the reassembly of parliament, demanded a clear statement from the government concerning its willingness to make peace, and complained about the legal position of the working people. The comments on the last point were actually sharp and vigorous, but in comparison with most of the speeches made at the workers' conference on November 5 they seem mild and restrained; the numerous government officials present at this assembly were compelled to listen to an unvarnished account of conditions in the country as labor's representatives saw them. The pent-up emotion of twenty-seven months burst forth in denunciations which Stürgkh would surely not have tolerated.[32]

A combination of repeated individual protests, the meetings just described, the repercussions of the assassination of Stürgkh, and the more enlightened attitude of his successor finally secured through imperial decree of March 18, 1917, the establishment of a comprehensive system of complaint commissions. The offices previously created had proved almost entirely unsatisfactory because of their limited jurisdiction, because of their failure to secure the confidence of the workers, and because of the further limitation on their jurisdiction imposed by the decree of September, 1916, already mentioned. The new commissions could exercise more authority in the matter of rendering decisions, could handle disputes concerning wages and labor conditions in concerns actually in the hands of the military administration or operating under the war service law, and could establish wages and all other labor conditions. Most important of all, they were required to fix wages which took account of the training and capacities of the workers as well as of the existing living and working conditions.[33]

Six weeks later another major demand of the workers was met: parliament assembled on May 30, 1917. The general importance of this event is obvious. Even the most optimistic opponents of gov-

[32] Cf. *Parteitag, 1917*, pp. 65–71 (in which the party conference of 1916 is reported), and Gewerkschaftskommission, *Bericht*, 1919, pp. 55–96.

[33] *RGBl.*, 1917, Nr. 122. The text of this decree is reproduced in Hanusch *et al.*, *op. cit.*, pp. 167–170.

ernment by decree would have hesitated, however, to prophesy the willingness of the legislative body to follow the lead of the Socialists in giving the government a stinging rebuke on a major issue. On July 6 the lower house unanimously refused its approval to the decrees that had abolished trial by jury and placed civilians under courts martial. One of the most drastic weapons of militarism and of the prevailing reaction was thus eliminated.[34] The chief credit for this achievement goes to Austerlitz, editor of the *Arbeiter Zeitung*. His brilliant and devastating attacks on judicial murders by the members of military courts deserve a high place in the annals of journalism.[35]

For a time the new bodies authorized to settle disputes seem to have operated quite satisfactorily, but on January 15, 1918, a number of Social Democratic members of parliament, the Trade-Union Commission and the metalworkers' federation filed with the central office of the complaint commissions a vigorous protest against recent tendencies. The evidence showed that the central office had sent out to the military chairmen of local commissions confidential orders to refrain from making decisions on collective demands for wage increases, as well as on requests for the establishment of minimum wages and minimum earnings. It was pointed out that on January 1, 1917, that is, under the previous system, a complaint office in Vienna had received orders to make wage changes effective as of the date of the decision, and that the stipulation under the new system that cases should be decided promptly was poorly observed. The petitioners had no difficulty in showing that these orders and practices were contrary to the spirit and to the letter of the decrees creating the commissions, and that such interference was destroying the confidence of the workers in the commissions' fairness and impartiality.[36]

But the workers had not waited for the presentation of formal petitions. Mention has already been made of the great shortage of food and of the complaints of workers' representatives against the inadequate distribuiton of what supplies were available. Before the war Hungary had supplied Austria with a large part of its foodstuffs,

[34] *Tätigkeits-Bericht*, Heft 9 (Wien, 1917), pp. 30–33; *Parteitag, 1917*, pp. 195–196.

[35] *Arbeiter Zeitung*, June 10, 1917, p. 1; June 15, p. 1; June 26, p. 1; June 27, p. 1; June 30, pp. 1–2; July 4, p. 1; July 5, pp. 1–2.

[36] Similar trouble developed in England and forced the government to make public apology. Cf. S. and B. Webb, *History of Trade Unionism* (New York and London, 1920), p. 642.

particularly cereals, but within a short time this traffic practically ceased. With the imposition of the "hunger blockade" by the Allied Powers the situation grew worse. As early as 1915 there were short stoppages of work, principally among miners, in protest against unsatisfactory and uncertain food supplies, as well as against Sunday work. In January, 1916, such strikes became more serious; in March of the same year a stoppage lasting nearly two weeks and involving thousands of miners took place. From this time on outbreaks increased in frequency and bitterness—and in the face of legal prohibition of strikes and the most brutal repressive measures of the military directors. The climax of these protests was reached on January 14, 1918, the day before the presentation of the petition just described.

The food supply office announced that the flour quota was cut in half. Beginning in Wiener-Neustadt a wave of strikes swept through the industrial centers. By noon of the sixteenth all of the big concerns in Vienna were closed. A deputation from the strikers had, on the morning of the fifteenth, informed the minister of food supply that the workers' major demand was for the cessation of hostilities. Furthermore, a joint declaration issued on the same day by the workers' party and the trade unions warned the government that there was no prospect of quieting the masses unless assurances were given:

1. That the peace negotiations in progress at Brest-Litovsk would not be allowed to collapse on any territorial issues, that the principle of national self-determination would be rigidly observed, that the representatives of the working class would be completely and promptly informed of the status of peace negotiations, and that those representatives would not be denied the opportunity of exerting the influence to which they were entitled on the course of such negotiations.

2. That the government would agree to a thorough reorganization of the food services with the object of making certain that the existing supplies be equitably divided.

3. That the government would approve of the introduction of general, equal, and direct suffrage in the cities and towns so that the control of local government could be taken from the hands of food profiteers.

4. That the government would restore to the workers rights impaired by the militarization of the factories.

There can be no doubt that large numbers of the working people desired a revolution; they believed that in no other way could the war be stopped. Their leaders, however, knew that the most probable result would be invasion from the north by German troops released from the Russian front and invasion from the south by an Allied army if, as probable, the Austrian soldiers ceased to offer resistance. On the evening of the nineteenth representatives of the strikers met with several cabinet members. The latter gave assurances that steps would be taken to meet all the points enumerated above. At ten o'clock the deputation reported to an assembly of working-class representatives and recommended termination of the strike. After a debate which lasted well into the morning of the twentieth this recommendation was accepted.

Although the January strikes were clearly a success in indicating a shift in the power relations of economic classes and in forcing promises of concessions from the government, they brought no significant improvement in general economic conditions; indeed, they could not. The need and misery resulting from lack of food, clothing, and fuel increased almost from hour to hour. The reports of the period are full of proof that the workers were physically unable to perform the tasks demanded of them. In the second half of June, 1918, strikes of metalworkers forced the payment of substantial supplements in wages to them, and later, to employees of other industries. The employers were reimbursed by the state for these extra payments. But the most important item in the concessions was the adoption of the principle that the height of the bonuses should be determined not by the worker's efficiency but by the number of his dependents. Everyone knew that this was only a temporary expedient; nearly everyone believed that only the restoration of peace offered any real hope for improvement. And, as had been true seventy-one years before, the stage was being set for revolution.

CHAPTER III

Foundation of the Republic

At a time more than twenty-five years after the event, and particularly in a book of this character, there is no need to describe in detail the final stages of the disintegration of the Habsburg Empire. The conflicting interests of the hodgepodge of nationalities within that political unit had been working toward its dissolution for decades; the war of 1914–1918 only hastened the process. Perhaps it is not too much to say that among the surprising features of the war period were the facts that the conglomerate army bore hardships and suffering as patiently as it had, that the militaristic and bureaucratic machine thwarted the centrifugal nationalist forces as well as it did, that the working class submitted to the harsh rule of the military in factory and shop with no more violent outbreaks than those previously described. But by mid-1918 the cracks in the edifice were obviously widening.

Nationalist Revolutions and the Breakup of the Empire

The last major offensive of the Austrians on the Italian front was a failure. The German army, which had many times saved its Vienna ally, was now under too great pressure to repeat this aid. In secret meetings of parliament sharpest criticism was directed against military chiefs and the continuance of the war. Even conservative members attacked the government on the ground that Tirolese troops—certainly amongst the most faithful and valuable—had had to suffer from hunger for weeks and months before the beginning of the last offensive.[1] The headquarters of the Sixth Army admitted that, "Any deserter, even if he has to hide himself in the woods, can have better food than the soldier in the front line."[2]

The reply of the government was particularly significant in that it stressed two forces working toward the impending collapse. First, Czech officers were accused of delivering plans of the offensive to the enemy; second, war prisoners returning from revolutionary Rus-

[1] Ludwig Brügel, *Geschichte der österreichischen Sozialdemokratie* (Wien, 1925), Vol. V, 344 ff.

[2] Quoted in Otto Bauer, *Die österreichische Revolution* (Wien, 1923), p. 72.

sia were charged with fomenting several mutinies. It is true that there were a considerable number of mutinies; but, as is at least equally important, it is also true that despite desperate shortages of food the Russian influence had not been able to bring about major movements or disturbances in the great industrial districts. Since the strikes in January, 1918, the workers had become more cautious, or were overawed by the large forces the government had held ready for emergencies, or both. In this connection, it must not be forgotten that even the left-wing Socialist leaders had warned in January that a revolution at that time was impossible. Although it is not intended to deny that after Friedrich Adler's assassination of Stürgkh, revolutionary sentiment rose rapidly, nor that after the fall of Czarism Austria became superfluous to her workers, the most active of the forces seeking dissolution of the empire were nationalistic.

Emperor Karl, however, was not yet prepared to make any important concessions to those nationalist forces. On September 14, without German consent, his government sent notes to the enemy powers inviting them to enter peace negotiations. Not the least important of his motives seems to have been the desire to salvage some sympathy for the dynasty by posing as one who had aided in bringing peace to a war-weary people. About two weeks later Prime Minister Seidler, whose stubborn pro-German policy had unnecessarily irritated the Slavs, retired; but when his successor Hussarek presented himself to parliament on October 1, there were no definite promises, only generalizations concerning reform and the creation of a federal state. As a matter of fact the decisive voices were being raised outside of Vienna. On September 29, Bulgaria signed an armistice, forcing Austrian troops to withdraw toward the north. On October 5, the "unity of all Slovenians, Croats, and Serbians in a national, free, and independent state" was proclaimed in Agram. Two days later the Poles announced their independence. On October 14, huge demonstrations of workers in Prague demanded the promulgation of a republic, and on October 27, the national council actually seized power in that city. Meanwhile, there were some interesting developments in Vienna the details of which, so far as could be ascertained, have never been published. They can be stated most satisfactorily by reproducing, with his permission, a memorandum from Professor Hans Kelsen to me.

It is a pleasure to comply with your request to state what is known to me on the basis of personal experience concerning the Lammasch government—the last government of the Austrian monarchy. First, however, I must call attention to the fact that I am making the following statements only from my memory since I do not have available various documents and some notes relating to this matter; I left them behind when I went from Geneva to the United States in 1940.

In the last years of the First World War I was legal advisor to the joint Austro-Hungarian minister of war (Stöger-Steiner). My particular task was the preparation of legislative bills that would be the basis of a separation of the up to this time common Austro-Hungarian army and the establishment of two independent armies, one Austrian and one Hungarian. This separation of the army was an old political demand of the Hungarians, and at the time of his accession as king of Hungary Emperor Karl had declared himself willing to make a concession in this direction. The juristic preparation of the separation of the army was, however, not my only duty. The war minister requested my advice in other legal and political questions also.

When the break-through on the Bulgarian front took place in September, 1918, and I came to the view that the war was finally lost for the monarchy and therewith the fate of the monarchy sealed, I worked out a memorandum the essential content of which was a plan, through an organization of the new states coming into being in the territory of the monarchy, to restore so far as possible the balance in Central Europe that would be destroyed by the unavoidable dissolution of the Austro-Hungarian monarchy and in particular to hinder the economic catastrophe that probably would be bound-up with the sudden disappearance of a great economic unity. The basic idea of the plan was this: to remove the existing Austrian cabinet of Hussarek von Heinlein and to put in its place a commission with full governmental powers the task of which would be to carry through the dissolution of the Austrian monarchy in agreement with the nationalities (German, Czech, Polish, and South Slavic) that were establishing themselves as independent states and in an economically as well as politically satisfactory fashion. The commission would be formed from representatives [*Vertrauensmänner*] of these nationalities under the chairmanship of a man of international reputation and pacificist opinion. In consideration of the legal structure of the entire monarchy the whole action was contemplated in the first instance for the Austrian half only. As chairman of this commission I proposed a friend then living in retirement in Salzburg, the former professor of criminal and international law and well-known pacificist, Heinrich Lammasch. The liquidation of the Austrian monarchy through a joint commission named by the Emperor and composed of representatives of the different nationalities should above everything else open up and further the possibility of drawing together the new national states into a Central

European federation of states or a federal state. The Emperor was to declare at the time of naming the commission that he considered such an organization of the forming national states to be a European necessity, that he was ready to take his place in some manner or other as the head of this federation of states or federal state, but that his person and his dynasty should not be a hindrance to the creation of the union.

My memorandum secured the approval of the minister of war who personally transmitted it to the Emperor. It seems that at first he found no time to study it or that other plans concerning the maintenance of the monarchy were more pleasing to him. In any case it was not possible during the next weeks to secure a decision from the Emperor on the proposals made in my memorandum. Not until the second or third week of October was I called one night by telephone from the military chancery of the Emperor and commissioned to go to Professor Lammasch and to ask him whether or not he was willing to negotiate with influential men as representatives of the different nationalities concerning the formation of such a government-commission and to assume the headship of this commission. This I did. I informed Professor Lammasch of the content of my memorandum. He was in full agreement with it. We drafted together a program of several points which should provide the basis of his negotiations and the content of a pronouncement from the monarch. Lammasch began to confer immediately. But his efforts had no success. He told me that he had, indeed, received approval in principle from the South Slavs, the Poles, and the Germans; but that Dr. Kramař, representative of the Czechs, had told him that he was not able to take part in such a combination. He could undertake nothing without the approval of the future government of Czechoslovakia, of Messrs. Masaryk and Benesch, who at that time, so far as I know, were in Geneva and to whom Dr. Kramař was about ready to go. It was between the 20th and 25th of October that Professor Lammasch came to me in my apartment to tell me that his mission had failed. He requested me to notify the Emperor, who was not then in Vienna but in Gödöllö (Hungary). I drove with Professor Lammasch in an official car of the ministry of war, which had been placed at his disposal, to that ministry to report to the Emperor by telegraph. To my astonishment I found Professor Josef Redlich in the car when we got into it. He likewise was a friend of Lammasch and presumably had advised him during his last negotiations. On the way from my apartment to the war ministry Professor Redlich endeavored to persuade Professor Lammasch not simply to lay down his mission but to propose to the Emperor the formation of a regular Austrian government that would take the place of the cabinet of Hussarek von Heinlein. Redlich's essential argument was that because of the great authority Lammasch had as a pacificist an Austrian government headed by Lammasch would ensure more favorable peace terms to the monarchy. At first Lammasch was not very much inclined to agree to this proposal. He asked me for my opinion; I argued against it; but finally he gave in to Redlich and asked me to inform the Emperor in this sense. In my office in the ministry of war Lammasch and Redlich drew up a list of ministers. Redlich was to be minister of finance. Lammasch said that he attached particular importance to placing one of his closest friends, Dr. Ignaz Seipel, professor in the seminary for Roman Catholic priests in Salzburg, in the cabinet, probably as minister for social welfare. At that time Seipel was still completely unknown politically. But Lammasch also expressed the misgiving that the naming of a Catholic priest as minister—a thing that had never occurred previously in the history of Austria—could make certain difficulties; and he seemed inclined, in order to anticipate possible anticlerical opposition, to take a man of Jewish origin into the cabinet. In this connection he thought of Dr. Julius Tandler as minister for health. But when it was called to his attention that Josef Redlich himself was of Jewish origin, he gave up the idea of proposing Tandler.

Since the conference took place in the war ministry, I thought it necessary to notify the minister of war. He also came to my office and was present during a part of the conversation between Lammasch and Redlich. As minister of war he was not a member of the Austrian but of the joint Austro-Hungarian government which was distinct from the Austrian as well as from the Hungarian government.

On the basis of my telegraphic report Lammasch was actually authorized by the Emperor to form an Austrian government. It was the last government of the Austrian monarchy. Redlich became finance minister; Seipel minister for social welfare. The government was in office only fifteen days [Oct. 27–Nov. 10], but practically speaking it carried on no governmental activities since at the same time the governments of the new national states had already begun to function. Worth mentioning is only the fact that the Lammasch government took an active part in the formulation of the pronouncement by which Emperor Karl renounced the exercise of his monarchial rights. If I remember correctly Dr. Seipel told me later that he personally had formulated the decisive words.

This is everything essential that remains in my memory concerning the Lammasch government.

During the course of the proposals and negotiations described by Kelsen, Emperor Karl had taken one step along the lines suggested. On October 16 he signed a manifesto announcing that Austria would be transformed into a federal state, that until this could be done by statutory enactment the existing arrangements remained unaltered, and that his government had been given the duty of preparing the way for the reconstruction without delay. As a matter of fact rumors, reports, and ambiguous denials of an impending change in the form of the state had been circulating for months. The manifesto, however, was a self-defeating document; it provided that the new order would in no way affect the integrity of the Hungarian crown. There is evidence that this concession was forced by the threat of the Hungarian government to close the border to the shipment of foodstuffs. In this way the South Slavs were deprived of any hope that they could acquire their independence within the scope of the monarchy.[3]

The practically universal answer to the manifesto was: too late! Factually, despite other desperate last-minute moves by Emperor Karl, the manifesto fixed the date of his empire's dissolution.[4]

The Revolution in German-Austria

In contrast with the classical examples of revolution, particularly the French and the Russian, it might be argued that the events of the closing months of 1918 in what became the republic of Austria do not deserve to be styled a revolution. There were no barricades, no Bastille, and practically no violent outbreaks of fury or acts of vengeance. The old regime vanished, wounded to death on the battlefield and deserted by the non-German peoples of the empire. In view of the Roman Catholic priest and political leader Seipel's subsequent statement, repeated a thousand times, of his determination to clean out the "revolutionary rubbish" of 1918 and 1919, it is interesting to read the contemporary comment of another priest that "If there was a revolution, German-Austria did not make it."[5] The two statements are not mutually exclusive in a strict logical sense, but there is a wide disparity between them in what the Germans call *Gefühlswert*.

In the 'forties of this restless century it scarcely needs to be said that the concept of revolution has lost much of the—probably seeming—precision it once possessed. The formation of the National Socialist state in Germany has created a new and strange species which science may classify as "counterrevolutionary revolution." But if this modern perversion of the traditional notions is put aside,

[3] *Neue Freie Presse,* October 18, 1918 (A.M.), p. 1; August 28 (A.M.), p. 1; August 29 (A.M.), p. 1. For other details supplementing Kelsen's statement, see Brita Skottsberg, *Der österreichische Parlamentarismus* (Göteborg, 1940), pp. 142 ff.

[4] As many readers with a special interest in this field have recognized, the immediately foregoing section of the text is greatly indebted to Professor Oscar Jászi's, *The Dissolution of the Habsburg Monarchy* (Chicago, 1929).

[5] Monsignor August Schaurhofer, "Zum Streit um die Legitimität Oesterreichs," *Das Volkswohl,* vol. 12, Heft 9–10 (1921), 243.

it is necessary to recognize that the tendency of reality to confound the elaborate concepts of the student of social science was also felt in the period of the great upheavals which accompanied and followed the conclusion of the war of 1914–1918.

A line of thought which leads back at least to the writings of Lorenz von Stein made the differentiation between political revolution and social revolution a fundamental basis of a sociology of revolution. As conceived by von Stein a political revolution implied the establishment of political equality, whereas a social revolution essentially meant abolition of economic inequality.[6] This conception was introduced *ad hoc* to cover the development of modern industrial society. Marxism largely accepted this dichotomy and the writings of Marx's followers made it popular with the masses in Germany. But non-Marxian scholars also did not refuse to think in terms of this distinction. In the everyday political terminology of Central Europe—a language which the historian cannot afford to ignore—political revolution came to mean the overthrow of absolute or half-constitutional monarchy and the introduction of a democratic republic; social revolution, the overthrow of private capitalism by the proletariat and the introduction of a "Socialist" economy. Whether the latter implied preservation of democracy or establishment of a proletarian dictatorship was another question. Moreover, the concept of revolution seemed to carry the idea of sudden changes, but this connotation was apparently better preserved in the case of political revolution. At any rate it was not infrequently maintained that a social revolution might be regarded not as a sudden change but as a long process. This development had its political meaning since it often reflected the attitude of moderate Socialists who stood for social evolution but who, for reasons of political convenience, did not wish to forego the use of a word which was dear to large masses of their adherents.

Was there a political revolution in Austria? To be sure the changes in the political structure of the country were sudden and drastic enough; if there is still some hesitancy to apply the term unreservedly, one reason is the deep-seated unwillingness of all factors concerned to overhasten the development. As already indicated, the

---

[6] Lorenz von Stein, *Geschichte der sozialen Bewegungen in Frankreich* (Leipzig, 1850), Vol. I.

monarchy was the victim of a collapse rather than an overthrow. Moreover, it is the opinion of some students that a further distinction should be drawn. For example, Professor Hans Kelsen, probably the outstanding political scientist of Central Europe in the twentieth century, differentiates between "legal" and "political" revolutions. In his judgment there was a legal revolution because the so-called Renner Constitution of October 30, 1918 (cf. below, pp. 56–57), was established with no regard to the rules of the old constitution concerning altering it. Politically, however, there was no revolution because of the coöperation between Lammasch and the new state council.[7] Since many other scholars do not draw this distinction and since the fact of collapse rather than overthrow of the monarchy is not really decisive, it seems at least permissible to speak of a political revolution in Austria.

The question of the social revolution is more complicated, and the opinions more divergent. Friedrich Wieser, the famous Austrian economist and sociologist, considered it obvious that no social revolution had taken place in his country. In taking this attitude he undoubtedly had in mind the fact that on the whole the private capitalist order of economy emerged from the storms of the transition period fundamentally unchanged.[8] On the other hand, a British observer of the events chose the title *The Social Revolution in Austria* for his presentation of the early history of the young republic.[9]

As will be shown, the relations between the social classes in Austria underwent material changes. Legal protection of the workers on a scale unheard of before, works councils, chambers of labor, and other institutions considerably restricted the freedom of entrepreneurs in a great many respects. These changes, apart from the modest attempts at direct socialization, were conceived by at least one leading representative of the Austrian labor movement as new forms of a partially socialized economy.[10] Whether they may justly be called a social revolution or not is partly a verbal issue; *partly* because, on the other hand, the view may be held that all these trans-

---

[7] Conversation with Professor Kelsen in May, 1944.

[8] Friedrich Wieser, *Das Gesetz der Macht* (Wien, 1926), p. 315.

[9] C. A. Macartney, *The Social Revolution in Austria* (Cambridge, 1926). Macartney's somewhat unique explanation of his use of "social revolution" appears on pp. 206 ff. Briefly stated the revolution was brought about "by the inordinate printing of paper-money."

[10] Karl Renner, *Wege der Verwirklichung* (Berlin, 1929).

formations of the economic and social order were not elements of a social revolution, but, on the contrary, had the direct effect of staving off the threat of social revolution. In the light of these considerations it seems precarious to apply the designation "social revolution" to events in Austria in 1918 and 1919. Nevertheless, and perhaps to some extent because of deficiencies in the English language, it has been customary for more than twenty-five years to speak of the "Austrian revolution." As a matter of convenience that term has been used frequently in this work. It is hoped that it is not too much to ask the reader to keep in mind the qualifications just set forth and to understand that for lack of a more accurate designation the words are employed to cover primarily the political changes in 1918 and, occasionally, both the political and social changes during the first two years of Austria's existence as a republic.

Although some overlapping cannot be avoided, it is a major purpose of the remainder of this chapter and of Part Two of the work, immediately following, to summarize the political events which transformed and solidified most of the German territory of the empire into the republic of Austria. Part Two also records the monetary inflation which cursed the early years of the new state and some of the steps toward general economic readjustment and stabilization. Part Three presents in detail those other events which in the opinion of a few observers justify the use of the term "social revolution." Throughout these sections particular emphasis will be on the activities and achievements of the various branches of the working-class movement. Because of the deliberate misrepresentation of many of those activities and achievements, another major purpose of Part Three is to set down precisely what Dollfuss, Schuschnigg, and the other Clerical Fascists mutilated or destroyed in attempting to establish their "Christian" state.

As has been indicated, the defeats of the armies of the Central Powers had released the national revolutions and thus brought to a culmination the disintegration of Austria-Hungary. But in this process Vienna and the German provinces had lagged behind Prague, Agram, Warsaw, and their surrounding territories. A partial explanation for this may be found in the unwillingness of the German element to give up the ruling place which it had held for centuries.[11]

[11] Cf. Joseph Redlich, *Emperor Francis Joseph of Austria* (New York, 1929), p. 364.

There were cross currents at work, however. Of the conservative parties the Christian Socials were intimately connected with the Habsburg state; in fact, its strongest support. The Pan-Germans desired union with Germany in order to ensure German rule over the numerically much stronger non-German nations in the old empire.

The position of the Social Democratic party, which embraced workers from all the nationalities in Austria-Hungary, was more complicated. It was noted that at Brünn in 1899, it announced its nationality program, demanding national autonomy; but that far from having any effect on Habsburg policy, this program could not halt the national struggle even within the party, so that in 1912 the Czech group severed relations with Vienna and thus destroyed the international unity of the Austrian Social Democrats.[12] Then, when Franz Joseph and his advisers decided upon a war which they visualized as more than anything else a war for the maintenance of the monarchy, the workers' party, by supporting the war for many months, virtually supported the monarchy. Nevertheless, the leaders did not disregard the necessity for thorough reforms; and Renner, the *Grossösterreicher* as Seipel styled him, worked diligently devising ingenious schemes for administrative changes that would have aided in the maintenance of the position of the house of Habsburg. Underlying these plans was a sound economic idea. Austria-Hungary represented a large economic entity. Its dissolution would sever economic bonds that had existed for a long time. Not the least hard hit by the displacements and readjustments that would follow would have been the workers whom Renner represented. But Renner underestimated the power of the nationalist centrifugal forces.

The position of Otto Bauer, the leader of the left wing of the party, was determined by his conviction that the crash of the mosaic Habsburg state could not be averted. In January, 1918, under his guidance a new "nationality program of the left" was adopted which "as far as it was possible under conditions of war censorship pleaded for the self-determination of the individual nations in each of the seven language territories."[13] According to this program, constitu-

[12] Cf. Otto Bauer, "Viktor Adler als Parteimann," in *Victor Adlers Aufsätze, Reden und Briefe,* Heft 6 (Wien, 1929), p. xxvii, and Deutsch, *Geschichte der deutsch-österreichischen Arbeiterbewegung* (Wien, 1922), p. 34.

[13] Cf. "Ein Nationalitätenprogramm der 'Linken,'" *Der Kampf,* vol. 11 (April, 1918), 269. The number of nations which lived within the borders of the monarchy varies

ent national assemblies in each of those territories were to adopt a constitution and lay down the principles of administration. For the German parts of the monarchy the program proposed anschluss with Germany. Thanks in part to this program, when the German political parties of the monarchy had to face the beginning of general revolution in the stormy days of October, 1918, the Social Democrats found it easier to steer a course. As early as the third of that month their representatives submitted to the German parties a resolution stating that the German-Austrian workers recognized the right of self-determination of the Slavic and Roman nations in Austria, offering to enter into negotiations with the other peoples concerning the transformation of Austria into a federation of free national communities, and insisting most emphatically upon self-determination for the German element.[14] Since the "bourgeois" parties found these proposals suitable as a basis of further discussion it may be said that the initiative had passed into Socialist hands. It is worth noting, however, that the resolution had not urged the formation of a republic. Union with Germany was the immediate aim; propaganda for it filled the editorials of the *Arbeiter Zeitung* in the first half of October. Negotiations with the other German parties dragged out. The Social Democrats demanded a "parliamentary revolution";[15] that is, a meeting of the German members of the Austrian parliament as a provisional national assembly, but it was not until October 21 that this took place. In this meeting a proclamation to the German people in Austria, moved by the Social Democrats, was passed unanimously. It laid down the principle of self-determination for those people, announced the decision to form an independent German-Austrian state, and claimed for that state the entire territory populated by Germans, particularly the Sudeten districts. A constituent national assembly elected on the basis of a general and equal franchise was to adopt the constitution of the new state. In the meantime the Provisional Assembly was to represent the Germans in Austria.

During the discussion Viktor Adler read a declaration of his party. After pointing out that the demands of the Brünn nationality program were now becoming facts and reiterating the claim to self-

according to whether the groups which later formed Czechoslovakia and the group of South Slavs are considered as unities or are divided.

[14] *Tätigkeits-Bericht,* Heft 11 (Wien, 1919), pp. 4 ff.

[15] Cf. Bauer, *Die österreichische Revolution*, p. 75.

determination, the declaration continued with a statement of possibilities. The new state might form a free federation of independent peoples with its neighbors if they so desired. If they rejected this union, or accepted it under conditions which did not conform to the national or economic needs of the German element, then German-Austria, being economically not viable, would be compelled to join the German Reich. "We demand for the German-Austrian state complete freedom to choose between the two possible unions." In any case the new state must be a democratic one. Furthermore, the party served notice that in the coming elections for a constituent assembly, and in that assembly, it would stand for the organization of German-Austria as a democratic republic. The Christian Social speaker stressed the point that his party clung to the monarchical form of government as a matter of principle, but promised that its influence would be used for democratizing German-Austria. The representative of the Pan-Germans likewise declared that they remained convinced adherents of constitutional monarchy.[16]

The only other action of importance to this study taken on October 21 was the election of an executive committee to represent the German people of Austria before the government of the emperor and the other nations.

In evaluating the significance of this first meeting of the Provisional Assembly two points must be stressed.

1. The two strongest conservative parties, which were later to become the rulers of the republic for many years, declared themselves to be Monarchists only three weeks before that republic was proclaimed.

2. The Social Democrats did not demand immediate proclamation of the republic and left the way open either for the maintenance of an "Austrian" state which would include many nationalities, or for union with Germany.

In the light of the long-standing demand of the workers' party for a change to a republican form of government and the clear-cut statement in its declaration that this change remained one of its

[16] *Stenographische Protokolle über die Sitzungen der Provisorischen Nationalversammlung für Deutschösterreich*, 1918–1919, Vol. I, 6–11. The Pan-German was apparently intentionally unclear in failing to distinguish between Habsburg and Hohenzollern. These proceedings are cited hereafter as Provisorische Nationalversammlung, *Protokoll.*

objectives, the question rises why it did not demand on October 21 the more or less immediate proclamation of a republic. As already noted, the Socialist workers in Prague had demonstrated for the republic a week earlier, and there is no doubt that those in Vienna could easily have been brought into the streets for the same purpose at this time.

The explanation of the hesitant attitude of the Socialist leaders is to be found in the generally uncertain state of affairs and in several specific factors. First, these leaders had to face the fact that, in contrast with the situation in the Slavic territories, strong political groups in German-Austria still clung to the monarchy. Second, most, if not all, of the influential figures in the party favored union with Germany, and it was by no means certain what state form that country would elect.[17] Third, the leaders clearly understood the effects of the years of war upon the minds of the masses. They feared the outbreak of pent-up passions, particularly in the event that the government attempted forcibly to suppress demands for immediate promulgation of the republic. They believed that the result could be only blind destruction, and this they desired to prevent at almost any price. As far back as July 24, 1918, a spokesman of the party, Leuthner, had declared in parliament: "The revolution you [the government] arouse among the soldiers is only the revolution of destruction . . . we fight for a higher and increased culture, fear and hate this form of revolution."[18] And so, with all this in mind, the party declaration kept the door open to various possibilities and confined its statements on the republic to a reaffirmation of the position that, though that political form remained the goal, the intention on October 21 was still to work for it through the orderly democratic process of ballots for a constituent assembly and in the assembly.[19]

[17] As is generally known, several important German Socialists violently opposed a republic; in fact, Scheidemann relates in his memoirs (Philipp Scheidemann, *Memoiren eines Sozialdemokraten* [Dresden, 1928], Vol. II, 313) that Ebert, who later became the first president of the German republic, severely criticized its proclamation on the very day of the proclamation.

[18] Brügel, *op. cit.*, Vol. V, 348, quoting minutes of a secret meeting.

[19] That the Socialist position and tactics were clear to responsible non-Socialists may be seen from their writings. Professor Viktor Bibl of the University of Vienna points out in *Der Zerfall Oesterreichs* (p. 556) that the loud demands for proclamation of the republic from the crowd in front of the meeting place of the Provisional Assembly on October 30 came "not from the Social Democrats but from German-Austrian middle-class citizens and students." Dr. Zessner-Spitzenberg, a Catholic legitimist, notes that on October 21 the republican form of constitution was viewed by Viktor Adler as "a long-run objective." *Das Neue Reich,* vol. 3 (July 31, 1921), 833.

As subsequent events revealed, these tactics of the party contributed greatly to the reorganization of the state without street fighting and practically without bloodshed. In the days following the first meeting of the Provisional Assembly the workers in the factories became stronger. Delegations from the factories appeared in the parliament urging Socialist members to hasten the proclamation of the republic. The military expert of the party, Julius Deutsch, spent day and night in the parliament building dealing with excited soldiers of the Vienna garrison sent by their comrades to offer their help in overthrowing the emperor's government by force. Although Deutsch advocated a "go slow" policy to these soldiers, he had worked for months to build up a secret organization in the army through which he was able to obtain continual information on what steps the government and the military authorities contemplated against revolutionary activities. In the last days of October, Deutsch and his friends even drew up plans concerning the occupation of government buildings by soldiers led by Socialists. It is interesting to note, however, that before the collapse of the monarchy the executive committee of the party was never informed of the existence of Deutsch's organization.[20] And because of the cautious tactics of the party, effectuation of some of the organization's plans never became necessary.

As should be clear from the references to the delegations of workers and soldiers, the emphasis placed upon the cautious policies of the leadership has not been intended as a minimization of the existing revolutionary pressure. That pressure was felt by the Socialists and their opponents alike. It helps to explain the facts that the initiative for the first meeting of the Provisional Assembly came from the workers' party, and that the most important resolutions, drawn by Otto Bauer, were passed unanimously by a house in which that party had less than one-third of the seats. Moreover, because of the increasing pressure of "the street," the influence of the Socialists rose rapidly. In these days began the crystallization of that situation which for years would be characteristic for the new republic; the parliamentary position of Social Democracy was continuously strengthened by forces outside the parliament.

At the second meeting of the Provisional Assembly on October 30,

[20] Deutsch, *Aus Oesterreichs Revolution* (Wien, n.d.), p. 9.

the first constitution of German-Austria—drawn up by Renner—was adopted. Its essential provisions were: the Provisional Assembly was the only legislative body; the Assembly elected from its members an executive committee, the state council, which was the supreme executive body and possessed all the rights previously exercised by the emperor; the three presidents of the state council, the director of the chancery of the state council, and the notary of the council formed an executive directorate; the state council appointed the ministers, that is, the government of the state.[21] In spite of these thoroughgoing democratic provisions the parties shrank from officially proclaiming the republic. The Social Democratic speaker again stressed his party's adherence to the republic, but it remained understood that it would be for the Constituent Assembly finally to decide the form of government. Since the emperor's court had feared that the proclamation of the republic would be effected on October 30, army headquarters had tried to arrange for the preceding day a kind of plebiscite for the dynasty among the troops. This appeal found no response. In the few cases where it actually reached the soldiers it only hastened the decomposition of the army.

Other important business carried through during the second meeting of the Provisional Assembly included the adoption of a note to President Wilson (informing him of the formation of German-Austria, describing the national conditions in the Sudeten districts, and claiming these districts for the new state) and the election of the state council and its three presidents. The Socialists had 5 seats out of 20 on the council and one of the presidential posts. The latter was occupied by Seitz. On the same day the council issued a proclamation to the "German people in Austria" announcing the creation of the independent German and Austrian state, and declaring that it would without delay appoint a government which would start peace negotiations and take over the administration of the German territories in Austria. The greater part of the proclamation was devoted to admonitions to preserve order and to abstain from violence.

[21] *Die Verfassungsgesetze der Republik Deutschösterreich* (Wien und Leipzig, Herausgegeben von Hans Kelsen, 1919), Part I, 11–16; *Staatsgesetzblatt für den Staat Deutschösterreich,* 1918, Nr. 1. The title of this State Law Gazette had to be altered because the Entente forced the country to change its name from *Deutschösterreich* to *Oesterreich.* This alteration, to *Staatsgesetzblatt für die Republik Oesterreich,* appears for the first time on October 23, 1919. Both titles are cited hereafter at *StGBl.,* followed by year and number of the law, order, or decree.

This second session of the Provisional Assembly lasted from 3 to 8 P.M. Immediately thereafter the state council met. By 3:30 A.M. it had organized itself, appointed Renner as "director" of its chancery and Sylvester as its notary, discussed the general political situation, and drawn up a tentative list of ministers. After only a few hours, at 10 A.M. of October 31, it assembled again and appointed a ministry of thirteen, including representatives from the three largest parties, but only two Socialists. The old party leader, Viktor Adler, became secretary of foreign affairs; the leader of the trade unions, Hanusch, destined to become one of the most important figures in the history of the next two years, became secretary of social welfare.[22] Among the more interesting of the less conspicuous phases of these developments were the facts that the proclamation to the Germans in Austria was drawn up and submitted to the assembly by Otto Bauer, the leader of the left who only a year before had strongly attacked those who were inclined to take part in a "bourgeois" government; and that on November 1 the Socialist party congress empowered, *post factum,* its members of parliament and of the state parliaments to participate in the government of the new state as long "as this seems necessary for safeguarding the democratic achievements of recent days."[23]

On October 31, 1918, Lammasch, the last prime minister of the Habsburg monarchy, informed the state council that he had been empowered to transmit to it the agenda, as far as they concerned German-Austria. On the same day the state council assumed the supreme military power in the new state, but refused at the same time to have anything to do with the conclusion of an armistice. Its reasons were that it wished to decline even any formal responsibility for the war and that it thus hoped to create a more favorable situation in the coming peace negotiations. The armistice was finally concluded on November 3 in Padua. It was an ill-starred conclusion of an ill-starred war: by some mistake of army headquarters the Austrian troops stopped their activities more than twenty-four hours earlier than did the Italians. The result was that the Italians brought in thousands of war prisoners and greatly accelerated the disintegration of the imperial forces. Up to then headquarters had still

[22] *Neue Freie Presse,* October 31, 1918 (A.M.), pp. 2–5; (P.M.), pp. 1–2.
[23] *Tätigkeits-Bericht,* Heft 11 (Wien, 1919), p. 13; (the proceedings of the party congress of 1918 were never published).

hoped to restore the old order in Austria with the help of the returning army. But the disappointment of such hopes was already a foregone conclusion. On October 30 large groups of soldiers had joined with workers who had left the factories to demonstrate in huge meetings in the Inner City of Vienna. It is not clear whether or not they acted upon a call of the party. Otto Bauer contends that they did, whereas, according to other reports, the masses came spontaneously.[24] The latter version seems to correspond much better to the general attitude of the party at the time.

At any rate there can be no doubt that the wildest instincts of the so-called lower classes were rising, and that the home-coming soldiers formed the most radical and dangerous element. Thousands of men of different nationalities, filled with bitterness against the old regime, crossed the country; the unorganized demobilization led to various disorders, plundering, and wild shooting affrays. The very first action of the new state had to be an effort to neutralize the dangers to the community of the existence of bodies of unoccupied, excited men. Many of the soldiers who had as prisoners seen the revolution in Russia tried to precipitate similar developments in Austria. Even the peasants, the conservative Roman Catholic peasants, were revolutionized by the war at least to the extent that large groups among them demanded the republic.[25]

At the time of the meeting of the state council on November 9 the reports of the proclamation of the German republic on that day had not been confirmed; but by the next meeting, November 11, the Social Democrats were faced with the practical impossibility of adhering to their announced policy of leaving the decision on the political form of the new state to the Constituent Assembly. As Renner pointed out to the council: "The consequence of those events [November 9 in Germany] for us is that the whole proletariat will unanimously demand the same policy from us. Thereby our posi-

[24] Cf. Bauer, *Die österreichische Revolution,* p. 83; and *Tätigkeits-Bericht,* Heft 11 (Wien, 1919), p. 12.

[25] On November 11 the Tirolese national council unanimously adopted a resolution declaring itself in favor of a republican form of government for German-Austria, authorizing the dispatch of a telegram to the state council in Vienna demanding that that body openly take similar action as soon as possible, and requiring the immediate publication of the resolution in all daily papers in Tirol. The telegram was signed by Schraffl, the Christian Social president of the council. The text of the resolution is reprinted in Dr. R. Granichstaedten-Czerva's monograph, *Tirol und die Revolution* (Innsbruck, 1920), p. 16.

tion is threatened in the highest degree. . . . The state council is based upon a coalition of the bourgeoisie, the peasants, and the workers in order to lead us out of the catastrophe. . . . You know how strong are the tendencies among the working class not to tolerate a coalition with bourgeois parties. My party held urgent council this morning and came to the conclusion that this coalition is to be maintained as long as possible, because it is the sole guarantee to preserve us from anarchy." Seitz spoke to the same effect. After a prolonged debate the state council adopted a draft submitted by Renner of a law concerning the proclamation of the republic to be passed by the Provisional Assembly the next day. Even at this late date three of the six Christian Social members on the council voted against the republic.[26]

November 11 acquired further significance because of Emperor Karl's manifesto to the people of German-Austria:

> Since my accession I have been untiring in my efforts to lead my peoples out of the horrors of the war, for whose outbreak I bear no blame.
>
> I have not delayed the restoration of constitutional existence and have opened to the peoples the way to their independent state development.
>
> Now as ever filled with unalterable love for all my peoples, I will not oppose my person as a hindrance to their free development.
>
> I recognize in advance the decision German-Austria takes with reference to its form of state in the future.
>
> The people, through its representatives, has taken over the government. I renounce every participation in the business of the state.
>
> At the same time I remove my Austrian government from office.
>
> May the people of German-Austria create and consolidate the new organization in harmony and in a conciliatory spirit. The happiness of my peoples was from the beginning the aim of my warmest wishes.
>
> Only internal peace can heal the wounds of this war.[27]

Although the foregoing statement has often been termed an abdication, it has also been argued that it was not so intended. As Professor Kelsen and others report, it was suggested to the reluctant and hesitating emperor by Ignaz Seipel, future leader of the Christian

[26] Brügel, *op. cit.*, Vol. V, 393–396. Renner's statement also mentioned police reports which gave evidence on plans "concerning the existence of this state council," including plans of an unnamed "rightist" movement to eliminate it. Cf. *Neue Freie Presse*, November 12, 1918 (A.M.), p. 3.

[27] *Neue Freie Presse*, November 11, 1918 (P.M.), p. 1. The frequently quoted translation in the *New York Times* (November 14, 1918, p. 2) is "free" to the point of inaccuracy in several respects.

Socials and at that time minister of social welfare in the Lammasch government. A typical piece of Jesuitry, it recognizes "in advance the decision" of German-Austria on the form of the state, withdraws the "person" of Karl "as a hindrance" to the "free development" of the people, "renounces" participation in affairs of state, but carefully avoids the use of the word "abdicate." Within two years Karl was attempting a putsch to reëstablish a Habsburg throne—an aim which his wife, Zita, and his son, Otto, have continued to follow with unflagging zeal until the present moment.[28]

As planned by the state council the meeting of the Provisional Assembly on November 12 adopted a law[29] by which the republic was proclaimed, the privileges of the Habsburg family abolished, and the parliamentary bodies of the monarchy dissolved. Furthermore, it was decided that the elections for the Constituent National Assembly were to be held in February, 1919, on the basis of a general, equal, and proportional franchise without sex discrimination. Finally, the German-Austrian republic was declared a part of Germany. Although the law was passed unanimously, the Christian Socials announced through Miklas, subsequent president of the republic, that they would have preferred a decision on the form of the state by means of a plebiscite of all adults of both sexes. They added, however, that regardless of the decision of the Provisional Assembly they would loyally subordinate themselves to the new state authority.[30] The details of the violation of this pledge by many of their most prominent leaders will fill scores of subsequent pages of this book.

After the transactions just outlined the members of the Provisional Assembly moved to the ramp of the parliament building in order publicly to proclaim the republic. Two presidents of the state council, the Socialist Seitz and the Pan-German Dinghofer, spoke to the huge crowds which filled the Ringstrasse; it may or may not be significant that the Christian Social president did not join his colleagues. Immediately after the speeches, members of the Red Guard tried to storm the parliament. In the wild shooting which followed two persons were killed and large numbers injured. This was, in fact, the first organized attempt of the Communist party to seize power and to proclaim the dictatorship of the proletariat. The ill-

[28] Cf. Imre Balassa, *Death of an Empire* (New York, 1937), p. 152.
[29] *StGBl.*, 1918, Nr. 5.
[30] *Neue Freie Presse*, November 13, 1918 (A.M.), p. 5.

prepared undertaking failed and its initiators subsequently tried to pretend that the whole affair resulted from a misunderstanding.

At this point, and again partly because of the success which propaganda for Otto Habsburg has found from time to time among self-styled democrats in high places, it is necessary to emphasize the obvious. The republic of German-Austria was not a continuation of the Austro-Hungarian monarchy nor of the Austrian monarchy. It has been shown that the leaders of the most active and powerful political group, the workers' party, had been forced by events in Germany to move more rapidly than they wished in changing the form of the state; but it must not be forgotten that they had been urged to it by Tirol, the province which for centuries had been considered a symbol of loyalty to the empire. In the words of an eminent Austrian historian: "The death struggle of the Danube Monarchy has come to its end. She was . . . gravely sick for a long time, sentenced to collapse. 'We were compelled to die,' said Ottokar Czernin, 'we could choose only the manner of death and we have chosen the most terrible.' One can dispute whether we could really have chosen and whether the end could have been even more terrible. But this is absolutely correct: the Habsburg Empire was no longer capable of life; it had become an anachronism."[31] Recognition of that incapacity for life was embodied in the change to a republic; fear of the incapacity for existence of the vestigial state was reflected in the simultaneous announcement that it was a part of a new German republic. The *Grossösterreicher* Renner even wished to designate the new country as the "Alpine republic." There remained, of course, some sympathy for the Habsburgs and the monarchic form, particularly in Christian Social circles in Vienna; the Catholic party as a whole desired to preserve the Austrian name. But such wishes were not the decisive factor. Clemenceau insisted that there must be an "Austria" to punish, and the Allies forced the new state to alter its name from "German-Austria" to "Austria," to sign a peace treaty, and to obligate itself to pay such indemnities as might be fixed by the International Reparations Commission. Among the paradoxical, not to say nonsensical, consequences of these developments was the fact that "Austria" was compelled to cede Moravia and Bohemia to Czechoslovakia—territory which the republic had never possessed.

[31] Viktor Bibl, *Der Zerfall Oesterreichs* (Wien, 1922), Vol. II, 558.

From the viewpoint of international law German-Austria cannot be considered as a continuation of the Austrian monarchy, much less of the Austro-Hungarian monarchy. Under international law it is not sufficient that the name of a state be preserved; it is also necessary for the idea of continuity that the geographical area and the population remain roughly the same. German-Austria had about 27 per cent of the area and 24 per cent of the population of the Austrian monarchy. So far as the makeup of the population may be used as a criterion of continuity, Czechoslovakia more nearly conformed. The truth is that the Austrian monarchy had disappeared by disintegration and dismemberment. But in the intervening years there have been numerous attempts to demonstrate that the social traditions of the monarchy were carried over into the republic and that it was a great misfortune that the political form was altered.[32] As will be shown in a subsequent chapter (see below, pp. 188–190), the first part of this argument is without foundation. With reference to the second part, it suffices to note that I am in complete agreement with the judgment of Professor Bibl quoted above. Only persons who for political, and occasionally economic, reasons are interested in the establishment of a Catholic Habsburg monarchy in Central Europe are interested in maintaining the political and legal fiction that the republic of Austria was a continuation of the Austrian monarchy. Such an establishment would only restore a focal point of infection—with all that that implies.

With the establishment of the republic only one problem was solved; there remained a multitude of others which were not even near solution. Contrariwise, it was precisely on the day of the proclamation of the republic that the imminence of the Bolshevist threat to it was revealed to the most skeptical. The increasing strength of this threat in the next several months made it the most acute issue of internal policy. Everything depended on the attitude of the Social Democratic party. The old leader, Viktor Adler, died on the eve of the proclamation of the republic. Otto Bauer was his successor in the government as minister of foreign affairs; he was to become Adler's successor as the chief leader of the party after a period of not quite two years in which Renner's influence was more dominant. Because

[32] For example, E. K. Winter, "The Rise and Fall of Austrian Labor," *Social Research,* vol. 6 (Sept., 1939), 316–340.

of Bauer's well-known and openly avowed left-wing sympathies it was feared that he might attempt to bring about a Bolshevik revolution in Austria; but, as the history of the subsequent months shows, he was determined not to lead his country in that direction. He regarded the events in Austria in the autumn of 1918 as primarily a national revolution, but also as containing elements of a social revolution not present in the actions of the Poles, Czechs, Slovaks, and Yugoslavs. The destruction of absolutism, the abolition of the remnants of the feudal system, and the victory of democracy were in his opinion the necessary conditions for the national emancipation of the German people; that is, its unification in one German state. Therefore, anschluss with Germany was actually what Bauer expected from, and desired to be the outcome of, the dismemberment of the Austrian empire.[33] To him this implied the rejection of the plans and dreams of Bolshevism. It is necessary to keep this fundamental position clearly in mind, for the ensuing struggle often compelled the party to tactical moves which could convey the impression that it had yielded to at least some of the demands of the Communists.

But not Bolshevism alone endangered the new-formed state. Desperate food conditions, and the throttling of the inflow of raw materials demanded prompt solutions. Unemployment—resulting from demobilization, lack of raw materials, and cessation of war industries—presented itself economically and politically as a complex and most urgent problem. And it was widely recognized even before the new state had been founded that its independent economic existence was highly dubious. In fact, the question, is Austria viable, was to be continuously discussed for the next twenty years; that is, throughout the whole lifetime of the first republic. The Provisional Assembly had adopted a temporary constitution, laws were passed, decrees issued; but the territory of the state to which these legal acts should apply was still unknown. In the north, the east, and the south the borders separating German-Austria from the Czech, Hungarian, and Yugoslav states were still to be drawn by the peace treaty or by force. Anschluss, it became clear at once, was to hang fire for the

[33] Otto Bauer, "Die alte und die neue Linke," *Der Kampf,* vol. 13 (July, 1920), 254. "We did not have to proclaim a new revolutionary slogan but to stick to the slogan proclaimed by the nationality program of the 'Left' as early as January 1918: the slogan 'anschluss with Germany!' " See also his *Oesterreichische Revolution,* pp. 109–115.

time being. Germany also feared to carry it through before the peace negotiations were brought to an end. As though this type of border difficulty were not enough, another variety soon demonstrated that the republic had inherited the worst vice of the empire. The centrifugal nationalist forces which had torn asunder the body of the old monarchy reappeared as "state particularism": the tendencies of the tiny provinces of German-Austria to become independent or to join one of the neighboring states.

With all these problems the workers' party had to deal immediately. In the Habsburg state, of course, it had also been necessary to take some position on important problems. But then the party had not been responsible for making and carrying through a policy; like all oppositions it exerted most of its energy in criticism. Now the situation had drastically changed. As already brought out, this party with less than one-third of the votes in the Provisional Assembly was actually the most important party. It had taken the lead in founding the new state, partly against open opposition from the other parties; it had insisted on the maintenance of a concentration government, against opposition from some of its rank-and-file members. Now it had to assume any and every responsibility for the policy of a state which was in fact its state.

The attempts of the Socialists to cope with the problems just enumerated, as well as with some others, will be discussed in Part Two. In turning to that discussion it is appropriate to recall the generalization with which this study was introduced and to amplify it by pointing out that for about two years following October 21, 1918, the history of the workers' movement and the general history of Austria are inseparable. Indeed, it is permissible to recast the oft-quoted phrase of a famous Austrian poet that the Austrian state during the Revolution of 1848 was in the camp of Radetsky's army (Thy camp, that is Austria), and to say that during the "revolutions" of 1918–1919 the newly erected Austrian state was in the camp of the Austrian Social Democratic Workers' party.

PART TWO: TOWARD POLITICAL AND ECONOMIC STABILIZATION

CHAPTER IV

Struggle Against Bolshevism

As pointed out in the preceding chapter, the changes that brought German-Austria into existence lacked many of the violent characteristics frequently associated with revolutions. As the form the new state was likely to assume became more definite, as the limits of what the most "radical" element in the concentration government—the Socialists—was willing and able to do became more obvious, another typical feature of revolutionary processes also became more obvious. In other words, forces that wished to push the developments further became more active. For the sake of brevity these forces may collectively be called Bolshevism.

Unfortunately the term Bolshevism, like revolution, is by no means unambiguous. In the passion of political struggles it has been applied to a great variety of things, sometimes quite unjustifiably. For the present purposes Bolshevism means the ideology and tactics of those groups which tried to remove the young Austrian parliamentary democracy in order to replace it by the dictatorship of the proletariat. The leading representative of these tendencies in Austria was the Communist party, organized among those radical groups which had themselves come into existence during the big strike of January, 1918. This party openly professed itself to be a Bolshevist organization, but Bolshevist ideas extended far beyond its limited membership. The idea of violence had been implanted in the minds of great numbers of Austrian workers by the four years of war. It was only natural that many Social Democrats among them were in favor of a proletarian dictatorship. The struggle against Bolshevism, therefore, was in the main the struggle of the Social Democratic party against the Communist party, but at the same time it was also a fight against the Bolshevist tendencies within the ranks of the former.

There are, of course, various ways of combating Bolshevism. The German Social Democrats chose the way of force and succeeded in smashing the Communist risings with the help of the old army. These events created two hostile parties among the German working class which fought each other with bitter hatred until the day both were swallowed by the counterrevolutionary victory of the Nazis. But an outstanding characteristic of the Austrian party was its will to preserve the unity of the workers' movement. This was the great bequest of its founder and leader, Viktor Adler. Therefore, although it was prepared to (and did) use violence *in extremis,* it very carefully tried to find a way to fight Communism, not by physical extermination of its adherents, but by a policy which would keep the workers within the Social Democratic organizations. Such a course was more difficult than that followed in Germany, particularly since it was exposed to misinterpretation. Nevertheless it was adopted and on the whole successfully carried through until the influence of Bolshevism as an independent political force was broken.

In the first days of November, Communist activities were mainly concentrated in the so-called Red Guard. This group organized a raid on the office of the editor of a bourgeois paper and searched some buildings, but because of lack of leadership, political experience, and any clearly conceived aim failed to do any real harm. As previously noted, the Red Guard's attempt to establish the dictatorship of the proletariat on the day of the proclamation of the republic was so ridiculous and so ill-prepared that the Communists later tried to disclaim any responsibility for it. Immediately afterward, however, they published leaflets charging the Socialists Deutsch and Glöckel with preventing the establishment of the rule of the proletariat in Austria.[1]

In the following months unemployment grew rapidly. In December, 1918, there were 24,503 unemployed in Vienna, 45,675 in Austria. In February, 1919, the respective figures reached 113,905 and 161,803; in May, 131,500 and 185,235.[2] These increases in joblessness were certainly a source of radicalism and might well have caused the Communists to believe their numbers were being augmented. Nevertheless they did not present any candidates at the elections to the Constituent National Assembly in February, 1919.

[1] Julius Deutsch, *Aus Oesterreichs Revolution* (Wien, n.d.), pp. 43–44.

[2] Karl Pribram, "Die Sozialpolitik im neuen Oesterreich," *Archiv für Sozialwissenschaft und Sozialpolitik,* vol. 48 (1920–1921), 634. (This journal is cited hereafter as *AfSS.*) It is true that to a certain degree the unemployment was artificial since the figures included many women who had returned to their households at the end of the war but continued to draw their unemployment benefits. Such niceties did not affect the propaganda use made of the data.

The Communists helped, however, to precipitate major disturbances in that month in the largest Austrian provincial towns, Linz and Graz. In both cities shops and warehouses were plundered. Military assistance was required to reëstablish order and the secretary of war, Deutsch, went to Graz. In the course of the disturbance six men lost their lives.

The most serious Bolshevist threat, however, was brought about by developments in the neighboring states of Hungary and Bavaria. On March 21, the dictatorship of the proletariat was proclaimed in Hungary. The democratic Karolyi government had resigned because of the territorial demands of the Entente. Interestingly enough, in the light of some Marxist teachings, the Communists had rapidly found large adherence in this little-developed country. The Socialists were pushed back and had to play second fiddle in a government under Communist leadership. Immediately Communist pressure upon the Austrian Socialist party increased considerably. It grew still stronger during the three weeks of soviet rule in Bavaria (April 7–May 2). But the Austrian Socialists were not taken by surprise. They had made their preparations subsequent to the elections of February, 1919. The first move had been to transform the loose concentration government which had included all the German parties of the old monarchy into a firm coalition with the Christian Socials alone, in this way maintaining the basic principle of their tactics as proclaimed by Karl Renner on November 11. The second was to meet the opposition within their own ranks against coöperation with a bourgeois party and at the same time to strike the Communists—who noisily repeated the slogan of the Russian revolution: "All power to the soviets!"—with their own weapon. Precisely put, they decided to use the soviets as a club against the Communists. To a world which has subsequently seen a pact between rulers whose politest terms for each other had for years been arsonist and murderer this may seem quite a simple trick, but in 1919 it did not. Moreover, unfortunately, it requires a somewhat lengthy explanation.

Workers' councils (soviets) had been founded in Austria during the January strike. They were created chiefly under the influence of the left wing of the Socialist party with the purpose of pushing it toward a more energetic peace policy. In November, 1918, they were formed all over the country. Originally, eligibility to them was based on membership in the Social Democratic party and subscription to the *Arbeiter Zeitung.* In the first months after the revolution the councils in Vienna and in the individual industrial localities and districts had almost no connection with one another; their activities lay chiefly in economic fields such as food supply, housing, and price control. On February 19, 1919, however, a meeting of the councils of Linz requested the executive committee of the party to summon a general conference of all councils in Vienna for March 1. By this time the growing Communist propaganda had crystallized the determination of the Socialist party to make its clever move.

The man who seemed predestined to execute this difficult and delicate task was Friedrich Adler. Adler enjoyed an almost unbelievable measure of popularity with the Austrian proletariat. His release from prison had been for months a major demand of the Austrian workers for he was generally regarded as the hero who had dared singlehanded to challenge the absolutism of the war government. After he had been given his freedom on November 1, 1918, the Communists immediately offered him the leadership of their young party. He rejected it. This refusal most materially influenced the fate of the Communist party, indeed, of the whole working-class movement in Austria. Prior to the Vienna conference of workers' councils, however, Adler proposed to the Communists a plan under which the constitution of the councils would be altered to admit them. This was a trap. However, the Communists did not recognize the plan for what it was and delightedly accepted it. Now Adler had solemnly announced that the new arrangements transformed the central conference of the councils into a "parliament of the working class"; that is, a working-class body comprising not only Socialist but also Communist delegates.[3] Despite the attractive phrase there was an all-important difference between the central conference of the councils and an ordinary parliament; and this difference was an essential part of the scheme, not to say plot, of the Socialists. The members of the councils were not to be elected on political party tickets. Furthermore, they were not to be bound by the discipline of any party. Thus, although factually the Social Democrats had a majority in the councils, and used it, the legalistically nonpartisan

[3] Cf. Adler's speech to the party congress of 1924; *Parteitag, 1924,* p. 212.

organization of the councils enabled them to weather some radical excursions in the councils without loss of authority. More important was the fact that through the councils the party could present its policy to the workers as one approved by the whole working class. This fact resulted from the circumstance that their majority in the councils generally enabled the Social Democrats to compel the Communists to obey what was called the "judgment of the proletarian democracy." Finally, the institution of the councils served as a vent for the criticisms brought by the workers against the coalition government and rendered the coöperation between the Social Democrats and the Christian Socials much smoother.

There is no doubt that this policy was dangerous. The party formally subordinated itself to the decisions of the councils. Certainly the moment could have come when the party itself would have fallen prisoner to the forces it had unleashed. The reason why this never became true will be made clear when the relations between the party and the trade unions and the specific part played within the whole working-class movement by the latter are discussed (see below, pp. 293–308). The point here is, of course, that through the moves outlined above the Socialists had completed a major step in their preparations for meeting the Communists.

Immediately after soviet rule had been established in Hungary Béla Kun's government addressed itself by telegraph "to all, all, all" requesting other countries to follow the example set by the Hungarian workers. Actually, the message was intended in the first instance for Austria; Béla Kun strongly hoped that the dictatorship of the proletariat would be established there within a very short time. The machinery just described was now put in motion; Béla Kun's request was answered by the central executive committee of the workers' councils on March 23. In that answer appear the following decisive sentences.

> You have appealed to us to follow your example. We should feel happy do so, but at this hour we regret not to be able to. In our country the food supply is exhausted. Even our scant bread supply is entirely based on the food trains the Entente has been sending us. Thereby we have become completely the slaves of the Entente. If we followed your advice today, Entente capitalism would with cruel inexorableness cut off our last supply and deliver us to the catastrophical ravages of hunger. We are convinced that the Russian soviet republic would do everything to help

us. But before its help could reach us, we should be starved. Therefore, we are in a much more difficult situation than you. Our dependence upon the Entente is absolute. . . . All our wishes are with you. With burning hearts we watch events and trust that the cause of Socialism will be victorious. Also, we are ready to fight and prepared to fulfill what historic necessity will demand.[4]

These effusive words should deceive no one; as previous and subsequent events show, the answer was actually a refusal and as such was soon understood in Budapest.[5] Nevertheless, a distinction was drawn between following the example of Hungary as a soviet state and giving it aid. Béla Kun's ambassador was received, a trade treaty was entered into, and considerable quantities of industrial products were sent from Austria to Hungary.[6] Naturally, these activities have been interpreted by opponents of the Social Democrats as proof that the latter desired to establish a proletarian dictatorship but were afraid to do so. An examination of the evidence in this and other sections of this book will, it is believed, demonstrate that the interpretation just stated is incorrect. At any rate, since Hungary was preparing for war against the Czechs and the Rumanians, and since it was of great strategic importance for her to secure the maximum degree of influence over Austria, that is, over Austrian industry and stores of arms, Béla Kun began preparations for a coup that would proclaim the dictatorship of the proletariat in Vienna.

Now the Austrian Socialists were sincere democrats in their aims, but at the same time they had a keen sense for questions of power. They saw clearly that without sufficient military force at their disposal they could be swept away within a short time either by a revolutionary movement from the "left" or a reactionary conspiracy from the "right." Against attempted violence they were prepared to use violence, but the huge military force of the Austrian empire had virtually ceased to exist in November, 1918. Therefore, in the first days of the revolution, Julius Deutsch began to build up a new army, the so-called Volkswehr or People's Army. Despite this name it was a professional army. The soldiers were paid six kronen a day. The organization of the new forces was to a great degree the work

[4] Quoted in Julius Braunthal, *Die Arbeiterräte in Deutsch-Oesterreich* (Wien, 1919), pp. 44–45.

[5] Cf. R. Bernasek *et al., Oesterreich, Brandherd Europas* (Zurich, 1934), p. 20, for a Communist evaluation of this reply as "refusing and excuse making."

[6] Otto Bauer, *Die österreichische Revolution* (Wien, 1923), pp. 137–138.

of the soldiers' councils which had arisen from Deutsch's secret military organization and which had soon achieved considerable power. In the October days the soldiers' councils even demanded that they be regarded as of equal status with the Provisional Assembly; they wanted to take part in legislation; they actually assumed some administrative powers. But when the new army, which in the beginning numbered scarcely more than five to six thousand men, was organized, Deutsch ordered new elections to the soldiers' councils; and his helpers gradually prevailed upon these groups to subordinate themselves in all important matters to the decisions of the workers' councils. Notwithstanding this the soldiers' councils remained an important part in the Social Democratic scheme. The officers of the old army were to a very large extent Monarchists; they watched the political development with poorly concealed disgust and hatred. The breakup of the monarchy had deprived them of their positions and destroyed their social standing. On the other hand, the commanding staff of the new army had to be chosen from old officers. Thus it became the chief task of the soldiers' councils to control the officers in order to prevent the new force from being used against the republic. At the same time, the Socialists made sincere efforts to reëstablish and improve military discipline in preparation for possible emergencies. They emphasized their position that the "control" functions of the councils were to be regarded as a transitory device.[7]

Another problem for the new army resulted from its overhasty creation: there were among the soldiers many men of dubious moral quality. This fact was especially emphasized by hostile critics. Deutsch slowly succeeded in eliminating these elements. Still other difficulties arose from the unavoidability of including Communists in the Volkswehr. Even the Red Guard was incorporated, and in the constantly fluctuating situation it temporarily proved politically impossible to prevent most of the Communists from becoming united in the notorious 41st Battalion. Radical influence remained great. In the first months after the formation of the republic, soldiers even more than workers were likely to succumb to the radical influence. Every action of the Volkswehr against the "left" had to be carefully

[7] Cf. J. Frey, *Revolutionäre Disziplin* (Wien, 1919), p. 10. Some light on the success of the efforts to establish discipline appears below, pp. 76, 77, 81, 114, n. 5, but of course criticism persisted.

mooted since the results could never be foretold with certainty. The extreme difficulty and complexity of the situation may be perceived from the fact that the strict prohibition against sending arms to Hungary was frequently disregarded by Social Democratic workers in the Wiener-Neustadt district, then practically on the border, and that these violations were winked at by at least some of their highest leaders.[8] As events of mid-April and mid-June were to demonstrate the skill displayed by Deutsch and his associates in dealing with complicated situations and partly unreliable material proved highly successful in days of real emergency.

Communist propaganda was successful in those groups among which there was naturally much discontent: the unemployed, the invalids, the home-coming war prisoners. Large and vehement demonstrations were carried out. Finally, committees which remained anonymous (an interesting side light on Communists who did not dare to operate under the name of their party) called a mass demonstration in front of the parliament building for April 17, Holy Thursday. In spite of the wild rumors which crept through the city, the first preparations of the government were inadequate. Several thousand people assembled on the Ringstrasse and, in faithful repetition of what the Red Guards had attempted in November, 1918, stormed the parliament building and set it afire. A struggle with the police ensued in which 5 policemen and 1 woman were killed, and 56 persons seriously wounded.[9] After several hours of disorder Deutsch resolved to call out the Volkswehr. The first detachment of troops also proved insufficient, but when reinforcements arrived, the police were withdrawn and the Volkswehr without great further difficulties dissipated the demonstrants, occupied the parliament building, and reëstablished order. The government and the creator of the Volkswehr, Deutsch, felt that a very risky undertaking had been successfully carried through.[10] No one in that excited time, with soviet governments in Budapest and in Munich, could have prophesied with any real feeling of certainty what the attitude of the Volkswehr would be. But the new army, as was recognized by the entire Vienna press, did its duty to the complete satisfaction of everyone except that band of civil-war mongers which took its orders from

[8] Bauer, *op. cit.*, p. 138.
[9] *Reichspost*, April 18, 1919, p. 2; *Parteitag, 1919*, p. 46.
[10] Deutsch, *op. cit.*, p. 100.

Budapest. The comments of the conservative Catholic *Reichspost,* frequently caustically condemnatory of the Volkswehr as a Social Democratic "party guard," are particularly interesting for the praise showered upon it.

> The Bolshevist rehearsal could not have found a worse reception among the people of Vienna. This fact is emphasized by the correct attitude of the Vienna Volkswehr. It is known that within the Vienna Volkswehr formations are to be found individuals who belong to the radical Socialist wing. Today two companies of the "Red Guard" from the Rossauer barracks performed their duty in maintaining the peace in the same faultless fashion as other Volkswehr groups, for example, the 26th Battalion. Against the Bolshevik mob the Volkswehr acted decisively; with reference to the public it conducted itself generally with a tact worthy of acknowledgment. In numerous places the Volkswehr people made use of their firearms against plunderers. During the evening the Volkswehr undertook the safeguarding of order and performed the assignment thoroughly. . . .[11]

Subsequent to the events just described the Communists in the central workers' council of Vienna moved a vote of lack of confidence in the Social Democratic members of the government, but they could muster only a small minority of supporters. Contrary to their hopes the workers' council approved a proclamation of the Socialist party's executive committee which strongly protested against the rise of violence that could lead only to the occupation of Austria by the troops of the Entente. At the same time the proclamation stressed the willingness of the Socialist ministers to resign; but only if ordered to do so by the majority of the workers' representatives, not by a few thousand noisy demonstrants.[12]

On the basis of the facts already presented it is clear that the Socialists were resolved to oppose Communist attempts to establish a proletarian dictatorship. But it is certainly true that they often succumbed to the temptation to pursue a double policy: on one hand, they tried to suppress Communist activities, as well as that could be done under the prevailing circumstances; on the other, they tried to avail themselves of the growing radicalism in order to intimidate the bourgeois parties and to reach their political aims. In fact, a great deal of the history of the social legislation of the

---

[11] *Reichspost,* April 18, 1919, pp. 2, 3.

[12] Braunthal, *op. cit.* pp. 45 ff.

republic reflects this second tendency. An especially good example was the action taken by the executive committee of the workers' councils when it believed that the parliamentary discussion of the works councils bill was being dragged out. Under pressure from Friedrich Adler the executive committee unanimously adopted a sharp and threatening resolution which contained the following sentences:

> The workers' organizations in German-Austria have always tried to carry through the revolutionary changes which have had to follow the war by negotiations and legal determination of the new forms. But we warn the bourgeois parties not to interpret erroneously this self-imposed restriction of the proletariat. There is inexorable resolution in the working class actually to make that step toward socialism which the defeat of Austrian and German imperialism has rendered possible. *No arithmetical accidents can stop the working class.* That there is a bourgeois majority in the committees of the national assembly cannot change anything in the real distribution of power in the state. The proletariat feels itself to be the decisive class in the state and is resolved to claim its due influence under any circumstances; it will not let itself be deprived of its rights by a few representatives of exploiting capitalism in the national assembly.[13]

This resolution roused a storm of indignation among the other parties in parliament. The Christian Socials protested against the intimidation of "the freely elected representatives of our Christian German people." The Pan-Germans spoke of a "criminal attempt to eliminate democracy, that is, the rule of the whole people." The situation was paradoxical to say the least. The Socialists, who were true democrats, threatened their enemies with dictatorial steps; the Christian Socials and Pan-Germans, whose adherence to democracy had been dubious in the past and would become still more dubious in the future, professed to be unflinching defenders of democracy and the parliamentary system. Two weeks later Friedrich Adler tried to undo the unfortunate impression of the resolution by a careful explanation of what was meant by the "arithmetical accidents." He argued that considering the separatist tendencies in Tirol, and, on the other hand, the possibility that the industrial German districts occupied by Czechs would finally be incorporated in German-Austria, the whole situation in parliament might change

[13] Quoted in *ibid.,* pp. 46–47. Italics mine.

and the Socialists attain a majority.[14] Compared with the plain words of the resolution this was undoubtedly a retreat, and the promptitude with which it was effected showed that the Socialists felt that this time bluffing had gone too far. Meanwhile preparations were under way for another test of Socialist policies and of the sincerity of their claims that they were firmly resolved to crush all attempts to establish the dictatorship of the proletariat or to destroy parliamentary democracy in Austria.

The defeat of the Communist coup on April 17 had induced Béla Kun to go to work more carefully. His representative, a certain Bettelheim, came to Vienna, dismissed the executive of the Austrian Communist party and established a secret "directory" which began to organize the putsch. The Communist plan was based upon the demand of the Entente that the number of men in the Volkswehr—which in the meantime had reached about 16,000—be reduced 25 per cent by June 15, 1919. Deutsch began the dismissals. Thereupon the Communists initiated a large-scale propaganda campaign among the soldiers, hoping to win over the army and thus to succeed in the coup which they planned for June 15. They arranged meetings in every battalion of the Volkswehr, a big protest assembly in the Concert House and, on June 5, a demonstration of the Volkswehr before the parliament building. Since the demand that the Volkswehr be reduced was naturally very unpopular among the soldiers and much disliked by the workers, the Communists succeeded in inducing a good number of Social Democratic soldiers to take part in the demonstration. In the general assembly of the Vienna soldiers' councils Deutsch had to face an unusually large minority (71 against 174) voting for a Communist resolution. When, moreover, the Social Democrats learned that arrangements were being made to occupy the Austro-Hungarian frontier with Hungarian troops, which, if necessary, could be led into Austria to support the Communists, they decided to strike. On June 12 they declared to the representative of the Entente that dismissals from the army had to be stopped. In view of the circumstances the Entente raised no protest. On the following day the workers' council of Vienna met. Friedrich Adler demanded that the Communists dis-

[14] Cf. Friedrich Adler, "Die Zufälle der Arithmetik und das Schicksal der Sozialisierung," *Der Kampf,* vol. 12 (May, 1919), 257 ff.

close what was planned for the next Sunday (June 15). When they refused, the council adopted a proclamation in which it strongly denounced the "small groups which, mostly under cover of anonymity," prepare a putsch.[15] The council stressed its claim that it was the only body entitled to organize mass action of the Vienna workers and protested against attempts to destroy the unity of the Volkswehr. On June 14 the Communists, again anonymously, issued an appeal to the soldiers stating that the hour of liberation for the working class had come, that the revolutionary workers of Vienna would demonstrate for the establishment of a soviet dictatorship on June 15, and that "every Volkswehr man was obligated to participate in this demonstration, weapon in hand." Furthermore, secret Communist instructions became known to the Socialists according to which the soldiers were supposed to support the workers during the street fighting.[16]

At this juncture the workers' council of Vienna, together with the executive committee of the national conference of workers' councils, issued another proclamation declaring the Communists responsible for the impending mischief.[17] In fact, in these days the workers' councils actually fulfilled the expectations the Socialists had cherished when they created them as a supreme country-wide organization of the workers. The Communists demanded the dictatorship of the workers' councils. But this dictatorship became impossible when the workers' councils themselves rejected it.[18] Had the Communists been an independent Austrian party they would have dropped their plans, but they were compelled blindly to obey the orders they received from abroad.

Now the Socialists again acted vigorously. On the night of June 14–15 the Socialist Eldersch, secretary of state for interior affairs, arrested 115 leaders of the Communist party. The next morning Deutsch occupied the Inner City with troops. The Communist 41st Battalion was confined to barracks and troops posted nearby were ordered to prevent it from leaving, if necessary by force. Despite Deutsch's precautions more than 5,000 men tried to storm police headquarters. A short clash ensued in which 20 persons were killed,

[15] Braunthal, *op. cit.*, p. 49; Deutsch, *op. cit.*, p. 103.
[16] *Reichspost*, June 17, 1919, p. 6; Deutsch, *op. cit.*, pp. 103, 104.
[17] Text quoted in Braunthal, *op. cit.*, pp. 50–51.
[18] Cf. Bauer, *op. cit.*, p. 139.

whereupon the crowds dissipated immediately. When the members of the Communist battalion learned what had happened they attempted to force their way to the street, but Socialist soldiers' representatives, revolvers in hand, successfully defended the gate of the barracks. The Communist revolution was at an end. And again the Volkswehr "party guard" had demonstrated that at a time of real emergency it was a guardian of republican institutions.

A fortnight later the second national conference of the German-Austrian workers' councils assembled in Vienna. The Communists moved: "The second conference of the German-Austrian Workers' Council resolves: (1) German-Austria is a soviet republic; (2) the executive committee is ordered to carry through all necessary measures to this effect."[19] It was only a rear guard action. In a long debate the majority of the conference severely criticized the Communist policy and approved the tactics of the executive committee. The acute Bolshevist danger was thus virtually banished from Austria. On August 1 the Béla Kun government was overthrown. A few weeks later Deutsch disbanded the 41st Battalion and thus eliminated the last Communist stronghold in Vienna.

Although the workers' councils were often sharply condemned the idea of "councils" was so popular at the time that one (the *Bürger-Ständerat*) was established by the bourgeois parties and another by the conservative Roman Catholic workers who were under the influence of the Christian Social party. Neither of these organizations ever had any real importance.[20] Similarly, numerous peasants' councils were created. Some of them achieved a degree of local importance and attempted working arrangements with workers' councils in the same community. Moreover, it is particularly significant that demands for incorporation of the councils into the constitutional system were often raised in non-Socialist quarters.[21] But the Socialists, who on the one hand always regarded the councils as a provisional institution, and on the other hand did not desire their transformation into *berufsständische* (corporative) bodies, rejected these plans. It will be seen later (below, p. 91) that so far as local administrative activities are concerned, the workers' councils cer-

[19] Braunthal, *op. cit.*, p. 16

[20] Cf. Leopold Kunschak, *Oesterreich 1918–1934* (Wien, 1935), p. 61; and Emil Lederer, "Die soziale Krise in Oesterreich," *AfSS.*, vol. 48 (1920–1921), 693.

[21] Cf., for instance, *Der österreichische Volkswirt*, vol. 12 (Oct. 11, 1919), 30.

tainly were guilty of a great number of arbitrary actions. On the other hand, the criticism that they were in themselves a kind of soviet system in the sense of the Russian constitution is clearly refuted by their history. In fact, it is necessary to recognize that they were a major instrument by which the Social Democrats were able to prevent the establishment of soviet rule in Austria.[22] As has been brought out, it became necessary on April 17 and again on June 15 to use armed force against the Communists, but the reliability of the Volkswehr as demonstrated on these occasions reflects the policy of the Socialists in the councils.

The motives which determined the whole anti-Bolshevist policy of the workers' party are easier to understand now than they were in 1918 and 1919. Under the leadership of Viktor Adler the party demonstrated that it was an essentially democratic organization; during the struggle with rising Fascist tendencies in the 'twenties and early 'thirties it continued to demonstrate its faithful adherence to democratic principles. But the growing radicalism of the masses in late 1918 and early 1919 forced the party, if it were to succeed, to put not reasons of principle but those of expediency in the foreground. The main argument urged against the proposals of Béla Kun and his Austrian sympathizers was, therefore, that an attempt to establish a dictatorial rule in Austria would be immediately quelled by the Entente, either by cutting off the food supply, or even, if necessary, by armed intervention.[23] This would mean the end of Social Democratic plans for organizing Austria as a democratic republic with a well-developed system of social legislation, strong trade unions in the factories, and a strong party in parliament. Furthermore, there was the danger that should the dictatorship of the proletariat be proclaimed in Vienna the agrarian parts of the state, most notably Tirol and Vorarlberg, would at once sever their connection with the capital. That quite apart from any questions of principles and

[22] That the Communists were under no delusions about what had happened to the workers' councils is clear enough. Their previously cited publication, *Oesterreich, Brandherd Europas,* states that Friedrich Adler, "changed the workers' councils into simple discussion clubs" (p. 18). Even stronger was A. Martynov, writing in *The Communist International* in 1925 (No. 16, p. 52). "Thus the Austrian Social Democrats got their wish with the help of a twofold deception of the working class. First of all they polluted its opinion by introducing into the Workers' Soviets a large number of officials (to strengthen their authority!) and then they formally subordinated the Soldiers' Soviet to these polluted Workers' Soviets on the plea that the People's Army is the armed force of the working class and must be subordinate to it."

[23] Cf. Bauer, *op. cit.,* p. 137; Deutsch, *op. cit.,* p. 86.

general political aims the party feared Bolshevism as establishment of the rule of the Communist party is also clear to everyone who understands the basic sociological facts concerning the will to self-preservation of social groups and bodies.

Incredible as it may seem, it must nevertheless be regarded as an established fact that in its struggle against Bolshevism the party did not obtain substantial and whole-hearted support from the ranks of the non-Socialist groups and classes. The reasons for this include not only the weakness of these groups but also their wish to see Bolshevism victorious in the hope that after a very short time it would be smashed and carry down with it the powerful position of the Social Democratic party.[24] This attitude naturally increased the role of the Socialists as the chief force against Bolshevism in Austria.

Years later two of the bitterest opponents of the workers' party gave credit to its leaders for the activities described above. Writing at a time when Dollfuss' field artillery was still firing on labor temples and laborers' apartments, Leopold Kunschak paid tribute to Renner as chancellor and Eldersch as minister of interior for suppressing the Communist risings in 1919.[25] Ernst von Streeruwitz, leading industrialist and at times president of the Austrian Association of Manufacturers and Christian Social chancellor of the country, wrote in his memoirs: "However one may judge the attitude of these [Social Democratic] labor representatives—without their intrinsic willingness for coöperation with the employers it would have been difficult to hold the Soviet waves at the Austrian boundaries when the Soviet republics in Munich and Budapest threatened us from both sides."[26]

[24] Cf. the speech of Seipel, "Die Märzrevolution im Reiche und wir," in 1920: "Repeatedly we heard voices saying that in the worst case there will be a few days of Bolshevism and then the people will come to their senses and the situation change." Ignaz Seipel, *Der Kampf um die österreichische Verfassung* (Wien, 1930), p. 81.

[25] *Christlichsoziale Arbeiter-Zeitung*, February 17, 1934, p. 1.

[26] Ernst von Steeruwitz, *Springflut über Oesterreich* (Wien-Leipzig, 1937), p. 213.

CHAPTER V

State Separatism

THE ECONOMIC geography of the German-Austrian residue of the old empire evinced two very different spheres. In the east lay Vienna, the huge industrial city. From it toward the south extended a long, narrow strip of industrial towns and villages including the factory district of Wiener-Neustadt. Farther to the south, over the Semmering Pass, lay the manufacturing and mining valleys of Upper Styria. The rest of Austria was agrarian, for the factories in Graz and Linz were but islands surrounded by rural areas. Because of the nearly two million inhabitants concentrated in Vienna the rural and industrial parts of the state were almost equal in population. The relations between these two parts of Austria, the "two Austrias" as they were dubbed by the well-known Austrian writer, Karl Kraus, became a serious problem at once. The reasons were manifold. In the first period after the revolution, however, the political opposition between predominantly Socialist Vienna and the non-Socialist country played a subordinate part. The war had radicalized the peasants. The republican movement among them was strong, for they retained little sympathy for imperial Austria. But there were weighty economic reasons which rapidly made smooth relations between Vienna and the provinces impossible. The capital city had sought its food principally in Hungary, Bohemia, and Moravia. As mentioned earlier, the Hungarian shipments ceased almost completely in the first months of the war. Since the revolution in Prague virtually no food trains had crossed the frontier between Bohemia, Moravia, and Lower Austria, so that Vienna naturally turned to the German-Austrian provinces for its comestibles. But here great difficulties arose. The war had done much damage to Austrian agriculture. The needs of the army had considerably reduced the supply of livestock. More than that the mountainous districts in the west did not produce enough grain and vegetables to nourish their own population for a period longer than a few weeks. When the breakup came only Upper Austria had food for several months in store. In Vienna were concentrated the so-called *Wirtschafts-Zentralen,* the huge machinery directed by bureaucrats in coöperation with businessmen that had been built up during the war to raise the necessary quantities of food and to provide for its quick and smooth distribution. Now this apparatus was directed against the Alpine provinces. It seemed as if the whole country was to be pilfered in order to maintain the huge parasitical city where industry stood still because of lack of coal and raw material. In the protracted struggle for food which ensued, the unity of the state and also the unity of the labor movement was severely threatened, for the workers' councils in the provinces tried to coöperate with the peasants in order to secure food for themselves. If it was impossible to reach this goal in a peaceful way they sometimes used violence. But both workers and peasants were strongly opposed to the city's demands for food and turned a deaf ear to the admonitions to preserve Vienna, the "heart of the revolution."[1]

---

[1] Julius Braunthal, *Die Arbeiterräte in Deutsch-Oesterreich* (Wien, 1919), p. 34. In the first months of the republic the Social Democrats were not anxious to give wide publicity to facts which obviously enough were in contradiction with Marxist teachings on the common interest of the whole working class. But they made no attempt to suppress them altogether. At the party congress of 1919 Seitz deplored the reluctance of the states to provide Vienna with food; Robinson, the party leader of Styria, who later became editor in chief of the workers' paper in that state, broke in: "Our party comrades are doing it, too!" (*Parteitag, 1919,* p. 153). At the same congress Bauer complained of workers who could see nothing but the food difficulties and thus promoted state separatism. (*Ibid.,* p. 160.) At the Austrian trade-union congress of 1919, Huppert, one of the leading men in the movement, declared: "We could observe to our painful surprise that even workers organized in trade unions lent themselves to furthering these separatist tendencies." (Gewerkschaftskongress, 1919, *Protokoll,* p. 394.)

When the Socialist Danneberg in his address to parliament in 1920 on the constitution demanded that Austria should at last become economically a united state, the Christian Social Gürtler broke in: "You had better tell this to the workers' councils." Danneberg replied: "We shall tell it to the workers' councils and you to the state governments . . . [controlled by the conservatives]. In many cases the workers' councils act in connection and agreement with the state governments." (Konstituierende Nationalversammlung, *Protokoll,* Sept. 29, 1920, p. 3391.)

Even as late as 1921 Bauer told the party congress the story of organized railroad workers in the states who prevented freight cars loaded with cattle and bound for Vienna from crossing state frontiers. And he added frankly: "I know that in the states they do not make this policy 'from above down,' but quite on the contrary, the masses demand such a policy." (*Parteitag, 1921,* p. 156. Cf. also, Otto Bauer, *Die österreichische Revolution* [Wien, 1923], p. 125: "The workers' themselves started . . . [the policy of preventing Vienna from getting food]. The workers' councils prevented the export of food from the individual states; their controlling bodies posted their pickets on the railroad lines.")

The *Oesterreichische Volkswirt* described the situation bluntly and accurately: "Virtually all the parties in the states agree that the workmen's councils actually make the restrictive measures of the states effective, and that the Social Democratic deputies in the state parliaments very willingly back every mutiny against the orders of the central government (for instance the recent occurrence in Upper Austria)." (*Der österreichische Volkswirt,* vol. 12 [Oct. 18, 1919], 51.)

The words "state" and "states" have been used to translate *Land* and *Länder* whenever the point under discussion involves a date subsequent to November 12, 1918; for

The pressing character of the food problem found expression in the earliest activities of the new political forms adopted in the states. Prior to the centralization reforms of Maria Theresia the provinces had enjoyed a large degree of independence, but subsequent to them the governors (*Statthalter*) appointed by the emperor were virtually omnipotent in local affairs.[2] The leaders in the Provisional Assembly desired to retain a centralist state: the Social Democrats because of their anschluss policy; many of the Christian Socials because of their Habsburg restorationist ideas; and most of the Viennese, regardless of party, because of their recognition of the city's need of a hinterland. This attempt was frustrated by the revolutionary movement in the provinces where the governors were removed and replaced by committees. In Styria, for instance, this took place on October 25; significantly enough the first responsibility of the Styrian committee was food supply. A prominent industrialist, Wutte, became economic commissioner and a Socialist, Eisler, vice-commissioner.[3]

Two days after the republic had been proclaimed, the Provisional Assembly adopted a law concerning the "assumption of political power in the states" according to which provisional state assemblies were to elect state committees and the latter elect state governors who were to assume all the powers and functions previously held by imperial governors.[4] Curiously enough, in the light of the desire of the Provisional National Assembly for a centralized state, the law did not establish the responsibility of the new state governors to the central authorities. Thereby the tiny states actually became independent republics, greatly fostering the ensuing separatist moves. In this situation Renner, the Socialist chancellor, thought it wise to demand from the states—*post factum*—declarations of adhesion. Some states, as for instance Lower Austria, never made such declarations; and those of the western states spoke of the rights of self-

---

matters prior to that date, "province" or "provinces" has been used. In strict accuracy the political subdivisions of the republic were not "states" until after the adoption of the constitution of 1920. Since there is no uniformity of usage among British and American writers, it seems simpler to employ "state" for the whole period after the collapse of the empire.

[2] Ignaz Beidtel, *Geschichte der österreichischen Staatsverwaltung* (Innsbruck, 1896), Vol. I, 30–34; Carl von Hock and H. I. Biedermann, *Der österreichische Staatsrath* (Wien, 1879), pp. 173–174.

[3] Otto Bauer, *op. cit.,* p. 105; Handrechter, "Ländersouveränität und Nationalversammlung," *Das Volkswohl,* vol. 11, Heft 2 (1920), 33 ff. No initials in original.

[4] Provisorische Nationalversammlung, *Protokoll,* Vol. I, 114.

determination and freedom of decision, so that the effects were somewhat contrary to what Renner had expected.[5]

The historical claims of independence brought forward by the states were far from convincing after their long years of never-questioned subordination to the central Habsburg government. State separatism as a widespread movement was rendered possible by the lack of national Austrian feeling among the Germans of the old monarchy. Strange as it may seem it is a well-established fact that the intellectual and material connections between Vienna and the Alpine provinces were never really deep and thoroughgoing. True, Vienna had been the economic center of the monarchy and her merchants and bankers had dominated the far-flung Habsburg territories, but the neighboring Alpine provinces had always lived an economic life of their own.[6] Therefore the national bonds among the provinces and the capital were rather poorly developed at the time of the revolution, so that it was possible for some of the states to argue that they had formed a part of the Austrian empire only on the ground of the so-called Pragmatic Sanction (1713) which formally established the unity of the lands of that empire under the Habsburg scepter. Now that the emperor had gone the ties with Vienna and the other provinces were dissolved. A distinguished Austrian writer shrewdly observed that this attitude was not that of a nation which regains its freedom, but of "servants who leave the house when their master dies."[7]

It is out of the question to present a detailed account of the sad history of the attempts to dismember further a small state, economically and politically more or less helpless. Only the most characteristic episodes of the separatist movement will be recorded. As already noted, the Socialists, led by Otto Bauer, demanded anschluss with Germany as the only possible solution of the Austrian problem and prepared to fight for it in the coming peace conference. In the first

[5] The Christian Social party in the states was the real beneficiary of these measures. With the fine irony of which he was so fond Seipel remarked almost ten years later: "It was not a bad idea of the first Austrian chancellor, the old Pan-Austrian Dr. Renner, to obtain from the states declarations of adhesion or at least to presume them.... He hereby established a part of the Austrian state feeling." Ignaz Seipel, *Der Kampf um die österreichische Verfassung* (Wien, 1930), p. 166.

[6] Cf. Josef Schumpeter, "Sozialistische Möglichkeiten von heute," *AfSS.*, vol. 48 (1920–1921), 354.

[7] Carl Brockhausen, "Die Staatsgewalt," *Geldentwertung und Stabilisierung in ihren Einflüssen auf die soziale Entwicklung in Oesterreich* in *Schriften des Vereines für Sozialpolitik*, vol. 169 (1925), 250. Cited hereafter as *Geldentwertung und Stabilisierung.*

months after the revolution the conservative forces in the states strongly opposed the idea of joining Germany, ruled at the time by Socialists. Conspicuously representative of this attitude was the tiny state of Vorarlberg, virtually separated from the rest of the country by the high Arlberg and bound to Switzerland economically as well as by similarity of dialect. It voted in May, 1919, 45,566 to 11,029 for union with that country.[8] At the same time the governor of the state, Ender, incidentally the man who fifteen years later drew up a new constitution allegedly based on the idea of Austrian independence and integrity, began negotiations with Switzerland concerning the incorporation of Vorarlberg into the Swiss Confederacy. The negotiations failed because, apart from the will of the Entente, the French Swiss did not want an increase of the German element. The case of Tirol was similar. The districts of German South Tirol were occupied by Italian troops. The government of the state hoped to preserve its unity by giving up unity with Austria. In the beginning of 1919 Tirol maintained for months an embassy of its own in Bern where negotiations with agents of the Entente were carried on. This embassy was led by the man who in 1920 became the first non-Socialist chancellor of Austria, Dr. Michael Mayr.[9] It provided the French statesmen with so-called proofs of the economic possibility of an independent Tirol. This material was later used against Renner when he tried during the peace negotiations to make clear that Austria could not be regarded as economically viable and demanded anschluss with Germany.

In the rest of Austria matters certainly were better than in Tirol and Vorarlberg, but they were bad enough. Lower Austria geographically surrounded Vienna and at this time was still governed with it by a common state parliament; consequently, it took no considerable part in separatist tendencies. But even here single districts visible with the naked eye from the tower of St. Stephen's Cathedral refused to share their food supply with the starving residents of the metropolis.[10] Separatist tendencies were almost negligible in Carinthia where the Vienna Volkswehr fought side by side with the local Heimwehr against the Yugoslavian army which tried to occupy the

[8] *Reichspost,* May 15, 1919, p. 5.

[9] *Tätigkeits-Bericht,* Heft 13 (Wien, 1920), p. 18.

[10] "Not only states, there are single districts, even at the gates of Vienna, which . . . declare: 'We grow potatoes, but we won't let any of them out.' . . ." Eldersch's speech to the trade-union congress, 1919, *Protokoll,* p. 410.

state in May, 1919. Styria, by virtue of its geographical position, did not threaten immediate separation, as had Tirol and Vorarlberg, but it did its best to thwart the Vienna policy whenever it could. One drastic example may illustrate the selfishness of its food policy. The Styrian authorities actually prohibited the transit trade in cattle from Yugoslavia to Vienna; being economically well-schooled the Styrian rulers argued that this trade would enlarge the demand for Yugoslavian cattle and thus Styria also would have to pay higher prices.[11] Customs duties on goods leaving the territory of a state were very common. At the party congress of 1919 the Salzburg party leader, Witternigg, defended the export duty on timber that had been introduced in his state. The same was true in Upper Austria. In addition, the state parliament there adopted a system of "transport permits," required for goods of any kind before they could leave the state. The fees prescribed for the permits were virtually another form of export duty. The Renner government appealed to the Constitutional Court, whereupon Dr. Max Mayr, a Christian Social politician in Upper Austria,[12] said in an address to the state association of master butchers in November, 1919:

> We know the decision already. We shall be degraded to slaves of the Vienna government and shall yield to the Viennese the last possessions we still own. . . . What are we going to do now? We will post gendarmes at the borders and seek to prevent the execution of the sentence. The [central] government, however, will say the gendarmes come under the jurisdiction of the [central] state . . . therefore nothing else will be left to us but that the people post themselves at the border and stop all illegitimate trade with Vienna. But for Vienna, Upper Austria would have food enough for ten months. . . . We have now voted in the diet not to go to Vienna, not to bow before the Viennese, not to carry on the law suit, in which we must fail right from the start, but . . . to write to the [central] government and to its chancellor that Upper Austria, proud of its sovereignty, does not recognize the law suit because the Vienna government was not entitled to bring it.[13]

And all this happened at a time when the population of Vienna lived literally on the brink of starvation. The situation may, perhaps, best be illustrated by the fact that the prewar daily milk consumption

[11] Cf. O. S. Phillpotts, *Report on the Industrial and Commercial Situation in Austria, Dated May, 1921*, British Department of Overseas Trade (London, 1921), p. 6, and J. van Walré de Bordes, *The Austrian Crown* (London, 1924), p. 7.

[12] Not the subsequent chancellor.

[13] Robert Danneberg, *Die Sanierungsgegner* (Wien, 1923), p. 12.

of 900,000 liters had fallen to between 50,000 and 100,000 liters.[14] More dramatic, but typical and revealing, was an incident that took place in the course of the disturbances of April 17, 1919. As reported in the conservative *Reichspost:*

During the shooting a policeman's horse was struck. The animal fell and the officer suffered an injury in consequence. In a trice, the crowd threw itself upon the prostrate horse; a sailor stabbed it and invited the people to take a cheap roast home with them. The horse was sliced up by the mob in less time than it takes to tell it. Men and women fought over the booty and shortly some people were seen hurrying away with pieces of the still smoking meat.[15]

Clearly enough neither the feeling of national nor of social solidarity proved strong enough to overcome the selfish and, in the long run, short-sighted policy of the states. Only the help of the Entente, which opened a 48 million dollar relief credit, only the work of Herbert Hoover's organization[16] spared Vienna from the fate of some Russian cities in the Volga districts during the famine of 1921. It is true that the help of the Entente would have been necessary even if the individual states had shown themselves ready to fulfill the duties of one part of a commonwealth toward the other parts. But there can be no doubt that the attitude of the states aggravated the situation most decisively. Much of the subsequent history of Austria can be better understood in the light of this attitude. In a country where half or more of the population could with perfect equanimity let a third of the inhabitants starve, grave civil disturbances and even civil war could easily be expected.

Closely connected with the problem of state particularism were

---

[14] Phillpotts, *op. cit.*, 1921, pp. 9–10.

[15] *Reichspost,* April 18, 1919, p. 3.

[16] What Hoover did for Austria, and, most notably, for Vienna, was once called "one of the greatest of the few manifestations of a world conscience which modern times have seen." C. A. Macartney, *The Social Revolution in Austria* (Cambridge, 1926), p. 102. Twenty years later the publication of secret documents of the 1919 Peace Conference officially put these activities in a different light. The text of these documents completely supports the summary generalizations in the United Press report on them that "Hoover and the World War I Allies considered food as a political weapon to block the spread of Bolshevism in hungry Europe," that Hoover was a "major adviser on political activities of governments in central and eastern Europe," and that "His discussion of food at meetings of the 'Big Five' of 1919 . . . never was disassociated from politics." The documents also show that Austria was threatened with a cessation of food shipments if she did not deliver arms to Czechoslovakia to use against Béla Kun's Hungary and that Hoover stressed the necessity of giving help to Austria so that she could pay reparations. U. S. Department of State, *Papers Relating to the Foreign Relations of the United States, The Paris Peace Conference 1919* (Washington, D. C.: Government Printing Office, 1946), Vol. VII, 174, 176–177; San Francisco *Chronicle,* May 19, 1946, p. 4.

the important *Schleichhandel* or black market difficulties; indeed, the restrictive policies of the states rendered that trade possible. And because of the desperate food shortage it became the most thriving "business enterprise" of Austria. The number of persons engaged in it, in defiance of laws and decrees both of central and state governments, was naturally never statistically ascertained, but must have amounted to many thousands. For different reasons the workers' councils in Vienna and in the states fought the black market bitterly. The former because, as they argued, it diminished the food supply coming to Vienna for distribution by government organizations; the latter because it increased the amount of food extracted from the states. In their attempts to put a stop to the illicit trade the workers' councils may be regarded as a partial substitute for the temporarily lacking democratic self-government of the communities, but the arbitrary methods they chose very soon met with general disapproval. The situation was clearly reflected in the following paragraph from the Coalition Pact concluded by the Social Democratic and Christian Social parties in the fall of 1919.

> The distrust of the population in the bureaucratic administration had the result that the council organizations, which arose after the revolution, have interferred with administrative activities and attempted repeatedly to exercise an activity which according to law belongs to the sphere of central and autonomous authorities. This fact had led in many cases to serious grievances. Fundamental rights, most notably the inviolability of one's domicile, were trespassed. Local council organizations have ordered traffic restrictions and confiscations on their own responsibility. Thereby, in many cases, the food service was hampered and especially the food supply to the large cities and industrial districts, particularly Vienna, rendered more difficult.[17]

Despite their support of laws and ordinances on the matter, the Socialists soon recognized that a major result of punitive measures against the black market was an increase in the profits from it. The consumer needed commodities so badly that he had to buy them at almost any price; consequently, he was generally prepared to pay for the greater risks of the profiteer and his higher costs, that is,

[17] This agreement of October 17, 1919, was signed by Otto Bauer and Matthias Eldersch for the Social Democrats and Ignaz Seipel and Johann Hauser for the Christian Socials. Cf. *Tätigkeits-Bericht,* Heft 13 (Wien, 1920), pp. 7–8. The chief newspaper of the Catholic party printed a text of the pact identical with that just cited; *Reichspost,* October 18, 1919, pp. 1–3.

bribes, entailed by the prohibitive measures.[18] When the left-wing elements in the Socialist party, supported by the Communists, contended that the "iron broom" of a proletarian dictatorship would quickly end the black market, Otto Bauer replied that it was clear to everyone who was barely acquainted with basic economic relations that since the illicit trade was a result of the scarcity of goods, it would disappear only when food conditions improved.[19]

At this time, when war and revolutionary upheaval had to a large degree weakened or destroyed the sense of morality within the population, the connection between the black market and state particularism[20] had another sinister aspect. Specifically, the black market became a source of income for many official circles in the states, for the bribes willingly paid by the profiteer were a welcomed addition to the lean wages of the civil servants. Thus the state bureaucracy had a special reason for supporting the system of trade restrictions which, as already noted, rendered the illicit trade possible. To a degree, therefore, Vienna's helplessness in checking the black market was but a new capitulation to state particularism.

As has been emphasized, the exaggerated state particularism of 1918 and 1919 arose from, and was deeply rooted in, the unfortunate food conditions prevailing in Austria. Those conditions enabled the particularist state governments to win the adherence of the large majority of their populations almost without regard to political opinion. It is necessary to point out that this adherence was used by the local governments in fields which had little or nothing to do with the food problem proper. A good example of this development is offered by the socialization attempts in Austria. Under the pressure of growing radicalism inside and outside of the country, the central government drew up a socialization scheme. The Socialists naturally took the lead in this matter, but the Christian Socials and Pan-Germans in Vienna also stressed their readiness to support the scheme.[21] The workers in the states welcomed it no less fervently than did their colleagues in the capital. One of its most important parts was the socialization of Austrian water power, despite the fact

[18] M. Hilferding, "Der Schleichhandel," *Der Kampf,* vol. 12 (May 17, 1919), 300 ff.

[19] Otto Bauer, "Die alte und die neue Linke," *Der Kampf,* vol. 13 (July, 1920), 257.

[20] Cf., for instance, the speech of the Tirolese deputy Abram to the party congress, *Parteitag, 1919,* p. 162.

[21] It must be said, however, that there were striking similarities between this attitude of the non-Socialist parties and the acceptance by the Socialists of the workers' councils.

that such a policy does not necessarily lead to a general attack against private capitalist economy. The lack of coal had reduced Austrian industry to a pitiful condition. The normal annual coal requirements of the country were estimated at from 13 to 15 million tons; the home output at approximately 15 per cent of the requirements.[22] There were months when the coal blockade was almost complete; in one notorious instance, in order to get one coal train over the Czechoslovakian border no less than five diplomatic *pour parlers* were necessary.[23] The coal situation was naturally closely connected with the food problem. It often happened that large quantities of food were available but could not be shipped to Vienna because of the lack of coal and means of transportation. At this same time, however, of an estimated total of 2,250,000,000 horsepower in "white coal" only 9 per cent was being utilized. It was calculated that by using this water power for electrification of the railways 450,000 tons of coal a year could be saved and 32 engines and 1,000 coal wagons diverted to other uses.[24] The Socialists were very anxious to initiate the scheme since they believed that upon it the recovery of the Austrian economy was largely dependent. But here state separatism set in; each state demanded that its water power be left to its sole administration. The federal constitution of October, 1920, conceded these demands. The unfortunate results for the Austrian economy are beyond any doubt, for the states were unable to obtain the necessary capital with which to construct the hydroelectric plants. But this was less important to the states than thwarting the Socialist policy in Vienna which, as they saw with deep distrust, was supported, or at least not sufficiently combated, by the non-Socialist parties in Vienna.[25] The state governments of Styria and Carinthia acted similarly on the issue of the socialization of the iron industry.[26]

---

[22] For somewhat varying estimates, cf. Karl Hudeczek, *The Economic Resources of Austria* (Vienna, 1922), p. 61; Gewerkschaftskongress, 1919, *Protokoll*, p. 378; Phillpotts, *op. cit.*, 1921, p. 35.

[23] Otto Bauer, *Die österreichische Revolution*, p. 118.

[24] Phillpotts, *op. cit.*, 1921, p. 12.

[25] To the preceding, cf. Otto Bauer, *Die Sozialisierungsaktion im ersten Jahre der Republik* (Wien, 1919), p. 11; Wilhelm Ellenbogen, Speech to the Trade-Union Congress, 1919, *Protokoll*, p. 378; R. Danneberg, *Verfassung und Sozialdemokratie* (Wien, 1920), p. 14 f.; H. Kelsen, *Verfassungsgesetze*, Part V (Wien, 1922), p. 7.

[26] Cf. Otto Bauer, *Die österreichische Revolution*, p. 178. In his speech to the party congress in 1919, Bauer quoted a prominent factory owner as saying: "We are not afraid of socialization; we shall hide ourselves behind the states." *Parteitag, 1919*, p. 160.

Typical of the mental attitude then prevailing in the states is the following quotation from the Pan-German paper in Styria. It constituted a more or less formal warning to the Entente and was published at a time when the government was doing all in its power to obtain credits from the Entente in order to secure food supplies for the winter of 1919–1920 and to stimulate general recovery:

> If, for example, through your [the Entente's] help the republic of Austria in spite of the present Socialist government should be able to restore the currency, to import raw materials, and to start the wheels of production turning again, then there would be the danger that the population would regard this as an undreamed of and incontestable success of the Socialist government, whereas it is actually only the work of the capitalist helper. The consequence would be undeniably a heightening of the Socialist wave.[27]

It is idle to apply the usual term of "high treason" to such an attitude. Hatred against Vienna, the republic, the workers' movement, and the Socialist-led government had become so strong in the states that it is scarcely an exaggeration to say that the concept of the new Austrian state as a political and economic entity superior to those single states had no place in the political ideas of the men who ruled them. As one of the leading economists of the country complained, the gulf between the metropolis and the peasant-petty bourgeois "hinterland" was "unbridgeable" and made a common state consciousness impossible.[28] In the first months and years of the republic the Austrian workers' movement was almost the only place where this "common state consciousness" found some shelter. Paradoxical as it sounds, and in spite of the anschluss policy, it is possible to argue that the origins of the "Austrian idea"—as professed fifteen years later by Dollfuss and Schuschnigg, who removed the workers' movement from the limelight of public life—can be traced back to the efforts and policies of the Social Democratic party in those first years. This can be better understood after I have dealt with three other important issues which were closely connected with state separatism: the federal constitution, anschluss, and the first Fascist attempts.

[27] Quoted by Danneberg, *Die Sanierungsgegner,* p. 10, from the *Grazer Tagblatt,* December 15, 1919.

[28] Gustav Stolper, *Deutsch-Oesterreich als Sozial- und Wirtschafts-Problem* (München, 1921), p. 106.

CHAPTER VI

Constitutional Settlement

THE CONSTITUTIONAL arrangements of October 30, 1918, as amended by the act of November 12, revealed all the features of a provisional regulation. Indeed, the author of one of the most painstaking studies of Austrian parliamentarism[1] concluded that the state council was of an "unclear and ambiguous character." This was the opinion of some of the members of the Provisional Assembly, for examples, Wolf and Hummer of the German nationalist group. Both charged that the state council was under no control, that is, irresponsible in the parliamentary sense; and Hummer even depicted it as the seed of an oligarchy which was no better than absolutism. To these and other criticisms Renner made vigorous replies, but it was generally agreed that the charge of absolutism against the state council was formally correct. Actually, the lack of control over it was compensated for by the fact that its members came from the assembly. The discussions led to the law of December 19, 1918, "altering or adjusting" the constitutional measures of October 30 and November 12. To meet the objection that the Provisional Assembly had too much power, the state council was given a suspensive veto, if two-thirds of a quorum of fifteen agreed to it, and was authorized to request changes in a law. However, a simple majority of the assembly could override the veto. The position of the director of the chancery of the state council was formally altered. Originally he had been looked upon as "help-organ" of the council, and, as representative of the presidents, had acted as chairman of the cabinet, had prepared in his office all laws and decrees relating to the constitution, and had performed other functions. These duties, as well as the use, from his first day in office, of the title of chancellor, had no basis in constitutional stipulations. Under the law of December 19, his duties and functions were prescribed, thus legalizing the existing factual situation. Moreover, he was made a responsible minister with the title of chancellor. Thus Renner became not only a responsible minister but also prime minister. Other provisions of the law

[1] Brita Skottsberg, *Der österreichische Parlamentarismus* (Göteborg, 1940), pp. 152–154, esp. p. 153.

altered the composition of the directorate of the state council and improved on the constitution of October 30, by setting forth precisely its field of activity. So far as the state council itself is concerned, it may be noted that its official documents (*Ausfertigungen*) now had to bear, not the countersignature of the irresponsible director of its own chancery, but the countersignature of the responsible chancellor or some responsible minister; thus the "control" was established. Since the exclusive power of the state council to issue executive orders or decrees under the October Constitution had proved impracticable, the various ministers were now given that power within their respective fields of competence.[2]

The constitutional stipulations were, of course, still provisional. They were appropriate for a period of general rebuilding of the state in which all existing political parties were to share. The institution of the state council in which each parliamentary party was represented corresponded to the extraordinary circumstances. But this "Constitution of Concentration" was to be replaced as soon as normally working democracy, that is, rule by the majority, was established. The first step in this direction was the election on February 16, 1919, of the long discussed Constituent National Assembly. The workers' party secured 69 seats as against 63 for the Christian Socials, 25 for a group of German nationalist and liberal parties, and 1 each for the Czech and Jewish nationalists.[3] Three days later the Socialist members of the new assembly submitted to the electorate and to the other parties a statement of the general principles on which they thought the permanent constitution should be based.

At this point it is necessary to describe the situation exactly. Although large groups of rank-and-file Socialists, expressing themselves particularly through workers' councils in the states, as well as local leaders, had gone along with and positively furthered separatist policies on the food supply issue, the attitude of the party on the constitutional question favored a centralized, not a federal state. One obvious explanation was that it did not wish to see the disin-

---

[2] *StGBl.*, 1918, Nr. 139; Skottsberg, *op. cit.*, pp. 156–163; H. Kelsen, "Die Verfassungsnovelle," *Neue Freie Presse*, December 20, 1918 (A.M.), pp. 3–4.

[3] Bundesamt für Statistik, *Statistisches Handbuch für die Republik Oesterreich* (Wien, 1920), vol. 1, p. 3; *Tätigkeits-Bericht*, Heft 12 (Wien, 1919), p. 1. The volumes of the *Handbuch* for 1920–1933 inclusive have the title as given here; no volume was issued for 1934, and the 1935 volume has the title *Statistisches Handbuch für den Bundesstaat Oesterreich*. For brevity, the *Handbuch* is hereafter cited as *SHfRO*.

tegration of the new nation, already so small that it was commonly designated as a dwarf state; but, in addition, there was the fact that the strength of the party was concentrated in Vienna (523,329 of its 1,211,814 votes for the Constituent Assembly came from there).[4] Again obviously, such concentrated power could be used much more advantageously in a centralized government. Nevertheless, the Socialist members of the assembly realized that it would be impossible fully to deprive the states of the independence they had secured in the days of revolution, and, consequently, their proposals included "comprehensive self-government in the states and the capital city Vienna." This concession was immediately qualified by the statement that certain principles must "notwithstanding" be firmly established in the constitution. And the first of these was that "national law is superior to state law." In other sections the statement of principles opposed the institution of a president, because of fear of Caesarist experiments, and favored a one-chamber parliament. Furthermore, abolition of bureaucratic administration, its replacement by a really democratic one, and the initiative and referendum were demanded. Nowhere in the document do the words "federal state" appear. Since the entire ministry, including the chancellor, was to be elected by the parliament, there can be no doubt concerning the desire of the Socialists to put that body in a dominating position. If the existence of a second house of parliament, representing the states, is an essential element of a federation, then the emphasis on a one-chamber body also emphasizes the opposition to complete federalism.[5]

On March 14, 1919, the provisional constitution was altered by a statute which embodied practically all of the major points of the Socialist proposals. During the same session another law[6] was passed reaffirming the republican character of the new state and repeating the declaration that German-Austria regarded herself as a part of the German Reich.[7]

---

[4] *SHfRO,* vol. 1, p. 3.

[5] The full text of the proposals appeared in the *Arbeiter Zeitung,* February 21, 1919, p. 2; it was reprinted in *Tätigkeits-Bericht,* Heft 12 (Wien, 1919), pp. 4–6.

[6] *StGBl.,* 1919, Nr. 179, 180.

[7] In the judgment of Dr. Skottsberg the first provisional constitution of October had translated the *theory* of sovereignty of the people into the *practice* of unrestrained rule of parliament. Like other commentators she realizes that the basic sentiment of the constitution makers, particularly the Socialists, was a deep distrust of the executive; for years the struggle over the rights of parliament had centered on the power to

Subsequent to the passage of the laws of March 14, Emperor Karl was asked by Chancellor Renner whether or not he was prepared to redeem his pledge to recognize the future form of the state. The emperor refused and left the country on March 23. As a retaliatory measure the Constituent Assembly confiscated the property of the Habsburgs and expelled all members of the family. In addition to its general importance this episode is significant in that it included a very unusual occurrence in Austrian parliamentary life, a split in the Christian Social party: the peasants' representatives voted for the expulsion of the Habsburgs, whereas the Viennese representatives left the meeting.[8]

Again these constitutional changes of March, 1919, were regarded as provisional (the parties agreed to draw up a comprehensive constitutional act to be adopted by the Constituent Assembly); but, as indicated above, they stressed, even more than had Renner's formu-

---

control the formation of the cabinet. The December amendments, she holds, contained the germ of a weak separation-of-powers principle; those of March restored the "extreme" rule of parliament, but also introduced the parliamentary system into the new Austria for the first time. "This coupling of two different systems gave to Austrian parliamentarism those weaknesses on which it slid to ruin." In order to function without friction parliamentarism needs an element of stability, a neutral head of the state, who "directs the change of ministers." The March legislation still failed to provide this. Moreover, none of the constitutional stipulations to this date provided for a dissolution of the assembly—not even by its own resolution, not to speak of dissolution by some other authority. (Skottsberg, *op. cit.*, pp. 187–188, 191, 237.)

Dr. Skottsberg says on page 187: "To bind parliamentarism by paragraphs is a ticklish business." Apparently, however, this is exactly what she wishes to do; her real complaint concerns "the little paragraphs that weren't there." Much more damaging to her conclusion on the weaknesses of the Austrian system of parliamentarism is the totally inadequate attention she pays to the internal forces that were determined to destroy it. Granting the existence of weaknesses, her emphasis is completely misplaced. Austrian parliamentarism "slid to ruin," not because of a "coupling of two different systems" in some paragraphs or of a failure to include others; but because bankers, industrialists, and landed aristocrats built the ways, in the form of Fascist private armies, on which it could slide and greased them with generous subventions. As will be demonstrated in subsequent Chapters, particularly VII and XXI, the evidence supporting this contrary conclusion has been published by conservative individuals who helped supply the funds. Perhaps the most important source, *Springflut über Oesterreich* by the industrialist and Christian Social chancellor, von Streeruwitz, is not even mentioned by Dr. Skottsberg though it appeared three years before her own work. It is evidently too much to say (see below, p. 99, the quotation from Seipel as counterevidence) that the bourgeois parties "never" wanted the "new parliamentary democratic state" set up in 1918; but, again partly in the light of efforts to induce the United Nations to recognize a government-in-exile composed of the remnants of Schuschnigg's last cabinet, it is extremely interesting that one of the members of that cabinet wrote the statement just quoted (Guido Zernatto, *Die Wahrheit über Oesterreich* [New York–Toronto, 1938], pp. 103–104). Without doubt the statement reflects accurately the opinion of many leaders of the bourgeois parties, including Schuschnigg.

[8] *StGBl.*, 1919, Nr. 209; Otto Bauer, *Die österreichische Revolution* (Wien, 1923), pp. 127 ff.; *Reichspost*, April 3, 1919, p. 2; and *Arbeiter Zeitung*, April 3, 1919, pp. 1, 3.

lation of October, absolute parliamentary democracy, or, as it was called in a rather meaningless perversion of terms, "the dictatorship of the parliament."[9] At the time the non-Socialist parties also went far in approving this thoroughgoing democracy, chiefly because it appeared to them as *digue et rampart* against the Bolshevist offensive. In 1920, during one of the last meetings of the Constituent Assembly, Seipel declared: "On March 14, 1919, it was necessary to proclaim that the democratic state had been established once and for all because . . . there was the danger that the democratic republic could be replaced by the dictatorship of one single class."[10]

In addition to being provisional this "parliamentary absolutism" was by no means absolute. One of the laws of March 14 was intended in part to curb the power of the states by giving the central government the right to appeal to the Constitutional Court against state statutes believed in Vienna to be unconstitutional. But since the responsibility of the governors of the states to the central authorities was nowhere established, one juristic basis of particularism was preserved. This is all the more remarkable because of the fact that the governors were also the organs of Vienna in the states. Thus the ensuing conflict over a permanent constitution which would solve this particularism problem was a struggle for the political entity of the Austrian state. Moreover, it was also a struggle for democracy; the unrestricted rule of the states meant the predominance of forces which evinced a waning enthusiasm for democracy as the contest continued. It is impossible to recite here the long and complicated story of this contest; but it is necessary to note the most important developments, to show the position taken by the working-class movement, and to indicate the results.

As early as November, 1918, work on a permanent constitution was begun in Renner's office. Professor Kelsen was, officially, to be the "consultant," actually, to do the greater share of the work. Partly because of the demands on the time of everyone concerned with other matters, for examples, the election campaign for the Constituent Assembly or the constitutional revisions of December and March; and partly because of differences between the two major parties concerning the nature of the constitution desired, progress

---

[9] Cf. Carl Brockhausen, *Geldentwertung und Stabilisierung,* p. 251.
[10] Konstituierende Nationalversammlung, *Protokoll,* September 29, 1920, p. 3375.

was slow. At the instigation of the separatist forces in the states a draft published by the *Reichspost* as "the Christian Socials' constitution bill for German-Austria" was introduced into the assembly in mid-May.[11] Just at this time Renner had to go to St. Germain to attend the peace conference. Before leaving he authorized Kelsen to prepare a complete draft. This was finished during the summer; in fact, by September 15 Kelsen had worked out five additional proposals. The basic principles of these conformed to the first; but there were some important differences on the matters of a "states' chamber" in the parliament, the president, and the bill of rights.

It has been shown that the first moves of the Social Democrats in the constitutional conflict were largely successful. During the many months before the constitution was adopted there was much shifting and changing of position. For example, the protecting wing extended over the organization of Fascist formations by some of the state governments forced Socialists who had at first favored separatist moves in those states to swing about and strongly support the idea of a unitary state. But prior to those developments the collapse of the soviet regimes in Bavaria and Hungary had brought an alteration of the power relations within Austria. The bourgeois parties no longer so greatly feared a radical move to the left by the Austrian Social Democrats, and consequently were less likely than ever to part with the strength they had secured in the states. For the same reason the influence of the workers' party outside Vienna was decreasing. This shift in power relationships found formal expression in the previously cited Coalition Pact concluded between the Socialist and Christian Social parties in the fall of 1919. It dealt with the constitution problem in some detail. Following are the most important paragraphs.

The draft of the new constitution is to be drawn up as soon as possible. Before its presentation to the national assembly the government will communicate, first with the two parties and then with the state governments. At the time of the preliminary deliberations on the draft in the national assembly a subcommittee of the constitutional committee will invite representatives of the states as experts.

The new constitution will constitute German-Austria a *federal state*[12] . . . Foreign policy, judicial legislation (civil and criminal law), and the

[11] *Reichspost,* May 15, 1919, p. 4; Konstituierende Nationalversammlung, *Beilagen,* Nr. 231; *Neue Freie Presse,* May 13, 1919 (A.M.), p. 3.

[12] Italics mine.

army are to remain the exclusive jurisdiction of the federal state, as well as economic legislation and administration, as far as this is required by the unity of the economic territory, social legislation, workers' insurance, and universities. The free traffic of goods within the federal territory must be safeguarded. . . .

The legislative function of the federal state will be carried out by the national assembly and a federal council. There is an agreement that the [constitution] bill of the chancellery of state, as far as the composition of the federal council and its functions are concerned, will follow the pattern of the German Reichsrat. If the federal council does not agree to a law adopted by the national assembly, a plebiscite shall be held. . . . With reference to the presidency, the present regulation shall be preserved by the bill to be drawn up by the chancellery of state.[13]

In further consideration of the reasons for the nature of the part of the pact dealing with the constitution it must be kept in mind that the substitution of Horthy for Béla Kun as ruler of Hungary greatly increased the danger of attempts at a Habsburg restoration. The well-known sympathy of large groups of Christian Socials for the old dynasty and the close connections between them and the politicians on the other side of the Leitha River were ample grounds for concern among the Socialist leaders in Vienna, so that they felt impelled to make significant concessions. The ambiguous formula "comprehensive self-government" used in March was replaced in the pact by the more precise term "federal state." Now there was to be a second chamber, composed of representatives of the governments of the states and put on a par with the first chamber. The resort to a plebiscite in every case of disagreement between the first and second chambers must be regarded as a concession to the Christian Socials in light of the fact that the Socialists had not succeeded in securing the adherence of the majority of the Austrian people even in February, 1919, when hatred of war, and of those who were thought responsible for it, caused thousands of non-Socialists to vote for the Social Democratic party. Finally, it is significant that nothing whatever was said about the position of Vienna, long the center of Socialist power in Austria and destined to become more important in this respect.

The foregoing stipulations distinctly reflect the first low phase in the postwar development of Austrian Social Democracy. The set-

[13] *Tätigkeits-Bericht*, Heft 13 (Wien, 1920), pp. 6–7.

back was, however, only temporary. Thanks in large measure to the powerful development of the trade unions the period of weakness was overcome; and, particularly with reference to the constitution, attempts were made to recover the lost positions. But the subsequent negotiations concerning the organic charter were difficult and slow. The continuous deterioration in the relations between the coalition parties was unfavorable to the resolution of the issue.[14] Coincident with the signing of the Coalition Pact a Christian Social member of the assembly, Michael Mayr, had been elected to the cabinet without portfolio but with the "personal task" of coöperating in the work of constitutional and administrative reform. From the various drafts of a constitution then resting in the chancellery he selected one which, with modifications, he used as a basis for negotiations with representatives of the political parties in the states.[15] Still the cabinet could not decide to take a decisive step; still the assembly waited for that step. This inactivity encouraged the states to start negotiations concerning the constitution among themselves–negotiations from which the central government would be virtually excluded. The chief objectives of the states were a constitution which would grant the utmost degree of autonomy to them and a states' chamber which would act as watchdog over the other house. For the purpose of crystallizing these ideas a conference of representatives of the states was summoned to meet in Salzburg in February, 1920; only one member of the government, Mayr, was invited, and he simply as a "private person."

At this conference the issue of federal state *versus* central state assumed great prominence despite the agreement to the former in the Coalition Pact. During the debate on February 16 the Socialist delegates declared themselves completely against the federal form, but in the vote this unity was not maintained. Carinthia, Salzburg, Tirol, and Vorarlberg were against federalization and for centralization without any reservations. A majority of the Upper Austrians favored a unitary state, but announced that if a majority decided for the federal principle they would accept it provided that certain

[14] H. Kelsen, *Verfassungsgesetze* (Wien, 1922), Part V, 59.

[15] Cf. *ibid.*, p. 56; and Skottsberg, *op. cit.*, pp. 192–193. Because of subsequent controversies concerning the authorship of the constitution of 1920 and because of Skottsberg's sharp criticism of Kelsen on more than one point, it is interesting to note that she accepts as unquestioned fact Mayr's use of a chancellery draft.

guarantees on democracy and economic unity were given. Styria voted for federalization unconditionally. Vienna and Lower Austria also favored the federal state, but made the reservations that economic development must be insured, particularly for Vienna, and that the new constitution must guarantee full democracy. The net result, clearly enough, was that working-class political leaders in the states were moving over to acceptance of a federation as the national leaders had already.

Among the representatives of the Catholic party and of the various German nationalists and liberals no split developed. All of them voted for the federal system without conditions or reservations of any kind.[16]

Mayr presented to the conference his modified version of the chancellery draft. It was much closer to the formulation of March 1919 than to the Christian Social proposals which he and his associates had offered to the Constituent Assembly in May of that year; but since the Socialists insisted that only the assembly was authorized to make decisions the conference turned into an exchange of ideas without binding effect. It was agreed, however, to hold another conference in the near future.

By the time the second conference met in Linz on April 20, 1920, the setting of the political stage had been considerably changed; a general strike of German workers in the preceding month had defeated the counterrevolutionary Kapp putsch. The balance of power shifted again to improve the position of the Socialists. Mayr brought in a further revision of his Salzburg proposals. The Pan-Germans presented a complete plan of their own. The representatives of the workers' party did not offer a draft as such, thus holding to the position that the conference was only for the purpose of exchanging ideas, but they did set forth a great number of amendments to Mayr's, which, taken together, actually amounted to a draft. The content of these amendments was almost identical with one of Kelsen's projects. Not even the Christian Socials were satisfied with Mayr's document; one of their most prominent leaders, Ender, declared that it was not a party draft and that it "absolutely does not correspond to our conceptions." The federal state issue had really been

[16] *Neue Freie Presse,* February 17, 1920 (A.M.), pp. 4, 5–6. Skottsberg's statement (*op. cit.,* p. 196) that the Socialists from all the states stood for centralization seems to rest on the debate and to disregard the vote.

settled but one die-hard Socialist from Upper Austria, Gruber, announced that the fight for centralization would continue. His party colleague from Vienna, Danneberg, replied that federal *versus* central state was not the decisive question, but rather the division of jurisdiction between the federation and the states.

Despite their sharp polemics against Mayr at Linz the Social Democrats showed a willingness to compromise on important points. The chief result of the conference was a relatively thorough reconciliation of the viewpoints of the Catholic and workers' parties, but long and tenacious negotiations remained.[17] This reconciliation was by no means sufficient, however, to relieve the antagonisms within the cabinet and the assembly. They exploded on June 10, 1920, in an interpellation by the Pan-Germans and a vituperative speech by the Christian Social, Kunschak. The immediate occasion was an order issued on May 25 by the Socialist army minister, Deutsch, concerning the soldiers' councils. His opponents made use of the fact that he had proceeded without laying the matter before the full cabinet and charged that the order was contrary to law. He contended that he had acted correctly. But behind this controversy were other much more basic ones related to the constitution, inflation, a proposed capital levy, and the organization of grain cultivation. The increasing pressure from the workers, formally expressed in the federal convention of workers' councils in early June, to dissolve the coalition, and the conviction previously crystallized among party leaders that it was no longer fruitful were probably the most important from the Socialist viewpoint. For these reasons the workers' deputies in the assembly greeted Kunschak's threat of breaking the coalition with a storm of applause. The next day their ministers resigned. Since the Catholic party had supported the Pan-German interpellation, the Socialists demanded that this *de facto* combination against them be turned into a new coalition cabinet of the bourgeois parties. It immediately became evident that the Christian Socials were very reluctant to form a government without the Socialists. Even Kunschak backed water in an article, "What Now," in the *Reichspost*. The liberal bourgeois press almost implored Renner to return to the

[17] Cf. Skottsberg, *op. cit.*, pp. 197–201; Kelsen, *op. cit.*, Part V, 57–59; *Tätigkeits-Bericht*, Heft 13 (Wien, 1920), p. 119; *Neue Freie Presse*, April 22, 1920 (A.M.), p. 3. There are certain significant differences in the reports cited. A comparison of them will show, I believe, that the statements in the text are correct.

chancellor's post. The upshot was the institution of a "proportional" cabinet containing representatives of all the parties on July 7.[18]

Contrary to what might have been expected the breakup of the coalition greatly hastened the proceedings on the constitution. The formation of the proportional government had been impossible until after agreement had been reached on parliamentary elections for October.[19] The leaders of the various parties understood quite well that if the Constituent National Assembly should dissolve without adopting a new constitution, not only would it have stultified itself, but also the states might attempt to prevent the election of the new parliament. Thoroughly dissatisfied, but without substantial hopes of materially influencing developments, the Pan-Germans had introduced their Linz draft of a constitution into the assembly on May 18. Immediately after the Linz meeting a committee, composed of Mayr and Fink, Christian Socials, Renner, Socialist, and Kelsen, went to work with the purpose of utilizing the *rapprochement* and preparing a draft that could be presented as the cabinet's. This proposal was published in the *Wiener Zeitung,* July 8, but was not brought to the assembly as a government bill because of the disruption of the coalition. Instead, the Christian Socials offered still another formulation on June 25. The Socialists came in with theirs on July 7. Except for a new section on the cities and towns it was identical with the program presented piecemeal at Linz. At this juncture the committee on the constitution of the assembly took the initiative and put a subcommittee to work. From the wealth of material it selected Mayr's Linz draft and that of the Social Democrats as the major bases. The result of the discussions was a document that was a compromise between these two with the inclusion of a few points from the Pan-German proposals. With insignificant alterations in language this formulation became the constitution of October 1, 1920. Although the final text of the new organic charter undoubtedly reflected compromises in all its parts it must also undoubtedly be regarded, especially in comparison with the various drafts offered by the states, as a victory over the forces of state particularism. For

[18] Konstituierende Nationalversammlung, *Protokoll,* June 10, 1920, pp. 2905, 2919; Julius Deutsch, *Aus Oesterreichs Revolution* (Wien, n.d.), pp. 140 ff.; Bauer, *Die österreichische Revolution,* pp. 214, 219–220; *Wiener Stimmen,* June 11, 1920, p. 1; *Reichspost,* June 13, 1920, p. 1; *Neue Freie Presse,* June 11, 1920 (A.M.), p. 1.

[19] For still another factor in the delay, see below, p. 124, n. 27.

example, it may be noted that the Christian Social draft of May 14, 1919, began with the words: "We, free peoples of the independent states . . . unite of our own accord and upon our free decision in the German Federal Free State Austria." The text of October 1 did not contain any such statement. Its juristic value would have been equal to zero, but it is symptomatic that such a proposal, which virtually denied the existence of the Austrian republic, could seriously be made. A much more decisive question was that of the composition of the second chamber or states' council (*Bundesrat*). According to the first drafts of the states each of them would have had the same number of representatives in the Bundesrat; that is, Vienna with its almost two million population and Vorarlberg with its 140,000 would have been represented by three delegates each. The Bundesrat's position, as far as legislation was concerned, was to be equal with that of the first chamber. That meant, under the specific circumstances, an absolute subordination of the whole legislative machine of the new nation to the will of the states. The final text provided for representation fairly closely in proportion to population; and, what was still more important, confined the participation of the second chamber in the legislation to a merely suspensive veto. (Articles 34 and 42.)[20] Another example of the tactics of the states is presented by a section of the Pan-German draft stipulating that even the bills of the government had to secure the approval of the Bundesrat before they could be submitted to the other house.[21] From the controversy on the make-up and powers of the Bundesrat it may clearly be seen that every victory over state particularism was, in fact, a victory of democracy over the attempt to establish minority rule through the apparatus of a particularist constitution.[22]

Of great importance was the unity of the "economic, customs, and currency territory" stipulated by Article 4. Traffic restrictions or

[20] For the text of the constitution, see *Bundesgesetzblatt für die Republik Oesterreich*, 1920, Nr. 1 (cited hereafter as *BGBl.*) or Kelsen, *op. cit.*, Part V, 1–52. An English translation appears in H. L. McBain and Lindsay Rogers, *The New Constitutions of Europe* (New York, 1922), pp. 256–292.

[21] This would have been nothing short of furnishing the Bundesrat with the right of the famous royal "pre-sanction" by which unconstitutional practice Emperor Franz Joseph had dominated the Hungarian parliament after the liberal reforms of 1867. Cf. Joseph Redlich, *Emperor Francis Joseph of Austria* (New York, 1929), pp. 360–361.

[22] How closely connected were the particularist tendencies and antidemocratic ideas is shown, for instance, in the criticism of the new constitution published by an outstanding Catholic magazine in Tirol shortly after the constitution act was adopted. Cf. Joseph Eberle, "Die neue Verfassung," *Das Neue Reich*, vol. 3 (Nov. 14, 1920), 125–129.

customs lines within the boundaries of the republic were prohibited. This was a blow against the very foundation of state separatism and met with strong opposition from the Christian Socials. They demanded that this stipulation not go into effect until August 31, 1922, but June 30, 1921, was finally agreed upon as the effective date.[23] Of great import, furthermore, were the facts that the governors of the states were at last made responsible to the federal government in their capacities as organs of the central administration, and to the state diet as state executives (Article 105). Thereby the previous anarchical state of affairs was terminated. On the other hand, the Socialists failed in their attempt to democratize the administration of the districts by substituting freely elected officials for the *Bezirkshauptleute* appointed by the state governors. The constitution included this reform, but it was never carried out.

On the whole the new constitution established or confirmed the parliament elected by general franchise as the supreme organ of the Austrian state.[24] The Socialists had successfully opposed all attempts to stipulate the election of the federal president by direct vote of the people. Remembering the history of the Second Empire in France they feared that this position might become the fulcrum for the restoration of the monarchy in Austria or for some other reactionary move. Considering the roles played by the presidents of Germany and of Austria (after the enlargement of the powers of the latter by the constitutional reforms of 1929) during the beginnings of Fascist rule in both countries, Austrian Socialists are convinced that their policy was certainly justified from the democratic point of view. According to the constitution the president was elected by both houses of parliament. His functions were largely decorative;

[23] Kelsen, *op. cit.*, Part V, 293; Danneberg, *Verfassung und Sozialdemokratie* (Wien, 1920), p. 13; Konstituierende Nationalversammlung, *Protokoll*, September 30, 1920, p. 3459.

[24] Primarily for this reason, but also for a number of others such as the differences in the powers of the states' chamber and of the president of the republic, I am unable to agree with the conclusions of Professor Malbone W. Graham that the final draft of the constitution conformed closely to the Christian Social proposals of May, 1919, and "that little of fundamental importance was altered, the modifications being only in matters of detail" (*New Governments of Central Europe* [New York, 1924], p. 166, n. 4). Skottsberg (*op. cit.*, p. 222) refers to the May, 1919, draft of the Catholic party as one of the only two that sought to weaken the power of the lower house and to divide the duty of forming a cabinet between it and the chief executive. The subsequent violent attacks of the Christian Socials on the 1920 constitution, leading to the revisions of 1929 and the establishment of the Clerical Fascist constitution of 1934, are scarcely consistent with Professor Graham's interpretation.

he could neither dissolve the parliament nor appoint nor dismiss a government. Moreover, the Socialists saw to it that the assembly included in the constitution the provision that members of reigning or formerly reigning families were not eligible for the presidency (Article 60).[25]

At the time of the constitutional struggles the Socialists hardly recognized the tremendous importance of the new position established for Vienna in the constitution more or less as a by-product of separatist tendencies. After the revolution Vienna remained, as it had been for centuries, an administrative unit with Lower Austria. The constitution of 1920 adopted a dualist construction for the city and the state so that their common state diet should be used only for matters pertaining to both territories. But it made the proviso (Article 114) that a "separate state of Vienna may be formed by concurrent laws of the city council of Vienna and the state parliament of Lower Austria." This separation was finally and formally effected on December 29, 1921, although for most practical purposes it had been true for more than a year. Vienna became city and state at the same time. The mayor of Vienna was also state governor; the city council, state diet; the city senate, state government.

Thus a legal construction was created which later developed into

---

[25] It is necessary to add that in the last stages of the constitutional struggle the Socialists found some support in the camp of the Viennese Christian Socials. Here, obviously, an interesting shift had taken place. In the first period of coalition there was real coöperation between the Socialists and the peasants' representatives in the Catholic party. Since state particularism, especially in its food policy, severely hit Vienna and its economic life, some of the Christian Socials living there inaugurated a more friendly policy toward the Socialists, and were even driven so far as to defend the very limited power assigned to the president by the constitution. Cf., for instance, Richard Schmitz, "Oesterreichs Bundesverfassung," *Das Volkswohl,* vol. 11, Heft 12 (1920), 360–364. "That in a democratic republic the political preponderance lies with the people, or with the men freely elected by the people, is a matter of course. The North American president with his supermonarchical power fits poorly in the relations of a small country; the bad experiences with Wilson's war and peace treaty policy do not speak for placing immense power in the hands of the president" (p. 363). Schmitz also made the interesting statement that "Austria must be prevented from complete dismemberment" (p. 361).

Another probable reason for this attitude was that at the time the anschluss movement in the states was beginning to gain momentum. From the point of view of a strong pro-Habsburg politician such as Schmitz a momentary compromise with the Socialists was certainly a lesser evil than irretrievable union with Germany. It will be shown, however, that in the coming years it was precisely the Vienna Christian Socials who were the chief enemies of coöperation with the Socialists, whereas attempts to collaborate with the Christian Socials in the states were several times fairly successful for short periods. Curiously enough Schmitz was to become one of the bitterest opponents of democracy. After the February, 1934, rising Dollfuss appointed him mayor of Vienna to replace the "freely elected" mayor, Seitz.

the strongest bulwark of the Austrian labor movement. In this later period the Social Democrats passionately defended the establishment of Vienna as a state and, largely without justification, described it as a most brilliant achievement of their statesmanship. During these same later years, the arrangement was fiercely attacked by the non-Socialist parties, most notably by the Christian Socials who used any and every means in order to denounce and combat what they called the "unnatural construction" of Vienna's existence as a city and state simultaneously. This fight for and against Vienna forms a large chapter in the postwar history of Austrian labor and, consequently, will be discussed in this book at some length. Here it is only interesting to note that if the Socialists had succeeded in forming Austria into a unitary state there might easily have been no "Red Vienna" in Austria, and that in 1919 and 1920 the most energetic demands for the separation of Vienna from Lower Austria came from anti-Socialist states. These states feared that otherwise there would have been one state so superior to the others in size, population, and economic power that it would have occupied a position similar to that of Prussia.[26]

The framers of the constitution were particularly interested in the establishment of a strong and independent judiciary. Regardless of party they wished to avoid certain arbitrary and irresponsible aspects of the imperial regime. To this end the Constitutional Court was given wide powers; in fact, in the opinion of one American scholar, "the doctrine of judicial supremacy is raised to a higher degree in the Austrian Constitution than in any other extant.[27] In this connection, however, it is interesting to note that though members of the Constitutional Court were chosen for life, its president, vice-president, half the members and their alternates were elected by the Nationalrat (people's chamber of parliament) and the other half and their alternates by the Bundesrat. The president of the republic had no voice in the matter.[28]

On three important matters the committee on the constitution of the Constituent Assembly was unable to agree; consequently, the 1920 basic charter does not define the boundaries of the jurisdictions of the federation, of the states and of the communities in matters of

[26] Ignaz Seipel, *Der Kampf um die österreichische Verfassung* (Wien, 1930), p. 231.
[27] Graham, *op. cit.*, p. 180.
[28] Cf. *BGBl.*, 1920, Nr. 1, Art. 82–94; 129–148.

taxation; it does not delimit the powers of the federation and of the state with reference to education; and it contains no codification of basic civil liberties—that is, no new "bill of rights." In lieu of this last the appropriate sections of three imperial statutes of 1862 and 1867 dealing with the protection of personal liberty, with the inviolability of the domicile, and with the general rights of citizens were declared to be "constitutional laws." Placed in the same category and probably also to be considered as a part of the bill of rights were the statutes expelling the Habsburgs and abolishing nobility, as well as the clauses of the peace treaty guaranteeing the rights of minorities (Article 149). Most of these matters, however, continued to be centers of bitter controversy, arising as they did from deep-rooted differences of conviction on the relation of State and Church and on economic policy. In all of Kelsen's seven or eight drafts of a constitution there had been a bill of rights, influenced greatly by the comparable section in the Weimar Constitution. The Christian Socials wished to maintain the stipulations of 1867 because of their protection of the rights of private property and of the position of the Church. Renner, on the other hand, had given Kelsen instructions to formulate this part of the constitution as close to that of Weimar as possible with the purpose of making socialization easier. In Kelsen's judgment the outcome was the first great victory of the Christian Socials over the Socialists.[29]

Despite its deficiencies, and particularly from the point of view of the Austrian labor movement, the 1920 constitution was one of the most momentous events in the history of the republic. It represented a decisive victory over state separatism and thus made the new Austria a political entity.[30] It strengthened Austrian democracy and thereby secured to the movement the necessary basis for its political, economic, and cultural development. Without the establishment of Austria as a political and democratic unit the labor movement in the states in all probability would soon have lost, along with political

---

[29] Conversations with Professor Kelsen. Cf. Konstituierende Nationalversammlung, *Protokoll,* September 29, 1920, p. 3378; Seipel, *op. cit.,* pp. 96–98; Kelsen, *op. cit.,* Part V, 64, 284, 285; Skottsberg, *op. cit.,* pp. 213–214.

[30] Other evidence of how close the young republic stood to the brink of dismemberment is shown by the fact that on the day before the adoption of the constitution in the Constituent Assembly the Christian Social Fink (vice-chancellor in the coalition governments) introduced a motion permitting the states to withdraw from the federation and become independent or join another country any time within ten years. Konstituierende Nationalversammlung, *Protokoll,* September 30, 1920, p. 3445.

freedom, the social achievements of the revolution. By the proclamation of the unity of the economic territory the constitution greatly contributed to the actual establishment of Austria as an economic entity. In contrast to the peasants and the middle class in the states, the leaders of the Austrian Socialist party clearly understood the importance of this issue. The modern economic system with its need for wide markets is incompatible with the existence of traffic restrictions corresponding to the period of feudalism and guilds. By fighting for the economic unity of the country the Social Democrats unquestionably did a great service to the restoration of the Austrian economy and thus to the improvement of the general conditions of the working class, as far as this could be done at all within the borders of the dwarf state German-Austria.

CHAPTER VII

Foreign Policy and Fascist Preludes

THE FOREIGN policy of the Social Democratic party after November, 1918, was largely determined by the idea that the dominant motive underlying the revolutionary movements in Central Europe toward the close of the war was the wish to attain national self-determination. For the German people this meant carrying through the great aim of the Revolution of 1848—the union of all Germans. The declaration on this issue already referred to was much more than a formality. Social Democracy hoped that within a few weeks it would be possible to effect anschluss and present the world with a *fait accompli.*[1] There is little room for doubt that had anschluss with Germany actually been effected at that time the Austrians would have been saved at least some of the worst economic troubles which were in store for them in the next decade. Very soon, however, it became clear that the big neighbor preferred not to overhasten the anschluss because she feared that this would have most unfortunate results in the peace-treaty negotiations. When, in January and March, 1919, Yugoslavia and Czechoslovakia began to stamp the kronen notes, Otto Bauer conceived the plan of proposing to Germany what virtually amounted to a currency union; but it was rejected for the same reason. At the same time, however, Bauer succeeded in concluding a treaty very favorable to Austria concerning the anschluss. It provided among other things that for a number of years after the union Austrian industry would still enjoy the protection of a customs tariff, whereas the German customs on all Austrian goods were to be abolished.[2] But this treaty had to remain secret "for the time being," and, naturally, never went into effect.

Bauer's foreign policy during his first months in office consisted chiefly of attempts to influence public opinion as well as official cir-

[1] Otto Bauer, *Acht Monate auswärtiger Politik* (Wien, 1919), p. 5: "This [the anschluss] would have been possible, if the whole people here had had a uniform, firm, and strong will in this matter. Then we could have dared in December or January simply to carry through the anschluss and confront the world with an accomplished fact without asking anyone." It will be recalled that after the death of Viktor Adler, Bauer had become state secretary of foreign affairs.

[2] *Idem, Die österreichische Revolution* (Wien, 1923), pp. 144–145.

cles in England and the United States. The French vigorously opposed him and launched in Vienna a comprehensive, well-financed propaganda campaign against anschluss. These seeds fell on fertile soil. In the first months after the revolution large groups in Austria were strongly against anschluss and others watched the development of the issue with calm indifference. The workers regarded the war as a product of nationalism and were much more interested in social than in national questions. Later, the fact that revolutionary risings of German workers were suppressed by somewhat excessive use of force was unlikely to increase the sympathy of their Austrian brothers for anschluss. Bauer, himself, had to admit that "there are many workers who say: 'We do not want to join a Noske Germany.'"[3] Thus the support Bauer got from his own party was not overly enthusiastic. Also, there were forces in the party which undoubtedly favored a policy of understanding with the succession states, primarily with Czechoslovakia. It is not surprising to find among the latter Karl Renner, the old "Pan-Austrian."

Among the bourgeoisie, too, there was a strong dislike, sometimes, indeed, a vicious hatred of anschluss. Their political reasons included fears of the Bolshevist danger in Germany, which then seemed quite threatening, and desires for a Habsburg restoration. The fact that the Christian Socials fought the elections of February, 1919, as a republican party is explained by political expediency. As the enthusiasm of the peasants for the republic cooled, the legitimist elements in the Catholic party regained the upper hand and swung it back toward its traditional position. In addition, the bourgeoisie had weighty economic reasons for their attitude, the most important of which was that the Vienna bankers having large funds and valuable connections in the succession states feared that anschluss would entail the immediate confiscation of their property there. As has been noted above, the separatist movement in the states did not, in the first half of 1919, take the form of an effort to join Germany. Even for the strongly nationalist Styria there are proofs that at that time its devotion to the anschluss cause was far from ardent.[4] Thus was voiced a curiously composed chorus of opposition to Bauer's foreign policy. It was stressed that this policy could result only in

[3] *Idem, Acht Monate auswärtiger Politik,* p. 6.
[4] Cf. Robert Danneberg, *Die Sanierungsgegner* (Wien, 1923), p. 5.

the imposition by the peace treaty of heavier burdens on Austria. The first draft of that document presented to Renner, leader of the Austrian delegation in St. Germain, fully confirmed these apprehensions. Austria was to lose not only the Sudetenland, the German districts of South Moravia and some parts of Lower Austria with important railway junctions, but also a large part of Carinthia, where in the spring the Carinthian Heimwehr and the Vienna Volkswehr had fought against the Yugoslavian invaders;[5] further, the German districts in the west of Hungary (later Burgenland) were to remain with Hungary, and South Tirol with Italy. At about this time it became clear that there was considerable dissension between France and Italy at the peace conference. Bauer swiftly tried to win the support of the latter country for the Austrian claims, even offering her the right of military domination of the Brenner Pass if South Tirol were alloted to Austria. This was refused, but Austria's position in the Carinthian and Hungarian questions was supported by Italy. According to the second draft of the treaty (July, 1919), a plebiscite was to be held in Carinthia,[6] and Austria was to be given parts of western Hungary. The last stipulation was unconditional; nevertheless the Austrians demanded that a plebiscite be held in the German-Hungarian districts[7]—a revelation of the difficult position of the Austrian government at the time. Bitter and scornful comments were subsequently made on this apparently odd demand.[8]

---

[5] The Vienna Volkswehr which was sent to Carinthia proved there that this army built up under most unfavorable circumstances and much abused as a body of criminals, or at least Communists, actually possessed a very considerable fighting value. In support of this conclusion may be cited the evidence in *Abwehrkampf und Volks-Abstimmung in Kärnten* (Klagenfurt, 1930), edited by Hans Lagger; and, more important, the testimony of Martin Wutte, industrialist, Pan-German politician, and bitter enemy of the Socialists:

"The detachments of the Volkswehr were composed of very different elements and had very different military value. Nevertheless it must be set down as established that to the greater part of it the defense of the Fatherland and of liberty meant more than everything else. This larger part of the Volkswehr bore the main burden throughout the whole Carinthian fight. It stood continuously in the front line and accomplished more than could have been expected from the whole Volkswehr organization. Disruptive attempts of individuals could not find fertile soil in the sound core of this part of the Volkswehr." (M. Wutte, *Kärntens Freiheitskampf*, Klagenfurt, 1922, p. 63.)

Wutte's unbiased statement is especially valuable in view of many sweeping generalizations such as that in C. A. Macartney's *The Social Revolution in Austria* (Cambridge, 1926), pp. 99–100: "... from the military point of view it [the Volkswehr] was a tragic farce."

[6] In October, 1920, the population voted in the ratio of 6 to 4 for Austria. *Neue Freie Presse,* October 14, 1920 (A.M.), p. 1.

[7] K. Renner, *Novemberverbrecher* (Wien, 1932), p. 53.

[8] Cf., e.g., Carl Brockhausen, *Geldentwertung und Stabilisierung*, p. 244.

The explanation is simple. At the time Béla Kun still ruled in Budapest. Under the prevailing conditions a rising of Austrian workers was quite likely if it became known that Austria had tried to increase her territory at the expense of Communist Hungary.

Despite these gains for the new republic it also became clear at this time that all hopes of inducing the Allies to consent to anschluss were vain. Thereupon Bauer and Renner met in Feldkirch and decided to abandon the anschluss issue and to attempt a *rapprochement* with France. Bauer resigned and Renner succeeded in obtaining further concessions in the third and final text of the treaty.[9]

The decisive change in Austrian foreign policy was accomplished at the right moment. The government established in Hungary after the overthrow of Communist rule threatened the Austrian democracy with no fewer dangers than had its predecessor. The restoration of Habsburg rule in Hungary, which remained formally a kingdom, became an actual aim of Hungarian policy. This development was viewed with friendly eyes by the pro-Habsburg wing of the Catholic party. Many Christian Socials entertained close connections with Hungary and hoped that after the restoration of the emperor there the reëstablishment of an Austro-Hungarian monarchy would be possible. In pursuit of the new foreign policy of the Socialists Renner tried to counteract these tendencies. In January, 1920, he went to Prague and concluded a secret treaty with Beneš. Under its terms Austria obligated herself to maintain a position of "friendly neutrality" toward Czechoslovakia in the event of war between that country and Hungary, whereas Beneš promised that Czechoslovakia would support Austria in the event of a Hungarian attack. The small part of these secret negotiations that leaked out aroused the strongest indignation among the Christian Socials and led to Kunschak's attacks against Renner in parliament. Without going into the details of the ensuing debate it is necessary to stress the fact that the *rapprochement* with Czechoslovakia, as well as the earlier change in

[9] It is interesting to note here the reason Bauer himself gave for his resignation. "Many have not understood why I resigned, for this country lacks a tradition of democratic policy. People were accustomed to see the emperor appoint some well-known person as his minister, and dismiss him as soon as he did not like him any longer. In parliamentary countries it is different. If there a minister tries something and then convinces himself that he can not carry it through, he says: another course must be pursued and I leave this to some one else." (Bauer, *Acht Monate auswärtiger Politik*, p. 10.) This statement is particularly significant in view of the countless attacks launched in later years against the allegedly antidemocratic character of Bauer's policy.

foreign policy at St. Germain, did not imply the renunciation of the anschluss as a general aim of party policy. The leaders simply thought that under the given circumstances it was vital for Austria loyally to execute the peace treaty.[10] The treaty with Czechoslovakia sought not only to prevent the destruction of Austrian democracy by a Habsburg restoration, but also to prevent a political connection with Hungary which would make union with Germany impossible. The foreign policy resolution of the congress of 1920 made the position of the party entirely clear.

> Anschluss remains the goal. As long as anschluss cannot be effected everything which later could stand in its way is to be prevented. Therefore, any union with Hungary or with other succession states is to be rejected. The restoration of the Habsburgs in Hungary is to be regarded as a threat to the independence and to the republican constitution of German-Austria. In order to prevent this danger German-Austria must coöperate with the other succession states.[11]

This policy initiated by the Socialists proved of actual value in March, 1921, when ex-Emperor Karl returned for the first time to Hungary. The coalition no longer existed, but Michael Mayr, the Christian Social chancellor, declared in the meeting of parliament on April 1 that the government would regard the restoration in Hungary as a threat to the peaceful development of the Austrian republic.[12] He thus sided with the Little Entente which put Hungary under strong pressure and compelled Karl to withdraw. Mayr belonged to the small anschluss wing of the Christian Social party. He was aided by the fact that West Hungary (Burgenland), which had been assigned to Austria by the peace treaties, was still held by Hungary. The feeling aroused by the issue helped to prevent the Habsburg wing of his party from converting the whole of it to a pro-Hungarian policy.

In subsequent months the Christian Socials became hesitant to defend the right of Austria to incorporate Burgenland. In order not to worsen their relations with Hungary they strongly opposed the occupancy of that territory by the Volkswehr when permission for it

[10] Cf. the Coalition Pact in *Tätigkeits-Bericht,* Heft 13 (Wien, 1920), p. 10.

[11] *Parteitag, 1920,* p. 101.

[12] *Stenographisches Protokoll, 31. Sitzung des Nationalrates der Republik Oesterreich,* I. Gesetzgebungsperiode, April 1, 1921, p. 1252. These proceedings of the lower house of the republican parliament are cited hereafter as Nationalrat, *Protokoll,* followed by date and page.

was at last given by the Entente. As a result the small detachments of gendarmery which did enter Burgenland met with the resistance of irregular Hungarian bands and were pushed back. In fact, on several occasions the army had to fight such irregulars who tried to invade Austrian territory. The Burgenland crisis was at last solved through the intervention of Italy, but not to the entire satisfaction of Austria. Close connections, almost amounting to an alliance, had already been established between Hungary and Italy so that Hungary secured a plebiscite in the part of Burgenland held under the supervision; that is, subject to the pressure, of Hungarian authorities. The capital of Burgenland, Ödenburg (Sopron), was thus lost to Austria. Before the Burgenland problem was settled, however, former Emperor Karl for the second time arrived in Hungary and started his march on Budapest (October 21, 1921). Socialist workers' representatives in Vienna issued the following proclamation:

> The meeting of representatives of the Viennese workers protests with indignation against the repetition of the attempt of Karl Habsburg to acquire the Hungarian crown. A Habsburg on the Hungarian throne means the strongest threat to the Austrian republic and the outbreak of bloody war in Central Europe.
>
> The meeting of representatives declares its determination to prevent any attempt at Habsburg restoration in Austria by every means at the disposal of the working class. The Austrian workers will never again tolerate the rule of a member of the blood-stained, murderous Habsburg family.
>
> In order to beat off the adventurous attempt of Karl Habsburg it is necessary to increase the fighting power of the Austrian army. Unmarried workers who have military training are urged to join the army without delay. No one must shirk the duty of defending our republic with arms in his hand.
>
> The representatives' meeting regards, further, the quick building up and reinforcement of the proletarian *Ordner*[13] as an efficacious protection against putsch attempts by the Monarchists.
>
> The meeting of representatives sends its fraternal greetings to all men who keep faithful guard on the border and assures them that in case of emergency the whole working class will fight on their side.[14]

But because of the influence of the Christian Socials the actions of the government during Karl's second putsch were much less ener-

[13] Literally: "Order maker" or "supervisor"; actually the word was used euphemistically in order to avoid the term "military organization" which undoubtedly would have better fitted the real state of affairs.

[14] *Parteitag, 1922,* p. 22.

getic than the workers' party desired. About all that can be said is that the Socialist interpellation and Seipel's speech in the parliamentary session of October 25 provoked turbulent scenes.[15] And when the Austrian government satisfied itself with a declaration of neutrality after the mobilization of the Czech army, the development of Austrian-Czech relations suffered a rather definite setback. Moreover, this action certainly caused a deterioration in the general position of Austria in the world. Hungary, on the other hand, secured a tangible improvement of her political situation through the putsch because Horthy, although he had corresponded with the emperor concerning the restoration and was informed of his plans,[16] quickly swerved around when he saw the attitude taken by the Little Entente, and defeated the legitimist troops.

Largely because of the display of force and energy by the Social Democrats during the Habsburg crisis the government woke up to the necessity of pursuing a more active foreign policy and of improving relations with the Little Entente. Consequently, Chancellor Schober concluded with Czechoslovakia in January, 1922, the so-called Treaty of Lana by which the essential stipulations of the Renner-Beneš treaty of 1920 were renewed, this time publicly. Although Schober strongly favored union with Germany he realized its impossibility at the time and believed that a temporary understanding with his neighbors against a restoration would aid in preventing that danger to anschluss. Later, when Germany was stronger, the objections of the Little Entente to a fusion of Germany and Austria might be overcome. Oddly enough the Pan-Germans regarded the treaty as an attack upon the anschluss. The evidence indicates that Seipel utilized their resentment shortly afterward to help overthrow Schober. Kunschak is certainly correct in styling this episode a "tragicomic incident."[17] Nevertheless, Austrian foreign policy continued on these lines, originally drawn by the Social Democrats, until June, 1922; then, after a short period of swift diplomatic moves, Seipel virtually permitted the foreign policy to be made by the League of Nations. This date marked the end of direct or indirect participation by the Socialists in the foreign policy of the republic.

---

[15] Nationalrat, *Protokoll*, October 25, 1921, pp. 2227–2229.

[16] Cf. Imre Balassa, *Death of an Empire* (New York, 1937), p. 239.

[17] L. Kunschak, *Oesterreich, 1918–1934* (Wien, 1935), p. 72. For further details on Seipel's role, see below, p. 167, n. 74.

Although anschluss remained their official policy, they realized the impossibility of carrying it through in the next few years. Shifting political developments also made anschluss appear much less desirable to the Socialists at times, so that for many years the party was scornfully designated as one "without foreign policy."

To sum up: it may be said that the Social Democratic foreign policy in the years 1918–1922 contributed significantly to the making of the Austrian republic.

(1) The Socialists succeeded to a great degree in preventing the dismemberment of the country originally planned by the authors of the peace treaty. Their untiring efforts saved a large part of Carinthia and Burgenland for Austria—efforts fully recognized by the people of these states.[18] Of course, the degree of success of this foreign policy must be appraised with regard to the balance of power then existing in Europe. South Tirol could not be regained nor the results of the distintegration of the old economic body of the empire undone.

(2) By initiating the pro-Czech policy the Austrian workers' party substantially reinforced Austrian democracy and diminished the danger of a reëstablishment of the monarchy.

Although these two achievements are sufficiently clear, the value of the anschluss policy is less certain. It may at least be argued that Bauer's persistent and exclusive anschluss policy had deteriorated Austria's position at St. Germain,[19] so that even the sudden change in July could not be of much help. And although the whole matter lies in the field of speculation it also may be argued that in the absence of the anschluss policy the French, from the beginning, would have associated the preservation of Austrian independence with the preservation of the working-class movement. As it was, most French politicians were profoundly suspicious of the Austrian Socialists

[18] In both states the Social Democrats became the strongest party at the first elections held after they had been finally attached to the republic. This fact is all the more astonishing because Burgenland had no industrial districts worth mentioning and Carinthia's were small as compared with those of Vienna, Lower Austria, and Styria. The disappointment of the Christian Socials was naturally great. Cf. Leo Volkmar, "Die Wahlen in Kärnten," *Das Volkswohl,* vol. 12, Heft 7–8 (1921), 212; and Hans Schmitz, "Zeitgedanken," *ibid.,* vol. 13, Heft 7–8 (1922), 194.

[19] Since the Catholic leader and convinced Monarchist, Seipel, was a natural enemy of anschluss, his opinion might have been biased; but there is no denying that he was one of the greatest diplomatic geniuses Austria ever produced. He was undoubtedly right when he warned against "putting everything on the one card of the anschluss." Cf. Seipel, *Der Kampf um die österreichische Verfassung* (Wien, 1930), p. 75.

and felt that their conversion to an anti-anschluss policy came much too late. Except for *Populaire,* the French press was for years generally unfavorable to the Social Democrats of Austria and in the decisive period of Dollfuss' chancellorship visualized him, not the Socialists, as the rock on which the Nazi wave would break. On the other hand, Paul-Boncour was keenly aware of the dangers. He told me that more than once during the time he was foreign minister of France he had urged Dollfuss to rule in a democratic fashion, that Dollfuss had agreed to do so, and that Dollfuss had also agreed not to attack the Austrian Social Democrats. Furthermore, the French statesman assured me that although the agreements to rule democratically and not to attack the Socialists were never reduced to writing, they were in the strictest sense "official" and not "personal."[20] But in January of 1934 one cabinet crisis in France was following another and one week before the Austrian civil war of February broke out Paul-Boncour definitely left the ministry. This fact and the circumstances described were of material help to Dollfuss when he decided to proceed to complete destruction of the independent workers' movement.

But during these early years when foreign policy was being used to solidify and stabilize the new nation crosscurrents continued at work. It has been shown that the change from monarchy to republic had been effected in a surprisingly peaceful and frictionless way. A high government official reports that for days the last ministers of the emperor and the ministers of the revolutionary government sat in neighboring rooms in the government buildings. The chief of the ministry staff appealed sometimes to one, sometimes to the other for instructions.[21] But however smooth this change was, there were, as already indicated in the chapters on state separatism and the constitution, strong forces opposed to the new form of government. As also noted, the Social Democrats became the strongest party in the Constituent Assembly. Although they suffered substantial losses in the elections to the first parliament in October of 1920, they still preserved the position of a strong minority which could prevent any act of the parliament if it seriously wanted to do so. Moreover, the Socialist trade unions embraced the overwhelming majority of

[20] Conversation with Joseph Paul-Boncour in San Francisco, May 17, 1945.
[21] Brockhausen, *Geldentwertung und Stabilisierung,* p. 242.

the workers. In view of these basic facts it seemed at that time rather hopeless to try to deprive the Socialists of their position by peaceful and democratic means. Separatist endeavors to dismember Austria were caused to a large degree by the wish to overcome the Socialist influence, at least within the narrower framework of the individual states. In tracing the earlier attempts of this sort it was pointed out that Vorarlberg wanted union with Switzerland, that Tirol wished independence, and that the majority of the states desired to obtain the greatest possible freedom from Vienna and the central government. When it became clear that the Bolshevist danger in Germany was rapidly waning the hopes of the separatist movement turned more and more definitely toward Germany. Especially when, after the Kapp putsch in Germany, rightist rule was established in Bavaria by Kahr, the tendencies toward union with that part of the Reich reached a climax in the states. Even earlier, December, 1919, Tirol and Salzburg had carried unanimous resolutions favoring "economic anschluss" to Germany. (The Salzburg resolution went further, stating the express desire for union with Bavaria.) The Entente, however, declared, by means of a very positive note of December 17, 1919, written by Clemenceau, that it would not tolerate any changes in the territorial or other stipulations of the peace treaty. This somewhat discouraged the separatist forces so that for a time they directed their efforts toward securing as much influence as possible for the states in the federal constitution.

The first Habsburg putsch in Hungary gave a new impetus to the anschluss movement in the states. On the one side, the events in Hungary strengthened the Socialists' position; on the other, they weakened the Habsburg adherents. In April, 1921, Tirol carried through a plebiscite on anschluss. Almost nine-tenths of the qualified voters participated and 98.8 per cent of them favored anschluss. Next, the diet of Salzburg passed a similar resolution, but chose to have the plebiscite held as a private undertaking of the parties. Although Upper Austria also decided to have an election, it was pointed out that the decision was to be regarded only as an expression of principle. Finally, Styria followed; on May 31 the diet there decided upon a plebiscite. In the meantime France, supported by England and Italy, made it clear to the government in Vienna that a continuation of the plebiscites in the states would lead to imme diate refusal of any credit. Since at that time of raging inflation in Austria the whole policy of the government was dominated by the need of foreign credits, this intervention of the Entente was decisive. The government tried to improve its political situation by asking Rintelen and Ahrer, the leaders of the Styrian Christian Socials, to join the government. Both of them refused. In order to counteract the anschluss movement in the states a law was passed by parliament authorizing an anschluss plebiscite to be held in the whole federal territory, but at a date to be fixed later. As was to be expected, it was never held. At the same time Chancellor Mayr's attempts to prevail upon the leaders of the state diet of Styria to withdraw the decision to hold a plebiscite were meeting with strong opposition. In fact, Mayr's attitude during the Habsburg putsch had determined the men in the states to get rid of him. This behavior seems to be inconsistent, since Mayr had opposed Karl's putsch on the ground that he was a sincere friend of the anschluss; now he was to be removed by an anschluss plebiscite. But the point is that state particularism was largely motivated if not dominated by hatred against the labor movement, so that the state leaders rather indiscriminately preferred anything to the existing state of affairs. In view of this basic fact it is interesting to note that the unconditional clinging of the Socialists to the idea of anschluss even induced Otto Bauer, during the negotiations, to defend in parliament the state plebiscites which were directed against his own party.[22] This was unquestionably bad party policy, but shows how seriously the Socialists took their nationalist policy.

The Mayr government was finally compelled to resign, whereupon an agreement was reached between the Christian Socials and the Pan-Germans to refrain from plebiscites during the next months. The plebiscite in Styria was never held.

The episode of the anschluss plebiscites was the last major action of state particularism. It showed once more the close connections between what can be called the foreign policy of the states and the internal political development in Austria. This becomes even clearer in the first attempts at building up right-wing private militias.

The idea of checking the development of the Social Democratic party and, at least to a degree, of undoing its achievements in the

[22] Nationalrat, *Protokoll,* April 15, 1921, p. 1340; June 22, p. 1491.

field of social legislation arose very early; in fact, very soon after the fall of the dictatorship in Budapest, rumors of a counterrevolutionary putsch began to circulate in Vienna.[23] At the party congress of 1919 Friedrich Adler stated that he was in possession of documents disclosing plans obviously drawn up by officers of the old army, and that these plans included details on exact military preparations, such as the occupation of bridges over the Danube.[24] But the forces of the Socialists in Vienna were obviously too strong; it was understood that to start an open struggle in the citadel of Socialism was too risky. Therefore, execution of the plans was never attempted; only a few relatively harmless demonstrations against the Polish Jews took place in Vienna, and the center of military activities against the existing regime was soon shifted to the states.

For the purposes in mind the conservative elements found already at hand the Heimwehr or Heimatschutz organizations. As previously noted these groups, particularly in Styria, Carinthia, and Tirol, had been formed primarily for exactly the purpose their names indicate—protection of the homeland against potential or actual aggression from neighboring states. Prince Starhemberg, one of their chief leaders, said that "early in 1919" they coöperated with "Socialist police troops" in clearing Linz "of its anarchist mischief-makers."[25] It was self-evident, however, that the Heimwehr might also be used against what the conservative elements considered at least an equal danger—the Socialists. Until the beginning of 1920 this second activity remained more or less underground; the participation of the Socialists in the government prevented it from assuming too obvious a character. Still, it is significant that the minister of interior, the Socialist Eldersch tried in vain to induce the Styrian government to dismiss a state commander of gendarmery who entertained relations with the Hungarian army.[26] And it is probably more significant

[23] Julius Deutsch, *Aus Oesterreichs Revolution* (Wien, n.d.), p. 127.

[24] *Parteitag, 1919,* pp. 168–169.

[25] E. R. Starhemberg, *Between Hitler and Mussolini* (New York-London, 1942), pp. 5, 6. Generally speaking, these memoirs are unreliable (for documentation of this statement see my discussion in *The New York Times Book Review,* November 8, 1942); but though the Fascist prince is making a definite attempt to rehabilitate himself, at the same time he makes innumerable admissions concerning matters which have long been disputed. His self-incrimination, as well as that of Schuschnigg in the latter's *My Austria,* will be cited to show the ideas and activities of men who have received support in England and the United States in their effort to return to power in Vienna.

[26] *Parteitag, 1920,* p. 19.

that when the coalition blew up on June 10, 1920, and a "proportional" government was formed, the Socialists, after a prolonged struggle, had to acquiesce in the loss of the ministry of interior.[27]

The states where the Fascist movement first gained momentum were Tirol and Salzburg. In February, 1920, while Kahr was still only a high official in the civil service in Bavaria, members of the Christian Social and Pan-German parties in those states asked the Bavarian military organizations and the Bavarian state government to help them organize against the "threat of Bolshevism" in Austria. Although Kahr evinced full and sympathetic understanding of the wishes of his brethren-in-spirit beyond the border, he stressed the fact that the government of Bavaria was not prepared to subsidize the movement officially. One of the leaders of the Bavarian military bands, Rudolf Kanzler, took the matter into his hands. Several conferences in Salzburg and Innsbruck followed. An Innsbruck meeting, on May 12, 1920, was held in the state capitol; those present included not only representatives of the local Heimwehr groups and the Bavarians, but also representatives of the police and even the state governor, Schraffl. The latter was somewhat apprehensive of the Bavarian plans, but finally acquiesced in the re-formation of the Heimwehr as a unified state-wide organization. To this he was persuaded by the Tirolese Christian Social and Pan-German representatives at the meeting who, in turn, received efficient help from a member of the Salzburg government also present. Three days later, May 15, 1920, the Provisional Statutes of the Tirolese Heimwehr were published. The Heimwehr was declared there to be a "nonmilitary organization." However, the purposes of the organization were stated to be: "protection against extraordinary dangers by which public security and order are threatened, especially by acts of violence against life and property," and extension of support to the authorities in safeguarding public security (Article 1). "The convocation of the Heimwehr," obviously a euphemistic term for mobilization, "will be carried out . . . as a rule upon request of the authorities of the public administration and security service

[27] On June 25 the negotiations between the parties were interrupted; at this time the formation of a proportional government was already decided upon, and only the question of the person of the prospective minister of interior remained for discussion. It took another week before the Socialists gave in and agreed to the appointment of Breisky—a man from the civil service. *Reichspost*, June 25, 1920, p. 1; July 2, p. 1.

or the gendarmery" (Article 9).[28] Richard Steidle, a Christian Social member of the Tirol diet, became leader of this organization.

The development in Salzburg was similar. Under Kanzler's continued management successful attempts at organizing the Heimwehren were undertaken in Styria and Carinthia. Also in Lower Austria, including Vienna, and Upper Austria steps in the same direction were made. On July 25, 1920, leaders of the Austrian groups from all states held a conference in Munich with Escherich, the leader of the Bavarian Orgesch (*Organization Escherich*). The roots of this essentially reactionary and antirepublican organization can be traced back to the stormy year 1919. The counterrevolutionary Kapp putsch of March, 1920, which in contradistinction to the rest of the Reich was successful in Bavaria, gave a strong impetus to Escherich's activities. Shortly after the putsch, the Orgesch was formally constituted. Kanzler became the right hand of Escherich and the work of his Orka (*Organization Kanzler*), as a part of the Orgesch, was concentrated on building up the Heimwehr in Austria. The attempt to spread the Bavarian organization over all Germany failed, chiefly because of the countermeasures of the Prussian government.

The Orgesch possessed large stores of arms. Under the terms of German law anyone who obtained knowledge of such depots but did not report them to the authorities made himself liable to severe punishment. Moreover, the Allied Commission had offered cash rewards for information concerning these secret stores. On the other hand, a special department of the Orgesch had been formed to deal with "traitors"; it committed a number of murders which in their cold cruelty occupy a disgracefully prominent place in the long list of crimes perpetrated by terrorist organizations in Germany. Under these circumstances the fact that at the aforementioned meeting in Munich the leaders of the Austrian Heimwehr subordinated themselves to the Bavarian Orgesch helps to explain the character of the Austrian movement, though it must be noted that its excesses in the early years never equaled those across the border.[29]

---

[28] Cf. for the text of the statutes, *Parteitag, 1921*, pp. 24–26.

[29] Cf. in the first place the uncommonly frank and revealing account given by Rudolf Kanzler in his *Bayerns Kampf gegen den Bolschewismus* (München, 1931), pp. 79, 81, 86–105, 248–251; furthermore: Günther Axhausen, *Organisation Escherich* (Leipzig-Berlin, 1921), pp. 12–18; Emil Julius Gumbel, *Verräter verfallen der Feme, 1919–1929* (Berlin, 1929), pp. 96–102; Bauer, *Die österreichische Revolution*, p. 231.

Nearly two decades later the Austrian Fascist Zernatto, secretary of the Fatherland Front and member of Schuschnigg's last cabinet, wrote with obvious pride of the early connections between the Heimwehr and the Orgesch and of the dreams that he and like-minded persons kept alive from 1919 on for the overthrow of the republic and the establishment of "the true state." As might be expected the ideas of this group were borrowed, at first, from Othmar Spann's book, *Der wahre Staat*. Moreover, the testimony of Jakob Ahrer, one of the organizers of the Styrian Heimwehr, shows that the movements in the various states were brought together "with the strong support of" the Orgesch and Orka. In the same passage Ahrer records his approval of the methods of the German bands.[30] It is worth noting that he was a Christian Social who was honored with the position of federal finance minister in 1924.

During the year 1920 arms were continually smuggled from Bavaria to Tirol and Salzburg and there distributed among the farmers for hiding;[31] and over a period of many months great quantities of arms of different kinds were stolen by the Heimwehr from the federal depots scattered throughout the country. Since these "thefts" included, on occasion, those of a large number of cannon, it is difficult to avoid the conclusion that at times they were committed with the tolerance of the authorities. For years these thefts were denied. Starhemberg not only admits them; he boasts of them in language similar to that used by a twelve-year-old lad in describing a successful raid on a watermelon patch. In January, 1921, the future vice-chancellor and some Heimwehr associates stole "twenty-one brand-new 10 cm. mountain-howitzers . . . all beautifully greased and in first-class condition." His only regret was that, "Unfortunately, we had to leave a few 15 cm. howitzers behind. . . ."[32]

Meanwhile, a joint demonstration in the form of a rifle match between the Orgesch and the Tirolese Heimwehr had been arranged

---

[30] G. Zernatto, *Die Wahrheit über Oesterreich* (New York-Toronto, 1938), pp. 76–78, 117; J. Ahrer, *Erlebte Zeitgeschichte* (Wien-Leipzig, 1930), p. 71.

[31] M. W. Fodor, *Plot and Counterplot in Central Europe* (Boston, 1937), p. 156. Fodor writes: "I saw in those early post-war years huge motor-lorries filled with rifles and ammunition going from Bavaria to Reutte and other places in the Tyrol."

[32] J. Deutsch, *Geschichte der österreichischen Gewerkschaftsbewegung*, Vol. II (Wien, 1932), p. 259; *Dokumente zum Wiener Schutzbundprozess* (Karlsbad [1935]), pp. 3–13; Starhemberg, *op. cit.*, pp. 7–10. Starhemberg's justification of this episode is that the artillery was soon to be taken over by the Italian Commission, that is, as part of Austria's disarmament; but he expressly states that it was taken "for the Heimwehr."

for November 20, 1920, at Innsbruck. Although the Austrian Socialist railroad employees struck and prevented the Bavarians from coming to Tirol, the plans gave opportunity for an airing of the whole situation in the lower house of parliament on November 19. In support of an urgent interpellation by his party the Tirolese Social Democrat Scheibein referred to the conferences between Heimwehr leaders and Escherich, as well as to the proposed demonstration, and charged that arms had been smuggled from Bavaria with the aid of Austrian state governments. Breisky, minister of the interior, in replying, mentioned the protest of the Allied Military Commission against the rifle match and the resulting request from the federal government to the state government either to forbid it or to deprive it of any official character. He added that because of the growing tension a second request had been made of the Tirolese authorities to take all necessary measures and "*perhaps*" to prohibit the demonstration; and pointed out that regulations against the crossing of the border by armed men were being intensified. More interesting is the fact that Breisky did not deny the charges of arms smuggling but said: "I may mention that a long time ago instructions were issued to submit the goods traffic to a strict supervision. These instructions have been emphatically reiterated today."

Scheibein then asked whether or not the government was prepared to give arms to the workers as it had to the Heimwehr. Breisky's reply was even more interesting, since he said that not everything which a representative of the people [meaning the governor of Tirol] does is done officially, and that at any rate the government was on the way to disarmament of the militant organizations.

The discussion was continued in a lengthy speech by the Socialist Deutsch. After referring to the coöperation between the Heimwehr and local officials, both city and state, he went on to the matter of arms smuggling, giving precise dates, the license number of an automobile seized in Innsbruck, the character of the weapons being transported, and similar details. The most convincing item in his indictment was the official report of a gendarmery inspector in Salzburg stating that every night between October 10 and 15, 1920, some 30 to 40 men had crossed from Bavaria bringing arms. Deutsch charged that the district officials had simply pigeonholed the report.

At the conclusion of Deutsch's remarks the president of the chamber reported that since no one else had asked to speak the debate was closed and the whole matter disposed of.[33]

The chief newspaper of the Christian Social party in reporting the interpellation and debate made no attempt to refute the Socialist charges but contented itself with accusing Scheibein of recounting fearsome fairy tales and making a parenthetical anti-Semitic jibe at Deutsch.[34]

The reasons for dealing with this matter at such length are obvious. In the nature of the case it is difficult to secure documentary proof of the activities of organizations which first in one way and then in another were attempting to destroy the republic. On this occasion, however, the Social Democrats had brought charges which were unequivocal, specific, and apparently well supported by documents or other reliable evidence. The newly formed Christian Social government was under obligations to refute these charges if it could; unless, perhaps, it believed that the successes of its party in the elections of the preceding month justified it in disregarding what may be called the etiquette of parliaments. The truth is that Breisky's answers were so evasive as to constitute a practical admission of the charges.

If the tactics of the Catholic party and its chief organ were to attempt to smother the whole controversy—and there is more than one indication that this is true—they did not succeed. The workers' party continued to hammer its charges on every occasion. Before long one of its representatives brought in another urgent interpellation, this time in the state diet of Styria: "On Saturday, March 5, [1921], the vice-governor of Styria, Dr. Ahrer, made a speech to a meeting of the Central Association of Manufacturers (*Hauptverband der Industriellen*) at which representatives of banks were also present, concerning the necessity of building up the Heimwehr in Styria and putting it in good fighting trim. For this purpose he demanded from the representatives of the major banks, industry, and large landowners there present a yearly contribution of five millions of crowns." According to the interpellation the request was granted after some hesitation, and after Ahrer had emphasized the need to fight Communist and Bolshevist dangers and the terrorization of the

[33] Nationalrat, *Protokoll,* November 19, 1920, pp. 47–54, esp. pp. 49, 50, 52, 54.
[34] *Reichspost,* November 20, 1920, p. 3.

workers. Ahrer declared in the state diet that he had requested this money not in his capacity as vice-governor, but as a private citizen.[35]

More important than this Styrian episode was a major move of the Association of Manufacturers in Vienna. Somewhat later; that is, on the first of December, 1921, there were great disturbances in the capital. Workers protested in the streets of the Inner City against rising prices, plundered shops and created general disorder. Under the impression of these events an emergency meeting of the Association of Manufacturers, bankers, and others was called late the same day. Fortunately for the historian the discussion at this meeting and the action taken have been recorded by the previously mentioned prominent industrialist and outstanding member of the Association, Ernst von Streeruwitz, who later became a member of parliament and chancellor of Austria. The meeting formally resolved to establish "self-aid" formations. "There began now the first consolidation of those forces which later on should form the Heimatschutz." In a previous passage Streeruwitz had pointed out that the Heimwehr had "double roots" in the peasant guards and in the industrialists' self-aid organizations. Some pages later he states that it is incorrect to say that "the Heimwehr has been a paid guard of the banks and of industry," but continues: "Indeed, industry has raised substantial sums of money in order to strengthen the Heimwehr movement, without ever denying it. Often enough I coöperated in these resolutions by counsel and vote." And in the next section he presents the real reasons for these activities. "Under the existing electoral conditions, however, the achievement of an appropriate representation and an appropriate influence [for industry in parliament] was not possible. Thus the idea developed . . . to solve the problem by instruments of force [*Machtmitteln*] created particularly therefor. Austrian industry furthered this development with the greatest vigor."[36]

At the risk of elaborating the obvious, certain conclusions from the foregoing quotations must be set down. First, the oft-repeated story that the Heimwehr was organized as a result of the riots of July 15, 1927, is false. Second, the real drive behind this private army was class interest. Third, that class interest could not secure

[35] Reprinted in *Parteitag, 1921*, p. 30. For facts concerning the development of the Heimwehr in more democratic Upper Austria, cf. J. Deutsch, *Die Fascistengefahr* (Wien, 1923), pp. 12–14.

[36] Streeruwitz, *Springflut über Oesterreich* (Wien-Leipzig, 1937), pp. 216, 212, 230, 242.

what it wanted "under the existing electoral conditions" (equal suffrage for adults of both sexes and a proportional representation system) and so it subsidized "instruments of force" in the shape of the Heimwehr.[37] Fourth, keeping in mind the fact that Streeruwitz published in late 1937, almost four years after the civil war of February, 1934, Austrian industry "furthered . . . with the greatest vigor" the destruction of parliamentary democracy.

The relations between the Heimwehr and the authorities and the states became ever more intimate. In November, 1922, the Socialist party council adopted a resolution protesting against these developments.

> . . . In Tirol, Salzburg, and Styria the Heimwehren have been granted the character of state armies . . . especially in Styria during recent days Heimwehren were even used by the state government for official proceedings against the workers and the governor of Styria has specifically conferred this function on the Heimwehren in an open meeting of the state diet; in Carinthia the Heimwehren serve as an instrument for threatening the activity of the Social Democratic governor. In Vienna there have been organizations of ex-service men [*Frontkämpfer*] for a long time; they are but reactionary storm troopers against the organized workmen. In the federal capital as well as in Upper Austria they were used by the chancellor [Seipel] as his bodyguards.
>
> Now in Lower Austria also the intention has been publicly expressed of carrying out the development of the Heimwehr in coöperation with the state government and the Christian Social governor. . . .[38]

An episode which occurred in the first part of November, 1922, throws some light on the precarious situation that was developing and also shows that the workers' groups were by no means confining themselves to parliamentary interpellations and party resolutions. Although, as usual in such cases, the reports are somewhat conflicting, the following account is essentially correct.

Workers in the Upper Styrian industrial town of Judenburg, having been informed that arms had been distributed among the peasants in the vicinity, decided to take countermeasures. Assembling in large numbers these workers, themselves armed, descended upon the homes of the peasants who allegedly had received arms,

---

[37] As early as October of 1920 the official organ of industry had broadly hinted at the desirability of such an organization: "The people . . . do not possess that physical power, such as for example the Bavarian *Reichspartei* has in the 'Orgesch,' and consequently is in a difficult position even if a bourgeois regime constitutes itself today. . . ." *Die Industrie*, October 23, 1920, p. 3.

[38] *Parteitag, 1923*, p. 25.

searched their premises and carried off a considerable number of rifles and pistols as well as some ammunition. Several days later about 200 members of the gendarmery occupied Judenburg under orders from the governor of Styria, Rintelen. That night six workers, among them the local secretary of the Social Democratic party, were arrested and taken to Graz. The excitement in Upper Styrian working-class circles was intense. During the discussion of the urgent interpellation of the Socialists on the matter in the national parliament, the bridge over the Mur River at Judenburg was occupied by armed forces—at one end the gendarmery, at the other the workers. Auxiliary detachments of federal troops were sent from Graz to Judenburg and reinforcements requested from Vienna. Heimwehr formations in the entire Mur Valley were kept in a state of preparedness. For some hours it seemed that fighting might begin at any moment, but the release of the arrested workers broke the tension and restored quiet.

In the course of the heated parliamentary debate on the interpellation, the Socialists admitted that the actions of the workers were illegal. They protested, however, against what they considered Rintelen's partiality, alleging that he had taken no action when reactionary students of the College of Mines in Leoben had for political reasons broken into workers' homes. Of more importance were the open admissions of a Christian Social deputy, the Roman Catholic priest Gimpl, that the peasants were being supplied with arms and that the governor of Styria regarded the Heimwehr as his bodyguard when he attended meetings. In reply to professions from conservative deputies that the Heimwehr was a harmless organization, Bauer emphasized the fact, which as he said, "no one in the house is able to controvert," that the formation was being "financed by a levy collected by the Central Association of Manufacturers and equal to 1 per cent of the total wage bill."[39] In the light of certain of the previously quoted statements from Streeruwitz, Bauer's assertion seems more than probable. And in the light of the determination of the industrialists, again as set down by Streeruwitz, to destroy parliamentary institutions by force, the characterization of the Heimwehr as harmless is ludicrous and mendacious.

[39] *Arbeiter Zeitung*, November 15, 1922, pp. 2–4, and November 16, p. 4; *Reichspost*, November 15, 1922, p. 4; Nationalrat, *Protokoll*, November 14, 1922, pp. 4705–4708, 4710–4712, 4719.

Despite strenuous efforts of the Socialists against it the arming of the Heimwehr continued relatively unchecked.[40] Although for the time being it was unable seriously to infringe upon the position of the Socialists, the Heimwehr continued eagerly at work preparing for the attacks which were unleashed several years later. The Socialists tried very hard to suppress the Heimwehr, but its connections with the former leaders of state separatism, who were still prominent figures in the states, helped it to weather storms of this kind.

The position of the Social Democrats has always been that the situation briefly sketched above left them no choice and that they were compelled to build up a military formation of their own. This organization was the Republican Defense Corps (*Republikanischer Schutzbund*). It was an expansion of the "order makers" and was limited at first to Vienna where it was constituted on February 19, 1923. Soon thereafter, April 12, it secured from the ministry of the interior and education approval for the charter and bylaws of an organization that covered the entire federal territory.[41] The conservative and reactionary groups have always insisted that their formations were created to put a check on Social Democratic "terror." In other words, each side claimed that it organized its military forces to meet the aggressions of the other. The truth seems to be that both Heimwehr and Schutzbund have a tenuous connection with the previously mentioned local defense corps which fought against the Slovenes in South Carinthia and the Hungarians in Burgenland, just as similar Bavarian corps provided a basis for the Nazi storm troops. Subsequently, differences in political and economic interests brought new alignments; Austrian industrial workers tended to join the Schutzbund, but peasants and others, the Heimwehr. The essential difference was that members of the Schutzbund—almost to a man—remained steadfast in their determination to defend the republic and democratic institutions, whereas the leaders of the Heimwehr groups had little patience with democracy in the beginning and lost even that little by 1929, at the latest. As for the rank and file of the Heimwehr, particularly the peasants, there can be no doubt that hundreds of them honestly believed the organization was engaged in a holy crusade against Bolshevism. In this attitude

[40] Cf. the evidence presented in J. Deutsch, *Wer rüstet zum Bürgerkrieg? Neue Beweise für die Rüstungen der Reaktion* (Wien, 1923).

[41] *Parteitag, 1923*, pp. 27, 35.

they were not infrequently encouraged by the local Roman Catholic priest. Further developments will be discussed in Part Five of this work which deals with the counterrevolution in Austria. At this point it need only be added that with the determination of anti-democratic business interests to finance the Heimwehr and the formation of the Schutzbund by the republicans began that unfortunate rivalry between party militias which was to become a chief feature of the life of the little country for years.

CHAPTER VIII

Socialization

The attempts at socialization undertaken in Austria during 1919 left scarcely any traces in the subsequent history of the nation's labor movement. Their interest and importance lie chiefly in the facts that they illustrate again the difficult political situation with which the Social Democratic party had to deal, and that they throw an interesting light on the line-up of forces which prevented the establishment of Bolshevist rule.

It has been shown that the theorists of the party regarded the Revolution of 1918 (1) as another step toward the completion of the national revolution of the Pan-German idea, (2) as containing elements of a social revolution, and (3) as the establishment of political democracy. Thereby only the basis was laid for a further development toward social reconstruction. Furthermore, these theorists held fast to the Marxist teaching that Socialism would become possible only when capitalism had reached a high stage of development in which it had the technical possibilities of providing a satisfactory existence for all members of society; but in which as a matter of fact there was an increasing concentration of wealth, because of the "law of capitalist accumulation," and a corresponding increase of "poverty, oppression, enslavement, degeneration, and exploitation" among the laboring masses. Whatever may have been true at other times, these conditions obviously did not exist in the first years of postwar Austria. As has been noted more than once above, the position of the workers was desperate enough, but industrial equipment was in good part antiquated and worn out; vital raw materials and coal simply were not to be had in anything like adequate quantities. In Renner's oft-quoted statement, "One cannot socialize debts."

If nevertheless, very soon after the revolution, the Social Democrats set forth a comprehensive socialization program, they did so because the general development abroad imperiously demanded such a policy. In Russia the Bolshevists without any preparatory work tried to build a completely socialized society at one grand stroke; later on, even they dubbed this period "war Communism" and reintroduced capitalist elements. But in the spring of 1919 the Russian attempt at a "lightning socialization" was exercising a great influence upon the minds of the workers in central Europe. And in some states bordering Austria socialization appeared to have become an accomplished fact. Notably, the Béla Kun government stipulated "by decree" the complete socialization of the Hungarian economy. Bavaria attempted the same thing during the short period of soviet rule there, and in the whole of Germany the socialization problem seemed to be treated most seriously. For Austria to ignore these facts would have meant preparing the way for Bolshevism. Thus socialization became one of the most important issues in Austria in 1919. The program of February 19 of the Social Democratic members of the Constituent Assembly demanded the "planned and systematic socialization of all the branches of national economy" which are today "ripe for this purpose," and the creation of a socialization commission which was to make proposals concerning the reconstruction of the Austrian economy.[1] The Socialists thus, as was to be expected, took the lead in such proposals. But the non-Socialist parties also hastened to include socialization in their programs. Only a fortnight later the Christian Socials adopted a program which included the statement that: "Transport and mining undertakings, as far as they serve the general needs [of the population], and those big industrial concerns which produce articles of mass consumption and in the nature of the case *easily attain a monopoly position,* shall be socialized by the central government, the states, or the communities." The Catholic party likewise demanded "without delay" a socialization commission composed of members of the Constituent Assembly, representatives of the states, and experts.[2] As is easily understandable, it laid especial stress on the participation of the states. Moreover, a limited program of socialization had never been alien to this party; Lueger had municipalized the public utilities of Vienna. Finally, the Pan-Germans drew up a program and stated in the Constituent Assembly their willingness to "coöperate and collaborate for socialization."[3] Obviously, socialization was "in style"; a large literature appeared suddenly and grew with mushroom rapidity. As Schumpeter stated, "everybody spoke of socialization." But as one of the leaders of the

[1] *Tätigkeits-Bericht,* Heft 12 (Wien, 1919), p. 5.
[2] *Reichspost,* February 28, 1919, p. 1. Italics in original.
[3] Konstituierende Nationalversammlung, *Protokoll,* March 14, 1919, p. 88.

movement, the Socialist Ellenbogen, confessed several years later, "a clear concept concerning the forms and conditions of Socialist production was scarcely to be found anywhere, and even the best schooled theorists of the party had to try to arrive at such a concept by hard mental work, without being able to come to an agreement."[4]

The best known of the attempts to formulate a plan for socialization in Austria is that of Otto Bauer, published as a series of articles in the *Arbeiter Zeitung* in January, 1919, and reissued as a booklet under the title *The Way to Socialism.*[5] Bauer's leading ideas, which actually became the basis of Austrian legislation on the subject, are as follows. Socialization is to be effected gradually. The key industries (coal, ore, iron, steel) are to be socialized first. The owners are to receive full compensation, the funds to be furnished by a general, strongly progressive capital levy. The reason given by Bauer for his proposal concerning compensation is an ethical one: it would be unjust to socialize certain types of industries while the owners of others remained in full possession of their rights. Socialized undertakings are not to be administered by the government—bureaucratic methods being inappropriate for management of an industrial undertaking—but by corporations created for the purpose (*Gemeinwirtschaftliche Anstalten*). The management of these corporations is to consist of representatives of the whole people (federal state), of the workers in the undertakings (trade unions), and of the consumers (either representatives of other industries, or, in the case of finished goods, of consumers' coöperatives). For the rest of industry, industrial syndicates (*Industrieverbände*) are to be organized on the same tripartite principle. These syndicates are to have the right to alter the production plans of individual undertakings, to try to prevent or diminish competition, to fix prices; in brief, to act as the management board of a cartel. Within the unsocialized undertakings the "autocratic rule" of the management is to be transformed by the democratic influence of workmen's committees in the factories. The socialization of the banks crowns the whole edifice of socialization.[6]

[4] Wilhelm Ellenbogen, "Die Gemeinwirtschaft," *in* Gewerkschaftskommission, *Bericht,* 1923, p. 32.

[5] Otto Bauer, *Der Weg zum Sozialismus.* Originally published in 1919, this booklet went through at least twelve printings.

[6] How unprepared the party was on this issue may be perceived from the fact that in the opinion of Karl Renner, the other major leader of the party, the socialization of banks should be the first step in the process. Karl Renner, *Die Wirtschaft als Gesamtprozess und die Sozialisierung* (Berlin, 1924).

The Constituent Assembly went to work on these general lines. On March 14, it adopted a law creating a socialization commission, and on the next day elected Bauer as president, Seipel as vice-president, the trade-union leader Domes, the Christian Social Kunschak, and the Styrian industrialist Wutte as members of the executive board of the commission. This executive coöpted a large number of persons as members, among them many non-Socialists. Since the inclusion of individuals who were not Socialists led to violent protests from the ranks of the workers,[7] Bauer was compelled to justify the action of the executive at some length.[8]

The activities of the commission were greatly hastened by the developments in Hungary and the following radicalization of the Austrian workers. On May 15, the law concerning the works councils was passed by the Constituent Assembly.[9] The connections between the councils and socialization were rather remote, as the law itself and especially the subsequent practice showed. Viewed from the most favorable angle they could be regarded only as a basis for schooling the workers for the management of factories; that is to say, to be part of a socialization in the very long run. "But it was politically very prudent to start this legislation with the law of May 15 . . . which met an old demand of the workers without involving a serious interference with capitalist economy. In this regard *all the parties* were very soon of the same opinion."[10] This statement of a high official in the ministry of social welfare and an outstanding scholar is of particular value because it indicates, from an impartial source, the motives of the socialization policy of all the parties.[11]

[7] Gewerkschaftskommission, *Bericht,* 1919, pp. 195–197. Members of the left wing of the party likewise criticized the attempt to carry out socialization in coöperation with members of bourgeois parties. Alexander Täubler, *Die Sozialisierung und der neue Geist der Zeit* (Wien, 1919), p. 17.

[8] *Arbeiter Zeitung,* April 9, 1919, p. 4.

[9] *StGBl.,* 1919, Nr. 283.

[10] Karl Pribram, "Die Sozialpolitik im neuen Oesterreich," *AfSS.,* vol. 48 (1920–1921), 647. Italics mine.

[11] The connection between socialization and works councils had another important aspect: the works councils were able in many instances to prevent the so-called wild socializations (actually, syndicalist attempts) of the factories by the workers. In this regard the following may serve as a good illustration. On April 7, 1919, there were riotous workers' demonstrations in the smelting works of the *Alpine Montan Gesellschaft* in Donawitz, Styria, against the high prices of the foodstuffs distributed by the works. A meeting of workers decided upon the dismissal of the director of the plant and the establishment of a managing commission consisting of two engineers and two workers. This body addressed itself immediately to Otto Bauer as president of the socialization commission with the demand that the works be socialized without delay. After protracted negotiations some of the demands of the workers concerning wages

Two weeks later, May 30, the assembly enacted a general statute concerning the procedure in expropriating economic undertakings; it stipulated that owners were to be compensated. But it was not until July 29, that an act was adopted regulating the formation of public corporations (*Gemeinwirtschaftliche Unternehmungen*) on the lines drawn up by Otto Bauer.[12] One of the more interesting provisions of this act was Section 37. It authorized the federal administration to require that in the organization of share-capital corporations the federation or other public bodies could participate in the capital of the concerns up to one-half under the most favorable conditions offered to anyone. In the event of an increase in the capital such public bodies could acquire shares until their portion equaled one-half of the total capital. Appreciable use was made of the rights thus established. Meanwhile, on May 21, Fink, the Christian Social vice-chancellor, had indicated briefly which undertakings the government was planning to socialize; that is, to expropriate and to turn over to the ownership and administration of *Gemeinwirtschaftliche Anstalten,* the main form of *Gemeinwirtschaftliche Unternehmungen.* He mentioned coal mines (unless production was reserved for local needs), the whole coal trade, iron-ore mining and pig-iron production, generation of electric current and the water power to be used for that purpose, the big forests, the timber industry, and wholesale trade.[13] Various schemes were drawn up for putting this program into execution, but not one of them ever got so far as adoption by the Constituent Assembly. With reference

---

and hours were granted; furthermore, it was decided to apply the works councils bill, which had not yet been passed by the Constituent Assembly, to the Donawitz smelter at once. The new works council undertook to do its best to secure an increase of production. Thus because of the works councils a "wild socialization" was actually prevented and peace restored. Cf. *Bericht der Gewerbe-Inspektoren Oesterreichs über ihre Amtstätigkeit im Jahre 1919* (Wien, 1920), pp. xlvii, 235–236 (the title of these reports varies; they are cited hereafter as Gewerbe-Inspektoren, *Bericht*); and Felix Busson *et al., Die österreichisch-Alpine Montangesellschaft* (Wien, 1931), pp. 168–169.

[12] *StGBl.,* 1919, Nr. 308, 389. In the spring of 1919 a few other laws generally characterized as "socialization" acts were passed. Among them was the "palaces act," officially called the "act concerning people's welfare places," according to which "castles, palaces, and other luxury dwellings" could be expropriated and used for general welfare purposes; in cases where the buildings were in the possession of *nouveaux riches* no compensation was to be paid. Furthermore, the so-called recolonizing act (*Wiederbesiedlungsgesetz*) should be mentioned under which large estates, composed of lands previously in the possession of peasants, could be expropriated and given back to them. Neither of these laws was of great practical import. For a survey of the socialization legislation, cf. Emanuel Hugo Vogel, "Die Sozialisierungsgesetzgebung Deutsch-Oesterreichs und ihre wirtschaftliche Bedeutung," *AfSS.,* vol. 48 (1920–1921), 74–147.

[13] Konstituierende Nationalversammlung, *Protokoll,* May 21, 1919, pp. 382–383.

to water-power resources, as previously explained (above, p. 93), state separatism coupled with lack of capital prevented socialization. The socialization of coal mining was of little importance, as compared with that of the coal trade. But here, as Otto Bauer frankly admits, private trade was so clearly superior in finding ingenious devices for getting supplies that socialization had to be postponed.[14] The attempt to socialize the *Alpine Montan Gesellschaft* was important for three reasons at least: it was the largest undertaking in Austria, it controlled the Austrian iron deposits which are among the most valuable in Europe,[15] and it was the strongest and most determined opponent among the industrialists of the labor movement. According to Bauer the socialization of the *Alpine* was rendered impossible by his colleague in the government, the minister of finance, Professor Joseph A. Schumpeter; that is, Schumpeter authorized the banker Richard Kola to make an arrangement with Italian interests whereby they would buy up large quantities of *Alpine* shares. The lira thus obtained were turned over to the finance ministry which was in urgent need of foreign exchange to buy foodstuffs and coal. Bauer continued: "Schumpeter supported this action although he knew that we had planned the socialization of the *Alpine Montan Gesellschaft*. He supported it without informing the other members of the cabinet of it. . . . This procedure on the part of Schumpeter led to a violent conflict within the coalition government in which Schumpeter sought and secured the support of the Vienna Christian Socials. . . ." The upshot of the affair, according to Bauer, was that the socialization plan had to be dropped, particularly after Italian intervention.[16]

The *Volkswirt,* though carefully pointing out that it was by no means enthusiastic for socialization at this time, observed that the communiqué of the "State Correspondence" on the matter "at least creates the appearance that the state secretary for finance is again making his own particular policy with reference to socialization, which is in contradiction with the general policy of the cabinet. . . ." This the journal considered to be "not permissible."[17]

---

[14] Otto Bauer, *Die österreichische Revolution* (Wien, 1923), p. 179.

[15] O. S. Phillpotts, *Report on the Industrial and Commercial Situation in Austria* (London, 1921), p. 10.

[16] Bauer, *op. cit.*, pp. 178–179.

[17] *Der österreichische Volkswirt*, vol. 11 (July 5, 1919), 750–751. The text of this communiqué appears in the *Neue Freie Presse,* June 28, 1919 (A.M.), p. 12.

In reply to my request for more information Professor Schumpeter wrote under date of August 7, 1944, giving me permission to quote.

All I can remember concerning the incident to which you refer is this. The Alpine-Montan Corporation, the largest iron producer of Austria and the owner of by far the most important source of iron ore in that country, naturally loomed large in all the plans of socialization that were discussed in 1918 and 1919. I have never been able to make up my mind how serious those discussions were considering that in the position of what was left of the Austrian state it was clearly impossible to carry any measure that would unfavorably affect any interest able to secure foreign support. Of this the leading men of the Socialist party were fully aware, but they found it difficult to make the point clear to the rank and file, which might easily have suspected prevarication behind any such argument. Under these circumstances, I find it perfectly understandable that Dr. Bauer, in the book from which you quote, repeated what then was a current rumor, although from my knowledge of him I absolve him from any charge of conscious dishonesty. But the fact is that I had neither a motive nor the power to initiate or to prevent any buying campaign on the stock exchange which was perfectly free. The banker you mentioned needed no authorization from me, nor would such authorization have helped him. All the minister of finance was concerned with was that foreign exchange acquired by means of sales of stock to foreigners should be duly delivered at the legal rate to the public treasury, a rule which was enforced as far as possible. To this, the criticism by the *Volkswirt* (I know of it only from your letter) must be reduced. I never published anything either officially or unofficially on the matter. . . ."

Socialist critics are not satisfied with Professor Schumpeter's explanation, particularly pointing out that Bauer repeated his charge of disloyalty to the cabinet four years after it allegedly had taken place. On the other hand, it must be noted that at the party congress of 1919, only a few months after the controversy under consideration, Bauer explained the failure to proceed to socialization in general terms of Austria's desperate economic plight and her dependence on foreign credit without reference to "preventive" action by individuals.[18] Whatever the reader's conclusions on the controversy, he probably can agree that the entire affair showed once more that a socialization action undertaken at a time of economic catastrophe was bound to encounter specific and practical obstacles which rendered its accomplishment difficult if not impossible.[19]

[18] *Parteitag, 1919,* pp. 202, 209.

[19] The foregoing paragraphs on the *Alpine* affair, except for two alterations explained immediately below, were submitted to Professor Schumpeter, with a request

Practical socialization work as Bauer and his party understood it was carried through in only one significant field, namely, in several former state undertakings that had produced supplies for the army. These factories, which otherwise would have been closed down, were organized as *Gemeinwirtschaftliche Anstalten.* The most important among them was the Arsenal in Vienna, a huge concern

---

for further comment, particularly on anything that seemed to him "inaccurate or unjust." (The alterations are the addition of a citation to the *Neue Freie Presse* on the communiqué of June 28 and the restoration of the sentence from Professor Schumpeter's letter of August 7 concerning the criticism of him by the *Volkswirt*. This sentence had been deleted from the draft sent him because in my first letter I had only indicated the criticism without quoting it precisely and because, therefore, the sentence was not to the point). On October 18, 1944, Professor Schumpeter wrote to me as follows:

"I certainly think that your pages convey an incorrect impression. I shall therefore restate more precisely what I said before. 1. I have never authorized, sanctioned, or suggested, anyone's purchase of stock in the Alpine Montan or any other corporation. 2. The idea of my doing so is absurd on the face of it, since no such authorization, sanction, or suggestion was required or would have induced anyone to carry out any such transaction. 3. I do not say this because I consider that such an authorization, sanction, or suggestion would have been wrong. On the contrary, I consider that, had I prevented a measure that could have only increased the difficulties of a difficult situation, this would have been a service to the country, the government and, above all, to the Social Democratic party. I say the above because it is the truth. 4. Nothing of this or of what I wrote in my first letter is in the least affected by that passage in the paper [the *Volkswirt*] you quote. I hope that this will clear up my position and end this correspondence."

Efforts to secure additional facts from printed sources and from other individuals proved of little use. In a later issue the *Volkswirt* referred again to differences within the cabinet on the whole issue of socialization; but emphasized the opinion that the chief hindrance to expropriating the *Alpine* was the state government of Styria which, on the basis of recent actions, would "probably" step in at the decisive moment. (Aug. 23, 1919, p. 891). About the same time the finance administration issued a formal statement that it knew nothing of the purchase of *Alpine* shares for foreign account until *after* the transaction had taken place (*Neue Freie Presse*, Aug. 22, 1919 [A.M.], p. 11). On the other hand, the British scholar, Macartney, who spent five years in Austria before publishing his book in 1926, states flatly that the plan to socialize the *Alpine* "was frustrated by the sudden action of the Finance Minister, a non-Socialist, in placing this concern in Italian hands." (*The Social Revolution in Austria,* pp. xi and 149.) He does not, however, cite any specific source.

Obviously, the results of efforts to clarify an old controversy are unsatisfactory. As is all too frequently true in such cases the investigator is confronted with categorical charges and categorical denials with no documents available. The only possible verdict is "not proved." Equally obviously, it would have been more agreeable to omit the whole episode; but to discuss socialization plans in the early history of the Austrian republic without mentioning the *Alpine* would have been equivalent to trying to swim without going near the water. Only one other point deserves mention. In my original letter to Professor Schumpeter I cited, from the larger number available, page references to four specific criticisms of him by the *Volkswirt* (vol. 11, pp. 750–751; 812, 813, 890–891), at least one of which was clearly directed to the *Alpine* affair. As already reported, he replied that he knew of this criticism "only" from my letter. It is, of course, a long time since 1919 and all of us forget things. Perhaps the reader will conclude that this is what happened. Considering the importance of the *Volkswirt,* the frequency and sharpness of its comments on Professor Schumpeter, the widespread discussion of the episode, and the temper of Austrian politics at the time, numerous Austrians will not share that conclusion.

which employed about 10,000 workers. Even here a primary motive for socialization was the fear that the sudden dismissal of thousands of workers would redound to the benefit of the Communist party.[20]

The collapse of the soviets in Hungary meant the virtual end of socialization attempts in Austria. Their political function was already fulfilled. The Coalition Pact of October, 1919, left scarcely any doubt in this respect. It limited socialization to further transformation of the war industry plants of the state into *Gemeinwirtschaftliche Anstalten,* but stressed the right of the state to claim a part of the shares of private joint stock companies on the occasion of capital increases by such private companies. Most significantly, the pact stated: "The socialization program formerly drawn up by the government remains valid, *but it is understood that the time and circumstances of its realization must be determined by the financial and credit situation.*"[21]

In accordance with the changed circumstances, the general attitude toward socialization underwent a remarkable transformation. Reference has been made to the socialization programs of the non-Socialist parties. A great number of outstanding scholars had published books on problems of socialization. Now, Seipel, the vice-president of the socialization commission, declared that "the mere existence of the commission exercises an unfavorable influence upon economic life because the fear of a socialization that may still be threatening does damage both to the working spirit of entrepreneurs and to the soundness of the undertakings."[22] Bauer emphasized the point that the fate of socialization depended on the general development of capitalism and admitted the possibility that capitalism might "recover for a few years."[23] At the same time Ellenbogen stressed the necessity of "slowing down the tempo of socialization" because of the desperate conditions of the Austrian economy.[24]

[20] "The danger was not to be ignored that the overhasty shutting down of some of these factories which had grown during the war time to gigantic proportions would lead to grave internal disturbances. This was decisive. . . ." Franz Leifer, "Die gemeinwirtschaftlichen Anstalten," *Geldentwertung und Stabilisierung,* p. 215. Cf. also Karl Renner, *Die österreichischen Arbeitergenossenschaften und ihre Kritiker* (Wien, 1926), p. 13.

[21] *Tätigkeits-Bericht,* Heft 13 (Wien, 1920), p. 11. Italics mine.

[22] Quoted in *Politisches Handbuch* (Wien, 1920), p. 245.

[23] Otto Bauer, *Die Sozialisierungsaktion im ersten Jahre der Republik* (Wien, 1919), p. 16.

[24] "We are a people of beggars, the country has been dismembered, the economic territory torn to pieces, the basis of recovery destroyed. . . . We are politically and eco-

As is already clear, the practical results of the Austrian socialization attempts were very limited. In 1921 there were eight *Gemeinwirtschaftliche Anstalten* proper and several undertakings of similar character.[25] The economic development of these undertakings was satisfactory for a few years; because of the inflation the state found it easy to furnish large credits. It was noted, however, that the strong influence of the works councils rendered the task of the management rather difficult and accounted for a wage policy which paid too little attention to the necessity of intensifying the labor process.[26] The stabilization of the currency in 1922 and the ensuing stabilization crisis were hard blows for most of the socialized undertakings, as was the cessation of credits from the state. Nevertheless, a few of the undertakings, partly with the help of the coöperative societies, managed to survive (cf. below, pp. 322–323). Although they were never of much importance they were compulsorily liquidated by the government after the defeat of the Socialist working-class movement in 1934. The history of the *Gemeinwirtschaftliche Anstalten* furnishes little or no valuable material concerning the economy of a socialized undertaking or of the value of tripartite management as conceived by Bauer.[27] It seems, however, that the advantage of an unbureaucratic management was sometimes more than counterbalanced by the dissensions of opinion among the different groups composing the management.

Thus the historical importance of the socialization attempts in Austria lies chiefly and almost solely in their relation to the struggle against Bolshevism.

---

nomically dependent upon enemies who have thrust upon us a peace treaty we will have to fulfill with set teeth. We must clearly understand that these brazen facts compel us . . . to reduce speed. . . . However wrong the contentions are . . . that socialization has been abandoned, it it true . . . that socialization . . . if it is not to be compromised by mistakes, can be effected only step by step." Gewerkschaftskongress, 1923, *Protokoll*, pp. 376–377.

[25] W. Ellenbogen, *Die Sozialisierung in Oesterreich* (Wien, 1921), pp. 21–28.

[26] Leifer, *loc. cit.*, p. 220.

[27] The praise lavished by Ellenbogen on the *Gemeinwirtschaftliche Anstalten*, which he contended—thanks to the selection of members of the staff from all strata of the people—were to be regarded as a "realization of the deeper sense of Plato's *Republic*," may be dismissed as boundless exaggeration. Cf. Ellenbogen, "Die Organisationsform der öffentlichen Unternehmungen in Oesterreich," *Moderne Organisationsform der öffentlichen Unternehmung* in *Schriften des Vereins für Sozialpolitik*, vol. 176, pt. 3 (1931), 93. Hereafter cited as *SVfS*.

CHAPTER IX

Inflation and Other Economic Problems

In his careful and comprehensive contribution to the Carnegie endowment series on the history of the war of 1914–1918 Gustav Gratz describes the collapse of the Austro-Hungarian monarchy as a "tragedy of exhaustion."[1] He shows how the war had largely cut off the external sources of Austrian food supply, sapped the strength of internal agricultural production, depleted the stores of raw materials, and thus exhausted the forces of the Austrian national economy. It was a pitiful inheritance that the young republic obtained from the empire. And those economic conditions were further aggravated and brought to a point where the physical existence of the people was endangered by the policy of the newly created neighboring states. Their old hatred against Vienna was coupled now with their desires to preserve foodstuffs for the needs of their own populations, to use their raw materials for building up what was called a "national industry," and, in general, to reorganize their own likewise seriously damaged economies. Except for foodstuffs, the coal supply rapidly became the most urgent economic problem in Austria. The new state had taken over about 12 per cent of the population of the empire, 30 per cent of its industrial workers, 20 per cent of the steam-boiler heating surface, but only one-half of 1 per cent of its coal supplies.[2] The blockade, first and foremost by Czechoslovakia, rendered industrial production in Austria almost impossible. All but one of the Styrian blast furnaces had to be put out, and of the twenty-four Martin steel furnaces only three remained in operation, so that production of iron and steel practically ceased. In consequence a very large part of the metal and machine industry came to a halt. Brick, lime, and cement works had likewise to put out their furnaces; the building industry came to an almost complete standstill.[3] Severe restrictions and prohibitions on the use of electric

[1] Gustav Gratz and Richard Schüller, *Der wirtschaftliche Zusammenbruch Oesterreich-Ungarns* (Wien, 1930).

[2] Cf. Friedrich Hertz, "Die Kohlenfrage in Oesterreich," *Der österreichische Volkswirt,* vol. 13 (Nov. 20, 1920), 120. The *Volkswirt* gives 22 per cent of the population, an obvious typographical error.

[3] Gewerbe-Inspektoren, *Bericht, 1919* (Wien, 1920), p. cxxix.

current were unavoidable; on some days the current had to be cut off entirely; very often there was no streetcar traffic in Vienna; railroad traffic was confined chiefly to food transport, so that passenger service became almost a rarity. These conditions, together with the grave slump in the war industries and the demobilization, resulted immediately after the revolution in large and rapidly growing unemployment which persisted well into the year 1919 (cf. above, p. 70). As early as November 6, 1918, a decree concerning unemployment relief was issued, and a few days later the first relief sums were paid out. The whole scheme was drawn up by a bipartisan commission of representatives of employers and employees. At that time unemployment relief was an absolute necessity, primarily from the political point of view; its role in preventing social anarchy in Austria can hardly be exaggerated.

Because of the generally desperate situation of the workers another decree of May 14, 1919, shortly after the Communist disturbances of Holy Thursday, compelled the proprietors of larger establishments to increase the number of their employees by 20 per cent and to maintain their work forces at the new level unless they received special permission from a bipartisan commission to lower that level.[4] However necessary these steps might have been, politically and also socially, it cannot be denied that they at least partly accounted for a phenomenon which became significant in the first months of the economic life of the new state: the terrible decrease in the intensity of labor, or, as it was called, *Arbeitsunlust* (work shyness).

In the volume cited above, Gratz does not refer to the situation of Austrian labor, but beyond any doubt four years of war had also led to the exhaustion of the physical strength of the workers. Although the hard military rule in the factories had prevented the complete breakdown of production for the duration of the war, the subsequent psychological reaction was all the stronger. The lack of coal and raw materials and the prevailing revolutionary unrest very often made it necessary to abandon the piece-wage system even where it had been generally adopted and to go over to time wages; piece wages could not be maintained in a situation where, for example, the irregularities in the supply of electric current caused interruptions

[4] *StGBl.*, 1918, Nr. 20; *ibid.*, 1919, Nr. 268.

in work lasting for hours. Thereby, too, the intensity of labor was considerably affected.[5] The further fact that the worker repeatedly had to leave his work in the factory and go into the country in search of food must be regarded as one of the many reasons for work shyness. Finally, it certainly was true that the general radicalization of the workers greatly increased their aversion to working for the "capitalist exploiters." Employers' complaints on the decrease in willingness to work began to be widespread very shortly after the revolution. In their press, employers emphasized chiefly the pernicious effects of the unemployment benefit system on the intensity of work. Less than two months after the proclamation of the republic the central paper of the federated manufacturers wrote:

> Complaints are piling up that laborers are leaving their work places, taking unemployment relief, and seeking a side-employment . . . partly in illicit trade. . . . It really looks as though we had forgotten how to work! . . . With the white-collar workers it is much worse . . . [they are the] employees who acquiesce in the shortest possible working time that is interrupted by the longest possible pauses for a mid-morning snack, smoking, and reading. . . . There is also, however, a sort of "peaceful Bolshevism" into which we more and more threaten to degenerate. It exists in the continuous soldiering on the job. . . .[6]

From then on for months the problem of work shyness maintained a prominent place in the articles in the employers' press and in the speeches of the representatives of industry.

The reaction of labor to these charges was in the beginning purely negative. The "chatter about *Arbeitsunlust*" was strongly condemned.[7] Although the desperate economic conditions soon compelled the Social Democratic party and the trade unions to change their attitude completely, it was only after the fall of the proletarian dictatorship in Hungary that they could openly take a strong stand for the necessity of increasing the workers' contribution to the restoration of the Austrian economy. In the Coalition Pact of October, 1919, the Socialists agreed that the "unemployment benefit must not be a reward for unwillingness to work."[8] This clearly implied that they recognized to some extent the validity of the charges of a causal

[5] Gewerbe-Inspektoren, *Bericht, 1919* (Wien, 1920), p. cxxiv.
[6] *Die Industrie*, January 10, 1919, p. 2.
[7] Cf. "Das Gerede über die Arbeitsunlust," *Die Gewerkschaft*, vol. 21 (Jan. 28, 1919), 13.
[8] *Tätigkeits-Bericht*, Heft 13 (Wien, 1920), p. 11.

connection between unemployment benefit and work shyness. In fact, immediately after the Béla Kun government had been overthrown, the minister of social welfare, Hanusch, made the terms for obtaining unemployment benefit more rigid and thus brought about a rapid decrease in the number of persons receiving it.[9] At the same time, the party and the trade unions began a serious campaign against *Arbeitsunlust.*

During the 1919 party congress Otto Bauer moved a resolution in which "the disparity between home production and consumption" was described as the most important reason for the existing economic distress. Instead of denying the fact of work shyness, as had been done before, Bauer expressly admitted it[10] and tried to explain its physical and psychological origins. According to the resolution, work shyness was to be overcome gradually by social legislation, by new methods of adjusting wages to rising prices, by retraining and colonization schemes, and, finally, by using the influence of the works councils to restore labor discipline in the factories. Against those who still spoke of "expropriation of expropriators" Bauer emphasized his conviction that "today the problem is to restore production so that there will be surplus product again"—certainly an unusual statement from a Socialist who was supposed to see in the existence of surplus value derived from surplus product the root of all evil.[11] This was clear enough, but the trade unionists were still more outspoken. At the congress of the metalworkers, leader Janeček moved a resolution protesting the attacks of the bourgeois press on the workers' "alleged unwillingness to work."[12] Although Janeček's resolution was finally adopted in order to avoid the impression that the trade unions were yielding to pressure, the speeches of the influential leaders left no doubt about their opinions. Hueber, the old veteran of the trade unions, expressly admitted the existence of *Arbeitsunlust* and declared that he had proposed methods of combating it at the recent bipartisan "industry conference." Ellenbogen, the newly appointed president of the socialization commission, stressed the necessity of decreasing the general misery by work.

[9] Karl Pribram, "Die Sozialpolitik im neuen Oesterreich," *AfSS.*, vol. 48 (1920–1921), 636.

[10] "The workers refuse to work for it [capitalism], or do their work in a joyless and unwilling way without the accustomed order and discipline." *Parteitag, 1919,* p. 201.

[11] *Ibid.,* p. 201.

[12] Gewerkschaftskongress, 1919, *Protokoll,* pp. 286–287.

He admitted that the war had demoralized a large part of the workers, he spoke of an "intoxication which had destroyed the sense of responsibility" and he tried to find a political formula with which to justify his appeal to increase the intensity of work: "Everyone's duty is to safeguard political freedom by fulfilling his duty in the economic process."[13]

The problem of work shyness has been dwelt upon at some length because of its close connection with the socialization program. Nothing would have been easier than to leave unchecked, or positively to encourage, the workers' tendency to "refuse to work for capitalism," as Bauer phrased it. Then the claim could have been advanced that private capitalism had demonstrated its inability to secure efficient labor from the workers, therefore, Socialism was necessary. In other words, at the same time that they were compelled to take a position on the question of unwillingness to work, the Socialist leaders were forced to choose between private capitalism and Socialism. They decided that in an economically wrecked country the former had to be repaired and maintained—at least for the time being. Their reason was that under the given circumstances the alternative policy meant literal starvation for thousands. Thus their decision for a definite and positive campaign against disinclination to work was but a necessary consequence of the abandonment of the socialization schemes. And the most curious fact of all is that the works councils were to be the major weapon of this campaign; organizations which were introduced as the first step of the socialization plan were now to be used to increase productivity in capitalist undertakings. Finally, the whole episode shows that the leaders of the party and of the trade unions had what the Germans call "the courage to be unpopular"; that is, to stand for a policy which was diametrically opposed to the wishes and momentary interests of the workers.[14]

In the fall of 1919, the economic outlook appeared extremely gloomy to the party leaders; they feared that the coming winter

[13] *Ibid.*, pp. 384 ff. Also very significant for a leader of a party which was so often described as the party of class war is the following sentence from his speech: "All of us, the whole people, employers and labor, brain workers and manual workers, politicians and economists shall have to take in hand the restoration of our economy" (p. 378).

[14] "The Social Democrats have abandoned unreservedly their original socialization program because particularly their radical leaders possess the clear vision, the knowledge of the world, and the moral courage by which one can tell a political leader from a demagogue." *Der österreichische Volkswirt*, vol. 12 (July 17, 1920), 790.

threatened to make the misery and sufferings of the population unbearable.[15] However, a slight improvement in the economic conditions set in at about this time. Unfortunately, the foundations of the coming upswing in trade were by no means sound since the change was brought about in the main by the progressive depreciation of the crown (*Krone*). It emerged from the war with its value diminished by one-third. After November, 1918, the breakup of the old economic unity, including particularly the stamping of crown notes by the succession states, greatly hastened the pace of depreciation. During the months of Bolshevist rule in Hungary there ensued an extensive flight of capital from Austria, prompted by fear of social disturbances. The almost complete cessation of exports and the burdensome conditions of the peace treaty, which destroyed confidence in the prospects of the new state to save its currency, combined to push the crown further down. Its rapid fall led to a big boom on the stock exchange in the summer of 1919. Huge profits were made there and the speculation fever seized large groups of the population. At first this development brought only some revival of luxury consumption. Toward the end of 1919, however, the exchange-rate curve with a mighty leap crossed the price-level curve for the first time, and thus created a disparity between the external and the internal value of the crown. Interventions on behalf of the crown in the middle of 1920 forced the rate of exchange curve below the price curve for several months.[16] But it must be noted that the price curve was based primarily upon certain commodities of vital importance like clothing which were scarce at the time. As far as other commodities were concerned the differential between the internal purchasing power of the crown and its value abroad opened new possibilities for Austrian foreign trade, although at first this revival affected relatively slightly the regular export business. The impoverished middle class sold shops, pictures, furniture, jewelry, books, and even clothing to the foreign buyers who flooded Vienna.[17]

[15] "Without wanting to be prophets we can already say today that this winter we are approaching the most dreadful catastrophe." Skaret's speech to the party congress of 1919, *Parteitag*, p. 143.

"We have to face a most difficult winter and we have no idea how we shall survive it." Adler's speech to the same congress, *ibid.*, p. 169.

[16] J. van Walré de Bordes, *The Austrian Crown* (London, 1924), p. 152.

[17] For vivid pictures of the state of extreme starvation in Vienna in the winter of 1919–1920, see *Chercheurs d'or* by the French writer, Pierre Hamp. His brilliant and devastating descriptions of the types of foreign merchants, industrialists, and profiteers

When the period of the world boom came to an end in the middle of 1920 and a prolonged crisis ensued, Austrian industry was again able to obtain coal and raw materials. Then, supported by the disparity in purchasing power, came the time of the great upswing for Austrian export industries. The huge expenditures of the state and its slowly and inadequately growing revenues necessitated continuous increases in the volume of notes in circulation. Thus the inflation proceeded unchecked and formed the basis of the so-called *Inflationskonjunktur.* The open connection between the upswing and the inflation was made fully clear by the foodstuff subsidies which were granted by the state. It was estimated that a worker producing in a day goods worth 320 crowns received 300 crowns in wages and another 100 crowns from the state in the form of subsidized lower prices; the food subsidies were thus actually subsidies to the manufacturers.[18]

What was the attitude of the labor movement to this development? Bauer's resolution at the party congress of 1919 proposed a capital levy in order to balance the national budget and to check rising prices.[19] But as soon as the temporarily favorable effects of the inflation became apparent, it no longer suited the Socialists—in this phase of the inflation—to attempt to stabilize the currency. Incidentally, the inflation also helped to bring the solution of the problem of work shyness. "The depreciation of the currency," wrote Bauer, "was the expedient . . . to lead the masses of workers, whom the war had torn from the workshops, back into the factories and to accustom them to regular work again."[20] In addition, Bauer described how the inflation had improved the food supply and the general conditions of Austrian labor.[21] In accordance with this general position, the stabilization of the currency was only very incidentally mentioned at the next congress of the party in 1920.[22] This attitude is more than difficult to understand today when the disastrous consequences of the inflation are well known and the devastation it caused in Central

---

who were attracted to Vienna by the wide price differentials are classics. These vultures bought anything and everything and made gold out of misery as Salzbach, the hero of M. Hamp's tales, proudly expressed it (p. 119).

[18] O. S. Phillpotts, *Report on the Industrial and Commercial Situation in Austria* (London, 1921), p. 19.

[19] *Parteitag, 1919,* p. 124.

[20] Otto Bauer, *Die österreichische Revolution* (Wien, 1923), p. 203.

[21] *Ibid.*, and p. 204.

[22] *Parteitag, 1920,* p. 102.

Europe is set forth in every textbook. At that time, however, when the *danse macabre* of the inflation had just begun, it seemed to many thinking persons the only way to lead the Austrian economy out of the crisis. Furthermore, as already brought out, the leaders of Austrian Social Democracy and of the trade unions believed that the existence of an *economically* independent Austria was absolutely impossible. Consequently, it is not improbable that even as far as they foresaw the consequences of inflation they accepted it because they thought economic collapse would make anschluss with Germany unavoidable. However far this idea played a part in their decisions, there can be no doubt that there was also a good deal of class selfishness in the attitude of the Socialists toward inflation. This attitude would have been impossible if no method had been found to adjust wages to the rapidly rising prices, but as early as the autumn of 1919 an expedient to exempt the workers to a considerable extent from the disadvantages of the continuous depreciation of the currency was discovered in the so-called index wage system. The question of the index wage and its applications very soon became, and remained for three years, such an important issue in the Austrian labor movement that all other social problems were more or less pushed into the background.[23] Since the real work on this problem was done chiefly by a joint committee representing entrepreneurs and workers, it is necessary to sketch briefly its background.

The coöperation between employers and employees in a central bipartisan board on various matters, particularly on social legislation, had been very important in the first months after the revolution. Between March and August, 1919, this fruitful coöperation was almost entirely interrupted, but when the threat of social revolution was removed both parties were very anxious to reëstablish it.[24] In November, 1919, Chancellor Renner called together the bipartisan "industry conference." A whole galaxy of economic problems was to be discussed at this conference, including, as mentioned above, the matter of unwillingness to work. Several subcommittees

[23] Emil Lederer, "Die soziale Krise in Oesterreich," *AfSS.*, vol. 48 (1920–1921), 687.

[24] Emmy Freundlich, a leader in the Socialist coöperative movement, in her speech to the trade-union congress remarked: "It is our ruin that we have not the parity [bipartisan organization] everywhere." *Protokoll*, 1919, p. 429. Incidentally, it is worth noting that here the "class war Socialists" appear as partisans of an idea which has a definite kinship to the *berufsständische* (occupational estates) theories which the Dollfuss and Schuschnigg governments were to use *against* the Socialists years later.

were created, but only the one concerned with the question of the adjustment of wages to prices did efficient work.

On November 26, Chancellor Renner submitted to this subcommittee a scheme according to which wages should be divided into two parts. One, to be called the basic wage, was to vary according to price movements; the other was to be made up of the additional earnings of skilled workers. The whole scheme was represented by the Socialists as the realization of an old plan formulated before the war by a party member, Adolf Braun.[25] His purpose was to counteract the effects of rapidly rising foodstuff prices in that period of agricultural protectionism. Although the trade unions were unable to induce the employers to agree to Braun's proposals in 1909, their tremendously increased strength forced acceptance of the Renner-sponsored plan in 1919. It remains probable that neither of the parties concerned realized at that time the whole import of the index system, and it is certain that the trade unions were at least as much concerned with the question of how to maintain money wages when prices declined again as with that on which the discussions began.[26] This desire to avoid a "freezing" of the miserable wartime wages, and possibly to gain something from the inflation, also explains why the trade unions hesitated to accept an absolutely mechanical system which would automatically raise and reduce wages in accordance with the purchasing power of money. Therefore, the bipartisan committee agreed only to the general lines of the new scheme. It was left to the collective agreements between trade unions and the employers in the individual branches of trade to work out the new principles in practice.

Meanwhile, that is, during 1919, collective agreements on conditions of employment had become so general that individual contracts between employer and employee were almost a rarity, except in very small establishments. On December 16, 1919, the metalworkers' trade union, the strongest in Austria, renewed such an agreement; the various family supplements and the lump-sum compensation for the depreciation of the crown previously made were abolished, and a sliding variation geared to price fluctuations introduced. The amount of the supplement or decrease was to be fixed every two

[25] Adolf Braun, "Lebensmittelteuerung und Gewerkschaftsbewegung," *Der Kampf*, vol. 3 (Dec. 1, 1909), 117–126.

[26] Cf. Pribram, *loc. cit.*, p. 676.

months by a bipartisan wage commission. This group was to establish a list of articles of food and other necessities and their prices on December 1, 1919, as the basis of a price index and to express the variation as a percentage of wages paid in the two preceding months. For December, 1919, and January, 1920, a more or less arbitrary increase was fixed at 33.3 per cent for male workers over twenty-two years of age, and at 15 per cent for male workers under twenty-two years and for all female workers.[27] In the following months the new system was gradually introduced into most of the collective agreements. The actual stipulations, however, varied considerably in accordance with the strength of the individual trade unions. The good and bad effects of the new scheme were manifold. That the adoption of it or something quite similar was unavoidable can scarcely be disputed in view of the development of the cost of living. An average workers' family in Vienna had to pay for a four-week supply of foodstuffs:

Date	Crowns
July, 1919	2,540.99
July, 1920	4,689.46
January, 1921	8,266.89
July, 1921	9,054.16
January, 1922	75,195.76
July, 1922	296,734.00[28]

From the theoretical point of view the effects of the index-wage system would not necessarily be contrary to those expected under the laws of a "free" market. But it is certain that the sliding-scale wages rendered it possible to adjust money wages to the purchasing power of money much more rapidly than a free market would have permitted.[29]

Almost needless to say, the system did not function absolutely automatically. Continuous negotiations were required because of claims that changes in the underlying list of commodities were necessary and because of the existence of several separate indexes with different figures. Then there was the question of whether the prices of the illicit trade should be taken into consideration, and, if so, to

[27] Benedikt Kautsky, "Löhne und Gehälter," *Geldentwertung und Stabilisierung*, pp. 113 ff.

[28] Felix Klezl, "Die Lebenskosten," *Geldentwertung und Stabilisierung*, p. 147.

[29] Cf. Richard Strigl, *Die angewandte Lohntheorie* (Wien, 1926), p. 95.

what extent. Furthermore, the whole system was much more thoroughly applied by, and worked more smoothly in, large-scale industry with its strong and well-disciplined trade unions. It was naturally more difficult to introduce it into small shops. For these reasons, the sliding-wage system as adopted in Austria by no means excluded wage controversies. But thanks to it these struggles assumed a definitely more peaceful form; strikes were of shorter duration and usually did not occur in big industries. On the other hand, there were bitter protests from the civil servants who were brought within the index system only toward the end of the inflation and only after they had gone on strike.[30] In 1919 and 1920 the increases in money salaries for this group had been irregular and inadequate so that their purchasing power had fallen to 14 per cent of the peace level.[31] In general white-collar employees were less favored by the sliding scale. The chief beneficiaries of it were the manual workers; and among them unskilled labor was favored in comparison with highly skilled. Particularly in the period of low intensity of labor, this situation was a very serious matter. The panegyrical statements of some Socialist leaders, who greeted the replacement of "efficiency wages" by what they called "social wages," cannot obscure the fact that the index system in its particular application in Austria hampered the efforts to combat work shyness and was in that respect in contradiction with the general policy of the party.[32]

The sliding-scale wage system had other disadvantages. It drove a wedge between the workers and other groups of the population. The intellectuals, including the members of learned professions, and large, and perhaps the most valuable, sections of the Viennese middle class were expropriated by the collapse of the crown. So far as—and this was true in the last period of the inflation—rising prices meant not only an increasing circulation and a falling rate of exchange, but also a general decrease of the social product, the workers safeguarded their income only at the expense of other, for the moment, economically even weaker groups of society. Furthermore, when the inflation boom had come to an end, the index wages to a certain degree

[30] Friedrich Gaertner, "Die Stabilisierung der österreichischen Krone," *Pläne und Versuche zur Währungssanierung* in *SVfS.*, vol. 165, pt. 2 (1923), 51.

[31] Arnold Madlé, "Die Bezüge der öffentlichen Angestellten," *Geldentwertung und Stabilisierung*, p. 135.

[32] Julius Deutsch, *Geschichte der österreichischen Gewerkschaftsbewegung*, Vol. II (Wien, 1932), p. 80.

prevented the relative rise of the value of money and furthered the process of the destruction of capital.[33] Again, there is no doubt that as the index system became more widely applied it furthered the rise of prices; the fear of the seller that the buyer would restrict his demand was progressively weakened.

Even from the point of view of the workers the system grew less and less satisfactory. As mentioned earlier, wages were adjusted every two months. When the pace of the inflation became so fast that huge changes in prices occurred literally from day to day, the long period between the adjustments often reduced wages to ridiculously low amounts.[34] Although this period was later shortened to one month, the gains to the workers were not great. These conditions led to continuous demands for readjustments. Very often strong unions succeeded in obtaining additional increases in wages for the elapsed period,[35] but again the workers in smaller shops suffered. Thus it can rightly be said that the whole period of the inflation was one uninterrupted struggle for wages. "There was," says the report to the trade-union congress, "one 'September week' when at the same time the following trade unions were engaged in negotiations concerning wages: metalworkers, chemical workers, coffeehouse employees, bank employees, industrial salaried employees, bakers, draymen, cab drivers, painters, tailors, shoemakers, fur workers, hatters, and miners."[36] But all these negotiations were lacking in aggressiveness

[33] On this point cf. Friedrich A. Hayek, "Kapitalaufzehrung," *Weltwirtschaftliches Archiv*, vol. 36, pt. 1 (1932), 94.

[34] "Thus, for example, the worker who obtained an increase in salary by the end of July, 1922, on the basis of the 41 per cent rise in costs of living in comparison with June, 1922, had to endure these wages until the end of August, despite the fact that by August 14, 1922, the further rise in prices amounted to 124 per cent as against the middle of July. . . ." Kautsky, *loc. cit.*, p. 118.

[35] Thereby, of course, the calculations of the employers were rendered nearly worthless. A few large firms consequently adopted wages fixed in foreign money, primarily in Swiss francs. Another reason for this policy was that in the course of time the index system had become extremely complicated—a situation clearly revealed by the following announcement of a new agreement in the *Metallarbeiter* of November 5, 1921 (the paper of the metalworkers' trade union). "Concerning wages, the following stipulations have been made: the old basic wage is now increased by 364 per cent rather than by 170 as formerly; then all other supplements are to be added and this sum forms the new earnings, which for workers over twenty-two years is to be divided by 1.52 and for those under twenty-two by 1.40. The result is the new basic wage, to which all workers over twenty-two years, and also workers under twenty-two years, as far as they are family providers, obtain a sliding supplement of 52 per cent. The rest of the workers get a supplement of 40 per cent to the new basic wage. On the fifteenth of every month this sliding supplement will be adjusted to the changed economic conditions by a special commission . . ." The increase in unproductive work which these stipulations meant for the wage bureaus of the factories can easily be imagined.

[36] Gewerkschaftskommission, *Bericht*, 1923, p. 93.

because the necessity of adjustment was recognized by both parties and the discussions referred only to the measure of this adjustment.[37] The political import of this fact is obvious enough. The whole process furthered appeasement in the field of social struggles and, to that extent, Renner's "happy idea"[38] fitted neatly into the general framework of Social Democratic policy.

The question of the precise degree to which the index system actually exempted the workers from the effects of the inflation cannot be fully answered. As might have been expected, this was one of the most controversial issues of the years of inflation. The employers argued that the real wages of the workers were higher than they had been before the war because at that time the metalworker, for instance, had to spend 80 per cent of his wages on "existence needs," whereas in 1921, he could satisfy them with only 50 per cent of his income.[39] Attacks against overvalorized wages played a great role throughout the period of inflation. Some of the calculations simply compared the percentage rise in the cost of living since 1914 with the rise in wages since 1914. Certain classes of workers badly underpaid in the prewar period naturally succeeded in securing higher increases because of the general equalizing tendency prevailing during war and inflation.[40] Reliable and impartial statistics were extremely difficult to secure at the time and very often the employers were alleged to have treated the highest wages paid in a branch of trade as average wages. On another occasion, the *Arbeiter Zeitung* charged that the industrialists had chosen prices for foodstuffs for 1914 that were too high and prices for 1921 that were too low, thus appreciably falsifying the real rise in the cost of living.[41] Without attempting to give final judgments on these various claims it remains certain that the balance of advantage between employers and workers shifted greatly from one to the other during the individual phases of the inflation period. In the summer of 1921, for instance, the trade unions were able to secure increases in wages which considerably exceeded those in the cost of living which had occurred

[37] Lederer, *loc. cit.*, p. 687.

[38] Hueber in his speech to the trade-union congress, 1923, *Protokoll*, p. 224, referring to the index system.

[39] Cf., for example, *Die Industrie*, February 19, 1921, pp. 1–2, and *ibid.*, June 25, p. 1.

[40] For instance, as was admitted by all parties concerned, agricultural workers' wages really crossed the so-called peace parity level. Cf. Kautsky, *loc. cit.*, p. 130.

[41] *Arbeiter Zeitung*, March 17, 1921, p. 5.

in the immediately preceding months. Thus wages were brought nearer to the gold parity, but they suffered another setback toward the end of the inflation when the insane speed in the rise of prices was coupled with a downward tendency in trade. One computation of the final results of the wage increases during the inflation indicates that the nearest approach to the "peace parity," generally between 70 and 80 per cent, was reached either by groups with very strong unions or by those which had been badly underpaid before.[42] On the whole there is little doubt that the sliding-scale wages—incompletely as they were adopted and in spite of their disadvantages—safeguarded the physical existence of the workers and thus rendered a great service to the Austrian economy.

It was noted earlier that the Social Democrats welcomed the inflation as a leverage to the belated upswing. At that time they realized only to a limited extent that this boom bore the germs of destruction within itself. After several months of sham prosperity, however, the adverse consequences of the inflation became apparent. Other countries began to protect themselves against Austrian "currency dumping" by high tariffs and import prohibitions. The faster the crown fell, the more difficult it became for the entrepreneur to secure the foreign exchange needed for the purchases of raw materials. From one turnover to another the working capital of industry became smaller and smaller. Restriction of production was the unavoidable consequence. Credit was dear, 20 per cent and more, and difficult to obtain. The rate of exchange rushed down so rapidly that the whirling note-printing presses were unable to maintain the pace. Thus the gold value of the continuously increasing circulation rapidly decreased, producing a grave tightening of money. Therefore, toward the end of the summer of 1921, the period of good trade, the *Inflationskonjunktur,* was approaching its end.

As in every inflation,[43] the rising national deficit continually pushed the whole machine of the Austrian economy in a vicious circle, or rather a vicious spiral, of currency depreciation. To stop the inflation meant, in the first place, to balance the budget—unquestionably difficult under the existing conditions. Some attempts to remedy the situation were undertaken by Grimm, who became min-

[42] Cf. Hueber's speech to the trade-union congress, 1923, *Protokoll,* pp. 225–227.

[43] Cf. Gottfried Haberler, *Der internationale Handel* (Wien, 1933), p. 53.

ister of finance in the fall of 1920 after the collapse of the coalition. But his efforts were almost entirely confined to endeavors to obtain foreign credits. In April, 1921, these efforts brought to Vienna a delegation from the League of Nations; it drew up a scheme according to which a foreign loan would be granted on the security of the customs, certain state monopolies, and a mortgage on all real property in the country. Since it was first necessary to secure from all signatories of the peace treaty a temporary relinquishment of their claims established by that treaty on some of the assets just mentioned, and since this could not be done despite protracted attempts, the loan was never granted. Notwithstanding this frustration of the scheme, it is worth noting that before it had been finally set up the delegates demanded that the Social Democratic party not only approve it but also undertake to fulfill the obligations involved should the party subsequently take over the government. Such a statement, written by Otto Bauer, was actually delivered. For the first time the party declared that it would lend its support to the endeavors to stabilize the currency and to balance the budget even at the cost of raising indirect taxes and abolishing the food-subsidy system.[44] The episode is significant, first, because it reveals the power and importance of the party at that time; and, second, because it shows that the supposedly revolutionary class-war party was prepared to give its help to the "government of the class enemy," and was deeply concerned with the development of the whole of the economy of the country. When subsequently the export trade began to get worse, the wheel was turned the full circle; the party and the trade unions fully realized the necessity of stopping the further depreciation of the currency at any price. "The inflation is a camphor injection. . . . But it is impossible to continue giving camphor injections unceasingly, if the organism is not to die from them."[45] In these words Bauer tried to explain his changed attitude toward inflation.

Meanwhile, the September, 1921, meeting of the League of Nations had confined itself to a mere regret concerning the delay on the Austrian loan and thus precipitated a new crash of the rate of exchange. In this emergency the organizations of the Austrian labor movement, that is, the party, the trade unions, and the coöperatives,

[44] *Tätigkeits-Bericht,* Heft 15 (Wien, 1921), pp. 18–21.
[45] *Parteitag, 1921,* p. 146.

submitted to the government on October 1, 1921, a memorandum since known as the Social Democratic Financial Plan—without doubt one of the most interesting documents ever produced by Austrian labor.

The financial plan,[46] the author of which was again Otto Bauer, disclaimed being a "Socialist" proposal, but rather one intended to indicate practical steps to be undertaken within the framework of the existing social order. It was stated that the only objective of the plan was to stop the inflation and thus to check the depreciation of the currency. This aim was to be reached by a set of measures designed to increase the state revenues shattered by the inflation, to decrease the enormously swollen expenditures, and to improve the credit of the country. In order to increase revenues the plan proposed: to reorganize the tax offices so as to enable them to enforce payments of the extremely large arrears; to revalorize the old capital levy; to impose an additional capital levy on large fortunes and on legal persons—in the latter case to be paid by "bonus shares"; to increase taxes on agricultural interests; to reorganize the taxation of industry through the creation of "tax unions" on which the state imposed the total sum of the tax, the distribution among the individual branches and undertakings to be performed autonomously; to reorganize the taxes on banking on the same lines; to create various trade and production monopolies, organized as *Gemeinwirtschaftliche Anstalten;* and, finally, to raise the tariffs on railroad, postal, and telegraph services. Expenditures were to be cut down by abolishing the food subsidies; by reducing the excessive staffs in the state offices, but only by agreement with the trade unions; by reorganizing the enterprises of the state, then hampered by bureaucratic administration, as *Gemeinwirtschaftliche Anstalten;* and, in general, by carrying on all the business of the nation in a more thrifty fashion. Since it was believed that this last could be ensured only if every branch of administration itself took care of providing the means it required, local administration was to be democratized. To improve Austria's credit position, the following measures were proposed: an internal loan, to be raised by requisitioning foreign money, exchange, and securities, and issuing therefor ten-year bonds, on which repayment was to be made in the original currency but on

[46] For the full text, cf. *Tätigkeits-Bericht,* Heft 16 (Wien, 1922), pp. 5–19.

which interest was to be paid in crowns with allowance for changes in the rate of exchange; severe fines for violation of exchange-control regulations; further endeavors to obtain foreign credits; advance readjustment of industry in preparation for the slump unavoidable after the crown became stabilized; and replacement of the vanishing export possibilities by increased economic activities of the national government (electrification of the railways, and so on).

By far the most interesting of all the measures proposed by the financial plan was the abolition of the food subsidies. These subsidies, once paid with the help of the foreign relief loans, had no inflationary effects at first. After this help ceased, however, they became an increasingly heavy burden on the state; in fact, the chief source of the inflation.[47] At the congress of 1920 the party still held that the continuation of the subsidies was necessary as long as wages and salaries had not reached the world market level.[48] The workers came to regard them as a customary part of their wages. Now the financial plan proposed to replace them by increasing money wages to compensate for the price rises which would result from their withdrawal. The very ingenious scheme directed to this purpose coupled their abolition with certain sociopolitical guarantees, particularly a system of pooled family and children allowances. Nevertheless, it was clear from the outset that the abolition of the subsidies was certain to worsen the position of the workers temporarily. The plan implied, therefore—and this was one of its most significant features—the intention of the party and the trade unions to overcome the resistance of the workers.

The impression aroused by the plan was favorable; even strongly anti-Socialist papers welcomed it.[49] Minister of Finance Grimm resigned and was replaced by Gürtler, who was on excellent terms with the Socialists. In close touch with them he started a new financial policy, first and foremost by preparation of a bill abolishing the sub-

[47] Late in 1921 it was computed that 250 billion crowns would be necessary for the subsidies in 1922. At that time the budget envisaged a total gross revenue from taxes, the railroads, the salt and tobacco monopolies—in short, from all sources—of only 208 billions. Cf. Otto Bauer's leading article in the *Arbeiter Zeitung,* December 6, 1921, p. 1.

[48] *Parteitag, 1920,* p. 102.

[49] Cf., for instance, the *Neue Freie Presse,* October 2, 1921 (A.M.), p. 3. "It is gratifying that Social Democracy at last has come out with its financial plan. From its experiences in sterile opposition Social Democracy has come to the conclusion that the present moment forces all citizens to resort to measures for the reconstruction of the state. It also seems gratifying that by and large the finance plan holds itself aloof from utopian party dictates. . . ." Needless to say the *Presse* made some criticisms of details.

sidies. This bill was to be introduced after the trade unions and the employers' organizations had reached an agreement upon the manner in which the subsidies should be taken over by industry. Here the chief problem was whether the abolition should be effected at one stroke or gradually. The financial plan advocated gradual elimination. The government and the employers preferred immediate action; they argued that gradual removal would never check the depreciation of the crown, since a huge amount of notes would still have to be printed. Although Bauer's discussion of the problem showed his awareness of the full weight of this argument,[50] he and the other leaders had to take into consideration the opinions prevailing among the workers. The firm organization of the party prevented an outbreak of open protest against the abolition scheme, but the fact of strong opposition is not to be denied. Some incidental remarks at the party congress of 1921 show it very plainly.[51] And these tendencies among the workers were greatly furthered by the propaganda of the Communists, supported by the popular radical press in Vienna which fought violently against "the madness of abolition."[52] Even the workers' councils were used by the Communists as a sounding board for their demands that the removal of the subsidy system be postponed until the workers had secured at least the prewar "standard of life"[53]—incidentally, this was a formula somewhat closely akin to the resolution of the congress of the Social Democratic party one year before. Nevertheless, the Socialists stood firmly for abolition.

Just at this time prices rose with appalling rapidity; between October, 1921, and January, 1922, the index leaped from 3.7 to 12.9.[54] The adjustment of wages to this development proceeded slowly and somewhat ineffectively. The rage of the masses of the workers now turned against the merchants and the *Schieber* (profiteers). There were several demonstrations in Vienna. On October 15, particularly,

[50] *Arbeiter Zeitung,* December 6, 7, 8, 1921, editorials.

[51] A representative from Wiener-Neustadt stated: "In the beginning some sections of the Wiener-Neustadt workers did not like the idea. But we succeeded in making it clear to the people, especially to the working class, in meetings, that for the time being nothing else is possible to procure provisions for the population" (*Parteitag, 1921,* p. 194). Another said: "Some of our comrades in the states are of the opinion that by this plan the party has given the bourgeois parties permission to destroy the dikes and to let the wave of high prices overflow the workers" (*ibid.,* p. 188).

[52] *Der Abend,* December 20, 1921.

[53] *Die Rote Fahne,* October 2, 1921, p. 1.

[54] Gewerkschaftskommission, *Bericht,* 1923, p. 23.

major disturbances, brought about by rising potato prices, took place in a working-class district. Six weeks later, on December 1, came the most violent outbursts—unparalleled even in the stormy years 1919 and 1920. The Floridsdorf workers marched into the city; shops and hotels were plundered. Several times the cry: "Down with the abolition of the subsidies!" arose from the ranks of the demonstrants.[55]

Against the passions of the workers and the demagogy of the Communists the leaders of the Social Democrats used their superior understanding of economic problems. At the party congress of 1921 Otto Bauer told the workers' representatives: "You yourselves pay the bread subsidies in the form of the present prices for potatoes and fat. We must say that to the masses if we want to be honest with them."[56] And to the Communists' demands in the workers' councils that the inflation be stopped by imposing taxes on property, Bauer replied "that even taxes on property must find a natural limit in the value of the property."[57] Nevertheless, the opposition of the workers made it impossible for the Socialists and the trade unions openly to defend the necessity of sudden abolition, a fact clearly revealed in another passage from the remarks of Eldersch at the party congress: ". . . we decline any responsibility for the effects of a sudden removal of the subsidies."[58] In 1921 this certainly was not the language used by the Socialists when they were resolved to prevent some measure at any price. Apparently, their plan was to let the government parties decide on immediate removal against sham opposition. But this failed because the Christian Socials declined to vote for abolition at one stroke unless the other parties would do the same.[59]

At last a compromise was reached. The subsidies on flour and fat

---

[55] In the city 174 shops and coffeehouses, of which 110 were in the Inner City, were damaged and partly plundered; 20 policemen and 26 civilians were injured. *Neue Freie Presse,* December 2, 1921 (P.M.), p. 2.

[56] *Parteitag, 1921,* p. 190. Since the purveyors of fats were receiving a subsidy it seems that Bauer or the reporter was in error, though there remains the possibility that Bauer was thinking of prices outside the regulated market.

Eldersch spoke to the same effect: "You have received cheaper bread and flour but . . . the wage which you have received . . . was worth less. Naturally, if we want to come to an economy such as exists in Soviet Russia at present where a luncheon costs 40 to 50 thousand rubles, then the state should go on printing notes. But the working class itself is interested that this state of affairs cease, for it suffers most under it" (*ibid.,* pp. 173–174).

[57] *Arbeiter Zeitung,* December 3, 1921, p. 2.

[58] *Parteitag, 1921,* p. 176.

[59] *Neue Freie Presse,* December 16, 1921 (A.M.), p. 2.

were to be stopped immediately, but that on bread—the most important one—was to be removed in five steps by May, 1922. The act embodying the compromise contained the sociopolitical guarantees demanded in the financial plan, as well as a provision transforming the children's allowances into a permanent institution after May, 1922. Although the judgment of the *Volkswirt* that the compromise really amounted to a sudden removal of the subsidies[60] is somewhat of an exaggeration, it remains true that the Socialists had agreed to a scheme that fell little short of removal of the subsidies. It could be argued, however, that the most important subsidy was to be eliminated in stages. In other words, they did what they knew was economically wise, but clouded the facts a bit for reasons of political necessity. On the day the act was passed the *Arbeiter Zeitung* published a party manifesto to the workers which tried to explain once more the necessity for the measure and to convince them that they must not resort to violence.[61]

It is interesting to compare the policy of the leaders of the Christian Social workers on this issue with that of the Social Democrats. When the financial plan was published the former welcomed the coming abolition of subsidies, claimed prior advocacy of the move, as did many others, and demanded that the government make prompt and energetic use of this concession of the Socialists.[62] After the act had been adopted, however, they wrote: "The financial measures the government and the National Bank have been compelled to undertake mean that a further rise in food prices will ensue. Moreover, a general rise in prices will be inevitable.... It must be assumed that the entrepreneurs will not fail to take their new expenses into consideration while calculating the prices of finished goods."[63] Such an inadequate comment, omitting any reference to the long-run benefits likely to result from the abolition of the subsidies, not only reveals a lack of economic understanding on the part of this group,[64] but also shows in which camp the demagogy was to be found on this occasion.

[60] *Der österreichische Volkswirt,* vol. 14 (Dec. 24, 1921), 302.

[61] "Not with an easy mind did we agree to the removal of the subsidies. We did it because we recognized that this step was unavoidable if a most terrible catastrophe was to be prevented . . ." *Arbeiter Zeitung,* December 23, 1921, p. 1.

[62] *Christlichsoziale Arbeiter-Zeitung,* October 8, 1921.

[63] *Ibid.,* January 7, 1922.

[64] Cf. Lederer, *loc. cit.,* p. 703.

The abolition of the subsidies was the only important measure from the financial plan which was adopted.[65] Nevertheless, confidence was considerably restored. In the beginning of 1922 it was possible to secure Czech and English credits and thus to check the further fall of the crown. But the government, which could not decide to embark upon a purposeful and energetic policy, left unused the valuable breathing spell of several months—and this in spite of a resolution by the Social Democratic members of the Nationalrat on March 16, 1922, offering to support the government in the financial reorganization on condition that measures to this end should be agreed upon with them.[66] After the credits had been exhausted the crown continued falling at an even more rapid and disastrous pace.

Although the financial plan did not check the inflation, its significance for the historian of the Austrian labor movement can hardly be exaggerated. It shows better than any theoretical propositions that the Austrian Socialists were deeply conscious of their responsibility toward the whole of society and that they did their utmost to save the economy of the country and to restore normal economic life within the framework of the existing political and social order. In attempting to reach their aims, they went far in risking their last asset, their popularity with the workers; they did all in their power to prevent dangerous social unrest and those grave disturbances which they deemed inevitable if the inflation were continued unchecked.

As already indicated, the fall of the crown in mid-1922 made the entire preceding history of the inflation look like a slight monetary friction. According to the private, but perhaps most reliable, index of the *Volkswirt*,[67] the cost of living developed from May to October, 1922, in the following way:

Date	Cost of Living (January, 1921 = 100)
May, 1922	1,988.78
June, 1922	2,726.18
July, 1922	3,671.52
August, 1922	7,132.22
September, 1922	16,548.40
October, 1922	20,550.80

[65] Instead of requisitioning foreign currency and exchange the government merely ordered their compulsory registration, a regulation which had little practical effect.

[66] *Tätigkeits-Bericht,* Heft 16 (Wien, 1922), pp. 60–61.

[67] *Der österreichische Volkswirt,* vol. 15 (Jan. 6, 1923), 367–368.

Segur, Gürtler's successor as minister of finance in the new Seipel government, tried to save the situation by a financial plan based chiefly on the creation of a note-issuing bank. When June brought another collapse of the crown the Social Democratic leaders appeared at the Ballhausplatz and informed the chancellor that unless drastic measures were taken they would not be able to hold the workers back. Thereupon the government secured the promises of the banks to put their funds of hoarded foreign exchange at its disposal for the creation of the note-issuing bank. Soon it became clear that the Segur-Seipel plan was "as complete a failure as its predecessors";[68] that it was out of date before its adoption in July.

Meanwhile, on June 9, Bauer had proposed a plan for a more or less definite currency union with Germany under which the latter would establish a bank of note issue in Austria. This was in line with his persistent anschluss policy, but also reflected his opinion that it would save the crown from annihilation. "For the mark can not go under completely; Europe would not tolerate that." As is well known, this judgment was promptly rendered ridiculous by the course of events. And although others with better claim than Bauer to expert ability in this field made equal or worse mistakes, his opponents lost few opportunities to jibe at him.[69]

By August the deficit was increasing at the rate of half a billion crowns a month. The populace was in a state of panic. Everyone spoke of the coming catastrophe, although most people had only vague ideas concerning the nature of a general collapse. Actually the day when the crown would lose its internal and external value completely appeared to be not far off. On August 7 the government urged Lloyd George to grant immediately a loan of 15 million pounds sterling to allay the social unrest that threatened the existence of the Austrian republic. The government furthermore declared that in the event of refusal of its request, it would, upon agreement with the parliament, declare that neither it nor any other government was able to carry on the administration of the country. Nevertheless, on August 15, London rejected the request, referring the Austrians to the League of Nations. Eight days later a conference of all Socialist labor organizations met in Vienna. The manifesto

[68] Phillpotts, *op. cit.*, 1923, p. 6.

[69] Cf., for example, *Christlichsoziale Arbeiter-Zeitung,* February 17, 1923, p. 1; June 2, p. 1; August 25, p. 1.

adopted by it pictures the situation in Austria in darkest colors. The most important point of the long proclamation was the cautiously worded declaration that the party was prepared to enter a coalition government in order to save the country from collapse.[70] A few weeks earlier this offer might have found a jubilant reception; as it was, the general reaction of the non-Socialist press was that the Socialists wanted a coalition at the price of the surrender of the bourgeois parties. The *Reichspost* did not even deign to reply. For, in the meantime, Seipel had acted and acted swiftly. He went to Prague, thence to Berlin, and finally to Verona. In each city he negotiated for the incorporation of Austria into Czechoslovakia or Germany or Italy. In Italy a far-reaching scheme, including a customs and currency union, was actually drawn up—to the highest discomfort of Czechoslovakia. Beneš now intervened in Paris and London. When Seipel went to Geneva in the first days of September he found a completely changed attitude. One month later, on October 4, the so-called Geneva Protocols were signed. Austria was to receive a loan of 650 million gold crowns on the security of Austrian customs and tobacco monopoly revenues. The government undertook to stop printing notes. Thoroughgoing reforms of the budget were to be carried out under the supervision of a commissioner general from the League; he was also to control the use of the loan for covering the deficit, which implied control over large parts of the administration. The Protocols furthermore contained a guarantee of Austrian independence by the League, and a corresponding undertaking on the part of Austria to preserve her independence. The parliament was to eliminate itself from any participation in carrying through the financial reconstruction by passing a law giving to any cabinet which might be in office during the next two years full power to take all measures, within the general limits of the program agreed upon with the League, that in the opinion of the cabinet were necessary to balance the budget in those two years. To make the point doubly clear this clause of the Protocols included the statement that the cabinet could take these measures without referring them to parliament.[71] Through this proposal to exclude parliament Seipel had

[70] *Arbeiter Zeitung*, August 24, 1922, p. 2. Also the editorial, "Die Bedingungen der Konzentrationsregierung," in *ibid.*, August 26, p. 1.

[71] For a summary and devastating denunciation of the Protocols, see the article "Genf" by Dr. Gustav Stolper, *Der österreichische Volkswirt*, vol. 15 (Oct. 7, 1922), 9–12.

secured the incorporation of a pet scheme which he had first published on May 26, 1919, and which had been sharply criticized by the conservative *Neue Freie Presse*.[72] His subsequent denial that his plan constituted an exclusion of parliament[73] from one of the most vital issues in the history of the republic deserves no credence. Not the least interesting aspect of the episode is its foreshadowing of the role Seipel was to play in the destruction of Austrian democracy.

On the other hand, and whatever may be thought of Seipel's methods, his campaign undoubtedly ended with a solution of the Austrian inflation problem. The stabilization of the crown was effected at last.[74] But what was the reaction of the labor movement?

When the party congress met on October 14, the Socialists faced an entirely changed situation. Their coalition offer of August 23

---

[72] *Neue Freie Presse,* May 26, 1919 (A.M.), pp. 4 and 1.

[73] Nationalrat, *Protokoll,* November 6, 1922, p. 4553.

[74] Years later, in February of 1930, there was a sharp interchange between the *Volkswirt* and Seipel over the stabilization and the overthrow of Schober. The journal had received information that during the Genoa conference of May, 1922, Chancellor Schober had secured promises of loans and advances which would have enabled his government to stabilize the crown at about 8,000 to the dollar instead of the nearly 80,000 under Seipel's arrangements a few months later. The journal charged the Catholic political leader with having used the Pan-Germans to put Schober out of office while he was returning from Genoa, with claiming the accomplishments of others for his own, and with hindering the work of others so that he might take the credit for being the savior of Austria. Seipel's letter of reply put the emphasis on a telegram from Schober announcing his success in Genoa; the accused denied the existence of the telegram and asserted that all the conclusions drawn by the *Volkswirt* collapsed. On March 7, 1930, Schober stated that parliamentary and other political difficulties made it impossible to bring about a quick decision. Then, on October 23, he was more specific, declaring in a public address that he had secured the promises of loans and advances, that he was told the loan would be granted only to him and his cabinet, that he transmitted this information to Vienna, but that on the return trip he read in the papers that he had been overthrown. He did not claim that the loans would have been adequate to stabilize the crown, did not mention Seipel directly in this connection, and did not offer to produce the disputed telegram.

Schober's biographer, Kleinschmied, who published at about this time, was more emphatic. He asserted that the decisive blow against Schober was struck just as he had "cleared the last stone away" that blocked the road to the reorganization of federal finances and the economy in general; that a great deal of the wealth of Austria could have been saved and the necessity for signing the Geneva Protocols avoided had the financial reorganization been left in Schober's hands; and that his overthrow, working through the lack of courage among the Austrian people and the revived courage of the speculators, gave the final push toward the currency catastrophe of the summer of 1922.

Although the facts concerning the stabilization remain clouded, it seems highly probable that Seipel, whatever his reason, helped to engineer Schober's fall. Even the contemporary editorial comment in the organ of his party offers support for this conclusion despite its denials. Cf. *Der österreichische Volkswirt,* vol. 22 (Feb. 8, 15, 22, Mar. 15, 1930), 501–502, 529, 557–558, 641–642; *ibid.,* vol. 23 (Nov. 1, 1930), 109–110; *Neue Freie Presse,* March 8, 1930 (A.M.), p. 12, October 24 (A.M.), p. 5; Oskar Kleinschmied, *Schober* (Wien, 1930), pp. 192–198, 274–275; *Reichspost,* May 25, 1922, p. 1; B. Skottsberg, *Der österreichische Parlamentarismus* (Göteborg, 1940), pp. 292 ff.

had lost all meaning. Seipel's tactical moves and his success in Geneva had put the Socialists in a very awkward position politically. In his main speech to the congress Otto Bauer set against foreign help a program of "self-aid" as the solution of the Austrian crisis. Specifically, he proposed that by compulsory loans from banks, bankers, and members of the stock exchanges, by revalorization of the old Segur loan, and by liquidation of the Austro-Hungarian bank the amount of 215 million gold crowns should be raised. With this sum in hand a breathing space of about eight months could be secured; during it, by increasing taxes on industrial and agricultural property, but also on the consumption of the masses, and by drawing up a scheme to reduce the number of civil servants, the budget could be definitely balanced. Thus the economy could be restored without impairing the independence of the country and without creating a new obligation to renounce union with Germany.[75]

But Bauer declared, and the congress agreed, that it was possible and permissible to overthow Seipel and to reject the Geneva scheme only if the party succeeded in causing a wave of general protest and indignation throughout the country that would permit the party to apply its own plan. The propaganda machine was set in motion. Its progress was not accelerated, however, by the reiteration of Bauer's charge that the bourgeois parties were willing to use foreign help against the workers in order to restore bourgeois rule.[76] In fact, the call found little echo beyond the ranks of the workers. Thereupon, without stopping its struggle against the Treaty of Geneva, the party resumed negotiations with the government. Certain points of the so-called Reconstruction Act were changed; for instance, the customs on foodstuffs were excluded, and the elimination of parliament was prevented by the institution of an extraordinary cabinet council as a special committee of parliament. This last was done by a constitutional amendment for which the votes of the Socialists were necessary. In view of this fact it was repeatedly said that the campaign against Seipel's *Sanierung* (reorganization of the national finances)—for years a major feature of the policy of the Socialists—was pure demogogy; in other words, that by their vote for the amendment they had accepted the implications of the Treaty of Geneva.[77]

---

[75] For the text of Bauer's address, cf. *Parteitag, 1922*, pp. 126–157.

[76] *Ibid.*, pp. 130–131.

[77] Cf., for example, Leopold Kunschak, *Oesterreich 1918–1934* (Wien, 1935), pp. 77 ff.

It can be argued, however, that the fact that the Social Democrats did not overthrow the Geneva arrangements is rather to be taken as a proof of their feeling of responsibility toward the state; nothing would have been easier than to confine themselves to mere criticism and "damn the consequences." They obviously preferred a constructive solution of the Austrian problem.[78] On the other hand, it cannot be denied that their way of putting the issue, "foreign help *versus* self-aid," together with their frantic efforts to use the ensuing stabilization slump as a propaganda weapon against the Seipel government, was inconsistent. The Social Democrats had repeatedly declared, in their financial plan of 1921 and subsequently, that foreign credits were indispensable for stabilization of the currency. At the party congress of 1922 Bauer was expressly asked to explain this inconsistency.[79] Although he replied that it was impossible to pay for credits "with the liberty of our country and the honor of our people" and reiterated his faith in his self-help proposals, it remains highly improbable that Bauer himself seriously believed that a restoration of normal conditions could be accomplished without foreign loans to the state. Certainly this was the common opinion in Austria at the time.[80] Furthermore, there is plenty of evidence that the Social Democrats were perfectly aware that the stabilization of the currency could not help bringing about a grave economic depression and severe unemployment in Austria.[81]

In spite of all this the Socialist movement for years to come used all the devices of its propaganda machine to put every sign of de-

---

[78] That the Socialists were not blind to the constructive value of Seipel's scheme may be perceived from a statement made two years later by Bauer to the congress of the metalworkers' union.

"As the Geneva treaty was being concluded, and, in fact, somewhat earlier than that, we Socialists said to ourselves: 'The most important thing for the whole future of the workers' movement is the stability of the crown.' When Dr. Seipel came back from Geneva, we knew: what matters is not the text of this or that article, but the execution of a policy which keeps the crown stable—prevents its falling, but also its rising." *Die Industrie,* August 9, 1924, p. 7. This employers' paper printed the complete text of Bauer's speech and declared itself in almost entire agreement with it.

[79] "With all due respect to the superior technical knowledge of comrade Bauer, I remind you of the fact that for a long time we clung to the opinion that Austria cannot be saved without foreign help." From the speech of Oskar Trebitsch, *Parteitag, 1922,* p. 163. Bauer's rejoinder appears in *ibid.,* p. 183.

[80] "When the ruin of the currency has once reached this degree there is scarcely any method of internal economic policy which could lead to its restoration." Lederer, *loc. cit.,* p. 704. As indicated above, Stolper vigorously disagreed. *Loc. cit.,* p. 9.

[81] Even in his speech to the party congress of 1922 Bauer had admitted that, "We shall not in any likelihood be able to avoid an industrial crisis whatever course be taken." *Parteitag, 1922,* p. 142.

pression, every increase of unemployment to the debit account of the Seipel government. This attitude is in such sharp contrast with that policy of serious and deep responsibility pursued by the party for years after the establishment of the republic that it calls for some explanation.

It has been shown that subsequent to the revolution the Social Democrats entered a coalition government with the Christian Socials because they thought this union indispensable in steering the ship of the new state between the Scylla of Bolshevism and the Charybdis of Habsburg restoration. When, under the pressure of the workers, the Socialists passed from "coalition" through "proportional" representation into "opposition" in the summer and fall of 1920, this opposition was of a peculiar character. Before the party left the government it had carried through the "military act" which legally recognized the soldiers' trade unions. Since these unions were under Social Democratic leadership, the party was certain that the army could not be used against the workers. Thus the strange situation arose that the opposition wanted to increase and strengthen the army, whereas the government stood for a reduction of man power. Furthermore, the governments after 1920 were much too weak; they wanted the coöperation of the Socialists. Several times the party was requested to rejoin the government, and hardly anything important was done without previous negotiations with it. Thus it was also possible that the opposition party issued a financial plan which was—at least partly—adopted by the government. This situation, abnormal as it was, assuredly preserved the maximum peaceful political development attainable in those unruly times; unfortunately it underwent a thoroughgoing change with Seipel's accession as chancellor. This man of extraordinary political and diplomatic gifts became the recognized leader of the Christian Social party, indeed, of the whole non-Socialist movement in Austria. As a prelate of the Roman Catholic Church and a convinced Monarchist,[82] prelate Seipel regarded it as his holiest and most patriotic duty largely to undo what Austrian labor had gained by the revolution, to destroy the powerful position of the anticlerical "godless" party, and to eliminate the So-

[82] A perusal of his articles written at the time of the Austrian revolution leaves no doubt in this respect. Cf. Ignaz Seipel, *Der Kampf um die österreichische Verfassung* (Wien, 1930), pp. 42–66, especially the article originally published in *Das Volkswohl*, vol. 9, Heft 10 (1918), 226, where Seipel speaks of "the Empire our hearts beat for" (p. 43 of the Seipel volume).

cialists' influence from affairs of state. The Treaty of Geneva was the first, and a very important, step on his way to this goal. The Social Democratic party found itself suddenly confronted by a strong and energetic government which not only did not care for Socialist collaboration but tried to prevent it as completely as that was possible at the time. Thus the labor movement was forced into actual opposition to the government. The participation of the Socialists in the government, which they had believed so near in the late summer of 1922 when Seipel seemed at the end of his tether, had now become impossible. The period of coöperation of classes so much lauded by Otto Bauer[83] came to an end. A period of sharpest struggle began which was to remain significant for the political life of the republic until the destruction of the independent Austrian labor movement in 1934. There can be no doubt that in this new situation the Social Democratic party acquired many features it did not possess before. Its radicalization was the unavoidable consequence of Seipel's policy. Only with these facts in mind can the fashion in which the party fought against the Treaty of Geneva and its consequences be understood. But here a certain qualification is necessary. Granted that the opposition into which the Socialists were forced was often fierce and ruthless; their party remained one with essentially democratic aims. One important point must not be forgotten: it was an opposition to a government, never to the state. The Austrian workers regarded the Austrian republic as their creation. They were always ready to defend it against any attack. With all the more distrust they watched this republic being ruled by a government whose adherence to republican ideals could reasonably be doubted. To a degree Austria was similar to France in the 'seventies of the previous century—"Une republique sans les republicains."[84] This situation bore the germs of a grave social disease in itself. France succeeded in emerging from the inevitable crisis (Boulanger) as a republic and a democracy. Austria was less fortunate.

[83] *Die österreichische Revolution*, pp. 242–249.

[84] Cf. Charles Seignobos, *Histoire politique de l'Europe contemporaine* (Paris, 1897), p. 189.

PART THREE:
DEMOCRACY CULMINANT

CHAPTER X

Social and Labor Legislation

FROM THE POINT of view of Manchester Liberalism social legislation, like every intervention with the free play of economic forces, is either superfluous or useless or harmful. Either the results of intervention would have been achieved anyway; or the intervention is defeated by economic forces; or the intervention defeats its own purposes and brings about a deterioration in the economic position of groups of people it set out to improve.

Under the terms of a strict liberal theory there was no space for a social problem as such. An Austrian economist aptly describes the liberal attitude as follows:

> If the workers want to work a long time this is to their interest because then they are able to earn more; every worker will think twice before he takes employment in an unsanitary undertaking, and he will decide to do so only if higher wages will compensate for the danger; if a worker sends his small children to the factory, he does so because then he is better able to provide for them, or perhaps because in the case of his own unemployment he could not provide food for them at all; if women work at night in factories, they do so because in this way they find a living; and if in the state of free competition the workers' conditions are unfavorable, they are still the best possible in the given situation. As soon as the national wealth renders the situation of labor more favorable workers will be able to force the adoption of better conditions by a free competitive struggle.[1]

In the 1940's it is scarcely necessary to stress the point that the history of practical social legislation has proved that this theory rests upon assumptions which make it inadequate as a basis for dealing with the complexity of reality. Even under comparatively "normal" conditions in economic, social, and political life, the economic weakness of large groups of workers, their lack of knowledge about employment possibilities, as well as other factors give rise to important frictions which call for intervention by the state. Such intervention seeks first to aid the workers; nevertheless, it is generally conceded to be in the interest of all social groups. In times of great upheavals,

[1] Richard Strigl, *Angewandte Lohntheorie* (Wien, 1926), p. 151.

however, when various social and political forces are unleashed and the whole body economic is subject to violent convulsions, situations arise in which measures by the state on behalf of the working class become of even more pressing import. In such periods, far beyond mere improvements in the position of one class, such measures become questions of life and death for the whole society. It is not difficult to show that this was precisely the situation in the crippled residual state of Austria after the collapse of the monarchy.

The soldiers of the old army streaming back to their native towns threatened an immediate catastrophe on the labor market. Demobilization was thus partly an economic problem, but first and foremost one of imminent political significance; the backflow of masses of highly excited men whom the war had taught to believe in force and violence was a continuous threat to social order. This was certainly a short-run problem. However, in addition, there was the general political problem of working people who had lived through four years under the discipline of war-regulated labor. The end of the war and the collapse of the authorities who represented in the eyes of the workers the suppression and exploitation of war industry were bound to lead to a strong and powerful reaction. The removal of the Habsburgs was thus regarded as the very first stage of the revolutionary development. The overthrow of the whole private capitalistic order—inextricably associated in the minds of the workers with war—should follow. Here, in the same way as in demobilization, but in an even more general sense, it was plain that the existing order of society could be saved from social revolution only by thoroughgoing social reform; that is, a wide system of social legislation. Apart from political considerations there were serious social and economic reasons which made such legislation a necessity.

First, the desolate wartime living conditions and undernourishment, aggravated by overexertion in the factories, had considerably reduced the physical strength of Austrian workers and thus had affected their productivity. Only by radical betterment of their living and working conditions could their physical condition be improved and their depleted working power restored. Closely connected with this situation is the problem of *Arbeitsunlust* discussed in Chapter IX. Only by making their work more attractive to them was it possible to induce large groups of workers to stay in the productive process. The totality of these reasons made imperative the extended social reforms which took place in Austria after the revolution. But on the other side there is little doubt that the men who created Austrian postwar social statutes did not conceive them as short-run measures, good only to bridge over a difficult situation. Much as the leaders of the Socialist party and the trade unions were opposed to a violent revolutionary solution of the social problem, they were firmly convinced that a wide system of social laws is an objective "devoutly to be wished." In fact, they were accustomed to use as a first measure of the long-run success of party and union activities the extent of material improvement in workers' conditions brought about by social legislation.[2]

During the formal existence of the Austrian democratic republic, 1918–1934, six periods in the development of social legislation can be discerned. These divisions are an adaptation and extension of those of one of the foremost authorities in the field, Karl Pribram.[3] They facilitate the organization of the mass of detail, but deviations from strict chronology have been made several times when considerations of logic seemed to require them. At first the periods were short, in accordance with the rapid development of revolutionary epochs, but became longer when a more stable situation was attained.

The first period ran from the beginnings of revolution in October, 1918, to March, 1919. It was the span in which speedy action was required unless demobilization and the sudden stoppage of war industry should lead to general chaos. The second extended from March through July, 1919, and covered the time when soviet dictatorships both east and west brought Austria to the brink of a Communist revolution. During it social legislation was par excellence the method to prevent violent outbreaks; naturally, therefore, it brought forth the most radical measures adopted which, like the Works Councils Act, represent a maximum of interference with the free decisions of the entrepreneur. The third period lasted from August, 1919, to October, 1920. In this interval there were two major developments: the most excessive measures adopted in the preceding period were withdrawn; and, much more important, the legislation issued in the first months after the revolution underwent a

[2] Cf., for example, Julius Braunthal, *Die Sozialpolitik der Republik* (Wien, 1919), pp. 4–5.

[3] "Die Sozialpolitik im neuen Oesterreich," *AfSS.*, vol. 48 (1920–1921), 615 ff.

general reorganization so that many hurriedly adopted or temporary acts were revised, improved, and made permanent. The fourth dates from October, 1920, to mid-1927. The disruption of the coalition government and the formation of a cabinet without the Socialists (after the interlude of the "proportional" ministry) meant a shift to low gear in matters of social legislation. In this period of almost seven years the opposition to social legislation, the so-called struggle against the "social burden," really crystallized and was carried on vigorously—without, however, recording any marked success against the strongly entrenched positions of the party and of the trade unions. When, in 1926, the stabilization crisis gave way to a new upswing in business, the impetus to attacks against the social burden was lessened. The beginning of the next period is marked by the general political reshuffling caused by the events of July 15, 1927. The deterioration in the position of the party and the subsequent increase in the strength of Fascist forces set the stage for the first real deterioration in the system of Austrian social legislation. The sixth period comprises the changes brought about by the Dollfuss government through its notorious emergency decrees during 1933, the year of the decisive decline of Austrian democracy, as well as those put through by the Schuschnigg regime after the murder of Dollfuss. Except for a few references to later events this chapter treats the development in the first four periods only. During that time the Austrian system of social legislation was created and underwent its practical test. The last two periods belong in an essentially different era, one of rising and victorious counterrevolution, and will be presented best as a part of the events of the era.

In October, 1918, a state department of social welfare was constituted. A fortnight later it took over the business of the Habsburg ministry of social welfare. This was the youngest among the ministries of the old empire, having been established as late as December 22, 1917.[4] With the Socialist trade-union leader, Ferdinand Hanusch, a new man and a new spirit took possession of this branch of state administration, the procrastination of which had become almost proverbial among the workers. But he certainly did not find a *tabula rasa* in the field of social legislation, even though most of

[4] In March, 1919, the state department of social welfare and the state department for people's health were united in the state department for social administration. *StGBl.*, 1919, Nr. 180.

the existing laws were more than thirty years old. Since they were the basis from which the reformatory work of the new state proceeded, a short survey of them is in order.

Social and Labor Legislation under the Habsburgs

Despite the development of the textile industry in the empire before 1800 there was no recognition by the Habsburgs of any obligation to protect their subjects against exploitation by the new industrialists for half a century. In 1842 a decree from the court chancery prohibited the employment in factories of children under nine years of age, limited to 10 the working hours of those between nine and twelve years, and to 12 those between twelve and sixteen years, and prohibited nightwork for those under sixteen.[5] The Revolution of 1848, which liberated the peasants, contributed scarcely anything to the improvement of the lot of industrial and handicraft workers. The following years of absolutist and semiabsolutist rule also present almost a vacuum as far as social legislation is concerned. By imperial *Patent* of May 23, 1854, the miners' benefit societies, which stemmed from the Middle Ages, became compulsory organizations for both mine operators and workers. The coverage included insurance against accident, sickness, invalidism, and old age, as well as benefits to survivors.[6] More important was the industrial code (*Gewerbeordnung*) of 1859. It reaffirmed the limitations on the labor of children and young persons and prescribed some regulations that enabled public officials to determine the state of labor conditions in factories,[7] but practically the spirit of *laissez faire, laissez passer* still reigned supreme. Even the Austro-Prussian War of 1866, though it deeply shook the Habsburg monarchy, did not result in any tangible activity in the field of social policy. It is true that the freedom of association and of assembly, granted by laws of November 15, 1867,[8] in intimate connection with the Liberal constitution which was enacted a few weeks later, indirectly furthered the ends of social legislation; nevertheless, the right of the workers to conclude agreements in order to achieve higher wages and more favorable working conditions was still hampered by statutes from the pre-Liberal

[5] Max Lederer, *Grundriss des österreichischen Sozialrechtes* (Wien, 1932), p. 16.
[6] *RGBl.*, 1854, Nr. 146, §§ 210–214.
[7] *Ibid.*, 1859, Nr. 227.
[8] *Ibid.*, 1867, Nr. 134, 135.

period, specifically, by the provisions of the industrial code of 1859 and by stipulations of the penal code of 1852.[9] A campaign was therefore started with the objective of bringing about the unrestricted right of coalition. The succession of meetings, resolutions, and petitions reached a climax in the previously discussed demonstration of about 20,000 workers before the parliament building in Vienna on December 13, 1869. Then came the high treason trial of leading demonstrants and the wholesale dissolution of workers' organizations in July of 1870. Meanwhile, however, a coalition act had been sanctioned by the emperor on April 7. This seemingly contradictory development should be noted because it became more or less typical in subsequent periods of greater activity in the field of labor and social legislation in the monarchy; these periods were very likely to be accompanied by intensification of political suppression and persecution of the workers and their organizations.

Outwardly at least the coalition act was prohibitive rather than permissive of certain activities. Article 2 declared as without legal effect, that is, unenforceable by resort to the courts, agreements among workers that sought by means of a strike to force higher wages or better conditions of employment from employers, as well as agreements (1) to support those who persisted in the original understandings to strike or (2) to injure those who withdrew from such original understandings. Article 3 went further and, in language similar to that of the anti-terror act adopted sixty years later through the efforts of the opponents of the "free" unions in the republican parliament, declared as illegal and punishable the use of intimidation or force (in connection with any of the types of agreements set out in Article 2) to hinder or to seek to hinder workers from freely deciding to accept work. The permissive or progressive value of the act consisted of the repeal of three sections of the penal code of 1852. These had made illegal and subject to penalty the agreements now listed in Article 2 of the law of 1870 and in their practical effect had been closely equivalent to an outright prohibition of strikes. Thus, as Lederer puts it, despite the "peculiar construction" of the law it did provide the unions with the "necessary elbowroom for development."[10]

[9] *Ibid.*, 1859, Nr. 227; *ibid.*, 1852, Nr. 117.

[10] *RGBl.*, 1870, Nr. 43; *ibid.*, 1852, Nr. 117, particularly §§ 479–481; *BGBl.*, 1930, Nr. 113; Lederer, *op. cit.*, pp. 228–229.

After the promulgation of the coalition act more than a decade passed before the matter of social and labor legislation was again seriously tackled. Then, in the first half of the 'eighties, began the comparatively short but most fruitful period for such legislation in the Habsburg empire. The impetus came from quarters which had but little contact with the workers' movement. The ideological leader of the new efforts was the conservative Austrian Baron Karl von Vogelsang whose "high merits" in this field were expressly recognized by the unifier of the Socialist workers, Viktor Adler.[11] It may be assumed, however, that the activities of Vogelsang would have borne little fruit had not the general political and economic development created the necessary prerequisites for the realization of some of his ideas. The heyday of Austrian Liberalism had come to a close in 1878. The lower middle class saw itself threatened by the competition of big industry. The workers found themselves exposed to severe persecutions under the rule of the Liberal Auersperg government. The Crown, after its reconciliation with the Church, was anxious to unite the high nobility, the Catholic peasants, and the middle groups which were hard pressed by big business, against Liberalism. An electoral reform was introduced by Prime Minister Count Taaffe, the chief exponent of the anti-Liberal policy, in order to mobilize the small businessmen against the Liberal bourgeoisie. Under the circumstances the enactment of certain measures of social legislation suited to a nicety this general line of policy. The social laws, applicable only to establishments of "factory" size, were bound to increase, at least temporarily, the competitive ability of small business. Moreover, anti-Liberals hoped by social legislation to stem the drive for the general franchise and to make even ruthless suppression of labor unrest politically tolerable to the masses.

In 1883 a parliamentary investigating committee was established under the leadership of Vogelsang. Problems of female and child labor, Sunday and holiday rest, and limitations on the working day were discussed. Even representatives of the workers had been invited; one of their leaders, Höger, demanded *inter alia* a ten-hour day.[12] The results of the committee's work influenced to a certain extent the contents of the laws adopted in the following two years.

[11] *Victor Adlers Aufsätze, Reden und Briefe,* Heft 4 (Wien, 1925), p. 148.

[12] J. Deutsch, *Geschichte der österreichischen Gewerkschaftsbewegung,* Vol. I (Wien, 1929), p. 192.

On June 17, 1883, a statute establishing a system of factory inspectors was passed.[13] The functions of the inspectors were restricted to supervision, reports, and expert statements. They were required to visit the factories and to report on workers' conditions and instances of disregard of the legal stipulations; but they were not allowed to assume any authoritative functions, and, most notably, they had no right to demand correction of the shortcomings they had been able to discover. The number of the inspectoral districts, each of them covered by one inspector, was ridiculously small. Even the greatest effort and endurance on the part of an inspector were inadequate to ensure any regular and complete check of the factories in his district. For example, the whole of Vienna formed one district, as did the huge territory of Galicia and Bucovina. During the first two years of the existence of their positions, moreover, the new officials were restricted by the small volume of social laws. On the other hand, despite perpetually insufficient financial resources and legal and administrative handicaps, they understood quite well how to turn out excellent work;[14] their reports were full of valuable suggestions concerning sanitary and protective innovations and represented a firsthand and highly trustworthy source for information on labor problems.

In March, 1885, after a year of parliamentary debates, an amendment to the *Gewerbeordnung* was adopted.[15] The most restrictive, that is, protective and useful stipulations, applied only to factories in accordance with the general political objectives of the government. Most important of the new regulations was the general limita tion of the working day to eleven hours (not to ten as had been provided in the original draft of the bill). Unfortunately, Section 96a establishing this limit contained several loopholes. The minister of trade was given power to designate trade categories which had "proved" their "particular needs" and to grant to them permission

[13] *RGBl.*, 1883, Nr. 117. The translation of the Austrian term *Gewerbeinspektor* presents some difficulties because of the unclear and changing content of the concept *Gewerbe* which sometimes is identical with "industry," sometimes is restricted to small shops in trade and handicraft, and sometimes covers the whole field of undertakings in production, commerce, and services. The translation "factory inspector" used here should be read with these facts in mind. For the earlier years it is almost precisely accurate; for later periods some writers prefer "industrial inspector" in line with the tendency to refer, probably too loosely, to railway transportation and even to agriculture as industries.

[14] Cf. Lederer, *op. cit.*, p. 375.

[15] *RGBl.*, 1885, Nr. 22.

to operate for an additional hour. The lists of such favored categories were to be reviewed every three years. Second, any entrepreneur was entitled to work his employees an indefinite number of overtime hours on three days within a month after simple notification to the subordinate industrial authorities. Furthermore, on the claim of an increased need for labor the employer might receive from the same authorities a permit to work overtime during three consecutive weeks; extensions past three weeks might be granted by higher officials. More satisfactory were the prohibition of the employment in factories of children under fourteen; the requirement that those between fourteen and sixteen were to be used only for easy tasks; and the prohibition of nightwork for women.[16] No limitations were placed on the hours of adult male nonfactory workers, but certain restrictions for the benefit of child and female labor were provided. The so-called truck system was prohibited.

For the political background of this legislation it is important to recall facts brought out in Chapter II. Its enactment was preceded and followed by a wave of persecutions against workers' associations. In January, 1884, martial law was proclaimed for Vienna and vicinity. This was the signal for general action against Socialist organizations all over the country. Vienna remained under martial law for more than seven years. A Socialist bill was submitted to the parliament in 1885 but was finally transformed into an Anarchist Act. These measures demonstrate that the Austrian government was keeping a watchful eye on the development in Germany and was eager to transplant south of the Bohemian forest the essentials of Bismarck's anti-Socialist policy.[17]

In 1887 and 1888 two other laws of major importance were adopted: the Workers Accident Insurance and the Workers Sickness Insurance Acts.[18] In both cases the upper house appreciably increased

[16] As mentioned earlier, nightwork in factories for persons under sixteen had been prohibited by decree in 1842.

[17] An outstanding historian of the Habsburg state in the nineteenth century says: "With all its defects, this legislation, at the time, represented a substantial advance and a genuine achievement on the part of the Austrian civil service which, in more than one department, carried out the grand political ideas of the conservative majority in masterly fashion. True, the same government repressed the social democratic movement among the workers with extreme severity, modelling its action in this as in other directions on the domestic policy of Prince Bismarck." Joseph Redlich, *Emperor Francis Joseph of Austria* (New York, 1929), p. 420.

[18] *RGBl.*, 1888, Nr. 1, 33. Although passed in 1887 the first law was not published until 1888.

the difficulties of the process of legislation. Old-age and disablement insurance was left out of consideration, and not until 1906 was a pension act passed for the group of salaried employees in private undertakings.[19]

With the laws enacted in 1883–1888 the time of intensive work in the field of social legislation in the monarchy was actually over. An attempt was made in 1886 to create chambers of labor, with power not only to give expert statements on labor problems, but also to delegate 9 members to parliament (as against 30 sent by the chambers of commerce); it led to no tangible result. This episode also must be regarded as significant for an understanding of the political situation out of which the social legislation arose. The desire to divert the workers' movement from the objective of the general franchise by means of social legislation is distinctly discernible. And these underlying motives also largely explain the setback in the development of such legislation after 1888. Political persecutions apparently did not succeed in breaking the independent labor movement. In fact, the termination of intensive social activity in the government and the parliament coincides with the previously discussed "Unity" party congress held in Hainfeld (December, 1888); that is to say, with the creation of a strong political labor party the declared immediate objective of which was the general franchise.

The foregoing statements have not been intended to deny the probabilities that there were other factors contributing to the practical suspension of progress in social laws after 1888. For one thing the Austrian empire was progressively developing in the direction of an industrial country. The nobility, which in the 'eighties had sat in their castles and watched with hatred the waxing financial and political power of the bourgeoisie, found themselves in the 'nineties increasingly involved in the processes of capitalist production. In the 'eighties they had been all in favor of limiting the profits and power of the Liberal upper middle class; in the 'nineties they began to believe that social legislation might prove disadvantageous to their own interests. Also in the lower middle class certain significant changes were developing. The process of industrialization was transforming it from a more or less economically independent group in society to a servant of the new industries. Over the years, the Chris-

[19] *RGBl.*, 1907, Nr. 1.

tian Social party began to lose much of the revolutionary—that is, anti-Manchester Liberal—impetus which it had demonstrated in the early 'eighties when Lueger first appeared on the political stage. The general shift from a free trade to a tariff policy in international commerce also favored a *rapprochement* between the employers in industry and the conservative parties. The result of these developments was that the progress of social legislation became much more dependent upon the pressure exercised by the Social Democratic party and the trade unions than upon any other political and social factors. In this connection should be mentioned the untiring efforts of these organizations, and particularly of the labor press (*Gleichheit,* then *Arbeiter Zeitung*), to see that what had been secured in social legislation was actually enforced. This task implied a steady criticism of the imperial authorities. They were to be "educated," as the favorite expression in the Socialist camp ran, to know, comprehend, and respect the law. Despite some success in these efforts it seems clear that the field for making real progress in the improvement of labor conditions shifted to direct bargains between the trade unions and the employers. The appreciable gains registered were, of course, confined to industries in which there were strong unions.

Apart from the various reasons already cited for the lack of progress in the field of social legislation there was the fact that the Reichsrat was progressively unable to work normally because of the increasing strife among the representatives of the individual nationalties. The almost continual obstruction certainly greatly hampered the development of social legislation. But, on the other hand, it may be inquired why the Crown, which made extensive use of the emergency powers in the famous Article 14 of the constitution, did not show the same readiness to proceed in matters of social policy by means of decrees.

As it was, very promising beginnings were prevented from bearing practical fruit. Toward the close of the century Minister of Trade Dr. Bärnreither, who had taken an active part in the social legislation of the 'eighties, created an office for labor statistics and attached to it a permanent labor advisory council (*Arbeitsbeirat*) which included men of high scholarly reputation (Philippovich, Hainisch, Mataja), representatives of the trade unions (Hueber, Smitka, Kunschak), and representatives of industry (Vetter and

Fillunger).[20] These and other well-qualified members of the committee did excellent work in collecting material and thoroughly discussing problems of social legislation. Several elaborate reports were submitted to the government, but only the extensive inquiry into working time in coal mines led to practical results; in 1901 the nine-hour day was introduced there.[21]

Legislative gains for salaried or white-collar employees provide another exception in the generally stagnant situation between 1888 and 1914, but here again the political motivation is discernible. By favoring the salaried group it was hoped that a wedge could be driven between them and the manual workers, thus weakening the trade-union movement and easing the position of the entrepreneurs in their shops. The old-age insurance law of 1906 for salaried employees has been mentioned. Four years later the general act concerning them was adopted.[22] This was a fairly modern statute by which paid holidays, salary payments during illness, discharge compensation, and notice periods were introduced. It was supplemented by the law of January 14, 1910, concerning closing times—likewise mainly applicable to white-collar workers. Finally, the law of January, 1914, may be cited; by it the conditions of salaried employees in agricultural undertakings were regulated.[23]

With reference to manual workers an enactment of May, 1911, extended the prohibition of nightwork for women from factories to workshops and construction concerns employing more than 10 persons.[24] Apart from some ordinances respecting lead poisoning and requiring "rest on Sundays" in the so-called continuous shops nothing else of appreciable importance was done. The long-standing wish of the workers for old-age insurance failed of adoption in parliament in 1911 after years of protracted discussions and intensive work. The representatives of the Galician peasants prevented the bill from becoming law.

The outbreak of the war brought disastrous consequences for the existing social legislation. Laws concerning rest on Sundays and holidays were suspended; permission to work overtime and to use women for nightwork was generously granted; the staff of the factory

[20] Lederer, *op. cit.*, p. 24.
[21] *RGBl.*, 1901, Nr. 81.
[22] *Ibid.*, 1910, Nr. 20.
[23] *Ibid.*, 1914, Nr. 9.
[24] *Ibid.*, 1911, Nr. 65.

inspection service was, to a large extent, used for military purposes. Moreover, the war industry law most seriously interfered with the social laws and rendered a large part of them completely ineffective. Even sickness and accident insurance provisions suffered greatly under this emergency statute.

Chiefly in the second half of the conflict, when the general unrest in the factories became dangerous to the continuation of the fighting, and indeed, to the existence of the state, certain relaxations of the strict wartime regulations and certain other concessions had to be made. In this connection the complaint commissions (March, 1917)[25] referred to in Chapter II may be recalled. Shortly before (February) the abolition of nightwork for bakers[26] had satisfied an old demand of the workers; the adoption of this principle had been rendered easier by prohibiting the production of white bread and rolls for the duration of the war. Along the same line was the tenants protection decree prohibiting arbitrary increases in rents and also arbitrary notices of the termination of leases.[27] Much earlier, in March, 1916, a thoroughgoing amendment to the civil code was promulgated by decree;[28] it contained *inter alia* the important prescription of Article 1154b by which continuation of wage payments during sickness of the worker was made obligatory for one week. The creation of a special ministry of social welfare has been mentioned. Any further extension of the scope of social legislation proved, however, unfeasible and the new ministry had to confine itself to preparatory work in various fields—especially provisions for the victims of the war, youth welfare, and the problem of employment organizations.

In summary of the development of social legislation under the rule of the Habsburgs it may be said that, most notably in the years 1883–1888, the foundation for a modern system was laid. What had been done by way of legal stipulations, and to a larger extent by way of preparatory work on bills which could not be brought to enactment so long as the monarchy endured, certainly proved of greatest value when the establishment of the republic removed the obstacles and opened the road to a new development. Nevertheless,

[25] *Ibid.*, 1917, Nr. 122.
[26] *Ibid.*, 1917, Nr. 54.
[27] *Ibid.*, 1917, Nr. 34.
[28] *Ibid.*, 1916, Nr. 69, esp. p. 152.

there seems little or no justification in speaking of a "social tradition of Austria" (meaning the work of the monarchy in this field) which was taken up and respected by the Socialists while they were the dominant political group in the new state. Ernst Karl Winter emphatically stresses this thesis of an "organic continuation."[29] He notes that Dr. Emil Steinbach, the man who elaborated the social laws adopted under Taaffe, stood very close to the emperor; he mentions the fact that frequently the same expert drafted the bills in the monarchy and in the republic; he stresses the idea that tenants protection—first adopted by imperial decree—"became the legal basis upon which the Social Democratic party established its political rule after the war"; and he concludes that none of the social reform laws passed by the republic would have been impossible in a constitutional monarchy.

As far as the example of tenants protection is concerned, it may be doubted whether it is really illuminating. What the Socialists used as an instrument of their policy was actually not the emperor's decree, which in itself would never have been sufficient for any more comprehensive purposes. Only because the subsequent inflation reduced the prewar rents practically to zero were the Socialists able to base their housing, and to some extent their general, policy upon this decree. But this is certainly a minor point. What may most seriously and legitimately be doubted is whether or not Winter is warranted in speaking of a "social tradition" in the Habsburg monarchy.[30] In the preceding pages it was shown how every period of more intensive social legislation was largely determined by special political constellations. This is true notably of the years 1883–1888 and it is not less true of the activities of the latter period of the First World War. In the intervals between these time limits there were

---

[29] Ernst Karl Winter, "Rise and Fall of Austrian Labor," *Social Research,* vol. 6 (Sept., 1939), 316–340, esp. pp. 324 and 337. Cf. also the development of the same train of thought in his *Arbeiterschaft und Staat* (Wien, 1934), pp. 19 ff.

[30] In his efforts to prove his thesis Winter goes so far as to contend that, "In Germany the discriminatory law against the Socialists continued from 1878 to 1890, *while not only did Austria abstain from a similar law* [italics mine], but the Social Democratic party emerged there in 1888 with the obvious tolerance and the indirect support of the Taaffe government." (*Social Research,* vol. 6, p. 319). This flatly contradicts Winter's own accurate statement that the Taaffe regime "copied the Bismarck legislation in its Anarchists' law" (*Arbeiterschaft und Staat,* p. 16). The period of martial law is mentioned neither in Winter's article, nor in his book. Second, German Social Democracy also was at the end of the period of suppression stronger than ever before. And, third, the police persecutions directed against the party congress in Hainfeld in 1889, to quote only one example, give little evidence of "obvious" toleration and "support" by the government.

years of almost complete standstill. Winter himself speaks of a "deadlock with regard to social legislation."[31]

It is, moreover, particularly interesting to quote here the opinion of two of the experts in the ministry of social welfare, since Winter refers to the fact, as supporting his general thesis, that such men remained in the same offices under the republic. Karl Pribram, one of the leading workers of the ministry states: "The old Austrian empire with its conservative tendencies preserved in matters of social policy a fearful reticence and confined itself in the main to following the example of neighbor countries with higher developed industry, in the first place of Germany."[32]

Max Lederer, another outstanding authority and one of the highest officials of the ministry, tells the story of a very moderate bill concerning child labor, drafted in 1913, which could not gain the support of the imperial minister of trade although it had been expressly approved by the Congress of the Society for the Protection of Child Workers in Salzburg in September of that year. Incidentally, the bill had been strongly supported before the congress in a paper presented by Michael Hainisch, later first president of the Austrian republic. And Lederer is justified in adding: "This too-far-going rejection even of moderate demands in the field of social policy was bound to have the result that after the revolution the stream of social laws—no longer kept back—could all the more easily overflow all dams."[33]

And this seems to be the important point. The question of the possibility of a constitutional monarchy permitting such social laws as those promulgated by the republic is irrelevant. For the empirical question of whether or not there is justification for speaking of a continuation of social traditions it is sufficient to ascertain that all efforts to pass these laws in the lifetime of the monarchy were doomed to failure, and that a comparison of the social legislation in prerevolutionary and postrevolutionary times certainly presents a case where the increased quantity per se means a change in quality.

[31] *Social Research,* vol. 6, p. 321.

[32] Pribram, *loc. cit.,* p. 615.

[33] *Arbeitsrecht und Arbeiterschutz,* eds. Max Lederer and Viktor Suchanek (Wien, 1925), p. 14; cf. also Lederer, *Grundriss des österreichischen Sozialrechtes,* p. 28: "In the last ten years of its existence the old state was unable to fulfill even modest social demands, like the introduction of the ten-hour working day for women, the regulation of child and home labor, the abolition of workbooks, and so on."

A genuine, that is to say, sociologically significant, tradition cannot live in the pigeonholes of a ministry where the social reform bills were buried in the time of the Habsburgs. Tradition is a phenomenon of mass consciousness. It needs the air of social reality. Only valid laws which form and transform the working and living conditions of the people can establish a "tradition." The following survey of the development of social legislation in the republic warrants the conclusion that a new and vigorous "tradition" in the social field was established by it.

Social and Labor Legislation in the Republic

FIRST PERIOD: EMERGENCY MEASURES

Unemployment.—Demobilization, collapse of war industry, and the blockade, not only by the Allies, but also by the succession states, hung over the new nation. The resulting unemployment became—apart from a short period during the inflation—one of the most characteristic features of the Austrian economic structure. The need to make provisions for men and women who were unable to secure by work their share in the national dividend was one of the very first problems which faced the leaders of the "residual" state. It was generally understood that the whole political situation had rendered this necessity absolutely inescapable and, consequently, the possible counterarguments on the lack of financial means weighed so little that, indeed, they were hardly uttered.[34] As early as November 4, 1918, District Industrial Commissions (*Industrielle Bezirkskommissionen*) were formed "in order to fight unemployment."[35] The functions of these commissions were comprehensive: to keep records of industrial shops which had dismissed large numbers of workers; to further the formation of bipartisan labor exchanges; to organize "mass transports" of workers to places of new employment, that is, to facilitate the mobility of labor; and to carry out the measures of unemployment relief. This last task became the most important one so that very soon the commissions were entrusted with the supervision of the whole benefit system. On November 6, by decree of the state council, that system was introduced for workers and exactly two weeks later extended to salaried employees. Soon thereafter

[34] Cf. Pribram, *loc. cit.*, p. 631.
[35] *StGBl.*, 1918, Nr. 18.

the extraordinary situation forced the inclusion of agricultural workers.[36] But this last was regarded as a temporary measure only, necessary to bridge over the first difficulties, and was abandoned for good in the middle of February, 1919. Incidentally, the lack of unemployment benefit in agriculture caused in later years a continuous flight from the land to the cities where unemployment was already rife and thus contributed to aggravating the situation.

The swiftness with which the unemployment-benefit scheme—the first ever adopted in Austria—was put into effect was astounding. On November 18 the first benefit payments were made. Largely because the system was an emergency arrangement it did not include features ordinarily associated with insurance, particularly not of private insurance. The state carried the whole burden of the costs.[37] The plan was, however, superficially related to existing social insurance arrangements. For example, the daily amount of the benefit was the same as that paid under the sickness-insurance law; namely, up to a maximum of 6 crowns. In practice this sum was paid to almost everyone. In addition the unemployed received one crown for each dependent. In February, 1919, the city council of Vienna began payments of 3 crowns a day to every unemployed person who had a family to support; in April, the central government granted 1 crown additional for every dependent of an unemployed individual living in Vienna; in May, Vienna matched this national allowance and also gave 1 crown to single males living alone, provided they were qualified for relief from the state; in June, the supplement for single males was allowed in particularly meritorious cases even if they were living with their families. The municipal supplements to the national relief payments reflected the increased power of the workers' party in the council following the temporary reallocation of seats in it in November, 1918, but even more, they indicated the strong pressure from the unemployed in the streets. These supplements were soon imitated by several larger towns. Because of them

[36] *Ibid.*, 1918, Nr. 20, 32, 73.

[37] There is no intention of implying that a system under which the state bears the whole cost can not be "insurance." The distinction between insurance and dole is not a matter of who pays the premium (or contributions to a fund), but rather of "the terms on which the benefits are dispensed. When the latter go to the worker as of right on proof of unemployment, it is insurance. When they go to the worker on proof of want or destitution plus unemployment, *i.e.*, at the discretion of the authorities in their estimate of his need, it is relief." B. N. Armstrong, *Insuring the Essentials* (New York, 1932), p. 517.

the total amount of relief for a man with, say, three dependents came very close to the prevailing wage rate, so that the difference between it and wages could easily be earned by occasional jobs or illicit dealings in foodstuffs.[38] This situation certainly could not be regarded as normal. It can be understood, indeed, only in the light of the tense political situation and the rising unemployment.

To a certain degree the rise in the number of unemployed on relief was directly connected with the growing radicalization of the masses, since the authorities felt induced to grant benefits to a

NUMBER OF UNEMPLOYED RECEIVING ASSISTANCE*

Date	Vienna	Austria
December 1, 1918	24,503	46,203
February 1, 1919	113,905	162,104
April 1, 1919	126,906	178,553

* *SHfRO.*, vol. 1, p. 63.

considerable number of persons who under normal circumstances would hardly be regarded as unemployed (e.g., women employed during the war who now returned to their households). When the frequently mentioned dictatorships were erected in Budapest and Munich, and when, in April, during employment disturbances, blood colored the Ringstrasse in front of the parliament building, the necessity for more energetic means of coping with the problem became apparent. On May 14[39] the government issued the decree (mentioned in another connection in Chapter IX) requiring every entrepreneur employing more than 15 workers in nonagricultural undertakings to increase the number of his employees by 20 per cent and to keep the number permanently at the new level, unless a deviation from that level was granted by special permission from a district industrial commission. These measures certainly meant a deep incision into an economic system essentially based upon the free decisions of entrepreneurs, and may be regarded as one of the most

[38] Pribram, *loc. cit.*, pp. 631–634. He incorrectly gives the date of the first payments under the new national system as November 15, 1918. Cf. *Die Gewerkschaft,* vol. 20 (Nov. 19, 1918), 262–263. For other details, cf. *ibid.*, vol. 21 (March 4, April 29, 1919), 35, 95; and *Die Gemeindeverwaltung der Stadt Wien in der zeit vom 1. Jänner 1914 bis 30. Juni 1919* (Wien, 1923), pp. 10, 221.

[39] *StGBl.*, 1919, Nr. 268.

radical measures in Austrian social legislation. Despite the widely differing opinions which might be cited, the material effects were actually rather limited. A report of the factory inspectors, for example, maintains in general that the decree "contributed extraordinarily to an improvement of the situation" on the labor market, but claims a specific reduction in unemployment of only 20,000. It expressed the additional judgment, however, that the measure prevented numerous discharges that otherwise would have taken place.[40] It seems probable indeed that the effects of the usual seasonal betterment in trade were unduly attributed to the decree. In a great number of cases the workers themselves tried to prevent additional employment. This through-the-looking-glass situation developed out of the fact that the distribution of foodstuffs was usually made in the factories. Though there were no strict quotas for a factory, the workers feared that a larger work force might mean less food per person. For this and other reasons, as already indicated, a far-reaching salutary effect on employment did not occur.[41] On the other hand, it should be recognized that the "orthodox" objections to such a measure, which undoubtedly impaired the efficiency of production, cannot be regarded as valid at a time when for political and social reasons the whole maintenance of production was endangered.[42]

In any case, it is generally recognized that the prohibition of discharges without approval from a district industrial commission prevented the labor market from being suddenly flooded and contributed a great deal to the general appeasement of the workers. The forcing of additional employment represented a "one time" act; the maintenance of the level of employment was originally conceived as a short-term measure valid for three months only. Curiously enough it was regularly extended from time to time and was not finally abolished until 1928. This example of the "inertia" of legal phenomena should not obscure the fact that the measure in question

[40] Gewerbe-Inspektoren, *Bericht, 1919* (Wien, 1920), pp. cxxviii–cxxix.

[41] Pribram, *loc. cit.*, p. 635.

[42] For the connection between the compulsory employment decree and the threat from Hungarian Bolshevism, see the frank statement of Otto Bauer in *Die österreichische Revolution* (Wien, 1923), pp. 163–164. Contrariwise, Bauer's claim that the law also prevented businessmen from withdrawing their capital from the process of production and, as it were, forced them to exercise their "entrepreneur functions" cannot be taken seriously. After all the right to close down the shops completely was by no means affected by the law. It is true, however, that demonstrative dismissals in protest against social legislation were rendered impossible.

was essentially a temporary one born out of the necessities of the "second period." Likewise of temporary character were measures of the "first period" which sought to prevent unemployment among white-collar workers. By decree of November 18[43] employers were compelled to reinstate former employees who had donned the uniform and now were demobilized. Provisions were also made for the upward adjustment of their prewar salaries so as to take into consideration the raises effected during the war. These stipulations were supplemented by prohibiting the giving of notice. By these regulations too a flooding of the labor market was to a certain degree prevented. After a short time the dismissal prohibition began gradually to be transformed into the requirement that a specific period elapse between the giving of notice and actual dismissal. This, together with the introduction of dismissal compensation, was later embodied in the Salaried Employees Act. Dismissal compensation was first introduced by the decree of June 2, 1919,[44] under which undertakings that had moved abroad were to compensate their salaried employees. This affected a large number of persons since many firms which formerly had their factories in Bohemia, Moravia, and other areas without the borders of new Austria had shifted their offices for a variety of reasons, for example, because of the new tariffs. The incidental purpose of the decree to slow down or even to stop this movement and thus to help preserve Vienna's economic position was achieved only to a small extent. But all the more important were the effects upon the "easing" of the labor market. It is also interesting to note from these examples how temporary measures dictated by necessities of the given situation developed later into lasting features of Austrian social law.

Hours of Labor.—The law concerning the eight-hour working day promulgated on December 19, 1918,[45] was likewise prompted by the desire to fight unemployment; as was expressly stated by Hanusch in presenting the bill to the Provisional Assembly, it would have been intolerable had some workers been compelled to work ten and eleven hours while their colleagues were starving. In fact, the whole measure was presented as an emergency device, and though it concerned one of the oldest demands of the trade unions was very cau-

[43] *StGBl.*, 1918, Nr. 27.
[44] *Ibid.*, 1919, Nr. 301.
[45] *Ibid.*, 1918, Nr. 138.

tiously limited. First, it was to expire with the ratification of the prospective peace treaty. This stipulation and Hanusch's comments on it reveal that he was anxious to forestall any unfavorable effects upon the Austrian economy. He stressed the general tendency toward introduction of the eight-hour day in Germany and Czechoslovakia; emphasized the idea that under existing conditions the question of competition with the Entente countries was to be discounted, since Austrian trade was out of contact with the world market; expressed his belief that the eight-hour day would be internationally introduced by the Peace Conference; and, finally, made the following very significant statement:

"Should the eight-hour day not be carried at the Peace Conference, that is to say, should a longer working time be decided upon, then our legislation also would be compelled to define its attitude to this question."[46]

The second limitation restricted the application of the law to factory workers.[47] Four weeks later, when the bill returned from the committee and was submitted to final debate, something very unusual happened. A representative of the Socialist party, Skaret, sharply criticized its limitations, ". . . do you really dare today to come to this working class with a law so limited, with its dreadful restriction of the eight-hour day to factory shops only . . . ?" Thereupon he moved to eliminate both restrictions.[48] In view of the singularly strong discipline within the party this attack on a bill which the Socialist Hanusch had certainly drawn in agreement with its leaders was indeed surprising. Hanusch saw himself in an uncertain position; he repeated that complete frankness was necessary as far as the time limit was concerned. If economically stronger countries and the trade unions therein were willing to work ten hours a day, Austria would scarcely be able to cling to the eight-hour day. But he agreed that it was not absolutely imperative to have a time limit in

---

[46] Provisorische Nationalversammlung, *Protokoll,* Vol. I, 124.

[47] The technical term of the Austrian law, *fabriksmässige Betriebe,* was admittedly lacking in the necessary precision. Generally speaking, a relatively large number of workers (more than 20), some use of machinery, and the utilization of the time and energies of the owner in managerial functions to the exclusion of manual labor were regarded as essential for the concept. Cf. W. Schiff, "Der Arbeiterschutz der Welt," *AfSS.,* vol. 16 (1920), 132–153, with Lederer, *op. cit.,* p. 278. In any case the whole field of undertakings in commerce and handicraft was not affected by the law. Cf. also the factory inspectors' complaint on the ambiguous character of the term "factory." Gewerbe-Inspektoren, *Bericht, 1919* (Wien, 1920), p. cxiv.

[48] Provisorische Nationalversammlung, *Protokoll,* Vol. I, 405, 406.

the law. A new statute could always adjust the working time to the requirements of a new situation. He likewise gave his consent to the extension of the bill to all firms in the country.[49] But the bill passed in the original form, Skaret's amendment being rejected. This in itself may be regarded as proof that the move of the Socialists was dictated by purely strategical motives: what they desired was to put the *odium* of the limitations on the shoulders of the non-Socialist members of parliament. For this purpose they also demanded a roll call vote. Now there is no doubt that in December, 1918, the workers' party was in a position to put through any law it really wanted, short of something like immediate socialization of the "instruments of production," in the form it preferred; nevertheless its parliamentary trick—and Skaret's amendment was nothing but a trick—was utilized by the trade unions to present the narrower scope of the law as a result of the non-Socialist tendencies in the assembly.[50]

On the other hand, it is again necessary to recall that at this time the Socialists stood on the threshold of a long and hard campaign against the threat of Bolshevism. If this struggle was to be carried out successfully, their influence upon the masses had to be preserved unaffected; in this sense, consequently, political moves such as the one just described may be regarded as being in the general interest of the community. The details of that move throw some additional light on Bauer's statement that in the matter of the eight-hour day "Hanusch proceeded with extreme cautiousness";[51] moreover, the conclusion seems justified that even though they were pushed by a strong revolutionary wave, the trade unions and the Socialist party did not desire to do anything which might have interfered further with the grave economic situation. An endeavor ruthlessly to destroy the despised private capitalistic system certainly cannot be deduced from their behavior in this instance.

As a matter of fact, the situation was probably never more favorable to the introduction of the eight-hour day in a most comprehensive fashion. Among others the undernourishment of the war years had the effect that the workers were simply physically unable to maintain their efficiency throughout a twelve- or even a ten-hour period. From the point of view of the entrepreneur this meant in

[49] *Ibid.*, p. 408.
[50] "Das Achtstundentaggesetz," *Die Gewerkschaft*, vol. 20 (Dec. 24, 1918), 282.
[51] Bauer, *op. cit.*, p. 165. Cf. also Lederer, *op. cit.*, p. 305.

the first place that, at least toward the end of the day, some of the scarce supply of coal was largely being wasted. Furthermore, the inadequate supply of raw materials in practically all industries would have led to a reduction of the working day even without legal interference so that the necessity for real readjustments arose chiefly in continuous processes. Generally speaking, therefore, the introduction of the eight-hour day was accomplished with a minimum of friction. Indeed, a contemporary report of the factory inspectors goes further, declaring that:

> The desolate conditions of industrial production after the war, which became more and more critical because of increasing raw materials and fuel shortages, compelled almost all undertakings to carry out thoroughgoing curtailments of operations. In most of them the workers could be employed only during a very much reduced working time or only on certain days of the week. It is therefore understandable that . . . at a time of such standstill of production, the introduction of the eight-hour working day or of the forty-eight-hour week in general was possible without significant difficulties.[52]

Despite these favorable circumstances the shorter schedule did not bring the increased productivity of labor which labor theory has always claimed and which numerous experiments have demonstrated; the previously cited factors, such as inability to secure regular supplies of coal or electricity, exhaustion of the workers, and "work shyness," weighed too heavily on the other side. It was no small achievement, under the "desolate conditions," that the reform did prevent a still larger decrease in productivity.

An exception to the smooth development pictured above resulted from an error that slipped into the law despite the cautiousness with which Hanusch had proceeded. Section 2 limited the hours of women and of children under sixteen to 44 per week. It had been bitterly opposed in the Provisional Assembly and had finally passed only because of some technical misunderstanding.[53] The unfavorable results appeared immediately. As stressed by industrial inspectors all over the country, this provision led to an appreciable fall in productivity since in many factories the skilled workers had to rely upon the simultaneous work of unskilled labor—in many cases women and apprentices. Thus four hours a week of the skilled workers' time

[52] Gewerbe-Inspektoren, *Bericht, 1919* (Wien, 1920), p. cxii.
[53] *Die Industrie,* February 25, 1919, p. 2.

seemed wasted. As early as February 12, 1919, Hanusch stipulated by decree[54] that shorter hours for women and apprentices should be observed only where this would not result in decreasing hours for adult male workers or decreasing employment opportunities for women and young persons. The trade-union leaders frankly admitted that a mistake had been made. In his speech to the trade-union congress of 1919 Pick, the leader of the salaried employees in commerce, declared: "At the time we did not realize the consequences of such legislation: the big unions had to tell us then that such a stipulation cannot be maintained."[55]

Although it belongs chronologically in the next period a law of May 14, 1919, may more appropriately be mentioned here. Under its terms nightwork for females under eighteen and for males under sixteen was forbidden generally, that is, not simply in factories; moreover, such severe restrictions were placed on the nightwork of males between sixteen and eighteen that they fell little short of a prohibition.[56] The absolute prohibition for males raised by two years the protection afforded under prior law.

Other Measures.—It is impossible to describe fully the work achieved in the field of social legislation in the first period, that is, the time between October, 1918, and March, 1919. The introduction of unemployment benefit and the limitation of the working day to eight hours represent the most important measures of permanent value. From the numerous other measures adopted, the law of January 25,[57] by which the workbooks and the old stipulations concerning breach of contract were abolished, is of particular interest. The workbooks represented a sort of workman's passport and as such had been a prerequisite for getting a job. From available sources it has been impossible to establish the earliest date on which they were used, but their practical equivalent became a legal requirement for miners at least as early as 1854.[58] The industrial code of 1859 made workbooks in the most precise sense compulsory for all industries and trades covered thereby; moreover, the language employed indi-

[54] *StGBl.*, 1919, Nr. 117.
[55] Gewerkschaftskongress, 1919, *Protokoll*, p. 339.
[56] *StGBl.*, 1919, Nr. 281.
[57] *Ibid.*, 1919, Nr. 42.
[58] *RGBl.*, 1854, Nr. 146, §§ 208, 209. Interestingly enough the regulations concerning clearance from one employer before securing a job with another were quite similar to those of the War Manpower Commission in the United States in the Second World War.

cates that they had previously been introduced in parts of the empire.[59] The abuses of them were of the same sort as those made notorious in the United States by, for example, the Lake Carriers Association; and so the unions had fought them for decades. The evidence is decisive that employers used them to blacklist politically or otherwise undesirable workers by entering ciphered warnings.[60]

The law on breach of the employment contract in Austria established the same unfair and one-sided situation against which British workers likewise had to wage a battle for generations. Specifically, if an Austrian employer discharged a workman without a legally valid reason prior to the time the arrangement was supposed to expire the only redress was the payment of wages and other compensations for the notice period, normally two weeks. If the worker quit prematurely without legal cause the employer could force him, through the proper officials, to return to his job for the unexpired period and could demand damages. Further than this the worker was to be "appropriately punished"—which meant a jail sentence. Again it has proved impossible to determine the early development of this situation; the description above reflects the industrial code of 1859.[61] The revision of that code in 1885 altered the wording but not the meaning of these provisions. The same is true for the workbooks.[62] Numerous efforts to eliminate these inequities[63] were blocked, usually in the upper house of parliament. Again we have an example to show that the working people were fortunate that Dr. Winter's "social tradition" of the Habsburg regime was not perpetuated in the republic.

Prohibitions and regulations of child labor of a much improved character were embodied in the statute of December 19, 1918. On the same day another law likewise improved the stipulations con-

[59] *Ibid.*, 1859, Nr. 227, *Anhang*, esp. § 4.

[60] The employer could also exercise considerable pressure on the worker by withholding the workbook, which had to be deposited with him, under some pretext when the worker desired to quit. In each of the years 1907, 1908, 1909, 1910 more than 3,000 suits were filed by the workers on this ground or because of unfavorable remarks the employers put into the books. *Verhandlungen des zehnten Verbandstages der Metallarbeiter Oesterreichs* (Wien, 1912), p. 115. For other details concerning the books and violations of contracts, see the entire speech of Dr. Ingwer at this metalworkers' convention, *ibid.*, pp. 106–123.

[61] *RGBl.*, 1859, Nr. 227, §§ 79, 80.

[62] *Ibid.*, 1885, Nr. 22, §§ 84, 85, 80–80 i.

[63] Cf., for example, Abgeordnetenhaus, *Protokoll,* XXI Session (1912), *Beilagen,* Nr. 1186.

cerning homework.[64] Both proved especially hard to enforce. Because of the strength of the unions no children were employed in factories and big shops in cities. In the country conditions were different, but even in cities circumventions of the regulations on the homework of children were all too frequent. As in other countries, Austrian experience showed that the best laws of this kind remain ineffective unless a thoroughgoing system of supervision has been organized. The provisions of the homework statute, by which *inter alia* the employers were required to post the wages and other conditions on the bulletin boards of their shops, were of little use when women of the ruined middle class increasingly took to homework as a consequence of the war and especially the subsequent inflation. In most of these cases a feeling of social degradation prevented the workers from divulging their rates of wages and labor conditions to the industrial inspectors.[65]

SECOND PERIOD: RADICALISM IN SOCIAL LEGISLATION

Vacations with Pay for Workers.—Of the laws passed in the second "radical" period of social legislation reference has been made already to some; for examples, to those on compulsory employment and the reinstatement of demobilized former employees. But whereas these were of merely temporary importance, two others of the period remained as permanent significant features of Austrian labor legislation.

The statute of July 30, 1919,[66] gave paid vacations to manual workmen. This was a complete innovation; in the monarchy only civil servants and salaried employees had been so favored. Workers, in the more precise sense of the German word *Arbeiter,* had had to work without interruption except for the unwelcome breaks caused by unemployment; the level of wages and the general policy of the employers had virtually precluded vacations for the workers in old Austria. As early as May, 1919,[67] workers under sixteen were granted by decree, as a temporary measure for the current year, a paid vacation of four weeks when this was urgently needed for health reasons. The law of July stipulated that every worker, except those in agri-

[64] *StGBl.,* 1918, Nr. 140, 141.
[65] Gewerbe-Inspektoren, *Bericht, 1921* (Wien, 1923), p. lxxxiii.
[66] *StGBl.,* 1919, Nr. 395.
[67] *Ibid.,* 1919, Nr. 262.

culture and some special categories, was entitled to a vacation of one week with pay after one year of continuous employment in the same establishment and two weeks after five years. Private agreements to evade or alter the terms of the law to the disadvantage of the laborer were null and void. The importance of this statute, especially under the given Austrian conditions, can hardly be exaggerated. It rendered it possible for the whole Austrian economy to replenish its reserves in physical man power—badly depleted by the overwork and undernourishment of the war. For the social reformers who were at this time in control of the ministry of social administration the matter had a broader aspect. To secure even a short period of holidays for the workingman meant, in the first place, a further step toward raising the whole class to a higher level of cultural life. According to their general plans one ultimate aim was that the worker should cease being simply a working machine—that he should be able to enjoy the loveliness of life, to travel, to see at least a bit of the wonderful natural beauty of his home country. As with the eight-hour day, the holidays on pay should enable the workman to have some free time which he could spend on his general education in the broadest sense of the word. They realized, of course, that what could be accomplished by formal juristic measures was not in itself a guarantee for the development of the working class to a higher social standard, but only a prerequisite. They also feared that free time gained in this way was too likely to be spent, or rather wasted, in the foul air of the wine and beer rooms in the outlying districts of Vienna and the small industrial towns in the provinces. Legislative enactment, therefore, needed to be supplemented by extensive and intensive cultural activities represented by organizations like the Friends of Nature (*Naturfreunde*) which provided facilities for the worker in the form of cheap excursions and cheap huts in the mountains; and, together with the various gymnastic associations, made provision for the development of healthy bodies. At the same time special organizations tried to make it possible for workers to visit the best theaters and concert houses of the famous art city of Vienna and thus make this art a possession of the whole people rather than of a small privileged group. In a later chapter a closer view of the whole panoply of these organizations will be offered. Here, it is important, by means of a particularly appropriate example, to stress the general significance of social legislation in the minds of its creators and to indicate that as such it was only a part in a vast program the gist of which is peaceful emancipation of the working class.

Works Councils and Trade Unions.—The second of the two most important laws of this period was regarded at the time of its enactment as one of the most radical acts; with it, in many quarters, truly revolutionary hopes were connected. The works councils measure of May 15, 1919,[68] has been referred to in earlier sections. It remains here to present briefly its main provisions and to discuss the specific problem which the creation of the councils constituted for the Austrian labor movement as a whole.

The functions of the new organizations as defined by the law may be considered under three main heads. There were, first, general social functions connected chiefly with observance of the stipulations of social legislation, including supplying information to the industrial inspectors and furthering the administration of institutions like factory housing, shop coöperatives, "saving brotherhoods," and so on. Second, what may be called trade-union functions; that is, in the main, observance of the terms of collective-bargaining contracts and conclusion of additional contracts for workers in the particular shop in which a council existed. Of particular importance here is the coöperation of works councils in fixing piece wages. After the period of general shortages in production had come to an end piece wages replaced time wages in almost all shops where the former system seemed applicable and thus rapidly became one of the principal concerns of the councils. Also in this group of functions it was the privilege of the councils to contest dismissals of workers when there was reason to believe they were made on political grounds or because of membership in a trade union. The members of the councils were given some independence of position by the provision that they might be dismissed only if they committed an act which generally justified immediate discharge. Otherwise the dismissal had to be approved by the conciliation office.

The third set of functions reveals the general situation in which the law was passed; they may be described as the managerial agenda of the work councils since they attempted to establish a certain

[68] *Ibid.*, 1919, Nr. 283.

degree of supervisory control over the production and management of the undertaking. Here belongs the provision under which councils in commercial undertakings with more than 30 employees and in all manufacturing concerns and mines were entitled to see the annual balance sheet and the profit-and-loss account of the firm, as well as the wage statistics. In joint-stock companies and similarly organized firms the works councils were entitled to attend the meetings of the boards of directors. In all types of concerns "the owner is authorized, and, upon demand of the works council, required to hold joint conferences each month on the improvement of the works and on the general principles of management." At the time the bill was passed these provisions were hotly discussed in press and parliament; Socialist propaganda did its best to describe them as important steps toward the establishment of a Socialist economy. Even as late as 1923 Otto Bauer attempted to present them as "germs of a future Socialist constitution of production."[69] If, however, these provisions of the law are freed from the obscuring influence of political declamations from both sides, the stipulations appear in a rather different light. Practically speaking the right of workers' representatives to be shown the balance sheet and the profit-and-loss account of a firm can scarcely be seriously regarded as a move toward Socialism. Whether or not it is a step in the direction of workers' participation in management depends upon prevailing accounting practices and the phraseology of the law. The first factor was particularly important in Austria where "hair dressing"[70] the balance sheet was sanctified by hoary business tradition. With reference to the second it is indisputable that a statute, for example the Wagner Act in the United States, can guarantee workers' participation in matters once generally considered the exclusive prerogative of management. That the Austrian enactment provided such a guarantee was likewise a hotly disputed question. There is some evidence that in addition to their demonstrative aspects the chief purpose of most of the provisions under consideration was to satisfy the wish of certain groups, mostly of salaried employees in small shops, to be able to use the knowledge of the annual profit-and-loss account as a supporting argument in their wage struggles.[71] On the other hand,

[69] Bauer, *op. cit.*, p. 182.
[70] Equivalent to the American term "window dressing."
[71] Pribram, *loc. cit.*, p. 653.

the overwhelming majority of businessmen in any country would consider a legal requirement that they discuss "general principles of management" every month "upon demand" of a works council as involving workers' participation in management.

Further examination offers every evidence that the problem of the works councils went deeper than the provisions of the law would indicate. The real issue was by no means exclusively a juridical one, but actually may be regarded as one of the most acute problems of the Austrian revolution. In fact, the whole character of the Austrian labor movement was at that time dependent upon the development of the new institution. With the creation of the works councils a new mass organization was added to the labor movement. Its particular strength was that it united men already brought together by the very process of production. The danger was great that it would become independent of the old units of the labor movement and develop into the dominant representative of the Austrian workers.

The problem which confronted the Austrian labor movement can be otherwise expressed in the antithesis of two catchwords which in the 'twenties of this century formed the centers for interminable discussions in Germany and Austria: "economic democracy" *versus* "shop democracy." Or, to use a more familiar term, it was the issue of "syndicalism" which was put before the traditional organization of the labor movement by the creation of the works councils. But though the term is warranted it should be noted that the "syndicalism" espoused by the Austrian works councils represented only certain particular features of that social philosophy. The system of *action directe* as expounded in the works of Sorel was essentially connected with the whole structural organization of trade unions, but to the extent that syndicalist tendencies became apparent in the Austrian labor movement upon the creation of works councils they appeared in spite of the wishes and ideas of traditional Austrian trade unionism. In the two decades of their close connection with the Social Democratic party before the First World War the unions had become strongly "politicized"; they came to regard parliamentary activities as the fulcrum of labor policy. It is true that the idea of a political strike was not foreign to them, but it is also true that in this respect they felt that they had to pay tribute to the party as a compensation for the political support it had been and was lending to them. And, to boot, they knew perfectly well that the party would never lightheartedly call a general strike for political reasons, though its leaders might use it as a threat and an instrument of pressure time and again in negotiations with their opponents.

But the more important difference lay elsewhere and concerned the whole conception of a Socialist economy. It is arguable—and, indeed, the history of trade unions gives large evidence to this effect—that they have been in themselves organizations indissolubly connected with the private capitalistic form of economy. But the character of the connection is perhaps best indicated by Professor Perlman's statement that "A labor movement must, from its very nature, be an organized campaign against the rights of private property. . . ."[72] as traditionally conceived. It stands to reason, however, that organizations like the Austrian trade unions, the members of which to an overwhelmingly large percentage at the same time held membership in a Socialist party, could not openly profess anti-Socialist opinions. But so far as they had to bind themselves to a Socialist program, they favored a system of socialization carried out by the central authorities in full order and discipline, with a minimum of interference with economic life; they were, therefore, most bitterly opposed to those elements of anarchism which constitute an essential part of the syndicalist system. Occupation of factories, such as took place in Italy, or the idea of the domination of each factory by the workers employed in it, was utterly abhorrent to the Austrian trade-union leaders. I am perfectly aware of the fact that it is easy to collect from various speeches of trade-union leaders, particularly in the time of the revolution, a number of quotations from which a much more radical attitude may seemingly be deduced. But this would be a deception. One of the main difficulties which faces any student of social institutions and, above all, a foreign observer, is to discern between the outward appearance and the real nature of the subject matter of his investigations.

Nothing is more revealing for the true character of the trade unions than the attitude they adopted toward the works councils. The relation between these two organizations was undoubtedly the most important problem in the development of the new institution.[73]

[72] S. Perlman, *A Theory of the Labor Movement* (New York, 1928), pp. 155–156.

[73] Cf. "Das Betriebsrätegesetz" (Introduction), *Die sozialpolitische Gesetzgebung in Oesterreich,* vol. 5, no. 1 (Wien, 1922), p. x.

The misgivings of the unions concerning the introduction and future development of works councils in Austrian industry were often frankly voiced by their responsible leaders. Before the trade-union congress of 1919 Domes said: "The Works Councils Act has frequently aroused the fear among the trade unions that now the works councils will take over functions that have been performed up to now by the trade unions."[74] To some extent these fears were expressed during the numerous negotiations which preceded the enactment of the law. The question of whether or not the councils should be authorized to negotiate collective-bargaining contracts was hotly discussed and met with the adamant resistance of the unions. It was argued that this idea, if adopted, would mean a step backward from the "branch" contract, that is, one covering an industry or trade, to the "shop" contract. This contention could have been met by the creation of a branch-wide organization of the councils, but to this the unions were likewise bitterly opposed for various reasons. As a matter of fact the original draft of the law had indirectly provided for such organization by stipulating that each works council had to maintain contacts with those of other undertakings in the same line of trade. In the socialization committee this provision was deleted; when it came before parliament as a minority amendment, it was rejected.[75] Consequently, Article 3 of the law, as mentioned before, granted the councils only the right to supervise and *not* to conclude collective-bargaining contracts.[76] Spokesmen for the unions insisted on including in the official explanation of the reasons for the law[77] a lengthy statement to the effect that the councils were but a continuation of the old institution of workers' deputies (*Vertrauensmänner*) in the shops; these had been at the same time representatives of the union organizations. Furthermore, it was indicated that the unions and the works councils were to coöperate.[78]

The speech of Domes, from which an extract was quoted above, and the ensuing debate in the congress throw additional light on the attitude of the unions toward the councils. This debate is all the more revealing because the rank-and-file delegates to the congress

[74] Gewerkschaftskongress, 1919, *Protokoll*, p. 368.
[75] Konstituierende Nationalversammlung, *Beilagen*, Nr. 164, p. 11.
[76] "Das Betriebsrätegesetz," *loc. cit.*, p. 4.
[77] Such an explanation had to be attached to every statute adopted in Austria.
[78] Konstituierende Nationalversammlung, *Beilagen*, Nr. 164, p. 9.

frequently presented not the viewpoint of the leadership, but, as members of works councils themselves, the interests of the latter. This indicated the extreme delicacy of the position of the unions and the gravity of the dangers they had to face. A good part of the difficulties arose from the fact that in spite of the alleged connection between the old deputies and the new councils the act made the latter obligatory for every concern with at least 20 employees, and even undertakings with between 5 and 9 had to elect 1 representative, and those with between 10 and 19, 2 representatives.[79] Both manual workers and salaried employees were included in the law, but the two groups had to elect separate councils. The consequence was that large groups of white-collar employees, who never before had been in touch with any labor organization and were completely unschooled in elementary questions of trade-union tactics and policy, were compelled to adopt the works council organization. It was only natural that not the laborers and craftsmen in relatively large-scale industry with a long trade-union education, but the new elements of workers in small shops and large groups of salaried employees, who up to the revolution had stoutly defeated all attempts to persuade them to join an organization, proved the most radical element, always ready to criticize adversely the cautious and "unrevolutionary" policy of the unions. Nobody could exceed the revolutionary ardor of such groups as, say, the actors from the Viennese theaters. "Very frequently persons have been elected to works councils," complained the representative of the union of industrial salaried employees, "who are radical 'shouters'," and do not understand that the "wage level depends upon the productivity of the undertaking."[80]

Another representative—again it was significant that he was the leader of the trade union of salaried employees in commercial undertakings—described the transformation of the general type of deputies under the influence of the Works Councils Act:

> The workers' representative has become entirely different. Formerly he was an idealist who by virtue of his calmness, judgment, and willingness to make sacrifices was enabled to represent the interests of his colleagues. Thereby he secured a certain authority. This has now become different

[79] *StGBl.*, 1919, Nr. 342. Article 19 of this decree clarified the ambiguous language of the statute.

[80] Gewerkschaftskongress, *Protokoll*, 1919, p. 389.

to some extent because in some shops through the free election not the old, cautious men were reëlected, but frequently those who had the ability to talk a lot and promised a great deal but had not yet the right tact and the right feeling about how far they could go.[81]

And these complaints from representatives of unions of salaried employees appear even more emphatically in speeches by leaders of workers' unions; they voiced their distrust of that whole group of white-collar employees who supported the employers up to the revolution and then suddenly shifted to an attitude of extreme radicalism.[82]

In contrast with the foregoing expressions of dissatisfaction must be placed the demands of those union members who were most closely connected with the works councils. They, too, professed dissatisfaction with the act to a certain degree; not because its scope was too wide but, as they alleged, too narrow. For example, they demanded that the approval of the works council should be made a prerequisite to engagements and dismissals of workers.[83] But in reply to these and other attempts aimed at the extension of the prerogatives of the councils the more conservative leaders of the unions answered with an unwavering "no,"[84] and took pains to explain that participation of councils in dismissals would put them in an awkward situation in times of business downswing when they would probably have to try to justify mass discharges or layoffs. The latter type of argument prevailed so that the resolution adopted by the congress concerning the relations between unions and councils was confined to emphasizing educational work for the councillors to be initiated by the unions.[85] At the same time publication of a special trade-union magazine, *Der Betriebsrat,* for the works councils was decided upon.[86]

In the following years the endeavors of the unions to force the

[81] *Ibid.,* p. 392.

[82] *Ibid.,* pp. 401–402; cf. also pp. 398–399 for the statement of Hammerschmied of the metalworkers: "A part of the workers were of the opinion that the Works Councils Act gave them complete power; that they were now, so to speak, the sole masters of the undertaking. This opinion, however, prevailed much less with the workers than with salaried employees."

[83] Janeček, representative of the metal trades union, *ibid.,* p. 404.

[84] Cf. the statements of Hueber: "I must warn you against starting a campaign for an amendment of the law now"; *ibid.,* p. 396; and of Domes: "Our law is the best that exists in this field," p. 406, as well as Domes' further remarks, p. 407.

[85] *Ibid.,* p. 373.

[86] *Ibid.,* pp. 390, 409.

councils to submit to their control were continued to ultimate success. In the same inconspicuous but effective way in which the unions had fought the workers' councils (cf. above, pp. 71–82) they managed to win influence with the masses of newcomers, frequently designated in Austria as "November-Socialists"; by untiring efforts they overcame the anarcho-syndicalist tendencies, educated the works councils, and transformed them into faithful instruments of the trade unions. This transformation was strikingly revealed at the trade-union congress of 1923. Neither in the report of the central *Kommission* to that congress nor in the debates was a word said about any friction in the relations of the unions with the councils. The latter were mentioned exclusively in order to defend them against attacks from entrepreneurs and groups generally opposed to Austrian labor and social legislation or in order to refer to educational work for their members.[87] It may safely be stated that as early as the end of 1922 the specific problem of the relations between the works councils and the trade unions was completely liquidated. To be sure the issue was to some extent revived more than a decade later in the fatal year 1933 when the final collapse of the whole labor movement was imminent. But this belongs to an entirely different era of the political and social history of Austria and will be dealt with in a subsequent chapter.

The development of the works councils in Austria was, therefore, largely determined by the fact of their domination by the trade unions. It moved along the lines of decreasing radicalism and increasing understanding of the responsibilities and necessities of the councils' position. In view of the bitter attacks which were subsequently launched against them as soon as the great campaign against "social burdens" started, it is pertinent to quote here several statements by observers who had the duty—and adequate opportunity—to watch their development in Austrian industry. These observers, the factory inspectors, were persons whose sound judgment, knowledge of the subject, and absolute political neutrality are beyond question.

[87] There was no lack of attempts by the employers to instigate trouble between the unions and the councils. "The institution of works councils meant no more and no less than a practically complete elimination and undermining of the trade unions.... They are the corollary of the workers' councils. Who wants to understand, will understand." *Die Industrie,* January 10, 1920, p. 1.

Even in the report for 1919, when the Works Councils Act was only a few months old, the chief factory inspector wrote:

> Dreaded by many entrepreneurs because of the possible illicit interference of the works councils with work methods, introduction of new machines, production in general, engagement and dismissal of workers, overrated by many workers who had hoped that the law would bring them unrestricted power over the shop, the Works Councils Act threatened to destroy peace in industry and lead to many violent conflicts. According to the reports of the factory inspectors such contingencies rarely occurred and, as far as they occurred, were swiftly remedied. . . .[88]

The extremely interesting information supplied by the factory inspectors emphasized the favorable effects of the coöperation of the councils, as well as the number of valuable suggestions they had been able to make concerning prevention of accidents and observance of the stipulations of social laws. However, some of the inspectors indicated the necessity for schooling the councils in order to fit them better for carrying out their functions. The report continued with the highly significant occurrence mentioned in Chapter VIII, that the establishment of a works council in a big iron works (Donawitz) contributed to the settlement of a strike; and cited the valuable assistance of the councils in general in restoring the badly shaken discipline in this undertaking.[89]

In their reports for the next year the inspectors were able to supply more details on the development. The councils successfully coöperated in determining wage rates, hours, and rest pauses; in improving safety measures and works housing conditions; and in handling the dismissals of workers forced by unfavorable business conditions.[90] The last point is of particular interest because it indicates that in this respect they were able to assume functions which had not been granted by the law and because of the warnings from the union leaders. My impressions, gathered in numerous conversations with representatives of both sides, are that in the large majority of cases the Austrian works councils proved a valuable instrument in this field. In spite of the highly controversial ques-

[88] Gewerbe-Inspektoren, *Bericht, 1919* (Wien, 1920), pp. lxvi–lxvii.

[89] *Ibid.*, p. lxvii. It is interesting to note the account of the general manager of the works, Rothballer, who described how Otto Bauer, then a cabinet member, tried to persuade the workers of this concern to abstain from unlawful acts. *Die Industrie,* April 20, 1919, p. 6.

[90] Gewerbe-Inspektoren, *Bericht, 1920* (Wien, 1921), p. xxxi.

tion of the closed union shop, there is warrant for saying that members of the councils gave assistance to the employers in explaining the need for discharges to their fellow workers and in selecting those whose dismissal would involve the least hardship and injustice.[91] In this fashion the councils contributed to a material improvement in the relations between employers and employees. They also aided appreciably in a great number of cases in the restoration of discipline in the factories, so much so that on some occasions, as was reported to the trade-union congress of 1919, the workers gave vent to the feeling that they were the "greatest sweaters."[92]

The works councils were, furthermore, very much concerned about securing the deficient raw materials and fuel for their firms in order to render possible the continuation of production. Cases were reported from some factories in Styria where the works councils induced workers to spend Sundays in a near-by mine digging the coal necessary for a week's work. Their endeavors to obtain raw materials led occasionally to conflicts with unions, coöperatives, and party officials. If this was syndicalism, it was by no means revolutionary syndicalism; in fact, at the same congress complaints were made that some councils had consented to their misuse by the employers. In clarification of these charges it must first be recalled that the government contributed largely to the distribution of raw materials by means of various central organizations. Representatives of coöperatives and of unions occupied important positions in these organizations. Frequently, therefore, employers preferred to have their works councillors come to Vienna and apply to their "comrades." Much to the distress of the latter the councils also very frequently attempted to protect employers accused of disregarding regulations. Emmy Freundlich reported to the congress:

> I was sometimes ashamed at the demands of the works councils. They used to come and say, "The jam prices must be raised to 20 crowns; other-

---

[91] I met a large number of men of an age well over thirty who held the approximate equivalent of a doctorate in economics; their *curricula vitae* were strikingly uniform on one point. After they had finished the *Gymnasium* they had found immediate employment with the big banks which were rapidly expanding at that time of inflation. In 1924, following the stock exchange collapse, the banks were compelled to reduce their staffs drastically. The young men were the first to go because, as they explained, the works councils decided after an inquiry into their personal and financial situation that as single men without dependents they should be. This situation caused an influx of students of somewhat unusual age into the courses in economics at the University of Vienna.

[92] Gewerkschaftskongress, 1919, *Protokoll*, p. 391.

wise we cannot get through our wage increases"; or: "Our firm is to be closed down because of infringement of the food regulations. But the complaint is unfounded. No such things ever happen in our shop." They simply back their employers. No employer appears now in the Food Supply Office [*Ernährungsamt*] when he wants an import or export license for a profiteering transaction. The works councillors come.[93]

The comments on this policy of the councils will differ in accordance with the individual standpoint of the critic, but in view of the facts it is impossible to believe that their attitude toward the employers was absolutely antagonistic.

To be sure, there was no lack of instances of bitter disagreement between councils and businessmen. The report of the factory inspectors for 1920 quotes the case of an employer who refused to transmit an official demand to the works councils with the remark that he did not know of any such institution;[94] as a counterpart may be cited the example of a council which ordered that passive resistance be started any time one of its wishes was not fulfilled.[95] But such cases were relatively rare from the beginning and decreased as time went on. The further evidence of the factory inspectors from the report for 1921 is decisive on this point.

As far as the relations between works councils and factory managers are concerned, there are certainly still today some managers who designate the works councils as instruments of a burdensome supervision; on the whole, however, the sharp disagreements have been considerably lessened and not rarely entrepreneurs express their satisfaction with the institution of works councils because the latter are particularly valuable helpers in maintaining peace and order and in settlement of wage conflicts. . . . Only in a few exceptional cases did the entrepreneurs declare that their works councillors were agitators.[96]

Even more positive is the entry for the next year:

The institution of works councils generally received only favorable reports. The relation to the entrepreneur is mostly good. It was pointed out by a number of employers that the action of the works councillors as mediators between the wishes of the workers and the employers on the whole makes itself felt advantageously and that it contributes to the maintenance of peace and order in the shop. Emphasis has been laid on

[93] *Ibid.*, p. 428.
[94] Gewerbe-Inspektoren, *Bericht, 1920* (Wien, 1921), p. xxxii.
[95] *Ibid.*
[96] *Ibid., 1921* (Wien, 1923), p. xxxii.

the valuable coöperation of the works councillors at the numerous negotiations which became necessary because of the great number of curtailments of operations and of dismissals of workers. They revealed in this connection understanding for the pinched situation in which industry was placed by the depression and contributed considerably to the resolution of the difficulties.[97]

At the risk of some repetition it must be noted that stress has been laid on the tenor of these reports because of the independent and highly qualified character of their authors and because, as will be shown in the latter part of this chapter, the subsequent campaign against the "social burdens" involved especially strong attacks on the councils and thus tended to cloud the impartial evidence on their merits and shortcomings.

In summary and appraisal of the activities of the works councils in the first years after their introduction the following points may be made. As was natural in a period of rapid depreciation of the currency they had to give most of their time to wage negotiations. The index system—as has been said before—did not work with such perfect smoothness as to make superfluous any considerable interference. On the contrary, questions arose concerning compensation for the depreciation during the time between increases of the index. Second, much of the energy of the members of the councils had to be spent in securing and distributing food and clothing for workers. Next, and quite important, were the arrangements made between the employers and the councils relative to changes in working time; that is, a distribution of the forty-eight weekly hours in a way that corresponded to the interests of the men and the needs of the employers. Here, and in other matters of varying significance, the councils succeeded in establishing themselves as an instrument which, by continuous negotiations on wishes and needs of the workers, eliminated a good deal of unnecessary friction. In this way what was called the "absolutism of the employers" was greatly mitigated and the mentality of the "master in his own house" replaced by a democratic spirit of mutual collaboration. This development continued, so that in the great majority of cases a state of smooth coöperation between the councils and the employers was reached. Almost needless to say, this situation not only did not impair the processes of production,

[97] *Ibid., 1922* (Wien, 1924), pp. 99–100.

but did contribute toward the intensification of labor and toward the restoration of that necessary discipline in the factories which war and unrest had so largely destroyed. But so far as democratization of the shops meant to some of the creators of the law and to large groups of workers at the time of its enactment something more than what have just been described as the chief activities of the councils; that is, so far as hopes were entertained that the law would become an instrument for securing to the councils any serious influence over the management of the factories, they failed of realization. What were designated as managerial functions of the councils never achieved any practical importance. Naturally the collapse of the socialization schemes played a large part in this result.

Pharmacists.—By no means so significant as the two statutes just discussed, but interesting because of its "interference" with "normal" managerial functions, was the law of July 30, 1919, regulating the wages of pharmacists. It required all owners or operators on lease of pharmacies, except those connected with some unit of government, to contribute to a wage-paying office (*Gehaltskasse*) and established a uniform remuneration system for all pharmacists. This included a base wage plus possible supplements for length of service, number of dependents, and differing costs of living in the various localities. Wages higher than the scale could be agreed upon but the employee's claim for the difference lay only against his employer, not against the central office.[98]

THIRD PERIOD: CONSOLIDATION

The period between the summer of 1919 and November, 1920, was primarily one of consolidation. In addition to numerous ordinances of the ministry of social administration, in the main extensions of various measures originally adopted as short-term emergency acts, several laws of major importance were promulgated.

Hours of Labor.—One of the most significant measures was the second eight-hour law,[99] December 17, 1919. In contradistinction to its predecessor it had no time limit. The prevailing, though by no means unanimous, opinion was that after the creation of the International Labor Organization and the adoption of the eight-

[98] *StGBl.*, 1919, Nr. 410.
[99] *Ibid.*, 1919, Nr. 581.

hour day at its first meeting in Washington in the fall of 1919 no special consideration need be paid to problems of international competition in this connection. Furthermore, the new statute was much broader in coverage. Whereas the first republican law had been restricted to "factories" (*fabriksmässige Betriebe*), the second extended to all concerns subject to the industrial code (*Gewerbeordnung*); that is, to all firms in industry and commerce, whatever their size. The new law also applied to banks, savings institutions, schools, railroad and steamship companies, and to editorial, legal, post, telegraph, and telephone offices.[100] Generally, only undertakings in agriculture and forestry remained unaffected by the all-round introduction of the eight-hour day.[101]

For overtime a supplement to the standard rate of at least 50 per cent was stipulated unless otherwise regulated by a collective agreement. Certain extensions of the normal working period, particularly those for unforeseen and irregularly recurring requirements of the firms, were permitted. In these cases a simple communication to the district administrator (*Bezirkshauptmann*) was sufficient. The same authority was entitled to grant individual permits to extend the working time in cases of pressure of work up to ten hours for no more than thirty days within one year. For seasonal undertakings the allowable number was sixty days. Furthermore, Article 6 of the act provided that the ministry of social administration could order exemptions from the general regulations of the law, such exemptions to be granted only after the appropriate organizations of employers and employees had been questioned and a special bipartisan committee permanently attached to the ministry had been heard.

It should be noted that this method of legislation by which the issue of exemptions from the law was left to the government contains a point of more general interest. The belief of the trade unions in their own strength and their firm conviction that they would be,

[100] For miners the eight-hour day had been previously established by statute of July 28, 1919, *StGBl.*, 1919, Nr. 406. Analogous regulations for bakers had been secured in an act of April 3, 1919, *ibid.*, Nr. 217, which in contradistinction to the general law applied also to shops not covered by the *Gewerbeordnung*. This act also reaffirmed the prohibition of nightwork (between 9 P.M. and 5 A.M.) in bakeries as originally provided for in the imperial decree of February, 1917.

[101] Control over the working time of agricultural workers was left to the so-called agricultural workers regulations (*Landarbeiterordnungen*) adopted by the individual states. Usually, however, these regulations instituted the provisions of the general eight-hour act only for forestry workers without making any stipulations for those in agriculture.

under any circumstances, in a position to prevent undesirable ordinances rendered possible a legal technique by which only short acts containing but few essential articles were required. This greatly simplified the proceedings; if the opposite method had been followed it would have been more difficult to carry through the same amount of social legislation in the two years following establishment of the republic. This was certainly an advantage. But, on the other hand, it reveals the fact that, dazzled by the huge influx of new members into the unions and the party, as well as by their generally predominant position in the state, the labor organizations regarded the given political situation as permanent. In view of the later development it may be said that this attitude also reveals a certain lack of historical perspective and some disregard for the sociological mechanism of revolutionary periods. In later years, consequently, the unions and the Social Democratic party were on many occasions unable to prevent the "perforation" of the social acts adopted in 1918–1920 by ordinances of ministers who, to say the least, were not unconditionally in favor of maintaining the system of social legislation.

The debate on the second eight-hour law discloses some interesting points. First of all the mere fact of a prolonged discussion on a social act merits attention. An examination of the proceedings of the Provisional National Assembly and of its successor the Constituent National Assembly up to the adoption of the law under discussion shows that in those first periods the social laws were carried through at top speed. After the short speech of the *rapporteur* a member sometimes spoke a few words in appreciation of the law; sometimes even this was omitted and the vote was taken without further delay. To be sure there were conflicts behind the closed doors of committee rooms, as was especially true with the Works Councils Act, but in the open house the machinery worked smoothly and only now and then were some prearranged amendments moved and accepted. Even the Pan-German opposition—itself composed of two groups, representatives of the cities and of the nationalist peasants—refrained from criticism; and even the law establishing paid vacations, later subject to violent attacks, was passed without any pretense of dissenting opinion on either side of the chamber. But the situation was different in the discussion of the eight-hour law. Dr. Wutte, leading Styrian industrialist and member of the Pan-German group, delivered a fierce polemic against the bill. He stressed the deplorable economic conditions in Austria and discussed the effects of the law upon her ability to compete in foreign markets. He asserted that it would have been a better proof of friendliness toward anschluss had the Socialists waited until a similar law was passed in Germany. The economic weakness of Austria, he argued, would make it necessary for her people to work ten hours a day even if the rest of the world worked only eight. He criticized the introduction of new national holidays (the Day of the Republic and the First of May) and declared that not a limitation but an extension of the working day was appropriate at a time when workers abroad were putting in overtime in order to provide their Austrian colleagues with foodstuffs. He submitted to the parliament a long list of industries and trades which, in his opinion, should be exempt from the law; he especially emphasized the necessity of confining the eight-hour day to shops in the towns, since those in the country which were satisfying the needs of agriculture ought to adapt themselves to the working schedules in agricultural undertakings. Furthermore, he urged the exemption of salaried employees in high positions (directors, work managers, and so on) and of the secretaries of the latter. Wutte's party colleague, Stocker, went so far as to demand the introduction of compulsory labor.[102]

In reply to this criticism Hanusch stressed particularly the political importance of social legislation.

> If the ministry of social administration had not organized its work in this far-seeing fashion, I do not know how we could have steered through the reefs when there were dictatorships in Budapest and Munich. Precisely because of the social legislation the workers could gain confidence in this state and in this government and only so was it possible to make them resistant to the temptation to proceed in the same way as in Bavaria and Budapest.[103]

This statement was typical of the new political period in Austria's postwar development. Before the collapse of the Red dictatorship in Hungary neither Wutte's speech nor Hanusch's frank words on the political effects of social legislation would have been possible.

[102] Konstituierende Nationalversammlung, *Protokoll,* December 17, 1919, pp. 1325-1332; 1344.

[103] *Ibid.*, pp. 1332–1334, esp. 1333.

The position of the Christian Socials is also worth mentioning. A representative of the Catholic workers, Spalowsky, made a long speech staunchly defending the bill; but a considerable number of his party colleagues were registered as speakers against it. Among them were prominent members such as Gürtler and Kollmann, both ministers of finance in subsequent cabinets. Before all of them could get the floor a motion to close the debate was carried; but, as customary, one additional speaker for and against the bill was allowed. Its opponents named the clerical deputy Partik to summarize for them. He offered amendments closely resembling those of Dr. Wutte and also voiced a general warning against the measure on the ground that it would reduce the aggregate earnings of the employees. Finally, however, he withdrew his amendments because of Hanusch's assurance that he would carry out most of the desired changes by way of ordinances.[104]

This lack of unity in the Christian Social party should be noted because it can be taken as one of the first indications of a shift from the generally democratic and social position it adopted after the war toward a more conservative attitude which *inter alia* implied more concern with the interests of the employers. Keeping in mind the reservations necessary in any attempt to symbolize general political shifts by labeling them with the names of certain persons, this incipient development in the clerical party may still be designated by the formula: from Fink to Seipel.

As far as the effects of the second eight-hour act were concerned, it must be said that to a considerable extent the law only confirmed the development which had taken place in the interval between December, 1918, and December, 1919. In the cities and larger industrial towns the shorter day had become almost general and certainly reached far beyond the restriction to "factory shops" stipulated by

[104] *Ibid.*, pp. 1322–1353, esp. pp. 1334–1341, 1349–1351. Prior to the meeting of parliament the Christian Social press gave considerable space to the same protests offered by the shopowners. The chief paper, the *Reichspost,* took less part in this campaign, but the evening paper, the *Wiener Stimmen,* lent rather vigorous support. Cf., for example, the issue of December 16, 1919, p. 3, in which it was stated that the introduction of the law would destroy the Austrian *Gewerbe,* in this case meaning the small shopowners in industry, trade, and handicraft. In fact, the paper went so far as to prophesy the destruction of the whole country as a result of the law. The *Volkswirt* was probably correct in surmising that the purpose of issuing this special evening edition of the *Reichspost* was to say in it everything which it was thought unwise to carry in the morning paper. *Der österreichische Volkswirt,* vol. 12 (Aug. 14, 1920), 856.

the first act. This was mentioned by the *rapporteur* in the parliament meeting, and subsequently confirmed by the reports of the factory inspectors.[105] To be more precise, it should be observed that in a great number of cases the eight-hour day was transformed by collective agreements into a forty-eight-hour week and the daily working time arranged so as to allow a free Saturday afternoon. In the case of salaried employees this arrangement for Saturdays was made as a rule without adjustments in the Monday to Friday schedule so that the working week of this group was limited to forty-four or forty-five hours. On the other hand, on the basis of testimony from my Viennese acquaintances, it may be noted that unpaid overtime work was very frequent in this category.

The real difficulties arose only in small shops in little towns and in the country, where cases of strict observance of the legal prescriptions were almost the exception.[106] But, on the whole, the eight-hour day became a characteristic feature of working conditions in Austria.

Conciliation Offices and Collective Agreements.—One day after the second eight-hour act was adopted the Constituent National Assembly passed a law concerning conciliation offices and collective agreements.[107] The former had their origins in the complaint committees established in the war industries in 1917. In the first days of the revolution these bodies were hurriedly transformed into conciliation offices by eliminating the military presidents and replacing them by judges who were likewise members. In the first months following this reform they had relatively little to do. There was a strong tendency among the workers to submit controversies even of a minor character directly to the department of social welfare. Cases involving greater interests and a large number of persons were referred to the head of the government, Karl Renner. New life permeated the conciliation offices when, in the spring of 1919, the Works Councils Act stipulated that they should decide disputes arising out of its application. There was at that time the alternative of submitting such controversies to the so-called industrial courts (*Gewerbegerichte*), but the workers' distrust of this monarchial institution finally determined the legislative action just mentioned.

[105] Konstituierende Nationalversammlung, *Protokoll,* December 17, 1919, p. 1322; Gewerbe-Inspektoren, *Bericht, 1919* (Wien, 1920), p. cxv.

[106] Gewerbe-Inspektoren, *Bericht, 1920* (Wien, 1921), p. lxxii.

[107] *StGBl.,* 1920, Nr. 16.

The offices were established as bipartisan organizations with equal representation of employers and employees and a president and vice-president nominated by the ministry of social administration. Their functions comprised: (1) the role of umpire in labor disputes; (2) the role of a court in disputes concerning works councils; and (3) a variety of matters connected with collective agreements. Such agreements had been almost completely ignored by the labor legislation of the prerepublican period. The chief obstacle to their development had been the fact that an employer was entitled even after he signed a collective agreement to introduce into individual contracts alterations to the disadvantage of the workers.[108] The efforts of the trade unions to alter this situation were partly successful in the case of strong organizations like those of printers and metalworkers. However, no legal provisions secured their position. The tremendous postwar increase in the influence and membership of unions led to a parallel development of collective agreements which almost completely replaced individual contracts in wide fields of industry and trade; the trend extended even into agricultural undertakings. The legal regulation of the institution became unavoidable. The extent and nature of that regulation, considering the power of the workers' party and their unions at the time, is in certain respects in sharp contrast to the antistatism of such an organization as the American Federation of Labor and of some academic theorists[109] in this field.

For the purpose of the law collective agreements were defined generally as written understandings between an occupational organization of manual or white-collar workers and one or more employers or an employers' association regulating those rights, obligations, and other matters arising out of the labor relationship that were of economic significance for it.[110] Conciliation offices were authorized to participate in negotiations concerning the drafting or alteration of agreements on motion of either of the parties or of a qualified public official.[111] Copies of all existing agreements had to be deposited with the appropriate conciliation office within two months after the day the statute became effective; subsequent agree-

[108] The German literature designates the possibility of altering a collective agreement by the technical term *Abdingbarkeit*.

[109] For example, Professor S. Perlman in his *A Theory of the Labor Movement*.

[110] *StGBl.*, 1920, Nr. 16, § 11 (2).

[111] *Ibid.*, § 12.

ments within fourteen days after their conclusion. The offices were required to give public notice of an agreement within eight days after it was deposited and to keep a register of the agreements.[112] Beginning with the day after that on which public notice of an agreement was given, and within the scope of its validity, its terms became a part of every contract of labor entered into between an employer and a worker or salaried employee. Special understandings, so far as they were not excluded by the collective agreement, were valid only if they were more favorable to the worker or employee or if they concerned matters not regulated in the agreement.[113] In other words, the purposes of the law were not to be defeated by "individual contracts" as has happened so often in the history of labor legislation. The conciliation offices were also authorized to participate in the negotiations concerning the drafting or alteration of an agreement when this was requested by either party or by a qualified public official.[114] But the most significant and extensive power given to the offices was that of bringing "outsiders" under a collective agreement, whether they were willing or not, on motion of the parties or an authorized public official. The procedure was that the office proclaimed as binding "regulations" (*Satzungen*) the entire agreement or certain provisions of it after proof that it or they had already acquired "predominant importance"; the regulations then became obligatory for all cases of employment essentially identical with those covered by the agreement. As with ordinary collective agreements that had been filed and publicly announced, the regulations became part of every individual labor contract and could not be evaded by special private understandings.[115] It is scarcely necessary to elaborate on the potentialities of such regulations for bringing into line what was designated in the Blue Eagle days in the United States as "the chiseling 10 per cent." That Hanusch was fully aware of these potentialities and their advantages to employers is clear from his remarks in the assembly.[116] On the other hand, it must be noted that there was no desire in the assembly to substitute directives from the conciliation offices for the free collective will of

[112] *Ibid.*, §§ 25, 13, 11.
[113] *Ibid.*, § 14 (1).
[114] *Ibid.*, § 12.
[115] *Ibid.*, §§ 16, 18. Cf. Lederer and Suchanek, *op. cit.*, pp. 35–36; 475–476; 1671–1676.
[116] Konstituierende Nationalversammlung, *Protokoll,* December 18, 1919, p. 1405.

employers and workers; these two groups could always withdraw themselves from the regulations by concluding a new collective agreement.[117] Since conflicts between regulations and collective agreements were thus made impossible, Hanusch was justified in speaking of the "elasticity" of the legal construction.[118] Not the least interesting aspect of the regulations is their reflection of the consciousness of strength among the free trade unions; clearly they made it possible for individual workers to enjoy the advantages of a collective agreement without being compelled to join a union.

As was stressed by the government when presenting the bill, the new offices were to be regarded as instruments of social peace.[119] Thus their work would prove one of the most important demonstrations by which the validity of the bipartisan principle was demonstrated and its prestige enhanced. It would be going too far to say that the bipartisan principle is under any circumstances opposed to the idea of class war. The struggle may continue. But under this principle not only was the form of the conflict deprived of its rude and primitive aspects, but also it naturally ceased to seek the extermination of the opponent.[120]

Chambers of Labor.—In some respects akin to the law just discussed was that of February 26, 1920,[121] by which chambers of labor, or, to use the exact wording, chambers for workers and salaried employees, were instituted. Both the conciliation offices and the chambers belong to that group of institutions designated by Palla as the "legal representation" of the working class.[122] In previous sections of this study reference has been made to attempts in the 'eighties to create chambers of labor as a substitute for the general franchise. The organizations created in 1920 had, of course, nothing in common with such purposes. Still another plan to create such bodies as bipartisan groups was discussed for some time in the mon-

---

[117] *StGBl.*, 1920, Nr. 16, § 17 (2); Lederer and Suchanek, *op. cit.*, p. 477.

[118] Konstituierende Nationalversammlung, *Protokoll,* December 18, 1919, p. 1405.

[119] Lederer and Suchanek, *op. cit.*, p. 466.

[120] It is interesting to recall the theoretical interpretation which Karl Renner gave to these new forms for settling industrial conflicts. He saw their importance in the fact that functions previously performed by the state (police, courts, government intervention) had been "regained" by society; hence, he termed them forms of socialization. Whatever the value of this construction per se it is a revealing shift in the concept of socialization. K. Renner, *Wege der Verwirklichung* (Berlin, 1929), pp. 57–59.

[121] *StGBl.*, 1920, Nr. 100.

[122] Edmund Palla, *Die Interessenvertretung der Arbeiterschaft in Oesterreich; Eine Denkschrift zur Errichtung der Arbeiterkammern* (Wien, 1921), pp. 29 ff.

archy. The Christian Social Spalowsky emphasized in parliament the difference between this idea and the final form of the Austrian chambers of labor.[123] Closer to the latter comes the previously noted labor committee established in the 'nineties by Minister of Trade Bärnreither, but in it the workers had to coöperate with representatives of the state bureaucracy and the activities of the group were restricted to labor problems proper.

In contradistinction to these early plans and forms of organization the labor chambers actually created were representative only of employees, that is, manual and white-collar workers.[124] The functions of the new bodies as set forth in the law were a close reproduction of those established for the chambers of commerce and industry by the amendments to their statute on the preceding day. In fact, a strong incentive for the trade unions and the Socialist party was the wish to demonstrate that in the republic workers were on a basis of perfect equality with other social groups.[125] In accordance with these desires and precedents the most important functions of the chambers of labor included the obligation to submit reports, expert statements, and proposals to legislative bodies and administrative authorities on problems of social legislation and the labor market and on all problems of industry, commerce, and handicraft which directly or indirectly concerned the interests of workers and salaried employees; most specifically, the chambers were expected to render expert opinions on all bills, laws, and other regulations referring to the above-mentioned matters. This stipulation of Section 2 was supplemented by the provision of Section 3, paragraph 2, under which ministries, state governments, and members of state governments were required to submit to the chambers all bills or particularly important ordinances dealing with the interests of industry, commerce, or handicraft, or with questions of labor relations. Speakers in parliament laid strong emphasis on the fact that by virtue of these stipulations the working class became legally entitled to raise

[123] Konstituierende Nationalversammlung, *Protokoll,* February 26, 1920, p. 1809. The speaker urged the necessity for clear terminology: "chambers of labor" covered the old scheme of bipartisan institutions whereas the modern Austrian chambers were chambers of workers. This terminological subtlety being of only historical interest, the more familiar name, chamber of labor, will be used.

[124] The fact that one chamber (although with separate sections) was provided for both groups, which in many respects have specific and, indeed, divergent interests, reflects the general Socialist idea of the solidarity of all wage and salary earners.

[125] Lederer and Suchanek, *op. cit.,* p. 1360.

its voice in matters which concerned practically the whole national economy.[126] Further important functions of the chambers were the collection of labor statistics; the prosecution of inquiries into the economic conditions of workers and salaried employees; the creation of institutions and organizations designed to improve the economic and social position of these groups; and the delegation of representatives to other organizations. The last activity was apparently intended in the first place to bring about coöperation with chambers of commerce, but also extended to various other institutions and authorities. During my first visit to Vienna, in 1930, I was the beneficiary of cordial coöperation between secretaries in the two chambers.

The funds for the maintenance of the new bodies were to be obtained by means of an addition to the sickness-insurance contributions, the so-called chamber of labor tax, to be paid by everyone included in that insurance scheme.

An important problem was the election of the members of the chambers. The qualifications for voting for them were somewhat complicated but, after some alterations, consisted primarily in being eighteen years of age, registered in the sickness-insurance system, and employed for at least two months in the area of the particular chamber of labor. The minimum age for eligibility to membership in a chamber was twenty-four. Difficulties arose, however, over the electoral methods. Understandably enough, however regrettable it may be on principle, the Socialists favored the majority system because it would have given them a monopolistic representation. Finally they agreed to a compromise under which the elections were to be carried out according to the rules of those to the National Assembly. This meant proportional representation with a certain slight bias in favor of larger parties. Spalowsky, the representative of the Christian Social workers, voiced his apprehensions in the assembly about the possible suppression of the minorities—at the elections and in the chamber itself—and obtained from the Socialists the public assurance that they would observe the "purity of the elections."[127]

As was to be expected from the comparative strength among the

[126] Konstituierende Nationalversammlung, *Protokoll*, February 26, 1920, pp. 1804, 1809.

[127] *Ibid.*, pp. 1810–1811, 1816.

workers of the trade unions of different political colors the Social Democrats became the uncontested masters of the chambers. Because the outcome was never in doubt the percentage of participation used to be rather low, especially if it is realized that at general parliamentary elections the turnout of wage- and salary-earning voters as a rule substantially exceeded 90 per cent. At the first chamber election (1921), of the 547,000 persons, including 25 per cent women, entitled to vote in Vienna, only about 64 per cent appeared at the polls. About 84 per cent of the ballots were cast for representatives of the free trade unions, 11 per cent for the joint list of the Catholic and Nationalist unions, and 4 per cent for the Communists. The Socialists received 114 seats out of 130, the Christian Socials and Nationalists 12, and the Communists 4.[128] At the elections in Graz the free trade unions obtained 58 seats out of 64 and the Christian-Nationalist group 6; that is, about the same percentage as in Vienna.[129]

The dominating position of the Socialist unions in the chambers of labor was maintained throughout almost thirteen years; its destruction at the hands of the Dollfuss government preceded by only six weeks the battles of February, 1934, in which not only Austrian Social Democracy but also Austrian democracy received their death blows. In this long period the chambers, particularly that of Vienna, did excellent work in various fields of labor problems. Their representatives in the bipartisan industrial courts were credited with unusual legal knowledge and understanding of the special problems involved. They displayed their greatest activity in preparing memoranda, not only on issues of social legislation, but also on almost every important question affecting the Austrian economy. Suffice it here to recall only their extensive papers on the economic reconstruction of Austria in 1922 and the series of essays on that crucial question of Austrian politics, the reform of the Tenants Protection Act. They tried with an appreciable amount of success to carry out the retraining of unemployed. Their periodical publications were and are worthy of every attention, particularly the Economic-Statis-

[128] This illustrates the statement made above concerning the method of vote computation: the Socialists received 4 per cent more seats than were warranted by their success at the elections, whereas the Christian-Nationalist group obtained about 3 per cent and the Communists 1 per cent less than they should have had in the case of absolute proportionalism.

[129] Pribram, *loc. cit.*, p. 671.

tical Yearbook (*Wirtschaftsstatistisches Jahrbuch*) which represents an invaluable source of information, the highly scholarly Journal of Social Law (*Zeitschrift für soziales Recht*) and the fortnightly magazine Labor and Economy (*Arbeit und Wirtschaft*). In addition there were the long series of inquiries into special problems such as homework, female labor, rationalization, and many others prepared by a staff of highly trained economists and social workers. The Vienna chamber built up a remarkable library on labor history and labor problems which rated as one of the best special collections in Europe. The Austrian unions learned to turn continually to the chambers of labor for information, advice, and support.

In spite of their achievements it is doubtful whether the purpose of the law to create labor institutions equal in every respect to the chambers of commerce was actually realized. If this equality was not attained it was not the fault of the act, but it remains a commonplace that a statute cannot do more than erect a formal construction. Its weight and value in terms of social reality depend upon the changing constellation of social forces. The slow but continuous shift of power in the state away from the workmen and toward the group opposing Social Democracy and their unions naturally weakened the position of the chambers of labor. The law compelled the ministries and the state governments to hear them on almost every economically important point of legislation. It could not compel those government bodies to pay heed. True, the memoranda of the chambers of labor continued to receive some attention; but, to name an approximate date, from the time of the second ministry of Seipel in 1926 their influence could not be compared to that of the chambers of commerce. This, however, is a general problem of all social legislation.

Journalists.—The law of February 11, 1920, the so-called Journalist Act[130] which was in a way a forerunner of the general law concerning salaried employees, attempted to do justice to the special position of the journalist, as well as to protect not only his material but also his spiritual rights. For the latter purpose the law provided that the journalist could demand his discharge in the event of a change in the political views of the paper or journal without forfeiting his claim to dismissal compensation. During his time of employment he was

[130] *StGBl.*, 1920, Nr. 88.

guaranteed an increase of salary at least once in five years until he reached the age of sixty and an annual vacation with pay of at least one month.

House Servants.—On the same day that the Constituent Assembly passed the Chambers of Labor Act it adopted another which is of particular interest because of the protection it sought to give to a group that is notoriously the victim of exclusion from the benefits of most social legislation. This statute was the House Servants Act.[131] The inadequacy of the old Servants Orders, which were much more concerned with the duties than with the rights of house servants,[132] together with the lack of organization among this dispersed and, usually, backward category of workers, led to working conditions which in many respects were highly deplorable. That even an attempt was made to provide the benefits of modern legislation for this group shows the wide range of the system of social laws erected by the Austrian republic. It is true, however, that the matter was not presented to the assembly as a government bill but was drafted by three Socialist members,[133] and that only after protracted discussions in the committee for social administration and a special subcommittee did it get to the floor. There it was opposed by the Pan-Germans on the ground that it was an unconstitutional interference with the competencies of the states.[134]

The validity of the law was limited to towns with a population over 5,000; its most important provisions referred to periods of rest, vacations, and illness. There were to be nine hours for rest daily, ordinarily between 9 P.M. and 6 A.M.; two additional hours were allowed for meals; every second Sunday the servant was permitted to leave the house for eight hours, beginning after 3 P.M.; and once a week four afternoon hours were reserved for the same purpose. After one year of continuous employment the house servant was entitled to a paid vacation of one week; after two years, two weeks; and after five years, three weeks. A fortnight was fixed as the notice period. The last stipulation could be changed by agreement to one

[131] *Ibid.*, 1920, Nr. 101.

[132] It is interesting to note here that disputes between house servants and employers were to be decided by the police. The new law replaced the police by ordinary courts without attempting to establish the jurisdiction of the bipartisan industrial courts in this field.

[133] Cf. Konstituierende Nationalversammlung, *Beilagen*, Nr. 130.

[134] *Idem, Protokoll*, February 26, 1920, p. 1824.

week but the preceding provisions were unalterable. In the event of sickness or accident the servant was entitled to two weeks' pay if the employment relationship had existed for two weeks, to a month's pay if it had been in force for six months.

The practical importance of the law remained small. Since households were expressly exempt from the control of the factory inspectors, even under the revised statute, there was neither an authority to urge obedience to the law nor a source of information for the cases of neglect. The representative of the house-servants' union, in her speech to the trade-union congress of 1923, complained that "in most cases the house servants are unable to avail themselves of the advantages of the law."[135] By an amendment of March 26, 1926, the original limitation of the statute was removed and its validity extended to the whole of Austria.[136] It may be doubted, however, whether any material change in the situation was thereby achieved. Apart from the other reasons mentioned, the great fluctuations of the personnel in this branch of employment rendered effective organization and persistent trade-union work extremely difficult. Thus a major support for satisfactory enforcement of the law was lacking; this is then another illustration of the fact that a certain degree of consonance between the development of social legislation and the strength of the union in the particular occupation is significant for the success of the former.

Unemployment Insurance.—Of paramount importance is the law of March 24, 1920,[137] by which a reform of the unemployment relief system was effected. It will be recalled that the scheme had been hurriedly patched together by the decrees of November, 1918; that originally the national state bore the whole burden; and that subsequently its efforts were supplemented by the larger cities. This burden on the central government was considerable. From November 18, 1918, to May 9, 1920, it paid out in relief the sum of 500 million crowns. It is, however, true, as Pribram and Lederer remark, that in comparison with other similar tasks the state had to fulfill during that period the cost of unemployment benefits may be regarded as small. For instance, the state subsidies for bread and flour in the short interval July to December, 1919, amounted to approxi-

[135] Gewerkschaftskongress, 1923, *Protokoll*, p. 291.
[136] *BGBl.*, 1926, Nr. 72.
[137] *StGBl.*, 1920, Nr. 153.

mately the same sum.[138] Under the circumstances Hanusch decided to carry out a reform of the system, which would include abandoning its provisional character and establishing it on a firm legal basis. His position was set forth clearly to the trade-union congress of 1919:

> I will say only that unemployment assistance in its present form is an impossible thing. This type is intolerable in the long run. But, on the other hand, I cannot simply strangle the present unemployment assistance. Shall the poor unemployed, who need the benefits, starve? It is necessary to create a legal basis so that not only the state, but three factors will contribute to unemployment insurance: the state, the employers, and the workers themselves. The workers themselves![139]

The emphatic conclusion reveals that Hanusch was prepared to meet opposition or actually had met some not recorded in the minutes. In itself this attitude furnishes another example of the general plan of Socialist policy which was anxious to take into consideration the needs of the state and the economy; otherwise stated, it throws an interesting light on the frequent charge of irresponsible demagogy as a characteristic of Austrian Socialists.

The statute passed by the Constituent Assembly without debate[140] carried the official title Unemployment Insurance Act. Doubts have been expressed, however, whether the arrangements adopted can be regarded as a true insurance system.[141] And regardless of any personal conception of the nature of a "true" insurance system it must be said that the official commentary on the original draft of the bill reflects a high degree of confusion in the minds of those who prepared it. It includes a mixture of criticism of the British arrangements, an acceptance of the insurance principle of spreading risks, the establishment of certain criteria that would indicate recognition of the idea that once those criteria are satisfied the unemployed person has a contractual right to benefits—"not in the form of crumbs of poor relief"—and then introduces as a further criterion a close

[138] Cf. Pribram, *loc. cit.*, p. 636; Lederer, *op. cit.*, p. 595; Hans Löwenfeld-Russ, "Lebensmittelpreise und Staatshaushalt," *Der österreichische Volkswirt*, vol. 12 (Feb. 14, 1920), 372.

[139] Gewerkschaftskongress, 1919, *Protokoll*, p. 348.

[140] Konstituierende Nationalversammlung, *Protokoll*, March 24, 1920, p. 2022.

[141] Cf. Karl Forchheimer, "Die Organisation der Arbeitslosenfürsorge in Oesterreich," *AfSS.*, vol. 48 (1920–1921), 709; and Lederer and Suchanek, *op. cit.*, p. 38. My complete disagreement with one of the main points of such objections has already been recorded (see above, p. 191, n. 37).

equivalent of a means test.[142] The result resembles the Louisiana Creole dish so aptly named "jumbalaya."

As announced by Hanusch, the cost of unemployment benefits was divided into three equal parts among the state, the employers, and the employees. The state advanced the whole amount paid out and was to be reimbursed for two-thirds of it by contributions from the others. The legal claim of the unemployed to benefits was against the state only. This pooled arrangement was a divergence from that envisaged in the repeatedly cited Coalition Pact of October 17, 1919, for under it the benefit system was to have been administered by the various branches of industry and trade.[143]

Generally speaking the law covered all persons who were compulsorily insured against sickness. The exceptions were the usual ones of agricultural workers, house servants, apprentices until the last year of their training period, and a few other groups that were in themselves not important except for the workers in "purely rural communities." An illuminating aspect of some of these exceptions is the proud announcement of a Roman Catholic journal that it was the "service of the Christian Social party" to have excluded the "unworthy and those not in need" from benefits. "In particular, the Christian Social party saw to it in the law that agriculture remained exempted from unemployment insurance—as not necessary considering the shortage of agricultural laborers—and that the industrial workers [*gewerbliche Arbeiter*] in rural communities were freed from unemployment insurance."[144]

Several stipulations of the 1920 law were stricter than the comparable preceding regulations. For example, employment of at least twenty weeks within one year instead of simple proof of unemployment was required as a condition of drawing benefits. The duration of compensation was limited to twelve weeks, but provisions for extension to twenty (subsequently thirty) weeks were also made. As under the original relief decree of November, 1918, the payments were related to those that might be drawn as sick benefits; that is, they amounted to 80 per cent for family supporters and 60 per cent for others of the minimum daily sick benefit that might have been

[142] Konstituierende Nationalversammlung, *Beilagen,* Nr. 680, esp. pp. 15–17.

[143] *Tätigkeits-Bericht,* Heft 13 (Wien, 1920), p. 11; Pribram, *loc. cit.,* p. 637 f.

[144] *Das Volkswohl,* vol. 14, Heft 10 (1923), 278.

drawn in the last employment.[145] Because of fluctuating economic conditions these percentages were changed by law or special order on numerous occasions. For example, an act of October 1, 1920, lowered them to 60 and 50; another, of March 17, 1921, raised them to 125 and 75; and a third, of October 21, 1921, set them both at 100.[146] For those with families to support the second amendment obviously meant an undue favoring of the unemployed as contrasted with the sick worker who is unable to make any small additional earnings.

About the time the law was passed the unemployment situation began to turn for the better so that hopes were entertained that the postwar slump would give way to "normal" conditions in trade. The beginnings of the inflation boom seemed to support this opinion. It was hard to foresee that the new republic was doomed to carry a load of mass unemployment almost throughout its existence. As it turned out, the problem of unemployment insurance preserved its place on the agenda of the parliaments from year to year; almost 30 amendments were enacted in the period up to 1933. Although some of them were "political" in the worst sense[147] so that it is more appropriate to treat them elswhere, it seems advisable to interrupt here the chronological presentation of the development of social and labor laws in general in order to sketch the outlines of this process of amending the Unemployment Insurance Act. Its outstanding feature was the progressive withdrawal of the state from its position as a contributor to the benefits funds. The institution of the Geneva scheme for the economic reconstruction of Austria was largely responsible for this development. The amounts to be refunded to the state were gradually raised from 66.6 to 80 and then to 84 per cent. Finally, by the eighteenth amendment of July 28, 1926,[148] the state discontinued its contributions entirely. In the meantime, however, the grave conditions on the labor market rendered it necessary to extend the duration of benefit payments beyond the maximum limit of thirty weeks. This was done by introducing a special scheme that permitted the payment of relief in accordance with the need and family status of the unemployed person but at

---

[145] *StGBl.*, 1920, Nr. 153, § 9.
[146] *Ibid.*, 1920, Nr. 473; *ibid.*, 1921, Nr. 171, 583.
[147] For example, the eighteenth amendment mentioned below.
[148] *BGBl.*, 1926, Nr. 206.

the "free discretion" of the district industrial commission. First enacted in 1922[149] as a temporary measure the scheme was prolonged at more or less regular intervals. This involved numerous changes in terminology, in the classification of the unemployed, and in the amounts of relief. For a long time the maximum relief could equal that of regular unemployment insurance benefits, subject to the "discretion" already mentioned. Subsequently, this maximum was set at a somewhat lower figure. The longer the period of average unemployment became the greater the number of unemployed who were shifted from normal benefits to relief payments, so that in 1932 there were approximately three persons on relief to two drawing benefits.[150] The contributions to the relief funds were regulated by the eighteenth amendment in such a way that 50 per cent were provided by the federation, the states, and the communities; the other 50 per cent came from supplementary contributions from workers and employers.

Other measures and proposals related to this field of unemployment compensation and relief merit brief attention. For example, there was the attempt to institute productive unemployment schemes in the fifth amendment to the insurance law (July 19, 1922);[151] these plans, however, remained chiefly on paper. Then there were more comprehensive programs such as that suggested by the joint memorandum (January 6, 1926) of the Socialist party, the free trade unions, the coöperatives, the Socialist members of parliament, and the free trade-union section of the chambers of labor in which proposals similar to the British Mond Plan were made; they never found any wide support in the government.[152] Likewise of some interest is the law of December 7, 1922, by which rent subsidies were granted to the unemployed.[153] Generally speaking other amendments to the unemployment insurance law from 1921 on were concerned with cuts of the benefit and relief rates. These aftergrowths resulted partly from the crisis and partly from the weakened position of the Social Democratic party and the trade unions.

Since it is not the purpose of this chapter to give an exhaustive

[149] The sixth amendment, December 15, 1922; *BGBl.*, 1922, Nr. 924.
[150] Lederer, *op. cit.*, pp. 597, 614.
[151] *BGBl.*, 1922, Nr. 534.
[152] For the text of the memorandum, cf. *Parteitag, 1926,* pp. 1–20.
[153] *BGBl.*, 1922, Nr. 883.

account of the whole development of social legislation in Austria, but rather to provide the reader with a general survey of its range and outstanding features, the juridic intricacies and the historic vicissitudes of the unemployment insurance statute must be left out of account.

Disabled Veterans.—Finally in this sketch of the third period may be mentioned the law of October 1, 1920, for the benefit of men disabled in the war.[154] Under its terms entrepreneurs were obliged to employ one such man for the first 20 workers and one further invalid for every additional 25 employed. This act was passed in the last meeting of the Constituent National Assembly. The following elections for the first parliament of the federal state of Austria marked the end of Socialist participation in the government. With the Constituent Assembly was also closed the great period in the history of Austrian social legislation. Thus the largest part of that legislation in the young republic was created within the comparatively short time of two years. This tremendous work would not have been possible without the intense coöperation of the trade unions and without the untiring energy of a selected circle of highly schooled civil servants. But first and foremost the system of social legislation in Austria is connected with the name of Ferdinand Hanusch, minister of social administration from the formation of the new state to the fall of 1920. It is therefore appropriate to conclude this section with a brief sketch of him.

The Role of Ferdinand Hanusch.—It may be said that in large measure the life of Hanusch reflected the rise of the whole class to which he belonged and to which he devoted the greatest part of his existence. Ferdinand Hanusch was born in 1866 the son of a Silesian weaver; the distressing economic conditions of the family did not differ appreciably from those described by Gerhard Hauptmann in his famous play, *Die Weber.* As a small child Hanusch knew the hard work at the loom which interfered with the scant education he received during five years in the *Volksschule* of the little town. Next came years of work in factories; then a period of extensive travels. Several times he was arrested as a tramp in Trieste, Bucharest, or Berlin and deported to Austria. He drank heavily, as did everybody in his environment. This was his life until in 1891 he joined a

[154] *StGBl.,* 1920, Nr. 459.

workers' organization in his native town. From then on he remained indissolubly connected with the Austrian labor movement. He worked first as secretary of a local trade union in Silesia and was then called to Vienna, where he became secretary of the central trade union in the textile business; after 1903 he acted also as one of the chairmen of the Central Trade-Union Commission (*Gewerkschaftskommission*). He was continually on the move. Traveling mainly through the northern parts of the monarchy he helped to transform the trade unions into a large and powerful machine. He took part in innumerable negotiations between employers and employees in the textile industry. As a participant in these activities and as a member of the *Kommission* he had vast opportunities to study thoroughly the whole field of labor problems. The improvement of the workers' standard of living became the sole meaning of his life. He hated every form of oppression and injustice. But there was nothing in him which would suggest wild revolutionary instincts. Quiet and unobtrusive, he carried, as year after year went by, the great burden of his work. By 1914 this highly gifted man, who had succeeded in the meantime in acquiring considerable general knowledge, was regarded as one of the best among the leaders of the Austrian unions. During the war he tried to mitigate, as far as this was possible, the hard lot of the workers under the iron rule of war industry. He took an important part, along with other members of the *Kommission* and representatives of the metalworkers, in the creation of the important "complaint commissions" referred to above. That he was chosen to carry out the highly responsible task of the chief administrator of the social welfare department was no surprise to anyone who knew him. He was considered the ideal man for the job, not only because of his tremendous energy, his knowledge of labor problems, his gift of organization, his ability to select advisors and experts, but also because of the great tact which he displayed in continuous mediations between the employers and the workers in those difficult times when radicalism was rife and a moderate workers' leader was swiftly styled a traitor to the high ideals of Socialism.

In the United States, with its old and strong democratic tradition, the rise of a man from the depths of misery to the very top of the social ladder does not seem particularly extraordinary. But it was different in the lands of Habsburg and Hohenzollern where an acute sensitivity to the watertight partitions between social groups prevailed. There the life of Ferdinand Hanusch appeared as something belonging to the legendary days of the French Revolution and was generally taken as a symbol of the rise of the working class from the place of a pariah to that of an equal member in a free society.[155] Just because of these facts the members of that class, so far as they knew it, were particularly appreciative of the tribute of a British scholar that Hanusch was "one of the most universally respected men in Austria" and that "The measures passed under his auspices during a few months did more to better the conditions of the masses than had previous decades of legislation from above."[156]

FOURTH PERIOD: LAST MEASURES AND STRUGGLE AGAINST SOCIAL BURDENS

"Since the Social Democrats have left the government, the old Austrian standstill reigns in the field of labor legislation."[157] Despite the high level of integrity and fairness which was one of the outstanding characteristics of Hanusch it must be said bluntly that this statement was not only inaccurate but also unjust. In the first place it is clear that the process of turning out one social law after the other cannot be maintained indefinitely. Sooner or later the point must be reached where the most enthusiastic reformist legislator has to admit that the development of the system is approaching its natural limits within a given economy and a given economic situation. In the Coalition Pact of 1919 the Socialists and the Christian Socials had agreed that the following measures were to be carried out: (1) a law on conciliation offices and collective-bargaining contracts; (2) a permanent law on the eight-hour day; (3) a reform of the unemployment benefit system; (4) the creation of chambers of labor; (5) a reform of the coalition law; (6) a reform of the factory inspection system; (7) a reform of the sickness- and accident-insurance statutes; and (8) the establishment of old-age and disability insurances.[158] As was shown in the preceding section, the first five of these

[155] Oesterreichische Gewerkschaftskommission, *Ferdinand Hanusch; Der Mann und sein Werk* (Wien, 1924).
[156] C. A. Macartney, *The Social Revolution in Austria* (Cambridge, 1926), p. 153.
[157] From the speech of Hanusch to the trade-union congress of 1923: Gewerkschaftskongress, 1923, *Protokoll*, p. 264.
[158] *Tätigkeits-Bericht,* Heft 13 (Wien, 1920), pp. 11 ff.

measures had been placed on the statute books before the Socialists left the cabinet in the fall of 1920. The reform of the factory inspection system was carried through in the period under observation. But with reference to point seven the ministry of Hanusch had accomplished practically nothing; the measures taken in this sphere were chiefly confined to adjusting the rates in the sickness, accident, and pension systems to the depreciation of the currency. Besides this only the inclusion of civil servants in the social insurance arrangements (act of July 13, 1920)[159] deserves mention.

In the speech cited above Hanusch obviously felt induced to defend himself at some length against the reproach of having neglected these important categories of social legislation. He described the difficulties which prevented him from achieving any material success. First, there were the disputes between workers and salaried employees which prevented the creation of a joint institution. On the other hand, such a joint arrangement—unified office (*Einheitskasse*) as it was called—was regarded as a prerequisite to the introduction of old-age and disability insurances. "The great building of social insurance was impossible because the basis of the unified organization was lacking." Next, no agreement could be reached because the Christian Socials naturally enough demanded a proportional representation in the workers' share of the administration. This share amounted to two-thirds, one-third being held by the entrepreneurs. The Socialists argued that under these circumstances proportional representation would have endangered the position of the workers. If, Hanusch explained, the "yellows" could secure only 17 per cent of the votes in the administrative bodies, then they together with the employers would have the majority in the management. Attempts to break this deadlock by reducing the share of the entrepreneurs to one-fifth and giving them four-fifths in the so-called control committee apparently failed too.[160]

Parts of Hanusch's explanations are far from convincing. The danger that the influence of the Socialist unions could be seriously impaired by granting proportional representation to the Christian and Nationalist groups was not grave. For one thing, not all of the non-Socialist unions could be justly designated as "yellow"—which

[159] *StGBl.*, 1920, Nr. 311.
[160] Gewerkschaftskongress, 1923, *Protokoll*, pp. 271–273.

in the political jargon of Germany meant fake labor organizations sustained by the entrepreneurs for their own benefit. For another, as the elections to the chambers of labor proved, the Christian and Nationalist unions obtained not more than 12 per cent of the votes and actually only 9 per cent of the seats. It may, therefore, be concluded that controversies among the free trade unions and their endeavors to obtain a monopolistic position in the administration were largely responsible for the fact that old-age and disability insurances failed of enactment in the periods of great reforms. Some Austrians well-informed in this field told me, however, that an important reason for the delay in establishing old-age pensions for manual workers was that they objected to the high contributions required.

As already stated, Hanusch's complaint concerning the standstill prevailing in this fourth period of Austrian labor legislation was also simply not consonant with facts. The parliament approved a series of important measures which became a vital part of the whole system. Among them were the reforms in factory inspection and the industrial courts. The former[161] extended the activities of the inspectors to all undertakings for which there were no special inspection services such as those for mines, railroads, and shipping. House servants and employees in the offices of notaries and lawyers, however, remained outside the compass of the inspections. The law relieved the financial difficulties which had hampered the activities of the inspectors in the monarchy and materially improved their organization with the intention of enabling them to fulfill adequately the enlarged functions resulting from the expanded scope of social legislation. Previously their authority in the shops had been confined to the right to inspect them; now they were empowered to give orders to correct conditions which were contrary to the law. In emergency cases they could force compliance immediately. Should the employer disobey any order the inspectors could bring him to book through the industrial authorities. Furthermore, inspectors were independently entitled, among other things, to grant permits for overtime work and for exceptional nightwork in the bakeries. Thereby their position in the factories and shops was materially enhanced.[162]

[161] *BGBl.,* 1921, Nr. 402.
[162] Lederer, *op. cit.,* pp. 375 ff.

The act of April 5, 1922, concerning industrial courts[163] simplified the selection of the members of the bipartisan bodies. Formerly they had been elected directly by the circles they represented; under the new law the chambers of commerce and the chambers of labor simply delegated them. More important was the authorization of a considerable number of additional courts. Up to this time large industrial districts like Linz, St. Pölten, Wiener-Neustadt, and others had been without the institution. Since the traveling expenses involved in going to the seat of one of these courts frequently compelled workers to resort to the ordinary courts, the purpose of the whole arrangement was being defeated.

The adoption of a new statute concerning salaried employees[164] on May 11, 1921, created a modern law for a group of employees that was disproportionately strong in Austria because of the special position of Vienna as a commercial and financial center. The new act, as compared with that of 1910, increased appreciably the number of occupations covered. In the matters of protection and benefits provided, it greatly extended those in existence. Only a few groups remained completely outside its scope: the salaried employees of the federal state, of agricultural undertakings, of the merchant marine, and of the railways; but actors and journalists also were omitted to the extent that they were better protected under their special acts. The definition of a salaried employee included three main groups: persons performing commercial services such as selling; persons rendering "higher services" of a noncommercial nature, primarily technicians; persons doing strictly office work. In practice almost every employee who did not do manual work—barring the groups mentioned above who were excluded or regulated by special acts—was to enjoy the considerable privileges of the new law.[165] Its provisions were to a large extent drawn from the ordinances of the government published in the early months of the revolution. The period

[163] *BGBl.*, 1922, Nr. 229.

[164] *Ibid.*, 1921, Nr. 292.

[165] As is probably taken for granted, the exact definition of "higher services" presented certain difficulties. There were some wider sociological implications of attempts to draw the lines since the evidence indicates that the law did not further the process of raising individual members of the working class into the higher white-collar group. For example, the work of, say, a foreman might or might not be regarded as a higher service. Cf. Eduard Stark, "Die sozialpolitische Gesetzgebung in Oesterreich von 1918 bis 1931," *Kölner sozialpolitische Vierteljahrsschrift*, vol. 10 (1931), 275; Lederer, *op. cit.*, p. 98; Lederer and Suchanek, *op. cit.*, p. 129.

the employee was allowed to stay in the shop after receiving notice, as well as the discharge compensations, was greatly influenced by those provisional regulations. The stipulations concerning paid vacations were very generous. After six months in the firm the employee was entitled to a vacation of two weeks in each of the first five years; this rest period became longer with the length of employment and reached five weeks after fifteen years. After two years with one employer time spent previously in the service of others was to be included in these computations. White-collar workers with academic degrees were even more favored since after one year of service they were entitled to include the years they had spent at the university and thus receive longer vacations. Payment of salary during illness was to continue for a minimum of six weeks; for those with longer service records such payment could be extended to a maximum of twelve weeks.

The bill did not meet with strong opposition in the Nationalrat despite a memorandum submitted to its committee by the employers especially opposing dismissal wages on the ground of a possible recovery of the currency. During the final reading of the bill the Christian Social speaker offered examples to show that closing down some shops would necessitate payments in discharge compensations far exceeding the capital of the firms concerned. The Pan-German speaker even declared such compensation to be "non-labor income," thus in a rather whimsical way adopting the current Marxist phraseology, but added that since these stipulations were bound to increase the willingness to work they might be considered as in the interest of the whole community. The Socialists moved the inclusion of a minimum salary; in view of the rapid depreciation of the crown this had little meaning beyond mere propaganda. The motion was rejected.[166]

Although the passage of this modern law is inconsistent with the allegation of a complete standstill in labor legislation, it should be recognized that it had a pronounced political background. The conservative legislators were moved not alone by consideration for the salaried employees as a part of the middle class—or should it be the "new middle class"?[167]—and as such at least to a degree potential

[166] Nationalrat, *Protokoll,* May 11, 1921, pp. 1411, 1413, 1416, 1422.

[167] Cf. Emil Lederer and Jakob Marschak, "Der neue Mittelstand," *Grundriss der Sozialökonomik,* vol. 9, pt. 1 (Tübingen, 1926), 120 ff.

voters for the non-Socialist parties; of no less importance was the endeavor, by granting special privileges to white-collar workers, to separate them politically and ideologically from manualists and arouse the envy of the latter.

The Salaried Employees Act was supplemented by one of September 26, 1923, concerning this group in agricultural undertakings; their conditions were generally adjusted to those established by the principal statute.[168]

In the same category was the so-called actors law,[169] by which Austrian labor legislation entered a *terra nova,* for Austria was the first country to adopt legal stipulations in this difficult field. The statute went so far as to establish regulations on such complicated questions as the cost of costumes. In addition it reduced materially the arbitrary actions of theater directors and put a curb on the agencies' "racket."

Of some special interest also is the law improving the conditions of house caretakers, who, like the concierges in France, were employed in every apartment building in Austria.[170]

The lot of apprentices was likewise improved by act of July 11, 1922,[171] under which a certain wage called apprentice compensation was to be paid after the completion of the first third of the apprenticeship. This was supplemented on March 26, 1926,[172] by a stipulation compelling the employer to keep the apprentice as a worker for three months after the expiration of the apprenticeship. Neither law could be circumvented by private agreement to the disadvantage of the apprentice.

Related to the pressing problem of mass joblessness was an enactment of December 19, 1925,[173] forbidding the employment of foreigners unless they obtained a special permit from the ministry of the interior or had established permanent residence in Austria before January 1, 1923. The terms of the law were extremely severe; for example, an absence from Austria for more than three weeks led to a forfeiture of the right to employment. Since the collapse of the monarchy had greatly increased the number of foreign citizens

[168] *BGBl.*, 1923, Nr. 538.
[169] *Ibid.*, 1922, Nr. 441.
[170] *Ibid.*, 1922, Nr. 878.
[171] *Ibid.*, 1922, Nr. 451.
[172] *Ibid.*, 1926, Nr. 74.
[173] *Ibid.*, 1925, Nr. 457.

living in Austria it was felt that the provisions of the law were extremely unfair to a great many of them. The act was adopted upon the energetic demands of the free trade unions; the non-Socialist parties secured only the possibility of exempting certain, not further specified, categories. The actual purpose of this move was to prevent the influx of cheap agricultural workers from Czechoslovakia to the farms and estates of Upper and Lower Austria. For the student of the political and social forces in the new country it is revealing to see that this law directed against foreign laborers was urged by a movement which was accustomed to profess most solemnly its adherence to the principles of internationalism.

The reorganization of the social insurance system actually began after the Socialists had left the government, but it was carried out with the continuous coöperation of their party and their trade unions. Of special importance was the amendment of October 21, 1921,[174] by which house servants, agricultural employees, and home workers were included in the compulsory sickness-insurance scheme so that practically every employee in Austria enjoyed the benefits of that institution. Subsequently, however, the competence of the federal parliament to pass a law concerning the insurance of agricultural workers was contested by the state government of Salzburg, and on June 27, 1924, the Constitutional Court decided that this provision was unconstitutional. Thereupon the diet of the state of Vienna adopted a duplicate of the federal act; but in the provinces, obviously the only areas where the insurance of agricultural laborers meant anything, laws less advantageous to them were passed. This anomalous situation was improved by a federal statute of 1928.[175] Another amendment of February 3, 1923,[176] confirmed the existing practice of continuing to provide sickness benefits in kind (hospital care, medicines, and so on) to unemployed persons for six weeks after they lost their jobs or ceased to pay contributions. More important, it extended the advantages of the system by providing that after these six weeks unemployed who were covered by unemployment insurance should continue to be eligible for sick benefits in kind as long as they drew unemployment benefits and even if they had been temporarily excluded from them. In none of the three contingen-

[174] *Ibid.*, 1921, Nr. 581.
[175] *Ibid.*, 1928, Nr. 235; amended by *ibid.*, 1929, Nr. 253.
[176] *Ibid.*, 1923, Nr. 73. Cf. Lederer and Suchanek, *op. cit.*, p. 1198.

cies, however, could they draw cash sick benefits. A significant step toward the concentration of the sickness-insurance funds was made by the act of December 28, 1926,[177] under which the number of types of workers' insurance institutions was reduced to five. This statute also fulfilled the wishes of the free trade unions for an administrative organization in these institutions in which the workers had four-fifths of the votes.

A long and difficult struggle preceded the passage on December 29, 1926, of the bill concerning the sickness, unemployment, accident, and old-age insurances of salaried employees;[178] in fact, the parliamentary treatment of the matter required more than three years. Its last stage was crammed with negotiations, proposals, and counterproposals; no less than 56 meetings of a special subcommittee, 34 meetings of the committee on social legislation, and 4 investigations were held before the bill was finally accepted. A Social Democratic threat of obstruction in parliament also played a certain part.[179] Particularly important was the protracted bargaining necessary to improve the old-age annuities as compared with those in the original draft of the law. Apart from numerous questions of detail, political problems such as the composition of the management played a great part, for the free trade unions made every effort to secure a representation corresponding to their strength among the salaried employees. The attempts to grant greater authority to the supervisory committees, in which the entrepreneurs were to hold a stronger position, also created much excitement, but were finally repelled.[180] On the whole the law brought about a great improvement in the organization of the system so that the contributions covered not only the sickness and accident, but also the old-age and disability insurances and annuities of the salaried employees.

Generally speaking the same problems were presented by the comprehensive bill on manual workers' insurance, but the atmosphere in which it was discussed was even more permeated with strain and excitement. The old-age and disability insurances which were to be incorporated in the new law represented the most ardent wish

[177] *Ibid.*, 1927, Nr. 21.
[178] *Ibid.*, 1926, Nr. 388.
[179] *Tätigkeits-Bericht*, Heft 21 (Wien, 1927), p. 50.
[180] Cf. the articles by Max Klein on "Die Angestelltenversicherung," *Arbeit und Wirtschaft*, vol. 3 (Dec. 15, 1925), 1043; and *ibid.*, vol. 5 (Jan. 1, 15, 1927), 5, 45.

of the Austrian manualists in this field. In the monarchy the bill had failed in the very last moment. Hanusch was unable to carry it through during his ministry, although, as has been shown, not without a considerable degree of guilt on the part of the free trade unions. Practically, however, the discussion of the problem never ceased; it played a major part in the electoral campaign of 1923. Time after time the Vienna workers marched over the Ringstrasse demanding an old-age insurance act and the slogan recurred regularly at the big demonstrations on the First of May and on the Day of the Republic. Periodically the Social Democratic party affixed huge posters to the walls and billboards in Vienna and in the provinces; on them was depicted an old worker stretching out his hands and asking: "How long shall I have to wait?" On November 10, 1925, the bill once again came up in parliament. Minister of Social Administration Resch used the following sentences in introducing it:

> The government has presented this bill because it was the general wish of the public to start discussions on the problem. The government is fully aware that at present the economy is unable to carry the burden which will result from the law. We can start thinking seriously about the practical introduction of workers' insurance when the economic conditions have improved so that we can with a quiet conscience lay this new burden on the shoulders of the economy.[181]

Was ever a bill presented by a government "in this humor"? In all probability it would never have been passed had not the Socialists used a situation embarrassing to the government to secure the promise that the committee would finish its work before March 15, 1927.

The final vote which made the bill into law[182] took place just three weeks prior to the general elections of that year. Again attempts had been made to alter the respective shares of the workers and employers in the management of the insurance funds, and again the old system had been preserved. The monthly rates of disability benefits were fixed for the best paid category of wage earners at either 84 or 56 Austrian schillings;[183] the higher rate applied to insured persons who had paid contributions for five hundred weeks; the lower, to those who had contributed for a shorter period. Requirements for drawing old-age annuities were the payment of five hun-

[181] Nationalrat, *Protokoll,* Nov. 10, 1925, p. 2762.
[182] *BGBl.,* 1927, Nr. 125.
[183] This amounted at the 1927 schilling-dollar rate of exchange to 11.8 and 7.9 dollars.

dred weekly contributions and the attainment of the age of sixty-five. The maximum rate of benefits for the highest group of wage earners was the same as in the case of disability insurance. The lowest rate was not to fall below 12 schillings monthly. Even if the differences in the purchasing power of the dollar and the schilling and in the standard of living are taken into consideration, the benefits seem exceedingly small and certainly did not reach the existence minimum. It should be noted, however, that they were to be paid whether the persons concerned were employed or not at the time they became eligible. In all probability these low rates would have resulted only in an addition to the wages of old workers, as far as they were still able to work, so that the law could scarcely have had any favorable effect on the whole distressing situation of the Austrian labor market. I say "would have" because, except for a minor and unsatisfactory provision discussed below, the act never went into effect. In the last weeks before the passage of the bill Seipel amended it by the introduction of a prosperity index. The Socialists charged that this was done at the demand of the Association of Manufacturers. The amendment stipulated that the law was to become effective only after the economic situation had reached a certain degree of recovery. The criteria of this recovery included a drop of the unemployment figure below an average of 100,000 for six months and specified increases in the volume of foreign trade, of agricultural production, and in the number of freight cars loaded.

The Socialists succeeded in removing the prosperity index during the short Streeruwitz ministry in the summer of 1929 by a statute which made the introduction of old-age and disability insurances dependent upon the achievement of certain budgetary economies.[184] In the period of rapid deterioration of economic conditions after 1929 these became impossible. In 1931 Resch attempted to make old-age insurance effective by drastic cuts in various branches of the social services, abolition of Article 1154b of the civil code, lowering of dismissal wages under the Salaried Employees Act, and the like. The rejection of this plan led to his resignation on April 14, 1931.

The minor provision of the law of 1927 mentioned above carried a partial introduction of old-age annuities in a different form. Unemployed or disabled workers over sixty were given a *Rente* amount-

[184] *BGBl.*, 1929, Nr. 247.

ing to two-thirds of their last unemployment benefits; this varied, according to the size of the family and the last wage earned, between 18 and 70 schillings a month—approximately 2.5 and 10 dollars. The annuity was to be paid in this amount for life. The sums required were advanced by the federal state but were to be derived finally as follows: 50 per cent from contributions of the employers and employees, one-third from the state where the insured person resided; and one-sixth from the federation. This scheme went into effect on July 1, 1927, and the first payments were made in October. On December 17, 1927, the plan was extended to aged house servants, the monthly *Rente* being fixed at 25 schillings. A year later the sum was raised to 30 schillings.[185]

The old-age and disability provisions of the law of 1927, even before the insertion of the prosperity index amendment, failed to fulfill the hopes the workers had connected with its adoption. The provisional scheme under which thousands of workers over sixty were thrown out of their former benefit schemes and put on the lower old-age rates met with passionate opposition among the workers.[186]

For the student of Austrian labor and of the functioning of Austrian democracy there is, however, an even more deplorable aspect of the passage of the insurance statutes of December, 1926, and April, 1927; namely, their "political" background. It has already been noted that the government was in an embarrassing situation. Specifically, the collapse of a great number of banks closely connected with the Christian Social party and the public scandal concerning them and the grave mismanagement of the Postal Savings Bank under the Christian Social minister of finance, Ahrer, rendered the position of that party extremely difficult in the fall of 1926. Despite the lack of documentary proof there is practically no room for doubt that under these circumstances Seipel, the chief of the new cabinet, proposed a pact to the Socialists: silence on the numerous cases of corruption among Catholic party leaders in return for the adoption of the insurance measures for the salaried employees and the manual workers. The editor of the *Volkswirt*, one of the best-informed and shrewdest observers of Austrian po-

[185] *Ibid.*, 1927, Nr. 125, § 268 (1); Nr. 368; 1928, Nr. 356.
[186] *Der österreichische Volkswirt*, vol. 19 (April 9, 1927), 739.

litical as well as economic affairs, openly charged that such a pact had been made, and his charges were not denied. Concerning the ethical quality of such an agreement between a Roman Catholic priest, professor of moral theology in the great University of Vienna, and a party which always stressed its desire to purify the political life of the country, nothing need be said. But the Socialists unquestionably got the worst of the agreement. Once the general excitement over the abysses of corruption had subsided, with the connivance and participation of the Socialists, Seipel did not find it imperative to listen to their wishes and insisted on passing the law in a form which amounted to little more than a demonstration. The Socialist press renewed its attacks against the Postal Savings Bank in December, 1926, but the right moment had been lost.[187]

Naturally, the Socialists could easily have prevented the adoption of the law concerning insurance for manual workers and postponed the matter until after the elections; in fact, this probably would have enhanced their position in the campaign and made it impossible for the Catholic party to use the act as a proof of the social tendency of the Seipel government. But it seems that their feeling of responsibility to the workers and some considerations of tactics came to the fore and prevented them from pursuing this line of policy. Old-age insurance in Austria had already a long and infelicitous history and the Socialists were afraid that after the elections the whole work would have to start anew. They assumed—wrongly as the subsequent development revealed—that it would be possible to improve the laws and to start after the elections the struggle for a reform of the old-age insurance. In other words, they decided it was advisable to get something on the statute books and then to work for its improvement.[188]

---

[187] Walther Federn, "Wahlen," *Der österreichische Volkswirt*, vol. 19 (March 26, 1927), 694 ff. The Social Democrats confirm this view to a certain extent: "The salaried employees insurance was so to speak a ripe fruit of the bank scandals." Indeed, keeping in mind the temporary cessation of the criticism of the scandals, it is difficult to see what other meaning this statement could have. *Tätigkeits-Bericht*, Heft 21 (Wien, 1927), p. 50.

[188] Cf. Matthias Eldersch, "Das Arbeiterversicherungsgesetz—eine Spottgeburt Seipelscher Sozialpolitik," *Arbeit und Wirtschaft*, vol. 5 (April 15, 1927), 309–312. Note also in this article the interesting statement that the discussions on the workers' insurance act would never have proceeded so rapidly but for the precarious situation in which Seipel found himself in the fall of 1926 (p. 312). My Socialist acquaintances in Vienna have interpreted this as an almost open admission that the pact as described above actually existed.

Attempts to include agricultural workers in the general act of 1927 failed. In the next year, however, an insurance law for them was adopted. It introduced, *inter alia,* a similar provisional scheme of old-age payments for unemployed workers over sixty-five and disabled workers over sixty; additional requirements narrowed the scope of persons benefited by these stipulations. On the whole this statute represents a combination of progressive and regressive elements.[189] The general benefits were less favorable and the influence of the employees in the administration weaker.

The foregoing section has been primarily a discussion of the outstanding measures of social and labor legislation adopted in the long period between the fall of 1920 and 1927 with occasional references to general political implications. In several instances, however, for the sake of convenience of presentation, laws have been treated which actually belong in the next period of such legislation. One result of this enumeration has been to show how the tempo of social enactment slowed down more and more as the years of the great upheaval in Central Europe receded into the past. Although, as noted earlier, it is unwise if not impossible for the legislative mill to grind out reforms in this field at the same rate indefinitely, it is possible to cloak opposition to all reforms in this argument. Needless to say, probably, the attitude suggested was not lacking in Austria. It came out from cover in the period 1920–1927 and under the designation "struggle against the social burdens" remained for several years in the forefront of the political life of the country. As has been shown in preceding sections, the political constellation in the early years of the republic, the inflation boom, and other extraordinary circumstances militated against the open avowal of this attitude so that the bulk of the social legislation was passed without any serious criticism, let alone any resistance, on the part of the entrepreneurs and the non-Socialist parties in parliament.[190] But toward the end of 1921, when it became increasingly clear that the inflation upswing was coming to a close, the first intimations of the ensuing struggle appeared. At the beginning the opposition was

[189] Lederer, *op. cit.,* p. 559; *BGBl.,* 1928, Nr. 235.

[190] Only the disappearance of the workbooks prompted the official journal of the manufacturers to a long article of regretful farewell. Its author maintained that the special conditions in Austria, namely the lack of national feeling, rendered the books necessary. *Die Industrie,* March 10, 1919, pp. 1–2.

extremely cautious. The first attacks, if they deserve this characterization at all, were carefully couched in the form of information concerning the abolition or relaxation of this or that social measure in foreign countries, mostly in Germany and Italy. Such information was spread regularly over the pages of the business magazine just cited. As early as November, 1921, however, the labor press acquired a confidential letter sent out by the Association of Manufacturers to its members. They were instructed to "interpret the Works Councils Act in a restrictive sense. . . ." and to forward to the Association any general claim of the councils even though they believed that such claim was in accordance with the law. The employers were required to refuse to acquiesce in a deduction of trade-union contributions from wages; furthermore, they were ordered to decline any coöperation with works councils and trade unions in the engagement and dismissal of workers. With respect to working time the employers were told as a matter of principle to negate any attempt to shorten the eight-hour day. Finally it was stressed that "Socialization tendencies, *may they come from the legislator* or from any other side," were to be rejected.[191] The italicized words reveal a mental attitude which should be noted as helpful for understanding some features of the development in Austria in subsequent years.

Comparatively soon, though, the campaign against the social burdens became visible in the limelights of public gatherings. At an extraordinary general meeting of the manufacturers association its president referred to "22 laws which were inflicted upon industry and the sole aim of which was to hinder production." There remained at that early time some industrialists willing to try to avoid the struggle. At the meeting just mentioned, for instance, Streeruwitz said he felt sure that a peaceful solution could be found and the relations between labor and industry improved. Interestingly enough he added that he could not find that the workers were entirely wrong in trying to avail themselves of the existing favorable situation.[192] But the protest movement could not be restrained any longer. "The legislative machine must be brought to a standstill."[193] "Our social policy is entirely wrong."[194] Unemployment insurance

[191] *Arbeiter Zeitung,* November 26, 1921, pp. 8–9.
[192] *Die Industrie,* March 3, 1922.
[193] *Ibid.,* April 4, 1922.
[194] *Ibid.,* April 29, 1922.

represents a danger for the whole economic life. Discharge compensation for salaried employees is impossible.[195] Almost every number of the manufacturers' journal now carried an outburst against the despised social legislation. At the general meeting of the association on January 18, 1923, the members were told: "Austrian industry has a social burden to bear which renders competition impossible even in countries with well-developed social legislation. . . . The social burden must be reduced!"[196]

It became customary for opponents to compute that burden as a percentage of wages. In 1923, for example, the current estimate was 22 per cent.[197] Several years later E. Weidenhoffer, secretary of the industrialists' association in Styria and member of parliament, published another computation intended to show that the aggregate burden of the social services equaled 25 per cent of the wage bill. In a sharply critical comment on Weidenhoffer's figures J. Jellinek came to the conclusion that the correct percentage was 9.5.[198] An examination of the data and the arguments indicate convincingly that Jellinek was correct. Only a few years ago even his figure would have seemed unwarrantably high to many Americans; but now (March, 1945), after the governor of California has formally proposed a compulsory system of prepaid medical care the costs of which will bring the total bill for social insurances to around 10 per cent of wages, the plan is receiving support from a number of the most conservative newspapers in the state.

The months immediately following the January, 1923, meeting of the Association of Manufacturers were filled with negotiations between its representatives and certain members of parliament. Then came sharp polemics between industry and the unions on the question of the eight-hour day.[199] The era of good feeling between the association and the trade unions which prevailed at the time of the "industrial conferences" seemed to be definitely over.[200] The

[195] *Ibid.*, Vienna Fair Copy, 1922.

[196] *Ibid.*, January 20, 1923, p. 1.

[197] Mentioned by Hanusch in Gewerkschaftskongress, 1923, *Protokoll*, p. 265.

[198] Cf. *Die Industrie*, February 17, 1928, pp. 6–8, and *Der österreichische Volkswirt*, vol. 20 (March 3, 1928), 623–626.

[199] *Die Industrie*, July 28, 1923, pp. 1–2.

[200] A certain change was discernible even at the time of the last conference. Concerning the first, *Die Industrie* wrote: "Especial significance must be attributed to the industrial conferences because here the representatives of the trade unions, that is, of the reasonable elements among the workers, joined hands with industry in order to

report of the *Kommission* to the trade-union congress of 1923 is crammed with information on employers' attempts to destroy social legislation. "The attacks of the employers against the eight-hour day have increased tremendously, especially in the last months."[201] During the discussions in the congress the old union leader, Anton Hueber, declared: "Woe to him who attacks the eight-hour day. I am very cautious and am in ill repute as a hindrance in some things, but on these questions I say nothing is possible except an iron No!"[202] Indeed, the need for a vigorous defense of the social legislation received major attention throughout the congress. A representative of the salaried employees in industry well summarized the situation: "The significant feature of this congress is that demands to extend and improve social legislation—the question what shall we do in order to obtain more social protection—do not play the main role they once did; this congress is but an outcry of indignation, and a defense against a plot to do away with our social achievements."[203] Hanusch called attention to a long list of proposals moved in parliament, all designed to weaken or abolish social acts.

> The motion by Heinl and Partik attempts nothing less than a reduction by half of the discharge compensations of those salaried employees who have been employed for more than three years. . . . In their attack against the salaried employees law the employers speculate that there could be workers envious of the ample protection accorded to the salaried employees. . . . There is further a motion that Article 1154b [of the civil code] which secures one week's pay to the worker in the event of illness should be abolished. This article is not even an achievement of the revolution . . . it was made effective during the war by a decree. The motion offered in parliament perforates the prohibition of nightwork and therewith the first breach in the social legislation is made.[204]

The indignation of the assembled delegates was reflected most clearly in the firm language of the resolution adopted by the congress.

---

salvage the country from common misery. The old organizations of the workers, we must admit it, were the beneficiary counterpoise against that company of hotheads and criminals who wanted to realize their wishes by means of violence." Two years later this paper stated: "We always have been skeptical toward industrial conferences. Either the government, or the Social Democracy, or both, want something from industry. . . . This time employment for jobless people was the platform. . . ." *Die Industrie*, November 8, 1919, p. 1; *ibid.*, October 15, 1921, p. 2.

[201] Gewerkschaftskommission, *Bericht*, 1923, p. 48.

[202] Gewerkschaftskongress, 1923, *Protokoll*, p. 224.

[203] *Ibid.*, p. 285.

[204] *Ibid.*, pp. 267–269.

The organized workers and salaried employees, who together with their families represent more than one-quarter of the population of this country, will resist resolutely and unyieldingly the recently growing attempts of the Austrian government, the employers, the bourgeois parties in the Nationalrat, and particularly the bourgeois press . . . to curtail or to destroy these rights of the workers.[205]

And so the struggle went on. The next year, 1924, was one of grave financial and social crisis. In the spring the swollen bubble of the Austrian stock exchange collapsed. The prices of securities fell rapidly and the movement assumed catastrophic proportions when it became clear that the bear speculations in French francs had proved a failure. The usual distressing consequences of such disturbances followed. A large number of banking houses disappeared immediately. Great restrictions on credit proved unavoidable. Unemployment increased. But there was a continuation of the rising tendency of prices which had begun after the stabilization and represented an adjustment of the internal purchasing power of the crown to its external value. Although credit restrictions slowed this movement, they could not check it. The real income of the workers decreased steadily and led to a great number of wage conflicts. With 380 strikes involving 6,925 undertakings and 265,667 strikers,[206] 1924 went down as a record year of social unrest. During most of the strikes, particularly in the four biggest conflicts (railroad employees, bank employees, miners, and metalworkers), the employers answered workers' demands for higher wages with counterdemands for modifications in social legislation.[207] The opposition to these demands among the working people was extraordinarily strong and went far beyond the Socialist organizations. At the time of the big metalworkers' strike the paper of the Catholic employees expressed the judgment that the employers stated their position concerning the eight-hour day in such a fashion as to arouse the solidarity of the whole working class.[208] Austrian Socialists now residing in the San Francisco Bay region confirm the paper's conclusion.

In the majority of cases the strikes of 1924 ended with victory for the workers—including the rejection of the counterdemands of the

[205] *Ibid.*, pp. 182–183.
[206] *Wirtschaftsstatistisches Jahrbuch, 1924,* p. 104.
[207] Cf., for example, *Neue Freie Presse,* September 3, 1924 (A.M.), p. 7.
[208] *Christlichsoziale Arbeiter-Zeitung,* September 20, 1924, p. 1.

employers. The metalworkers, for instance, secured wage increases varying between 10 and 20 per cent.[209]

Thus the attempts to reduce the "social burden" at the time of major strikes proved a failure. In addition, the employers' representatives in parliament proved unable to carry through the desired amendments. The Socialists were still powerful enough to prevent the various motions from appearing on the agenda of the Nationalrat. In this situation the employers conceived the ill-starred plan of addressing themselves to foreign governments; that is, to the League of Nations. In August and September, 1924, a delegation from the League was in Vienna to study the financial situation of the country. To it the Association of Manufacturers submitted a memorandum. After a long survey of the alleged overtaxation of industry the paper dealt with the social burdens which had likewise been imposed upon it, stating that

> a social policy out of accordance with present economic conditions increases the cost of production. Yet it should be a fundamental principle that social policy must always be adjusted to the economic situation of the country, and the fact that the latter is worse in Austria than anywhere else should have been taken into consideration. Especially a large number of legal stipulations must be removed which in the present situation of industry have to be regarded as an absolutely unjustified social burden. In no case can Austrian industry bear burdens which are unknown in countries which have won the war.

Then followed a long list of social acts and stipulations which were regarded by industry as special impediments to production: Article 1154b; paid vacations for manualists; unemployment benefits, which had been constructed as a *Rente* paid by the state; the Salaried Employees Act with its paid vacations and discharge compensations which ruined the credit of Austrian undertakings; the Works Councils Act. Concerning the latter the authors of the document remarked: "There was not a single case in which thanks to this act the workers had taken greater interest in the undertaking. The works councils turned out to be defendants of the shortest run interests of the workers; they did not confine themselves to a representation of material interests but included also political interests,

[209] It is interesting to note in passing that during their strike the electric current was cut off one night in the Inner City of Vienna, apparently in order to exercise pressure on the employers.

even though the latter might not be consistent with the interests of production." A special section concerned the eight-hour day: "This mechanical restriction of working time cannot be maintained when in Germany, which is our strongest competitor in neutral markets, the eight-hour working day has been abolished."[210]

It stands to reason that the memorandum provoked the strongest criticism from the camp of organized labor.[211] But the general reception also was more than cool. Industry's representative, Reiner, declared in parliament that he had had no knowledge of the document before its appearance. The Social Democrats described it in the same place as a scandal.[212] The *Volkswirt* carried an incisive comment, emphasizing the incompatibility of the memorandum with national dignity. It pointed out, furthermore, that had Austrian industry had the intention of scaring off international capital and inducing a capital flight from Austria, it could have concocted no better method than the publication of this memorandum.[213]

From the point of view of international politics the business leaders chose the least favorable date. Édouard Herriot was the premier of France and Ramsay MacDonald the prime minister of England. It was highly unlikely that these two men, at the time virtually the masters of the League of Nations, would have felt ready to join in a campaign against the Austrian Socialists.

The obvious exaggerations of the memorandum also left an unfavorable impression. Its sharp criticism of the works councils was, for instance, scarcely consistent with the statement published by the secretary of the Association of Manufacturers, Dr. Margaretha, only a few months earlier: "The worst abuses of the works councils system, as we observed them in the first years of the introduction of this institution, have been more or less overcome and it must be credited to many works councils that at least they have no intention of hampering production."[214]

But perhaps the most illuminating commentary on its usual sweeping attacks on the burdensome character of social legislation

[210] *Neue Freie Presse,* August 31, 1924 (A.M.), pp. 7–9.
[211] Cf., for example, J. Hannak, "Eine denkwürdige Denkschrift," *Arbeit und Wirtschaft,* vol. 2 (Sept. 15, 1924), 753–758.
[212] Nationalrat, *Protokoll,* September 2, 1924, pp. 1518, 1502.
[213] *Der österreichische Volkswirt,* vol. 16 (Sept. 6, 1924), 1478.
[214] *Die Industrie,* April 19, 1924, p. 8.

is provided by the Association of Manufacturers itself. In the report on its activities for the last half of 1924 appears this statement:

> The principle that every further sociopolitical burden on industry must be stopped is all the more difficult to carry through since in some fields of social insurance, particularly sickness insurance, we still have from the period of inflation a rather far-going situation of inadequate insurance the elimination of which would certainly be necessary in order to bring the insurance benefits up to a purpose-serving level.[215]

With the memorandum to the representatives of the League the public struggle against the "social burdens" had reached its climax. Immediately afterward the intensity of the campaign subsided. At Christmas, 1924, Streeruwitz solemnly declared that "as far as the eight-hour day is concerned neither the industrialists nor business and tradesmen in general even think of attacking it."[216] In the following years, nevertheless, the voice of industry protesting against these "burdens" could frequently be heard in the press, in speeches in parliament, and in various investigations. On the other hand, such fierce attacks on social legislation as those launched in the years 1922–1924 did not recur. This did not mean that industry had abandoned the struggle; the strategy only was changed. Instead of trying to alter the legislation the employers undertook to evade the laws or to avail themselves of some imperfect legal formulations to attain the same objective. Repeatedly, for example, the notice stipulations of the Salaried Employees Act were circumvented by indefinite extension of the "probationary month." Sham discharges and reëngagement of employees were used for the same purpose. Sometimes the laws were directly broken; particularly the act prohibiting nightwork for bakers was frequently violated. The annual reports of the factory inspectors always carried references to continuous attempts to avoid this legal prescription, and that for 1924 related an amusing case in which the bakers of a certain town organized an insurance system under which fines for nightwork imposed on one firm were to be borne by all the bakers of the place.[217] When the severe depression of 1924–1926 began to lift the employers found an unexpected ally in their endeavors to extend hours, namely the

[215] Hauptverband der Industrie Oesterreichs, *Tätigkeitsbericht über das zweite Halbjahr 1924*, p. 15.
[216] *Die Industrie*, December 24, 1924, p. 7.
[217] Gewerbe-Inspektoren, *Bericht, 1924* (Wien, 1925), p. 118.

workers themselves, who were anxious to increase their earnings by long hours whenever work was available at all and thus to compensate themselves for their recent losses.[218]

It remains true, however, that within a period of about nine years (1918–1927) all these cases of neglect, disregard, evasion, and violation of the social laws were kept within comparatively modest limits. When the political decline of the Socialist movement began, and when, some time later, the outbreak of the great crisis weakened the resistance power of the workers to an unprecedented extent, then the employers were able to apply new and more effective means in their struggle against the system of social legislation. For one outstanding example, they were successful in establishing company unions. In addition, the old weapons in the employers' arsenal could now be used in a larger field and with incomparably greater success. Discussion of these developments, however, exceeds the framework of the present chapter.

As far as was possible without writing an entire volume[219] on the subject the foregoing survey has sought two chief objectives: to show how a comprehensive and well-organized system of social legislation was built up by the Austrian labor movement in the years following the establishment of the republic; and, second, to make the reader understand that this system was created not only in order to make a human investment in the Austrian economy, not only to save the Austrian laborer from physical decline, and to make the life of the whole class freer and happier, but also to save Austrian democracy from assault by the blind forces of a ruthless dictatorship from the left.

---

[218] *Ibid., 1927,* p. 95, and *ibid., 1928,* p. lix.

[219] Satisfactory presentation of the details of the legislation would require such a volume; they have been omitted because the other details discussed are more important for the general purposes of this study, and because they are available in numerous sources such as the reports of the International Labor Office.

CHAPTER XI

Trade Unions

THE OLD SLAVS believed that our world rested upon the backs of three huge whales. Not as a matter of mythology but of principle and practice the Austrian working-class movement rested upon the threefold unity of the political party, the trade unions, and the consumers' coöperative societies. It is evident from the discussion to this point, and will become ever clearer in subsequent sections, that the movement was predominantly political throughout its history. This tendency was even more enhanced after the establishment of the republic and, most notably, in the years after 1923. Indisputable as this is, the role played by the Socialist or "free" trade unions in the tragic drama of the republic must not be underrated. Their horizon and the amplitude of their activities were greatly broadened by the outcome of the First World War. In the years after the revolution they almost became governmental institutions. Through Ferdinand Hanusch they reigned supreme in the ministry of social administration. Their will weighed heavily with the cabinet of Renner, and, at times, their influence on the decisions of his government was overpowering. The new functions which accrued to them, the new tasks they had to face, were not only a result of their greatly increased membership. The loss of the old internal market rendered the export problem a question of life and death. Particularly after the stabilization crisis the trade unions never lost a keen interest in problems of national economic policy, notably in matters of foreign trade. The employment interests of the unions largely influenced the line of action of the Social Democratic party and their wishes may be easily traced every time it took a stand in parliament on questions of tariffs and quotas, on commercial treaties, on budgetary appropriations, and the like. This did not mean that the unions exercised "pressure" upon the party. The specific Austrian situation where both organizations were traditionally thought of as "two sides" of the same movement, to use one of Viktor Adler's favorite expressions, had long replaced pressure by continuous coöperation.[1] It is safe to say that this coöperation went far beyond the specific interests of the trade unions. There were periods of relatively short duration when the unions and the party did not see eye to eye and compromise solutions had to be found in arduous negotiations, but on the whole the unions readily left the general political leadership to the party—without, however, eclipsing themselves.

Given this state of affairs, the futility of segregating in one chapter a discussion of the attitudes and actions of the unions on a wide variety of topics becomes evident; consequently, that discussion has been and will be presented in the appropriate sections. The present chapter is confined, in the main, to an analysis of the data on the size and structure of the Socialist unions and a treatment of their specific problems of internal organization. Even the question of their relations to other unions, in Austrian political parlance the "terror question," will be more conveniently dealt with in Chapter XXI. Nevertheless, the concluding part of this chapter will elaborate certain aspects of the Socialist organizations and bring out more plainly their specific characteristics.

Statistical Survey

Because of the civil war of early 1934 comprehensive data concerning the free trade unions for the year 1933 were never published by them; the Austro-Fascist regime that destroyed them did not see fit to publish those data; consequently, almost all free union statistics of republican Austria are limited to the years 1919–1932. The basic facts on the number of organizations and members are given in the table, page 258. Those for 1918 are included to indicate the great increase in membership immediately after the war. The decreases in organizations reflect in part the results of centralization efforts; those in membership are discussed below and in Chapter XIX.

A general picture of the quantitative structure and development of the more important Socialist unions is provided by the table, page 259. The years 1921 and 1932 represent the high and low points for years in the republican era for which data are available; 1927 is a median or more "normal" year.

[1] Cf., for example, *Victor Adlers Aufsätze, Reden und Briefe,* Heft 7 (Wien, 1929), pp. 164, 175. For the expansion of trade-union activities, cf., for example, Viktor Stein, *Der Arbeit zur Wehr und Ehr', Kurze Geschichte des österreichischen Metallarbeiterverbandes* (Wien, 1924), p. 73.

The small military organization has been included in the table on page 259 because of its general interest as the first soldiers' trade union in the world. As will be evident from subsequent sections, its decline resulted from the political development of the country. Some other relatively small groups, such as the typographers and pressmen, the clothing workers and the shoe workers, have been

NUMBERS AND MEMBERS OF FREE UNIONS*

Year	National unions	State or regional unions	Total	Locals	Members
1918	48	15	63	2541	412,910
1919	55	17	72	2885	772,146
1920	51	14	65	3238	900,820
1921	51	13	64	3545	1,079,777
1922	49	14	63	3579	1,049,949
1923	47	8	55	3372	896,763
1924	45	8	53	3119	828,088
1925	45	8	53	3050	807,515
1926	43	9	52	3246	756,392
1927	43	8	51	3268	772,762
1928	41	8	49	3068	766,168
1929	40	8	48	3060	737,277
1930	38	7	45	3024	655,204
1931	37	7	44	2586	582,687
1932	37	6	43	2631	520,162

* *Jahrbuch 1932 des Bundes der Freien Gewerkschaften Oesterreichs*, p. 37, cited hereafter as Gewerkschaftsbund, *Jahrbuch*. The membership figures include only persons in unions affiliated to the national organization or federation and so reported to the *Bundesamt für Statistik* (Federal Bureau of Statistics). Actually there were in various years from 20,000 to 40,000 members of groups sympathetic with or proclaiming themselves as "free" unions but not attached to the national body. They will be included in a subsequent comparison of the main types of unions (p. 271), but since no continuous record of them could be offered it seemed best to reproduce here the report in the official union yearbook.

listed because of their strength despite small membership, or the contrast they provide with their counterparts in the United States. The miners were important in themselves at the beginning of the period, but it seems appropriate to emphasize their absorption by the metalworkers. Leaving out of account the soldiers' union, the other 21 unions listed were only some 40 or 60 per cent of the total national unions in 1921 and 1932, respectively, but they included 90 or 91 per cent of the grand total membership. Stated otherwise, the 10 largest unions of 1921, about 20 per cent of the total national groups, comprised just under 61 per cent of the members. From this obvious disproportionality between the number and the size of the

MEMBERSHIP IN SELECTED FREE TRADE UNIONS*

Organization	1921	1927	1932
Agricultural workers	71,031	34,088	29,642
Bank employees	22,158	8,439	6,374
Building service employees	22,211	18,535	[a]
Building trades workers	88,453	59,856	37,390
Chemical workers	43,998	35,249	28,726
Clothing workers	15,892	7,166	6,290
Commerce, salaried employees in	41,238	27,949	26,741
Federal, state, and municipal employees	21,465	49,380	40,860
Food industry workers[b]	39,244	42,128	32,783
Hotel employees[c]	36,966	23,293	14,293
Lumber and wood workers	37,592	18,058	10,081
Manufacturing industries, salaried employees in	47,959	31,553	23,762
Mercantile and transportation workers[d]	58,254	42,722	33,299
Metalworkers	170,609	119,037	81,428
Machinists	7,125	[e]	
Military union	20,469	7,679	655
Miners	32,092	10,916	[f]
Post-office employees	13,838	13,644	9,965
Typographers and pressmen	7,836	13,538	11,777
Helpers	5,159		
Railway employees	106,732	88,489	55,021
Shoe workers	14,097	5,305	2,917
Technical union	16,358	14,364	6,604
Textile workers	56,095	38,007	17,865
Others	82,906	63,367	43,689
Total	1,079,777	772,762	520,162

* Data for membership appear for 1921, in Gewerkschaftskommission, *Bericht*, 1923, pp. 83–84; for 1927, in *ibid.*, 1928, pp. 73–74; for 1932, in Gewerkschaftsbund, *Jahrbuch*, 1932, p. 38.

[a] Left free trade unions in 1928 (Gewerkschaftsbund, *Jahrbuch*, 1928, p. 99).

[b] Includes tobacco workers, bakery workers, butchers. (Gewerkschaftskommission, *Bericht*, 1923, p. 83.)

[c] Includes coffeehouse and restaurant employees.

[d] This was an amalgamation of several groups in which actually the transport workers predominated numerically. In 1923 it adopted the misleading name *Freier Gewerkschaftsverband*. At that time it had seven largely autonomous sections (*Arbeit und Wirtschaft*, vol. 2 [Dec. 15, 1924], 1041).

[e] The machinists became a part of the metalworkers in 1926 (Gewerkschaftskommission, *Bericht*, 1928, p. 108).

[f] The miners became a part of the metalworkers in 1930 (Gewerkschaftsbund, *Jahrbuch*, 1930, p. 57).

remaining associations grew the grave problems of reorganization and concentration.

Throughout the whole period, but especially in the first years, the metalworkers' union was by far the largest. The absolute importance of the metal industry in Austria and the concentration in it of the greatest Austrian undertakings account for this preponderance. Needless to say there were significant implications for the character of the trade unions as a whole. The metalworkers had developed a certain radical tradition. After the revolution they were of all unions the most genuinely interested in works councils and socialization. They had instituted the regular congresses of works councillors in their industry and the central executive of trade unions, although fundamentally opposed to the idea, had to put on the best face possible.[2] After the events of July, 1927, they backed the position taken by Otto Bauer against a coalition government.[3] The influence of this mighty trade union, which was generally exercised toward achieving even greater unity between the party and the unions, can be traced throughout the postwar history of Austria. Separatist tendencies in the unions would have had to break the resistance of the metalworkers, an arduous and probably impossible task.

The percentage distribution[4] of male and female members in the free trade unions was as follows:

Year	Male	Female	Year	Male	Female
1919	74.98	25.02	1926	77.80	22.20
1920	76.11	23.89	1927	77.36	22.64
1921	75.78	24.22	1928	78.14	21.86
1922	77.83	22.17	1929	78.12	21.88
1923	77.26	22.74	1930	78.31	21.69
1924	76.94	23.06	1931	77.95	22.05
1925	76.98	23.02	1932	77.92	22.08

On the whole these figures reveal only minor shifts; they reflect to some extent the fact that at the time of crises the percentage of female employment rose and at the time of upswings fell. But it is interesting to note that in the only year for which data could be found, 1934, the percentage of females to the total gainfully employed was almost 34.[5] Keeping in mind the considerations just stated, the indications are that the free unions were not attracting so large a group as might have been expected. In this respect political reasons apparently were decisive. As will be shown, the percentage of women in Catholic unions was appreciably higher.

[2] *Die Gewerkschaft*, vol. 26 (Feb. 22, 1921), 69.
[3] *Arbeit und Wirtschaft*, vol. 5 (Oct. 15, 1927), 853–856.
[4] For 1919–1922, Gewerkschaftskommission, *Bericht*, 1923, p. 86; for 1923–1927, *ibid.*, 1928, p. 77; for 1928–1930, Gewerkschaftsbund, *Jahrbuch*, 1930, p. 59; for 1931–1932, *ibid.*, 1932, p. 36.
[5] *SHfRO.*, vol. 15, pp. 15, 18–19.

The relation between workers and salaried employees also reflects a rough relation to the phase of the business cycle. Adjustment of the work force to fluctuations in trade is generally carried out more promptly among its manual than among its white-collar members; consequently, the long crises which plagued republican Austria were relatively less disadvantageous to salaried employees. This is shown by the following table:

PERCENTAGES OF MANUAL WORKERS AND SALARIED EMPLOYEES IN FREE UNIONS*

Year	Manual workers	Salaried employees	Year	Manual workers	Salaried employees
1919	68.51	31.49	1926	64.05	35.95
1920	69.67	30.33	1927	65.19	34.81
1921	70.44	29.56	1928	65.15	34.85
1922	68.91	31.09	1929	65.35	34.65
1923	67.82	32.18	1930	64.20	35.80
1924	68.11	31.89	1931	63.75	36.25
1925	64.64	35.36	1932	63.47	36.53

* For 1919–1922, Gewerkschaftskommission, *Bericht*, 1923, p. 87; for 1923–1929, *ibid.*, 1928, p. 78; for 1928–1932, Gewerkschaftsbund, *Jahrbuch*, 1932, p. 48.

The sociological and political implications of the strong and increasing share of salaried employees in the membership of trade unions are obvious. The psychological attitude of a middle group, except in times of extraordinary mental shifts, is not propitious for direct action. This fact should be kept in mind; it furnishes one of the reasons for the long and fateful hesitations of the trade unions and the party to take up the gage of battle thrown down repeatedly by Dollfuss and the Heimwehr in 1933.

Somewhat akin in its effect was the development of membership in Vienna and the rest of the country. (See p. 262.)

Partly because of the relatively greater rise of unemployment outside of Vienna, partly for other reasons, such as the persistent attacks of the *Alpine Montan Gesellschaft* in Styria on the free unions, those unions were to some degree losing their grip on the workers in the provinces. This too was a serious development since its effects were to enhance the isolation of Vienna and to weaken the general position of labor in Austria.

The free unions described above possessed a richly developed press. It was a long tradition with the working-class movement in

Austria that every organization, whatever its size, should have a paper or magazine. Thus the smallest unions prided themselves on the ownership of an organ. This situation had its unsound aspects;

Distribution between Vienna and the States of Membership in Free Unions*

Year	Vienna	States	Year	Vienna	States
1919	55.34	44.66	1926	55.76	44.24
1920	50.91	49.09	1927	55.84	46.16
1921	49.71	50.29	1928	55.26	44.74
1922	48.50	51.50	1929	55.64	44.36
1923	50.70	49.30	1930	56.20	43.80
1924	53.58	46.42	1931	56.97	43.03
1925	55.34	44.66	1932	57.94	42.06

* For 1919–1922, Gewerkschaftskommission, *Bericht*, 1923, p. 85; for 1923–1927, *ibid.*, 1928, p. 76; for 1928, Gewerkschaftsbund, *Jahrbuch*, 1928, p. 103; for 1929, *ibid.*, 1929, p. 73; for 1930, *ibid.*, 1930, p. 74; for 1931, *ibid.*, 1931, p. 55; for 1932, *ibid.*, 1932, p. 41.

the existence of a number of the papers was little more than a reflection of the difficulties experienced by those who attempted a reorganization of the movement—a symbol of craft consciousness.

Periodical Publications of the Free Unions*

Year	Number	Year	Number
1919	51	1926	54
1920	49	1927	53
1921	50	1928	52
1922	52	1929	51
1923	52	1930	47
1924	54	1931	46
1925	54	1932	47

* For 1919–1922, Gewerkschaftskommission, *Bericht*, 1923, p. 113; for 1923–1927, *ibid.*, 1928, p. 112; for 1928–1930, Gewerkschaftsbund, *Jahrbuch*, 1930, p. 180; for 1931–1932, *ibid.*, 1932 p. 73.

About half of these publications appeared monthly; about one-third, fortnightly. In 1930 there were 18 in the total of 47 that had attained the respectable age of between thirty and forty years; 10 of between twenty and twenty-nine years. One paper was sixty-four years old.[6] It is understandable that the relatively long life of these papers made them dear to the hearts of many a trade-union member, whatever their current value as means of propaganda and education and regardless of the facts that they contained a great deal of similar material and involved a considerable waste of union funds.

In 1925 the Socialist unions introduced a special section for ap-

[6] Gewerkschaftsbund, *Jahrbuch*, 1930, pp. 178–179.

prentices. The salaried employees in commerce and the metalworkers accounted for the majority of the total membership in this section which developed as follows:

Membership in the Apprentice Section*

1925	7,142	1929	15,416
1926	9,605	1930	17,316
1927	10,907	1931	15,964
1928	14,164	1932	14,076

* Gewerkschaftsbund, *Jahrbuch*, 1932, p. 134.

After completion of their apprenticeship most of the members of this section became ordinary members of the union concerned. The metalworkers transferred in this way: 1,325 members in 1927, 1,564 in 1928, and 1,249 in 1929, for a total in this period of 4,138. Their experience led them to the conclusion that the section was a good device for securing the new generation for the union organizations.[7]

The financial status of the free unions had deteriorated greatly in the years of inflation. Beginning with 1923 they energetically reorganized their budgets. Membership dues were raised, or distributed in a more purposeful fashion. Although the plan differed in individual unions, two systems predominated: fixed and variable contributions. The former was adopted by the majority of the big unions. The fixed fees were either equal for every member, as in the railroad unions; or were 25 or 30 per cent lower for women, as in the metalworkers and food industry organizations; or, finally, were arranged in three or four classes according to the wage level of the individual workers, as in the chemical industry. This last arrangement approaches closely the second main system, that is, of variable contributions. Under it dues were levied in terms of wages for a time unit (the building trades collected weekly fees equaling wages for one hour), or as a variable percentage of the wage. Several unions of salaried employees used this method.[8] Dues averaged about 2 per cent of wages. This was high, particularly in the light of the low standard of wages in Austria. The free unions, however, staunchly supported the view that a union which collected inadequate dues and was consequently unable to give efficacious aid to its members was not worthy of the name.

[7] *Die Lehrlingsbewegung im österreichischen Metall-Arbeiter Verband, Ihre Stärke, ihre Leistungen und Aufgaben* (n.p., n.d. [1930?]), pp. 7, 13.
[8] *Arbeit und Wirtschaft*, vol. 5 (Jan. 15, 1927), 51–54.

The improvement in the revenues of the Socialist unions after the reorganization of the contribution system appears below.

These larger funds enabled the unions to meet the increasing expenditures of the stabilization crisis. The year 1928, one of relative upswing, showed the highest revenues and the lowest percentage of expenditures since 1924. Although the effects of the crisis on budgets

REVENUE AND EXPENDITURE OF THE FREE UNIONS, 1923–1932*
(in millions of schillings)

Year	Revenue	Expenditure	Expenditure as per cent of revenue
1923	9.6	6.9	71.9
1924	14.9	10.5	70.4
1925	20.6	16.9	82.0
1926	21.5	16.9	78.5
1927	22.4	19.1	85.5
1928	25.2	19.5	77.3
1929	25.3	22.6	89.3
1930	23.4	22.5	95.8
1931	21.1	23.8	112.9
1932	20.3	20.1	99.4

* For 1923–1925, Gewerkschaftskommission, *Bericht*, 1928, p. 79; for 1926–1932, Gewerkschaftsbund, *Jahrbuch*, 1932, p. 49.

were serious it is clear that the unions were strong enough to stand a few years of deficit. It was not from the financial side that the danger came; the Labor Bank (*Arbeiterbank*) where the trade unions deposited a substantial part of their moneys was one of the last sound banks left in Austria.

Because of the free unions' policy of collecting high dues and giving good service in return, a summary of revenue and expenditure in schillings per member is of interest.

Year	1923	1924	1925	1926	1927	1928	1929	1930	1931	1932
Revenue	10.72	18.03	25.48	28.40	28.93	32.89	34.38	35.80	36.20	39.49
Expenditure	7.70	12.62	20.90	22.29	24.74	25.44	30.69	34.30	40.86	39.23

In 1931, for example, unemployment benefits amounted to about 25 per cent of the total expenditure per head. This was more than three times in absolute figures per member what it had been in 1927 and more than six times the amount of 1923. Average disbursements per head for help in cases of sickness, incapacity, death, emergencies of various sorts, and for legal protection rose from 63 groschen in 1923 to 4.38 and 8.60 schillings in 1927 and 1931; that is, about seven- and fourteenfold.[9] Obviously enough these expenditures involved a severe strain on the unions.

Financial strength and large membership of an individual union did not always go together even if some small but traditionally wealthy unions such as the printers are not considered. For example, a comparison in these respects as of 1929 of the 10 principal unions gives the following results.

MEMBERSHIP AND FUNDS OF THE TEN LARGEST FREE UNIONS IN 1929

Organization	Membership[a]	Funds[b] (in 1,000,000 S)	Rank in membership	Rank in funds
Agricultural workers	33,041	0.10	IX	IX
Building trades workers	64,200	4.06	III	III
Chemical workers	35,415	3.24	VIII	IV
Federal, state, and municipal employees	46,739	0.67	IV	VI
Food industry workers	42,531	5.00	V	II
Manufacturing industries, salaried employees in	31,594	0.04	X	X
Mercantile and transportation workers	42,492	2.64	VI	V
Metalworkers	118,315	6.21	I	I
Railway employees	86,923	0.50	II	VII
Textile workers	35,836	0.29	VII	VIII

[a] Gewerkschaftsbund, *Jahrbuch*, 1929, p. 70.
[b] *Ibid.*, p. 87.

Thus for agricultural workers, building workers, salaried employees in manufacturing industries, and metalworkers, the rank in both columns is identical. The most striking difference appears in the railway employees. The meagerness of the resources of the agricultural and textile workers, and salaried employees in industry is emphasized by contrasting them with the chemical workers; all four unions had about the same numerical strength. The subsequent depression effected considerable shifts. Organized metalworkers lost their dominating position as far as the funds were concerned. Food industry workers took first place in this respect (end of 1932) with an absolute increase that carried them past the 6 million schillings mark. Those in public employee, chemical, and mercantile and

[9] Gewerkschaftskommission, *Bericht*, 1928, p. 79, and Gewerkschaftsbund, *Jahrbuch*, 1932, p. 61, for all figures on expenditure per member.

transportation organizations also improved their financial position in spite of the crisis.[10]

In the International Federation of Trade Unions the Austrians occupied an honorable position. In 1928, for example, Austria figured in third place, after Germany and England, but preceding France, Czechoslovakia, Belgium, and Sweden.[11]

The evolution of trade unions other than the free or Socialist organizations may be indicated more briefly. As brought out in Chapter II, the most important competitor of the free group was the Christian trade unions.

MEMBERSHIP IN CHRISTIAN TRADE UNIONS, 1918–1929*

Year	Total	Male		Female	
		Absolute	Per cent	Absolute	Per cent
1918	20,556	12,161	59.2	8,395	40.8
1919	30,725	16,365	53.3	14,360	46.7
1920	64,478	32,681	50.7	31,797	49.3
1921	78,737	46,693	59.3	32,044	40.7
1922	78,105	46,722	59.8	31,383	40.2
1923	79,377	49,617	62.5	29,750	37.5
1924	80,128	49,833	62.2	30,295	37.8
1925	77,200	47,230	61.2	29,970	38.8
1926	76,122	46,968	61.7	29,154	38.3
1927	78,906	49,975	63.3	28,931	36.7
1928	100,087	67,288	67.2	32,799	32.8
1929	107,657	74,148	68.9	33,509	31.1

* Franz Hemala, *Geschichte der Gewerkschaften* (2d ed.; Wien, 1930), p. 268.

These figures from one of their leaders picture a trend of growth punctuated by great advances in 1920 and 1928. Taken at their face value they certainly indicate for the period after 1922 a more favorable development than that of the free unions. This impression is heightened by the data for the next three years. (See table, p. 267.) It seems, therefore, that even in the Great Depression the Catholic organizations revealed a much stronger power of resistance than their Socialist rivals. It should be noted, however, that in both 1921 and 1922 they had reported to the Federal Bureau of Statistics "about" 70,000 members of 11 state and regional Christian unions

[10] Gewerkschaftsbund, *Jahrbuch,* 1932, pp. 52, 53.
[11] *Ibid.,* 1931, p. 316.

which did not adhere to their central *Kommission.* In 1925 they reported "about" 50,000 such members in only 7 state or regional organizations.[12] Later issues of the *Handbuch* do not mention these members, but Hemala reports that in 1928 the task of bringing into

MEMBERSHIP IN CHRISTIAN TRADE UNIONS, 1930–1932*

Year	Total	Male		Female	
		Absolute	Per cent	Absolute	Per cent
1930	111,939	76,747	68.6	35,192	31.4
1931	108,420	76,197	70.3	32,223	29.7
1932	100,606				

* *Wirtschaftsstatistisches Jahrbuch, 1930/31,* p. 173; *ibid., 1931/32,* p. 166; *SHfRO.,* vol. 14, p. 172. No data on male and female members in 1932 could be found.

the *Kommission* those groups previously outside it was practically completed so that only about 15,000 remained unincorporated. If members of this type are included, the figures for the years just mentioned become:

1921	149,000	1925	127,000
1922	148,000	1928	115,000

For years subsequent to 1928 the situation could not be clarified completely, but it seems most probable that the increases reported in 1929 and 1930 actually reflected chiefly the process of absorbing most of the 15,000 reported by Hemala in 1928 as still outside the *Kommission.* If this is correct, the figure 100,000 for 1932 represents very closely the total membership in Christian unions and indicates a drop of almost exactly one-third from the high point in 1921. During the same period the Socialist unions had dropped from 1,079,777 to 520,162, almost exactly one-half. In short, the revised data do not support Hemala's statement[13] that "ten years of struggle and persecution have led the Christian trade unions of Austria upwards"; but they do support the conclusion that those unions had maintained their membership more satisfactorily than had the Socialists. As already noted (above, p. 29) the Catholic unions had a high percentage of nonindustrial members—teachers, clerks, and, in later years, soldiers. This composition was doubtless partly responsible for their greater stability of membership.

[12] *SHfRO.,* vol. 4, p. 105; *ibid.,* vol. 7, p. 127.
[13] *Op. cit.,* p. 268.

Hemala was not the only spokesman for the Catholic unions who chose to minimize or disregard the significance of membership reported to the Federal Bureau of Statistics but not attached to the *Kommission.* For example, a prominent leader, Hans Schmitz, brother of the Clerical Fascist mayor of Vienna after February, 1934, compared data for 1925 and 1930 for members in the competing central organizations to show that the Socialists had lost 152,311 whereas his group had gained 34,739.[14] From men who were forever emphasizing the religious aspect of their labor organizations and damning the Social Democrats for operating on an unspeakably low ethical level this method of writing is, to say the least, interesting.

The high percentage of women is not surprising in a Catholic organization. Since this circumstance is connected with the fact that female members were to a large extent employed in small establishments (textiles) or in domestic service, the social weight of this membership appears smaller. The rise of the government-fostered Catholic unions of soldiers and policemen is the chief explanation for the changes in the ratio of males to females in later years.

A comparison of the financial strength of the Catholic and free unions shows the former in an inferior position. In 1924 their average revenues per member were 6.53 schillings as against 18.03 in the Socialist organizations. Their total revenues in 1924 amounted to 522,913 schillings and expenditures to 471,598. In 1929 the comparable figures were 1,612,090 and 1,121,229,[15] or about 15 and 10.40 schillings, respectively, per member as against 34.38 and 30.69 in the free unions. The Socialists charged that it was the policy of Christian unions to assess low fees in order to attract members, and that consequently they were unable to take due care of their members and their needs.

General differences in policy between Catholic and free unions are, of course, of major importance. While in Austria in 1936–1937, I discussed this matter at length with representatives of various shades of opinion. Dr. Hemala repeatedly made the point that there were actually only two things that kept the two groups apart: religion and the philosophy of the class struggle. With this view Kunschak agreed. Incidentally, they both insisted that membership

[14] H. Schmitz, *Im Gleichen Schritt* [Sonderabdruck aus dem *Katholischen Almanach,* 1932] (Wien, 1932), p. 14.

[15] Hemala, *op. cit.,* p. 268.

in their unions was open to adherents of any religion, not alone to Roman Catholics. Many spokesmen for the Socialist unions accepted Hemala's main points but usually stated that in their judgment the Church in Austria was not so much a religious as a political organization. Most of them carefully pointed out that there were certain "highly honorable" leaders in the Christian unions, but went on to say that as organizations they were "yellow." They claimed that the record over decades proved that whenever it came to a real issue the Catholic organizations always gave in to the employer and made deals which would keep them in his good graces. Needless to say Hemala and his associates vigorously denied this charge; indeed, they went out of their way to bring it up and showed plainly that it was a very sore point with them.

In contrast to the situation in the Socialist camp the Christian unions proclaimed in the constitution of their central organization that they were politically neutral.[16] In my conversations with him, Hemala also repeatedly insisted that his unions were independent, completely independent, of the Christian Social party. As proof he offered the fact that the Christian union of postal employees had struck against Seipel's wishes and, of course, against the government which was in the hands of the Catholic party. This, he claimed, was a mark of distinction that clearly set off the unions he represented from the free unions. By this type of reasoning, however, it can be demonstrated that Socialist unions in Vienna were independent of their party; in fact, Hemala discusses in some detail a strike of Socialist streetcar workers there in June, 1922, although the leaders of the union and "the Social Democratic party had used all measures to hinder the outbreak of the strike."[17] The trams were owned and operated by the municipality; the city council was about two-thirds Socialist, a position of power which the Christian Socials never even approached in the parliament. Hemala could have argued with much more reason that the members of his party were largely middle-class persons whose economic interests were often in conflict with those of Christian trade unionists so that a greater degree of independence might have been expected from them than from the free unionists who made up the bulk of the Socialist party. Obviously

---

[16] Printed in 6. Kongress der Christlichen Gewerkschaften Oesterreichs, 1929, *Bericht und Protokoll,* p. 175.

[17] Hemala, *op. cit.,* p. 166. For other instances of the same sort, see below, p. 358.

enough he was barred from this contention by his repudiation in principle of anything that smacked of the Marxist class struggle.

The so-called German National unions reported steady increases in their relatively small membership until 1926; after that the figures were fairly stable.[18]

1919	35,132	1926	50,858
1920	38,538	1927	47,857
1921	40,163	1928	51,247
1922	43,087	1929	47,250
1923	45,364	1930	49,559
1924	46,882	1931	49,645
1925	47,019	1932	53,376

This membership consisted almost exclusively of Pan-German higher railroad employees and salaried employees. After about 1930 it came more and more under Nazi influence.

The table (p. 271) gives a general view of the relative strength of the different trade-union groups in Austria in four selected years.

In striking contrast to anything ever attained in the United States the grand total of union members in Austria in the peak years 1921 and 1922 equaled approximately 21 per cent of the entire population, 31 per cent of the population eighteen years of age and over, and 51 per cent of the total non-independently gainfully employed.

The so-called neutral unions in the table (p. 271) refer in the earlier years primarily to such organizations as that of the petty officials of the central government[19] and in the period after 1927 primarily to the Independent union that was dependent upon the *Alpine Montan Gesellschaft* and to a less extent upon like-minded "union-busting" industrial and financial concerns.[20]

The obvious conclusion from the comparative figures was, of

[18] *Wirtschaftsstatistisches Jahrbuch, 1931/32,* p. 164; *SHfRO.*, vol. 14, p. 172. A discrepancy in the figure for 1919 between the *Jahrbuch* and the *SHfRO.*, vol. 2, p. 115, was resolved by choosing the former because it was the result of a later inquiry and because in earlier years the Federal Bureau of Statistics apparently had some difficulties in securing the coöperation of these unions. It reported that it could get no figures for 1920, 1921, and 1922. *SHfRO.*, vol. 3, p. 102 and vol. 4, p. 104.

[19] Gewerkschaftskommission, *Bericht,* 1928, p. 127.

[20] Julius Deutsch, *Geschichte der österreichischen Gewerkschaftsbewegung,* Vol. II (Wien, 1932), pp. 112 and 222, makes contradictory statements concerning the date on which the employers founded what are designated in American usage as "company unions." The first page cited refers specifically to the *Alpine* and 1919; the second to employers generally and to the period (Jan., 1927–July, 1929) that he is discussing. Other sources indicate that the free unions were not particularly concerned over the "independents" and their connection with the Heimwehr until some time after July 15, 1927. Gewerkschaftsbund, *Jahrbuch,* 1928, p. 174; *ibid.*, 1929, p. 257.

Relative Strength of Trade-Union Groups in Austria

Groups	1921		1925		1928		1931	
	Number	Per cent	Number	Per cent	Number	Per cent	Number	Per cent
Free trade unions[a] (affiliated with *Kommission*)	1,079,777	85.1	807,515	77.1	766,168	75.6	582,687	72.2
Other free trade unions[b] (not affiliated)			20,000	1.9	40,100	4.0	24,500	3.0
Catholic unions[c] (adjusted)	149,000	11.8	127,000	12.2	115,000	11.3	108,420	13.4
German national trade unions[d]	40,163	3.1	47,019	4.5	46,882	4.7	49,645	6.2
Neutral unions[e]			45,000	4.3	45,000	4.4	42,000	5.2
Total	1,268,940	100.00	1,046,534	100.00	1,013,150	100.00	807,252	100.00

[a] Gewerkschaftsbund, *Jahrbuch*, 1932, p. 37.

[b] For 1925: Gewerkschaftskommission, *Bericht*, 1928, p. 128 (estimate for 1926); for 1928: Gewerkschaftsbund, *Jahrbuch*, 1931, p. 207; for 1931: *ibid.*, 1932, p. 96.

[c] Cf. above, pp. 266–267.

[d] Cf. above, p. 270.

[e] Same as [b]. No data for years before 1925 could be found for this group although some units of it existed earlier. Obviously this distorts the percentage comparisons to some extent.

These specific years were chosen in order to give the Catholic unions the benefit of members reported to the Federal Bureau of Statistics but not affiliated to their *Kommission*; and also to give the free unions the benefit of some of the years in which they too noted in their own publications members of sympathetic but unaffiliated groups.

Comparisons similar to that above appear in Gewerkschaftskommission, *Bericht*, 1928, p. 128; Gewerkschaftsbund, *Jahrbuch*, 1931, p. 207; *ibid.*, 1932, p. 96. They were not utilized because they took no account of the unaffiliated Catholic members, a trick very similar to that for which Hemala and Schmitz were criticized above.

course, already clear: throughout the republican era the free unions preserved their position as an overwhelming majority of the organized workers in Austria—this in spite of severe losses which were partly of economic and partly of political nature. It is also not too much to say that their close connection with a powerful political party and their greater internal cohesiveness actually rendered it possible for them to carry out over many years a policy of sovereign neglect of other groups. Usually the other unions had to follow the lead of the free organizations in spite of the bitter antagonism which existed between them. This was true not only in the field of collective-bargaining contracts, but also in the work of the chambers of labor. Once the unfortunate decision had been made, chiefly under the influence of the papal encyclical *Rerum Novarum,* to push the development of Catholic workers' economic organizations, stiff-necked attitudes on both sides contributed in some degree to the final destruction of an independent labor movement by the Dollfuss-Schuschnigg-Starhemberg variety of Fascism. As has been indicated and as will be shown more completely, the determination of powerful economic interests to do away with parliamentary democracy and reduce the workers to impotence was the decisive internal factor, but without going too far into the realm of speculation it may at least be said that the prospects of successful resistance were weakened by the willingness of many Catholic union leaders to see their rivals destroyed in the hope that they would replace them.

Industrial Unionism

In an industrial society where businessmen do lip service to the ideal of private competitive capitalism but prove by their predilection for gentlemen's agreements, trusts, and monopolistic trade associations that they favor competition chiefly "for the other fellow," economic organizations are perforce essentially fighting units. As such they have to face the problem of integration. A trade union is no exception. It has to set definite limits to the tendencies toward differentiation; it must never allow them to develop into disintegration. What is more, it has to elaborate those schemes of differentiation which best safeguard the integration of will and resources. Clearly, there is no scheme which will not require readjustment over long historical periods, *pari passu* with the changing environment. Such a problem of revising the whole structure of their organization was presented to the Austrian trade unions after the establishment of the republic initiated a new era in their history. On the face of it, the problem was by no means specifically an Austrian one. In most of the industrial countries of the world similar questions had to be met; they became well known as the struggle between industrial and craft unionism. In each country, naturally, there were certain specific peculiarities.

It was, of course, no accident that the Austrian revolution gave a powerful impetus to attempts at reorganization. The rapid influx of new members raised "difficulties of growth." The fight between the American Federation of Labor and the Committee for Industrial Organization, so far as it was a struggle over reorganization, may likewise be viewed as a problem of expansion. This expansion took the form of the creation of a rival organization and destroyed the unity of American trade unionism. It has been shown that disunity already existed in Austria, though the dissidents were much weaker than in America. At any rate, postwar expansion did not result in significant additional organizational splits in the Danubian republic.

The first attempts to build a common shelter for the scattered trade-union groups proper and the various workers' educational clubs, which to a large extent were carrying out trade-union functions, were made in the early 'nineties. Most important of these attempts was the resolution of the first trade-union congress in 1893. It envisaged the erection of a centralized union system along the lines of industrial organization. At that time the supreme organ of the trade unions, the *Kommission,* was hardly one year old. The congress formally approved its creation and transformed it from a provisional to a permanent body. This action did not alter its precarious juridic position; indeed, it never was sanctioned under the Austrian law on associations. As a result, it was from time to time the victim of certain chicaneries on the part of the police.

More important was the fact that despite formal recognition by the congress the young central organ needed appreciable time before it could influence decisively the process of organizational development in individual unions. Meanwhile, spontaneous evolution was going on; that is, more and more central trade unions, representing aggregates of craft organizations, were being established under the name of "empire organizations." The *Kommission* found itself unable, probably also unwilling, to check this development. Understandably, its members were the prominent leaders of the craft branches; equally understandably, they were not enthusiastic about demoting themselves. More momentous was the consideration that in many instances local organizations were opposed to the necessary integration; in acquiescing to the retention of the craft structure the *Kommission* followed the road of minor resistance. Three other factors appeared to push in the same direction. First, was the backward stage of the industrialization of the country; the great number of small handicraft shops preserved a high degree of craft consciousness. Second, the organizations of enterpreneurs were still in their beginnings so that the unions were not yet faced by industry-wide associations of employers. Finally, and probably of greatest importance, was the fact that the Austrian trade unions from the very outset opened their doors to semiskilled and unskilled labor, including women. In contradistinction to British and American unionism the tendency to exclusiveness remained almost foreign to the Austrian unions.[21] Most likely the explanation for this difference lies in the close connection of the unions with a political party that naturally accepted all the voters it could get, but the connection itself was only one of the results of the belated development of a working-class movement. When the unions began to build strong organizations the "aristocratic" tradition of the British "New Model" of the 1860's had already received a body blow from the success of the dockers' strike of 1889. Only the metalworkers, the strongest Austrian union, approached the industrial structure, and even it was far from being a perfect representation of the type.

By the time the republic came into being the situation had been drastically altered. One incentive to an immediate reorganization of the unions was the great advance in industrial concentration which had taken place a few years before 1914 and had been intensified by the war. A large modern undertaking, employing representatives of a great variety of skills, made the old craft unions seem antediluvian and inefficient for collective-bargaining purposes. Second, the employers had become well organized; the Association of

[21] Deutsch, *op. cit.*, Vol. I (Wien, 1929), p. 229.

Manufacturers in particular was a powerful body. It was based upon industrial branch organizations so that, in the event of conflicts and so long as the unions did not follow suit, an indefinite number of them faced a unified employers' organization that needed no instruction in the art of playing off one against another. After 1918 the mushroom growth of collective-bargaining contracts naturally increased the feeling that the multiplicity of contracting partners on the employees' side should be removed.

These two arguments in favor of reorganization were not uniquely Austrian. They reflected an international development. The implications of the Works Councils Act were a different matter. In preceding chapters the struggle of the trade unions to keep these councils in check was described. During its course the union leaders became convinced that the subordination of a works council to the orders of the unions was rendered much more difficult if the individual councillor was virtually a representative of several trade unions. The existence of several masters was likewise bound to enhance the independence of the council as a whole. Thus the idea arose of making the "shop organization" (*Betriebsorganization*) the basis of the entire trade-union superstructure. The tremendous growth of the unions after the revolution had led to a great number of mutual encroachments. Jurisdictional disputes, or boundary disputes as they were termed in Austria, called imperatively for a permanent settlement. It was believed, with unwarranted optimism, that a reorganization on industrial lines would make such disputes impossible and thus eliminate all their damaging effects upon the unity and cohesiveness of the movement. Finally, there was the previously noted rapid expansion in the scope of union activities after the revolution. With the increased importance of the unions in the state, with the necessity of appearing much more frequently than before as a united body in various negotiations and discussions, it seemed that a greater centralization was unavoidable.

In this process of centralization craft consciousness was judged to be an antiquated psychological attitude, more in consonance with the periods of medieval handicrafts or early industrialism than with the environment of modern capitalism. Not craft consciousness but class consciousness was the slogan of the day. Since the class was the true basis of the movement, since it was believed that during the coming struggle for power, and, most notably, during the coming attacks upon democracy, the Austrian workers would have to act as one man, even the dualism of party and trade-union organizations seemed to some to be contrary to the supreme goal of unification. Nevertheless, and despite the tendency, particularly after 1923, to recognize the party as the virtual leader of the movement, the idea that the trade unions should be fully reduced to auxiliaries of the party never went beyond the narrow circles of party youth. It was only after the catastrophe of February, 1934, when these circles began to play a dominant role in the illegal movement, that for a brief period the necessity for a trade-union organization was seriously questioned. But without coming anywhere near such radical solutions the immanent consistency of the class-struggle principle demanded a unification of the trade-union forces. The statutes of various trade unions frequently emphasized the "solidarity of the whole working class," and the "scientific recognition of the irreconciliable opposition of interest between the classes."[22] From this point of view craft consciousness seemed to be a "foreign body" in the ideology of a class movement. The logical sequence would have been the creation of a "Unity" trade union and voices in favor of this most radical centralist solution were raised from time to time through the whole period 1919–1933.[23] But the way toward such a unity union was long; indeed, considerably longer than was understood for years following the Austrian revolution. Even the more modest efforts aimed at a reorganization along the lines of industrial unionism proved an arduous task, which, in many respects, remained unsolved in spite of all attempts and in spite of all reasons which spoke for enforcing the reconstruction.

The first trade-union congress after the revolution put the problem of reorganization in the center of its proceedings. Proposals from various unions urged the adoption of the industrial type. Among them was a joint motion prepared by 8 unions, including those of the most important metal, textile, and railroad workers, which demanded the introduction of a "shop organization."

"The congress recognizes that for the purpose of unified leader-

[22] See, for example, the constitution of the union of salaried employees in manufacturing industries, quoted in Richard Seidel, *25 Jahre Bund der Industrieangestellten Oesterreichs* (Wien, 1931), p. 77.

[23] Gewerkschaftskongress, 1931, *Protokoll*, p. 79.

ship in wage conflicts and for the attainment of an all-embracing organization, all workers employed in one plant should be permitted to belong to only one trade union. The criterion for membership in one of the existing unions is the product of the plant, not the nature of production or of the process of production."[24]

The *Kommission* submitted a motion which recognized the "shop organization" as the higher form of union structure and demanded the greatest possible unity in the negotiation of collective agreements. Concerning industrial organization the resolution was confined to suggesting means of accelerating the development by making it obligatory for trade unions to join an industrial union if and where the latter already existed within the branch in question. No attempt was made to provide methods for forcing the formation of *new* industrial unions. The resolution simply proposed that the *Kommission* should "work for a systematic development" by which the various trade unions would finally be organized in 16 industrial unions; one of them to be reserved for white-collar employees. Thus, from the outset, there was no attempt to carry out the scheme of industrial unions with complete consistency.[25]

This cautious resolution, which, very significantly, avoided a definition of the concept of industrial union and left open the principles upon which new delimitations were to be made, was accompanied by an equally cautious speech from Anton Hueber. The old war horse of the movement vigorously espoused the cause of industrial unionism, but pressed the point that such a reorganization could not be carried out by force or majority resolutions.[26] Apparently the opposition to the new scheme was expected to be determined. Indeed, the ensuing debate demonstrated considerable resistance to reorganization; it was, however, of a peculiar kind. The interest shown in this debate was amazing. Between the last (1913) and the present (1919) congress lay the fateful period of war and revolution; nevertheless, the report of the *Kommission* on these meaningful years was almost neglected. But when the congress turned to the question of reorganization no less than 44 individuals asked for permission to speak, and before the debate was closed 26 had expressed their views on industrial unionism.

[24] *Idem.*, 1919, *Protokoll*, p. 299.
[25] *Ibid.*, pp. 296, 298.
[26] *Ibid.*, p. 303.

Representatives of small unions opposed the new plan. They were attacked by members of those unions which assumed that with reorganization they could swallow up the opposing little groups, which, as was said, "live only on their old tradition."[27] On closer scrutiny, however, the attitude of the big groups was far from devoid of ambiguity. To be sure, they eagerly paid lip service to the idea of industrialism. But every one of them wanted the assurance that the reorganization would be so carried out as to make it the pillar of the new union and place the affiliated, formerly independent, unions under its leadership. For this reason the speaker for the comparatively large union in the food industry stressed the age of his organization, reminded the delegates that in the thirty-three years of its existence it had always fulfilled its obligations, and suggested that the greatest caution should be observed in order that the structure of the original organizations would not be shaken.[28]

The debate left the general impression that nobody would oppose reorganization if his particular union were declared an industrial union. The hotel and *café* employees secured such a concession, for in the final resolution their organization was recognized as an industry group and thus the number of the planned industrial unions was increased from 16 to 17.

As could be expected from the tenor of the debate the tempo of reorganization in the following years was slow. Nevertheless, several amalgamations took place. The association of workers in the building trades absorbed 8 different unions, including such groups as brick and stoneworkers, roofers, carpenters, and painters. Three unions joined the food industry association; the salaried employees in bookshops joined the union of commercial employees. A few other unifications of varying importance were carried out. In addition, several industrial coalitions were concluded. Through them individual trade unions, without relinquishing their independence, agreed upon common action in the event of need.[29]

More important than these amalgamations were the fierce boundary disputes which, unfortunately, characterized the period between 1919 and 1923. No less than fifty-one disputes were submitted to the *Kommission* and almost all national unions were involved.

[27] *Ibid.*, p. 307.
[28] *Ibid.*, p. 311.
[29] Gewerkschaftskommission, *Bericht*, 1923, pp. 109–111.

A great deal of trouble arose out of the attitude of the small union of machinists (about 7,500 members) which violently resisted attempts to force it into any of the groupings which had been envisaged as units of the new organization. The metalworkers claimed that the machinists should join them. This attitude is worth noting for two reasons. First, because it shows that the idea of "industrialism" was easily confused with simple centralization. It stands to reason that the machinists union, which frequently had but one or two members in individual shops, should not be devoured by any single body but be distributed among most of the new industrial associations. Second, because it shows plainly that the boundary disputes were created not only by the process of rapid expansion, which incidentally came to a close in 1921, but also and perhaps even to a greater extent by the specific plans of reorganization.

A special role in the long series of these disputes was played by the so-called *Technische Union,* a group in which several branches of state workers were organized. The organization demanded that all workers employed in undertakings belonging to the state should join it and claimed that this was in accordance with the principle of "industrialism." The lack of a clear definition of this concept was again proving unfortunate. The opponents of the *Technische Union* retorted that the identity of the employer had nothing to do with the basic idea of industrial unionism; but the union's representative fought vigorously for his view and supported it with general arguments borrowed from Marxist theory. Since the state was nothing but a representative committee of the ruling classes, it was imperative that the strongest possible union be formed to oppose it as employer. It had been said time and again, the speaker continued, that the great disadvantage of craft unions lay in the fact that given the modern organization of industry several unions had to deal with one employer. The *Technische Union* held that its plan of organization would remove precisely this drawback in an extremely important field. This position involved it in bitter conflicts with the union of agricultural workers and the union of chemical workers because of its attempts to incorporate workers in state forests and salt mines. Again, attempts at building up correctly and incorrectly conceived industrial unions led to boundary disputes. In one case the policy of the *Technische Union* even induced part of the workers in federal tobacco factories to form a small new organization which placed itself in opposition to the free unions. The problem of the *Technische Union,* which incidentally had a close parallel in Germany,[30] remained for several years a focus of disturbance. On more than one occasion the central paper of the trade unions urgently appealed to them to cease the "internal war."[31] But the appeals were of little avail. The *Kommission* worked hard to mediate between the "hostile brothers." Usually it had to be satisfied with a provisional settlement.[32] Sharp complaints and criticisms were frequent and the instigators of some of the disputes were accused of "trade-union demagogy" and of efforts to capture members of other unions.[33]

Thus, in spite of the amalgamations carried out in the meantime, in spite of the well-functioning groups in the building, textile, and food industries, which may be considered as industrial unions, the prospects of reorganization were generally dark on the eve of the congress of 1923. As one of the outstanding leaders in the movement confessed at this time: "The resolution of the last congress, by which industrial unions were characterized as the form of organization to be attained, found little attention."[34] A little earlier another prominent leader had at last suggested a definition of an "industrial union" in the following terms: "an association of workers according to the principle of identity or similarity of materials used in production."[35] This formulation was as good as any other; and probably better, because wider, than the "product principle." It is clear that in view of the multiplicity of industrial forms in practice no definition could be ideal in the sense that it would exactly fit the reality. Whatever the chosen arrangement a number of groups would not *eo ipso* find their place in it. Therefore, what mattered was to agree upon a definition and then have the will not only to pursue it logically to the end, but also to make the necessarily arbitrary decisions concerning the groups whose position was left ambiguous by the definition. It may be doubted that this will was existent. Uniform

[30] Karl Zwing, *Geschichte der deutschen Gewerkschaften* (Jena, 1928), pp. 73–74.
[31] For example, *Die Gewerkschaft,* vol. 24 (Jan. 31, 1922), 33.
[32] For example, *ibid.,* (May 23, 1922), 171.
[33] *Arbeit und Wirtschaft,* vol. 1 (June 15, 1923), 425.
[34] Stephan Huppert, "Die Aufgaben des Gewerkschaftskongresses," *Arbeit und Wirtschaft,* vol. 1 (June 1, 1923), 353.
[35] Eduard Straas, "Gewerkschaftliche Zeitfragen," *Arbeit und Wirtschaft,* vol. 1 (May 1, 1923), 277.

shop organization was hardly separable from the general scheme of reorganization; nonetheless, Straas, a partisan of industrialism, suggested that the question of organizing the industrial shop as a unity or along the lines of craft representation was still unanswered.[36] This uncertainty on a most decisive problem was significant.

The resistance against "industrialism" and the centralization implicit therein seemed to grow stronger as a certain spontaneous centralization, by way of the growth of some unions, apparently made headway. Of 63 national, state, and regional free unions existing in Austria in 1922 the 6 largest included a little more than 50 per cent of all organized Socialist workers and salaried employees.

The 1919 congress had instructed the *Kommission* to carry out the reorganization. Four years later this central organ was looking hopefully to the congress for a complete solution of a problem which apparently was too great for its powers. But were not its hopes an illusion? The congress certainly had the power to pass a sweeping coercive resolution which would make further disputes, once the supreme organ of the unions had spoken, impossible. But this presupposed a readiness to refrain from a compromise solution and to enforce a decision; in short, to do something which for a number of reasons the Austrian trade unions did not want to do.

Again, at the 1923 congress, no less than seven motions concerning reorganization were presented by various trade unions. No one of them opposed the ideas of industrial unionism or of "shop" organization; in fact, some of them urged the hasty completion of the reforms. But probably the most significant was the proposal of the machinists' union, responsible for so much of the jurisdictional squabbling in the intervening four years. On the one hand, this resolution demanded the establishment of a "Unity" trade union based upon thoroughgoing centralization. On the other, it referred to the difficulties of shop organization, intimating that it had proved a failure where and when introduced, emphasized the necessity for putting an end to internal strife, and wound up by demanding the establishment of the machinists' union as a "special group" which should be added to the 17 industrial organizations envisaged by the resolution of the last congress.[37] This attitude was by no means con-

[36] *Ibid.*

[37] Gewerkschaftskongress, 1923, *Protokoll*, pp. 176–177.

fined to the machinists. In general, the small unions were fully prepared to approve the industrial union scheme with the condition that every one of them would become an industrial union, thus duplicating the developments at the 1919 congress.

Domes, the leader of the great metalworkers' union, took a prominent part in the discussion. In a concise and impressive way he reiterated the arguments for industrial unionism and pressed the point that a uniform shop organization, which made the whole crew members of one union, was the indispensable prerequisite. But he hastened to add that no sudden abolition of craft unions was contemplated.[38]

No less than 35 speakers took part in the debate, which revealed a new and intriguing problem. The "industrial union" of the building trades had succeeded in uniting in its ranks not only the workers, but also the salaried employees in those trades. It seems natural to assume that, with the basic idea of industrialism clearly in mind, this development would have been warmly welcomed by all those genuinely interested in the new plan. But the opponents of this idea were not restricted to unions of salaried employees. Another representative of the metalworkers, Stein, reminded the delegates of the hard struggle which had been necessary before the unions had succeeded in liberating white-collar employees from the old prejudices and traditions of a middle-class group. "If you want," he exclaimed, "to push the salaried employees . . . back into the yellow swamp they came from . . . then go ahead and create today a common organization of manual workers and salaried employees."[39]

It is necessary to do justice to Stein's argument. The quantity of imponderable social values bound up with the position of a salaried employee in Austria should not be underrated and can be only incompletely understood in the United States. Scarcely anywhere else in the civilized world, even in Germany, long the butt of jokes in this respect, were titles and social standing held in such high esteem as in Austria; in her cities the vernacular carefully distinguished between workers and "better people." On the other hand, the workers' love for their higher placed colleagues was by no means untempered. For one thing, they envied the more extensive social

[38] *Ibid.*, pp. 302–305.
[39] *Ibid.*, p. 309.

legislation given the salaried employees. For another, they remembered the wartime when the white-collar men had to act as underlings of military management in the factories. After 1918, cases were not rare in which embittered workers laid hands upon the members of the salaried staff in the factories in order to avenge past grievances.[40] With this background a rather good case could be made for abstention from attempts to press the white-collar groups into the manualists' unions, but the good case undoubtedly was bound to have bad effects on the prospects for reorganization. Salaried employees represented almost one-third of the membership of the free unions. Under these circumstances a dualistic construction of the industrial unions would, of necessity, detract a great deal from the ideal of industrialism.

The debate was heated. But, again faithful to their traditions, the unions were anxious to avoid a "majoritization" of the minority. Protracted negotiations went on in the privacy of committees elected for the purpose. On the question of shop organization two extreme views were presented by friends and enemies of the scheme. Between them stood a group of delegates who favored shop organization, but with the condition that manual and white-collar workers be organized separately. The ideas of this intermediate group prevailed and were expressed in the final form of the resolution on matters of organization. A second question, related of course to that just discussed, was the lengthy proposal of the *Kommission* concerning the organizational composition of the free unions with particular reference to the issue of industrialism. This proposal again reduced the number of prospective industrial unions to 16, but reserved 2 of them for salaried employees; that is, those in private and in public employment. The congress decided to postpone final decision on the division into industrial groups, referring it back to the *Kommission* and giving the *Kommission* the task of working out the division in consultation with the "sections." The results were to be laid before a conference of the executive committees of the unions and the conference was given full authority to make a final decision. The previously mentioned general resolution on the whole matter authorized the *Kommission* to carry out decisions reached by itself and by the conference of executive committees as well as to uphold

[40] Seidel, *op. cit.*, p. 75.

the resolutions passed in 1919. In short the problem had once more been deposited in the lap of the *Kommission*.[41]

The period between the congresses of 1923 and 1928 was again one of various attempts at amalgamation; they did not, however, result in a thoroughgoing reorganization of the movement. According to the report of the *Kommission* to the 1928 congress a "valuable" fusion of the unions of machinists and metalworkers was effected.[42] As mentioned before, valuable this amalgation might have been, but not from the point of view of "achieving industrial unionism," and this was clearly expressed in a speech to the congress by a delegate of the building trades union.[43] Five or six other amalgamations took place. *Inter alia* the small union of chimney sweepers was at last prevailed upon to join the building trades union.

But on the whole the results were meager. In 1927 the 6 largest unions comprised just short of 52 per cent of the whole membership so that the remaining 45 unions had only 48. There were still very small organizations like that of the artificial flower makers with 549 members or of the commercial agents with 265. It was true, however, that the number of workers' unions had considerably diminished between 1917 and 1927, from 49 to 30, whereas the number of salaried employees' unions had strongly increased. On the other hand, as the example of the machinists demonstrates, not every centralization could be welcomed from the point of view of industrial reorganization. That the number of trade-union newspapers or magazines did not diminish in the years 1923–1927 is comprehensible under the circumstances. In fact, this indicator of the degree of centralization showed an increase of two in the years immediately after 1923.

The poor success in the field of reorganization again induced several trade unions to enter more or less loose agreements for the purpose of coöperation. Five such "cartels" came into existence in this period; their importance was minor. As in the preceding in-

[41] Gewerkschaftskongress, 1923, *Protokoll,* pp. 184–185, 188–189, 337–343. It is worth noting that the large mercantile and transportation workers' union dissented and refused to vote for the resolution on shop organization because it accorded special treatment to salaried employees. They chose the mild form of abstention to manifest their disagreement.

[42] Gewerkschaftskommission, *Bericht,* 1928, p. 108. The amalgamation took place in 1926.

[43] Gewerkschaftskongress, 1928, *Protokoll,* pp. 420–421.

terval between congresses, the number of jurisdictional disputes was deplorably high. The first pages of this sad chapter were again filled by the *Technische Union.* Its conflicts with several trade unions reached such an intensity that the *Kommission* found itself unable to deal with them. Significantly enough the supreme authority of the executive committee of the party had to be invoked twice; it aided in finding a compromise solution. Another dispute between the union of civil servants and that of city employees likewise provoked much excitement and was only partly settled despite the cartel agreement finally effected by the two organizations. Apart from these "great wars" a number of small conflicts were breaking out and keeping the central organ busy throughout the period. "It is in the long run impossible," complained Hueber, "that the *Kommission* has to spend a great deal of its time on boundary disputes."[44] Yet there was only one way to stop the conflicts and to achieve reorganization on an industrial basis: to make clean-cut authoritative delimitations between the unions by unambiguous order from above. Since the industrial principle had been approved time and again by overwhelming majorities or unanimous votes in individual unions or in the congresses, such action could have been defended against any charge of authoritarianism. But since it was generally and clearly understood that the resolutions of the congress of 1923 had not brought the practical solution of the problem any closer,[45] it seemed that an increase of the power of the central organs of the movement was indispensable. And in this respect the congress of 1928 accomplished a great deal.

The new organization created in 1928 abolished the old and never formally legalized *Kommission* and replaced it by a federal executive committee. This body was the supreme administrative organ of the likewise new Federation of Free Trade Unions of Austria. The functions and powers of the executive committee were generally more comprehensive and stronger than those of its predecessor. Every effort was made to realize the hope that its members would consider themselves to be and would act as representatives of the federation as a whole rather than as members and representatives of the particular interests of their original unions. An entire

[44] *Arbeit und Wirtschaft,* vol. 6 (June 15, 1928), 539.

[45] Cf. Johann Schorsch, "Der zehnte ordentliche Gewerkschaftskongress," *Arbeit und Wirtschaft,* vol. 6 (May 1, 1928), 370.

system of subordinate organs was created and the dependence of the new state executive groups upon the federal executive committee clearly established. The finances of the federation were put on a solid basis by the institution of a regular contribution per member from all affiliated branch organizations.[46]

Less gratifying from the labor point of view were the debates in the 1928 congress on the problem of industrial unions. In many respects they were but a repetition of old arguments and a rechewing of old problems. Once again mutual charges of procrastination and obstruction were brought forward. Endless disputes over technological questions of production were cited at the congress, for example, that between the textile and chemical unions concerning waterproof materials. The former claimed that since modern methods of fabrication did not involve chemical processes, the workers in question rightly belonged to it.[47] With great vigor numerous speakers scourged the conservative tendencies of the unions and the personally selfish attitudes of many of the leaders of small organizations.[48]

The importance of the last-named source of resistance should not be underrated. That people who for two or three decades had been chiefs of independent trade unions were unwilling to acquiesce in their own relegation to subordinate positions is psychologically understandable. It is all the more so for anyone who has learned to appraise correctly the extent to which oligarchic tendencies unavoidably arise even within the framework of the most democratic institutions. Only the determination to sacrifice such interests could open the road to reform. But this determination apparently was lacking. After a long speech exposing the inadequacy of the previous policy the representative of the *Kommission* said: "There is no sense in applying compulsion." And he added, "It would be inexpedient to set definite time limits for reorganization."[49] He had to bear silently the criticism of a delegate who expressed the simple truth that no reorganization ever would be possible so long as this task

[46] Gewerkschaftskongress, 1928, *Protokoll,* pp. 242–250.

[47] *Ibid.,* p. 357.

[48] *Ibid.,* pp. 353, 354, 357, 359, 360, 367, 368. The amount of almost incredible obstinacy a small union could develop in opposition to the reform is most clearly revealed by the shoemakers. Heinrich Moller, *Geschichte der Schuhmacher Oesterreichs, 1871–1931* (Wien, 1931), pp. 482–490.

[49] Gewerkschaftskongress, 1928, *Protokoll,* p. 340.

was coupled with the wish to save all the vested interests of the existing arrangements.[50] This defense of vested interests and an appreciable amount of the stolid bureaucracy that characterized large sections of German and of American trade unionism in the late 1920's was frankly admitted to me by several Austrian leaders, particularly by one who had had at that time the advantage of three years' residence in the United States. In 1928 the most trenchant criticism was offered by Domes, who in his capacity as a prominent member of the *Kommission* was largely and personally responsible for the doldrums into which the reform plans had fallen. ". . . for thirty-five years we have been arguing about the industrial groups, but so far no one has explained in a concrete way what an industrial union looks like, out of what elements it should be put together."[51] And this was essentially true. After a decade of effort the republican Austrian trade-union movement presented a confused picture. Most of the unions were still organized on the craft principle; some others were built upon the principle of identical material used in production; in others again, the product was the principle of differentiation; in unions of civil servants, identity of employer was the basic principle.

In 1928, for the first time, the *Kommission* submitted to the congress a plan in which not only the names of industrial unions, but also the branches to be embraced by the individual industrial groups were listed. This was progress, although such a plan should have been elaborated in the early stages of discussion, not after ten years. After several amendments had been proposed the congress was unable to agree; consequently, it referred the plan to the federal executive committee with power to start new negotiations with the national unions and to effectuate the scheme. The only limitation was that the original idea of differentiating between private and public employers should be avoided. To this extent at least the project approached a greater degree of consistency. At the same time it remained clear that at best the reorganization would require further years of assiduous work. The congress, it is true, empowered the executive to carry out amalgamations of small unions within one year; on the other hand, it recommended for unions not yet ripe for

[50] *Ibid.*, p. 347.
[51] *Ibid.*, p. 384.

the industrial form the method of "industrial cartels."[52] It almost seemed as though, despite all plans and intentions, the resolution of referral was the winding sheet of the idea of industrial unionism in Austria.

In the following years, it must be admitted, several amalgamations were effected. Three groups united in the leather industry workers; the miners joined the metalworkers. These two fusions were clearly of importance and remained among the few triumphs of the reformers. The furworkers joined the tailors, the glassworkers became a part of the union in the chemical industry. When the congress of 1931 met in September the number of free unions had been brought down to 45 (by the end of the year to 44 because of the action of the furworkers) of which 7 were local organizations. The report to the congress of the federal executive committee contained a scant nine lines on its efforts to further the development of industrial unionism. In explanation it referred to the multiplicity of its tasks. Delegate Härting of the salaried employees in industry commented tartly that it was high time for action—"at the various trade-union congresses we have adopted enough resolutions"—and recommended some initiative and serious activity on the part of the executive. But, in the words of the official yearbook of the unions, 1932 brought only "discussions and negotiations."[53] Thus the attempts at reorganization bogged down. The destruction of the independent trade-union movement by the Clerical Fascists in 1934 came long before the erection of the new structure had approached the stage of completion.

This lengthy discussion of the problems of reorganization is necessary, and not only because of the major role it played in the history of the trade-union movement. Particularly after 1923, when the primate of the party was established, the trade-union wing, as modern psychology would style it, almost "fled" into reorganization. In addition, the meager results of the protracted attempts seem significant for an understanding of the spirit and of the destiny of the whole working-class movement. Always and under all circumstances that movement was apprehensive of dangers which might destroy its unity. Therefore it had developed a theory in which its whole

[52] *Ibid.*, pp. 475–479.

[53] *Idem*, 1931, *Protokoll*, pp. 56, 113; Gewerkschaftsbund, *Jahrbuch*, 1931, p. 205; *ibid.*, 1932, p. 96.

history after Hainfeld appeared as one unbroken chain. Therefore it had adopted the specific policy of radical phrase coupled with reformist action. Therefore it had developed a technique of compromise solutions in which it reached a genuine mastery. And these elements were instrumental in frustrating to a large extent the progress of Austrian unions to a new and better form of organization.

To be sure, compromise and democracy are not only connected; compromise is an essential element in democracy. The role of a minority in a democracy consists largely in influencing, under certain circumstances coercing, the majority into a solution acceptable or at least less inacceptable to the community or the organization as a whole. This lesson of democracy the Austrian movement had learned thoroughly; indeed, it may be argued, too thoroughly. For there are situations where an obstinate minority may prevent the whole organization from taking a necessary course of action, thus frustrating the will of the majority and jeopardizing the progress or even the existence of the organization itself. In such cases the majority must find the force to impose its will upon the minority. But the danger of a split? Within certain limits this danger was real in the trade-union movement, and probably much more real than it ever was in the Social Democratic party. The party organization was naturally much more homogeneous than that of the unions under the *Kommission* or the federation. Under both arrangements there remained a multiplicity of once independent and still more or less autonomous organizations. Moreover, a midget party is usually doomed to insignificance. A small trade union, if absolutely independent, may be at a comparative disadvantage; but under favorable conditions may nevertheless be able to do a substantial amount of successful work for its members. To force industrial unionism upon the whole movement, which implied the dissolution or transformation of organizations with a long history of their own, might have engendered a split even in Austria where unity had become a creed. Was the reorganization worth the split? Whatever the correct answer, it is clear that despite their approval of it in numerous votes the Austrian unions recoiled from going the whole way in putting it into practice. Even after due allowance is made for the danger that some unions might have chosen to follow their own path, it also seems clear that the democracy of the Austrian trade unions was pushed to a point where democracy itself was jeopardized by their inability to act.[54] This situation plus the dangers resulting from oligarchic leadership, which had almost caused a split on the reorganization question, are two facts important for the later discussion of the reasons for the defeat of the Austrian working-class movement in 1934.

Although, as stated before, this chapter is not primarily concerned with the general problems of unionism, it is appropriate to indicate the attitude of the "free" organizations toward some of them and thus to bring out more clearly the specific characteristics of the dominant element in the Austrian trade-union movement.

The Closed Union Shop

A primary objective of trade unionism is the replacement of contracts between individual workers and employers by collective-bargaining agreements. The strength of a union, as well as of the trade-union movement of a country, can be measured in considerable degree by the number of collective-bargaining agreements entered into and the number of employees covered by them. Admittedly, the statistical data on these matters in Austria are not satisfactory. However, a comprehensive survey was made in 1927 by the Federal Bureau of Statistics. It revealed the existence of 2,737 agreements, covering 147,596 enterprises with 1,007,723 employees. The agreements generally covered whole occupational groups within smaller or larger geographical areas and only infrequently individual plants. The individuals protected by the agreements equaled approximately 80 per cent of the manual and white-collar workers in private industry in 1927,[55] but were a little

[54] As the reader recognizes, this argument, at least superficially, edges uncomfortably close to those employed by a Führer or a Duce in attempting to discredit the whole institution of parliamentary democracy. The basic distinction between the arguments, however, may be expressed in the old formula that a sufficient difference of degree becomes a difference of kind. Otherwise stated, the purpose of the strong executive argued for in the text is to put into effect *decisions that have been reached in a democratic fashion;* the purpose of a "leader" is to dictate decisions, with or without the approval of a rubber-stamp "legislature." On examination, the charge by Fascists of all colors that democratic parliaments are unable to reach decisions almost always resolves itself into the fact that they do not reach decisions agreeable to those Fascists.

[55] *SHfRO.*, vol. 10, pp. 143, 159. Because there had been no census of the gainfully employed since 1923, the comparison is between the persons covered by collective agreements and those covered by sickness insurance. The latter group, as has been noted, was almost synonymous with the gainfully employed. See also Gewerkschaftsbund, *Jahrbuch*, 1928, pp. 65–67.

less than the aggregate number of trade unionists. As is probably taken for granted, some union members worked in shops where there were no agreements and some nonmembers were covered because of the Collective Agreements Act of 1919 (see above, p. 219); nevertheless, the data are an impressive indication of the extent to which Austrian labor, through its unions as helped by its political party, was able to secure joint determination of wages and working conditions.

Along with other European groups the Austrians placed much less emphasis on the "closed shop" than the American movement did.[56] This issue came to the fore chiefly in the time of growing reaction when it was declared by the enemies of labor to be the main weapon of the "red terror." The foregoing statements have not been intended to deny that the Austrian free trade unions, like organized labor in other countries, wanted job control and were anxious to draw all workers of a plant into their organizations. As far as could be ascertained, however, this goal was accomplished more by other pressures of the traditional sorts upon unorganized workers or workers belonging to one of the Catholic or Pan-German unions than by means of formal closed-union-shop agreements. Not that such contracts did not exist; for instance, as early as 1908 it was reported that a brewery in Lower Austria had entered into an agreement by which it bound itself to hire machinists, coopers, and various classifications of skilled brewery workers only from the union.[57] Other contracts provided that no unorganized worker should be employed (as against the obligation to employ only workers from a specific union), and in still other instances the employer had to hire his personnel from a specifically designated, often union-influenced, employment office.[58]

By and large, however, the unions were satisfied if they were recognized as bargaining agents for their members. At least during the earlier years of the twentieth century this goal was achieved because, practically speaking, the unions were the only source for obtaining skilled workers.[59] In later years, and particularly after the First

[56] William M. Leiserson, "Closed Shop and Open Shop," *Encyclopaedia of the Social Sciences*, vol. 3, pp. 568–570.

[57] Deutsch, *op. cit.*, Vol. I, 446.

[58] Max Lederer, *Grundriss des österreichischen Sozialrechtes* (Wien, 1932), p. 234.

[59] Deutsch, *op. cit.*, p. 445, citing a report of the ministry of trade in 1909.

World War, the fact that the great majority of workers was organized made it more or less imperative to negotiate with the recognized representatives of the union and most of the employers accepted this fact. Nevertheless, the free trade unions probably would have pressed more energetically for written agreements establishing their exclusive right to furnish workers from the ranks of their members had not the legality of such contracts been questionable.[60] These doubts were demonstrated to be soundly based in 1927 when the Supreme Court (*Oberster Gerichtshof*) declared as "contrary to good morals" and unenforceable an agreement providing that a motion-picture machine operator might be hired only from the placement office of the union of stage and cinema personnel. The Court held that such an arrangement "results in a monopoly of a private association with sliding *numerus clausus* and in the exclusion of the competition of equally qualified applicants for work."[61] As pointed out in the discussion of this decision in the trade-union journal just cited, the Supreme Court had practically outlawed the same or similar provisions in other collective-bargaining agreements. In the absence of an instance for further appeal the next step to clarify the situation had to come from the legislature. This step was the enactment of the "antiterror" law on April 5, 1930; it will be discussed at some length in Chapter XXI. Here it suffices to say that the majority of the parliament, against the vehement opposition of the Social Democrats, voted to outlaw all types of closed-union-shop agreements, as well as agreements excluding from employment persons not belonging to a union or belonging to a particular union or to a voluntary association. In addition, the new law strengthened the provisions of the criminal code and the law of April 7, 1870 (*Koalitionsgesetz*), against coercing workers to join or to quit an organization.[62]

As pointed out above, one of the reasons for the rareness of written closed-union-shop agreements in Austria was their questionable legality. Other contributing factors were the close relation between the free trade unions and the Social Democratic party and the strong class consciousness of the workers. These factors not only made unions hesitant to enter into too close a relationship with employers

[60] Lederer, *op. cit.*, p. 234.
[61] On May 10, 1927; cited in *Arbeit und Wirtschaft*, vol. 5 (Aug. 1, 1927), 645.
[62] Lederer, *op. cit.*, p. 234.

or their organizations, but also made workers more susceptible to the appeal to join a union. Thus it was possible to enlist in the unions the great majority of employees in manufacturing industries without the aid of a closed-union-shop clause in the collective-bargaining agreement. The same goal was achieved in the small shops by the obligation of every journeyman to belong to the journeyman section of his guild, an organization which was generally dominated by the free trade unions. Finally, it must not be overlooked that many working conditions which, at least until recently, had to be established in the United States almost entirely by collective-bargaining and union contracts were fixed in Austria by legal enactment. All these circumstances go far to explain why the closed-union-shop issue was so much less stressed in Austria than in this country. The observation that "The degree of insistence by unions on the closed union shop policy thus varies with their ability to make gains secure by other means"[63] is unquestionably supported by Austrian experience.

Unions and Party

The connection between the political labor party and the trade unions of a country is seldom entirely free from precarious aspects. What have been traditionally regarded as trade-union functions proper further an attitude of acceptance of or "reconciliation" with the given economic arrangements and seldom point beyond them. This tendency seems to many writers "natural" with respect to the unions, although the records of some of the so-called reformist labor parties reveal the same process. Depending frequently upon the political attitude and temperament of the writer, the process, or drift, is characterized as return to reality, *embourgeoisement,* or sheer treason to the emancipation ideals of workingmen. The broader basis of political labor parties, their traditional ideologies, the phraseology to which they become accustomed, and the wider character of the political struggle are likely to dissimulate this transformation. But just this dissimulation tempts some writers to construe an essential difference between the trade union and the political labor movements.

An outstanding example of the tendency just mentioned is pro-

[63] Leiserson, *loc. cit.,* p. 570.

vided by the publications, prior to the late 'thirties, of Professor Selig Perlman of the University of Wisconsin. According to the most elaborate of them,[64] trade unionism represents the "native," or "home grown" ideology of the workers as a "manual scarcity group." The trade union, Perlman argues, deals with the individual laborer and his real interests, whereas the "labor" of the political party is a mere philosophical abstraction invented *ad hoc* by a person essentially foreign to the true labor movement. This individual is Perlman's much despised "intellectual," defined as "the educated non-manualist, who has established a contact with the labor movement, either indirectly, through influence acquired over trade union bodies, or else as a leader of labor in his own right, as Lassalle was in Germany and as the leading Communists are in Russia today" [1928]. Perlman classifies intellectuals in three groups, "revolutionary," "ethical," and "efficiency"; but for all of them "labor" is an "abstract mass in the grip of an abstract force"—an instrument for the achievement of their plans.[65] Numerous passages in his castigation of them call to mind the whimsical adage of the nineteenth century which ascribed the perturbing events of the French Revolution to the disruptive influence of the "intellectuals" of the pre-revolutionary epoch: *"C'est la faute à Voltaire, c'est la faute à Rousseau."* Curiously enough, in the light of his strictures on the intellectuals and their abstract nonsense, Perlman comes to deplore the lack in American labor of "class consciousness"—the very incarnation of intellectual abstractness.[66]

The difference between the trade union and the political labor movements that Perlman reported in 1928 rested upon his interpretation of the history of labor in Russia, Germany, England, and the United States. But it must be emphasized that he came out with a theory of *the* labor movement applicable in all essential respects to the developments in *all* industrialized countries. Precisely because his interpretation has been so widely accepted in the United States

[64] *A Theory of the Labor Movement* (New York, 1928).

[65] *Ibid.*, pp. 280, 282–283, x, 6, *passim.*

[66] In his contribution to H. A. Marquand, *Organized Labour in Four Continents* (London, New York, Toronto, 1939), p. 387. Even in his *Theory* Perlman gives credit to the German intellectual for leaving "upon the labor movement an indelible imprint of idealism and of an unquestioned class solidarity . . . a solidarity which has survived, *to the great advantage of the movement. . . .*" On the other hand, "American labor, which has never come under his [the intellectual's] influence, largely remains even today in the stage of *mere* craft consciousness" (p. 300). Italics mine.

and used as a measuring rod by which to determine whether or not specific developments reflect the mentality of manualists or intellectuals, it is indispensable to examine the validity of his interpretation as applied to Austria. This examination, because of his geographical coverage, his conviction that he has discovered a theory of *the* labor movement, and his reliance on examples from the four countries named, particularly from the United States, necessitates the inclusion here of matter which would otherwise be inappropriate.

Obviously the interpretation by Perlman of German labor history is the most immediately pertinent to this story. In essence his version is that that history was one of conflict between the intellectuals and the Social Democratic party on one side and the manualists and trade unions on the other. By this he does not intend to deny, of course, that the mass of the membership in both groups was made up of the same individuals, nor that prominent trade-union officials were real leaders in the party. As a part of the evidence for his conclusion Perlman lays emphasis on the battle of resolutions between the congresses of the unions and the party in 1905. Because of the inclination among party left-wingers to resort to the general strike and the political mass strike for certain purposes the trade-union meeting adopted the following resolution:

> The congress emphatically rejects all attempts definitely to determine the tactics of labor by means of propaganda for the political mass strike; all organized workers are hereby put under the obligation to combat it with all their power. The congress further refuses even to discuss the general strike as advocated by anarchists and by individuals without any understanding of the economic struggle; the workers are strictly warned against permitting such ideas to divert them from their every day work of strengthening their organizations.

Perlman states that the shot at economic illiterates in the resolution was directed against "the intellectuals in the Party leadership." Be that as it may the party assembly replied with an equally blunt resolution:

> The convention declares that in the case of an attack upon the universal, equal, direct and secret suffrage or upon the right of combination, it becomes the bounden duty of the entire laboring class to defend itself with every available means. The convention declares a most comprehen-

sive use of the strike *en masse* as one of the most effective weapons for the repulsion of such a criminal encroachment on the rights of labor, as well as for conquering additional basic rights.[67]

Generally speaking, Perlman's account of the battle of the resolutions is supported by that of Paul Fröhlich, a warm admirer of Rosa Luxemburg and her left-wing position. Fröhlich brings out, however, as Perlman does not, the fact that a number of revisionist and reformist politicians such as Bernstein, Stampfer, and Eisner likewise advocated the use of the general strike against attacks on the franchise, or even in order to extend the general franchise to the German states and thus consolidate German parliamentarism. Fröhlich also indicates more clearly the idea that the trade-union convention was dominated by the suspicion that the radicals within the party would utilize a general strike to stage a movement similar to that which at the time was shaking the Russian empire. These radicals scornfully derided the idea of a "general strike pledged to remain within legal limits" as a "military demonstration with unloaded guns."[68]

In passing it may be noted that an attempt was made in England in 1918 to create a separate trade-union party in order to protect the unions and their aims from the alleged influence of radical intellectuals on the Labour party. The proposal was rejected by an overwhelming majority. Perhaps it does not go too far to epitomize the attitude of that majority in the statement of a London printer: "I would no more sneer at a man because he is a doctor than I would sneer at a man because he is a docker."[69]

Shortly after the exchange of resolutions in Germany negotiations seeking to effect a compromise began. They culminated in the Mannheim Agreement of 1906. Under it party and trade unions agreed to coöperate on all common questions of importance. In Perlman's judgment: "Thus the trade union movement won equal rights at last, and the 'superior' intellectual radical had to capitulate before the embattled trade unionist."[70] His entire discussion shows unmistakably that in 1928 he believed the capitulation to be one of

[67] Cf. Perlman, *op. cit.*, pp. 96–98. The texts of the resolutions are quoted from *ibid.*
[68] Paul Fröhlich, *Rosa Luxemburg* (London, 1940), pp. 152 ff.
[69] Trades Union Congress, *Fiftieth Annual Report* (London, 1918), pp. 251 ff. esp. p. 254.
[70] *Op. cit.*, p. 100. Cf. also p. 303.

the happiest events in the history of German labor. In the opinion of other observers his emphasis is misplaced and his conclusion erroneous because he fails to evaluate properly the defeats of the revisionists by the radicals (in this case synonymous with the orthodox group), particularly at the party congress of 1903. Professor Sturmthal, for example, writes: "This was perhaps the most fateful event of pre-World War socialism. Out of the Reformist defeat emerged the pressure-group mentality of European labor . . . no serious activity for political objectives was possible. The main attention of the labor movement was focused upon trade-union problems, to the neglect of basic political and even economic issues."[71]

Perlman's elaboration of his classification of intellectuals into "revolutionary," "ethical," and "efficiency" has no niche for the German revisionists. The truth is they fit very poorly, if at all, into his categories; at any rate, they are dismissed with the almost contemptuous observation that "it was not the 'revisionist' intellectual but the trade unionist . . . who delivered a critical blow to the leadership of the labor movement by the revolutionary intellectual."[72]

As already suggested, the struggle within German labor which held the center of the stage after the failure of Bismarck's anti-Socialist law was not one between the "home grown" ideology of the "manualists" and the "revolutionary" ideology of the "intellectuals," but rather that between orthodoxy and revisionism. As is generally known, the writings of Bernstein were one of the chief expressions of revisionist thinking and became more or less the "Bible" for revisionists. Although the orthodox group was victorious at the party congresses of 1899 and 1903, those victories were actually only temporary; it was becoming more and more evident that the gap between the revolutionary formulae and the practical needs of the political labor group was widening. The need for closing this gap found formal recognition in the reversal of the party's attitude toward state social insurance and in the instructions concerning the introduction of bills given to members of the Reichstag at the party congress of 1906. Then the war, the Russian Revolution, the split of the Social Democrats into Majority and Independent wings, and the rise of the Communists again widened the gap.

---

[71] Adolf Sturmthal, *The Tragedy of European Labor, 1918–1939* (New York, 1943), p. 18.

[72] Perlman, *op. cit.*, Chap. VIII, esp. p. 303.

With reference to the role of the trade unions in these developments it must be said, contrary to Perlman's interpretation, that most of the men and women who formed the vanguard of German organized labor were party members first and union members second. If any German trade-union leader had attempted to divorce the free union movement from the Social Democratic party—for instance by forming a separate labor union group in the Reichstag—he would have been swept out of office by the indignation of his own followers. All authors, both German and foreign, who fail to realize this basic fact, overestimate the significance of such controversies as that of 1905 over the question of the political mass strike. It was the character of the issue, not the threat of separation, that caused the advocates of the mass strike in the party to yield to the opinion of the union leaders. If a strike had been called, the task of carrying out the party strategy would have fallen upon the unions, and since the union leaders did not believe in the plan, they could not have led the proletarian army to victory. Moreover, many party leaders were themselves skeptical about the mass strike and probably glad to justify their own abandonment of the plan with the disinclination of the union leaders to share the responsibility.

Although the free trade unions could never have cut the ties between themselves and the Social Democratic party, and never wished to do so, it is probable that few of the top union leaders were entirely satisfied with the kind of party-union relationship that historical conditions had produced in the Reich. The staffs of the unions and of the party formed two rival bureaucracies—the term is not to be understood here in any deprecatory sense—and it was only human that the unionists sometimes wished to play a greater part than that of second fiddle in determining the legislative policies of German labor. Undoubtedly, many of them looked with envy upon England where the Trades Union Congress, as the parent body, possessed at least the theoretical right to control the party. On some occasions German unionists expressed their resentment over the predominance of the party so sharply that a threat of separation might be read into their statements, but in view of the basic conditions such bitter words should not be taken at face value.

Although most of the trade-union leaders were revisionists before 1914, they were of the Bernstein-Frank type rather than of the

Hildebrand-Quessel faction. They believed in gradualism and in the national state, but not in the kind of nationalism which the party rejected by expelling Hildebrand in 1912, and which was frequently expressed in the *Sozialistische Monatshefte*. Moreover, some prominent unionists stood on the radical side, for instance Joseph Simon, president of the shoemakers' union and leader of the radical minority in the otherwise revisionist Bavarian party organization. After 1918, the majority of the union leaders took even more decidedly a center position because it gave them a better chance to mediate in conflicts of political sentiment among the members. Unity of the trade-union movement was the primary aim of most union leaders. On one vitally important occasion the vote of the union leaders in the councils of the party brought the decision for a turn to the left; the rejection of the compromise on unemployment insurance in the spring of 1930 was due to the insistence of the trade unions. As a consequence the Social Democratic Chancellor Müller had to resign and the Socialists went into opposition against his successor Brüning.

Some attitudes and trends in the German labor movement must be explained by reference to the specific state of political democracy in the Weimar Republic. On the one hand, a superficial stabilization aided in creating the delusion that democracy had been secured forever. On the other, the permanent division of the working class into Socialist and Communist camps kept alive among some trade-union leaders that desire to avoid the political struggle of which there were evidences at the time of the orthodox-revisionist conflict; among other leaders it led to an attitude of attempting to mediate between the parties of the left. To repeat, however, it is completely erroneous to present, as valid for all industrialized countries and at all times, the desire to avoid the political struggle as the true expression of "trade union mentality." To oppose Socialism and violent revolution as the way to it is one thing. There the unions may find themselves in absolute conformity with a middle-class reformist political party that intends to work within the limits of a system of private capitalism. To favor Socialism but oppose violent revolution is another thing. This was the position of the German trade unions. And they expected to attain Socialism through the workers' party; that is, after that party had secured a majority in the Reichstag. Thus it is only by emphasizing a distinction between trade unions and radical parties, say the German Social Democracy in the early 'nineties or the Communist party in the 'twenties, that an artificial difference in nature between them and a labor party in general can be maintained. Again it is necessary to point out that the revisionist Social Democratic party in Germany scarcely fits into Perlman's theory and to add that the same is true of the British Labour party. Indeed, his lengthy defense of his interpretation of British developments,[73] conflicting as it does with most other interpretations, can be viewed as a more or less unconscious admission of the incongruity.

As I hope I have demonstrated, it is necessary to treat the problem of relations between trade unions and a labor political party not in the blue air of general considerations but as a function of the special historical situation obtaining at a given time. And in some passages in various publications Perlman has done this. Like other writers he carefully points out the relation to the problem of the multiplicity of political units in the federal system of the United States, of the character of its constitution, and of the power of its Supreme Court to declare laws unconstitutional. In 1928 he was convinced that these factors made it especially arduous for a political labor party to attain any lasting success. But it would seem that the degree of democratization achieved in a country is equally if not more important. Whatever their aims trade unions may thrive and prosper only in a truly democratic state. If democracy has such strong traditional foundations in a country that recourse to undemocratic ways of solving political, social, and economic problems seems excluded, it may be argued that the working class is justified in abstaining from the creation of a political party and limiting itself to the furtherance of unions, coöperatives, and perhaps other organizations which would pay relatively little attention to political activities. But in immature democracies such as Germany and Austria, permanently threatened by forces of reaction, where preservation of liberty is attendant upon continual vigilance, the situation is different. In such cases lack of the most direct participation in political life on the part of trade unions is contrary to their elemental interests and may aid materially in their final destruction. ". . . whatever hardships or even crises the future may be holding in store for

[73] *Ibid.*, Chap. IV.

the German labor movement—its experience, both in the past and in recent years, has amply prepared it to cope with them."[74] These words of Perlman's printed in 1928 are remarkable not simply because they turned out to be bad prophecy. They are significant because they reflect a belief in the security and permanence of German democracy—a suicidal belief which contributed to the coming annihilation.

More broadly speaking, the truth seems to be that Perlman's researches into American labor history led him to present in 1928 a "theory" of a "natural" or a "normal" development of working-class movements that is strongly reminiscent of similar concepts in economic theory in general. As already suggested, most divergencies from this ideal pattern were treated as "exceptions" or laid to the discredit of pernicious "intellectuals." In other words, it appears that unless a labor movement in a given country would fit fairly precisely into the American mold as Perlman found it shaped by Gompers and associates it was not "organic" or "home grown." Not the least startling of the results of this method of analysis is Perlman's categorical statement that for American labor "to make socialism or communism the official 'ism' of the movement, would mean . . . deliberately driving the Catholics, who are perhaps in the majority in the American Federation of Labor, out of the labor movement, since with them an irreconcilable opposition to socialism is a matter of religious principle."[75] There is no evidence I know of that would indicate that American Catholic workingmen are more devout and hence more likely to observe this religious principle than their Austrian brothers; in fact, the traditions of Austria might suggest the opposite. But as shown above the Socialist unions in republican Austria comprised from 75 to 85 per cent of the total organized workers despite the fact that the population was always 90 or more per cent Roman Catholic. And these same workers made up the overwhelming majority of the Socialist party that polled around 40 per cent of the votes for parliament and 60 per cent and better for the city council of Vienna.

At the outset of this section it was noted that Perlman's *Theory* had been selected as the "outstanding example" of numerous at-

[74] *Ibid.*, p. 122.
[75] *Ibid.*, pp. 168–169.

tempts to construe an essential difference between the trade union and the political labor movements. These attempts almost invariably draw the moral that wise labor leaders will seek to prevent the rank and file from going into independent political action, particularly if it is contaminated by any variety of Socialism. Stated otherwise, and despite the title of his 1928 volume, Perlman held at that time that experience had demonstrated that the "labor movement" *ought to be* almost completely restricted to a "trade union movement." Not only political parties but coöperatives were condemned. As was also indicated above, however, his conclusions underwent some change in the next decade. This change resulted from the "veritable revolution" in the political system of the United States in the spring of 1937 when the Supreme Court upheld the Wagner Act and thus "endowed the national government with a far-reaching jurisdiction over industrial relations. . . . Henceforth, disregarding the possibility of a reversion to type, political action ceased to be a blind alley for labour. . . ." And in other passages he writes that *"the political weapon has become the unions' paramount weapon"* so that, "by a curious reversal, the existing disruption in labour's economic organization [the A.F. of L.-C.I.O. war] threatens catastrophe to its political influence, after which, although it would be a manifest exaggeration to claim that 'all would be lost,' yet an opportunity, perhaps unequalled in all American labour's history, might thereby be irrevocably missed."[76]

Whether or no others agree that the Supreme Court staged a "revolution" in 1937 is immaterial. What is important is the fact that in his *Theory* and other early writings Perlman fails to give proper weight to similar specific circumstances. For example, though he explains the failure of American labor to develop a political organization partly on the ground that workers received the franchise so relatively early in our history, he reveals no appreciation of the fact that the struggle for that right may be, indeed, almost surely is, more important for the rise of labor parties in Central Europe than the teachings of "intellectuals."[77] Nor is there any indication in any of his publications that American labor might have performed a real service to the country by fighting for a political

[76] Perlman in Marquand, *op. cit.*, pp. 326, 399. Italics mine.

[77] Probably the most illuminating illustration of Perlman's failure to make the connection suggested in the text appears in *A Theory of the Labor Movement*, p. 291, n. 1.

division that would put most of the reactionaries and honest conservatives in one camp, most of the liberals and radicals in another, and thus hasten the elimination of that hypocritical situation which has prevailed for most of the past fifty years under which the differences between the major parties have rarely, if ever, exceeded the differences within each of them. On the contrary, he wrote in 1945 that "So far nothing has happened [in the United States] to upset the conviction that pressure politics and control of a major party through infiltration are the real vehicles rather than a political party in competition with the old parties."[78] Many European labor groups may rightly claim for themselves, particularly after about 1900, that they did fight to perform precisely the service suggested above. As will be shown in subsequent chapters, such elements in the work of the Austrian Socialists as tenants protection, housing, and the agricultural program were parts of this fight. And most commentators seem agreed that the elections of 1945 prove that British labor has gone far toward winning it—after abandoning "pressure politics" and "infiltration" of, or collaboration with, a major party.

Other developments in the history of Austrian labor underscore its characteristic divergences from the Perlman pattern, particularly from his thesis of the conflict between the trade union and the political mentality.

In the economically backward Habsburg monarchy the labor movement had been spared the dangers of sweeping victories in the early stages of its evolution. In 1891, when Bebel, under the impression of the tremendous success of the Socialists in the Reichstag elections of the preceding year, told the German party congress that few of those present would not live to see the ultimate victory,[79] Austrian labor was still facing another fifteen years of dramatic struggle, not for the majority in parliament, but for the general franchise. And it was thirty years after Bebel's statement before the Austrian movement entered into the period of "great expectations" for an early democratic victory. By that time the children's disease of underrating the importance of trade unions had been long overcome. Paradoxical as it sounds, the belated attainment of the general

---

[78] T. C. T. McCormick (ed.), *Problems of the Postwar World* (New York and London, 1945), p. 42.

[79] *Protokoll über die Verhandlungen des Parteitages der Sozialdemokratischen Partei Deutschlands,* 1891, p. 172.

suffrage was beneficial to the unity of Austrian labor. The absence of smashing political victories prevented the rise among the party membership of any tendency to neglect the trade-union movement. On the contrary, the protracted fight for the ballot helped to create the tradition of tested alliance between the political and economic wings. It is significant that the public life of the recognized leader of the Austrian unions, Anton Hueber, began with a speech for the general franchise.[80] During almost forty years of leadership he remained a warm friend of the most thoroughgoing collaboration between party and unions. Every time he felt that a strain was developing in the relations between the two organizations, he used all the weight of his powerful and venerated personality to eliminate it. His solemn injunction to the trade-union congress of 1923 to remain faithful to Viktor Adler's legacy of a united movement is only the most frequently cited instance.[81] Most of the leaders of the Austrian unions were members of the Social Democratic party from the first days of their public activities. In fact, in many cases membership in the party preceded that in a union and this created in the earlier days of labor history the feeling that it was the Social Democrats who were preëminently active in building up the unions.[82]

In the period immediately after the revolution frictions between unions and party reached their greatest severity. The central magazine of the former reprinted in February, 1920, two articles from branch papers criticizing the political wing; it added editorially the threat that under prevailing circumstances "the trade unions will do best to go their own ways."[83] This was a most unusual step in a movement whose long tradition had been to conceal disagreements as much as possible in the privacy of closed conferences. At that time the discontent of the unions with the works-council policy of the party must have been very great indeed. Several months earlier an editorial in *Die Gewerkschaft* had clearly stated that with the successful revolutions in most of Central and Eastern Europe a year

[80] *Die Gewerkschaft,* vol. 23 (Sept. 27, 1921), 350.

[81] Gewerkschaftskongress, 1923, *Protokoll,* pp. 237–238.

[82] As one example of this general fact see the autobiographic sketch of Franz Domes, leader of the metalworkers and next to Hueber one of the most affectionately respected men in the movement, in *Denkt an gestern, Denkt an morgen . . . ! Worte der Alten an die Jungen zum 40. Geburtstag des österreichischen Metallarbeiterverbandes* (Wien, 1930), p. 35.

[83] *Die Gewerkschaft,* vol. 22 (Feb. 3, 1920), 27.

behind them the workers there should see to it that the emphasis was shifted from the political to the economic field, and that the trade unions now had a greater opportunity to think about tasks which heretofore had been deemed, erroneously, to be the exclusive domain of the political party.[84]

But despite these dissensions there was nothing even at this time which would indicate the aversion of the trade unions to political activities by the working class; quite the contrary. It must be noted that even the editorial just cited did not call for abstention from politics but for the right kind of policy; that is, such as would be agreeable to the unions. When the 1919 congress of the German trade unions declared the Mannheim Agreement nugatory, the national organ of their Austrian counterparts expressed doubts about whether this shift away from Social Democracy would prove useful to the unions.[85] Significantly, the paper also emphasized the lack of any efforts to find a common basis upon which a unanimous vote could be reached. This was not the way things were being done in Austria. Even more noteworthy is the fact that the Austrian unions not only clung to the idea of unity between the party and themselves, but also were strongly opposed to any suggestion of abandoning the theoretical ideas of Marxism which formed the traditional ideological basis of the party. When Alfred Striemer, editor of the works council magazine in Berlin, began to advocate the liberation of the union movement from the theories of surplus value and exploitation, he was violently rebuked in the Austrian trade-union press.[86]

An examination of the role of the "intellectual" in the Austrian working-class movement shows that it, likewise, can scarcely be fitted into the terms of Perlman's theory. He could, of course, find a few quotations from leaders of that movement to support his strictures. The most frequently cited is that of Engelbert Pernerstorfer in 1915. This old stalwart blasted the "little handful of academicians" who had formed a "closed clique" and arrogated to themselves the position of a supreme court with power to decide what was true Socialism. He also emphasized the charge that "this little handful is made up not simply of academicians, but exclusively of

[84] *Ibid.*, vol. 21 (Oct. 28, 1919), 241–242.

[85] *Ibid.* (July 15, 1919), 150.

[86] Jakob Brod, "Gibt es noch einen Mehrwert?" *Die Gewerkschaft,* vol. 24 (July 25, 1922), 257; also *Arbeit und Wirtschaft,* vol. 1 (Oct. 1, 1923), 742.

Jews."[87] Even more detached observers found in the attitudes of Friedrich Adler, Otto Bauer, Julius Deutsch, and Friedrich Austerlitz some of the traits for which Perlman criticizes the intellectuals in the labor movement. But, as noted earlier, all these men, Renner, and other "intellectuals" in the Socialist movement were given generous credit by their political opponents for preventing the Bolshevization of Austria in 1919. And as will be seen in subsequent chapters there were numerous other "intellectuals" such as Breitner, Danneberg, Tandler, and Glöckel whose practical work in taxation, tenants protection and housing, welfare, and education should absolve them from any charge that they conceived labor as an "abstract mass in the grip of an abstract force." Had Perlman had an opportunity to talk with the workers in the Vienna districts of Floridsdorf, Ottakring, or Favoriten, than whom he would have to search far to find equally good examples of what he calls "working people in the real," and thus to learn their appreciation of the municipal apartments, the health and recreational services, and the reformed schools of the Socialist administration—secured and maintained precisely because of the emphasis on political activity—had he learned at first hand the veneration of these workers for many of their "intellectual" leaders—and "veneration" is scarcely strong enough for Viktor Adler and Seitz—he might have found it more difficult to write so confidently of the "basic contradiction" between the mentality of "manualists" and "intellectuals." But so far as can be ascertained from his *Theory* he talked only with American workers while preparing it. Is it too much to conclude that in the course of a prolonged polemic against the abstractions and generalizations of "intellectuals" he has been guilty of a number of sweeping generalizations that involve the neglect of essential historical facts? As already indicated, however, the reader will have a broader basis for judgment after reading additional chapters in this study.

No doubt the specific political situation in Austria explains to a considerable degree the fact that the frictions between party and unions in 1919 and early 1920 were smoothed out so that the alliance, or actual unity, among them in the republic proved even better cemented than in the monarchy. In Germany, for several years re-

[87] As might be expected from the usual Jew-baiting tactics of the Christian Socials, they took great delight in quoting Pernerstorfer. See, for example, Franz Hemala, *Die Sozialdemokratie* (3d ed.; Wien, 1922), p. 86.

actionary attacks upon democracy could be couched in terms of a struggle against the radical left party. The absence of a noteworthy Communist movement in Austria rendered it unavoidable that such attacks were directed against the labor movement as a whole and most notably against the Social Democratic party. Under these circumstances the antidemocratic forces had to try to make men believe that the Austrian labor movement was bent upon dictatorial aims; or to claim that they stood for a better and truer form of democracy, that is, the corporative or "occupational estates" (*Berufsständische*) state; or both. This was a position which left much less room to these forces for clouding their essential antidemocratism. Their real aim of destroying the democratic constitution could be clearly perceived and the continuous danger for labor to lose with democracy the very ground under its feet could not fail in general to enhance the unity of the working-class movement and in particular to bring the party and the unions closer together. But apart from this general consideration which, however, as years went by, and particularly after 1927, increasingly dominated the political thinking of the labor organizations, the close coöperation between party and unions during the republican era was carried on in manifold practical ways.

Here may be recalled the previously mentioned general problems of economic policy in which the unions were deeply interested, as well as the parliamentary treatment of social and labor legislation. It was probably clear before this that conceptions generally obtaining among American trade unions in the days before the Great Depression were not accepted by their Austrian counterparts. The philosophy expressed by Gompers as "voluntarism," with its rejection of social legislation except, for example, as a protection against the competition of various types of substandard workers, had been rejected long before the republican era in Austria. On the other hand, as shown in the chapter on social legislation, the Austrian unions in later years had occasion to regret the fact that in the period of revolution they were overly reliant upon their strength and therefore approved a legal technique which coupled short general laws with detailed ordinances by the cabinet. The struggle against the "social burden," the necessity to be eternally vigilant against breaches of the law, certainly proved factors strong enough to prevent any weakening of self-reliance on the part of the trade unions, so often described as the natural consequence of social legislation. To maintain and continually to adjust the system of unemployment insurance, for one example, was vital to the trade unions in their efforts to safeguard the wage level.

But apart from these great general fields of continuous collaboration, parliamentary pressure was frequently of value to the unions in their most specific task, namely, wage conflicts. Two instances may serve as illustrations. In May, 1926, the union of agricultural workers found itself involved in a serious dispute of this character. The employers rejected proposals for a peaceful settlement; nevertheless, the union hesitated to resort to the strike weapon because the law for the protection of native labor did not apply to agriculture so that the danger of a "scab" invasion from Czechoslovakia was very real. In this situation the party refused to continue the negotiations on agricultural tariffs and thus forced a compromise solution. A second instance is provided by the strike at the *Alpine Montan Gesellschaft* in 1925. This time the party delayed the enactment of the duty on iron impatiently urged by the Austrian iron producers and thus materially aided the union of metalworkers in their negotiations.[88] Cases like those just cited certainly were instrumental in creating the feeling of mutual confidence and reliance between the political and union wings. Through them the members of the latter could convince themselves of the advantages of parliamentary activities, but their willingness to support the party in its struggle for democracy was just as much the product of general reflections as of the practical experiences of the movement. Thus the trade unions did not hesitate to support the political general strike of July, 1927; thus they threw their full weight into the "warning of 700,000"[89] when an antidemocratic reform of the constitution threatened in 1929; thus, in 1933, they for some time kept urging the party to launch the open struggle against the Dollfuss government. More about their policies will be said later. Here it seemed important only to sketch their general character and to emphasize the fact that it cannot be grasped with the help of some general theories but requires understanding of the specific historical and political situation in which they had to perform their work.

[88] *Arbeit und Wirtschaft,* vol. 4 (Aug. 15, 1926), 651.
[89] Deutsch, *op. cit.,* Vol. II, 235.

CHAPTER XII

Coöperatives

WITHIN THE "threefold unity" of the Austrian working-class movement the coöperatives[1] were the smallest and least important element. The early history of the movement reveals that the obstacles to their development were manifold. First of all they did not fit into the rigid ideology originally adopted from the teachings of Ferdinand Lassalle and Karl Marx. The iron law of wages as expressed by the former implied the uselessness of attempts to improve working-class conditions by raising the purchasing power of wages, since in the long run the only result of such attempts would be a proportional decrease in wages. Consumers' coöperatives had no place within this system. Toward the end of the last century, chiefly because of the successful development of the trade unions, Lassalle's teachings lost a great deal of their former influence upon the minds of the workers. During the same period Marx's theories gradually became the gospel of the Austrian labor movement.

For Marx the worker as consumer was of little interest. His most famous volumes were an analysis of the industrial worker's position in his capacity as producer of surplus value. In them there is at least one reference to workers' productive associations,[2] but no mention of consumers' societies despite their successful development since 1844 in the country of Marx's exile. One of the early resolutions of the First International (Congress of Geneva, 1866), which usually reflected Marx's personal opinion, warned the workers against organizing consumers' coöperatives which "only touch the surface of the present economic system."[3] Furthermore, scientific socialism, as Marx and Engels were accustomed to designate their theory, regarded the development of society as determined by general laws that inevitably lead to the collapse of capitalism. This basic concept, construed to reduce the voluntary activity of men to a relatively minor role, was likewise scarcely likely to further the coöperative

---

[1] Grateful acknowledgment is hereby made to Mr. Oliver Grover, manager of the Labor Bank of Austria throughout its entire independent history, for his help with this chapter.

[2] Karl Marx, *Das Kapital* (Moskau, 1933), III, pt. 1, pp. 481 ff.

[3] Hermann Fleissner, *Genossenschaften und Arbeiterbewegung* (Dresden, 1911), p. 9.

movement. Economic development itself was supposed to lead the capitalistic system into a deadlock. At the same time this development organized the forces of the working class, which, "when the death knell of the capitalistic society strikes" would overthrow the state, regarded as an oppressive instrument of the ruling classes. Thus the whole policy of the labor movement, as far as it was inspired by the economic and sociological theories of Marx, had to be concentrated upon overthrowing the power of the state by revolution. The first step to this revolution was to be the conquest of the franchise by the workers, which Lassalle, of course, had emphasized—perhaps even more strongly. For only within the framework of a democratic state, it was argued, would the working class be able to collect its forces and lead them into the final battle against capitalism. Thus the struggle for political power assumed a predominant position within the Austrian labor movement, and the political party became its most important organization. The trade unions, by fighting for higher wages and better working conditions, rendered most valuable services to the party's activities, efficiently organizing the proletarian army and providing it with the powerful weapon of the general strike. Consequently, as shown in Chapter II, the history of the modern working-class movement in Austria was for many years primarily the history of the struggle for suffrage. And as also brought out in that chapter, there was one more reason for the overwhelming importance of politics in Austria: the continuous struggle among the different nations living within the borders of the empire. Workers as well as other citizens became thoroughly steeped in politics, a situation which has remained the outstanding feature of Austrian labor to the present day. Apparently the general ideas prevailing within the movement left no room for an adequate development of coöperatives. If, nevertheless, a coöperative movement arose and began a promising development, the explanation must be that there was an undeniable and genuine need for protection of the interests of the worker as a consumer which proved stronger than general conceptions and theories.[4]

---

[4] The present survey is confined to the development of the workers' consumers' coöperatives. Although many producers' associations were inaugurated, they were never able to record any real achievements. In Austria as in other private capitalistic lands, except, to some extent, France, their structure proved unable to adapt to the cyclical movements of general trade or to resist the tendency to become private part-

Workers' Coöperatives in the Empire

The earliest consumers' coöperative societies in the German parts of Austria were founded toward the end of the 'fifties of the nineteenth century, but generally proved unsuccessful. The sound principles of the Rochdale Pioneers, which gave such a mighty impetus to the British movement, were then unknown in Austria. In 1861 a group of civil servants organized a consumers' society that was the predecessor of the First Viennese Consumers' Coöperative Society (*Erster Wiener Konsumverein*) and under that name lasted for many decades.[5] The first workers' group that acquired a stable status was formed on October 9, 1864, by 26 weavers in the Vienna suburb, Fünfhaus, under circumstances which had an astonishing resemblance to those of the foundation of the society in Rochdale. Exactly one year later its charter was approved by the authorities but not until 1873 did it formally assume a name: First Lower Austrian Workers' Consumers' Coöperative Society in Fünfhaus (*Erster Niederösterreichischer Arbeiter-Konsumverein zu Fünfhaus*). Meanwhile, in 1865, a Workers' Savings and Consumers' Coöperative Society had been founded, also in Fünfhaus.[6] The basic Rochdale idea, sales at market prices with a subsequent rebate in proportion to purchases, was adopted soon thereafter.[7]

---

nerships. Most of them failed after a short existence crammed with internal arguments and financial troubles.

Source material for this survey, though not so rich as that for some other sections of the study, was found in quantities reasonably adequate for the purpose. Particularly for the period prior to the formation of the republic liberal borrowings have been made from the summary accounts of Emmy Freundlich and Andreas Vukowitsch. The former devoted the greater part of her life to the coöperative movement and was generally considered to be one of the two or three outstanding Austrian figures in that movement for many years. Examples of such accounts are: E. Freundlich, *Die Genossenschaftsbewegung im Lande und der Gemeinde Wien* (Wien, 1930), pp. 71; *idem, Die Geschichte der österreichischen Genossenschaftsbewegung,* in *Oesterreich und seine Genossenschaften* (Wien, 1930), pp. 30–81; A. Vukowitsch, *Geschichte des konsumgenossenschaftlichen Grosseinkaufs in Oesterreich* (Wien, 1931), pp. 81; *idem, 30 Jahre Zentralverband österreichischer Konsumvereine* (Wien, [1932]), pp. 43 + ix; *idem, Besonderheiten und Entwicklungstendenzen der österreichischen Genossenschaftsbewegung,* in *Oesterreich und seine Genossenschaften,* pp. 82–95. These works are cited hereafter as: Freundlich, *Genossenschaftsbewegung;* Freundlich, *Geschichte;* Vukowitsch, *Geschichte;* Vukowitsch, *30 Jahre Zentralverband;* Vukowitsch, *Besonderheiten.*

[5] J. Deutsch, *Geschichte der österreichischen Gewerkschaftsbewegung,* Vol. 1 (Wien, 1929), p. 87.

[6] Subsequently the first group dropped the designation "in Fünfhaus" and the second took it over. Cf. Freundlich, *Genossenschaftsbewegung,* pp. 4–5, 21; *idem, Geschichte,* p. 31 and Vukowitsch, *30 Jahre Zentralverband,* p. 5.

[7] Freundlich, *Genossenschaftsbewegung,* p. 6.

Progress of the movement was, at least on the surface, satisfactory. In 1865 there were 52 consumers' coöperatives in all of Austria; by the end of 1872 there were 540. Part of this development was only a reflection of the feverish boom of the period, commonly referred to as the "promotion era" (*Gründerzeit*). Since many of the societies lacked a sound financial basis as a result of overinvestment, they were swept away by the collapse of trade in 1873. The value of their buildings sank rapidly and even those that survived the crash were compelled to sell a good part of their property, to close down many branches, and to restrict activities in general. Among the survivors were the First Lower Austrian and the Fünfhaus societies. Centered on them a slow but steady development began.

The public at first paid little or no attention to the coöperatives; but the tax officials, apparently suddenly discovering their existence after some years, began to make trouble. For example, in 1874, they demanded that the First Lower Austrian pay certain taxes covering the decade since its activities had begun. Only with great difficulty could installment payment of the arrears be arranged. Four years later a retroactive assessment of almost 17,500 gulden in enterprise and income taxes was made on the same society. A direct appeal to Emperor Franz Joseph brought some relief. The Fünfhaus organization had similar difficulties and likewise took its case to the emperor. It secured a reduction of about 32,000 gulden in the taxes levied on it for the years 1874 to 1880 and a statement from Franz Joseph that he was thoroughly convinced of the advantages to the workers of the coöperatives and would support them as far as it lay in his power.[8]

In this connection it may be mentioned that when the First Lower Austrian society wished to buy land and construct a building in 1870 it secured a contribution of 500 gulden from the emperor.[9] There is little reason to doubt that he and some of the high officials of the empire regarded the coöperatives as a sound remedy for anarchistic and socialistic tendencies among the workers, but this attitude did not percolate sufficiently far downward; consequently, the societies suffered from a great deal of persecution from lower-rank authorities. Although another significance of these events is fairly obvious, it should be emphasized; they show that at a time when the workers'

[8] *Ibid.*, pp. 8–9; 29.
[9] *Ibid.*, p. 7.

political movement was extremely radical, strongly republican, and in some segments even anarchistic, the workers' coöperative societies adopted a quite different attitude toward the emperor and the state.

Together with other coöperatives (agricultural, as well as middle-class credit groups), the workers' organizations belonged to the General Federation of the coöperative societies (*Allgemeiner Verband der Erwerbs- und Wirtschaftsgenossenschaften Oesterreichs*) which had been established as early as 1872.[10] The quiet development of these groups went on for several years, their membership and financial strength gradually increasing. In the beginning of the 'nineties the first faint signs of joint action by the coöperatives and the political movement can be traced. The former, although reluctantly, agreed to close their stores on May Day, 1890, at noon.[11] Such joint action was partly stimulated by the rise of the Christian Social party which rapidly developed into the strongest political unit in Vienna and the German provinces. Its membership consisted largely of small traders who strongly resented the competition of the coöperatives. In the parliament two Christian Socials even introduced a motion aiming at their complete prohibition.[12]

But the decisive incentive to the labor movement to take greater interest in these societies resulted from the outcome of the parliamentary elections of 1897. Prior to these elections, as noted earlier, a so-called general electoral body (*Allgemeine Kurie*) had been formed, in which for the first time large masses of workers were entitled to vote. Since the Christian Socials won the votes of the Vienna middle class, the elections in Vienna ended in absolute failure for the Social Democrats. The disappointment of the workers was great and their anger against the small traders and grocers whose votes rendered the victory of the Catholic party possible expressed itself in increased patronage for the coöperatives. All over the country more societies were founded and it became clear that the other parts of the labor movement would have to take a new stand toward the rising third branch.

As early as 1896 motions had been submitted by local organizations to the party congress urging it to recognize the coöperative

[10] Vukowitsch, *Geschichte*, p. 10.
[11] Freundlich, *Genossenschaftsbewegung*, p. 10.
[12] *Ibid.*, p. 12.

societies as an "important link in the chain of labor organizations."[13] The party leader, Viktor Adler, tried to carry through a noncommittal resolution slightly encouraging members to take part in the activities of such associations; but the resolution actually adopted ran: "The congress declares: the party as such has nothing in common with the foundation of consumers' and producers' coöperative societies."[14] The next year's congress held a great debate on the same issue. The charges raised against the coöperatives (selling at market prices, unwillingness to give their funds to the party) evidenced but little understanding of the true importance of the movement. Schuhmeier's resolution opposing party participation in coöperative activities carried the day by 40 votes to 34.[15] In 1899 the congress very reluctantly adopted a resolution which, although still declining any and every party responsibility for them, recognized that well-managed consumers' coöperatives "under certain circumstances might be of some use to the working class."[16] It further recognized that the interests of the organized workers often rendered it necessary for them to exercise their influence in such societies.

These resolutions demonstrate how unwillingly the party recognized the new branch of the labor movement. And this in spite of the impressive achievements of the coöperatives affiliated with the Belgian Social Democratic party; in spite of the fact that Karl Kautsky, then the outstanding and most respected theorist of continental Socialism, warmly emphasized the importance of consumers' coöperatives in a pamphlet published as early as 1897.[17]

As already brought out, however, the actual development proved stronger than paper resolutions; the impetus of the 1897 elections had been decisive. More and more coöperatives were founded and managed by members of the party. Unfortunately, many of them had little or no financial basis; by the end of 1901 the situation of a large number had become desperate.[18] A thoroughgoing reform was unavoidable. Attempts were made to induce the First Lower Austrian society to take over the Viennese groups which actually were on the edge of ruin. But that old and carefully managed organiza-

[13] *Parteitag, 1896,* p. xvi.
[14] *Ibid.,* pp. 115, 181.
[15] *Ibid., 1897,* pp. 194–208, esp. p. 207.
[16] *Ibid., 1899,* pp. 112–113, 119.
[17] *Konsumvereine und Arbeiterbewegung* (Wien, 1897).
[18] Freundlich, *Geschichte,* p. 42.

tion declined. With the assistance of the party the Consumers' Coöperative Society *Vorwärts* was created on March 24, 1902, by amalgamation of five highly unsound societies, and actually became the party's coöperative. Since further hesitation in recognizing the new branch of the labor movement was impossible, the 1903 party congress took final action on the issue. Even then, despite the commitments to the *Vorwärts,* opposition persisted. A delegate named Rousar repeated the whole list of charges which had ever been raised against the coöperatives; he alleged that if they provided foodstuffs cheaper, then "we know that where the food is cheap the wages are low" (the iron law of wages was evidently not quite forgotten); he quoted facts concerning societies which delivered goods of bad quality; he argued that payment of dividends (rebates) aroused "predatory property instincts" and declared finally: "They point to England and Belgium where the movement is said to have been successful. But I have quoted facts from Austria, where it was not. In the same way you could point to Africa, where palms are growing. But they cannot prosper on our soil."[19] The decisive section of the resolution which was finally carried ran:

> The greater strength of the political and trade-union organizations of the Austrian proletariat now renders it possible to place coöperative organization also in the service of the labor movement. The kind of coöperative organization which is possible today in all those places where the political and trade-union groups have attained a considerable degree of preparedness to strike and of efficiency (and only there) is the consumers' coöperative society. The advantages of a well-managed consumers' coöperative for the economic interests of its members are obvious. But the true importance of the consumers'-coöperative movement lies in the services it is able to perform for the working class (to increase the workers' standard of life by elimination of the middlemen, to regulate the local and then later the national prices for foodstuffs, to establish coöperative production, to fight cartels and trusts, to render material support to the political and trade-union organizations).[20]

The close connection between the political and coöperative movements thus established was to last until the destruction of the party in 1934. Very soon after the 1903 congress a new Central Federation of Austrian Coöperative Societies (*Zentralverband österreichischer*

[19] *Parteitag, 1903,* pp. 183 ff.
[20] *Ibid.,* pp. 183, 189.

Konsumvereine) was formed.[21] Such a federation had been attempted as early as 1896, but proved unsuccessful because of mismanagement. In the next year the Central Federation succeeded in enrolling those consumers' coöperative societies which had hesitated to leave the old General group of 1872. This shift was not made for political reasons, but rather because the societies rightly felt that their interests could not be safeguarded within the General Federation which embraced all kinds of coöperatives. In Germany also the consumers' groups formed their own central organization. In both cases the different interests of "buyers and sellers" were decisive.[22] The new federation proceeded efficiently toward centralization and unification of the activities of the coöperatives; furthermore it did regular auditing work as prescribed by the coöperative law amendment of 1903. In 1905 the Austrian Coöperative Wholesale Society was created and thus the foundations for the further growth of the movement were completed.[23]

The effects of the party's agreement to the incorporation of coöperatives into the working-class movement were twofold. On the one hand, a rapid increase in membership ensued. Especially the *Vorwärts* was regarded by the Vienna workers as an institution of their own—a feeling which became the true source of its strength. But, on the other hand, it cannot be denied that the existence of the *Vorwärts* for many years greatly jeopardized the very existence of the whole coöperative movement in Vienna. The *Vorwärts* had from the outset debts amounting to many hundred thousand crowns, resulting from the amalgamation of several societies standing on the edge of bankruptcy. Hence it was compelled to attempt to compensate for this original handicap by feverish activities. New branches were founded in rapid succession; investments greatly exceeded what would have been prescribed by sound business policy. In order to attract new masses of members the rate of rebate was usually much too high and not at all justified by the actual profits. The older societies, although their financial basis was much sounder, were

[21] In 1919 the name of the central organization was changed to Federation of German-Austrian Consumers' Coöperative Societies, but in 1931 was again altered to restore the formulation of 1904. Vukowitsch, *30 Jahre Zentralverband,* pp. 15–18, 27, 40.

[22] Cf. Franz Oppenheimer, "Käufer und Verkäufer, Ein Beitrag zur wirtschaftlichen Kollektivpsychologie," Vol. 24, n.s., Schmoller's *Jahrbuch fuer Gesetzgebung, Verwaltung und Volkswirtschaft,* 1900, pp. 1369 ff.

[23] Vukowitsch, *30 Jahre Zentralverband,* pp. 18–19.

likewise endangered by the policy of the *Vorwärts*. The evil of overlapping, resulting from the continuous and reckless increase of the number of branches, became worse and worse. In order to check the competition of the *Vorwärts* the older societies were compelled to adopt its tactics, so that their prices became much too low, their rebates much too high for safety. Furthermore, the rapid rise in the cost of living which swept over Central Europe in 1907 reduced the purchasing power of the workers and rendered the position of the societies still more difficult. The workers unreasonably expected the societies, still far short of a dominant position in retail trade, to be able to combat the private merchants who continuously raised prices and to offset the general tendencies. In order to meet these desires the Wholesale Society imported cheap frozen meat from Argentina, but the transaction proved a failure and involved serious losses. Meanwhile the disappointment of the party, which instead of drawing money from the *Vorwärts* was compelled to finance the coöperatives, led to the foundation of a large bread factory, *Hammerbrotwerke,* in Schwechat near Vienna. For reasons explained below it was continuously in want of money, and the large amounts of its bills of exchange taken over and endorsed by the Wholesale Society (which actually was in charge of this party undertaking) considerably weakened the financial position of the former. In spite of all endeavors it was impossible to overcome the continuous shortage of capital.

In summarizing the development of the coöperative societies before 1914 it may be said that after many years of distrust and opposition the moral and material support given the movement by the party greatly increased the membership and made the idea of coöperation popular with the workers. On the other hand, the desire for political prestige which had led to the foundation of the *Vorwärts* and the policy adopted by this society undoubtedly did much damage to the whole coöperative movement. On the eve of the war the situation had become desperate; the collapse of the whole movement was imminent; the manager of the *Vorwärts* committed suicide.[24]

War conditions soon greatly improved the financial position of the societies, but at the same time they brought about considerable

[24] Siegmund Kaff, *Politik und Geschäft* (Wien, 1926), pp. 26–27.

changes as far as coöperative principles were concerned. The Austrian bureaucracy proved utterly incapable of solving the economic problems raised by the war. Although the Austrian state had looked forward to this war for many a year, the army's supplies of foodstuffs, blankets, shoes, and so on, were inadequate and government purchasing agents were prepared to pay any price. The frightened civilian population also tried to effect as large purchases as possible. Very soon Hungary, the monarchy's most important agricultural district, stopped sending foodstuffs to Austria. The self-administered communities were helpless. Even in the first year of the war corn meal had to be used for bread production. In spite of all efforts to ensure adequate provision for the workers employed in war industries (prices were fixed and controlled by the state) the food conditions became intolerable. An embargo was laid on the available stock of flour and grain; later, the entire harvest of 1915 was confiscated. Needless to say a rationing system was introduced. Soon it covered all consumption goods except a few items such as salt and vegetables. More than that, every inhabitant of the country was compelled to cover all his needs from a designated store, operated by a private merchant or a consumers' coöperative. The stores received goods only for the customers thus bound to them. The result was a tremendous increase in membership in the societies, but a membership that was practically, though not strictly legally, "compulsory."[25] But the needs of workers in war industries were still inadequately met. The military administration decided to make more direct use of the self-help organizations of the workers. In 1916 the representative of the Austrian metal trades union, Domes, was invited to the war ministry where he received a kind of ultimatum: either the workers' organizations would undertake to supply foodstuffs to the workers in war industries in Vienna or the ministry would militarize the workers, confining them to special barracks and providing them with soldiers' rations. The latter would have meant the complete abolition of what little remained of the activities of the trade unions; therefore, Domes and Renner, who since 1911 had become the actual leader of the Austrian coöperative societies, drew up and submitted the following scheme to the government. The Wholesale Society together with the four big workers'

[25] Freundlich, *Geschichte*, p. 56.

consumers' societies in Vienna would undertake to organize the food supply for the workers in war industries, on condition that the same food rations would be supplied to the whole membership of the workers' coöperatives. The proposal was agreed to, with the understanding that for the duration of the war no further increase in membership would take place. The coöperators willingly agreed to this stipulation, since they did not want to share their privileges with people who came to the coöperatives only under the pressure of urgent wartime need.[26]

The implications of this arrangement for the coöperative societies were manifold. There had been a decisive betterment in their financial standing since the outbreak of war; the depressing shortage of capital under which they had labored for years decreased rapidly; the *Hammerbrotwerke* had obtained large orders and loans from the military administration. Now their organization of the food supply by order of the state brought many material advantages to them: further state credits, good relations with the state, and cessation of the various persecutions to which they had been subject for so many years. On the other hand, the system of closed membership and rationing meant not only that the total supplies that most members were entitled to receive were strictly prescribed, but also that their choice was restricted. Payment of rebates stopped altogether. Under the abnormal conditions of the period, this change met with no objections; people were happy enough to get food and did not quibble about rebates. But it must not be overlooked that in this fashion the whole nature of the societies was deeply affected. Of consumers' democracy as embodied in the principles of the Rochdale Pioneers there was not much left. It is even doubtful whether the societies as they existed during the war could have been spoken of as coöperatives at all considering that "the attraction of new and additional purchasers" by a consumers' coöperative society is to be regarded as of the essence of its business.[27] Nevertheless, when it was later charged that the societies had departed from the true coöperative sphere as delimited by the Rochdale Pioneers, Renner was not without justification in replying that they had had no prescription whatsoever concerning the attitude to be taken during

[26] *Idem, Genossenschaftsbewegung,* pp. 41 ff.

[27] Sidney and Beatrice Webb, *Consumers' Coöperative Movement* (London, 1921), p. 9.

the time of a world war; that practices were determined by conditions.[28] In any case, one of the wholesome consequences of the war period was that the competition and overlapping between the single societies ceased completely when hunting for new members became impossible. For the first time real collaboration among the societies began and thus the foundations for the merger which was to be effected after the war were laid.

The chief effect, however, of the First World War was that the coöperatives became the only flourishing branch of the labor movement. The Social Democratic party was built up on the principles of internationalism. It was supposed to fight against war with any and every means it had at its disposal. When it willy-nilly accepted the war policy in the summer of 1914, the groundwork was laid for a grave ideological crisis which at times even jeopardized the unity of the party. Moreover, its best men, many of its leaders, and the majority of the local representatives had to enter the armed services. As noted in Chapter II, the chief field of party activity, the parliament, was suspended for just over three years. Although the trade unions suffered less, many of their representatives had been called to the colors, the rights of their members and of all workers were drastically curtailed, and the militarization of factories made dealings and negotiations almost impossible. With the coöperatives it was quite the other way around. When the man went away his household remained and in many cases the wife of the soldier went on buying in the coöperative society as she had before. If, on the one hand, the war destroyed the principles of consumers' democracy, on the other, it put the societies into a very favorable position and enabled them to carry on more efficiently than ever before their main practical business, that is, providing their members with commodities. The war which almost destroyed the political and trade-union branches of the labor movement brought salvation to the coöperatives and rescued them from the deadlock into which the years preceding the war had brought them. To understand the relations between the coöperatives and the party the reader should, throughout the discussion that follows, keep in mind these developments.

[28] Karl Renner, *Die österreichischen Arbeitergenossenschaften und ihre Kritiker* (Wien, 1926), pp. 11–12.

Workers' Coöperatives in the Republic

The collapse of the Austrian monarchy was a severe blow to the coöperative movement. The overwhelming majority of the societies were lost to the new republic, particularly the strong and well-organized units in Moravia and Bohemia which went to Czechoslovakia. There were also some absorptions of small by large associations. The totals were 498 in 1917 and 103 in 1920 for the two "Austrias."[29] When, after difficult negotiations, the division of property was carried through the result was lamentable for the Austrian coöperatives. The Wholesale Society had to hand over to its newly founded counterpart in Czechoslovakia its recently built cannery—the first serious step of the society toward coöperative production.[30] The number of members, however, did not diminish; on the contrary, the desperate food situation and the continuance of rationing after the revolution brought about a tremendous influx of new masses of "compulsory" members. Republican Austrian societies, although one-fifth of the number of imperial Austrian societies, had 503,622 members in 1920, or almost one and a half times more than in 1917.[31] The close collaboration of the movement with the central economic organizations (*Wirtschafts-Zentralen*) of the state continued, but the large and sudden unemployment in war industries and the blockade of Austria by neighboring countries rendered the task of supplying foodstuffs to the population almost insoluble. The disorder was great. In many places the newly founded workers' councils actually controlled the food supply. Illegal confiscations of food by these councils were frequent. When, in the spring of 1919, the works councils were created, they too did everything in their power to secure sufficient food for the workers in their factories. Sometimes they acted through the coöperatives; sometimes, and more often, they simply went to members of the government and urged them to put the necessary quantities at their disposal. Thus, besides the coöperatives, a large number of different groups, councils, and committees were actually assuming the functions of distributive societies and doing their work. It took some time before a degree of order could be restored, and the relations between

[29] *Parteitag, 1919,* pp. 98–99; Freundlich, *Geschichte,* p. 59.
[30] Vukowitsch, *Besonderheiten,* p. 83.
[31] Freundlich, *Geschichte,* p. 59.

the coöperatives and the new organizations, in the first place the works councils, put into a clearly drawn framework. In this connection the coöperative works councils subcommittees established in the factories in accordance with an idea of Otto Bauer's were of first importance, since through them the tendency to rash actions on the part of works council members was gradually restrained by the coöperatives.

Had the socialization scheme drawn up by Otto Bauer become a reality the coöperatives would have broadened the scope of their activities, for under it they would have represented the consumers on the management boards of the new *Gemeinwirtschaftliche Anstalten,* and some branches of industry would have been leased to the Wholesale Society of the consumers' organizations or to the agricultural organizations.[32]

In spite of all the falsifications of coöperative principles during the war and the revolution, the leaders of the movement still felt that it had its own program of socialization; consequently, the socialization plans adopted by the party, and to some extent incorporated in statutes, aroused no enthusiasm among them. It is significant that in the party congress of 1919 the only sharp opposition to Bauer's proposals came from the coöperatives.[33] Wilhelm, secretary of the Central Federation, urged that the attempt to unite conflicting interests (state, workers, employers, consumers) in the management of a socialized undertaking could not but lead to a collapse of the whole system. Years later Renner said: "If it has not become generally known yet, I can state it now without hesitation: Among the members of the coöperatives there were more doubters than adherents of socialization. But, of course, the coöperatives maintained discipline and disturbed nothing."[34]

In the course of developments *Gemeinwirtschaftliche Anstalten* were established with the actual participation of the coöperatives, for example, the shoe factory, *Vereinigte Leder- und Schuhfabriken* and the textile mill, *Aktiengesellschaft für Textilindustrie.* Another participant in the shoe concern was the state, which placed credit, buildings, and other facilities at its disposal. The third partner was the farmers. Through their coöperatives they were obligated

[32] Otto Bauer, *Der Weg zum Sozialismus* (Wien, 1919), pp. 10, 12.
[33] *Parteitag, 1919,* pp. 211–213.
[34] Renner, *op. cit.,* p. 13.

to provide raw leather and hides. The state and the consumers' coöperatives were to undertake the distribution of products. In varying degrees all three participants proved unable to carry out their parts of the plan. After many difficulties, many organizational reforms, and considerable sacrifices by the Coöperative Wholesale Society, which finally acquired the majority of the shares, the shoe factory was transformed into a successful undertaking, the largest part of the production being sold in coöperative shops.[35] The textile concern likewise went through many organizational changes, but after ten years of financial ups and downs had to be liquidated in 1930.[36] The coöperatives took part, without capital participation, in the management of a number of other socialized concerns such as the Arsenal, but withdrew after a few years.[37] These experiences are of little importance from the coöperative point of view.

The most serious damages suffered by the coöperatives in the early years of the republic resulted from the inflation. Their activities, particularly in 1921, developed feverishly; purchases of goods were rendered easy by the subsidy system under which the state acquired foodstuffs and sold them to the societies at less than cost. Every unit—and many new ones were founded at this time without sufficient financial basis—tried to get the largest possible quantities of commodities from the state at the greatly reduced prices, and payment was usually effected much later after further depreciation of the currency. The general desire to get rid as soon as possible of money that was losing its purchasing power led to overinvestment which would not have occurred under normal conditions. But after the game went on for a period lasting approximately until the fall of 1921 the devastating effects of inflation became more and more obvious. The state's subsidies system had to be abolished in the beginning of 1922. Now prices rose wildly, that for flour, for instance, tenfold in one day. In spite of the comparatively large credits which the state gave to the Wholesale Society its working capital was unable to meet rising requirements. At the same time the false boom in Austrian industry, consisting largely in dumping goods and capi-

[35] Vukowitsch, *Geschichte,* pp. 58–60; 70.
[36] *Ibid.,* pp. 59 ff., 70 ff.; Freundlich, *Geschichte,* p. 61.
[37] Freundlich, *Geschichte,* p. 61. Her statement that the coöperatives participated as shareholders in only two *Gemeinwirtschaftliche Anstalten* is misleading. One of these, the textile concern, was a fusion of two others in which the coöperatives had participated. Cf. Vukowitsch, *Geschichte,* pp. 59 and 70.

tal on other countries, reached its end. Increasing unemployment rendered the situation of the coöperatives still more difficult. The central economic control organizations of the state were dissolved one after another, so that the societies lost a support to which they had become accustomed. The frequent attempts to continue the collaboration through trade companies and in other ways generally failed. As soon as the rationing of commodities, chiefly food, was abolished, thousands of members, whom only the war and the post-war conditions had brought into the movement, left it. And only the depreciation of the currency disguised the great decrease in aggregate turnover that resulted. The end of the inflation left the coöperatives in a desperate condition. The single favorable result of that period was that in 1920 the four Viennese Workers' Consumers' Coöperative societies were at last merged into one large organization—Consumers' Coöperative Society of Vienna and Vicinity (*Konsumgenossenschaft Wien und Umgebung*).[38] Competition between the Vienna societies which had been stopped only by the war was thus prevented from starting again.

After the stabilization things grew still worse: export trade was almost completely paralyzed; demand for industrial products sank from month to month; speculative activity on the stock exchange led to a certain recovery in luxury trade, but it scarcely touched the coöperatives. On the other hand, just because of the feverish speculation, shortage of credit became the central problem. Tremendous paper profits on the stock exchange rendered it possible for speculators to pay any rate of interest. Sometimes 2 per cent and more were paid for a single week. Such rates were, of course, out of the question for the coöperatives, particularly in the light of their decreased turnover. Both large and small societies were threatened with collapse. In this grave state of affairs the foundation of the Labor Bank prevented disaster (cf. below, p. 341). Funds raised by it saved the movement from catastrophe, despite individual failures, but naturally these funds were not adequate to overcome the effects of the crisis and of the special structure of the Austrian national economy.

The position of the coöperatives was rendered extremely difficult by developments in retail trade which badly overcrowded that occu-

[38] Vukowitsch, *30 Jahre Zentralverband,* p. 31.

pation. The bulk of the war refugees from the eastern parts of the monarchy tried to make their living in this fashion. Seipel's scheme of currency stabilization implied dismissal of 100,000 civil servants. Actually only 80,000 of them were dismissed, but a great number felt induced to start some little business. Their competition was hard to fight, since most of them regarded their shops as a source of supplementary earnings, a pleasant addition to their pensions. They had, furthermore, no obligations under the extended protective and social legislation because they and their family members carried on the business. For them the wage account did not exist.[39]

The coöperatives, which in the first part of the inflation had overextended their scale of business, were now in the time of crisis and sinking turnover unable to avail themselves of the advantages that large undertakings offer in periods of good business. When the artificially inflated balloon of the rates on the stock exchange suddenly burst in the spring of 1924, a new and still more tremendous wave of unemployment swept over the country. The economic crisis in Austria actually had become permanent. As one result the reconstruction of the coöperative movement was rendered more difficult. The war and still more the inflation had introduced methods of doing business which often did not measure up to the rules of ordinary honesty and decency, let alone the principles of the coöperative movement. By the end of 1923 the secretaries of the Central Federation of the coöperatives, Kaff and Wilhelm, left their posts because of divergencies of opinion between them and the leaders of the movement. Soon afterwards they began publication of a series of articles and pamphlets[40] containing grave charges against a large number of these leaders and their administration of the most important undertakings run by the coöperative movement. The *Hammerbrotwerke*—the bread factory which belonged to the Social Democratic party—was also attacked. Among the numerous allegations the following were the most serious: balance sheets were unwarrantably altered to compensate for previous losses (*Stafa* department stores);[41] invoices were faked in order to cheat the tax

[39] *Idem, Besonderheiten*, p. 87.

[40] Among the most important were: Siegmund Kaff, *Der Brotwucher, seine Ursachen und seine Gönner* (Wien, 1925); *Politik und Geschäft* (Wien, 1926); *Der Sozialismus als Ware oder der "wahre" Sozialismus* (Wien, 1926).

[41] Kaff, *Der Austrobolschewismus als Hüter der "Gesetzlichkeit,"* p. 90.

authorities (coöperative in Innsbruck which, according to Kaff, obtained the desired invoices from the Coöperative Wholesale Society);[42] a coöperative institution (underwear and clothing factory) took part in the French franc speculations with losses that were absorbed in large part, but concealed, by the Wholesale Society and *Stafa* in order to prevent further losses to individuals involved;[43] other invoices were faked to create a hidden reserve that was used for personal expenditures by a manager of coöperative concerns (director Lorentz of *Stafa* and other undertakings);[44] attempts were made to induce a civil servant to break his oath by disclosing secret contracts which seemed of some importance for competitive purposes (by Emmy Freundlich);[45] the true financial position of the coöperatives in prewar times was disguised (by Renner and Eldersch).[46]

The underlying facts in the *Hammerbrotwerke* affair seem to be as follows. Unfortunately, the factory was situated not in Vienna but in a little industrial place some miles away. One reason for this, according to the Social Democrats, was the refusal of the Viennese building office, under orders from Lueger, the Christian Social mayor, to grant a permit for its erection within the city. However, the poor location meant considerable additions to transportation costs and induced the party to build a huge establishment with the hope of offsetting these costs by the advantages of large-scale production. This, in turn, involved the investment of large funds, as well as the continuous difficulty of finding buyers for the whole production so that the full capacity of the plant might be utilized. As mentioned before, credit needs of the *Hammerbrotwerke* forced the whole coöperative movement, especially the Coöperative Wholesale Society which had to manage the concern, into a difficult position. Moreover, the *Hammerbrotwerke* produced a certain amount of resentment within that movement. The First Lower Austrian Workers' Consumers' Coöperative saw the existence of its own bakery highly endangered. It bitterly criticized the *Hammerbrotwerke* on the ground that it had nothing to do with coöperative prin-

[42] *Ibid.*, pp. 213 ff., esp. pp. 217 and 221. Cf. *Der österreichische Volkswirt*, vol. 19 (Dec. 11, 1926), 287.

[43] Kaff, *Politik und Geschäft*, pp. 51–52.

[44] *Ibid.*, pp. 50, 52.

[45] *Ibid.*, pp. 56–57; *idem, Der Sozialismus als Ware oder der "wahre" Sozialismus*, pp. 27–28.

[46] *Idem, Politik und Geschäft*, pp. 20–21, 23–24, 26.

ciples—it did not produce goods for the organized coöperative membership, but for sale to private merchants.

The Socialist-owned bakery emerged from the war in a relatively sound position. During the inflation times it provided about one-quarter of the bread consumed in the capital city. The party thought that the hopes cherished when the establishment was founded were now going to be fulfilled. But after state control ceased it became clear that the factory was unable, because of the fundamental error of uneconomic location, to keep down the price of bread in the Vienna market. On the contrary, partly because of their better organization and location, partly because of their successful speculation in grain, the private bakeries were able to realize a greater profit although selling bread at the same price as the Socialist concern. There is little doubt that these profits were excessive; in fact, Kaff charged that the *Hammerbrotwerke* also made abnormal profits. This would have been strange behavior indeed for a Socialist party, but it has been impossible to determine the truth. At least it is known that after the charges had been aired in the Vienna press, the management of the factory asked the party to audit the accounts and check the calculations by which the selling price of bread was determined. In October, 1924, the auditors made a preliminary report to the party's executive establishing the fact that the distributed dividend amounted to only 0.102 per cent of the turnover, but admitting that certain amounts were used for investments and upkeep, and that in this respect further examination of the accounts was necessary. On the real point at issue the auditors confined themselves to the statement that for the time being it was impossible to speak of any disproportionate profits.[47] No further report was ever published, and in January, 1925, the party surprised the public by announcing that the *Hammerbrotwerke* had been sold to Siegmund Bosel, a notorious profiteer, to whom the party some time previously had sold 40 per cent of the concern. What had happened was this. In the fall of 1924 the Ramek government was formed. At about that time some banks run by the Christian Socials got into difficulties, and the civil servants demanded increases in salaries to compensate for the steady rise of the cost of living. The government was not willing to comply with these demands but attempted to

[47] *Parteitag, 1925*, pp. 47–48.

pacify the civil servants and at the same time to divert attention from the Christian Socials' banking misdeeds by hitting at the Socialists. Hence it started investigations of the price of bread in Vienna which led to the arrest and trial of one Fried, managing director of the largest private bakery in Vienna. It was obvious that the next step would be a similar attack against the *Hammerbrotwerke*. Rumors of the imminent appearance of Kaff's first pamphlet might also have quickened the proceedings; at least it is an interesting coincidence that the sale was effected just one day before the said pamphlet left the printing press. That the sale was carried through in the greatest haste may be perceived from Renner's statement when dealing with the question why the bakery, for which so many sacrifices had been made, was delivered at last to a private capitalist and not sold to the coöperatives: "We had not the time . . . to summon the representatives of the coöperatives and to ask for the opinion of the great number of organizations concerned."[48]

There is one more aspect of the whole issue. If the *Hammerbrotwerke* was really unable to compete efficiently with other factories, then what interest had Bosel in taking it over? If it was only to free the party from an embarrassing situation, then the question arises whether there were any counterservices Bosel could expect the party to do for him which really would point in the direction of an illicit political connection. The available material gives no satisfactory answer to that question. After the sale of the bakery the central party organization attempted to prevent the foundation of new undertakings by subsidiary party groups and to get rid of some others which were more or less a political burden. At the next party congress, 1925, Danneberg pointed out that during the inflation the incentive to enter business had become very strong indeed and that many party functionaries had felt induced to raise money for it in this way. In consequence, various undertakings had been founded which had no necessary or logical connection with a political organization.[49]

No concrete reply was ever made to most of the various charges brought forward by Kaff. On the contrary, it was several times admitted, directly or indirectly, that at least some of the charges or

[48] Karl Renner, "Prinzip in der Praxis," *Der Kampf*, vol. 18 (Feb., 1925), 43.
[49] *Parteitag, 1925*, p. 189.

some parts of particular charges were based on facts. Such instances appear in Renner's[50] sarcastic comments on Kaff's bad luck in publishing his pamphlet against the *Hammerbrotwerke* after it had been sold and in dealing with the misdeeds of Lorentz, the president of *Stafa,* in another pamphlet which appeared after he had been forced out of this position. On another occasion Renner issued a long statement in the name of the Central Federation. He specifically excluded any discussion of accusations concerning events prior to and during the war and replied to only three charges from Kaff. His answers shed some additional light but definitely leave the impression that he was making rather lame apologies and admitting at least parts of the accusations.[51] During one of the numerous libel suits involving Kaff and leaders of the coöperative movement, the *Arbeiter Zeitung*[52] likewise admitted that the general points of Kaff's charges were correct, and was content to point out that individuals who had been guilty of incorrect dealing were dismissed as soon as the management of the coöperative organizations was informed of what had happened. Throughout the whole controversy, which raged for years, such figures as Renner, Eldersch, and Freundlich were vigorously defended. Support for them also came from the *Volkswirt:* "Unfortunately," carried away by his passions, Kaff chose to use his experience of forty years in the movement too much for accusations of corruption against outstanding Socialist politicians "which, however, find no support in the great amount of material brought forward." Later the journal became more critical, correctly pointing out that Social Democracy had made the grievous error of attempting to conceal some "failures" and thus permitted them to ripen into "cases."[53] It should be noted, moreover, that a director of the *Stafa* now living in the United States categorically denies any falsification of its balances, and that the state prosecutor quashed the proceedings in the alleged tax-evasion case from Innsbruck.

As has been indicated, when action had been decided upon energetic steps were taken with the purposes of purifying the coöperative movement and adapting it to the somewhat more normal general economic conditions—"normal" only as compared with the wild

[50] Cf. Renner, *Die österreichischen Arbeitergenossenschaften und ihre Kritiker,* p. 2.
[51] *Arbeiter Zeitung,* January 16, 1926, p. 5.
[52] *Ibid.,* January 29, 1927, pp. 5, 6.
[53] *Der österreichische Volkswirt,* vol. 18 (Jan. 16, 1926), 411; *ibid.,* vol. 19 (Dec. 11, 1926), 287.

days of inflation and stock exchange speculation and within the permanent crisis that began in 1924.

In the first years after the foundation of the Labor Bank the coöperatives still had to rely upon comparatively large and not easily obtainable credits from private banks and business firms. Since the burden of interest payments especially handicapped the movement, vigorous efforts were made to induce members to pay up their shares and to place their savings with the consumers' societies. As far as deposits are concerned the efforts were reasonably successful, as aggregate deposit data show.[54]

Year	Schillings
1923	3,667,000
1925	11,585,000
1927	16,003,000
1929	19,476,000

Less successful were the attempts to increase the capital. Payments on the shares flowed in extremely slowly and were to a great extent counteracted by the increasing number of societies selling their goods not for cash but on a more or less long-term credit. In spite of all efforts the aggregate paid-up capital in 1927 amounted to only 2,000,000 schillings whereas more than 3,300,000 schillings had been extracted from the coöperatives by sales on credit.[55] In this connection it should at least be mentioned that after the war the coöperatives in a number of countries where the movement was strongest departed from the principle of cash payment, as for instance, Great Britain, Holland, and Czechoslovakia.[56] On the other hand, valuable reforms concerning the wage system were carried through that reduced the percentage of wages to turnover.

Of great importance for the reconstruction of the movement was the problem of the dividend or rebate on purchases. During the war and early postwar years when the members badly wanted goods and were prepared to pay any price for them, the fact that no dividend was paid had no importance whatever. But when normal conditions were restored and more than half of the members had left the coöperatives the dividend became a necessity again; it was reintro-

[54] Vukowitsch, *Besonderheiten,* p. 86.

[55] Verband deutschösterreichischer Konsumvereine, *Jahrbuch, 1927* (Wien, 1928), p. 27. Cited hereafter as Konsumvereine, *Jahrbuch.*

[56] International Coöperative Alliance, *Agenda of the XIII International Coöperative Congress at Vienna, 1930,* pp. 181 ff.

duced by some societies in the states even before the consent of the central organization had been secured. In 1925, the largest of the coöperatives in Vienna and its environs began to pay a dividend amounting to 1 per cent of the turnover. This rate was certainly very small compared with that paid by British societies—which usually averaged around 10 per cent[57]—but in the typical conditions of Austrian pauperism it represented a strong inducement to many to become members of the coöperative and to increase their purchases. In order to prevent competition among the societies in dividend rates the rule was adopted in 1928 that they were not to exceed 2 per cent. At the same time the membership lists were thoroughly revised and "paper soldiers" (the name used for members who were only on the lists but never bought anything) were removed.[58]

Of much importance was the merger of the consumers' societies with the Foodstuff Stores of the railway employees. These stores had been established by the railway companies before the war of 1914–1918 with the purpose of sidetracking demands for salary increases; they developed during the war into organizations independent of railroad administration and run by the employees themselves. Technically the merger presented many difficulties because of the credit system of the railway stores in which purchases were never paid for in cash but deducted from wages twice a month. Furthermore, the stores enjoyed lower freight rates than their competitors. After long negotiations the federal railway consented to pay a considerable amount as redemption for the abolition of this privilege.[59] The process of affiliation dragged on for about seven years and was not quite accomplished so far as Vienna was concerned even in 1933. The general result of the merger was to increase greatly the strength of the movement.

The practices of the tax authorities impeded the development of the coöperatives to some extent. After the power of the bourgeois parties had grown stronger and they had succeeded in securing increasing influence over the administration, cases of unfair treatment became frequent. The reports of the general meetings of the Central Federation are crammed with complaints from coöperatives all over the country. Under the law of 1924 they were entitled to deduct

[57] S. and B. Webb, *op. cit.*, p. 296. The Scottish rate was higher, as were prices.
[58] Vukowitsch, *30 Jahre Zentralverband*, pp. 35, 36.
[59] Freundlich, *Geschichte*, pp. 67–68.

1 per cent of their turnover from the yearly "surplus" and to pay the 12 per cent corporate income tax from the remaining amount. These surpluses were, of course, determined locally, and each society endeavored to adhere to the Rochdale principle of selling at customary market prices in its locality; but for reasons set forth in the debates at the meetings of the Central Federation unavoidable deviations appeared. It became common practice for hostile tax officials to take advantage of such deviations as the basis for a ruling that parts of the profits were being distributed by the societies in "lower" prices charged their members; by arbitrarily including these parts of the profits the tax offices managed to eliminate the privileges of the law. It was significant for the general development in Austria that this illegal practice found support in the courts.[60]

The methods just described could not, however, seriously hamper the favorable development of the coöperatives which, with the beginning of 1927, was furthered by some general economic recovery in Austria. This upward tendency reached its peak in 1929, also the best year of the movement. Between 1925 and 1929 the aggregate turnover of the consumers' societies rose from 133,845,977 to 160,816,807 schillings; the net profits from 674,442 to 3,082,025 schillings.[61] The Consumers' Coöperative in Vienna and Vicinity contributed 36,000,000 schillings to the 1925–1929 turnover. This coöperative, even after the elimination of its "paper soldiers," still remained in the late 'twenties and early 'thirties a powerful organization of around 60,000 members as contrasted with 37,000 in 1919. It operated its own bakery, and later a dairy, a coffee-roasting establishment, a macaroni and noodle factory, and other departments.[62] The development of this society may be regarded as a refutation of the opinion very common among coöperative theorists at the turn of the century that metropolitan areas are destined to remain "coöperative deserts." The Coöperative Wholesale Society was likewise developing in a more than satisfactory manner. Its turnover increased from 70,770,269 schillings in 1925 to 95,239,277 schillings in 1929.[63] Large department stores were established throughout

[60] Konsumvereine, *Jahrbuch, 1925–1926,* p. 22; *ibid., 1927,* pp. 31, 80–89.
[61] Freundlich, *Geschichte,* p. 81.
[62] Konsumgenossenschaft Wien und Umgebung, *Geschäftsbericht für das Jahr 1931,* vol. 67, pp. 15–20, 24.
[63] Grosseinkaufsgesellschaft österreichischer Consumvereine, *Bericht,* 1925, p. 63; *ibid.,* 1931, table I (following p. 75). Cited hereafter as GöC, *Bericht.*

the country with favorable results for the textile division; particularly the linen and clothing factory flourished. Together with the city council of Vienna the Coöperative Wholesale Society ran the "butchers' stalls" and the *Wihoko* concerns. The latter company supplied the coöperatives with firewood, coal, and coke. Furthermore, the Wholesale Society owned a combined bakery and macaroni factory in Salzburg, a sausage and smoked-meat factory in Linz, and a bakery in the same place. These last two were created by the local unit of the Social Democratic party but subsequently got into difficulties and, when taken over by the Wholesale Society, were in a deplorable condition. The persistent efforts of the wholesale organization finally achieved entirely satisfactory results in these cases also. In these transactions the Labor Bank participated actively, thus further justifying its foundation.

The crisis which began in 1929 naturally checked the further development of the coöperatives. Unemployment increased and soon reached a scale never before known even in this country of chronic structural crisis; general purchasing power sank rapidly. Nevertheless the coöperatives showed amazing powers of resistance. It was to be expected that the turnover would decrease, but considering the fall of prices and the tendency among the working class to go over to the use of substitutes, the decrease must be regarded as a small one. Deposits generally maintained their levels or sank only slightly; capital payments increased even in 1932—the year of the big slump. The Wholesale Society, its factories and its undertakings, except the textile mill, proved strong enough to stand the storm; in short, all branches of the movement, distributive, productive, and credit organizations, demonstrated their stability. Evidently the dangers and errors and illnesses of the war and inflation periods had been overcome. The coöperative movement stood on a sound economic basis; it was not the economic but the political crisis which was to bring grave dangers and changes.

Workers' Coöperatives and the Social Democratic Party

The relations between the coöperatives and the Social Democratic party became even closer after the war than they had been before. Leading men in the societies were dispatched by the party to the highest positions in the state and in the city council of Vienna.[64] In Vienna as well as in the small industrial towns and villages all over the country the same men were the local leaders of the party and of the coöperatives. As long as state control over necessities was maintained, the societies continued to play an important part in providing the workers with foodstuffs and textiles. On the recommendation of Otto Bauer, the party created the so-called coöperative subcommittees of the Austrian works councils, thus establishing a close contact between the most active part of the party membership and the coöperatives (cf. above, p. 322). As shown earlier, the societies had been scheduled to participate as consumers' representatives in the abortive socialization attempts (*Gemeinwirtschaftliche Anstalten*) undertaken by the party. In the agricultural program of the party,[65] which ascribed much importance to the agricultural coöperatives, the necessity of collaboration between those institutions and their workers' counterparts for the purpose of eliminating the private traders was carefully stressed. Otto Bauer, the author of the agricultural program, pointed out, however, that the complete elimination of the powerful private traders by the coöperatives without the help of the state must be regarded as an impossible task.[66] Still more important in this respect was the general program adopted by the party the following year. The societies were declared to be "socialized enterprises"; further, since they were serving the interests of the whole working class in the "period of transition" from capitalism to socialism, their growth was to be solicitously stimulated.[67]

But in spite of this close connection in theory and practice, it must not be overlooked that there were some more or less powerful undercurrents creating conflicts and divergencies of opinion between the party and the coöperatives. First of all there was the development of the latter during the war. The intense pacifistic sentiment which dominated the party even before the collapse of the monarchy and caused its members to despise the war, was again made manifest in wide circles of the membership by a certain amount of feeling

[64] Renner became chancellor; Eldersch, minister of interior (an important post because it gave control of the police and the gendarmery); Speiser and Kokrda, members of the Vienna council.

[65] *Parteitag, 1925,* pp. 155–169; useful summary in C. A. Macartney, *The Social Revolution in Austria* (Cambridge, 1926), pp. 270–281.

[66] *Parteitag, 1925,* pp. 158, 255.

[67] *Ibid., 1926,* p. 191.

against the societies which but for that war would have collapsed—the war had proved to be for the societies a release from almost all their troubles. Furthermore, the period of conflict and inflation, of profiteering and wild speculation which went on after stabilization until the crash on the Viennese stock exchange in April, 1924, followed by the wave of political corruption which swept over the entire country, had left the masses of workers with strong prejudices against business activities in general. During these years "business" had been too often associated with swindling and all sorts of dishonest tricks. In departing from strict adherence to the principles of consumers' democracy during the war the coöperatives undoubtedly rendered an invaluable service to the Austrian people; but the connection with the state implied thereby, and the reliance upon credits coming from without the movement that were recalled suddenly when the inflation was over, brought the societies into difficulties.[68] These difficulties, coupled with the economic crisis, weakened the movement considerably and pushed it into the background, whereas the prosperous economic activities furthered by the party in Vienna won the admiration of the workers. Finally, after losses in the elections of 1920, the party continuously increased its adherents among the Austrian people. Had it succeeded in obtaining another 350,000 votes,[69] it would have obtained a majority in parliament and had the whole machinery of the state at its disposal. This prospect seemed to open opportunities compared with which the modest work of the coöperatives appeared slight and unimportant. The party did the utmost to get those additional votes; its need for them was the immediate incentive for the formulation of the agricultural program, designed to win the peasants, and for the renewal and intensification of the process of catering to petty entrepreneurs. The party founded as a class party seemed to be on the road toward transformation into a peoples' party. As a matter of fact the Social Democratic Association of Small Businessmen and Handicraftsmen (*Verband der sozialdemokratischen Handels- und Gewerbetreibenden*) had been founded, under a different name, as early as 1898. Before 1914 the association was ostensibly neutral politically, but its meager success is reflected in a membership in

[68] In 1925, Renner spoke of eleven years of wrong policy of the coöperative movement, that is, from 1914 to 1925. Konsumvereine, *Jahrbuch, 1923–1924,* p. 9.

[69] Cf. Danneberg's speech to the party congress, *Parteitag, 1925,* p. 227.

that year amounting to hardly more than 500. In 1919 its open proclamation of adherence to the party resulted in a large and rapid increase in membership, a development furthered by the practice of the Vienna city council in favoring the members with orders. Especially during the electoral campaign of 1927, party members were often invited to do their shopping with the Social Democratic traders. As a matter of course these tactics did not meet with the approval of the coöperatives. For instance, at the general meeting of the Central Federation in 1925, Schnöpf, a prominent leader of the movement, complained that the "threefold unity" did not exist any longer, that the Social Democratic traders also seemed to belong to the movement, that the party—or single sections of the party—while collecting members' fees, distributed lists of names of Social Democratic merchants.[70] In 1927, with unfavorable impressions of the party tactics during the campaign fresh in mind, these complaints became still more urgent. One of the leaders of the Styrian coöperative movement, Korp, reported that a list of "recommended firms" including greengrocers and other small merchants had been posted on the entrance doors of the labor temple in Knittelfeld—a building that had been constructed chiefly with money from the local coöperative. The speaker continued indignantly:

> We coöperators must put the decisive question before the party: Where does your policy lead? Can you assume the responsibility for confronting party comrades with this conflict of conscience—whether they should do their shopping with the Social Democratic merchant or with the near-by coöperative society? It has already happened in some localities that when we have gone to the housewives to secure support for the coöperatives they have said, "We don't know what we should do; Comrade Merchant is also politically organized; we should support him also."[71]

And even more indignation and prolonged debate was aroused by the alleged neglect of the coöperatives by the party press, particularly the *Arbeiter Zeitung*. The official representative of the party had a difficult time in defending it against attacks coming from all sides.

Quite typical of the none too friendly attitude prevailing at this time in party circles was an article by Ernst Fischer, "Class Struggle

[70] Konsumvereine, *Jahrbuch, 1923–1924*, pp. 29–30.
[71] *Ibid., 1925–1926*, p. 77.

and Competitive Struggle."[72] He quoted examples of coöperative societies the breakdown of which had damaged the party's reputation and protested against the continuance of any connection between party politics and business, arguing that by association with coöperative societies the party moved dangerously close to the capitalistic system. The same copy of the magazine, however, carried a reply written by Korp, "Party, Business and Coöperative Movement," which revealed the mistakes and misunderstandings contained in Fischer's attack.[73]

This summer of 1927 may be regarded as a turning point in the relations of the political wing to the coöperative movement. The events of July 15 suddenly changed the general position of the party; it was driven back into the defensive. Everyone realized that the hopes of obtaining a majority in parliament were not to be fulfilled in the near future. The attacks against the working-class movement compelled the single branches to move closer together; dissensions between the party and the coöperative movement ceased. With the rise of the Heimwehr movement in the states, especially in Styria, the coöperatives won a new importance; a good number of the shopkeepers in the small industrial towns supported the Heimwehr so that the workers were only too glad to exercise economic pressure upon them by trading in the coöperatives. Naturally the party made vigorous propaganda urging the workers to join the coöperatives and to patronize them. In other words, as in the very beginnings of the movement after the elections of 1897, the pressure of events brought it about that the coöperatives were used by the party as a political weapon. This improvement in relations was marked by the appearance of Otto Bauer at the next general assembly of the Central Federation in 1928. Although his name was never mentioned in any complaint or criticism by the coöperatives he was supposed to think little of their value. In his remarks before the assembly he emphasized the importance of the coöperatives for the entire labor movement.[74] The address made an excellent impression upon the audience and one of the following speakers referred to it as "almost an historic act." In the following years of constant attacks against all divisions of the Austrian labor movement the good rela-

[72] *Der Kampf*, vol. 20 (Sept. 1927), 426.
[73] *Ibid.*, p. 429.
[74] *Partei, Gewerkschaft und Genossenschaft* (Wien, n.d.), pp. 7 ff.

tions between the coöperatives and the party were maintained until the destruction of the legal existence of the latter in 1934.

Workers' Coöperatives and Trade Unions

At the 1928 meeting of the Central Federation just mentioned a representative of the trade unions also expressed their appreciation of the achievements of the coöperatives. As a matter of fact the relations between the two groups had always been reasonably satisfactory. The charges raised in the early days concerning exploitation of workers by the societies had long since ceased, and the trade unions even preceded the party in officially recognizing the value of the coöperative movement. It remains true that, especially in the first years, there were many major and minor conflicts involving wages and working conditions. Even at the end of 1921, when the coöperatives found themselves in a very difficult position because of the destruction of their working capital by the continuing inflation, the idea arose that their funds might be replenished if all Austrian workers would agree to work overtime for a few months and contribute their additional earnings to the societies. This "attempt to abandon the eight-hour day," as it was styled, was flatly refused by the trade unions.[75]

As long as inflation persisted, wage questions were regulated more or less automatically by the index system. In the second period of the inflation, when state control over the food supply was abolished and foodstuffs became available everywhere, the decrease in the number of members who were actually buying considerably affected the turnover. This development, the just-mentioned impact of inflation on working capital, and other factors, combined to make the whole matter of labor relations more urgent. As a matter of principle the coöperatives felt obligated to observe the prescriptions of social and labor legislation much more strictly than any private firm. The expenditure implied was substantial. Although the workers' consumers' societies, for instance, were formally exempted from the requirement of having works councils in their undertakings (this exemption was adopted by parliament at the urgent request of the agricultural coöperatives), they raised no question concerning the election of such councils.

[75] Cf. *Die Gewerkschaft,* vol. 24 (Jan. 17, 1922), 18; "Gedenket der Konsumvereine!"

Other issues involved workers' efficiency and wages. As brought out before, the efficiency of all grades of labor, including white-collar employees, greatly decreased during the early period of the republic. This tendency went so far that clerks in general were often compared with civil servants—and the small amount of work done by these bureaucrats has been proverbial in Austria for generations. The stabilization crisis forced the immediate dismissal of some employees. This was done by agreement with trade unions, but the question of cutting wages was much more difficult. Before the war wages amounted to less than 6 per cent of the turnover of the coöperatives; after the war they rose to 7½ per cent on the average and reached 9 and even 11 per cent in some cases.[76] As early as 1923 proposals had been made to abandon the existing system of straight time wages and substitute for it a plan under which employees would receive a basic time wage that was supplemented in accordance with a previously determined scale. This scale was itself related to the degree by which the turnover exceeded a certain prescribed amount. Although the new basic time wages were to be lower than the existing wages, this reduction was to be more than compensated for in the case of an efficient worker by the supplements he would receive. But the scheme met with strong opposition from the trade unions so that its introduction was materially delayed.[77] At the general assembly of the Central Federation in 1925 the subject was dealt with at some length and Renner emphasized the necessity of changing what he called the "labor constitution" of the coöperatives. The strong competition of the private traders, said Renner, "compels us, let me state it frankly . . . to apply to the trade unions—not to any individual trade union but to the Central Executive Committee" and to ask them, not for a reduction of wages, but for the establishment of a system "which would couple maximum efficiency for the coöperatives with maximum earnings for the employees."[78] The resolution finally adopted demanded a wage system which would stimulate among the employees interest in the highest sales turnover in the distributive shops, and the highest production in the manufacturing establishments. After long and difficult struggles the coöp-

[76] Konsumvereine, *Jahrbuch, 1923–1924,* p. 18.

[77] Cf. E. Freundlich, "Die Konsumvereine Oesterreichs im Jahre 1923," *Arbeit und Wirtschaft,* vol. 2 (Sept. 1, 1924), 747.

[78] Konsumvereine, *Jahrbuch, 1923–1924,* pp. 43–45.

eratives succeeded in spreading the efficiency principle throughout almost the entire movement.[79] Although unfortunate conflicts arose and the wage question remained a center of them, negotiations were usually carried on in an atmosphere of mutual understanding and cordiality so that it was possible to arrive at compromises satisfactory to both parties. After the deepest period of the depression had been passed toward the end of 1926, and the beginning of 1927 brought a slight improvement in the general situation, the problem lost much of its former gravity.

Of decisive importance for the relations between coöperatives and trade unions was their close collaboration in the Labor Bank. By providing advantages to both groups (higher interest for the trade-union deposits, lower interest for the coöperative borrowings) this institution aided in the solution of many problems which might otherwise have assumed a much more threatening character. Also, the occasional help given by the coöperatives to the trade unions, such as the sale of commodities at lower prices to union members on strike, proved very helpful in settling the issues arising between them.[80] The party program adopted at Linz in 1926, without actually restricting the right to strike of the workers employed by the coöperatives, had strongly advised them to use peaceful mediation and arbitration as methods for settling conflicts.[81] Because of the mutual respect developed in the fashion heretofore described this advice was followed during the remaining years of the existence of the free trade unions.

THE LABOR BANK

The persistent difficulties before the war of 1914–1918 of the *Hammerbrotwerke*—the bakery owned by the party and the coöperatives—had led to the foundation of the Credit Union of Austrian Workers' Associations (*Kreditverband der österreichischen Arbeitervereinigungen*). Its purpose was to concentrate the available funds of the workers' organizations, primarily of the trade unions, and to put them at the disposal of the *Hammerbrotwerke* and the Coöperative Wholesale Society.[82] Beginning in 1910 a number of small banks were founded in Styria, Carinthia, Salzburg, Tirol, and

[79] Vukowitsch, *30 Jahre Zentralverband*, p. 38.

[80] Cf. *Arbeit und Wirtschaft*, vol. 4 (Jan. 15, 1926), 71, on the strikes in the small miners' villages of Kroith and Bleiberg.

[81] *Parteitag, 1926*, p. 192.

[82] Freundlich, *Geschichte*, p. 52.

Upper Austria, and in the industrial district of Wiener-Neustadt. The most important of these provincial banks was the Styrian *Alpenländische Volkskreditbank* which developed in a completely satisfactory fashion. As mentioned before, the stabilization of the currency brought the coöperative organizations into an extremely difficult position. The inflation had meant heavy losses for them; their working capital was exhausted. The last period of the inflation had been accompanied by a grave credit crisis, which in the first years after the stabilization grew steadily worse. Interest payments on the money borrowed by the coöperatives rose threateningly. In this situation the realization of the plan long cherished by Karl Renner to found a coöperative bank became an unavoidable necessity. The *Arbeiterbank* was founded on June 22, 1922, and began operations on January 3, 1923. It was not, however, a bank formed exclusively by coöperatives like that of the British Wholesale Society. Such an institution would have had to take over the deposits of individual members in the savings departments and the temporarily liquid funds of the single coöperative branches, thus separating the trading operations from the fiscal operations, but the grave crisis of the societies[83] rendered such an organization impossible. Hence the new institution was founded as a coöperative and trade-union bank, the consumers' coöperatives and the unions acquiring 40 per cent each of the shares. An additional 10 per cent was placed with various enterprises of the Social Democratic party and the remainder with the credit coöperatives.[84] The original capital was extremely small, only 10,000 schillings, but during the first year (1923) of operation it was increased to 200,000. The new bank made it possible to transfer the large funds of the trade unions from private financial institutions and make them available to the coöperatives; actually, the average maximum of these deposits varied from 30 to 40 per cent of union funds. On principle and for practical reasons the manager of the bank urged the unions not to place all their funds in it. There was the possibility that the government might close the institution for short periods and that this might happen when a strike was going on. Second, there was no desire to antagonize private banks with some of which the Labor Bank had

[83] Cf. Karl Renner, "Die Krise der Genossenschaften," *Arbeit und Wirtschaft,* vol. 2 (April 15, 1924), 305.

[84] According to Austrian law it was necessary to organize as a joint-stock company.

good relations. Nevertheless, the absolute sums deposited by various types of workers' organizations were large. Increases in capital followed rapidly, so that the value of the paid-up shares amounted to 500,000 schillings in 1924; 1,000,000 in 1925; 2,500,000 in 1927, and 4,000,000 in 1930. The scale of the bank's operations grew accordingly, as may be perceived from the following table of the yearly balance.[85]

Year	Schillings	Year	Schillings
1923	4,853,000	1928	50,032,000
1924	14,782,000	1929	58,762,000
1925	23,961,000	1930	67,567,000
1926	28,432,000	1931	65,260,000
1927	39,161,000	1932	64,105,000

Changes in deposits during the same period are shown on page 343.[86]

The management of the bank proceeded very cautiously, particularly because the first fifteen months after it opened its doors were a time of wild boom on the stock exchange. The prices of securities skyrocketed until April, 1924; the collapse brought catastrophic losses to hundreds of industrial and banking firms. As a matter of principle the board of directors formally resolved not to acquire stocks for the bank's own account. Its securities' account consisted solely of federal loans and certain city loans of which it had to buy small amounts. The result was that the ensuing period of "bank mortality" did not affect it at all. It also managed then and later to maintain a high rate of liquidity, oscillating around 30 per cent. This was difficult because representatives of the unions, the party, and the coöperatives were forever making demands and pointing to the high rate of liquidity. The board rejected many of these requests, often contrary to the wishes of Renner, the bank's president. For a time the institution confined itself to the task of being the clearing house of the labor movement. In this way both the trade unions and the coöperatives drew profits from the bank, the former receiving higher, the latter paying lower rates of interest.

[85] Andreas Korp, "The Fate of the Austrian Arbeiterbank," *Review of International Co-operation,* vol. 28 (May, 1935), 163.

[86] Karl Renner, "Ten Years of the Arbeiterbank," *Review of International Co-operation,* vol. 26 (June, 1933), 236.

The aggregate gain resulting from this policy for the two groups was calculated in 1928, after five years of the bank's existence, to be 1,700,000 schillings.

In the opinion of the creators of the *Arbeiterbank* these activities had a deeper significance than mere help for the coöperatives in their passing difficulties. According to Renner's theory the work done by the bank was the logical continuation of the coöperative

Year	Schillings	Year	Schillings
1923	4,455,000	1928	44,974,000
1924	13,894,000	1929	53,276,000
1925	22,276,000	1930	59,119,000
1926	26,641,000	1931	56,204,000
1927	34,604,000	1932	54,314,000

development which started by "socializing" the distribution of goods, then extended its activities into the sphere of production, and now finally was taking the first steps in socializing "credit"—the labor movement was becoming its own moneylender.[87]

Through its close connection with the coöperatives the bank was gradually led into an extension of its activities. For example, in the spring of 1924 it participated with the Wholesale Society in the reorganization of the *Stafa* department store, each acquiring 50 per cent of the shares. This was strictly a part of the socialization of distribution, but the *Stafa* organization included two other sections. One was a credit institution of civil servants. They were among the lowest paid of white-collar workers but any loan to them was absolutely secure. Practically speaking they could not be discharged and were entitled to a full pension after thirty-five years of service; nevertheless, the major banks were not interested in making the small loans they frequently needed and so it had become notorious that they were among the most unfortunate of the victims of loan sharks. Their *Kreditinstitut* was also in difficulties. Ultimately the majority of its shares became the property of the bank, the Wholesale Society, and the *Stafa* department store. The bank provided most of the money for the loans, increased the business about tenfold and reduced the interest rate to less than 20 per cent of what it

[87] Karl Renner, *Wege der Verwirklichung* (Berlin, 1929), p. 99.

had been. The third component of the *Stafa* complex was the *Gara,* an organization which gave loans for purchases from the department store. The loans were not cash but a drawing account on which the customer paid low interest. The time of the loan was from twelve to eighteen months. In 1933 *Gara* had about 40,000 individual accounts.

Another field of expansion for the Labor Bank was the so-called Russian business. Soon after the Austrian revolution representatives of the Russian coöperatives came to Vienna to organize connections between the societies of the two countries. For many months no tangible results could be achieved, but after the foundation of the bank more progress was made. On June 7, 1923, the Austro-Russian Trade and Industry Syndicate was formed in Moscow.[88] The original capital was 300,000 gold rubles. It was divided equally, that is, so far as ownership was concerned, between the Russian government and the Austrian group; but the latter were required to pay for and turn over to their associate gratis shares in the amount of 75,000 gold rubles. In other words, the Austrians obligated themselves in the agreement to supply three-quarters, not one-half, of the original cash. They also obligated themselves to provide a credit of one million gold rubles. Their financing was to be done by an Austrian syndicate in which 26 per cent of the total original capital was to come from *"Gemeinwirtschaftliche Unternehmungen"* (chiefly the Arsenal), the consumers' coöperatives, and the Labor Bank and 24 per cent from private banks. On August 22, 1923, the joint Austrian-Russian syndicate formed the *Ratao,* the Russo-Austrian trading company. Negotiations with private banks finally brought the Export and Industry Bank and the *Depositenbank* into the Austrian syndicate.[89]

Actual trading operations still hung fire because the Russian government felt compelled to put limitations on imports and because the *Depositenbank* failed to supply some of the needed funds. The reason for this failure became evident in mid-1924 when the bank collapsed. Thereupon the Arsenal proposed to the Labor Bank that it take over the shares of the Arsenal and the *Depositenbank* in

[88] Freundlich, *Geschichte,* p. 77; *Der österreichische Volkswirt,* vol. 15 (June 23, 1923), 1062.

[89] *Arbeit und Wirtschaft,* vol. 1 (July 15 and Nov. 15, 1923), 527, 855; *Der österreichische Volkswirt,* vol. 15 (Sept. 15, 1923), 1397.

Ratao. After more protracted negotiations the original *Ratao* was liquidated and another concern of the same name formed. The Wholesale Society and the workers' bank came out with 26 per cent of the total capital and the private *Credit Anstalt* with 24. The other 50 remained with the Russian government.[90]

In 1927 the Wholesale Society and the Labor Bank organized the Russo-Austrian Export and Import Corporation, *Russex*. Its function was to deal with private industrial firms interested in Russian business, neither of its founders being engaged in such operations. In practice the *Russex* was interposed between Austrian manufacturers and *Ratao,* thus securing double commissions from the sales effected. This business implied greater risk because Russia might have ceased honoring the bills. Moreover, it aroused criticism in coöperative circles since the operations were of a "capitalist" character and had no relation to coöperative principles. On the other hand, the trade unions continuously demanded extension of the business, particularly after the general economic collapse of late 1929.

During 1929 the licenses from the Russian government of *Ratao* and of *Russawstorg,* another mixed Austro-Russian trading company financed from the Austrian side by private capital, expired. The former was relicensed, with a doubled capitalization, but the affairs of the latter were wound up.[91] The *Ratao* was liquidated in late January of 1934 at the request of the Russian government. It had always been contrary to Soviet principles to get credits through such mixed companies and by this time the necessity for them had disappeared. *Ratao* got back its capital investment, in gold, from the Russians.[92]

Available reports on the importance and achievements of *Ratao* are to some degree conflicting, even from working-class publications. One of them stated in November of 1925 that subsequent to the

[90] GöC, *Bericht,* 1925, p. 10; *Arbeit und Wirtschaft,* vol. 2 (May 15 and July 15, 1924), 409, 619; *ibid.,* vol. 3 (Nov. 15, 1925), 983; memorandum supplied by Mr. O. Grover, former manager of the Labor Bank.

[91] O. S. Phillpotts, *Economic Conditions in Austria,* Revised to November, 1929 (London, H.M. Stationery Office, 1930), p. 26.

[92] One other concern related to the Russian business merits brief mention. This was the *Osteuropäische Warenverkehrs-Gesellschaft,* commonly referred to as *Ostexport* or *Ostex*. It was organized in 1931 by the central association of Russian coöperatives, the Austrian Labor Bank and the Austrian Coöperative Wholesale Society. Its purpose was to export goods from Russia to those countries in which the Soviet Union did not have its own commercial representation. By 1933 all its shares had been taken over by the Russian government. GöC, *Bericht,* 1931, p. 69; E. C. D. Rawlins, *The Financial and Economic Position of Austria* (London, H.M. Stationery Office, 1933), p. 34.

reorganization necessitated by the collapse of the *Depositenbank* the new company was enjoying a lively trade; but another, referring to the same period, wrote of unsatisfactory fulfillment of hopes. The next year this second publication spoke of the "quite insignificant deliveries" that *Ratao* had been able to make to Russia. After still another twelvemonth, however, it reported that the fiscal year 1927–1928 had ended very satisfactorily.[93] A source outside the labor movement states that in the spring of 1926 the Russian business was divided among the official Russian trading agency and the two mixed companies, *Ratao* and *Russawstorg;* that the volume of the first was "many times" that of the second and third combined; and that the volume of *Russawstorg* was about double that of *Ratao.*[94] The failure to renew the license of *Russawstorg* in 1929, whereas the capital of *Ratao* was doubled, resulted from the facts that the former lacked the finance capital that had been promised in the original contract so that the Russians were dissatisfied with it and that the latter was giving them the service they wanted. Official data, that is, those from the Federal Bureau of Statistics, are unsatisfactory on the point of the relative importance of Russian trade to total Austrian exports. They do show, however, a rise in the value of exported "machines and apparatus" (excluding electrical machinery) from 6.8 million schillings in 1926 to 19.1 million in 1929.[95] These figures represent 10 and 22 per cent, respectively, of the total value of this category of exports. Some machine factories were operating almost exclusively on Russian orders, and though their volume in absolute figures may seem small, they surpassed by far the exports of these items to any other country. During the next four years this business practically disappeared, dropping from 10.3 to 10.1 to 4 million schillings in 1930, 1931, and 1932 and not being reported separately in 1933.[96] The general situation is reflected by renewed complaints in 1931 from coöperative circles in Austria that Russian orders were not coming through satisfactorily and by a broad hint that the Soviet government was thereby in danger of not fulfilling its contractual obligations to *Ratao.*[97]

---

[93] Cf. *Arbeit und Wirtschaft,* vol. 3 (Nov. 15, 1925), 983, and GöC, *Bericht,* 1925, p. 10; *ibid.,* 1926, p. 13; *ibid.,* 1928, p. 14.

[94] *Der österreichische Volkswirt,* vol. 18 (March 13, 1926), 645.

[95] *SHfRO,* vol. 8, p. 94, note 6; *ibid.,* vol. 11, p. 103, note 7.

[96] *Ibid.,* vol. 12, p. 104, note 6; vol. 13, p. 119, note 10; vol. 14, p. 116, note 5; vol. 15, p. 129.

[97] GöC, *Bericht,* 1931, p. 13.

In two other cases the *Arbeiterbank* exceeded the sphere of coöperative operations, and in both political considerations were essential. Beginning in 1928 it financed the *Kiba* which operated several of the largest moving-picture theaters in Vienna. The predominant ideas were to improve the quality of films shown and to give the Social Democratic party a new means of influencing public opinion. By the time the independent working-class movement was destroyed the *Kiba* owned some 13 theaters and did the booking and operating for 25 more. These were scattered throughout Austria and included two first-run houses in Vienna. For the booking and operating activities *Kiba* received a commission; in other words, it was not financially responsible for about two-thirds of the theaters with which it was connected. In order to be independent of commercial distributors it set up its own distribution company. It was the first to introduce "talking" pictures into Austria; their success contributed materially to its expansion. As with other coöperative and Labor Bank ventures this one was accused of corruption. According to the manager of the bank the facts were as follows. The bank hired as manager of *Kiba* a private theater owner whose father was a party member. After some years reports were circulated that he was accepting private commissions for leasing films for *Kiba*. Investigation substantiated the charges, the manager was discharged, and a Labor Bank official appointed in his place. The bank, however, lost no money on the moving-picture business; on the contrary, it received satisfactory interest on the funds put into it.

The second of these extracoöperative operations was the acquisition of the *Inva,* a large printing establishment where a number of dailies and weeklies were printed. Through this participation the Social Democratic party acquired control of two important dailies and edited them on political lines. The Labor Bank credited the *Inva* with large sums on the security of machinery worth, again as reported by the manager of the bank, four times the amount of the loans. The concern was actually overburdened by its debts and carried on a rather precarious existence for some five years before it was destroyed by a hostile government after February, 1934.

The economic crisis which began in 1929 naturally affected the Labor Bank, but caused no vital damage. The Heimwehr scare of 1929, which led to the collapse of the *Boden Credit Anstalt,* and the struggle for constitutional reform had already brought about some withdrawals of deposits. Then, the intensification of the political crisis resulting from increased Heimwehr activities, the necessity for financing strikes, and the introduction of the regulations concerning dealings in foreign exchange in the fall of 1931 brought further withdrawals. Some of the unions, fearing that the Labor Bank would be one of the first victims of a political change, placed their funds elsewhere. Short-term foreign credits had to be paid back. Finally, the steadily increasing unemployment, which weakened the financial position of the trade unions and seriously affected the activities of the coöperatives, hampered the further expansion of the bank—a fact which appears clearly in the balance-sheet totals given above. But, on the whole, the activities of the Labor Bank were thoroughly successful, so that even the ruthless liquidation after the events of February, 1934, did not result in losses to its creditors.

Workers' Coöperatives and Municipal Activities

The extent and importance of the work done by the Social Democratic city council in Vienna affected the activities of the coöperatives in various ways. The housing policy proved of particular value since the big apartment houses usually contained special premises for the branch societies. And since a huge complex such as Karl Marx Hof or Schlinger Hof formed a more or less closed settlement, the majority of the tenants tended to patronize the coöperative shop almost exclusively. This was even more true in the "garden settlements" built either entirely by the municipality or by some coöperative building society with its help. Since most of these settlements were in outlying districts, far from the markets and better shopping streets, the coöperative branch always became the only marketing center of the place. It is no wonder, therefore, that branches in such colonies as Rosenhügel or Laaerberg had the greatest turnover figures and comparatively the largest membership in Vienna.[98] In some instances, however, the Social Democratic Association of Small Businessmen and Handicraftsmen succeeded in obtaining business

[98] Otto Bauer, *Partei, Gewerkschaft und Genossenschaft,* p. 7: "There is no doubt that the conglomeration of large masses of workers in the new apartment palaces, built by the Viennese working class through the community, is to be regarded as one of the basic conditions of the progress of the coöperatives in this city."

quarters for its members in the new apartment houses. The inevitable, and understandable, results were bitter complaints and criticism among the Viennese coöperators.[99]

There was another, perhaps more important, implication of the Viennese housing policy for the coöperatives. This policy had been rendered possible by the maintenance of the legal tenants protection which kept rents on a very low level, and this in turn permitted the imposition of the housing tax, the proceeds of which were used entirely for building purposes. As one result of this system the market value of Viennese buildings was held considerably lower than their construction costs. Since the societies had invested heavily in buildings and land, they were seriously affected by the impossibility of mortgaging such property on satisfactory terms and thus extending their very limited credit basis; but since the tenants protection law was one of the supporting pillars of the Social Democratic policy in Austria, sharp criticism of it was hardly possible. Nevertheless, it is worth noting that representatives of the coöperatives frequently and carefully pointed out these implications of the law for their business activities.[100]

Apart from the housing policy and its implications there was a certain competition and overlapping between coöperative and municipal activities which led to some resentment in coöperative circles. During the early 'twenties a few of the smaller communities attempted to organize the provision of foodstuffs for their inhabitants. Although these attempts generally failed, they caused a degree of bitterness. The coöperatives also established an insurance agency which evolved quite satisfactorily and was to be transformed into an independent organization. But competition of the Insurance Company of the City of Vienna rendered further development impossible so that the societies had to agree to a compromise restricting the activities of their agency to coöperative institutions only.[101]

Replying to criticisms made by the coöperatives in the states against the Viennese societies Emmy Freundlich said:

None of you have in your movement in the provinces the severe competition of the city of Vienna. . . . If the coöperatives meet with difficulties

[99] Konsumvereine, *Jahrbuch, 1925–1926,* p. 82.

[100] Cf. Renner's speech to the general meeting of the Central Federation, *in* Konsumvereine, *Jahrbuch, 1925–1926,* p. 28, and Vukowitsch, *Besonderheiten,* p. 85.

[101] Renner *in* Konsumvereine, *Jahrbuch, 1925–1926,* p. 42.

in Vienna the reason is that the people of this city administer a large social institution [the city itself] which is able to give them tremendous advantages. We are not able to provide the Viennese women with diapers . . . we cannot give them lots of things which the city council can very well [give]. That is, in my opinion, the chief reason for the progress of the political organization in Vienna, which is much larger than outside of this city, but it is also the explanation for the fact that the economic organizations [coöperative societies] find it more difficult to succeed in Vienna than in the rest of Austria.[102]

Just because the welfare work done by the city so completely overshadowed similar services rendered by the coöperatives, the latter were handicapped in a field the cultivation of which goes far to explain the popularity of the British coöperatives among their members.

The real trouble was that prior to the First World War the coöperatives were the only institutions concerned with the economic activities of workers viewed as consumers. The so-called "coöperative" Socialism felt that it was being driven back by the successful policy of "municipal" Socialism. Against these tendencies the coöperatives tried to emphasize the greater importance of voluntary self-help among workers as contrasted with the "compulsory" Socialism of the states or the communities.[103] On the whole, however, the coöperatives found understanding and support in the city administration of Vienna. This was demonstrated not only by the important undertakings operated jointly by the Coöperative Wholesale Society and the city (*Fleischbanke* G.M.B.H. and *Wihoko*), but also by the fact that up to January 1, 1934, the effective date of a Dollfuss cabinet decree prohibiting certain types of coöperatives from selling to the nation, the states, the communities, and to institutions such as hospitals and gasworks operated by any unit of government,[104] the Coöperative Wholesale Society supplied a very large part of the needs of the city administration and its enterprises for foodstuffs and textiles. Since Dollfuss drew a large part of his support from the peasants, and since their agricultural- and forestry-product coöperatives did substantial business with public bodies, such coöperatives were carefully excluded from the prohibition. The account of the decree in the main Catholic paper, likewise a

[102] Konsumvereine, *Jahrbuch, 1925–1926,* pp. 58–59.
[103] Renner *in* Konsumvereine, *Jahrbuch, 1925–1926,* p. 105.
[104] *BGBl.,* 1933, Nr. 502.

strong supporter of Dollfuss, makes it clear enough that a major purpose of the cabinet's action was to disturb relations between the Vienna city hall and the coöperatives.[105]

EDUCATIONAL AND PROPAGANDA WORK OF COÖPERATIVES

The consumers' coöperative movement reaches far beyond the mere provision to its members of cheaper and better commodities. In the language of the Webbs its "social and political significance . . . lies in the fact that it provides a means by which, in substitution for the Capitalist System, the operation of industry may be . . . carried on under democratic control without the incentive of profitmaking, or the stimulus of pecuniary gain."[106] This wider conception of the movement implies that unlike private trade it cannot confine itself to the usual methods of advertisement and propaganda. The fundamental idea of the movement makes a considerable amount of education and teaching necessary. During the First World War and the early years of the republic, educational work in the Austrian movement was naturally pushed into the background and neglected. The tremendous task of supplying food to the huge membership did not leave time or energy for other activities. Also, it is to be kept in mind that the temporarily "compulsory" character of the membership, falsifying the originally democratic idea of the movement, tended to weaken whatever proselyting zeal was left in the leaders. The restoration of more normal conditions after the stabilization of the currency made it possible to start educational activities anew. First of all special attention had to be paid to the badly neglected coöperative press. The papers founded in the prewar period, *Der Konsumverein* and *Für unsere Hausmutter* (For Our Housewives–a coöperative family magazine), were published very irregularly in the years of the war and in the first months after the revolution; finally they ceased publication. In 1920 a new semimonthly, *Der freie Genossenschafter,* was founded. It attempted to be both a paper for coöperative employees and functionaries of the movement, as well as for the masses of members. The difficulties from the educational point of view are obvious. In 1925 an effort was made to meet these difficulties by alloting alternate issues to the special interests

[105] *Reichspost,* November 9, 1933, p. 7.
[106] S. and B. Webb, *op. cit.,* p. vi.

of the two groups. The continuing dissatisfaction is shown by the facts that the big consumers' coöperative society in Graz started publishing its own paper, that in 1929 *Der freie Genossenschafter* became a pure "functionary paper," and that a new monthly "family paper," *Für Haushalt und Heim* (For Household and Home), was founded.[107]

More important than the press question was the development of a Women's Organization quite similar to the Women's Coöperative Guild created by the British movement. The purposes of this organization were both educational and social: lectures on cooking, sewing, and housekeeping, as well as general addresses on the purposes and ends of the movement, were given; social afternoons, teas, and theater parties were arranged. In the lectures on housework the demonstration of the commodities sold by the coöperatives was coupled with the demonstration of new and better methods of food preparation, so that the overworked and overstrained working-class women might learn to perform their tasks more quickly and efficiently. Other lectures were on choosing and arranging the furnishings for the small apartments in which the workers lived. Since the coöperative department stores sold furniture, a business motive was present; but it remains true that this furniture was of a light and practical sort that did not require much space and was easy to clean. Again the purpose was to reduce the amount of housework to be done. At the same time the worker was introduced to a type of apartment more spacious and better ventilated as compared with the older dwellings usually crammed with heavy old-fashioned furniture full of dust and germs. This type of work by the coöperatives had implications for the cultural and sanitary conditions of working-class life closely resembling the endeavors of the trade unions and the party to shorten working hours and ensure a sound currency. A glance at the *Arbeiter Zeitung* with its columns of announcements of meetings and lectures shows clearly the continuous and earnest efforts made by the coöperatives in this direction.

As propagandists for the movement, the members of the Women's Organization proved invaluable. They visited members whose purchases were low; they tried to persuade former members to come back to the coöperative; they urged the advantages of membership

[107] Vukowitsch, *30 Jahre Zentralverband,* pp. 29, 32, 37.

upon persons who still hesitated to join. In the last endeavor the close connection between the party and the societies proved particularly helpful. Women active in the coöperative movement were usually party members and so could work for it in the meetings of local Social Democratic women's organizations and in the weekly meetings of local party sections. The self-sacrifice and enthusiasm of these "missionaries" is attested by the reports of 500 to 700 visits to housewives made by a single member of the Women's Organization within six months; their success, by further reports of 50 to 70 new members brought in within three months by individual members.[108]

However, this almost religious devotion to the cause was supposed, like charity, to begin at home. A coöperative employee was expected to be, not only a good salesman or bookkeeper, but also to have a thorough understanding of the significance and ends of the movement. Courses were conducted regularly in Vienna and in Styria; summer schools were established. In them theoretical issues were carefully analyzed, but practical questions of coöperative law, taxes, and propaganda work were also emphasized.

Worthy of more space than can be given it was the propaganda work done by the coöperative works councils subcommittees in the factories, the costs of which were borne by the societies. Their chief purpose was to establish a closer connection between the coöperatives and the factory workers, and the success achieved was substantial.

Finally, in this summary of propaganda and educational activities, must be mentioned the publication of a large number of pamphlets on general subjects, such as, "Party, Trade Union, Coöperative," as well as on special questions, for example, "How to Read a Balance Sheet." These publications were issued chiefly by the central coöperative organizations and the very active group in Styria.

As was shown in the concluding paragraph of the second section of this chapter, the coöperatives withstood the great depression remarkably well. Mistakes of the earlier periods had been rectified and some necessary house cleaning carried through. The effects of the political changes of 1934 will be discussed in Volume II, Chapter XXIX.

[108] Freundlich, *Geschichte,* pp. 70 ff.

CHAPTER XIII

Tax Reforms in Vienna

"Wien, Wien, nur Du allein
Sollst stets die Stadt meiner Träume sein . . ."

TO MANY still living the sentimental old song brings memories of Habsburg Vienna; their dreams are of the brilliant balls in the Hofburg or Schönbrunn, of the New Year's Eve performances of *Die Fledermaus* in the opera, of pleasant hours in the *Heurigen* of Grinzing, of *café* life in the *café* capital of the world—a Vienna still suffused with the splendorous rays of a Canaletto. To another group their city of dreams seemed for almost a decade even more completely submerged in the successive tides of Fascism that swept over it. For fifteen years after the proclamation of the republic of Austria they spoke proudly of "the new Vienna" which they were building on the "wreckage" of the imperial city. In the intervening years this second group has been scattered literally to the four corners of the earth. Some of its members spent many months in the prisons or concentration camps, first of Dollfuss and Schuschnigg, then of Hitler; they have seen important leaders die in those concentration camps, or in exile. Some abandoned all hope of witnessing the completion of their ideal Vienna; from *émigré* centers others continued the attempt to keep alive at least that ideal.

In a very definite sense, however, the members of this second group of dreamers believed in materialism as Francis Hackett once explained the term. They too believed in "all the proceeds of a healthy materialism—good cooking, dry houses, dry feet, sewers, drain pipes, hot water, baths, electric lights, automobiles, good roads, bright streets, long vacations away from the village pump, new ideas, fast horses, swift conversation, theatres, operas, orchestras, bands . . ." And above everything they believed with him "in them all for everybody." They had no desire to see Vienna lose its preëminence in music and medicine, but they were more than desirous that tuberculosis should cease to be designated in Central Europe as "the Vienna sickness." Many of them had lived in the miserable quarters so devastatingly described in Philippovich's famous work on Vienna housing; most of them had been trained in a school system which was primarily designed to produce docile subjects of the temporal and ecclesiastical lords of the old empire. Without minimizing the efforts of this second group—working-class leaders—in other fields, it remains appropriate to focus attention on those in which they concentrated their energies: housing, social welfare, and educational reform. With these topics the three succeeding chapters are concerned. The results attracted the attention of housing experts, social workers, and educators throughout the world. Naturally such a program required large sums of money. The methods by which these sums were raised will be considered in the immediately following pages.

The plight of Vienna when the Social Democrats assumed full and formal control of its administration in May, 1919, was desperate. In addition to the facts set forth in previous chapters the following judgment from qualified observers may be submitted: "At the end of the war, the City of Vienna was perhaps in a more difficult position than any other town in Europe. Stocks were exhausted, repairs had not been carried out for several years and a considerable proportion of the population was in need of public assistance. The financial position was made more difficult by the rapid depreciation of the currency."[1] Further light is thrown on this difficult position by the facts that during the fiscal year 1918–1919 (ending June 30, 1919) the city had borrowed 179,500,000 crowns, or more than one-third of its total expenditures of 515,700,000, and that in July, 1919, *Der österreichische Volkswirt* was commenting upon a deficit of 401,000,000 in a total proposed budget for 1919–1920 of 820,000,000 crowns.[2] As indicated in the foregoing quotation and developed at length in Chapter X, a major reason for the heavy expenditures was the burden of relief. In Vienna the number of unemployed persons receiving assistance jumped from 24,000 in December, 1918, to 131,000 in May, 1919. And unemployed workers were, of course, by no means the only group which demanded help from public funds. The general poverty which had engulfed all classes forced into bread

[1] See the report presented to the Council of the League of Nations by W. T. Layton and Charles Rist, *The Economic Situation of Austria* (Geneva, 1925), p. 158.

[2] *Die Gemeindeverwaltung der Stadt Wien in der Zeit vom 1. Jänner 1914 bis 30. Juni 1919* (Wien, 1923), pp. 57, 58; *Der österreichische Volkswirt,* vol. 11 (July 5, 1919), 748.

lines hundreds who had at one time considered themselves the "bread-givers" to thousands.

A recapitulation of other factors complicating the problems of the Socialist administration in Vienna is helpful for an appreciation of the magnitude of those tasks. They included the intense bitterness and radicalization of the workers, the strikes and demonstrations for better treatment and for peace following the Russian collapse, the economic warfare waged by other succession states among themselves and against Austria, the depreciation of the currency, and the establishment of soviet regimes in Bavaria and Hungary. In the strikes and demonstrations the workers had been encouraged, sometimes led, by men who in 1919 became officials of Vienna. Even if these men had not on principle been ready to take a "liberal" attitude on all matters of relief they would have been compelled to do so for political reasons. Peace was not bringing to the masses what they had hoped. Bread had to be provided even though circuses were impossible. And, again as a matter of principle, the city council was under obligations to make upward adjustments of the wages and salaries of its own employees at least adequate to meet rising living costs.

Stated in other terms the tasks of the new Socialist administrators of Vienna were to aid the national coalition government (which their party colleagues dominated) in avoiding a Communist revolution, to reorganize a practically bankrupt city, and then to *rebuild* that city in the literal and the figurative meanings. In a sense the inflation of the currency was an advantage in meeting these tasks, since it reduced the service on the debts and then wiped out the greater part of them; but, on the other hand, it imposed the additional problem of evolving a tax system that would be as near inflation-proof as possible.

The first task involved the expenditure of tremendous sums for welfare work and relief, partly through the previously described municipal supplements to the national unemployment-relief system. Exact amounts do not appear in the available data, but rough calculations indicate that during the calendar year 1919 the city expended on cash unemployment relief something over 10 per cent of its total disbursements for the year. Other items, could they be included, would certainly bring the ratio much higher.

Before proceeding to an examination of the methods used in attempting to solve the other major problems it is necessary to sketch the broad outlines of the sources of revenue of imperial Vienna. Between 45 and 50 per cent of the total came from taxes on rents, about 20 per cent from profits of the municipal monopolies (water, gas, electricity, trams), approximately 11 or 12 per cent from consumption taxes on meat, alcohol, and other comestibles, 15 per cent or better from a tax on industrial enterprises, and the remainder from a variety of taxes all of minor importance. Classified in another fashion, for the year 1913, only 44 per cent of the revenues came from monopoly profits and strictly city taxes, whereas 52 per cent were derived from surtaxes on imperial taxes collected in Vienna, and 4 per cent from the city's share of certain other national taxes.[3]

For a workers' party administration the continuance of such a system was impossible. Close to 80 per cent of the revenues had come from sources such as rent, food and drink, and the monopolies on which the laborer had to expend the greater part of his income. Moreover, there was the very practical consideration that the proceeds of the rent tax seemed destined for extinction. In 1917 rent increases had been prohibited by the imperial government. By the time the Social Democratic city council took over in the spring of 1919 the crown had depreciated to 18 per cent of its 1914 value in Swiss francs and by January, 1920, to 3 per cent. For reasons to be explained later (Chap. XIV), it was felt necessary to retain the rent laws. And as time passed the necessity for formulating an elastic or "inflation-proof" revenue system became more pressing.

The individual to whom this duty was primarily entrusted was Hugo Breitner. To most Americans Breitner would be an incredible combination; a shrewd, practical, successful banker, and at the same time a hundred-per-cent Socialist. To Austrians he was god or devil, though many of those who held the latter view admitted that in financial matters he was a genius. Without detracting in any way from the credit, or blame, which should go to Breitner, it must be noted that he was most ably assisted by Robert Danneberg and that he was always generous in giving credit to Danneberg.

[3] Cf. R. Danneberg, *Das Neue Wien* (Wien, 1930), pp. 10, 11 and *idem, Steuersadismus?* (Wien, 1925), pp. 10, 11. The second citation is to a reproduction of the itemized sources of income of Vienna and their amounts in 1913 and 1925. A similar table in somewhat less detail appears in Layton and Rist, *op. cit.*, p. 169.

In Breitner's own words the questions were: "Who should pay the costs of the war; who should pay the taxes, the poor or the rich?"[4] Because of the general position of the Social Democrats and their attitude on the origins of the war, their policy was, of course, to do everything possible to throw more of the tax burden on the well to do. But for the first two years the new administration also had to borrow and its handling of city employees in certain situations and of the municipal monopolies during the early years might have been characterized as more "capitalistic" than "socialistic." Specifically, there were wage conflicts between the Socialist administration and the Socialist workers in the gasworks, the fire department, the hospitals, and on the streetcars. The tramway strike lasted a week, June 26 to July 3, 1922, and was as vexatious as any strike stopping a public utility. Dr. Deutsch stated that the question was whether or not one group of workers should secure advantages for itself at the cost of the whole proletarian class.[5] For the purposes here, there are at least two other issues.

It had been commonly charged that even if it desired to do so a workers' party government in Vienna would not seriously resist any demands made upon it by the trade unions for fear of wrecking itself. In the instances just cited this contention was demonstrated to be incorrect. Second, Breitner and his associates had been exerting every effort to reorganize financially and to restore physically the municipal monopolies. In fact, the *Volkswirt* nine months earlier had accused Breitner of indirectly taxing the masses by "reckless" increases in the prices of gas, electricity, and streetcar tickets.[6] A comparison of the increases in these prices since 1914 with the increase in the cost of food for a family of four in Vienna at the time the charge was made shows that the latter was greater.[7] The real point, however, is that in rearranging working schedules on the trams with the results of reducing wages and bringing about the strike the managers of this city enterprise were doubtless influenced by Breitner's advice and his desire to rehabilitate the system. Moreover, beginning in the middle of 1923, the charges for gas, elec-

[4] H. Breitner, *Kapitalistische oder sozialistische Steuerpolitik* (Wien, 1926), title page and p. 3.

[5] Cf. Julius Deutsch, *Geschichte der österreichischen Gewerkschaftsbewegung,* Vol. II (Wien, 1932), p. 139; and *Christlichsoziale Arbeiter-Zeitung,* July 8, 1922, p. 1.

[6] *Der österreichische Volkswirt,* vol. 13 (Sept. 24, 1921), 975.

[7] *SHfRO.,* vol. 2, p. 103.

tricity, and street railway transportation were one after another materially reduced as compared with prewar rates. Nor should it be forgotten that by a law of December 22, 1923, in sharp contrast with prewar days, water in the amount of 35 liters per head and per day was supplied free of charge to domestic consumers, that this arrangement persisted as long as the Socialists were in power in Vienna, that the price of water for industrial purposes was drastically reduced, and that even after an increase in 1929 this price was still 58 per cent below what it had been before 1914.[8] In short, Breitner carried on a steady policy of strengthening the position of the municipal enterprises. Within a few years their physical equipment had been improved, prices had been markedly decreased, the number of patrons and total consumption of the products and services greatly increased, and a beginning made in the accumulation of the surpluses which were to prove extremely useful in 1933. Whether these accomplishments be judged by Socialist or bourgeois standards they seem highly praiseworthy.

It proved possible to retain all of the lowest prices reached, except for increases in streetcar fares on October 4, 1927, and July 1, 1929, and the previously noted increase for water for industrial use, until after the world depression set in; even the last increases under Socialist control, forced by the deepening of that depression and the financial assaults of the Dollfuss government in 1933, did not bring the charges back to 1913 levels except in the average cost of tram tickets where the prewar and 1933 figures are almost identical.[9]

Meanwhile a new tax system was being evolved. The basic principles upon which it was planned to erect this new system were the taxation of "luxury," the use of direct rather than indirect taxes, and the use of progressive rates. The rapid depreciation of the cur-

[8] Danneberg, *Das Neue Wien*, pp. 72, 74, 75, 76; *Landesgesetzblatt für Wien*, 1924, Nr. 14, §§ 8, 10; *ibid.*, 1925, Nr. 14; *ibid.*, 1929, Nr. 33. This collection of statutes is cited hereafter as *LGBl. für Wien.*

[9] For a record of the prices of gas and electricity beginning with January 1921, see the successive volumes of the *SHfRO.*, esp. vol. 2, p. 103; vol. 4, p. 87; vol. 5, p. 92; vol. 11 p. 143; vol. 15, p. 169 for the changes. Tram tariffs were altered several times after 1929. These changes can be traced in the issues of the *Wirtschaftsstatistisches Jahrbuch* for *1927*, p. 359; for *1928*, p. 354; and for *1932/33*, pp. 307 and 308. The "average cost of tram tickets" has been used advisedly since the numerous types of tickets render any discussion in terms of a basic fare unrealistic. If, however, the most frequently sold ticket is utilized as a basis for comparisons, there was a great increase between 1926 and 1933—from 24 to 35 groschen. Partly because jobless workers were carried without charge when reporting to the unemployment offices, the "average" was kept down.

rency prompted the adoption of two compensatory devices. The rates of numerous taxes were set at a percentage of some computation base, such as theater admission prices or wages, which was increasing as the value of the crown decreased. Second, many taxes were collected at frequent intervals, every month for example, and payments delinquent by five days were increased by 25 per cent. Since such changes could not be introduced overnight, the new administration was forced to all sorts of stopgaps, including increased prices at the public baths, increased slaughtering fees at public abattoirs, and short-term loans.

The first application of the luxury principle, in the amusement tax law of June 17, 1919, was actually only a modification of a statute of March 24, 1918, which had been preceded, beginning in the fall of 1916, by the voluntary collection by most of the theaters and moving-picture houses of Vienna of a 1 to 6 per cent supplement to ticket prices to be turned over to the city for poor relief.[10] Attempts of July, 1919, and April, 1920, to introduce a tax on "passenger automobiles" and taxis shattered on the objections of the central government that they should be taxed by it rather than by local authorities. Since it was not possible until July of 1921 to overcome these objections, the Social Democrats were thus prevented for two years from applying their principles to a tax object which was certainly a real luxury in postwar Austria.[11]

During the remainder of 1919 the crown continued to drop (from the equivalent of 18 Swiss centimes on July 1 to 3.4 centimes at the end of the year). In late October the majority in the city council carried through changes that introduced a tax on land values in general, raised the levy on capital gains, increased the tax on wine and beer by 500 per cent, and drastically altered the tax on rents. These changes brought forth a violent attack from the official organ of the Catholic trade unions on the grounds that they interfered with the development of a housing policy of benefit to workers and that they were indirect taxes. The second charge was, of course, directed against the alcohol levies. It disregarded completely the estab-

[10] *Die Gemeindeverwaltung der Stadt Wien in der Zeit vom 1. Jänner 1914 bis 30. Juni 1919,* pp. 67, 69–70.

[11] Cf. *Der österreichische Volkswirt,* vol. 11 (July 5, 1919), 752, and *Christlichsoziale Arbeiter-Zeitung,* July 19, 1919, p. 2. The Christian Social members of the city council objected to the tax on taxicabs despite the lower rates for them. See also, *Arbeiter Zeitung,* February 5, 1921, p. 6, and *LGBl. für Wien,* 1921, Nr. 32, 158.

lished Socialist policy, as expressed to me on scores of occasions, of "trying to get the workers out of the stinking little beer rooms." As subsequent events were to prove, the workers' party actually put into effect a housing program that was of much more benefit to their group than anything their critics had ever contemplated. The plan was slow in formulation, but there can be little doubt that the rent tax changes of 1919 were an important step in this formulation; they began the transformation of the levy from a general purpose one, highly unsocial in its incidence, to a specific purpose one. This is not to deny the fact that at the time the emphasis was on the desire to effectuate the principles of "luxury" and progressive taxation rather than on any connection with a still nebulous housing program. Previously the rent impost had been collected at uniform rates on all rents, and since the provincial and imperial governments also assessed such taxes, the burden had become so great that even before the war 42 per cent of the rent paid was actually taxes. The alteration freed four-fifths of the apartments, houses, and business places of the city from the tax. The remainder paid taxes ranging from 5 to 50 per cent of their rent, the latter category including only 402 tax objects.[12]

Despite the measures just mentioned the crisis in city finances remained acute. Unlike the federation, Vienna was under legal restrictions on its taxing power and was not able to meet its obligations by means of the printing press. New taxes or increased rates on existing ones were imperative, and during 1920 a number of proposals along these lines became law. The new taxes included those on rented rooms, on saddle and carriage horses, on household servants in excess of one, on food and drink sold in luxury establishments, on licenses to operate businesses, and on wages and salaries. Rates were increased for the taxes on annual rents above 2,000 crowns, on surtaxes on land taxes, and taxes on income from investments, annuities, savings deposits, and so on, and on the supplements to the general and the specific taxes on business enterprises and the yield therefrom.[13] Other subsequent changes included the introduction of taxes on automobiles, luxury goods, posters, news-

[12] Cf. *Politisches Handbuch* (Wien, 1920), pp. 294, 295; *Christlichsoziale Arbeiter-Zeitung*, November 8, 1919, p. 1; *Der österreichische Volkswirt*, vol. 12 (Dec. 13, 1919), 211 ff.

[13] *Der österreichische Volkswirt*, vol. 12 (Aug. 7, 1920), 839.

paper advertisements, fire insurance premiums, consumption of gas and electric current, sales at auction, and one or two others of no significance.[14] The tax on luxury goods had to be abandoned at the time of the introduction of a general turnover tax (*Warenumsatzsteuer*) by the federation. The prewar taxes on comestibles were dropped as was the tax on rents because they became worthless,[15] but the latter reappeared as the house-construction tax (*Wohnbausteuer*) in 1923. By 1923 the tax system of Vienna had assumed the form which, with quite minor differences, it was to retain until the Social Democrats were forced out of the city hall.

Now it happens that the prospective income of Vienna according to the budget proposals for 1913 and 1925 was almost the same. The former reflect the policies of the Christian Social administration in the last prewar year; the latter those of the Social Democrats after stabilization of the currency and crystallization of the reforms. From the details of the proposals it is possible to draw some comparisons and conclusions. The figures for 1925 have been expressed in gold crowns to facilitate the comparisons. (See tables on pp. 364 and 365.)

Of the eighteen strictly municipal taxes of 1925 those classified as luxury taxes—on autos, horses, dogs, servants, amusements, and luxury food and drink—supplied 22,400,692 crowns, or 22 per cent of such taxes and just under 15 per cent of the total tax revenue. As a matter of fact this computation understates the proportion of luxury taxes, since the house-construction tax was so arranged that some 3,500 "luxury" apartments, palaces, and business establishments paid almost exactly double the aggregate tax paid by over half a million tax units in the lowest brackets.[16] The transfer of the part of the house-construction tax paid by the approximately 3,500 units just mentioned into the "luxury" category would mean that about 31 per cent of the strictly municipal taxes and about 21 per cent of the total tax income was coming from luxury sources. From

---

[14] The most convenient summary giving citations to the collected statutes of Lower Austria and of Vienna, will be found in, *Die Gemeindeverwaltung der Bundeshauptstadt Wien in der Zeit vom. 1. Juli 1919 bis 31. Dezember 1922* (Wien, 1927), pp. 175–217.

[15] Danneberg, *Das Neue Wien*, p. 11.

[16] The exact amount of the taxes paid by the "luxury" units cannot be computed on the basis of the data available. The statements in the text are based on the facts that at the end of 1928 there were 3,470 units which paid 44.57 per cent of the total house-construction tax and 527,731 units which paid only 22.66 per cent, and that the scale of rates was identical in 1925 and 1928. Cf. Danneberg, *Das Neue Wien*, pp. 23, 24.

the foregoing statements it is doubtless clear that the house-construction tax was steeply progressive.

Of the six luxury taxes those on dogs and horses were of relative unimportance fiscally. The levy on automobiles was of importance but was rather generally accepted. The remaining three—on servants, amusements, and luxury food and drink—as well as that on horses, were bitterly attacked. Allegedly, these attacks were based on economic grounds; actually, they were, in varying degrees, "political piffle."

Although most of the comment on these criticisms has been reserved for later passages in this chapter where they will be more easily understood, it may be appropriate here to dispose of what is without much doubt the best example of "political piffle"; namely, the charge against the horse tax brought by the authoritarian Schmitz regime which came into power in February, 1934. According to it the levy was responsible for increasing unemployment.[17] Since the tax imposed upon private owners an annual burden of $35 or less per animal it was obviously not enough to exert any influence upon a person financially able to maintain a saddle or carriage horse. And since, at a constant rate, the proceeds increased from 56 to 65 thousand schillings between 1925 and 1928, it seems clear that grooms and saddle and harness makers were not adversely affected.[18]

The tax on house servants became law in August, 1920. It did not apply to the first servant and was steeply progressive. Rates were changed twice to compensate for the depreciation of the currency and a third time, in December, 1923, as a matter of tax policy. This third tenfold increase remained effective from January 1, 1924, to January 1, 1934. It set the rates at 50 schillings a year for the second servant, if female, 300 for the third, and so on by 250 schilling increases per servant as compared with the preceding servant. Male servants were taxed at double the rates for female and were com-

[17] *Wien im Aufbau: Finanzwesen* (Wien, 1937), pp. 5, 12. This is one of a series of seventeen elaborately printed and beautifully illustrated brochures issued by the Clerical Fascist administration of Vienna at the close of its third year in power. The general title is *Wien im Aufbau*. Each brochure has a subtitle such as *Finanzwesen, Wohlfahrtswesen,* or *Schulwesen*. Among other purposes it was intended as a reply to *Das Neue Wien,* the four-volume work which the Socialists published in 1926 and subsequent years.

[18] *Wirtschaftsstatistisches Jahrbuch, 1925,* p. 68; *Statistisches Taschenbuch . . . Wien,* 1929, p. 45.

Budget Proposals for Vienna, 1913*
(in gold crowns)

	CITY TAXES PROPER	
1	Rent tax, 8¼ heller on each crown of rent	30,523,889
2	Provincial beer tax	4,797,869
3	City levy on brandy and similar beverages	2,278,951
4	Dog tax	466,751
	Total	38,067,460
	SURTAXES ON CENTRAL GOVERNMENT TAXES	
1	House-rent tax	41,879,261
2	Land tax	144,908
3	Tax on business enterprises and proceeds thereof	25,546,360
4	Tax on interest (securities, savings accounts, etc.)	848,862
5	Tax on salaries	993,178
6	Consumption tax (food and drink)	9,958,775
7	Real-estate transactions, fees	1,590,905
8	Race, pool, and bookmaker levy	667,872
	Total	81,630,121
	SHARE IN PROCEEDS OF CENTRAL GOVERNMENT TAXES	
1	Real-estate tax	4,290,925
2	Beer tax	1,425,783
3	Brandy tax	1,196,403
	Total	6,913,111
	REVENUE FROM NET PROFITS OF MONOPOLIES	
1	Gasworks	5,804,081
2	Electrical works	9,747,319
3	Streetcars	2,750,000
4	Water	12,903,655
	Total	31,205,055
	Grand Total	157,815,747

* For the material in the tables, p. 364 and p. 365, see Robert Danneberg, *Steuersadismus?* (Wien, 1925), pp. 10, 11; and W. T. Layton and Charles Rist, *The Economic Situation of Austria* (Geneva, 1925), p. 169.

BUDGET PROPOSALS FOR VIENNA, 1925
(in gold crowns)

	CITY TAXES PROPER	
1	Welfare tax	41,666,666
2	Rented rooms (hotel) tax	3,125,000
3	Real-estate value increment tax (special assessment)	4,166,666
4	Billboard tax	416,666
5	Advertisement tax	1,736,111
6	Contributions of persons insured against fire to the costs of the fire department	1,319,444
7	Tax on voluntary auctions	298,613
8	License tax	104,166
9	Land tax	388,888
10	Recording and inspection duties	250,000
11	House-servants tax	1,944,444
12	Automobile tax	3,263,888
13	Horse tax	39,583
14	Dog tax	486,111
15	Amusement tax	8,333,333
16	Luxury food and drink tax	8,333,333
17	Water-power tax	1,805,555
18	House-construction tax	22,638,888
	Total	100,317,355
	SURTAXES ON CENTRAL GOVERNMENT TAXES	
1	Real-estate transactions, fees	493,055
2	Race, pool, and bookmaker levy	555,555
	Total	1,048,610
	SHARE IN PROCEEDS OF CENTRAL GOVERNMENT TAXES	
1	Total (no details given)	49,250,833
	Revenue from net profits of monopolies	Zero
	GRAND TOTAL	150,616,798

puted at the end of the list. The sharply progressive character of the tax entailed, in 1928 for example, the payment of 291,237 schillings by the household most seriously affected—that of Rothschild.[19]

The previously noted amusement tax was usually collected in relation to the admission prices but sometimes in a lump sum. The basic rates were altered on several occasions prior to 1921 but thereafter remained almost unchanged until the end of 1925. During this period they ranged from 10 per cent on tickets for the opera, theater, and some concerts to 50 per cent on those for horse races and prize fights.[20] It may seem surprising that the levy on movie admissions was 40 per cent at this time (it was subsequently lowered). The explanation lies partly at least in the fact that the city fathers hoped to encourage attendance by workers at the opera and concerts and to discourage it at film houses. Behind this attitude was the unquestionable desire already noted that good music should be available "for everybody," but apparently there was a certain political opposition to the usual Hollywood production. Of what use for the training of good trade unionists and Socialists were these vapid travesties with their inevitable osculatory happy ending?

The luxury food and drink tax had also been authorized in August, 1920. Actually, the tax was not on champagne, for example, as a luxury, but was collected at fixed percentages on the amounts paid for food and drink served to patrons of "bars, cabarets, varieties, concert *cafés,* concert restaurants, *Heurigen und Buschenschenken,* liquor and breakfast rooms, and further in public houses which—in the light of the prices asked, the social position of the customers, the equipment, favorable situation or comfort offered—may be considered as luxury establishments." The tax was also collected in "places subject to the amusement tax" which sold food and drink—in practice, primarily legitimate theaters and movies.[21] The rates varied from 2 to 15 per cent at the discretion of tax officials, the highest rate affecting only a small group. The Socialists claimed that this discretion was exercised in the light of the relative luxuriousness of the tax objects; their opponents that it was of a purely

[19] *Landesgesetz- und Verordnungsblatt für Niederösterreich,* 1920, Nr. 725 (cited hereafter as *LGuVBl. für Niederösterreich*); *LGBl. für Wien,* 1922, Nr. 20; *ibid.,* 1923, Nr. 2; *ibid.,* 1924, Nr. 5; Danneberg, *Das Neue Wien,* p. 15.

[20] *LGuVBl. für Niederösterreich,* 1919, Nr. 163; *LGBl. für Wien,* 1921, Nr. 126.

[21] *Die Wiener Gemeindeverwaltung,* Heft 1 (Oct. 1923–Sept. 1924), pp. 32–33; *LGuVBl. für Niederösterreich,* 1920, Nr. 727.

arbitrary and political character.[22] Though there may have been isolated and exceptional cases of unfairness in the administration of the tax, it is interesting to note that the more responsible critics of the Socialist regime with whom I talked either did not bring the charge or considered it of little significance, and that the succeeding Schmitz government did not even mention it in the previously cited violent attack on the finance policies of Breitner.[23]

The table on page 365 shows that the largest single source of revenue among the strictly city taxes was the welfare tax (*Fürsorgeabgabe*). This had been introduced in the summer of 1920[24] following a period of severe fluctuations in the value of the currency and at a time when relief needs were great and promised to be greater. It was collected monthly from all employers, including those of domestic servants, at an initial rate of 2 per cent on their wage and salary costs; but by 1925 had been increased to 4$\frac{1}{16}$ per cent for all except banks which paid 8½. Although the tax was originally designed to meet pressing welfare needs it had, prior to 1925, ceased to be a "purpose" tax.[25]

On the face of it this levy was in outright conflict with the principles of progressive and luxury taxation which would put the burden on the well to do. Of course the law stipulated that the employer only should pay and that he should not transfer the tax to his workmen in any way, but orthodox economists and tax experts are ordinarily not impressed with the probable effectiveness of such regulations. Without attempting any detailed discussion of the shifting and incidence problems involved, it may at least be pointed out that there are some reasons for believing that the employers actually paid the tax and tried to pass it on to the consumer whenever possible. The Socialist trade unions were particularly strong in Vienna and the Socialist party had an overwhelming majority in the city council. Both groups could be relied upon by the workers to exert severe pressure on any employer who attempted to evade the law.

In another respect also the welfare tax was important since it was well designed to help meet one of the previously stated tasks of the

[22] Cf., for example, Eduard Jehly, *10 Jahre Rotes Wien* [1930?], p. 25.
[23] *Wien im Aufbau: Finanzwesen, passim.*
[24] *LGuVBl. für Niederösterreich,* 1920, Nr. 728.
[25] Robert Danneberg, "Die sozialdemokratische Gemeindeverwaltung in Wien," *Die Gesellschaft,* vol. 1 for 1925, p. 245.

new administration, namely, the evolution of a more or less inflation-proof revenue system. It is clear that the strength of the trade unions and of the party, working through the index system, provided some guarantee that wages should be forced up at a rate not lagging too far behind compensation for currency depreciation. This situation and the monthly collection of the tax tended to increase this part of the municipal income at a pace with rising paper-crown costs.

Brief examination of items 2 to 10 in the strictly city taxes will show that they are exclusively levies on business and property. The tax on advertisements was based on the charges made for them and was strongly progressive. Since it affected most severely newspapers which were politically opposed to the Social Democrats, there were frequent and bitter charges that its purpose was political, not fiscal. Though the Socialists denied the charge in this form, it is entirely probable that their sincere convictions that a great deal of advertising is economically stupid and wasteful and that large advertisers exerted a corruptive influence on news and editorial policies had something to do with the introduction of the tax.

There remain the water-power and house-construction taxes among the strictly municipal imposts. Although the origin, incidence, and progressive character of the latter have been sketched it is probably worth adding that for scores of thousands of typical workers' apartments the tax amounted in 1925 to only 10 or 15 cents a month and that about 500,000 of the 600,000-odd dwellings and business establishments paid 50 cents a month or less. These figures represent taxes of from 1/19 to 1/16 of the prewar taxes.[26] The water-power levy was actually a tax of 1½ per cent on the consumer's gas bill and 4 per cent on his electric current bill. It was introduced in the fall of 1922 just at the worst part of the inflation when the Vienna banks refused to extend further credits for the construction of hydroelectric power plants in which the banks were themselves interested. There can be no doubt that this tax violated the principles of the city administration; but since, as already stated, the prices of gas and electricity were soon greatly lowered and since without the tax construction activities would have been terminated, the administration considered itself justified.[27]

---

[26] Danneberg, *Steuersadismus?*, p. 30, and *idem, Das Neue Wien,* p. 24.

[27] Danneberg, "Die sozialdemokratische Gemeindeverwaltung in Wien." *Die Gesellschaft,* vol. 1 for 1925, p. 248; *LGBl. für Wien,* 1922, Nr. 152.

Reference to the tables on pages 364 and 365 will show that the surtaxes on national levies which had provided a little more than half of the city income in 1913 had been reduced under the republic to about 7/10 of 1 per cent of that income in 1925. In partial compensation for this loss the municipal share of certain central government imposts was much greater in 1925 than in 1913. The combined proceeds of the surtaxes and the "shares" in 1925 was only about 57 per cent of what they had been in 1913, however. And the source which had provided 20 per cent of the total income in 1913—profits of the municipal monopolies—had been wiped out by the different policy of the workers' party government.

There can be no doubt that Breitner and his associates had largely succeeded in shifting the burden of the exclusively city taxes upon the relatively well to do and the rich. At least 60 per cent, and probably more, of this revenue came from luxury, broadly defined, property and business.[28] Although the workers did not pay the remainder of the municipal levies by any manner of means they were still contributing substantially to total city income. A few of them kept dogs, many used gas and electricity, practically all lived in dwellings affected by the house-construction tax. But these were small items as compared with the workers' contributions to those taxes collected by the republic of which Vienna received a share. The outstanding example was the general turnover tax, the type of levy that notoriously affects most severely those groups which have to spend practically their entire incomes on consumption goods.

Further reference to the table on page 364 will show that six sources of the revenue of Christian Social Vienna provided about 119,700,000 gold crowns, or 75 per cent of the total. These six—the two on rents, the two on beer, that on comestibles and the profits from the municipal monopolies—bore most heavily on working people. It is obvious, of course, that this does not mean that the workers paid three-fourths of the taxes in 1913; but it is equally obvious that there had been a tremendous shift in the burden by 1925.

[28] Twenty-two per cent was derived from the six luxury taxes, 9 per cent from "luxury dwelling" house-construction taxes, and 11 per cent from business and property taxes concerning which there can be no question. As pointed out earlier, it is probable that a great part of the welfare tax was also actually paid by business. But if less than half of it was so paid the estimate of 60 per cent in the text is warranted.

As her entire history demonstrates republican Austria was a country in which economic issues were particularly likely to become political issues. And just because Breitner and his associates had succeeded in effecting a major shift in the burden of Vienna taxes the conflict concerning them was certain to become extraordinarily bitter. Derogatory terms such as "tax Bolshevism," "welfare inflation" and "tax sadism" were among the printable characterizations of the Socialist policy. The replies were equally pungent. In 1925 Danneberg had published his pamphlet, *Steuersadismus?,* already cited. In the middle of March, 1926, the leader of the Christian Social opposition in the city council, Leopold Kunschak, vigorously attacked the majority's tax policy as "overtaxation"; and described the results as "taxing away of business capital, limitation of production and employment." Proof of overtaxation he found in the following argument. The strictly municipal levies brought only 83,427,100 schillings in 1923, whereas the budget estimates for these taxes for 1926 was 153,798,000—an increase of 86 per cent. To this should be added, however, the sums allocated to Vienna from federal revenues (the assumption being that had the allocation not been made the city council would have tried to raise these sums). The aggregate amount meant an average annual burden for every man, woman, and child in Vienna of 131 schillings, or the equivalent of three weeks average income for a skilled manual worker.[29]

About two weeks later Breitner made a lengthy reply. His argument admitted only that Kunschak could do correctly a problem in long division—"everything else is false." The whole point of the Socialist system was that taxpayers of varying abilities contributed in accordance with those abilities. The luxury taxes and many of the others were paid almost exclusively by the "upper classes," so that they should not have been included in the "division" at all; and the house-construction tax, which did affect everyone, was steeply progressive, in sharp contrast to the 1913 system under which every crown of rent, whether paid on palace or hovel, was taxed at exactly the same rate. For the worker living in a cheap apartment a major practical result was that in 1926 he paid for the entire *year* in house-construction tax only 60 per cent of what he had paid for rent taxes in 1913 in one *month.* The application of the welfare,

[29] *Christlichsoziale Arbeiter-Zeitung,* March 20, 1926, p. 2.

house servant, automobile, and house-construction taxes to the Vienna Rothschild family meant that its eight members paid as much in them as 6,016 persons would according to Kunschak's "division." Eight night clubs paid taxes equal to 7,738 of his tax units, and two newspapers in advertising taxes the same as 15,602 of those units. Under the assumption that the Christian Socials could realize their ideal tax legislation, abolish all levies on particular objects and include them in a general turnover tax such as that of the federation, then Kunschak's "simple division" would be in order; under the Vienna system of 1926 it had no sense. The very fact that the local leader of the Catholic party which had ruled the city so long was attacking the Social Democratic tax policy with such bitterness was proof enough to Breitner of his success.[30]

Meanwhile, the Socialist *Arbeiter Zeitung* had carried several attacks on Kunschak's speech, particularly on March 21 and March 28, which were little, if any, short of vicious. He was characterized as "the choirmaster of the impotently raging gang" and likened to a dog baying at the moon; his statements were in one place compared to the bomb of a circus clown which turns out to be only a cleverly shaped bit of paper, and in another flatly called lies.

To these attacks and to Breitner's speech Kunschak retorted in the *Christlichsoziale Arbeiter-Zeitung* of April 3, 1926. He accused the Socialist paper of making no attempt at a factual rejoinder and Breitner of circling away from the Christian Social indictments "like the devil from the holy water font." But after this unquestionably effective introduction, Kunschak's remaining three columns are somewhat disappointing. Part of them are strangely reminiscent of "the flowers that bloom in the spring"; they "have nothing to do with the case." To Breitner's statement of fact that scores of thousands of workers, clerks, and even petty officials paid an extremely low house-construction tax, Kunschak replied that the way in which the tax affected the poor and the poorest could be seen from the fact that students in five "student homes" paid from 26 to 145 schillings per capita each year in this levy. According to a university student of the period now in America, some of these "homes" were clubs

[30] Hugo Breitner, *Kapitalistische oder sozialistische Steuerpolitik* (Wien, 1926). Other passages of the speech dealt with the reductions in the prices of gas, electricity, and streetcar transportation previously discussed, and still others with the rent laws and housing policy which are discussed in Chapter XIV.

in which extremely wealthy students lived and others were given to students rent free on condition that the tax be paid. In any case what relation is there between Kunschak's statements concerning a handful of students and the freeing of the masses of Vienna workers from the burdens of the old rent taxes?

Another paragraph of Kunschak's reply comes at least dangerously close to the "limited love of truth" of which he accuses Breitner. In this passage he refers to a meeting of unemployed house servants in which their "terrible need was established," and states that: "This need is in great part the consequence of the house-servant tax." But the available data lend no support to this explanation. According to them, the number of Vienna households and clubs employing two or more servants for the years designated was as follows.[31]

Year	Number	Year	Number
1920	5,905	1927	6,820
1923	7,312	1928	6,584
1924	7,822	1929	6,340
1925	7,816	1930	5,960
1926	7,256		

A much more probable explanation of the decreases which took place after Kunschak's article appeared is the gradual deepening of the general crisis in Austria which began after the collapse of the French franc speculation in May, 1924. Furthermore, since the annual tax on the second servant amounted to only 50 schillings if the servant was female and 100 if male, there is serious doubt whether or not it could have exercised any restraining influence on a household financially able to hire two servants. And since the city was spending so much of its income on apartment building and huge extensions of its welfare activities, there is no doubt that these activities more than compensated for whatever minor increases in unemployment among servants the tax on them might have caused.

In still other passages Kunschak alleged that the reduced prices charged by the municipal monopolies were primarily the result of

[31] The figure for 1920 was secured by a special enumeration of the employers affected; cf. *Statistische Monatsschrift*, 3d. ser., vol. 2 (Wien, 1920), p. 207. The figures for 1927–1930, inclusive, appeared in the issues of the *Wirtschaftsstatistisches Jahrbuch 1927*, p. 442; *1928*, p. 438; *1929/30*, p. 494; *1930/31*, p. 447. Data for the intervening years were supplied by a tax official of Vienna who stated that it was impossible in 1937 to ascertain the facts for 1921 and 1922. All figures are as of December 31, except that for 1920 which was of September 23, and for 1930 which was "November."

technical improvements and the disappearance of funded debts as a consequence of the depreciation of the currency. This argument completely disregards the facts pointed out by Breitner and others on innumerable occasions that rationalization and technological changes had gone even further in Germany than in Austria, that these improvements were open to all, that Germany too had suffered an inflation, but that nevertheless Vienna prices for gas and electricity were lower than in the overwhelming majority of European cities, including Austrian towns controlled by Christian Socials.

For a time after the Kunschak-Breitner duel—or squabble—the political aspect of taxes was less prominent. Then, during the debates on the city budget in December, 1926, and January, 1927, but always with an eye on the impending elections of April 24, 1927, the verbal pyrotechnics blazed up again. The *Neue Freie Presse* ushered in the new year with several articles of importance. One, filling over three pages, summarized world economic events during 1926. The section on Austria complained of general economic losses, decreases in the values of bank and industrial stocks, and "along with this the pressure of taxation, particularly that of the city of Vienna, experienced only a very small moderation." Another, of one and one-half pages, "Vienna in the Year 1926," contained the following gibe at municipal taxes: "Although it appears at the moment as though the worst stage of lassitude in the theaters has happily been overcome, one cannot shake off the impression that sooner or later only the luxury tax would reveal that once upon a time there was such a thing as luxury in Vienna, and that the amusement tax would considerably outlive all amusements." On the next page but one, however, appeared a half-column story, "Vienna on New Year's Eve," including the following:

> The festive note appeared by seven o'clock in the evening. Attendance at the evening performances was far and away better than in the recent weekdays; some houses were already sold out by the beginning of the evening. The midnight performances that lasted until one and one-thirty in the morning, although there were not less than ten on the Viennese stages, were without exception completely sold out. Even the movies which had secured the appearance of popular Vienna stage darlings were full. In the large hotels, restaurants, and coffeehouses of the Inner City, in which jazz bands frequently played the farewell dance of the old year, there was not a vacant table.

The remainder of the account was taken up with similar comments. The large dance halls, inns, and coffeehouses of the outlying districts were, literally translated, "pump-full." Something new in New Year's Eve entertainment was the huge mob in the Prater. Restaurants with and without dance floors were overflowing; side shows, the scenic railway, and similar amusement places were brilliantly lighted and drawing crowds as though it were summer; the famous Prater Ferris wheel kept turning until the first gray of morning appeared. And back in the heart of the old city the foot traffic on Kärntner and Rotenturm streets was so thick that people had to stay on one side if they wished to go in one direction and on the other if they wished to go in the opposite direction.[32]

Perhaps these extracts from the New Year's issue of the stock exchange sheet of Vienna are entirely consistent, but perhaps the outsider may be pardoned a little skepticism. Further examination of its files may, again "perhaps," heighten or dispel whatever skepticism has arisen. The morning edition for January 5, 1927, reported a meeting of trades people, petty manufacturers, moving-picture theater owners, industrialists, concert hall, hotel and restaurant proprietors, and others on January 3 to protest city taxes. The complaints of these groups were directed against the taxes on luxury food and drink, on amusements, and on rented rooms. It was charged that the first had forced 70 concerns into insolvency during the preceding two years, that the second had compelled 80 establishments to close their doors, that as a result of the third "the necessary tourist trade is completely paralyzed," and that thousands of workers were being forced into unemployment. The afternoon edition of the *Presse* for the same day carried an editorial approving these protests under the heading: "The Success of the Tax Vampires." It referred to the "Breitnerism under which Vienna sighs so much" and to the "*great suffering of entrepreneurs under the city taxes.*"[33] On the matters of the rented rooms tax and of the consistency of the *Presse* it is interesting to note that the previously cited article "Vienna in the Year 1926" had called attention to the fact that though Vienna was not yet a tourist center "in the grand style" and was not overcrowded with foreign millionaires, nevertheless the tourist trade

[32] *Neue Freie Presse,* January 1, 1927 (A.M.), pp. 23, 11, 13.
[33] *Ibid.*, January 5, 1927 (A.M.), p. 8; (P.M.), pp. 1 and 2. Italics in original.

was no longer a matter of committee reports so that the city had "decisively profited" from the "democratization of travel traffic" and "had become in the past year to an extensive degree a convention city."

As for the "thousands" who were being forced out of work by the taxes, it may be noted that particular complaint was made concerning musicians, theater employees, cooks, waiters, and others employed in *cafés* and restaurants. There is no doubt that there was great unemployment among musicians and that the president and the secretary of the Socialist trade union of stage employees bitterly denounced Breitner and the amusement tax as being responsible for the "need and misery" resulting from lack of work for its members;[34] but for the hotel, *café,* and restaurant employees the official statistics show that unemployment in Vienna increased from an average of 4,406 to an average of 4,668 between 1924 and 1926, or about half of 1 per cent, and then decreased steadily through 1929 to an average of 3,449. In other words, a group supposedly suffering severely from Vienna tax policy was generally in much better position than Vienna or Austrian workers as a whole.[35] And as for the business failures most complained of, those of establishments affected by the luxury food and drink and amusement taxes, it may again be said that the crisis which began in the late spring of 1924 probably had a great deal more to do with such failures than did the taxes.[36]

Protest meetings continued thick and fast. On January 6, 1927, the *Presse* reported one of January 4 of the "Central Organization of Tradesmen and Small Producers and of the Free Professions of Austria," directed "against tax tyranny." The chief speaker, Karl Lossmann, denounced "the city administration's tax nonsense that already bordered on sadism" and added that "Saint-Germain inflicted terrible wounds upon us but that is surpassed by far by the unheard of tax tactics of the community of Vienna" which are slowly but surely destroying the entire group of small producers and the whole middle class. Throughout January several such reports and editorials appeared each week. Most of them were directed against

[34] Quoted in *Christlichsoziale Arbeiter-Zeitung,* April 3, 1926, p. 2.

[35] Cf. C. A. Gulick, "Vienna Taxes Since 1918," *Political Science Quarterly,* vol. 53, 537 ff. for a more detailed discussion. The figures were taken or computed from the *Wirtschaftsstatistisches Jahrbuch, 1924* ff.

[36] Cf. *Der österreichische Volkswirt,* vol. 17 (Nov. 8, 1924), 146.

the taxes already mentioned and that on newspaper advertising, but at least one attacked the house-construction tax. The occasion was the rejection by the Administrative Court, the highest federal body having jurisdiction in such cases, of the appeal of Count Lanckoronski against the house-construction assessment on his palace of 28,700 schillings a year. The palace housed a famous art collection which had always been open to the public. When Count Lanckoronski announced that because of the court decision he would have to remove his art treasures from Vienna, the *Presse* bewailed the great loss for the cultural life of the city—a new victim of the Socialist tax policy. That these editorial tears were premature is demonstrated by the fact that in Vienna ten years later Count Lanckoronski's secretary stated that the collection had never been removed and had always been open to the public during this period. On the other hand, it is true that Rothschild abandoned his gardens because of the heavy incidence of the house-servant tax on him, that they were little if any less famous than Lanckoronski's art collection, and that the cultural loss to Vienna was great.

Some of the complaints were, of course, worthy of more serious consideration. Among these was that of a deputation claiming to represent 4,500 unemployed hotel, inn, and coffeehouse employees. These workers urged that Breitner reduce the amusement and luxury food and drink taxes, reported that the employers had undertaken that each of them would employ two or three additional men if taxes were materially reduced, and argued that such reduction would permit the reëmployment of 3,000 men. Breitner replied that there was no guarantee that the employers would not discharge the men again a short time after the taxes were reduced, and that since the city council had social tasks of great importance to fulfill a reduction of taxes could not be considered.[37] In this connection it should not be forgotten that late in 1925 the city council had reduced the tax on hotels (rented rooms) by two-thirds and had also considerably reduced the taxes on various types of amusements.[38]

[37] For the articles and editorials discussed in the text, as well as others, see the *Neue Freie Presse* throughout January, particularly the issues of January 6 (A.M.), p. 8; 21 (P.M.), p. 2; 22 (A.M.), pp. 1–2, 17; 23 (A.M.), p. 14; 24 (P.M.), pp. 1, 2; 27 (A.M.), p. 8; 28 (A.M.), p. 7.

[38] Cf. *LGBl. für Wien,* 1922, Nr. 137 with *ibid.,* 1925, Nr. 61; and *ibid.,* 1921, Nr. 126 with *ibid.,* 1925, Nr. 60. For examples, the tax on operetta tickets was reduced from 30 to 23 per cent; on movie tickets from 40 to 28.5 per cent; on horse racing and boxing from 50 to 33.3 per cent.

Moreover, as shown above, this group of employees was more fortunate than Viennese or Austrian workers in general on the matter of unemployment.

During the bombardment from the bourgeois press, for the *Reichspost* and other papers had joined with the *Presse,* the batteries of the *Arbeiter Zeitung* had been far from silent. The largest shells were directed not against the issue of unemployment but rather against the federal fiscal policies of the Christian Socials, the allegations of overtaxation and welfare inflation, and the "real purpose" behind the whole agitation. That real purpose was the emasculation or destruction of the tenants protection laws and the housing program of Vienna.

As has previously been indicated, the chief complaint against the Catholic party's tax system was that despite a progressive income tax it emphasized indirect consumption taxes which hit the poor man the hardest, so that what appeared to be uniform rates were actually regressive and antisocial. In this counterattack Breitner's speech of January 31, 1927, and an article in the *Arbeiter Zeitung* of the same date are noteworthy. Since the Christian Socials had protested against increases in the tax income of Vienna in the period between 1923 and the 1927 proposals, Breitner pointed out that in the same period the customs duties had increased from 113 to 206 million schillings and the sugar tax from 2.8 to 10.3 million. Then he called attention to certain changes in different types of turnover taxes: that on stock exchange transactions had amounted to 15 million in the 1924 budget and 2 million in 1927; that on banking transactions had dropped from 15 million to 300,000 in the same period; and that on dealings in foreign currency had fallen from 10 million to 250,000. But the general turnover tax on almost all goods and on numerous services ranging from those of the obstetrician to the undertaker showed an increase from 44 million in the 1923 budget to 212 million in that for 1927—an increase of 480 per cent. As one other example of the administration of the last-mentioned tax, Breitner cited the action of the finance minister in raising the rate on flour from 6.5 to 7 per cent on the same day that he reduced it from 8 to 7 on imported automobiles. In the light of these facts, asked Breitner, is it any wonder that the bourgeois press is so loud in its praises of the central government's understanding of the needs of "the economy" and that the banks contribute so gladly to the Christian Social campaign fund?[39]

Although the editor of *Der österreichische Volkswirt* wrote that Breitner's address was not lacking in demagogy, particularly in its references to the financial turnover taxes, he added that Breitner could justly say of himself that he "administered with conscientious fidelity"; and that in the editor's opinion, measured against the fighting tactics of the Christian Socials, Breitner's demagogy was "almost scholarly method."[40]

Just what is demagogy cannot be determined in a test tube. During a political campaign party spokesmen and party publications utilize those methods which they believe will secure or hold votes. From this point of view the workers' daily in Vienna was always effective, and rarely more so than in the article mentioned above, a summary of which follows. The story begins in the delivery room of a hospital.

As he left his mother's womb his first glance fell on a tax official of the finance ministry. "Not a step farther," said the official, "before you have paid the turnover tax on the wages of the midwife."

"Gladly," said the infant, "but you forget the turnover tax on the lighting."

"By no means," replied the official, and presented a list of taxes on lights, disinfectants, powder, and everything conceivably used in connection with birth.

"Yes, this is correct," remarked the infant; "hope you have not forgotten anything. By the way, what about my mother's milk?"

"We don't tax that directly," explained the official; "the tax has already been levied on all your mother's food."

Then the official departed, but not for long. He came back to tax the doctor's fees during childhood illnesses, clothes, toys, school books, and so on, and so on. Soon the finance minister had enough money to reorganize a few bankrupt Christian Social banks and to protect others from smashing.

One day, after the child had become a young man in his 'twenties, he said to the tax official: "I'm worried that some day you won't come to visit me; that would be terrible."

But the official quieted him with the assurance that he could rely on his presence—even on the day of his burial to collect taxes on the coffin.

Thereupon a heavy stone fell from the heart of the young man and he resolved to go to some amusement center for a really "big" evening. To

[39] Hugo Breitner, *Seipel-Steuern oder Breitner-Steuern?* (Wien, 1927), pp. 8–10.
[40] Vol. 19 (Feb. 5, 1927), 494.

his great pleasure he met his old friend there and paid his turnover taxes, but as he was putting his purse away another official came. This gentleman explained that he represented the city of Vienna and wished to collect the amusement tax; the proceeds went to build hospitals and recuperation homes. But at this the young man became very angry and exclaimed: "Too much is too much! Since the day of my birth I have paid turnover taxes on every necessity of life in order to give the finance minister enough money to reorganize smashed banks and make presents to big capitalists. I have never protested against this burden; in fact, I have carried it easily and with pleasure. Now, however, if the city taxes my amusements to create welfare establishments, it will spell my economic ruin. To hell with Breitner!"[41]

The polemic concerning overtaxation was again precipitated by Kunschak. This time he was able to show that strictly municipal taxes had risen 94.4 per cent by comparing the proceeds in 1923 with the budget for 1927. The *Neue Freie Presse* supported him editorially, emphasized the fact that this huge increase had taken place during a period of terrible slump, of bankruptcies, and of collapse of security prices on the stock exchange, and reproached the city council, which was spending tremendous sums for social purposes, because it was not willing to help other classes of the population. The theaters and the night clubs, said the *Presse,* were badly in need of aid.[42]

The *Arbeiter Zeitung* replied the next day with figures showing that federal taxes had increased between 1923 and 1927 by 97 per cent. After quoting the headline of the editorial in the *Presse,* "New Facts against Breitner," it continued: City taxes "up 94 per cent—terrible—that scoundrel Breitner"; national taxes "up 97 per cent—admirable—fine finance minister is Herr Kienböck."

During the following week anti-Breitner speakers charged that the *Arbeiter Zeitung* had "intentionally forgotten" to mention the fact that Vienna received a big slice of the federal taxes, that it had omitted the municipal beer tax in computing city revenues, and that an accurate comparison would show that federal taxes had risen only 68.7 per cent, whereas municipal levies had gone up 106 per cent.[43] Some weeks later the Christian Social electoral manifesto again made comparisons of federal and municipal budgets. Perhaps

[41] *Arbeiter Zeitung,* January 31, 1927, p. 5.
[42] *Neue Freie Presse,* January 22, 1927 (A.M.), pp. 1, 2.
[43] *Ibid.,* January 25, 1927 (A.M.), p. 4; January 28 (A.M.), pp. 14, 15.

the best comment on this aspect of the controversy appeared in *Der österreichische Volkswirt,* April 9,[44] where it was noted that these types of comparisons "really say no more than if we should reproach the municipality because it did not maintain an army." The truth is, of course, that both the city and the federation had been compelled to increase taxes; but it cannot be denied that the workers' party had made a good case for its position that the real overtaxation was inflicted by the federation, since its taxes were in large part regressive. And as one of the shrewdest and ablest of the foreign observers of the work of the Vienna Socialists in housing, welfare, sanitation, and school reform pointed out: "It is true that the richer classes were obliged to pay high taxes to maintain this work; but even these taxes were only a fraction of what London capitalists must pay, proportionately as well as absolutely."[45]

During the years in which the conservative parties and their journals had pressed the charge of "welfare inflation" there had been numerous replies, but again this campaign of 1927 produced the one most frequently mentioned, even ten years later. Its author, Dr. Wilhelm Ellenbogen, began with a vivid picture of conditions toward the close of the war: "the long polonaise of nights through which mothers stood before empty grocery stores," the reduced flour and meat rations, food substitutes of all sorts, lack of apartments, children freezing because of tattered clothing and lack of shoes, infants dying because of scarcity of milk, and on top of all this the empty, plundered treasuries of the state and the cities.

With the trains came hundreds of thousands of hungry, enraged soldiers from the fronts that had broken, rifles and machine guns in hand. "Revenge" was the one idea that filled the brains of millions of desperate men and women—revenge on the criminals, parties, and persons, who had brought this limitless misery on them and their families. "His majesty's minister for social administration, Dr. Seipel, implored us, Viktor Adler, Seitz, and me," for help in order that Vienna might not become a mass of fire-blackened ruins.

Then came the Social Democratic municipal administration which proceeded vigorously in the work of saving parents, and above all the children, from physical and spiritual misery and degra-

[44] P. 738.
[45] M. W. Fodor, *Plot and Counterplot in Central Europe* (Boston, 1937), p. 211.

dation. And now these activities which have been greeted with wonder and gratitude by all the rest of the world are "spat upon by the mouthpiece of the Austrian financial and industrial plutocracy [the *Neue Freie Presse*] with the epithet 'welfare inflation.' The whole unfeeling cold-heartedness of the money-bag men spurts out of all the pores of this poisonous word."

Most of the remainder of the two-column article is taken up with short paragraphs comparing the statistics of prewar years and of 1925 on mortality rates in general and by particular causes such as "epidemic and other infectious diseases," tuberculosis and puerperal fever, and presenting other statistics on tubercular "welfare institutions," school dental clinics, and municipal institutions for alcoholics. Each paragraph closes with a sarcastic "and this is welfare inflation."

"What is this welfare activity of the municipality other than the application of the Scriptural words, 'Come unto me all ye that are weary and heavy laden.' But if Christ should come today and speak these kind and noble words, then Herr Kunschak together with his Jewish leader Ernst Pharisäus Benedikt, would call out to him: 'Welfare inflationist! The wages of the masons are far too generous. Crucify him, the tax sadist!!'"[46]

Perhaps this, too, is only demagogy. But it is more probable that the correct explanation lies in Ellenbogen's deep and bitter conviction of the hypocrisy of the leaders of the Christian Social party—a party which the *Volkswirt* characterized during this campaign as the opposite of Christian and social.[47]

For proof of the fourth point in their counterattack; namely, that the whole agitation against Breitner's taxes had as its real purpose the destruction of the tenants protection laws and of the housing program, the Socialists were able to offer the general record of the Christian Social party and specific quotations from its leaders and supporters. In the last preceding election the Catholic party had campaigned in favor of drastic modification of the rent laws, and though it was more careful in 1927, the results of its proposals would have been much the same. Among the quotations from conservative sources, the *Arbeiter Zeitung* used most effectively a resolution

[46] *Arbeiter Zeitung*, February 27, 1927, pp. 1, 2. Benedikt was editor of the *Presse*.
[47] *Der österreichische Volkswirt*, vol. 19 (March 12, 1927), 630.

adopted at a meeting of January 24: "Since those engaged in crafts, small manufacturing, and trade visualize in the apartment-building activity of the city of Vienna the real cause of high taxation, they demand the complete cessation of apartment building from tax money after the completion of the apartments already begun and authorized."[48]

Throughout the budget debate and the following campaign, despite some sharp criticism already cited, the *Volkswirt* strongly supported the Breitner tax policies. Nothing, it said, could indicate better the poverty of ideas in the bourgeois parties and their journals than their attack on precisely that position in which the Socialists were most impregnable. The municipal fiscal policy was characterized as energetic, conscious of purpose, and thrifty; the policies of the federation and numerous states (controlled by the Christian Socials) as "planless, putrescent, and despite all stinginess, wasteful." The federation had flung away millions of schillings of the people's money for the benefit of smashed banks; the city had not lost a schilling of its tax money. In fact, the more the city budget and the criticism thereof was studied, the more the reader became convinced that the root of that criticism was that the city was building dwellings. Since the editor of the *Volkswirt* approved of the housing policy, though not of all the Socialists' ideas on tenant protection, he believed that the whole criticism was invalid; and since many if not most of the petty manufacturers and trades people who had protested against the housing program and the retention of the rent laws were just the ones who directly benefited from low rents paid by their customers and themselves, he had serious doubts concerning the "seriousness of the whole tax storm." On several occasions during the campaign the *Volkswirt* stated that the bourgeois parties had united in "a class war from above," but perhaps its best shot was the charge that the Roman Catholic prelate, Chancellor Seipel, had reached the "summit of demagogy" in discovering the reason for widespread unemployment and economic crisis in Breitner's taxes.[49]

Since the workers' party maintained its approximately two-thirds

[48] *Arbeiter Zeitung*, January 25, 1927, p. 1.

[49] *Der österreichische Volkswirt*, vol. 19 (Dec. 4, 1926), 260; (Jan. 8, 1927), 382; (Jan. 29, 1927), 465; (Feb. 19, 1927), 550; (April 30, 1927), 821. The general position of the *Volkswirt* was that the real issue of the national election, held on the same day as that in Vienna, should have been union with Germany.

control of the city hall and slightly improved its position in the parliament, whereas the Catholic party was losing 1 vote in the municipal council and 9 in parliament (3 to the Socialists, 4 to the Landbund, and 2 to its partner in the coalition government, the Pan-Germans), there can be no doubt that Seipel and Kunschak had suffered a serious defeat. In less than three months, however, the deplorable events of mid-July[50] had put the Social Democrats on the defensive. It was, of course, out of the question for the conservatives in the city council to force reductions in municipal taxes, but because they controlled the Nationalrat it might be possible to hamstring their opponents in another fashion. This possibility lay in the fact previously mentioned that a number of taxes collected by the federation were divided among it, the states, and the communities. Since Vienna was both state and city after December 29, 1921, its share of such taxes was quite important. At this point, then, it is necessary to trace briefly the earlier developments in this phase of the tax problem.

The first statute of the republican era regulating the division of joint taxes was passed March 3, 1922.[51] The chief practical aspects of the law of immediate interest here are, first, that the states and communities lost almost all the revenue previously derived from surtaxes on federal levies and received in lieu thereof a share of the joint taxes; second, that they were to lose entirely by the end of 1926 the contributions previously made by the federation to the wages of their employees. It is necessary, moreover, to note that the central government retained varying percentages of different taxes and that the share of certain taxes on consumption going to an individual town or city was determined with reference to its inhabitants as weighted by an arbitrary scale in which the lowest unit of 500 population or less was multiplied by twenty and the highest of over 50,000 by seventy;[52] that is, according to the "graduated population key."

In April of 1923 the general turnover tax[53] went into effect. After an increase in the basic rate from 1 to 2 per cent in 1924 this tax pro-

[50] Cf. Chapter XX.
[51] *BGBl.*, 1922, Nr. 125.
[52] Cf. R. Danneberg, "Die deutschösterreichische Finanzverfassung," *Der Kampf*, vol. 15 (July, 1922), 208, 209, for a reproduction of the table and scale prepared by the finance ministry setting forth the details of the division.
[53] *BGBl.*, 1923, Nr. 121.

vided for years about one-third of the total amount raised in joint taxes. Since the basis on which it was divided among the states, cities, and towns was obviously extremely important, there was a series of storms in parliament and in party publications concerning the proper "key." Others proving unsatisfactory or impracticable it was finally agreed, in the fourth amendment to the tax division law,[54] to base the division of the turnover tax until 1930 on the "graduated population key."

Meanwhile, late in 1923, the government had introduced amendments to the tax division law which would have deprived the other governmental units of any share in the income and property taxes. The opposition, not only from the Social Democrats in Vienna, but also from some Christian Socials in the states, was so great that it was necessary in June, 1924, to compromise on a plan under which the federation deducted for its exclusive use 50,000,000 schillings in 1924, 1925, and 1926 and 40,000,000 in subsequent years before distributing the shares.[55] During the debates the League of Nations commissioner, Zimmerman, criticized the Vienna administration for its opposition to the law and was in turn criticized by the *Volkswirt* for his failure to see that, generally speaking, the other states were always trying to increase their shares at the expense of the metropolis.[56]

In 1925, however, another amendment to the division of taxes law brought "better stipulations" from the Socialist viewpoint in the sharing of that part of the income taxes deducted before receipt of said income (*Abzugseinkommensteuer*) and of the turnover tax. On the other hand, in an accompanying measure, the federation secured until December 31, 1930, far-reaching veto powers over the authority of states and communities to levy taxes.[57] Again in 1926 there was a squabble over the fifth amendment to the law. The government claimed that in order to meet rising unemployment-compensation costs it needed to retain all the proceeds of the taxes on alcoholic drinks and of the capital levy. It proposed to allow the states to introduce their own alcohol taxes. The Socialists charged that the real purpose of the move was to secure funds to assist certain

---

[54] *Ibid.*, 1925, Nr. 287.
[55] *Ibid.*, 1924, Nr. 185, p. 516.
[56] *Der österreichische Volkswirt*, vol. 16 (April 12, 1924), 844.
[57] *Tätigkeits-Bericht*, Heft 19 (Wien, 1925), pp. 24, 25; *BGBl.*, 1925, Nr. 287, 270.

"Christian Social banks" which were in difficulties. Finally the states were given the right to levy a tax on beer only. As the *Volkswirt* suggested, it would have been more intelligent simply to increase the federal beer tax.[58]

Although Vienna had suffered no financial losses worth mentioning from the various amendments to the tax division law through 1926, subsequent events, culminating in the Dollfuss decrees of 1933, were to prove that the fears of its Social Democratic rulers were entirely justified. In spite of the weakened position of the workers' party following July, 1927, the attack was somewhat slow in getting under way, however, for again some Christian Social leaders in the states were skeptical of Finance Minister Kienböck's plans for a "more uniform financial policy" in those states.

The proposals of the government actually brought into parliament in July, 1928, involved primarily changes in the tax division law and the financial constitution. The former would have altered the basis of allocation of the turnover tax from the "graduated population key" to population, and cost Vienna 23,000,000 schillings a year. The latter would have reduced the compensation which Vienna and Graz received for collecting certain federal taxes from 3 to 1 per cent of the amount collected and cost the capital city about 5,000,000 schillings annually. During the negotiations Kienböck stated that he had other plans in mind which would have brought the total yearly loss to Vienna to about 35,000,000; further, he confirmed the prevailing conjecture that his purpose was to hinder the house-building program of Vienna. The proposal concerning the division of shares was, of course, a crass violation of the agreement of 1925 which was to last until 1930, and a significant demonstration of the immaturity of parliamentary democracy in Austria. Moreover, as the *Volkswirt* pointed out, it was just the sort of "tax Bolshevism" which the bourgeois party leaders were always charging against the Social Democrats. Granted that the original basis of allocation was arbitrary, the proposal was even more so in its application to the turnover tax, since it disregarded the obvious fact that that tax much more seriously affected the resident of Vienna than it did a peasant.

After months of debate the government withdrew its proposals

[58] *BGBl.,* 1926, Nr. 340; *Der österreichische Volkswirt,* vol. 19 (Nov. 27, 1926), 233, 234.

concerning the tax division law and the financial constitution and agreed to legislation authorizing all the states to increase their beer taxes from 6 to 9.8 schillings per hektoliter. Vienna, however, was to deliver the additional proceeds thus realized to the other states and cities.[59]

To this point it may have seemed to some readers that the attitude of the Socialist majority in the city council was simply one of bull-headed refusal to pay attention to the demands for tax reductions, and that the very number and persistence of those demands indicate that there was some basis for them. My judgment on the latter point has already been noted in part and is developed at greater length toward the end of this chapter. The imputation of unreasoning stubborness can be demonstrated as unwarranted by a thirty-minute examination of the tables of contents of the volumes of the law gazette of Vienna. In addition to the changes previously cited the following may be noted. The taxes on subtenants and on trucks were abolished in 1923 and 1925, respectively. The amusement tax was reduced in June, 1926. Between December 23, 1926, and December 23, 1927, there were other reductions in the amusement levy, and the welfare, hotel, and automobile taxes, as well as the penalty for late payment of taxes, were decreased. The welfare tax reduction was unimportant—from 4 1/16 to 4 per cent—but as far back as 1924 it had been cut from 4½ to 4 1/16. Only part of the amusement places benefited, but some of the decreases amounted to 30, 40, and 50 per cent of the former rates. In 1928 there were very substantial reductions in the value-increment tax. As related above, the attacks on the "Breitner system" did not lessen, however. Late in 1929 further decreases were made in the welfare, billboard, amusement, automobile, advertisement, hotel, and luxury food and drink taxes. The welfare tax modification applied only to financial institutions and the reductions in the last two cases were given only on condition that the sums not paid to the city be used entirely for investment purposes. Nevertheless the savings to taxpayers were substantial. For example, the automobile tax had been lowered by the two cuts of 1927 and 1929 from 150 schillings for each horsepower as computed

[59] *Der österreichische Volkswirt,* vol. 20 (July 21, 1928), 1193–1195; *ibid.,* vol. 21 (Oct. 20, Dec. 22, 1928), 54, 300; *Jahrbuch der österreichischen Arbeiterbewegung, 1928,* pp. 95, 96, 113–116, 234, 235; Nationalrat, *Protokoll, Beilagen,* Nr. 196, 261, III Gesetzgebungsperiode; *BGBl.,* 1928, Nr. 358.

for tax purposes to 60 schillings for each of the first seven horsepower, and the billboard tax by one-third.[60]

Obviously not satisfied with the change in the luxury food and drink levy, a group of café and restaurant owners appealed to the Constitutional Court, alleging that it conflicted with constitutional stipulations concerning the imposition by the federation and by a state or a community of a similar tax. The decision developed at some length the point that there was a difference between the federal turnover tax and the city tax prior to July 17, 1925. On the ground that the revision of the latter on that date had excluded the luxury concept, and thus eliminated the difference, the court ruled the Vienna tax partly unconstitutional; because of the impending modification of the tax division statute, it also ruled that the offending section might remain in force until January 1, 1931. The exact language of the city laws shows that the term "luxury establishment" (*Luxusbetrieb*) had been replaced by the phrase "undertaking which stands out" (*Unternehmung die sich . . . hervorhebt*), but it also shows that the tests by which it was to be determined whether or not a concern belonged in the "luxury" or "stand-out" class had remained almost to the letter identical. To most laymen and many lawyers the decision seemed to have more political than judicial basis. Nor was this impression lessened when the Constitutional Court some months later handed down decisions in similar cases from Tirol and Salzburg which a contributor to the *Volkswirt* characterized as in contradiction to the Vienna findings. The revisions of the tax forced upon the city in early 1931 changed it from a luxury to a mass levy, abolished assessment at the discretion of tax authorities in favor of a system based on the monthly turnover in the establishments covered, and greatly reduced the amounts paid by exclusive clubs and first-class hotels, restaurants, and *cafés*.[61] Although these changes cost Vienna some tax revenue, the whole controversy concerning them was overshadowed by that concerning the seventh revision of the tax division law.

[60] *LGBl., für Wien,* 1923, Nr. 30, p. 29; 1925, Nr. 59, p. 74; 1926, Nr. 30, p. 38, Nr. 49, p. 80, Nr. 52, p. 81; 1927, Nr. 1, p. 1, Nr. 14, p. 17, Nr. 20, p. 25, Nr. 22, p. 27, Nr. 31, p. 37, Nr. 44, p. 65; 1928, Nr. 24, p. 63; 1930, Nr. 2–8, pp. 2–6.

[61] *Neue Freie Presse,* February 7, 1930 (A.M.), p. 6; *LGBl. für Wien,* 1922, Nr. 82; *ibid.,* 1925, Nr. 34; *ibid.,* 1931, Nr. 6; Franz Urban, "Verfassungswidrige Doppelbesteuerungen," *Der österreichische Volkswirt,* vol. 23 (Jan. 31, 1931), 467; *Jahrbuch der österreichischen Arbeiterbewegung, 1931,* pp. 254–255.

As is already clear, the ramifications of the struggle over the division of the proceeds of the joint taxes, chiefly the turnover and alcohol levies, extended throughout the economic and political structure of Austria. In the language of the *Volkswirt* the conflict was nourished by the fact that in 1929, for example, Vienna received almost exactly 50 per cent of that part of the proceeds going to the states and communities though it had only 28.5 per cent of the population. The bitter opposition to the housing program in the metropolis on both economic and political grounds continued to find expression in attempts to reduce the income of the city and thus hamstring the program. Heimwehr plans to overthrow the parliamentary system (discussed in detail in Vol. II, Chap. XXI) caused the Social Democrats to face the necessity of working out a settlement and demonstrating that they were prepared to make real concessions to avoid civil war. As 1930 wore on and the depression deepened the whole tax problem was thrust more and more into the foreground, but it is doubtful if workers' party leaders were entirely prepared for the drastic proposals finally made public in the bills laid before the Nationalrat by the new Ender government on December 18, 1930.

In presenting the measures, Finance Minister Juch made it clear that their major objective was to take revenue from Vienna and give it to the other states. After pointing out that the government was not offering simply amendments but rather a fundamental long-term reform based on the experience of the past ten years, he declared that the former system had favored the stronger states at the expense of the weak. The new system was to rest on a consideration of the needs of the states rather than the geographical areas from which the taxes came. Perhaps the old system was justified in normal times, but in days of crisis there must be solidarity; the strong must help the weak. Therefore a scheme which gave half of the joint taxes to Vienna and half to the other states, cities, and towns must be replaced by one on a 35 to 65 ratio. Despite the reference to the unfairness of distributing the joint tax proceeds on the basis of their place of origin, the government proposed to retain that basis for direct taxes and for taxes on changes in the ownership of property. For the alcohol and turnover taxes, however, a new "key" was planned: the number of school children.

Danneberg replied for the Social Democrats. He charged, in general, that the bills constituted a "March on Vienna" as real as that the Heimwehr had been threatening, that they were designed to deprive Vienna of "all financial possibility of existence," and that they meant destruction of the federal principle. More specifically he estimated that they would deprive the metropolis of 42 million schillings a year for the benefit of the other states and of an additional 6 million for the benefit of the federation. He granted that the question of a proper basis for distributing the joint taxes, again particularly the turnover and alcohol taxes, was difficult; but stated that if the existing scheme was unsatisfactory his party was ready to return to the old surtax plan. Then he pointed out that the authors of the bills had apparently searched around for the "key" which would be most disadvantageous to Vienna. He asked why school expenditures or welfare expenditures had not been selected, and found the answer in the facts that on the welfare basis Vienna would get 76 per cent of the joint taxes but on the proposed school-children measure only 18 per cent. Furthermore, he noted that in the central government there were numerous opportunities for savings, particularly in the ridiculously overstaffed army with 1 officer for every 11 men and with 29 generals sitting in the war ministry. Danneberg granted that the state of Lower Austria was being treated unjustly under the existing arrangements, but insisted that if any governmental units were in need of help the cities and towns deserved most consideration. He granted likewise that there was great need for solidarity; but reminded his hearers that the plea for it came with particularly poor grace from those states which in the first years of the republic, when the situation was much worse, had tried to cut themselves loose from Vienna and did everything they could to prevent food from reaching its starving people.[62]

Whatever the merits of Danneberg's arguments may be the government held the whip hand. It will be recalled that under the tax division amendment of 1925 the applicability of the "graduated population key" to the turnover tax was to terminate on December 31, 1930. Now it happened that the statute concerning emergency benefits for the unemployed also expired on that day. Since the nego-

[62] *Der österreichische Volkswirt*, vol. 22 (July 5, 1930), 1094; Nationalrat, *Protokoll*, December 18, 1930, pp. 98–111.

tiations between the parties on the tax revision bills were getting nowhere, the government extended the emergency unemployment benefits only four weeks. Subjected to this pressure the Social Democrats, through Danneberg as spokesman, offered on January 9, 1931, a compromise solution. The plan proposed, first, an unweighted population basis for the distribution of that part of the turnover and alcohol taxes going to the states, pointing out that this had been for years the method demanded by the other states. Second, the plan accepted the government proposals concerning certain deductions from Vienna's share of business enterprise taxes and personal income taxes. In the third place, Danneberg offered 14 per cent of the city's share of the joint taxes in its capacity as a state as a contribution toward the administrative expenses of the other states. This was in lieu of the government's demand for a flat sum for the purpose. On the other hand, the Socialists rejected the proposal to divest Vienna and Graz of their right to collect federal taxes. Moreover, they demanded certain guarantees including a promise from the government that any agreement reached would remain in force for seven years; that during this period the old Vienna taxes might be retained, but that as an offset the veto powers of the central authorities acquired in 1925 would also be retained; that Vienna could levy a food and drink tax in modified form; that the national government give the city a subsidy for at least 2,000 dwellings; and that a large part of what Vienna had given up should go to the benefit of the state that was in greatest relative need of an adjustment, namely, Lower Austria.

After sixteen days of further negotiations two formal protocols concerning the whole set of issues were signed, one by the government and four of the parties represented in parliament, the other by the government and the city of Vienna. They and the law based on them followed closely Danneberg's proposals except for the government's reservation of the right to introduce when it saw fit a bill depriving Graz and Vienna of their power to collect federal taxes, the provision that the agreement was to last only five years instead of seven, and a couple of other minor points. It will be shown later that the government and the Catholic party had no scruples whatever against violating its solemn pledges and the law embodying them. Here it remains to add that the Socialists estimated the revenue loss to Vienna at about 29 million schillings and that the *Volkswirt* estimated it at approximately 27.5 million.[63]

The general significance of the compromise solution of the 1930–1931 conflict over taxes lies largely in the fact that it was a compromise. The government receded from several of its original proposals; in particular it did not deprive Vienna of so much revenue as at first demanded. This was a victory for the Ender-Schober group over the Heimwehr extremists. The Social Democrats made concessions and thus demonstrated that if it were possible they were still determined to settle controversies on the parliamentary plane. It was noted above that the government held the whip in being able to stop the emergency unemployment benefits; but, as on previous occasions, nothing would have been simpler for the workers' leaders than to let that whip be applied and use the ensuing resentment as a basis for agitation. Given the existing temper of the Heimwehr leaders, such tactics might easily have led to civil war. In the second place, it had proved possible to retain the Vienna tax system almost intact. The abolition of the discretionary assessments under the food and drink levy had the disadvantage, from the Socialist viewpoint, of destroying its luxury character; but it had the advantage of removing one of the most important grounds for complaint against the tax.

The next attack on the Vienna tax system is more appropriately discussed in detail in connection with the destruction of the Social Democratic party as a legal institution and the disappearance of Austria as a democratic republic. Nevertheless, remembering the violence and bitterness of the attacks on that system, it should be noted here that the Clerical Fascists who replaced the Social Democrats in the city hall proved capable of only a few important perversions of it. Except for a small group, Vienna taxpayers in 1937 were unanimous in the opinion that the authoritarian system was definitely worse than that of the Socialists—"and they don't build any houses."

In attempting a general evaluation of Breitner's taxes the foregoing facts should be kept in mind. It is taken for granted, however, that individual judgments will be largely influenced by the answer

[63] *Jahrbuch der österreichischen Arbeiterbewegung, 1930,* pp. 178–183; *BGBl.,* 1931, Nr. 46; *Der österreichische Volkswirt,* vol. 23 (Jan. 31, 1931), 457.

to the basic question: What is the function and purpose of taxation? To the degree that the individual favors the conscious use of taxes to bring about economic changes conceived as socially advantageous, he will be more likely to approve of the Vienna system of 1919–1934. If he favors a scheme that is limited chiefly to maintaining fire and police protection, paving and cleaning the streets, and similar matters, he is, of course, likely to disapprove. As is probably clear by this time, I lean toward the judgment of such an expert as Professor R. M. Haig that, "As a practical matter the arguments in favor of the narrow view of the function of taxation are being rapidly undermined by the course of events."[64]

Throughout the preceding pages the reader has doubtless noticed that the most common charges against the municipal taxes were that they increased unemployment, restricted production, and hampered the formation of capital. To these should perhaps be added the complaint that a poor country like Austria could not afford heavy taxes, though this idea is somewhat tied up with, if not implied in, the others. Concerning this last point little need be said except that as formulated by Austrian politicians it was at best a plausible half-truth. They would have been well advised to ponder another judgment of Professor Haig's: "Some countries are rich and others are poor, yet the poor may require larger revenues to finance their activities than the rich."[65]

The unemployment issue has been discussed in relation to specific taxes. A more general treatment requires the examination of the available official figures. The table on page 393 gives such data for the years 1919–1933; that is, for the period during which the Social Democrats controlled the municipal administration.

It will be recalled that early in 1927 there was a particularly forceful series of attacks on the Breitner system. Conservative parties and their publications pointed to the facts that there had been a tremendous increase in the average number of registered unemployed in Vienna between 1924 and 1926—from 57,000 to 100,000, or about 75 per cent—whereas the similar increase in Austria outside Vienna was from 69,000 to 104,000 or only 50 per cent. They explained these facts on the ground that the obviously bad unem-

[64] *Encyclopaedia of the Social Sciences,* vol. 14, p. 533.
[65] *Ibid.,* p. 540.

ployment situation throughout the country was aggravated in Vienna by the taxes. Naturally, this was denied. Socialists and their defenders argued at the time that the proper basis for comparison was not the number registered as unemployed but the number receiving public assistance, chiefly through unemployment insurance benefits, since it was these unfortunates only who were really put-

AVERAGE NUMBER OF UNEMPLOYED PERSONS IN AUSTRIA AND IN VIENNA, 1919–1933*

Year	Registered at employment offices			Receiving assistance		
	All of Austria	Vienna (number)	Vienna (per cent)	All of Austria	Vienna (number)	Vienna (per cent)
1919	......	......	.....	147,192	111,796	75.95
1920	......	......	.....	32,217	26,396	81.93
1921	32,419	23,567	72.70	12,055	9,551	79.23
1922	75,540	50,786	67.23	46,917	30,591	65.20
1923	144,974	76,479	52.75	110,352	62,741	56.85
1924	126,572	57,152	45.15	95,442	46,574	48.80
1925	173,345	85,944	49.58	150,331	72,283	48.08
1926	204,388	100,336	49.09	178,937	83,810	46.84
1927	203,265	95,970	47.21	173,362	81,073	46.77
1928	186,723	82,644	44.26	158,377	68,872	43.49
1929	195,570	82,606	42.24	165,551	67,487	40.77
1930	244,386	102,254	41.83	207,859	82,718	39.80
1931	303,365	125,580	42.13	254,606	96,728	37.99
1932	379,285	161,933	42.92	309,642	115,539	37.31
1933	405,745	184,742	45.48	331,027	130,817	39.52

* *Wirtschaftsstatistisches Jahrbuch, 1929/1930*, p. 83; *1931/1932*, pp. 426, 428, 440; *1932/1933*, p. 414; *1933/1935*, pp. 399, 406, 407.

ting a strain on the finances of the country. On this basis unemployment had increased 80 per cent in Vienna between 1924 and 1926 but 90 per cent in Austria outside the city. Years later some Socialist spokesmen reverted to the "registered unemployed" basis and pointed out that between 1923 and 1929; that is, the dates marking the inauguration of the municipal building program and the beginning of the world depression, the number of such persons increased only 8 per cent in Vienna, whereas in the remainder of the country they increased 64.9 per cent. By now the reader may have reached the conclusion that if the proper years and the proper measure of unemployment are selected it is possible to "prove" astonishingly conflicting findings. But the more careful representative of the Socialist viewpoint insisted on a more detailed examination of the figures. The really significant thing, he argued, was the trend of unemployment: what had happened to Vienna's share of total unemployment? From the percentages recorded in the table it is clear that on the registered-unemployed basis the proportion of the city decreased fairly steadily from 1921 through 1930 except for 1925 and 1926. On the unemployed-receiving-assistance basis the figures are more striking. After an increase between 1919 and 1920 the percentage in Vienna dropped every single year without a break through 1932. And the proportion in 1932 was less than half what it had been in 1920.

To the claim that these data offer proof that the tax policy, chiefly as it worked through the housing program, was reducing rather than aggravating unemployment several objections were urged. In the first place, more than half the decrease in Vienna's proportion of the unemployed receiving assistance took place before 1924; in other words, before the building operations could have had any appreciable effect. Probably more important were the general considerations that the factors contributing to unemployment in metropolitan Vienna and in the remainder of Austria, with its high percentage of agricultural and forestry workers, were by no means the same, and that the influence of governmental endeavors to reduce unemployment was difficult if not impossible of isolation from other influences and factors. In reply, the Social Democrat granted the difference in factors but contended that it supported his position. All of Austria was in a most deplorable economic condition. Agricultural interests, however, had fared appreciably better than most others. The inflation had liberated the peasants from their debts. Since the Catholic party drew its chief strength from them and looked upon itself as their representative, it included high agricultural duties in its general protective system. Thereby the farmers actually secured a safe market although the greater part of industry, for reasons already explained, had lost its market. Therefore, it was argued, the maintenance of the purchasing power of agriculturists would lead to the expectation that the employment situation in the states would be more favorable than in Vienna. But, as the figures show, the relative position of Vienna definitely improved until a year *after* the world depression began. The Socialist contention that this trend finds its explanation in the policies of the city council and that those policies could not have been carried through without the taxes is certainly more than plausible; in fact, to the highly competent editor in chief of the *Volkswirt* it appeared conclusive as early as the spring of 1927.[66] However the reader may evaluate the decisiveness of the arguments from Socialist quarters, two points seem clear: Breitner's critics were much less convincing in their attempts to prove their *general* charge that his tax system aggravated the unemployment situation in Vienna than were his supporters in their attempts to prove that his system ameliorated that situation; the contentions of the critics concerning the effects of *particular* taxes were sometimes nothing short of ridiculous.[67]

The claim that taxes, and particularly such taxes as the Vienna welfare, advertising, billboard, luxury food and drink, hotel and amusement levies, restrict production and generally interfere with business is, of course, a hardy perennial. It flourishes vigorously in the wealthiest country of the world as well as in a poor one like Austria. Moreover, no one would deny that such taxes can have the results complained against. The difficulties lie, first, in ascertaining at what tax rates these results begin to appear; and, more important, the relative advantages which may be derived from the use of the tax receipts as against the losses that may result from interferences with particular lines of business or even with restrictions on the production of particular commodities. Here, again, the basic question concerning the purpose of taxation appears. The Vienna Socialists viewed as major purposes the housing, welfare, and school programs described in the next three chapters. It should be kept in mind, however, that they looked forward to a long-run gradual transformation from private capitalism to Socialism. As a part of this general program the Vienna group invested large sums in an appreciable number of private businesses.[68] Such practices certainly favored some industries more or less at the cost of others, but the Socialists considered this help more justifiable than the subsidies

---

[66] *Der österreichische Volkswirt,* vol. 19 (March 26, 1927), 694.

[67] The discussion above reflects some modification of the position which I took in the previously cited article, *Political Science Quarterly,* vol. 53 (Dec. 1938), 537 ff. Generally speaking this modification is in the direction of more credence to the claims of the Socialists; it resulted from the discovery of additional evidence, particularly the article in the *Volkswirt* just cited.

[68] *Statistisches Jahrbuch der Stadt Wien 1929* [2. Jahrg.], pp. 304–305, gives a list of such enterprises.

by the central government to the Danube Steamship Company, for example. To the extent that tax revenues were used for these investment purposes they aided rather than interfered with business.

The usual method of "proving" the charges relating to restrictions of output and interference with business was to list concerns which had gone bankrupt, or given up the struggle for fear of bankruptcy, allegedly because of the taxes. Anti-Socialist publications of all sorts frequently generalized to the same effect. In addition to the references above, mention should be made of Eduard Jehly's widely circulated pamphlet, *10 Jahre Rotes Wien* (*10 Years of Red Vienna*). It was apparently issued as a reply to a number of self-laudatory and in some instances far from modest Socialist publications. Jehly states that between 1923 and 1928 there were over 3,000 bankruptcies and almost 14,000 judicial adjustments of debts in Austria, most of them in Vienna. The number of legal seizures to satisfy debts in the capital alone increased from 56,000 in 1923 to 228,000 in 1928. Jehly claims that the municipal tax policy so sharpened the crisis that but for it many of these cases might have been avoided.[69] But, as in almost all the other instances which it has been possible to find, there is no attempt on Jehly's part to prove the connection between the taxes and business difficulties. It is not intended to deny by this the difficulty, perhaps impossibility, of establishing such a connection; the point is that the critics satisfied themselves with sweeping generalizations. If an attempt is made to get away from such generalizations the result is that to a large extent the problem becomes one of determining whether a tax or a group of taxes which a particular employer had to pay *actually was* the last straw which broke his financial back. No evidence has been found that the critics made any real attempt at such an analysis and I could not. As has already been indicated and as the citation from Jehly admits, the major explanation for business failures and other difficulties is most probably the practically constant state of crisis in postwar Austria. It was a standard joke that the two chief crops of the little country were political stories and crises. To this unhappy situation must be added the speculative fever that began during the inflation, persisted for several years, and often took the form of unwise business ventures. Then there was a small army of former civil servants and bank clerks, released as a result of the shrinkage in jobs, who used their

[69] P. 15.

dismissal compensation or small pensions to set up a shop. Thousands of them had no business in business. In connection with the validity of the immediately preceding explanations a statement from Franz Egkher, president of the Café Owners Association, is revealing. His group had been most vociferous in its denunciations, not only of specific taxes but of the whole system. Nevertheless, in commenting on the court decision in the luxury food and drink tax case, Egkher declared that Vienna coffeehouses were doing poorly because, first, there were too many of them in relation to the population; and second, the purchasing power of the patrons had sunk markedly.[70] In other words, in the field where he was particularly competent, this vigorous critic of Breitner put in the first rank precisely those explanations of business ills just suggested.

Since it has been pointed out that the Vienna system succeeded in shifting the burden of taxes in large degree from the masses to the well to do and to business, there has obviously been no idea of suggesting that there is no evidence supporting the position that that system restricted production or particular business activities. On the contrary, it seems clear that the welfare tax in particular worked somewhat in this direction, and that such levies as those on advertising, billboards, hotels, fire insurance, and automobiles did likewise in varying measures. The point of the discussion has been that the pernicious influence of the taxes was grossly exaggerated and that the volume and character of the protests were out of any relation to their foundation in fact.

Before turning to the last charge, namely that the taxes hindered formation of capital, it seems advisable to give some attention to another aspect of the issue not discussed heretofore. The problem whether the municipality should finance its investments from taxes, as it usually did, or from loans played a large part in the heated political discussions. The opponents of the tax system violently demanded that Breitner stop the "economy killing" taxes and float loans. As has been stated directly or indirectly several times, Breitner's system undoubtedly was in many respects class taxation. Therefore, the attacks against it were in the main an expression of certain class interests just as was the no less passionate defense of it by the Socialists. As usually happens in such cases, representatives of the

[70] *Neue Freie Presse,* January 23, 1930 (A.M.), p. 2.

conflicting interests were anxious to sublimate the issue by recourse to general axioms of the theory of public finance. The enemies of the system contended that covering current investments by taxation was in contradiction to established doctrines. This, of course, was in itself wrong. What actually may be regarded as a recognized principle of a sound budget is that ordinary expenditures should be covered from tax proceeds, whereas for extraordinary expenditures extraordinary sources of revenues, that is, loans, should be made available. Since the center of the storm was the housing program the problem became that of whether or not the building of houses by the city council was to be considered as ordinary expenditure; in other words, whether the program was an emergency measure or a permanent feature of municipal activities. This, however, is not essentially a problem of theory, but rather of policy.

There is little if any doubt that the Socialist administration intended to become the landlord of an increasing per cent of the mass dwellings in Vienna. The leaders pursued this policy because prewar experiences had convinced them that a system of private ownership was particularly unable to cope with the problem of mass housing. Once they came to regard their building activities as lasting, the problem taxes *versus* loans became simply a matter of arithmetical computations. It was clear that because of the satisfactory condition of its budget the city was able to float loans on comparatively favorable terms. The proceeds of the housing tax could guarantee interest payments for a loan of from 350 to 450 million schillings, varying with the year selected as the basis of the computation; but raising the loan would, of course, tie them up for some twenty years or more. Since these proceeds formed only about 40 per cent of the total expenditure on housing, including the acquisition of land, this procedure would obviously render it possible to save the economy the remaining 60 per cent and thus partly alleviate the strain. But it was not less clear that since the city was spending about 100 million a year on housing and wished to continue at that rate at least, it would have faced every four years or so the alternatives of stopping the building, of increasing taxes, or of increasing rents in order to obtain the money for the next four-year period. There is general agreement among impartial observers that the first alternative was impossible in the given conditions; public housing on a large scale was imperative for some time. Continual increases in taxation would have been unfeasible and building activities would have ceased. Raising rents would in all likelihood have led fairly promptly to a development similar to that in Germany, where there proved to be no effective demand for dwellings let at high rents, so that the social intent of the scheme would have been frustrated.[71] The city council held—and this was the core of the whole policy—that building was justified only on the principle that part of the building costs were nonrecoverable. Financing building from taxes was the only procedure consonant with that principle and the intentions of the city council.[72] The situation was somewhat different for other investments of the city. Here Breitner proved by no means adamant in his opposition to loans. After careful preparations which included waiting until after the financial reputation of Vienna had long been restored, he floated in 1927 a loan of 210 million schillings on conditions that under the existing circumstances must be regarded as very favorable.

It is not too much to say, therefore, that the conflict over taxes or loans actually meant: continuation or abandonment of the city investment policy. This issue is obviously connected with that concerning the restriction of production, interference with business, and general "economy killing" effects so frequently ascribed to the Vienna taxes; but it is also closely bound up with the previously mentioned charge that they hindered the formation of capital, or, as sometimes formulated, that they increased the general tendency of Austrian industry and trade to live on their capital. In fact, in this last charge the whole spectrum of strictures launched against the city taxes was concentrated as in the focus of a concave mirror. And it cannot be denied that it is easy to reason plausibly in general

[71] A contrary view is held by Dr. C. O. Hardy in *The Housing Program of Vienna,* p. 116. Though he was clearly conscious of the social purposes of the plan, he did not, in my judgment, allow them the weight they deserve on this issue of rentals.

[72] For a closer examination of these intentions, cf. Chapter XIV, n. 71. More specific computations of the sort sketched above appear in the *Wiener Wahlhandbuch,* Heft D, 1932, pp. 48–49; Hugo Breitner, *Kapitalistische oder sozialistische Steuerpolitik* (Wien, 1926), p. 14; and E. K. Winter, "Wiener Wohnbaupolitik," *Hochland,* vol. 28 (May, 1931), 125–126. Dr. Winter's generally highly laudatory comments on the housing program are particularly interesting in light of the facts that he was an ardent Monarchist, a Christian Social, and third vice-mayor in the Schmitz administration. *Der österreichische Volkswirt* consistently supported the taxation method of financing the buildings. Cf., for example, *ibid.,* vol. 18 (Sept. 18, 1926), 1410; *ibid.,* vol. 24 (May 28, 1932), 847–848: "That Breitner remained inexorable, did not float loans but covered the building cost from taxes is his greatest merit."

terms: increases in public expenditure imply high taxation; high taxation increases the cost of production; increased cost of production makes unemployment rise. Since the unemployed must be taken care of, there are again increases in public expenditure which lead to higher taxation, which again increases the cost of production, and so on, until the economy reaches a state of general bankruptcy at the end of its downward journey along the vicious spiral. "The end comes when the whole capital is consumed."[73] But this argument, which in its boundless generality applies to any attempt to improve the shortcomings of a system of—politically—unrestricted competition by measures of social policy, must be applied with special caution to the specific tax system of the city of Vienna in the specific conditions of Austria. Nor is this true only because no person endowed with an adequate sense of proportion could reasonably argue that, compared with the lasting structural effects of the dismemberment of the empire, the unfavorable results of the city tax policy were a quantity sufficient to be taken into account in this respect.[74]

In the shattered countries of Central Europe after the war the tendency to what was called state capitalism became very marked. This development may be approved or disapproved, but it is impossible to refuse to see the fact that capital formation progressively ceased being an exclusive affair of private economy; certain expenditures of public bodies had to be increasingly considered as capital formation. In this respect especially the policy of the city of Vienna was outstanding if compared with that of the central government. The terrible waste of public funds by the federation,[75] most notably in the years 1925–1926, makes it impossible to put its public expenditure and that of the capital city on the same level.[76] For several years before 1929 the "value-increasing" investments of the

[73] Cf. Fritz Machlup, "The Consumption of Capital in Austria," *The Review of Economic Statistics,* vol. 17 (1935), 16–17.

[74] When Nicholas Kaldor contends ("The Economic Situation of Austria," *Harvard Business Review,* vol. 11 [Oct. 1932], 23–34) that collapse of the empire and, after 1929, the effects of the world slump are per se insufficient to explain the economic plight of Austria, and stresses the disastrous effects of the credit policy of the banks with respect to industrial firms, he is unquestionably right; but he seems to overlook or underestimate the fact that a direct road leads from war, breakup of the monarchy, losses of markets, inflation, and the postinflationary bubble of the stock exchange boom to the unsound conditions which developed both in banking and in industry.

[75] *Der österreichische Volkswirt,* vol. 24 (May 28, 1932), 848.

[76] As for instance, Professor Machlup does, *loc. cit.,* p. 17.

latter amounted to almost 40 per cent of its total expenditures.[77] By the end of 1927 about 30,000 persons were employed by the municipal enterprises, several of which were producing building materials for the new dwellings (cf. Chap. XIV). Apart from this, it will be recalled that the city participated in a number of undertakings; many of these were likewise suppliers of various building materials.[78] A large share of the taxes thus returned to the economy as part of the despised "public expenditure." Further, since building activities are a particularly "labor intensive" line of production, there is, as stated before, some merit in the claim that those activities materially aided the employment situation. Thus the policy of the city council also helped to reduce unproductive public expenditure and so decreased the general cost of production.

It was also argued that the houses created by the city represented genuine capital formation despite the fact that (reasons explained in detail in Chap. XIV) it abstained from charging rents which included more than maintenance and running costs. Here the profits on the invested capital were conceived as paid to the economy as a whole in the form of higher productivity of labor. This gain to the economy was also claimed for a large part of the welfare activities of the city. The isolated existence of Austria was regarded as a temporary state of affairs. If the incorporation of the country into a larger economic unit could be achieved or the tariff policies of the succession states could be overcome, collection of higher rents and utilization of the houses as a basis of credit would become possible and the huge investments justified even from the point of view of private capitalistic accounting. On the basis of this reasoning the Socialists believed themselves warranted in demanding that their critics drop the halo of sanctity which they had placed around private capital formation.

Furthermore, it should not be overlooked that under postinflation conditions there was a widespread reluctance among private entrepreneurs to embark upon capital investments. By financing the creation of public capital through taxation the city council in many cases carried out capital formation which otherwise would not have

[77] Friedrich Hertz, "Kapitalbedarf, Kapitalbildung und Volkseinkommen in Oesterreich," *SVfS.*, vol. 174, pt. 4 (1929), 63.

[78] Benedikt Kautsky, "Kapitalbildung der Oeffentlichen Hand seit dem Kriege in Deutschland und Deutschösterreich," *SVfS.*, vol. 174, pt. 4 (1929), 246.

taken place. With this in mind Goldscheid wrote that the city worked like an exemplary social savings and insurance institution.[79] Whether and to what extent there were instances in which city taxes actually hampered capital formation or increased consumption of capital is not ascertainable, but the opinion of an extremely competent observer, who on the whole was opposed to the principle of public capital formation, is worth noting. He wrote in 1929, when the Breitner system was at its apex, that although it would perhaps be an exaggeration to say that dangers for capital creation resulting from the municipal tax policy were already present; nevertheless, because of the tendency of Vienna to further public capital formation at the cost of private, such apprehensions might not be unfounded at some time in the future.[80] Even with the welfare levy, which was said to affect employment unfavorably,[81] it could also be argued that it was one of the factors which induced entrepreneurs to embark upon rationalization schemes. By dispensing with some workers they partially evaded the tax. To the extent that this contention is sound the welfare duty contributed toward enhancing the productivity of Austrian industry and toward improving its competitive position, particularly against German industry. Nor should it be overlooked that Breitner's method of reducing taxes on condition that businessmen employ the resultant "savings" as capital investments in their undertakings amounted to compulsory formation of private capital under pressure.

Therefore, it seems not too much to say that many favorable effects of the municipal tax system could be seen and felt by the vast majority of the Viennese population. The contentions concerning the unfavorable effects are at best attempts to demonstrate the *probability* that certain undesirable economic conditions could be ascribed in part, along with a multiplicity of other causes, to that system. This probability was never established to a degree which made the criticism significant except in a political sense. Here an almost paradoxical aspect of the entire controversy is reached.

[79] Rudolf Goldscheid, "Steuerverwendung und Interessenpolitik," *SVfS.*, vol. 174, pt. 1 (1928), 20.

[80] Alexander Spitzmüller, "Das österreichische Steuersystem des Bundes der Länder und Gemeinden und die Kapitalbildung," *SVfS.*, vol. 174, pt. 4 (1929), 292.

[81] That the case against the welfare tax was greatly exaggerated may be perceived from Spitzmüller's cautious formulation: "That it contributes to a large degree, or even that it contributes at all, to the increase of unemployment, is not proved; but in the nature of the case this is by no means absolutely impossible." *Ibid.* p. 277.

Whatever the degree of truth in the general criticism of the Vienna tax system, it is a notorious fact that this criticism was pressed by precisely that political group which was most obviously vulnerable to a counterthrust. As early as 1925 Layton and Rist remarked that "the Vienna system has to a very great extent been copied by provinces with a Christian Socialist majority."[82] Although it is not precise to say that the Vienna "system" was copied, it is true that practically all the taxes hotly attacked by the Christian Socials

WELFARE TAX AS A PERCENTAGE OF THE TOTAL REVENUE FROM TAXATION
STATE BUDGETS, 1929*

Burgenland	16.53	Styria	27.60
Carinthia	29.13	Tirol	19.26
Lower Austria	24.41	Upper Austria	15.65
Salzburg	15.06	Vorarlberg	41.54

* Finanzministerium, *Die Landeshaushalte nach den Vorauschlägen für das Jahr 1929.*

in Vienna were, under their administration, quietly being collected, up to March, 1938, in large areas of Austria. The most conspicuous example is offered by the welfare tax. If the budgets for 1929 are compared it is perceived that in Vienna this tax played an outstanding part since 39.27 per cent of the aggregate strictly city-and-state tax revenue was derived from it; but the above figures show that in the other states it was likewise one of the supporting pillars of their systems.

The much criticized hotel tax was adopted in all states except Tirol; the luxury food and drink tax was collected in a series of towns in Styria and Tirol; the amusement tax existed in all states; the billboard tax was by no means confined to Vienna, and the advertisement tax was being collected not only in Vienna, Linz, and Graz, but also in non-Socialist Salzburg.[83] This enumeration is far from being exhaustive. In the words of Szende, "There is no city tax in Vienna which did not exist in other states, or cities and towns with non-Socialist administration."[84] His statement is slightly exaggerated, because the servant tax was applied outside of Vienna only in the

[82] W. T. Layton and Charles Rist, *op. cit.*, p. 168.

[83] Spitzmüller, *loc. cit.* pp. 272–282.

[84] Paul Szende, "Der Staatshaushalt und das Finanzsystem Oesterreichs und Ungarns," *Handbuch der Finanzwissenschaft*, vol. 3 (Tübingen, 1929), p. 212.

Socialist-controlled municipality of Graz. But Szende is unquestionably right when he adds that only in Vienna was the progressive principle applied so sharply, and that nowhere else was so much regard for "small people" and their everyday needs shown by the taxing authorities.

With these facts in mind it must be noted again that the attacks of political opponents were allegedly based on grounds of high principle; the arguments were borrowed—and perverted—from textbooks on public finance. But at the time of one of the hottest debates on the issue Kienböck, the Christian Social minister of finance, excused the developments because the states were in a "difficult position" and therefore had "established their tax systems in conformity with the Vienna example."[85] It remains difficult to comprehend why the sloppy budgeting of the states[86] gave them a better title to certain forms of taxation than the strict budgetary order and the social purposes of its expenditures gave to Vienna. To repeat: the real forces behind the drive against the Vienna tax system were the desires to shift the heaviest part of the burden back where it had been "in the good old days," to stop the housing program, and to weaken greatly, if not to destroy, the working-class movement—particularly in its political aspect.

Finally, in any evaluation of the Breitner tax system, account must be taken of its relation to the type of democracy which was the ultimate goal of Austrian labor. Granting that to some students of politics and economics the Austrian working-class formulation of that goal seems self-contradictory, it remains true that the clearest and most accurate characterization of the objective is: democratic Socialism. This implied rejection of violence, and, more specifically, rejection of the dictatorial methods which had become popular with considerable sections of European workers after the Bolshevist revolution in Russia. In pursuance of the democratic policy the Austrian Socialists sought to secure a majority in parliament by which they could gradually carry through a scheme of socialization. Obviously the first step in this program required time; the way to a majority is long. Consequently, adherence to democratic Socialism made imperative a demonstration to the masses that during the

[85] Cf. his address before the *Oesterreichische Politische Gesellschaft* as reported in the *Reichspost* for January 28, 1927, p. 3.
[86] *Der österreichische Volkswirt*, vol. 19 (Jan. 8, 1927), 382.

long period of struggle for final acquisition of power it was still feasible to achieve substantial gains for them. Previous chapters have shown that such gains were secured through social legislation and by means of the coöperatives. But equally or more important, because of the scope of the work and its somewhat more direct relation to the ultimate goal, was municipal Socialism, a specific form of democratic Socialism.

The principal ideas of Vienna municipal Socialism were, by taxes on the propertied classes, first, to effect a more equalitarian distribution of real income through the housing program and various forms of welfare work; and, second, to extend the scope of municipal undertakings and of participation in private enterprises so as to secure the ultimate socialization of a part of the latter, as well as to influence the whole private capitalistic economic body. In this connection it must not be forgotten that the city was the largest purchaser in Austria.

The most important limitation of such a program is probably obvious; for a relatively long time its continuance depended upon the existence of private capitalistic enterprises and private capitalists that might be taxed. During this period the program did not seek the destruction of private capitalist elements, but rather the building up of Socialist economic organizations in the lap, so to speak, of private capitalist society. Thus municipal Socialism may be viewed as a logical inference from the general conception of democratic Socialism. But democratic Socialism derived strength from a vitally functioning municipal Socialism. This interaction meant, among other things, that *Das Rote Wien* greatly fostered the reformist attitude of Austro-Marxism. In the first place, the practical achievements in Vienna made impossible adherence to the traditional position: we have nothing to lose but our chains; we have a world to win. Second, as already indicated, the tax system made the Socialists take an interest in the prosperity of taxpayers—that is, primarily of capitalist undertakings—and this meant a revision of the former attitude toward crises. Therefore, the simple fact that practical achievements were being realized without revolution reinforced the reformist attitude and gave the leaders a feeling of confidence that that attitude was being justified. This fact also went far toward destroying the effectiveness of the revolutionary propaganda of the

Communists and explains in large degree the weakness of their party.

On the other hand, it would be unwarranted to fail to call attention to the circumstance that the successful work of the Vienna Socialists created a countercurrent; that is, it stimulated the desire of the workers to see a thoroughgoing revision of the existing economic order. To that extent the effects of the policy of the municipal administration might easily have worked toward a radicalization of the rank and file had not such tendencies been led into democratic channels by Otto Bauer's policy of attempting to secure a parliamentary majority (see Chap. XIX).

CHAPTER XIV

Municipal Housing and Tenants Protection

THE FUNDAMENTAL interrelations of social life make it difficult to treat a special problem in isolation. This is particularly true of tenants protection in Austria. The history of the postwar republic presents hardly any other example where a particular issue was so closely, indeed, almost inseparably, woven into the whole fabric of political, social, and economic development. Tenants protection formed the basis of the housing policy of Vienna and was thus one of the most important prerequisites to Socialist activities in that city. But the recognition of this relation falls far short of an adequate comprehension of the role of tenants protection in Austrian politics. Two of the five general parliamentary elections held in the lifetime of Austrian democracy, 1918–1933, were fought largely on this issue. Tenants protection was directly connected with one of the most delicate questions of the political labor movement in Austria—the middle-class problem. There is evidence now, and to spare, that the relation between the labor movement and the middle classes was the most vital question for democracy in Central Europe and that it largely accounted for the momentous political changes which took place in the period of the Great Depression. To a very appreciable extent the strength of the Socialist party in Austria, demonstrated by its brilliant and seemingly irresistible development in the years 1923–1927, is to be attributed to its attitude on tenants protection. This led to remarkable repercussions on the whole nature of the policy of the party and to a certain extent influenced its structure; its traditional proletarian character became less pronounced. A witticism current during the electoral campaign of 1927 urged the organization to change its official name from Social Democratic Workers party to Social Democratic Tenants party of Austria. There were grains of truth in this advice, since for some time tenants protection seemed to be the device which would transform the workers party in the narrow sense of the term into a "people's party," enable the Socialists to win a decisive victory at the polls, and thus obtain the majority in parliament.

What the student of this development finds most striking is its character—in many respects accidental and, as it were, spontaneous. The historic prerequisites of tenants protection and housing policy are to be found, of course, in the general housing conditions in prewar Austria, most notably in prewar Vienna. These conditions created certain specific psychological attitudes between tenants and houseowners. Both the conditions and the attitudes must be understood as a basis for comprehending postrevolutionary developments; consequently, the next section is a sketch of the situation under the Habsburgs.

Housing Conditions Prior to 1914

> Considering . . . that in the last few years the wretchedness of housing has reached a level unheard of before; that today all classes of the population have come to regard it as a grave public calamity; that unless energetic steps are undertaken to fight it large classes of the population will within a very short time find themselves left to economic and social disorganization; that because of the general housing scarcity and, most notably, because of the pressing shortage in small dwellings . . . the rents exceed the financial ability of the middle and working classes . . . considering further that the housing scarcity and, particularly, the high rents and general housing conditions have brought about a situation in Vienna which must be regarded as highly undesirable in moral, sanitary, and political respects; that housing conditions as they exist for instance in Zwischenbruecken and in Brigittenau [Viennese districts] are not consonant with the dignity of a big city—a commission to remedy housing destitution should be instituted.

The above statement, written in the stiff formal language considered the appropriate style in the preceding century, appears in a motion submitted to the city council of Vienna, May 19, 1871.[1]

'Seventy-one—this year fell within that period of feverish prosperity which gave so great an impetus to the further transformation of "Biedermeier Vienna" into a large industrial center. Already, however, a serious economic maladjustment had become obvious. Although times of heightened business activity attracted new masses of workers from the country to Vienna, they implied also a high

[1] Quoted by Rudolf Weiss, "Wohnungsfrage und Bodenrente," *Der Kampf*, vol. 20 (May, 1927), 217.

interest rate so that capital found more profitable employment than the building of mass dwellings. And, as Professor Philippovich pointed out more than twenty years later in his famous study of Vienna housing, large apartment buildings seemed to exercise only moderate attractive power for capital even when a normal interest rate on the investment was secured.[2] The result was a highly deplorable lag between the influx of people into the city and the rate at which additional accommodations were provided for them. The 'eighties and the 'nineties of the last century were years of particularly rapid growth. Between 1890 and 1900 the population rose by more than 22 per cent, from 1,364,548 to 1,674,957.[3] In these years the workers' quarters grew and assumed their present appearance of a broad ring forming the periphery of the capital.

The appalling misery of the proletarian dwellings found their classic description in the report of Philippovich. It is more appropriate, however, to abstract from his most dreadful examples of workers' quarters in the capital city of Austria: dark cellar rooms with water-covered walls; toilets used by 120 persons; habitations which in his words were scarcely adequate as stalls for domestic animals.[4] There were several thousand such dwellings in the city, but they did not represent the typical apartment of a Viennese worker. It consisted usually of one room and a kitchen. Opening on a narrow gangway on each floor of the court side of the house were ten, fifteen, sometimes more, kitchen doors; thus the kitchens usually lacked any direct light. From the kitchen a door led to a room of about 150–180 square feet. Usually two, seldom more, of these apartments per floor had an additional narrow room with only one window, called in Vienna a *Kabinett*. Along the gangway were a few toilets, each of them used by the occupants of two or more apartments. There was one water faucet for the common use of all tenants of a floor. A glance through the "court" column of Viennese newspapers of any period shows that this faucet was the place of origin of a good number of insults, in words and deeds, which led to libel suits.

---

[2] Eugen von Philippovich, "Wiener Wohnungsverhältnisse," *Archiv für soziale Gesetzgebung und Statistik*, vol. 7 (1894), 256.

[3] E. Oberhummer, "Die geographische Lage Wiens," *Wien sein Boden und seine Geschichte* (Wien, 1924), p. 145.

[4] *Loc. cit.*, p. 227.

The housing census of 1917 revealed that the number of "small" apartments, that is, those of maximum size: kitchen, one "room," and one *Kabinett,* was 405,991; and that this was no less than 73.21 per cent of the 554,525 dwellings in Vienna.[5] In the seven typically workers' districts of Vienna the "small" apartments constituted about 90 per cent of the aggregate number of dwellings; in four of these districts the percentage exceeded 90. The census taken in 1919 disclosed the degree to which these apartments were provided with facilities of different kinds; in it, however, dwellings consisting of one *Kabinett* only, or a *Kabinett* and kitchen, were considered separately. Among the "small" apartments (distinguished in 1919 from the "*Kabinett* apartment" by the fact that it had one "room" and possibly a kitchen or a *Kabinett* or both, in addition) 15.25 per cent had no kitchen, 39.3 per cent no storage room in the cellar,[6] 92.1 per cent no toilet, 95.32 per cent no water faucet, and 76.8 per cent neither electricity nor gas.[7]

The legal building prescriptions in Vienna were based on the building ordinance of 1883, itself largely a repetition of the earlier ordinances of 1868, 1859, and 1829. Under these regulations the buildings might cover 85 per cent of the lot; cellar dwellings were not prohibited; and the number of floors was not regulated in accordance with the width of the street. Favored by the rapidly increasing demand in the growing city, the building capitalists used every inch of space allowed by the generous limits of the ordinance. In doing so they acted to a large extent under the pressure of land speculation which was the main beneficiary of the growth of the city. Speculators who held the land for, say, the ten years between 1890 and 1900 were sure to make profits of 1,000 to 1,200 per cent; the few operators who held lots during the last fifteen years of the century made 2,400 to 2,900 per cent in profits.[8] In Vienna all the well-known devices of land speculation were found, such as the donation to the community of a small part of a large plot on condition

[5] Salomon Rosenblum, *Die sozialpolitischen Massnahmen der Gemeinde Wien* (Bern, 1935), p. 89. The reader should keep in mind the fact that neither in conversation, nor in publications concerning housing, nor in official statistics did the Austrian consider the kitchen a "room."

[6] This implied the payment of higher retail prices for coal.

[7] Rosenblum, *op. cit.,* p. 90.

[8] Paul Schwarz, "Die Entwicklung der städtischen Grundrente in Wien" in *Neue Untersuchungen über die Wohnungsfrage in Deutschland und im Ausland, SVfS.,* vol. 94, pt. 1, section 1 (1901), 83.

that a church be erected there; the consequences were considerable rises in the value of adjoining lots and increased profits to speculators.[9]

The result of these conditions was, on the one hand, erection of dwellings of insufficient size with inadequate and unsatisfactory provisions for light, ventilation, and sanitation. On the other hand, they led to rents which Austrian commentators criticized as taking an exorbitantly high part of the workers' income. As Philippovich brought out, moreover, these rents were in some cases even more expensive per square meter in the poor worker's dwellings in the outskirts than in the luxurious apartments on the lovely Ringstrasse.[10] Estimates of how much of a worker's income had to be used for rent vary between 1/8 and 1/4. The labor statistics office in the imperial ministry of trade arrived at 13.7 per cent;[11] Philippovich speaks of rents up to 25 per cent of the wages;[12] and Benedikt Kautsky, taking the wages of a skilled worker at 35–50 crowns and those of an unskilled worker at 20–30 crowns a week, notes that it was generally assumed before 1914 that 20–25 per cent of those wages went to the landlords.[13]

The variations in the estimates result in part from the fact that computations were based in one case on the aggregate income of a worker's family and in the other case on the earnings of the *pater familias*. Apart from this the opinion has been ventured that the estimates of the labor statistics office did not take into due consideration the income and rent conditions of unskilled labor; moreover, it studied only 119 families. However this may be, it remains significant for landlord-tenant attitudes that it was a typical statement of workers in republican Vienna that in prewar times one week's wages had to be laid aside every month to cover the tribute to the houseowner. Of this rent more than 40 per cent was turned over to the central government and the city as taxes; about 5–6 per

[9] Cf. Adolf Damaschke, *Aufgaben der Gemeindepolitik* (Jena, 1922), p. 129; and "Wohnungswesen," *Wiener Wahlhandbuch 1932*, Heft D, p. 32.

[10] *Loc. cit.*, p. 239.

[11] Cf. Hans Türr, *Die Wohnungsprobleme Oesterreichs vor und nach dem Kriege* (Berlin, 1933), p. 128.

[12] *Loc. cit.*, p. 241.

[13] Benedikt Kautsky, "Die wirtschaftlichen und sozialen Folgen des Wohnungsrechtes in Oesterreich"; *Beiträge zur städtischen Wohn- und Siedelwirtschaft, Wohnungsfragen in Oesterreich, SVfS.*, vol. 177, pt. 3 (1930), 62. In 1901 American workers were paying an average of 18.12 per cent of their wages for shelter. *Eighteenth Annual Report of the United States Commissioner of Labor* (Washington, D.C., 1903), p. 101.

cent was spent by the landlord for administrative costs; 7–10 was used for maintenance. From the remaining 44–48 per cent about one-half went to service the mortgage loans,[14] which equaled more than 50 per cent of the aggregate value of the houses in Vienna. In this fashion an average of something like 20 per cent of the gross rent formed the net income of the landlords. Computed otherwise this was a comfortable but by no means excessive interest on the capital outlay. The mass of tenants, however, were naturally inclined to regard the situation from a different angle. The gross rent, which swallowed a large part of the worker's income, either compelled his wife to go to the factory[15] or made it unavoidable that the family sublet parts of their tiny apartment; both methods were regularly used simultaneously. By the first, the whole family life of the workers was seriously affected. By the second, the consequences were almost as undesirable. Subtenants and "bed tenants"[16] became a permanent feature of a great number of the smallest apartments. In the years just prior to the First World War the number of bed tenants in Vienna was estimated at from 60 to 70 thousand.[17] This meant that about 17 per cent of the families in the small dwellings had a stranger in their midst; very often one of the family members had to share a bed with him.

The results, in their sanitary, moral, and cultural aspects, were appalling. The crowded ill-aired rooms were breeding places of disease. There was, as Philippovich showed, a direct correlation between the degree of overpopulation in the apartments of a district and its rate of mortality. The inadequate habitation slowly killed its occupants. Few secrets of life remained hidden from children growing up in such surroundings. Young girls slept in the same room as the bed tenant. A disproportionately large number of incest cases dealt with by the Viennese courts originated in these "homes."

---

[14] Robert Danneberg, *Was wird aus dem Mieterschutz?* (Wien, 1924), pp. 13–14.

[15] Cf. Werner Sombart's statement (*Der moderne Kapitalismus*, vol. 2 [Leipzig, 1902], p. 494) that the rise of land rent in the cities was one of the prominent reasons which forced the female members of workers' families to look for jobs in factories and shops.

[16] A subtenant in Austria rents a separate room from the tenant; a bed tenant (*Bettgeher*) rents only a bedstead in a room occupied by family members.

[17] Kautsky, *loc. cit.*, p. 63. In 1900, 66,246 bed tenants were counted in Vienna. The number of subtenants was 86,708, or, including all family members in this group, 104,463. From the social point of view the latter figures are less revealing since they included, for example, a considerable number of students in the University and other schools of Vienna. For figures, cf. Ludwig Vogler, "Wien," *Verfassung und Verwaltungsorganization der Städte, Oesterreich, SVfS.*, vol. 122 (1907), 6.

Professor Philippovich, who, without support or encouragement from any source, tried in his personal inquiry to measure the depths of this misery, summarized his impressions in these frequently quoted words:

> The dwelling is only a cover against the grimness of the weather, only a bedstead for the night which provides—in the narrow space, lacking air, cleanness, and quiet, into which the people are pressed—rest only to a completely exhausted body. The life of this class of the population moves uneasily between this bedstead and work and worries. There is complete lack of everything that we are accustomed to regard as the basis of a healthy middle-class life: the independent existence of the family, the special attention to the fundamental needs of everyday life, to the sick and to those particularly needing care, protection of modesty by separation of the sexes, concealment of the parents' sexual life from the children, and educative attention of the parents for their children in the hours of rest and relaxation. These dwellings offer no comfort and no relaxation; they have no attraction for those who come home tired after work. Whoever was born in these places or sank into them must degenerate and wither, bodily and mentally, or grow brutal.[18]

The author carefully points out that the inhabitants of these apartments are by no means poor people in the sense of a group without regular income. What he describes are the "homes" of a whole class which has its specific and important place in the social mechanism.

It may be said, however, that the worst plight of the unhappy resident in Vienna workers' districts began when bad trade or even normal fluctuations in the demand for labor caused some interruption in the regular inflow of wages. The houseowners were unwilling to wait for rent payments. Partly because of the pressure of their own obligations to mortgage credit institutions, partly because of the natural wish to preserve their net incomes,[19] they were impelled to an inconsiderate and, indeed, ruthless attitude. The law undoubtedly supported them in the matter of prompt payment of rent by stipulating a notice period of only two weeks. Moreover, landlords were entitled to seize the belongings of tenants to satisfy claims for unpaid rent. Once in the street, the workers' family had to solve the difficult problem of finding other accommodations. The Philippovich study noted that the proportion of empty dwellings

[18] *Loc. cit.*, p. 236.

[19] For years they were, for example, responsible to the authorities for that part of unpaid rents that actually were taxes on tenants.

was more unfavorable in the categories of "small" dwellings than in the others. As years went by this situation deteriorated further. Vacancies of 3 or 4 per cent were usually regarded as a necessary minimum in order to secure a smooth satisfaction of the existing demand. In 1914 only 1.39 per cent of all Viennese dwellings stood empty and in the class of small apartments the percentage was only 0.89.[20] This was but an expression of the fundamental fact that private enterprise had proved unable to organize an adequate supply of dwellings, so that the existing landlords enjoyed a quasi-monopolistic position in the market. The more the tenant was compelled to cling to his apartment the more ready was the landlord to give notice for any reason and frequently without reason at all. The landlords came into the comfortable position of being able to select their tenants carefully. In these years it became increasingly difficult for families with several children to find any accommodations. The number of persons who were compelled to seek refuge in the "homes for the roofless" grew considerably.

"The letting of dwellings to a large number of 'small people' of dubious solvency, questionable cleanliness and lacking a sense of order is . . . not a pleasant business," wrote Herkner.[21] This is undoubtedly true. Or, as Hoss, the Christian Social acting-mayor of Vienna, once observed in the city council: "It is understandable from the point of view of the landlords that they are not readily prepared to take into their new houses people who–it is certainly very sad and unpleasant to say it–do not bring in any furniture but a number of children instead."[22] The landlords naturally regarded the house primarily, in the large majority of cases solely, as a source of income. Nobody could expect any appreciable number of them to apply principles of social policy in their business lives. But for the masses of tenants the landlords, likewise "naturally," appeared as

[20] Rosenblum, *op. cit.*, p. 88. In Ottakring, a typical proletarian district of Vienna, the ratio was only 0.28 per cent. Cf. Nationalrat, *Protokoll,* February 10, 1922, p. 3077.

[21] H. Herkner, *Die Arbeiterfrage,* Vol. 1: *Arbeiterfrage und Sozialreform* (8th ed.; Berlin and Leipzig, 1922), p. 603.

[22] Proceedings of the meeting of the city council of October 17, 1911, as quoted by Alois Huber, *Weg mit dem Mieterschutz* (Wien, 1923), p. 6. Also of interest is a speech in the postwar Austrian parliament made by Pölzer, the Social Democratic leader in Favoriten, one of the Vienna districts most unsatisfactory in housing conditions. He recalled that in prewar times he had been compelled to advise workers' wives to conceal from landlords the true number of their children because otherwise it would have been impossible for them to find a dwelling. Nationalrat, *Protokoll,* February 10, 1922, p. 3091.

the personified cause of their troubles. It was the landlord who was responsible for the inadequate dwellings, for the high rents. It was the landlord who doubled the insecurity of their existence, who at any time could deliver them to the horrors of homelessness; it was the landlord who, to borrow a term from Sombart, transformed them into "modern nomads."[23] Whoever had the opportunity to speak with Viennese workers on their housing conditions in prewar times realized how much revengeful hatred had accumulated in their hearts against the "rent vultures" and "house tyrants"—a hatred growing out of major grievances and perhaps in no less degree out of the everyday harassments inherent in the situation. Thus were created the psychological prerequisites of the housing policy in postrevolutionary Austria.

It was stated above that nobody could expect the landlords to act as if they were honor members of the *Verein für Sozialpolitik*. But one could expect that the city council of Vienna would regard improvement of housing conditions as among its first duties. This was not so, unfortunately. From the first appearance of Philippovich's study complaints of the inactivity of the municipal legislature were reiterated in most publications on the subject.[24] In the forefront of the complaints were those against the antediluvian standards of the building ordinance of 1883. When the first Christian Social mayor, Lueger, came into office in 1897 he promised immediate action. His first committee was unable to agree. The second met and debated for seven years. Its report was sent back to it by the city council for "further study." After thirteen years in office Lueger died. His administration had accomplished exactly nothing with reference to his pledge. His successor finally pushed through some amendments to the code in 1911, but they were not of a material character.[25] On October 17 of the same year the council approved a resolution, offered by the vice-mayor, providing for the participation of the city in a limited liability company which was to build at once 250 emergency dwellings for homeless families. The council provided 200,000 crowns, one-third of the capital, in cash; obligated itself to make certain installations, such as sewers and

[23] Sombart, *op. cit.*, p. 328.

[24] Cf., for example, the report of Professor C. J. Fuchs in *SVfS.*, vol. 132 (1910), 71.

[25] Cf. C. O. Hardy, *The Housing Program of Vienna* (Washington, D.C., 1934), pp. 132–135.

streets, that were estimated to cost 150,000 crowns; renounced some fees it normally collected; and agreed to compensate at 4,000 crowns a year for an unstated period a hospital fund which would lose income by the arrangement. Even this drop in the bucket was accompanied by the solemn declaration that the city was acting "without recognition of a legal obligation to provide for houseless families."[26]

During the First World War, apparently in reply to the current crop of complaints, the mayor of Vienna wrote that before the war the city had built "not less than 3,000 small dwellings," that "if today no direct emergency in the small-dwelling situation exists in Vienna, this is exclusively thanks to the building activity of the municipality," and that further construction of this sort had been stopped only by the war. He made it clear, however, that in principle he considered such activities unwise.[27] Critics of this particular project emphasized the facts that the apartments were actually constructed by the municipal streetcar, gas, and electric undertakings for the exclusive use of their employees and that the funds came primarily from the pension funds of those employees. In other words, this was no attack by the city proper on the whole problem. The critics claimed that the action was prompted by the wish to have the residences of the workers near their places of employment, and that this motive indicated that housing conditions in prewar Vienna already presented certain hindrances to the mobility of labor.[28]

Finally, it should be mentioned that in 1913 a small-housing bureau was instituted in the city council offices. It provided employment for four officials, but did not perform any activities worth recording. The same has to be said of a city council committee which was set up in the same year.

Very important, on the other hand, were the continuous land purchases of the council. By the end of 1918 the municipality owned 4,690 hectares, about 17 per cent of its area. These purchases could have alleviated the wretched housing conditions in the metropolis

[26] A. Weber, "Wiener Wohnungs- und Sozialpolitik," *Das Neue Wien,* vol. 1, p. 204; *Neue Freie Presse,* October 14, 1911 (A.M.), p. 11; October 17 (A.M.), p. 12; October 18 (A.M.), pp. 11–13. The varying statements in secondary sources concerning the amount of the contribution of the city probably reflect varying estimates of the sums lost in fees or paid to the hospital fund.

[27] R. Weiskirchner, *Städtische Wohnungspolitik* (Wien, 1917), pp. 15–16.

[28] Cf. Weber, *loc. cit.;* and Rosenblum, *op. cit.,* p. 105.

had they been used by the city fathers for the purposes of an energetic building policy. As it was, they restricted the existing supply of land, decreased building activities, and drove up rents. Thus the purchases aggravated the general situation. The city levies on rent, constituting about two-thirds of its tax revenues, were discussed generally in the preceding chapter. Here it should be emphasized that such heavy ungraduated taxes certainly contributed toward an intensification of "housing misery" (*Wohnungselend*) in Vienna. To the extent that the city used the tax money for investments, such as new streets and lighting, it increased the land rent and thus increased the rent payments of the tenant as well as his burden of taxation.

The composition of the Vienna city council must be regarded as mainly responsible for its almost absolute neglect of the housing problem. The system prescribed for municipal elections in the empire days was rightly styled by a Catholic scholar as "mythological."[29] Prior to the reform of 1900 there were three electoral bodies, or *curiae,* each of which elected one-third of the city council. The first group was composed of owners of large fortunes and a handful of high dignitaries of the state and the religious confessions; the second was made up chiefly of professional men; the third body was reserved for the lower middle class. In the election of 1896, when the Christian Socials first came into power, the qualified voters in the respective *curiae* were as follows: first, 5,500; second, 25,800; third, 51,500. Thus only 82,800 inhabitants of Vienna were allowed to take part in the elections to the council; and the decisive majority of the voters, assembled in the third group, was a priori represented by only one-third of the members in that council. The masses of the workers were deprived of any representation. The reform of 1900 introduced a fourth electoral *curia;* the voters in it, and only in it, were required to have lived in Vienna for three years prior to the elections. Moreover, all voters in the first three bodies were allowed to vote again in the fourth. Finally, the first three *curiae* elected 46 representatives each, whereas for the fourth body, comprising 283,614 voters, only 20 seats were reserved. This system secured an overwhelming majority for the Christian Social party: in the first elections held after the reform of 1900 it obtained 136 seats from a total of 158. Only two members of the city council were Social Democrats.

[29] E. K. Winter, "Wiener Wohnbaupolitik," *Hochland,* vol. 28 (May, 1931), 123.

What is most revealing for this study is that among the 158 members of the council, no less than 77 were houseowners in Vienna.[30] This fact makes understandable the attitude of the city council toward the housing problem. It explains, for instance, why all efforts to introduce a new building ordinance on more modern principles regularly failed in the council.[31] But the artificial strength of the landlords in that body naturally increased the antagonism between the workers and the landlords. The former regarded general manhood suffrage as one of their main objectives. The undemocratic system in Vienna continued unaffected even after 1907 when that suffrage was made the basis of parliamentary elections. It required a revolution to make the city council of Vienna a truly democratic institution. So far as in the consciousness of the workers the despised legislative organ of Vienna became a "landlords' council" the personal grievances of the individual assumed the larger aspect of political class hatred.

The description of prewar housing conditions has been confined to the capital not only because it was the only really large city of what later became the Austrian republic, but also because it was virtually the only place in that new political unit where the Social Democratic party carried out its far-reaching housing policy. However, the conditions in the provincial cities did not differ so much as might be expected from those in Vienna. In fact, the evil of overcrowded dwellings was even more pronounced outside the capital, as may be judged from the table on page 419.

The ratio of empty dwellings, however, was on the whole more favorable in the provinces. Two additional points deserve mention. In many of the cities of the provinces, as for instance in Graz, the largest of them, the development of separate working-class districts lagged considerably behind that in Vienna; large masses of people still lived in what was called a *Hinterhaus*. It was usually separated

[30] L. Vogler, in *SVfS.*, vol. 122 (1907), 9–10, 13–16. "The landlords' associations influence the selection of candidates [for the city council elections], since they declare they will support only such candidates as are willing to support the program drawn up by these associations. The political associations [parties] frequently get in touch with landlords' associations before they nominate their candidates (especially in the first electoral body)." *Ibid.*, p. 14.

[31] I do not intend to leave the impression that in my opinion a new building ordinance might have favorably influenced the housing conditions to any appreciable extent. In all likelihood, it would have worked the other way round by rendering construction more expensive, reducing the flow of capital into this line of enterprise, and further increasing rents.

by a courtyard from the front part of the building. The latter—very different in the quality of its residences and in its outward appearance—was occupied by well-to-do people, whereas the *Hinterhaus* was the dwelling of workers and lower middle class. This had certain important sociological implications. Furthermore, the courtyard between the front house and the *Hinterhaus* was usually fairly large, so that a smaller area of the lot was occupied with buildings. Together with a smaller number of floors than was common in Vienna, this arrangement improved the housing conditions from a sanitary point of view. A second feature of provincial dwellings, especially

AVERAGE NUMBER OF PERSONS IN APARTMENTS OF ONE LIVING ROOM*

City	Number	City	Number
Vienna	2.36	Steyr	2.51
Atzgerdorf	2.50	Salzburg	2.15
St. Pölten	2.63	Graz	2.35
Wiener-Neustadt	2.53	Knittelfeld	2.88
Linz	2.39	Leoben-Donawitz	2.93

* Kautsky, *loc. cit.*, p. 63.

in the smaller industrial towns, were "factory houses" erected by the industrial firms. Since hardly anywhere were they provided in sufficient quantity the taking of bed tenants was the general rule. This was all the more serious because the dwellings normally consisted of only one room, without a separate kitchen. The high average figures for Leoben-Donawitz and Knittelfeld in the preceding table result from the large number of such company houses there. The city and town councils in the provinces were elected in the same undemocratic fashion as in Vienna. But even if this had not been true the lack of funds would have rendered it impossible for them to venture upon any comprehensive housing plans.

The central Austrian government did but little to bring about a betterment of housing conditions. A law of 1892, stipulating that workers' dwellings which met certain requirements were to be freed from taxation, proved a failure because the construction of such higher standard accommodations was not profitable enough. Several housing acts passed by the Austrian parliament after 1910 were concerned chiefly with the formation of a Housing Welfare Fund, with reduced taxes on new buildings, and with long-term community land leases. The general objective of these laws was the furtherance of coöperative building; their practical results in the short time remaining before the outbreak of war were very limited.[32] The idea of direct building activities by a city council or any public body was foreign to this legislation.

Twenty years before the beginning of the First World War Professor Philippovich closed his study on Vienna housing with an earnest appeal:

> If everything is allowed to stay as it is, if we put our hands in our laps, then the ghastly devastating effects of our housing conditions on life, health, and the mental development of the population will continue. Time and again diseases will break out and carry their destructive germs far beyond the precincts of the poor classes; sick people will become a burden to the communities; the dead bodies of those who had to die before their time will raise their mute complaint and will provoke in the hearts of the living deeper hatred against the owning classes and our order of society than the most eloquent agitator ever could produce; the moral feelings of the people will be extinguished and choked by the rougher instincts of animal life. Not only humaneness, compassion with the suffering of our fellow men, but also sober reflection and enlightened *raison d'état* make it imperative to intervene and organize in a sensible way the basic condition of all orderly physical and psychical life—the dwelling of the people.[33]

The warning was a cry in the desert. The few efforts undertaken in imperial Austria, in the Vienna of Lueger and his successor, were insufficient to palliate, let alone to cure, the social disease of "housing misery."

In closing this section one other important aspect of the housing conditions of prewar Vienna must be mentioned. Philippovich was certainly correct in stating that slum housing favored an anticapitalist attitude among the people compelled to live in those dwellings. But he probably went too far in regarding them as "breeding places of anarchism."[34] On the other hand, certain functional relations between housing conditions and the strength of the Socialist party cannot be overlooked. As Michels has pointed out, separate workers' districts in large cities are likely to favor the development of class

[32] This was admitted even in the generally sympathetic report of Karl Forchheimer. Cf. "Die neue wohnungspolitische Gesetzgebung Oesterreichs," *AfSS.*, vol. 36 (1913), 545.
[33] *Loc. cit.*, p. 264.
[34] *Ibid.*, p. 237.

consciousness among their inhabitants to a much stronger degree than is true in the *Hinterhaus* or in the cellar and mansard dwellings in an apartment house in a central district where some daily contact between the classes is still preserved.[35] This undoubtedly played a part in making the Socialist party in Vienna relatively stronger as compared with Austrian provincial cities like Graz. In his leisure hours the Viennese worker fled the desolate barrenness of his quarters. Frequently his way led him to the beer and wine houses which were so abundant in the proletarian districts, but often it was because the worker felt that his residence was in no proper sense a home that the Socialists were able to form an army of devoted and industrious functionaries who put every minute of their free time at the disposal of the party. Thus was created the formidable mechanism the possession of which so strikingly distinguished the Socialist political organization from all other parties in Austria.

War and Housing Problems

ORIGINS OF TENANTS PROTECTION

The war brought a certain relaxing of the housing-market situation. The ratio of empty dwellings in Vienna rose from 1.39 in 1914 to 1.49 in 1917; though the data are not available there is reason to believe that the ratio was even more favorable in the intervening years. This improvement was confined to small apartments, as shown in the table on page 422.

The divergent movement resulted from two sets of facts. On the one hand, the mobilization of the heads of families in small dwellings frequently induced the women to abandon the apartment altogether and to return to their parents or other relatives for the duration of the war. In such instances reduced tension in the market was achieved at the price of an actual deterioration of housing conditions. Nevertheless, the sagging demand for small dwellings compelled the landlords to acquiesce in some reductions of rents in a great number of cases. Whether, as Türr claims, the patriotic sentiments of houseowners had anything to do with this economically well-understandable action, is hard to say.[36] On the other hand, the irruption of Russian troops into the eastern parts of the mon-

[35] R. Michels, "Psychologie der antikapitalistischen Massenbewegungen," *Grundriss der Sozialökonomik,* vol. 9, pt. 1 (Tübingen, 1926), pp. 255–256.
[36] Türr, *op. cit.,* p. 55.

archy brought a large flow of refugees from Galicia to Vienna. The demands of this group, belonging chiefly to the middle class, accounted partly for the reduction in the number of empty dwellings in all categories except "small." The transformation of such dwellings into offices for the military administration also decreased the supply.

PERCENTAGE OF EMPTY DWELLINGS IN AGGREGATE NUMBER OF DWELLINGS OF SPECIFIED CLASS*

Class of Dwellings	1914	1917
Large	4.33	1.07
Medium large	2.89	1.04
Medium small	1.67	1.40
Small	0.89	1.60

* International Labor Office, "European Housing Problems since the War," *Studies and Reports*, Series G (Housing and Welfare) No. 1 (Geneva, 1924), p. 356.

Almost needless to remark, building activities were gravely affected by the war. In the provinces they ceased almost instantly. In Vienna, 13,988 dwellings were built in 1913. Although hostilities began in the middle of the building season of 1914, 9,586 were completed in that year. In 1915 the number dwindled to 4,794; in 1916 to 962; in 1917 to 342; and in 1918 to 85;[37] that is, there was a virtual standstill in residential construction. Nevertheless, the high mortality, the tremendous decrease in the number of marriages (after a temporary sharp increase in 1914), and the reduction in income of families whose "earners" had to join up combined to prevent the stoppage of building activities from being too severely felt on the market for dwellings in the "small" category. As said before, this did not mean any real improvement in housing conditions. In fact, the opposite was true so that the imperial government had to undertake measures for tenants protection.

As early as the second year of the war, when a general rise in prices set in, there was a pronounced tendency among landlords to raise rents and to give notice to those of their tenants whose diminished incomes could not be stretched to cover them. Attempts were also made to combine several small dwellings into one large

[37] Figures of the municipal building office; reproduced in R. Danneberg, *Kampf gegen die Wohnungsnot!* (Wien, 1921), p. 2.

apartment in order to meet the demand for large accommodations. For some time this continued unchecked. But as the war dragged on and misery and general unrest increased throughout the country, the government began to feel that continued evictions of the families of soldiers might develop into a dangerous situation as well as impair the fighting power of the army. As the Christian Social Resch pointed out in the republican parliament, "if the prohibition against giving notice had not been introduced . . . there would have been social disturbances."[38]

Tenants protection was established by three decrees. The first, issued on January 26, 1917,[39] was by no means a general norm, since it applied only to apartments and business premises bringing in less than stipulated amounts of annual rent which were themselves different in five categories of towns and cities. Furthermore, the decree was not *eo ipso* valid for the whole country since the minister of justice was authorized to name by special decrees the communities in which extraordinary increases of rents had taken place and in which, therefore, the new regulations should be applied.

The essentials of tenants protection were the limitations on the landlord's rights to raise rents and to give notice. Like other countries, Austria proceeded on the principle that each of these restrictions would be practically ineffective without the other.[40] Rent increases were allowed only to the extent of actual rises in the maintenance and administrative costs of the house, in house taxes, and in interest on mortgage loans. For families of soldiers any increase of rent was prohibited "if it would endanger their livelihood." In the language of the decree, notice could be given only "for important reasons." As instances of such reasons the following, among others, were cited: refusal of the tenant to pay the rent, continued neglect by the tenant of the rules of the "house order," and the landlord's personal need for the dwelling. The decree was issued as a provisional emergency measure[41] to expire December 31, 1918.

By the end of 1917 about 120 cities and towns of the German part of Austria had been placed under tenants protection. The continuing general rise in prices and the waxing political tension necessi-

[38] Nationalrat, *Protokoll,* February 10, 1922, p. 3047.
[39] *RGBl.,* 1917, Nr. 34, pp. 92–97.
[40] Cf. *Encyclopaedia of the Social Sciences,* vol. 13, p. 293.
[41] Cf. Moriz Sternberg, *Die Wohnungsgesetze* (Wien, 1928), pp. 2 ff.

tated a second decree, promulgated on January 20, 1918, and valid for the whole territory of the monarchy.[42] Its most important feature was the extension of the tenant's protection against eviction to all apartments and business premises, whatever their rent. The stipulation concerning the landlord's personal need for a dwelling was changed to require proof that he would be put to severe disadvantage if he did not obtain the apartment in question. Moreover, a landlord who had acquired a house after January, 1918, was entitled to claim it (or an apartment in it) for his personal use only if his advantage from getting the apartment was greater than the tenant's disadvantage from losing it. This represented a substantial protection for the economically weaker party. By another change affecting rents, tenants in apartments with rents exceeding the limits set by the first decree were given certain protection; namely, rent increases had to be "appropriate" in view of the "special circumstances of every case." This, of course, was much more elastic than the regulations protecting tenants in cheaper accommodations against increases in rent. An attempt was made to safeguard the interests of subtenants in unfurnished rooms through a stipulation that their rent was not to exceed the proportional amount of the rent paid for these rooms by the main tenant to the landlord, but since the majority of rooms were sublet furnished this regulation never assumed any large importance and the subtenants virtually remained outside the scope of tenants protection.

As had been provided by the first decree, all litigations arising out of these new rules, most notably the extent of permissible rent increases, were to be decided by special rent offices instituted by the communities.

The second decree also was to have expired at the end of 1918, but in the very midst of the collapse of the monarchy the field of tenants protection was regulated anew by the third order.[43] It was rendered imperative by certain developments on the market. Theoretical considerations as well as practical experience indicate that interferences with the free market, if they are to be effective, must be thoroughgoing; otherwise, numerous evasions become inevitable. There were two major loopholes which threatened to frustrate the

[42] *RGBl.*, 1918, Nr. 21.
[43] October 26, 1918, *RGBl.*, 1918, Nr. 381.

efforts of the authorities. First was the appearance of the so-called apartment redemptions (*Wohnungsablösen*); that is, bonuses paid to the old tenant and to the landlord by a new tenant. The number of transactions in this new line of trade had been growing steadily. Second was the tendency of rents charged to subtenants to lose relation to the rent paid by the main tenant. The new decree attempted to cope with both types of evasions by flatly prohibiting the taking of redemptions and by stipulating that the charges for furniture and services put at the disposal of the subtenant must be "appropriate." These changes, being prohibitions and as such only negative measures, were of themselves insufficient to cope with the evasions. Of the further innovations brought by the decree mention should be made of a certain relaxation of the limitations on notices. The most important among them was that "company" houses were exempt from such restrictions. The stipulations concerning rent increases were left unchanged. Since the first decree had established the principle that tenants protection did not apply to buildings begun after January 27, 1917, and since this remained unaltered, the whole system was confined to the stock of houses existing on that date. The third decree had no time limit. Whether this was so because the decree represented an attempt to create a modern rent law by permanently replacing the antiquated stipulations of the civil code[44] or because, as Schneider seems to think, the point was forgotten in the haste of those trying days[45] is an issue which must remain undecided.

So much for the changes brought about by the specific war conditions and the imminent collapse of the empire. The strain of an extraordinary situation had induced a government which in the past had rejected even a milder reform to adopt a radical system of tenants protection. Although in its legal essentials this system was to remain unchanged for many years to come, the subsequent economic cataclysm completely altered its meaning.

---

[44] Sternberg, *op. cit.*, p. 7.

[45] Josef Schneider, *Der Tod von Wien,* Wien (n.d.), p. 4. It is rather improbable that the authors of the decree considered the freezing of rents at the prewar level a wise permanent measure. On the other hand, Schneider's reference is far from clear. He seems to believe that tenants protection came into being as a *law* enacted by *parliament* in 1917 without time limit. Since it is known that two *decrees* of January, 1917, and January, 1918, were to expire on December 31, 1918, Schneider seems to be factually wrong in more than one way.

Housing Problems in the First Years of the Republic

CONSEQUENCES OF WAR AND PEACE

The breakup of the monarchy and the establishment of new states and new citizenships naturally led to considerable shifts in population. The census of 1920 revealed that between 1910 and 1920 the inhabitants of Vienna decreased from 2,031,498 to 1,841,326, that is, by 190,172.[46] It would be wrong, however, to assume that the drop had any far-reaching effects upon the housing market. This anomalous result derived partly from the fact that different groups of people were moving in both directions. Large numbers of Czech laborers left Vienna. Many of them had lived as subtenants and bed-tenants, so that their departure lessened the density of occupation in small dwellings but did not materially increase the supply. On the other hand, the majority of those who returned to Vienna were Austrian civil servants who had been expelled by the governments of the succession states. They appeared on the market as a demand for additional dwellings.

The rate at which new households are founded is obviously of major importance for the problem. During the war the number of marriages was greatly reduced. As soon as peace was restored there was a rush to the altar, as the number of marriages in Vienna show.[47]

Year	Marriages	Year	Marriages
1914	22,294	1919	25,049
1915	14,648	1920	30,137
1916	13,583	1921	28,208
1917	13,431	1922	26,734
1918	16,389		

If the three full war years 1915–1917 are compared with the three full peace years 1919–1921 it is seen that the yearly average of marriages in the latter exceeded that in the former by 13,911. In prewar times the number of new dwellings was 45 per cent of the number of marriages.[48] This ratio probably was not sufficient in itself, but the postwar marriages were concluded after years of almost complete standstill in building activities—a state of affairs which three years of peace did not change much. In 1922 the net increase in dwellings

[46] *SHfRO,* vol. 2, p. 6.
[47] *Ibid.,* vol. 2, p. 17; vol. 5, p. 17.
[48] J. Bunzel, "Wohnungsmarkt und Wohnungspolitik," *SVfS.,* vol. 177, pt. 3 (1930), p. 106.

in Vienna was almost exactly that of 1916 and the aggregate increase in the years 1917–1921 was only about 200 dwellings larger than that of 1916 or 1922. Thus an anomalous number of marriages was accompanied by a likewise anomalous stabilization in the number of dwellings. One special point appears worth mentioning in this respect: all over Europe the war led to decided shifts in moral concepts and customs. Especially among the working-class population there was an important increase in the number of couples who founded a new household without seeking sanctification of their

Age	Increase	Decrease
0–9	....	−132,229
10–19	....	−48,916
20–29	....	−62,191
30–39	....	−17,057
40–49	+43,437	....
50–59	+19,178	....
60–69	+10,088	....
70–79	....	− 542
Over 80	....	− 1,863

status from the Church or confirmation from secular authorities. After the war, therefore, the number of marriages became a less safe index and rather underrated the demand for new dwellings.

Also important were the shifts which took place in the age distribution of the population. The falling birth rate and the high infant mortality during the war, losses on the battlefields, and deaths from privation caused considerable displacements. The above table shows by age groups the shifts in the population of Vienna between 1910 and 1920.[49] Keeping in mind the fact that the net decrease in this decade was 190,000, it is clear that the overwhelming part of it, 181,000, came from the age group 0–19 the members of which did not constitute a demand for separate apartments. On the other hand, as the International Labor Office report points out, "the figures show a particularly large increase (72,703) in precisely those age groups to which heads of families and householders belong."[50]

[49] International Labor Office, "European Housing Problems," *Studies and Reports*, p. 359.

[50] *Ibid.*, p. 360.

REDISTRIBUTION OF AVAILABLE HOUSING SUPPLY

All the factors discussed above worked together to sharpen and intensify a housing shortage that had been severe before the war. On December 31, 1918, the number of free apartments in Vienna was 315, or 0.056 per cent. Since among the more than 8,000 vacancies in 1917 there had been many not appropriate for dwellings, it is clear that these figures implied the complete disappearance of even halfway satisfactory empty dwellings. As will be shown in the next section, there were some efforts to further building activities soon after the armistice; but the emphasis, because of the general economic breakdown, certain theoretical considerations, inflation, and tenants protection, had to be elsewhere. Not creation of new dwellings, but redistribution of the already available space to cover the most urgent housing needs of the greatest possible number of persons was the immediate problem. The relations of this problem to economic breakdown and to inflation are obvious; to the theoretical points I shall return. Here it is important to note that the very existence of tenants protection made attention to the redistribution problem all the more pressing. If rents were kept down in relation to the development of the general price level, then the tendency would be for the larger apartments to be retained by the tenants even though they were not absolutely needed. On the other hand, as mentioned before, tenants protection naturally implied the danger of a "black market" in dwellings. In consonance with the usual expectations of economic theory, price fixing, also in this special case, threatened to remain useless unless supplemented by a thoroughgoing scheme of rationing. This rationing was carried out primarily by requisitioning of dwellings.

Before the establishment of the republic only two measures had been adopted which even pointed in the direction of the subsequent legislation on requisitioning. A decree of March 28, 1918, forbade the use of premises appropriate for dwelling purposes in any other way, as well as the amalgamation of two or more apartments into one. The practical effects of this ordinance became visible only under the republican government. The other regulation, October 23, 1918, required landlords to notify housing departments of every vacant dwelling in their properties.[51]

[51] *RGBl.*, 1918, Nr. 114, 368.

A decree of November 11 of the republican[52] state department of social welfare authorized the communities to set up special committees with power to act in providing accommodations for homeless people. The utilization of military buildings, barracks, hutments for war prisoners, hospitals, and the like was particularly emphasized. Funds were provided by the new state council. But the process of demobilization was to prove a long and painful one. It was at once clear that measures of far larger scope were required.

On November 13 the state council adopted an executive order concerning the requisitioning of housing.[53] Under its terms landlords were compelled to inform the municipal authorities of all cases in which two dwellings were held by one person or in which the space was not completely utilized. Those authorities were empowered to requisition all such dwellings, as well as vacant ones and quarters previously used as habitations but diverted to other employment after the outbreak of war. Furthermore, the municipalities obtained the right to put the requisitioned dwellings or parts of dwellings at the disposal of persons who either belonged to the community in question[54] or had impelling reasons to live there. If landlords failed to supply the required information within the stipulated time the municipal authorities were authorized to inspect their properties. Should need arise Minister of Social Welfare Hanusch had power to make these regulations more severe.

A week later, November 20, the state council issued an executive order concerning the requisitioning of land and buildings which was designed to maintain control over such properties as had already been leased by public bodies for military, economic, or welfare purposes during the war.[55] On February 4, 1919, the Provisional Assembly authorized by statute the expropriation of land and the buildings thereon when necessary for "improving the housing conditions of the less well-to-do population."[56] A number of other laws, decrees,

[52] Although the republic was not actually proclaimed until November 12, the new political unit of German-Austria had been functioning since October 30 under the Renner Constitution of that date. For the text of the decree, see J. Brod, *Die Wohnungsnot und ihre Bekämpfung*, Pt. II (Wien, 1919), pp. 6–7; for the use made of it see, *ibid.*, pp. 30–33.

[53] *StGBl.*, 1918, Nr. 22.

[54] Under the citizenship laws every Austrian was assigned to a community which was regarded as his home community.

[55] *StGBl.*, 1918, Nr. 31.

[56] *Ibid.*, 1919, Nr. 82.

and orders[57] of similar purport were issued during the first months of the republic, but the foregoing adequately demonstrate the main features of the program.

After a short time it became evident that the adaptation of the stipulations of the order of November 13 to the special conditions prevailing in the individual communities would render its execution more efficient; consequently, by a decree of April 9, 1919,[58] Hanusch simply transferred his powers in this respect to the state governments. Since landlords still displayed great ingenuity in circumventing parts of the regulations, another executive order of August 11 tightened them up.[59] The state authorities made extensive use of the orders of April 9 and August 11. For example, on June 30, Lower Austria stiffened the regulations by a decree based on suggestions of the Vienna housing department. Thereby the number of dwellings requisitioned in Vienna in the second half of 1919 was almost exactly three times as great as in the first half. In addition, 1,710 single rooms were requisitioned.[60] Even more severe was the decree of the governor of Vienna on March 31, 1921,[61] which introduced the principle of "general requisitioning" of every dwelling that became vacant in the capital. *Inter alia* the additional principle was laid down that in a dwelling with more than three rooms the others were to be regarded as "superfluous" if the total number of rooms exceeded the number of inmates by more than one. If one person occupied a dwelling with three rooms, one of them was superfluous. The decree utilized past experience and also paid consideration to the rulings of the Administrative Court.[62]

With the help of the decrees just mentioned, the city council of Vienna worked out a comprehensive system of providing dwellings for homeless or inadequately accommodated people. The number of dwellings requisitioned in 1919–1925; that is, during the period of the validity of the regulations, is shown by the table on page 431.[63] In addition to entire dwellings, as indicated, a great number of

[57] Cf. Brod, *op. cit.*, Pt. II, *passim*, for a convenient summary of them.
[58] *StGBl.*, 1919, Nr. 223.
[59] *Ibid.*, Nr. 418; Brod, *op. cit.*, Pt. II, pp. 9–10.
[60] *Die Gemeindeverwaltung der Bundeshauptstadt Wien in der Zeit vom 1. Juli 1919 bis 31. Dezember 1922* (Wien, 1927), pp. 389–390.
[61] *LGBl. für Wien*, 1921, Nr. 26.
[62] Weber, *loc. cit.*, p. 243.
[63] *Wirtschaftsstatistisches Jahrbuch, 1925*, p. 78.

rooms of various sorts were requisitioned. In 1921, for example, the total of these was 26,671.[64] The data in the table show clearly the effects of the March, 1921, decree on the number of requisitioned dwellings. The decline beginning in 1923 was caused partly by some relaxation of the rules (brought about by new legislation at the end of 1922); and partly by the natural limitations of a redistribution scheme. Altogether 44,838 dwellings were requisitioned. The number is certainly large and indicative of the energy displayed by the city council. If, however, the number of requisitioned dwellings in 1919–1922 is taken as a percentage of the number of marriages which took place in the same period, it is found that that

Year	Number requisitioned	Year	Number requisitioned
1919	4,914	1923	6,014
1920	5,975	1924	5,068
1921	9,385	1925	3,790
1922	9,692		

percentage is approximately 27. This contrasts most unfavorably with the previously noted percentage of 45 in prewar times—itself also insufficient. A large proportion, 55 per cent, of the requisitioned dwellings or parts of dwellings was given to the subtenants living in them prior to the requisitioning. This practice simplified the procedure but had some undesirable concomitants. For example, people frequently paid considerable sums to main tenants in order to induce them to sublet rooms.[65] The municipality of Vienna often gave the owners of "luxurious" apartments which could not be easily transformed into small dwellings the choice between requisition and payment of a comparatively large redemption. The sums thus acquired became a special city building fund.[66]

A very important consequence of the requisitioning system was that it enabled the city council to organize the exchange of apartments on a large scale. Because tenants protection had reduced the mobility of labor to the freezing point such exchanges proved very useful, especially after 1920 when the economic upswing rendered a higher mobility necessary. The municipality facilitated them

[64] International Labor Office, *op. cit.*, p. 379.
[65] *Ibid.*, pp. 379, 382.
[66] *Ibid.*, pp. 378–379.

by a special *Exchange and Subletting Gazette*. If the tenants concerned were in agreement on the transaction the landlords had to acquiesce; otherwise, the apartments would have been requisitioned and the exchange carried out by the municipality. In this sense, therefore, the requisitioning decrees were a necessary supplement to tenants protection.

The municipality went even further in this direction and facilitated the removal of persons who wanted to abandon their apartments, but lacked the necessary funds. In such cases the city helped by taking care of the shipment of belongings, by indemnifying the tenants for their general removal expenses, and even by payments of premiums of about 100 schillings. In 1923–1925, 231 apartments were provided in this way at a cost of 150,590 schillings.[67] Though this was certainly of very moderate importance, it showed again that will to alleviate the existing housing conditions which so favorably distinguished the postwar administration in Vienna from its predecessor.

On the whole the mere redistribution of the existing stock of dwellings so as to provide accommodations for a larger number of people proved successful within its natural limits. To be sure the number of apartments which were "bought" and "sold" surreptitiously was still substantial. In the fall of 1922 the housing department of Vienna issued an urgent statement appealing to the public spirit of the citizens and warning them against selfish actions which would unfavorably affect the general housing conditions.[68] Despite the implications of this appeal it remains true that the evasions only slightly impaired the beneficial effects of the redistribution system. The city council could proudly refer to the fact that the average number of persons accommodated in the Vienna "homes for homeless" in 1924 was about 46 per cent smaller than in 1913.[69] Within a few years after the establishment of the republic, however, the Socialists were more than ever convinced that the erection of new dwellings in large numbers was the only method by which the housing shortage could be combated effectively. The problem remained: who was to start building?

[67] Weber, *loc. cit.*, p. 248.
[68] *Arbeiter Zeitung*, November 28, 1922, p. 3.
[69] Weber, *loc. cit.*, p. 242.

PUBLIC BUILDING ACTIVITIES TO 1922

In the early years of the republic, the Social Democrats endeavored to make the central government carry out an energetic policy of promoting building activities. The new country's share of the old imperial Housing Welfare Fund was reconstituted by a law of January 25, 1919, as the State Housing Welfare Fund of German-Austria. On April 15, 1921, it was transformed into the Federal Housing and Settlement Fund.[70] The fund's purpose was to bear the "nonrecoverable building cost" (*verlorener Bauaufwand*)[71] in the erection of small houses, residential settlements, and certain buildings for social purposes. It was stipulated that municipalities which budgeted money for building were entitled to an equal sum from the fund. The aggregate of these subventions was, of course, limited by the total assets of the fund. The resources of the fund were provided in the main from contributions by the federal government and from a special tax which all employers had to pay for each of their workers or salaried employees. The Social Democrats participated eagerly in the formulation of the act of 1921, but their special wishes concerning the broadening of the expropriation law, and the requisitioning of undertakings in the building-materials trade were not accepted by the majority.[72] In the subsequent months of inflation the act was amended several times because it became necessary to increase the contributions. On one of these occasions the Socialists endeavored to put through a stipulation that the only municipalities entitled to receive help from the fund were those in which housing taxes were being collected, but the attempt failed.[73]

On the whole, the activities of the fund did not come up to the expectations, more properly, illusions, which had been cherished. Since the inflation was primarily the expression of a deficit in the budget, it appeared to be an illusion to hope for any substantial financing of building operations so long as the rapid depreciation of the crown continued. During 1921 and 1922 about 5,500 dwellings were begun (and in most instances finished) with the assistance

[70] *RGBl.*, 1910, Nr. 242; *StGBl.*, 1919, Nr. 45; *BGBl.*, 1921, Nr. 252.

[71] "Nonrecoverable building costs" are explained as "that part of the capital invested in house-building which does not bear interest in the form of rent" in International Labor Office, *op. cit.*, p. 390.

[72] *Tätigkeits-Bericht,* Heft 15 (Wien, 1921), pp. 84–85.

[73] *Ibid.*, Heft 16 (Wien, 1922), p. 111.

of the fund. The end of the inflation instead of improving actually deteriorated the situation. Under the strict control of the League of Nations the Austrian state had to limit subventions to the fund to absolutely inadequate sums. Moreover, ministers of finance in the stabilization period, Kienböck as well as his successors, were opposed to public schemes for promoting building activities. Thus the aggregate number of dwellings indirectly created by the fund all over Austria up to 1928 was 8,654[74]—certainly a moderate contribution to the solution of the Austrian housing problem.

The activities of the city council were also severely hampered by the inflation. As shown in the chapter on Viennese finances, the council drastically altered the municipal rent tax in October, 1919, approval being given by the diet of Lower Austria on December 18.[75] Partly to attempt to keep pace with the inflation and partly to make the rates more steeply progressive this statute was amended on August 4, 1920, and March 4, 1921.[76] Shortly after the second modification; that is, on March 18, 1921, the city council created the Housing and Settlement Fund the chief sources of which were to be the proceeds of the rent tax and subventions from the federation. It should be noticed that though revenues from the rent taxes were being used to further building, the texts of the measures did not stipulate such use.[77] This situation was altered by a new rent tax law (not an amendment) adopted by the city council on February 10, 1922, and effective May 1, 1922. It required that the proceeds be expended for the construction and maintenance of houses and for settlement purposes. Subsequently it was announced that 60 per cent should go for new houses, 10 for repairs, and 30 for settlements. In other words, this was a "purpose" tax. A commission was elected by the council to administer it. The housing and settlement fund was abolished.[78]

During the period January, 1919–July, 1923, the efforts of the municipal administration increased the number of habitations in Vienna by 6,926. But only 3,604 were in new buildings, incidentally of low quality in every respect, and the financing of these buildings

[74] Kautsky, *loc. cit.*, p. 73.
[75] *LGuVBl. für Niederösterreich,* 1920, Nr. 10.
[76] *Ibid.*, 1920, Nr. 726; and *LGBl. für Wien,* 1921, Nr. 34.
[77] *Die Gemeindeverwaltung der Bundeshauptstadt Wien in der Zeit vom 1. Juli 1919 bis 31. Dezember 1922,* p. 385.
[78] *Ibid.*, p. 386; *LGBl. für Wien,* 1922, Nr. 59, 60, 64.

had been effected to the extent of three-fifths by the Federal Housing and Settlement Fund. Of the remaining 3,322 dwellings, 1,376 were little settlement houses erected with the assistance of the city council, and about 2,000 were provided by the construction of hutments, the adaptation of barracks for dwellings, and the addition of superstructures to old houses.[79]

Although with all these measures the city council had scarcely begun the building activities which became famous throughout the world in subsequent years, certain preparations were made. Throughout the whole period of inflation, land in considerable quantities was purchased, particularly land which was available for immediate building. City brickworks were rationalized and equipped with modern machinery to increase their capacity by two and one-half times. The city fathers acquired an interest in enterprises producing important building materials; they founded a concern which was to produce flooring, doors, and windows in mass quantities; they purchased a lime kiln which was to make them independent of private purveyors.[80] The previously cited rent tax, effective May 1, 1922, was intended as a part of these preparations, but before its effectiveness as a source of building funds could be determined the crown finally collapsed in September. On January 20, 1923, the city council passed the house-construction tax (*Wohnbausteuer*), effective February 1, but did not formally decide upon its precise building plans until September 21.[81] Thus, although the workers' party was committed to direct construction of housing early in 1922, after less than three years in power, it did not announce its exact program until more than four years had passed.

As indicated, a major reason for this groping approach to what later became the very core of the council's policy was the extreme difficulty of formulating comprehensive plans in a period when the depreciation of the currency rendered any economic foresight impossible and when the most solid economic activities of necessity assumed the character of daring speculations. But another point deserves stress in this connection.

The Social Democratic party, which acquired the overwhelming

[79] International Labor Office, *op. cit.*, pp. 390–397.
[80] Cf. Breitner's speech reported in *Arbeiter Zeitung*, September 19, 1923, p. 6.
[81] For details, cf. below, pp. 449–453; for the text of the tax law, cf., *LGBl. für Wien*, 1923, Nr. 30.

majority in the city council as soon as the democratic electoral system was introduced, was in its basic doctrines, of course, a Marxian party. Chapter XXVII (Vol. II), on the theoretical conceptions of the Austrian labor movement, will show that the special brand of theory it developed—the so-called Austro-Marxism—was essentially a continuation of revisionist ideas. Revisionism always preached the active participation of Socialists in municipal work. It would seem then that Social Democracy in Austria under the leadership of Viktor Adler would not have held to the abstinence or boycott policy toward municipal policy and municipal ownership favored by orthodox Marxism. But it may be said that, on the whole, the development of Austrian Social Democracy toward a revisionist attitude was effected step by step and, significantly, it was usually a practical problem which brought about the abandonment of some orthodox dogma. Unfortunately, the reactionary electoral system in the municipalities of prewar Austria prevented the Socialists from obtaining an adequate representation in city councils; consequently, they tended to confine their activities in them primarily to criticism.

As is probably taken for granted, there were foreshadowings of the later policy. For example, a conference of representatives of workers' sickness funds in 1904 laid down nine principles for combatting "housing misery." Item 6 was: "Construction of apartment houses with small, cheap dwellings on city ground under the municipal administration's own management."[82] And at the city council meeting of October 17, 1911, when the 250 emergency dwellings were provided for, a Socialist member moved the expenditure of 10 million crowns for housing.[83] But these were only foreshadowings. In matters of municipal policy, and particularly housing policy, Austrian Social Democracy in 1919 had largely preserved the theoretical views of earlier Marxism.

These views found their classical expression in the articles Friedrich Engels had published on the housing question a half century earlier. In them he had endeavored to show that "housing misery" was only a secondary evil of capitalist society; that the bad housing conditions of workers were only the expression of the fact that they were an oppressed and exploited class. The central problem was the fact of the appropriation of surplus value. Only the abolition of

[82] Brod, *op. cit.*, Pt. I, p. 5.
[83] *Neue Freie Presse*, October 18, 1911 (A.M.), p. 12.

capitalist society would, according to Engels, put an end to the deplorable housing conditions, chiefly by changing the location of industries and thus disintegrating the big cities and by overcoming the rift between town and country. To be sure, Engels distinguished this general phenomenon of "housing misery" from a special acute housing shortage. He believed that it might be possible to adjust the supply to the demand in a way more consonant with the interests of the masses of tenants. But he did not leave any doubt about his conviction that such improvements could be but imperfect and temporary.[84]

Further evidence that Engels' views on the subject still exerted great influence on the minds of the Austrian Socialists at the time the revolution put before them new practical problems which called for quick solution appears in the fact that then and for some years to come the phrase "Only Socialism will dispose of housing misery" was commonly employed. On the other hand, although Brod's pamphlet, published under the auspices of the party in 1919, included the statement that Engels' observations still applied, "word for word," it also recommended direct municipal building activities. "Only when the city administrations themselves build apartment houses and let them to the renters can private land speculation and housing usury be checked." It is beyond dispute that Brod favored this program within an economy that remained capitalistic, for he wrote in high praise of results achieved under it in England and Germany. "The system has stood the test brilliantly and deserves to be copied in all cities."[85] This is not to say flatly that Brod was inconsistent. On the contrary, his observations provide an excellent example of that continuous process by which revisionists attempted to adjust orthodox Marxist dogma to the practical needs of a Socialist workers' movement. Engels' words were still law, but his distinction between permanent "housing misery" and a special acute shortage could be extended into a distinction between remedies.

Finally, it is important to note the attitude of Otto Bauer. His program of socialization, drawn up early in 1919, placed upon the towns and cities the responsibility for solving the housing problem.

---

[84] Engels' articles were published in *Volksstaat* in 1872, then issued as a separate pamphlet. Friedrich Engels, *Zur Wohnungsfrage* (Hottingen-Zurich, 1887), esp. pp. 11, 51, 53.

[85] *Op. cit.*, Pt. I, pp. 4, 8.

To this end it was necessary "only" that the federal state give them the legal means; namely, the right to expropriate building land and rent houses within their limits. The owners "must naturally be compensated by the communities." This would be done by bonds carrying a fixed rate of interest. But there was no expectation that all communities would immediately proceed to socialize all building ground and rent houses. Once they had the legal power they might acquire the land, the buildings, both, or, by implication, neither; decision would be made in the light of what seemed most advantageous. Bauer gave considerable space to a "right to a dwelling" which everyone would be able to maintain, if necessary by a suit in the courts. He also wrote of democratization of the house administration, of establishment of tenants' committees, and of fixing the rents in small apartments so as to cover only the cost of maintenance and administration. Certain of these suggestions were carried out in later years. But most interesting in the present connection are Bauer's evaluations of the conditions under which it would be advantageous to a community to expropriate land or houses and his conclusions on the implications of a "right to a dwelling." If it seemed probable that the population in a given place would decrease, no advantage was likely to accrue from land acquisition. If, however, the "right to a dwelling" were recognized every community would be compelled to take care that building activity was adjusted to the demand for housing. This would also force a growing community to exercise its right to expropriate land and either build itself or confer the building lease on an individual or on a coöperative building association. Interestingly enough, because of later developments, Bauer offered no suggestions on the method by which house construction would be financed by a municipality.[86]

In the foreword to a later printing of his pamphlet, in which the text unfortunately remained unaltered, Bauer stated frankly that it had been "thrown together in haste" under the pressure of many other duties.[87] This may explain his lack of precision on some points; nevertheless, it seems clear that socialization of the existing stock of dwellings was foremost in his mind in 1919 and that he was still under the influence of Engels. The housing problem was to be solved in the general process of socialization. The very fact, how-

[86] Otto Bauer, *Der Weg zum Sozialismus* (Wien, 1919), pp. 22–24.
[87] *Ibid.* (Wien, 1921), p. 2.

ever, that in a program of socialization he could leave it open to the communities to expropriate land or buildings as circumstances dictated probably indicates that he was on the way to the advocacy of direct municipal house construction within a capitalistic society. By the fall of 1921 another party leader, Danneberg, was writing that the city must build on a large scale and that a special house-construction tax must be introduced to finance the project.[88]

It may seem that the foregoing section has placed too much emphasis on theoretical considerations, but theories always played a large role in the Austrian Social Democratic party. The orthodox Marxian or Engelsian attitude formed a handicap which had to be overcome before the party could put its full weight into the constructive housing schemes of the city council of Vienna.[89]

THE REFORM OF 1922

Before proceeding to a description of the city council's large-scale building schemes some attention must be paid to the reform of tenants protection. This reform, carried out a short time after the stabilization of the crown, reshaped the machinery of tenants protection in a way that eliminated the essential shortcomings which had become apparent during the inflation, transformed the emergency measure of wartime into a more lasting system, and made it a basis capable of supporting the far-reaching plans subsequently evolved by the council.

As previously noted, the wild slide of inflation in 1921–1922 finally brought the Austrian crown to 1/14,400 of its prewar value. The effects of this monetary catastrophe profoundly changed the meaning of the stipulations of the imperial decrees concerning tenants protection. In 1917 and 1918 it had been the purpose of the government to prevent landlords from making war profits at the expense of tenants and to protect the latter against arbitrary notice the former might have given in order to realize such profits. The depreciation, however, created a new and unforeseen situation.

---

[88] *Kampf gegen die Wohnungsnot!*, pp. 10, 12.

[89] It is significant that as late as the middle of 1921 the *Arbeiter Zeitung* (June 2, 1921, p. 2) gave conspicuous space to an article by Friedrich Hertz, "Wohnungsfrage und Sozialismus," in which the author argued that it was inevitable that in the years to come the "living space" enjoyed by workers would be narrowed. It was not customary with the labor daily to put its columns at the disposal of opinions not shared by the editorial board.

First, it completely eliminated the net income of the landlord by reducing the rent proper to an infinitesimal sum. This development produced more cheers than tears because of the long-standing antagonism of most tenants toward individual landlords and toward landlords as a group. Although interest rates had not sufficiently compensated capitalists in general for the loss in the value of money through depreciation, landlords remained in a more favorable position than did the owners of some other kinds of property. Just because of the interest situation, however, it may be doubted that the disappearance of landlords' income exercised any generally unfavorable economic effects. On the other hand, there can be no doubt that the problem of the maintenance of the existing stock of dwellings was becoming ever more urgent.

It will be recalled that the landlord was empowered under the regulations concerning tenants protection to raise the rents to the extent of actual increases in his expenses for maintenance, administration, taxes, and interest on mortgages. In the beginning the following procedure was adopted: the landlord demanded the increase and if the tenant refused to pay it the landlord was entitled to give notice; thereupon, the parties applied to the rent office and if the latter found the increase in order the tenant had to leave the apartment. The fear that in this way many tenants would become homeless in a period of growing social unrest induced the imperial government to change the procedure by the second decree—published, significantly enough, at the time the big strike of January, 1918, threatened to cause the immediate collapse of the state. Under the new stipulations the tenant obtained the right to consent to an increase of rent *after* the decision of the rent office, and thus retain the dwelling. If there had been no rapid depreciation of the currency this provision could have been justified on the ground that it provided additional protection to the economically weaker party. As it was, an untenable situation was created. In the majority of cases the tenants naturally were anxious to tolerate no increases in rents without previous approval by the rent office. In so doing they obeyed their momentary interests—and who, in the years of inflation, gave thought to long-run considerations? Moreover, in proceeding in this way, the tenants were gladly seizing the opportunity to take revenge on the landlords for past grievances. The result was that the number of controversies coming to the rent offices increased so rapidly that it proved impossible to deal with them without very considerable delays. In 1921 between 230 and 250 thousand cases were submitted.[90] These figures fell little short of 50 per cent of all apartments in Vienna. When, after weeks and months of delay, the office reached its decision the originally proposed rent increases for the whole house frequently represented the value of a loaf of bread. The tenant lived practically gratis so far as shelter was concerned, but the maintenance of the house was gravely jeopardized.

On February 10, 1922, the Schober government submitted to parliament a bill providing that the rents of 1914 should be raised fourfold and that the executive committee (*Hauptausschuss*) of parliament should be empowered to adjust rents to rising prices not oftener than twice a year. The right to give notice was to be expanded in some respects. The most important feature of the bill, which had no time limit, was that it did not endeavor to restore the net income of the house owner.[91]

The Social Democrats offered their own bill which proposed the introduction of tenants committees in each house, apparently in some analogy to the works councils. If these committees should agree to rent increases to cover maintenance and administrative costs and secure the approval of the "tenants assembly," such increases would go into effect without reference to the rent office. The bill further proposed the creation of a special building maintenance commission, composed of technical experts, tenants, and house-owners, which was to decide on the necessity of major repairs. If the owner refused to follow its decisions, compulsory administration of the property was recommended. Finally, the right of the landlord to give notice so that he might use the dwelling himself was to be additionally restricted.[92] Although the tenants committees may be viewed as an unrealistic approach to the problem of securing increases in rents necessary to maintain the houses, it is more probable that they were in considerable part a device intended to bring the workers around to acceptance of such increases. The economic development in 1922, particularly the continuing depreciation of the

[90] Nationalrat, *Protokoll*, February 10, 1922, p. 3073.
[91] *Ibid.*, 1922, *Beilagen*, Nr. 723, p. 22.
[92] *Ibid.*, Nr. 742.

currency, helped to remove hesitancies which the party might still have felt in supporting a reform which was decidedly unpopular with the masses of townfolk. After long negotiations in a committee of the Nationalrat a compromise was reached and the bill was finally passed on December 7, 1922.[93]

The rent under the new law was not one fixed sum, as in prewar times, but was made up of four components. The only one of these which was constant, the so-called basic rent, was fixed formally at 50 per cent of the prewar rent. But because of the depreciation and because of the formula that "crown is crown," this meant in strict accuracy only 1/28,800 of that rent. From the viewpoint of the landlord, Türr is certainly correct in calling it a "farce."[94] However, by this stipulation the landlord was put in about the same position as the owner of state bonds. This meant that for the time being the net income of the houseowner remained eliminated, but that his claim to it was recognized as a matter of principle. The Christian Socials had insisted on inserting this point into the law.

The second component of the rent was the maintenance rent, set at 150 times the amount of rent in 1914. Special conciliation offices were to be instituted by the municipalities in order to help the parties concerned in coming to an agreement on further increases of maintenance costs; for the cases in which these offices proved unsuccessful special bipartisan rent commissions were to decide whether and to what extent it was necessary to raise the maintenance rent. The law established certain auditing or checking rights of the tenants so that they could satisfy themselves that the amounts granted for maintenance were properly used by the landlords. The tenants could also compel the landlords, through the rent commissions, to carry out necessary maintenance work. Apart from these individual increases the possibility of a general increase of the maintenance rent was provided. For these purposes the political parties agreed on a curiously decentralized system which in subsequent years gave rise to major difficulties. State rent commissions were to be instituted in each state; representatives of the chambers of commerce, chambers of labor, tenants' organizations, and landlords' associations were to sit on them under the chairmanship of a

[93] *BGBl.*, 1922, Nr. 872.

[94] *Op. cit.*, p. 96. Paper crowns had been stabilized at the rate of 14,400 to one gold crown and the schilling equaled 10,000 paper crowns.

professional judge. To the degree that increases in the cost of building materials and in wages of building-trades workers took place after November 1, 1922, the commissions were entitled to change the original provision of the law and to raise the maintenance rent in the respective states.

The third component came from the individual tenant's proportional share in the administrative and operating costs of the house such as water and sewage charges, chimney-sweeping costs, garbage fees, and wages of the caretaker. Fourth, the proportional share in taxes imposed on the house was to be added to the rent.[95] The regulations concerning the landlord's right to give notice were reformed on the basis of experience and, if anything, rendered more severe.[96]

The new scheme, effective February 1, 1923, involved an appreciable increase in the tenant's expenditure. In this month the housing-cost index rose to 346 as against 166 in the preceding month (1914 = 1). This was certainly still negligible in comparison with the general living-cost index, which reached 9,601 in February, 1923 (1914 = 1);[97] but in the economic conditions prevailing then, when the stabilization of the currency severely curtailed the export possibilities of industry, every increase in expenditure was sharply felt so that the transition from almost no rent to the payments established by the law was rather sudden. The Social Democrats, who voted for the law, together with the Christian Socials and Pan-Germans,[98] tried hard to explain to the workers the absolute neces-

[95] If a worker's small dwelling with a prewar annual rent of 360 crowns is used as an example, then the amount of aggregate annual rent paid by the tenant under the 1922 law, and under the (actually unrealistic) assumption that no increases in maintenance rent were effected subsequently, was:

	Schillings
Landlords' rent proper	0.18
Maintenance rent	5.40
Running costs and taxes, about	15.00
Total	20.58

At the rate of exchange existing after the stabilization this means about 3 United States dollars annual rent. Cf. International Labor Office, *op. cit.*, p. 366, where a similar computation is given for a dwelling with 1,000 crowns prewar rent. The amount of 10 schillings given there for the third item of the computation seems to be very much on the low side so that it was increased here even for the smaller apartment with 360 crowns prewar rent. To the amount of 20.58 schillings computed above about 20 per cent "cleaning money" paid to the house janitor should be added. It is, moreover, necessary to keep in mind that the maintenance rent was raised rather rapidly after 1922; in the less substantially built workers' houses the increases were greater than in the better districts of the city.

[96] Cf. Sternberg, *op. cit.*, p. 21.

[97] *SHfRO.*, vol. 4, p. 90.

[98] Only the Agrarian party refused to vote for the law, a fact of major political importance in the struggle against tenants protection. (See pp. 460 ff.)

sity of providing for the maintenance of the houses;[99] and to make them understand, as had been clearly stated by the report of the parliamentary committee,[100] that "the maintenance of the houses is not so much an interest of the landlords but an interest of the people (tenants)."

To summarize, the law was a significant reform designed to eliminate the most important shortcomings of the situation prior to its passage. The net income of the landlord beyond his actual expenditure on the house remained "confiscated," to use Türr's expression.[101] Adopted in a moment when the stabilization of the currency seemed to warrant restoration of normal conditions, the law possibly may reveal the intention of the legislators to make tenants protection a permanent feature of economic and social life in Austria: as previously noted it had no time limit. In this it differed from another passed on the same day by which the decrees concerning requisitioning of dwellings were put on a statutory basis.[102]

The second law just mentioned had become necessary because the decree by which Hanusch had transferred his powers to the state governments was about to be ruled unconstitutional by the Constitutional Court. As was to have been expected, the landlords had waged a bitter struggle against the requisitioning decrees; finally they had succeeded in discovering a weak spot in the machinery. The nullification decision of the Constitutional Court on December 11, 1922, also rendered illegal the decrees issued, on the basis of Hanusch's ordinance,[103] in the individual states, including Vienna. The second law of December 7 involved certain relaxations of the severe requisitioning system which had been adopted in Vienna, but still preserved this necessary supplement of tenants protection in its main features. However, it was to expire at the end of 1925.

The introduction of tenants protection in Austria during the war was in itself nothing exceptional. Measures to restrict the right of

[99] E.g., Robert Danneberg, "Der neue Mieterschutz," *Arbeit und Wirtschaft*, vol. 1 (Jan. 15, 1923), 63: "Tenants protection does not mean gratis housing." Cf. *idem, Was wird aus dem Mieterschutz?* p. 12.

[100] Nationalrat, *Protokoll*, 1922, *Beilagen*, Nr. 1308, p. 1.

[101] *Op. cit.*, p. 96.

[102] *BGBl.*, 1922, Nr. 873.

[103] Cf. *Neue Freie Presse*, December 11, 1922 (P.M.), p. 5; December 12 (A.M.), p. 8. There is some reason to believe that the Constitutional Court delayed its decision in this question until the housing reforms were passed by the parliament so that undesirable developments on the market in the interval could be prevented.

the landlords to raise rents and to terminate leases proved unavoidable in almost every European country. Some discrepancy in the movement of the rent index and of the general cost-of-living index could be observed years after the war in all those countries. But among them the national units shattered by inflation occupied a special position and, in the latter category, Austria stood out as the land with the most incisive and thoroughgoing system of tenants protection. "There is no other country in which the right of the landlords to give notice is so restricted as in Austria," wrote Danneberg after the adoption of the reform act.[104] As years went by and one country after another relaxed its legislation and restored the free market in this sphere, Austrian tenants protection became "the most radical legislation" of this kind.[105] In no other country was there so strong a tendency for tenants protection—an emergency measure—to develop into an instrument of social welfare of first importance. In no other country was there so serious an attempt to make tenants protection a basis for a far-reaching housing policy—a policy which was expected by its authors to change completely the housing system of a metropolis of 2 millions. Tenants protection pushed down the prices of land in Vienna; in some extreme cases they were as low as 4.2 per cent of the prewar level.[106] This enabled the city to acquire sufficient and appropriate plots. Though tenants were not relieved to the full extent of the landlords' loss of income, their huge savings did provide a source which could be tapped to some extent for the funds needed by the city for its building policy. Tenants protection rendered this policy possible; but the converse relation was also true, and only the building policy of the city could render tenants protection possible as a long-term institution. The causes and effects of this interrelation will now be examined more closely.

Building Activities of Vienna, 1923–1933

The Problem of Housing Shortage and the Aims of the City Council's Policy

As explained, the Social Democratic leaders gradually realized that a comprehensive program of construction executed by the city council was necessary to alleviate, or even to prevent the accentua-

[104] *Der neue Mieterschutz,* p. 62.

[105] Danneberg, *Das Neue Wien* (Wien, 1930), p. 53.

[106] J. Jellinek, "Baukostenindex," *Der österreichische Volkswirt,* vol. 20 (Nov. 26, 1927), 238.

tion of, the housing shortage in Vienna. It is advisable here to comment briefly on the much-used and misused concept of housing shortage. There are, in fact, no less than three different, though interrelated, conceptions of this term. Strictly speaking, from the point of view of the theory of a free economy, the problem of shortage itself is not present. This theory recognizes the fundamental scarcity of all economic goods, including human dwellings, but a shortage in the sense of demand exceeding supply in the long run appears from this standpoint impossible: temporary shortage would be adjusted by price movements with the subsequent reduction of demand and increase of supply. If the free market is restricted and prices (rents) fixed lower than they would be on the free market, then a shortage in the economic sense would certainly appear eventually. In this case the simple advice has been given: remove all restrictions from the housing market; whereupon, all housing shortage will disappear, equilibrium will be restored to the market, and peace to the mind of the orthodox theorist.[107] Against this concept it is hardly necessary to reiterate the history of housing conditions in prewar Vienna where, for a number of reasons, *but without any interference with the free market,* there was "an acute housing shortage."[108] And this condition had persisted over a period which would seem to qualify as a "long run." Even people willing to pay the market price found it extremely difficult to obtain a dwelling.

For the men shaping the policy of the Vienna city council, a return to the free market meant return to prewar housing conditions, and this made them very skeptical of the liberal economists' proposals. Nevertheless, these men could not ignore the fact that those theorists were right in maintaining that the low level of rents prevailing under tenants protection tremendously increased the extent of the demand for dwellings and thus was responsible for what was called the artificial housing shortage in Vienna. However, their evaluations of this phenomenon differed widely from those of the liberal economists. The reason was that their conception of housing shortage

---

[107] Cf. Friedrich Hayek, "Wirkungen der Mietzinsbeschränkungen," Verhandlungen des Vereines für Sozialpolitik in Königsberg, 1930, *SVfS.*, vol. 182 (1931), 268; and W. T. Layton and Charles Rist, *The Economic Situation of Austria* (Geneva, 1925), p. 42.

[108] *Der österreichische Volkswirt,* vol. 15 (Oct. 28, 1922), 100; Emil Pfersche, "Das Mietrecht in Oesterreich," *SVfS.*, vol. 95 (1901), 333: "Creation of new apartments in large numbers for the poorer classes can undoubtedly be accomplished only by public institutions, since private capital has proved unable to solve this task."

was based on an essentially different principle. It may be called a "physical" notion of shortage, or one conceived in terms of what the Germans style *Sozialpolitik*. Years before, Philippovich had worked for certain minimum measures of dwelling accommodations elaborated by hygienists and regarded by them as necessary to ensure a healthy life and a normal rate of mortality for the inhabitants. This "objective" conception is altered in the course of historical development, with general changes in knowledge, in ideas, and in the material resources of society. It is also altered by the aims and requirements of policies. In order to raise the educational level of the masses, as the Vienna city council hoped to do, the dwellings of the poorer classes must give the children living in them the opportunity for quiet and concentrated homework, and must also give the adults the opportunity for self-educational reading in the hours of *"dopo lavoro."* And, finally, this concept has an important economic aspect. Removal of housing shortage in this sense implies increased productivity from healthier and happier laborers. Economic theory runs in terms of interest accruing to the individual capitalist upon individual dispositions. The gains secured by investments in human capital are not tangible from the usual theoretical point of view. But this does not impair the reality of those gains. Here the housing problem is but a part of the general problem of social legislation. The acuteness of this problem was hardly anywhere else so important as in Austria where the skill of the industrial workers and of the fine handicraftsmen represented one of the foremost assets left to the "residual" country and where the value of this asset had suffered so severely in the years of privations and misery.[109]

Closely connected with the above concept is the use of the term "housing shortage" in the "subjective" sense. The chieftain of an African tribe may live in conditions viewed as utmost misery by the European observer but regarded as palatial luxury by the owner. There is little doubt that the revolution which increased so tremendously the power consciousness of the Austrian workers contributed a good deal toward changing their ideas of housing standards, toward making them realize more completely the degrading housing con-

[109] This general train of ideas closely approaches the theory formulated by Rudolf Goldscheid and styled by him "human economy" in contradistinction to "commodity economy"; cf. Goldscheid, "Steuerverwendung und Interessenpolitik," *SVfS.*, vol. 174, pt. 1 (1929), 45.

ditions of prewar times, and thus toward producing considerable shifts in their demand schedules. The low rents of the tenants protection system naturally furthered this development.

Since tenants protection rendered it less necessary for the workers to take bed tenants, their number fell rapidly. In 1910, 22 per cent of the single-room dwellings were sublet to bed tenants; in 1919, only 6.93 per cent.[110] The subtenants became confined chiefly to middle-class apartments where their absolute number increased markedly. The general density of population in Vienna dwellings decreased from 4.23 in 1910 to 3.49 in 1923.[111] "To a large extent the workers' dwellings today [1922] differ from prewar times. They do not enjoy dwelling luxury, but families of 5 to 8 persons sleeping in one single room as well as bed tenants have become rarer. This is one of the very few advantages war and postwar have brought us."[112] The Social Democrats in the city council completely shared this opinion of the *Volkswirt.* They viewed with gratification the fact that what Lassalle once called the "damnable lack of wants"[113] (*verdammte Bedürfnislosigkeit*) of the workers was vanishing more and more. They regarded it as their duty to provide a housing standard which, beyond the improvements already reached, would approach more closely the new demands of the masses. They realized, moreover, that the favorable effects of tenants protection were confined primarily to those who were accidental possessors of dwellings at the time of the introduction of the system. The creation of new apartments was a problem of life and happiness for new generations in years to come. They knew, finally, that in spite of the undoubted betterment there were still more than enough cases of bitter housing misery in Vienna.[114]

To remove the housing shortage by restoring a free market and increasing the density of occupancy in the dwellings, as suggested

---

[110] *International Labor Office, op. cit.*, pp. 380–381. These percentages are not comparable with those on p. 412 above, partly because of the difference between "small" and "single-room" dwellings, but are satisfactory to show the trend.

[111] Bunzel, *loc. cit.*, p. 107.

[112] *Der österreichische Volkswirt,* vol. 15 (Oct. 28, 1922), 101.

[113] F. Lassalle, *Arbeiterlesebuch, Reden und Schriften,* vol. 2 (Berlin, 1893), pp. 543–544.

[114] During the years of inflation and long thereafter anyone who arrived in the capital city by one of the main railroad lines could see, as the train approached the station, rows of coaches bordering the tracks that were used as dwellings by those unable to find more suitable accommodations.

by liberal economists, would not have eliminated housing shortage as conceived by the city council of Vienna, but would have increased and aggravated it. Private construction was ruled out by high cost of building and exorbitant interest rates. The federal government could and would not lend any serious help to promotion of building schemes. If building was to be resumed in the capital it could be done solely by the municipality.

THE CITY HOUSES

On September 21, 1923, the Vienna city council passed a resolution authorizing the construction of 25,000 apartments during 1924–1928 at an average rate of 5,000 apartments a year.[115] Since general parliamentary elections were scheduled to take place a few weeks later, the political opponents of the Social Democrats received the announcement with skeptical scorn and suggested freely that the building program was nothing but a campaign promise liable to be forgotten on the day after the elections.[116] But the promise was more than kept. By the end of 1927, that is, after only four years instead of five, the announced program of 25,000 had been completed except for 348 dwellings. In 1927—again before the general elections—the city council raised its 1923 program to 30,000 dwellings and resolved to construct a further 30,000 apartments in the years 1929–1933. The table on page 450 shows the development of the municipality's building activities.

Because of a great deal of misrepresentation of the accommodations, almost entirely unfavorable, it is important to explain in some detail what kinds of dwellings were constructed. The large majority of them were in big tenement houses, usually much bigger than the

[115] *Arbeiter Zeitung*, September 22, 1923, p. 6.

[116] Subsequent to the decision of the city senate on the building program (which preceded the above-mentioned resolution) Mataja, a Christian Social member of parliament, commented in a public address: "The Social Democratic city administration is coming out with a program to build 25,000 small dwellings. If the city is really going to build, I certainly shall approve it. But I merely object to their coming out in an electoral campaign and saying: Now I am going to build 5,000 small dwellings every year. I should suggest that the Social Democratic party save this excellent 'electoral kit' of 25,000 apartments until the dwellings have really been built. Then they may present themselves to the voters. . . ." *Reichspost*, September 14, 1923, p. 5. A resident of Vienna at this time, subsequently a member of the faculty at the University of California, remembers a Christian Social cartoon placarded all over Vienna; it pictured an astounded Viennese standing in the Prater under the trees, every bough of which was adorned with little wooden birdhouses, and saying: "And we thought they meant building houses for *us!*" On another placard a man was depicted looking at the sky through a huge telescope and searching in vain for the dwellings of the city council.

so-called mass apartment house in Vienna. On the other hand, no more than 50 per cent of the lot was built upon except in very rare cases; usually less than 50 per cent was used. This gave space for huge courtyards with gardens and playgrounds for children. An open-air bathing basin for them was a common feature. In the first period of regular city building, 1923–1927, the dwellings were in

MUNICIPAL BUILDING ACTIVITIES IN VIENNA, 1920–1933*

Year	Total number of dwellings	Suburban cottages
1920–1923	2,950	1,422
1924	2,478	975
1925	6,387	380
1926	9,034	486
1927	6,753	89
1928	4,584	458
1929	5,003	239
1930	6,575	601
1931	6,180	283
1932	5,098	277
1933	3,625	47
Total	58,667	5,257

* The figures have been taken, for the period 1920–1932, from *Statistisches Taschenbuch . . . Wien*, 1932 (Wien, 1933), p. 22; for 1933, from C. O. Hardy, *op. cit.*, p. 57. Dr. Hardy obtained the 1933 figures directly from the statistical office of the city of Vienna. For 1920–1932, Hardy used the source first cited in this note; however, the total figures for suburban cottages in the table above differ from his. He was obviously misled by an error in addition in this column of the *Taschenbuch*. Furthermore, owing to a typographical error, his total figure of dwellings for 1927 is 6,763 and not 6,753 as in the *Taschenbuch*. Dr. Hardy complains of some discrepancies in the official statistics which I also found troublesome; see, for examples, the lower figures given for the years up to 1931 inclusive by the *Wirtschaftsstatistisches Jahrbuch*, *1924*, p. 46; *1925*, p. 77; *1926*, pp. 417–420; *1927*, p. 450; *1928*, p. 434; *1929/30*, p. 504; *1930/31*, p. 448; *1931/32*, p. 404. For the purposes of the present exposition the exact number of dwellings erected in each year is of less importance.

the main of two types: a smaller one of 38 square meters and a larger one of 48 square meters space. From 1927 on four types were constructed. Each type had a small entrance hall and a toilet; the three largest had a kitchen. Otherwise they may be described as follows. First, apartments of 21 square meters for single tenants consisting primarily of one room. Instead of a kitchen they had a gas plate in the hall. Second, apartments of 40 square meters with a living room and one bedroom. Third, apartments of 49 square meters with a living room and two bedrooms. Fourth, apartments of 57 square meters with two large rooms and one small room. With very few exceptions all of these dwellings were sunny. A water faucet and a gas cooking stove (or plate) were in every dwelling. No more than four apartments were placed on one landing. All windows opened either on the streets or on the wide courtyards. Living and bedroom floors were hardwood except in a few early houses; toilet and kitchen floors were waterproofed. Many apartments had balconies of considerable size. Gas or electric connections were installed from the beginning; both were characteristic of the later apartments. Each dwelling was allotted a definite cellar or garret space that could be locked.[117] The larger houses harbored various additional facilities for the residents, as may be illustrated by the example of the huge Karl Marx Hof. With its 1,400 apartments and 5,000 inhabitants this complex occupied a tremendous area of which only 18.4 per cent was built upon,[118] had a length of more than a kilometer, and represented a little town in itself. Apart from the housing accommodations the building contained: two laundries with the finest and most modern equipment, two kindergartens, a youth center, a library, a school dental clinic, a health insurance office with medical facilities, a pharmacy, a post office, 25 shops of various sorts, and two bathing establishments with 20 tubs and 30 showers in each.[119]

In addition, the city council ventured some interesting experiments; for instance, the erection of a large building with small apartments and a common kitchen intended for working couples.

In appraising these dwellings it must be remembered that they should not be compared, for instance, with the modern dwellings of the better paid groups of wage earners in England or in this country. A fair comparison would be with the prevailing type of prewar building in Vienna; that is, with the vast majority of workers' dwellings in postwar Vienna. This was one major reason for the lengthy description of prewar housing. Such a comparison reveals the tremendous progress achieved by the city council. The half-dark kitchen, in which the worker's wife had to spend a large part of her life, disappeared. Light and sun entered all parts of the new dwellings. Windows no longer opened on gangways or on those narrow

[117] Cf. Bunzel, *loc. cit.*, pp. 129–132; *Das Neue Wien,* vol. 1, pp. 191–303; Rosenblum, *op. cit.*, pp. 127–131; Danneberg, *Das Neue Wien*, pp. 64–65; *Die Wohnungspolitik der Gemeinde Wien* (Wien, 1929), p. 54.

[118] *Statistisches Taschenbuch . . . Wien*, 1932, p. 22, note: total area 156,000 square meters; occupied by buildings, 28,700 square meters.

[119] *Blätter für das Wohlfahrtswesen der Gemeinde Wien*, vol. 30, (May–June, 1931), 142–148.

stone wells called "light yards" in Vienna for which the name "darkness yards" would have been more appropriate. A source of disease and inconvenience, the common toilet, was eliminated, as was the source of infinite squabbles, the common water faucet in the gangway. By building more staircases and eliminating the gangways a typical undesirable characteristic of the poor peoples' houses was removed. The hardwood floors greatly facilitated cleaning work. Thanks to the large courtyards, the streets, with their various physical and moral dangers, ceased being the playgrounds for the children.

There is little doubt, however, that the dwellings were too small, especially in the period 1923–1927 when the small type of 38 square meters formed about 75 per cent of the total being built. This situation improved appreciably after 1927. Moreover, special apartments of about double the common size were erected for professional men, particularly physicians. But, on the whole, even in later years, the city did not consider it possible to build commodious dwellings, or even to approach the 60 square meters which were considered by many as the proper size for an average worker's apartment. Financial limitations and the wish to increase the number of habitations as quickly as possible determined the policy of the city council in this respect. The same considerations forced it to abstain from building a bathroom in each apartment and to confine itself to the construction of common bathing facilities in the larger houses and of bathing establishments in various quarters of the city. The best known of the latter was the modernly, not to say extravagantly, equipped Amalienbad in the densely populated Favoriten district of Vienna. These deficiencies were all regrettable; and there is certainly justification for saying that from the point of view of an ideal social policy the dwellings did not present an adequate solution of the mass housing problem; but in the Austrian economic environment they should be regarded as the maximum of what could be achieved.

A special movement, largely supported by the propaganda machinery of the Social Democratic party and of the coöperatives, endeavored successfully to introduce into workers' dwellings modern types of furniture which were at once space and work saving. For examples, the large double beds which frequently occupied more than half of the living space in a worker's apartment were gradually replaced by modern divans, the heavy outmoded buffets by lighter and more practical cupboards.[120]

As appears from the table on page 450 the number of dwellings built by the city council in small suburban cottage settlements formed about 9 per cent of the total number. In the beginning the municipality put the land at the disposal of coöperatives organized among public utility workers and advanced 85 per cent of the building costs, accepting mortgage securities. The remaining 15 per cent was usually covered by the physical work of the prospective tenants. Later, the city authorities wrote off these "debts in kind" as irredeemable and began to provide the entire building costs. A special company, *Gesiba,* was founded and charged by the city council with the task of building and administering the settlements. The *Gesiba* also built some settlements for people with larger incomes. A certain initial payment was required, the remainder due in installments running fifteen to twenty years. The average cottage house, or "one family house" as it was called in Vienna, had two floors with a total area of about 62 square meters. As extremely important advantages over the apartments it usually had individual bathing facilities and a small kitchen garden. After 1928 a smaller type of only 45 square meters was given preference so that the living area in the cottage and the "city house" became about equal.

The important problem of selection among the thousands of would-be tenants who besieged the Vienna housing office was met by introducing in 1922 a system of points based on the degree of urgency of need for better accommodations and other criteria. Thus, for example, Austrian citizenship was rated at 1 point; residence in Vienna since birth at 4; each child under fourteen at 1; each child over fourteen at 2; pregnancy past the six month of the wife of the applicant at 1; subtenancy, except with parents or parents-in-law, at 2; severe disability, such as blindness, at 5; unfit-

[120] It is interesting in this connection to mention the results of an investigation of the sleeping conditions of children undertaken by the municipal authorities of Vienna a few years after the Socialists had been forcibly ousted from the city hall. Concerning the general conditions of bedrooms the author of the report stated that in private houses, 79 per cent of the bedrooms were found in a neat state, 18 per cent were disorderly, and 3 per cent badly neglected. In city council houses, the respective figures were: 89 per cent, 10 per cent, and 1 per cent. Such were, in spite of the equality in social and economic position of the tenants, the effects of the city dwellings on the willingness of the occupants to take proper care of the apartment. Cf. F. Breunlich, *Kinder ohne Bett, so schlafen Grosstadtkinder* (Wien, 1936), p. 39.

ness of dwelling for occupancy at 5; and legally upheld, without fault of the tenant, notice from the landlord at 5. Applicants with at least 10 points were placed in the first category; from them was selected a special list of emergency cases to be provided with a dwelling as quickly as possible. Persons having 5 to 9 points were assigned to the second group. This point system was the foundation of the claim that objective criteria, easily verified by the officers of the housing department, were the basis of allocating the dwellings.[121]

Since, as has been frequently noted, almost every question in Austria tended to assume a political character, it was not surprising to find that critics condemned the Socialist claim as a swindle and declared that it was practically impossible for anyone but a "party comrade" to secure a dwelling. And since I, like other investigators, had neither the time nor the resources to make an extensive field survey that might have yielded a satisfactory answer, it is possible only to record agreement with one of my predecessors. "We doubt very much if the task of allocation has been performed in Vienna very differently from the way it would have been performed in an American city. Outside Utopia one cannot anticipate that the public administration of extensive properties occupied by voters can be kept free from partisanship." It is, moreover, extremely interesting to note that nearly a decade after this charge of "political" assignment of housing had become a standard weapon in the arsenal of the Catholic party precisely the same charge was brought against its administration of municipal houses in Innsbruck by the agricultural block in the diet of Tirol.[122] Probably needless to say the members of this group were not Socialists.

The rents per square meter were about the same in both the cottage and apartment types of city buildings. They varied, however, from about 11 groschen to 30 groschen per month and per square meter according to the quality of the dwellings, the location of the building, its remoteness from transportation lines, and the general equipment of the house. Since the quality of municipal houses was continuously improving the rents in the newer ones were usually higher than in the older. None of them, naturally, were under the restrictions of tenants protection and so the city was entitled to

[121] Weber, *loc. cit.*, pp. 230–239.

[122] Hardy, *op. cit.*, pp. 95–96. He cites the organ of the Association of House and Land Owners for October 4, 1931, on the Innsbruck situation.

charge, as far as the law was concerned, any rent it pleased. But the municipality decided to adjust its rents to the general level existing in old houses under the rules of tenants protection. This implied that the rents charged were supposed to cover only the maintenance cost and the running expenses connected with the house. The building cost was regarded as nonrecoverable cost and no attempt was made to include it in the rents. Computed in this way the rent for the most frequent type of city apartment amounted in 1929 to about 7 shillings a month, including the house-construction tax.[123] This rent of approximately 1 dollar a month was possible because the city council financed its building program from the proceeds of taxes. As already noted, the principal tax used for this purpose was the house-construction tax effective February 1, 1923. The tax was strongly progressive, as may be perceived from the fact that although there were in 1929 about 600,000 dwellings and business houses in Vienna subject to it, some 3,000 of them contributed 40 per cent of the proceeds.[124] The tables on page 456 give a picture of the magnitude of those proceeds, of the city expenditures on housing, of the relation of those expenditures to the aggregate investments of the city, and of the role of the housing tax therein.

The second table shows that the housing tax covered, at the peak of city building, only about 40 per cent of the expenditure. Thus the inscription, "Built from the Proceeds of the House-Construction Tax," which adorned every one of the city houses was not literally correct. Presumably, the inscription was intended to emphasize the fact that the financial cornerstone of the city houses was this progressive and generally popular tax. In fact, at least part of the remaining 60 per cent had to be provided by the proportional welfare tax, the most questionable among the municipal levies. The table reveals, furthermore, that, on the average, expenditure on housing formed about three-fourths of the total investments of the city. Finally, from both tables, it is seen that not until 1932, when the

[123] Cf. Bunzel, *loc. cit.*, p. 133. P. Vas, *Die Wiener Wohnungszwangswirtschaft von 1917–1927*, referred to by Bunzel, estimates the average annual rent at 94 schillings, or about 7.85 schillings per month.

[124] E. K. Winter, "Wiener Wohnbaupolitik," *Hochland*, vol. 28 (May, 1931), 125. Cf. the more detailed data for the same period from Bunzel, *loc. cit.*, p. 124: 86 per cent of the "tax objects" contributed 23.55 per cent of the tax; 13.5 per cent of the "tax objects" contributed 34.81 per cent of the tax; ½ per cent of the "tax objects" contributed 41.64 per cent of the tax.

growing depression severely restricted revenues, did the city decide to adjust construction expenditures to the proceeds of the housing tax, at the same time reforming the levy so as to increase its proceeds.

PROCEEDS OF THE HOUSE-CONSTRUCTION TAX*
(*in 1,000 schillings*)

Year	Amount	Year	Amount
1923	3,370	1929	36,403
1924	14,638	1930	36,258
1925	37,913	1931	36,385
1926	38,474	1932	43,530
1927	36,283	1933	50,844
1928	36,194		

* *Wirtschaftsstatistisches Jahrbuch, 1924*, p. 42; *1925*, p. 67; *1927*, p. 437; *1928*, p. 427; *1929/30*, p. 489; *1930/31*, p. 443; *1932/33*, p. 385; *1933/35*, p. 458.

INVESTMENTS OF THE CITY OF VIENNA, 1926–1933*

Year	Total investments in 1,000 schillings	Investments in housing		Percentage of total expenditure on housing represented by house-construction tax
		In 1,000 schillings	As percentage of total investment	
1926	144,340	116,764	80.9	32.9
1927	124,386	92,528	74.4	39.2
1928	115,877	88,957	76.8	40.7
1929	120,970	88,225	72.9	41.3
1930	123,583	93,143	75.4	38.9
1931	100,177	80,707	80.6	45.1
1932	47,256	43,319	91.7	100.5
1933	35,248	24,087	68.3	211.1

* *Wirtschaftsstatistisches Jahrbuch, 1927*, p. 436; *1928*, p. 426; *1929/30*, p. 488; *1932/33*, p. 387; *1933/35*, p. 459.

The policy just described rendered it possible to keep rents on a very low level and to avoid the results of the housing policy in Germany, where the rents were so high that a large part of the small apartments remained vacant.[125]

In this connection must also be mentioned the virtual builder's monopoly enjoyed by the city for several years. As brought out above, the city, even before the adoption of the house-construction tax, had been acquiring in part or in whole various concerns con-

[125] Cf. the speech of "bank director Astor of Berlin" in "Verhandlungen des Vereines für Sozialpolitik in Königsberg 1930," *SVfS.*, vol. 182 (1931), 304, also, Winter, *loc. cit.*, p. 120.

nected with the building-materials industry. The vigorous prosecution of this policy enabled it to build as cheaply as possible and to check the offers it received from other concerns by comparisons with the costs in its own partially and completely owned firms. As a consequence of its general position it was able to prevent the creation of price cartels in building materials and to break up some existing ones.[126]

The city continued to purchase land so that the 4,690 hectares inherited from the old administration were increased by the end of 1928 to 7,910 and by the end of 1929 to 8,206. This last figure was about 30 per cent of the total area of the city.[127] Most of the purchases were being quietly carried out by various agencies in order to keep land prices on a low level. The activities of the city council in this field were severely hampered by the lack of an appropriate land expropriation law. The existing statute of February 4, 1919, made the expropriation dependent upon so many conditions that it proved useless in the majority of cases.[128]

By the end of 1933 the city of Vienna administered altogether 66,270 dwellings and 3,697 business premises. Since the dwellings census of 1934 revealed 613,436 habitations in the capital, this means that roughly 11 per cent of its homes belonged to the city as a result of the postwar building policy.[129] Other results of this census are of greatest interest since they make apparent and specific certain improvements introduced by the housing policy of the workers' party administration in the mass dwellings of the city. Fortunately, for the purposes of comparison, there was in 1919 a thorough study of a sample of 20,000 dwellings covering all sizes in all districts. It included questions concerning the "equipment" of the dwellings; that is, the presence or absence of water faucet, gas and electric connections, bathroom, toilet, and so on, that had not been asked in 1917 but were in 1934. Thus it is possible to contrast the situation in the year the Socialists acquired a majority in the city hall with that shown by a census taken six weeks after they were thrown out.

[126] Cf. *Statistisches Jahrbuch der Stadt Wien*, 1929 (2. Jahrg.), pp. 304–305; B. Kautsky, "Kapitalbildung der öffentlichen Hand nach dem Kriege in Deutschland und Oesterreich," *SVfS.*, vol. 174, pt. 4 (1929), 241–242.

[127] Bunzel, *loc. cit.*, p. 127 f.; *Statistisches Taschenbuch . . . Wien*, 1928, p. 3; 1929, p. 3.

[128] Cf. E. Hein, "Die Bodenpolitik der Gemeinde Wien," International Housing and Town Planning Congress, *Papers*, I (Wien, 1926), p. 5, and Hardy, *op. cit.*, p. 79.

[129] *Statistisches Jahrbuch der Stadt Wien*, 1930–1935, pp. 92, 94.

The comparison will be confined to "small" dwellings since this was the group on which the housing reformers had concentrated their attention. The 1934 census defined the group as including dwellings from 0.0 to 1.5 rooms. The apparently absurd classification of an apartment as having zero rooms is, of course, explained by the fact that under Austrian terminology halls, bathrooms, and kitchens were not "rooms." In 1934 no less than 3,803 or 0.85 of 1 per cent of the small dwellings, were rated at 0.0; that is, they usually had only a kitchen. In such small dwellings lived 6,686 persons. Another 54,325 apartments, 12.5 per cent of the small dwellings, consisted typically of a *Kabinett* only and, as previously, were rated at 0.5 of a unit or room. Here lived 116,615 persons. The group rated at 1.0, the one-room (Zimmer) dwellings, amounted to 227,731 or about 51 per cent of the small dwellings and housed 616,473 individuals. The largest accommodation included in the "small" category consisted primarily of a room and a *Kabinett* and was classified at 1.5 units. There were 155,527 of this type. They made up 35 per cent of the whole category and gave lodging to 497,247 persons.[130]

It will be recalled that in 1919 the so-called *Kabinett* dwellings were not included as a part of the "small" dwellings but placed in a distinct class; consequently, it would seem inaccurate to compare the equipment in the category of "small" dwellings as differently defined in 1919 and 1934. As a matter of fact, however, the degree of equipment in the *Kabinett* class of 1919 was far below that in the "small" class of the same year, so that such a comparison definitely *underrates* the salutary effects of the policy of the city council.[131]

In 1919, 84.75 per cent of the small apartments were provided with a kitchen; in 1934 this percentage had risen to 90.5; in 1919, 6.2 per cent of these apartments had a hall; in 1934, 17 per cent; in 1919, 7.9 per cent had a toilet inside the apartment; in 1934, 20.5 per cent; in 1919, 2.67 per cent had gas *and* electricity installed; in

[130] H. Pawlik, *Wie wohnt der Wiener* (Wien, 1937), pp. 10–12.

[131] On the other hand, the picture may be slightly shifted in favor of the city council in that this comparison includes small dwellings which were built by other persons or bodies. Up to 1930, however, the city was practically the only builder, particularly of small dwellings. Under the 1929 law promoting building (see below, p. 497 f.) slightly more than 7,000 dwellings were built in Vienna and a part of them were built by the city council. From the remainder, a very large part did not belong in the group of small apartments at all; furthermore, under the 1929 act dwellings up to 60 square meters were to be regarded as "small." This so considerably diminishes the number of small dwellings as defined in the census of 1934 that the influence of other than city council dwellings on the comparison may be regarded as insignificant.

1934, 71 per cent; in 1919, 76.8 per cent had neither gas nor electricity; in 1934 only 9.5 per cent;[132] in 1919, 4.68 per cent had water faucets inside the apartment; in 1934, 19 per cent.[133]

These figures speak an eloquent language. They tell a cheering story of increased comfort, health, and happiness—of a successful campaign against housing barbarism.

Struggle against Tenants Protection and City Building

First Phase: 1922–1923

The first clash in the long-drawn-out battle against tenants protection and municipal housing took place as early as the beginning of 1922. The occasion was offered by that reform of the Vienna rent tax that definitely transformed it into a "purpose tax." The fury of the attacks launched by the Christian Social party against the beginnings of the city housing policy clearly foreshadowed subsequent developments. For example, the chief organ of that party characterized the tax as "unsocial to a criminal degree."[134] Kunschak called it the "most brutal and violent form of taxation."[135] There was much talk about "housing Bolshevism" and "war against the tenants."[136] The press of the supposedly conservative and law-abiding Christian Social party went so far as to instigate the tenants to refuse to pay the tax.[137] Strident though these voices were in condemnation, they faltered or became mute on the matter of an alternative solution to the housing difficulties. The one, and very significant, exception was Seipel, by this time the virtual leader of the Catholic party. He did not confine himself to complaints against the oppressive burdens put on the tenant and the probable ineffectiveness of the tax but stated that,

> The private houseowners must obtain again the possibility of living from the proceeds of the rents and of drawing adequate interest on the capital invested. Only in this way will building revive, whereas the measures planned by the Social Democrats will completely kill building activities and certainly further hasten the decay of the existing houses.

---

[132] This development also reflects a policy of the city council; namely, the sale of gas and current at low prices and the provision of facilities of installation by the city enterprises.

[133] Cf. *Statistisches Jahrbuch der Stadt Wien,* 1930–1935, p. 92; and Rosenblum, *op. cit.,* p. 90.

[134] *Reichspost,* February 10, 1922, p. 8.

[135] *Wiener Stimmen,* February 23, 1922, p. 3.

[136] *Ibid.,* January 31, 1922, p. 2; *Reichspost,* same date, p. 5.

[137] *Wiener Stimmen,* February 11, 1922, p. 3.

The Social Democrats are completely forgetting what impression it must make abroad if they hoist the socialization flag in Vienna again and again.[138]

This was a clear program: the former acting president of the socialization commission rejected the "hidden attempt at socialization"; he linked the housing policy of the city council with the problem of tenants protection, and proposed the restoration of the landlord's income. The "revolutionary rubbish" had to be removed.

As indicated, the clerical party as a whole had not yet reached this clear-cut view on the subject. In a parliamentary speech delivered only a few days later, Ramek, subsequently Christian Social chancellor of the republic, said: "We have reached the conviction that tenants protection is not a temporary measure, but must remain for the future, as far as we can foresee it, a permanent part of our legal order."[139]

In December, 1922, on the occasion of the reform of the tenants protection law, the Christian Social speaker Resch was more careful; he did not stress the lasting character of tenants protection, rather confining himself to remarks on the absolute necessity of the restrictions on private property involved in the measure. In fact, only the Social Democratic speaker declared that the system of tenants protection was to continue more or less indefinitely. The Pan-German speaker declared that he considered it would be necessary to reform the law again as soon as it had been promulgated.[140] The bill was carried by the votes of the three major parties with only the Agrarian League dissenting. But when the bill reached the Bundesrat a curious intermezzo took place. The Christian Social *rapporteur* moved its approval. Thereupon another Christian Social, Rintelen, the governor of Styria, made a strong attack against it; speaking for himself and a group of his friends he declared that it was impossible to vote "yes." He denounced bitterly the injustice of a system which deprived so many persons of the fruits of a laborious life; he spoke of rich people living in the houses of impoverished landlords and paying only the legal rent. He claimed to know that the Nationalrat had passed the bill only to breach the wall of tenants protection.[141]

[138] *Reichspost,* February 1, 1922, p. 3.
[139] Nationalrat, *Protokoll,* February 10, 1922, p. 3072.
[140] *Ibid.,* December 7, 1922, pp. 5003, 5007, 5009.
[141] Bundesrat, *Protokoll,* December 13, 1922, pp. 759–761.

Apart from considerations of principle, Rintelen was prompted to this attitude, so contrary to Austrian concepts of party discipline, by two facts. The first and major fact was the fear that the Agrarian League, mainly rooted in Styria, would avail itself of the situation to the political disadvantage of the Catholic party. The second was the fury of the landlords.

When the more or less final draft of the proposed reform became public in the fall of 1922 the landlords of Austria organized a strike. Their measures were to include: cutting off the water supply except in the basements; leaving the staircases and gangways in darkness in the evenings; refusing to collect rents, pay taxes, and clean the sidewalks; removing from the houses telephone wires, mailboxes, and even the cross wires supporting the streetcar cables.[142] The police were compelled, "with full appreciation of the difficult conditions in which the houseowners find themselves," as Schober put it, to call their attention to the illegal character of these measures.[143] The Social Democratic party issued a proclamation urging the tenants to form house committees and threatened that the tenants would take over the administration of the houses. The *Arbeiter Zeitung* compared the "landlords' strike" with the "stock exchange strike" which had taken place in Vienna some time earlier, and stressed the fact that the former Christian Social vice-mayor of Vienna, Hoss, had signed the declaration of intention to cease tax payments.[144] Under the combined pressure the landlords canceled a part of their plans. The strike was confined to Vienna; even there it comprised only a small group of landlords and virtually broke down on the first day.[145] Although the *Reichspost* had given much space to the strike, it declared, after the collapse, that the conditions under tenants protection were untenable and paternally criticized the landlords, for the first time, for having organized the strike without "getting in touch with *the party which is supposed to represent the landlords* in the parliament."[146] This significant admission reflected the growing influence of Seipel in the party; it reflected, furthermore, a defeat for the postwar democratic tendencies in the Christian Social

[142] *Reichspost,* October 2, 1922, p. 4.
[143] *Ibid.,* October 3, 1922, p. 5.
[144] *Arbeiter Zeitung,* October 3, 1922, pp. 1, 2.
[145] *Reichspost,* October 4, 1922, p. 6.
[146] *Ibid.,* October 6, 1922, p. 5. Italics mine.

party and its reversion toward prewar traditions. After the reform was passed the *Reichspost* interpreted the fact that the law had no time limit as showing that early amendment would therefore be possible.[147]

For some time the problem of tenants protection was shifted into the background. Beginning with the spring of 1923 the political parties carried on energetic preparations for the general elections to be held in October. The position of the Christian Social party was very promising. The inflation had been anathema to every class of the population. The stabilization had brought a shrinkage of export industries, but the stock exchange was still active and prevented too rapid a spread of depression. With its leader, Seipel, the clerical party shared the glory of having "saved the country from catastrophe." The Social Democratic party was politically in a much weaker position. To be sure, many of the dismissed civil servants—and no less than 100,000 were supposed to be discharged under the Geneva Treaty—were unlikely to give their votes to the parties of "reconstruction." But the loudly trumpeted slogans of the workers' party against national slavery could scarcely find much resonance in a country where there was so little genuine national feeling, so that the Socialists had every reason to look forward to the coming elections with a feeling of apprehensive uneasiness. Then, in the summer of 1923, Seipel's speech to a mass meeting in Wiener-Neustadt radically altered the situation. This speech has become famous in the political history of Austria and the parts dealing with the immediate problem deserve to be quoted *in extenso*.

> There is one field where we have not been able to make much progress so far; this is the field of our dwelling and rent law. We had numerous negotiations on the subject and I confess it frankly—*somebody may use it for electoral agitation against me; I am not afraid of it*—that the present state of *our tenants protection cannot exist for eternity*. Once upon a time it was necessary; however, in my judgment it could have been abolished much earlier, soon after the end of the war. But at that time it was not got around to and now consideration must be paid to the large masses of those who do not have so much income that they can again pay relatively as much for the dwelling as before. But this is certain: the big housing shortage, which has brought it about that we have many homeless people and thousands living in railroad carriages, will not cease *until*

[147] *Ibid.*, December 8, 1922, p. 3.

in the laws on dwellings and rent we return to conditions similar to those which existed in prewar times. If the houseowner cannot live off what the house brings, then I cannot demand that he keep the house in proper shape or that somebody starts building new dwellings. For this purpose we need at present, as in the past, private initiative. A municipalization, a socialization of house property would not help. To be sure, we cannot suddenly exact from the tenants a valorized rent, that is to say, to make them pay as much in gold crowns as they paid in peace times, because they simply are unable to pay it. To speak of only one group of the population—so long as we cannot pay our civil servants well enough so that they do not have to worry about their dwellings, we can proceed only gradually, only step by step. *According to my firm conviction it will be one of the first tasks of the new parliament, not indeed to upset suddenly our dwelling and rent legislation, but in agreement with tenants and landlords to establish those standards on which in this sphere also we can come back to normal conditions.*[148]

The effects of this speech can hardly be overestimated. The workers' party immediately began a great offensive with the slogan: "Seipel wants to destroy tenants protection." Social Democratic placards posted everywhere announced that Seipel's victory would mean the end of that protection, the restoration of prewar conditions and a rent 15,000 times higher (in paper crowns) than the peace rent. With great skill and persistence the Socialists sought to transform the elections of October 21 into a plebiscite on tenants protection.[149]

The Christian Socials were stunned at first by this turn; their replies to the attacks were surprisingly weak. They dismissed as silly the Socialist talk of a rent of 15,000 crowns per prewar crown, but they did so by saying that nobody ever spoke of an *over*valorized rent and that the landlords would be glad if they obtained the peace rent.[150] *Peace rent,* however, meant 14,400 paper crowns per peace crown. In addition, Seipel laid some stress on the fact that he had never spoken of a *sudden* restoration of peace rents. On the other hand, with a persistence which requires some special explanation, he launched an attack against the second pillar of tenants protection—the restriction of the landlords' right to give notice. After saying that the landlords never had asked the Christian Social party

[148] "Die Bedeutung der kommenden Wahlen," *Reichspost,* July 25, 1923, p. 3. Italics mine.

[149] Cf. *Arbeiter Zeitung,* July 26, 1923, p. 1; October 21, 1923, pp. 2–3; and numerous issues between these dates.

[150] *Reichspost,* September 13, 1923, p. 2.

for a restoration of the unrestricted right of giving notice, he proceeded: "But one day, sometime in the future, it shall again be as it was: the landlord will be able to choose his tenants and the tenant to choose the landlord or the house where he wants to live."[151]

The tenant of an apartment house in Vienna never had much freedom in choosing a landlord after his own heart. Economic conditions were such that in the groups of dwellings studied here, only the landlord as a rule could afford to pick and choose. Remarks like Seipel's gave new weapons to the Social Democratic party and kindled to a blazing fire the endemic hostility of the Austrian tenant against the landlord.

The elections ended with what must be described as a substantial victory for the workers' party since it gained votes and seats. (Cf. below, pp. 689–690.) Tenants protection had proved one of the most powerful weapons of the Austrian labor movement.

Seipel had lost a battle. By throwing tenants protection into the electoral campaign he had forfeited a highly probable victory. What were the motives of this man who more than once gave evidence of his high diplomatic gifts and unusual political skill? To understand his attitude, a brief review of history is necessary. In May, 1923, the Agrarian League had moved in the finance committee of parliament the immediate and complete abolition of tenants protection. The Christian Socials were "put on the spot." They split; 3 of their party members on the committee voted against; 9 for the motion. Thus it was passed and brought to the Nationalrat, but there it was pigeonholed in the justice committee.[152] The Agrarian party, however, continued to time its moves cleverly. The tenants protection bill had been under consideration since January. Now came the period when, in view of the forthcoming elections, the landlords—to use Seipel's words—"attempted to push us [the Christian Socials] to sudden and radical measures in this field, without paying due consideration to the needs of other groups of the population."[153] Nevertheless, an agreement was reached early in July by which the houseowners consented to withdraw their demands pending the electoral campaign. There is little doubt that the clerical party purchased this with-

[151] *Ibid.*, September 15, 1923, p. 5.
[152] *Arbeiter Zeitung*, May 8, 1923, p. 3; L. Kunschak, *Oesterreich 1918–1934* (Wien, 1935), p. 80; *Tätigkeits-Bericht,* Heft 17 (Wien, 1923), p. 70.
[153] *Reichspost*, September 15, 1923, p. 5.

drawal by promising a reform early in the next parliament.[154] Not to be outdone the Agrarian League again stepped forth as the champion of the landlords and made even greater promises to them at one of their meetings in Graz. Their association showed an inclination to urge the members to support the League. Thereupon the Christian Social paper in Graz, the *Grazer Volksblatt,* launched a moving appeal to the landlords in which it spoke of the old friendship between Lueger and the landlords, and did not forget to mention Rintelen's speech in the Bundesrat.[155] The state governors urged Seipel to make public and binding promises to the landlords; otherwise, they argued, radicalization of this group and heavy electoral losses would ensue.[156] Thus Seipel decided on the course which in all likelihood destroyed his dream of a two-thirds majority in the Austrian parliament. This policy was subsequently sharply criticized within his party. "Seipel's compliance with the governors' demands very soon proved a bad mistake. It would have been more advisable to put the rent reform on the agenda of the newly elected house without touching the issue during the electoral campaign."[157] The morality of this advice may be doubted, but not its political value. At any rate, the foregoing shows that it is not correct to put the entire blame—as Kunschak does—on the shoulders of the Socialists who "shamelessly misinterpreted a remark of Seipel's."[158]

Whether Seipel's policy really was a mistake is not the point here. The phrases in his speeches concerning a return to normal conditions were not cleverly chosen, to say the least. They only proved that Seipel's knowledge of what "normal" prewar conditions meant to the masses of the electorate in Vienna was very limited. But, as

[154] The *Reichspost* for July 9, 1923 (pp. 2–3), carried a report of a landlords' meeting under the title: "Temporary withdrawal of the houseowners' demands." After references to the negotiations which had taken place, to the inopportunity of agitating the question before the elections, and to the dissatisfaction of the landlords with the Christian Socials and the Pan-Germans, the paper quoted the president of the central organization of houseowners and chief speaker at the meeting as follows: "We must consider how far the position of the landlords would be deteriorated ... by inconsiderate tactics.... We must see to it that in the next elections the bourgeois parties pull in a large majority. This means for the moment to set aside our demands in the interest of the state. To take this action reflects no weakness on our part but rather that we have come to a more clever tactic from which we expect a betterment of the present hopeless conditions of the landlords."

[155] Quoted by *Arbeiter Zeitung,* July 25, 1923, p. 4.

[156] Spectator Noricus [probably Gürtler], "Von Seipel zu Schober," *Das Volkswohl,* vol. 22 (March, 1931), 201–209.

[157] *Ibid.*

[158] Kunschak, *op. cit.,* p. 80.

already suggested, it is more important to understand what motives prompted him to adopt this policy. Both earlier and later, Seipel demonstrated that he was well able to withstand any pressure put upon him. If he did not, in this case, the reasons lay deeper. As a conservative statesman, Seipel felt it necessary to preserve for his party the traditional adherence of a group which may be regarded as the representative of a conservative middle class par excellence.[159] It may be argued that this connection was more valuable in the times of the electoral privilege system than in the days of democracy. But Seipel was not a democrat; he preferred to weigh votes rather than count them. And it certainly may be argued against Spectator Noricus that in the long run Seipel's policy might have proved the more successful one.

But this matter of timing—whether or not Seipel should have acted in the summer of 1923—is unimportant in comparison with the fact that he certainly felt a deep impelling urge to act. It was not primarily to "dry the tears of the landlords," as the Socialists alleged. Seipel feared that much more was at stake. He realized that the preservation of tenants protection meant the continuation and expansion of the city council's building policy. And this meant growing Socialist influence in the city. The city council, once the landlord of a large part of Vienna, might beome so powerful as to be unconquerable. To stop city building by abolishing tenants protection and thus to check the growth of the Socialist labor movement—this was Seipel's real motive; it was the basis of his moves in the next legislative period of the Austrian parliament.

SECOND PHASE: PARLIAMENTARY STRUGGLES

The power consciousness of the Social Democratic party had been tremendously increased by the victory at the elections. If prior to the polling, the Christian Socials could hope to reduce the Socialist position in parliament to less than one-third and thus free the road for constitutional reshaping of the state, after it, the Socialists could see the possibility of obtaining the majority in parliament at the next or at the second subsequent election. They examined the results of that polling and came to the conclusion: "If we succeed in

[159] Cf. Theodor Brauer, "Mittelstandspolitik," *Grundriss der Sozialökonomik* (Tübingen, 1927), vol. 9, pt. 2, p. 398.

diverting from the bourgeois parties only 320,000 voters and gaining them for our party, then we shall obtain the absolute majority in the parliament; then we can govern Austria."[160] But these voters could hardly be found in the ranks of the working class. The Social Democratic party had succeeded in coming very close to exhausting this main source of its power. Further gains from the small groups of Communist and Catholic workers were unlikely. The 320,000 votes had to be sought to a large extent from the middle class. Here tenants protection seemed to be the appropriate lever. Furthermore, this method seemed very happy indeed from the point of view of the party, in that it allowed a middle-class policy which was absolutely consonant with basic party principles; that is to say, with the policy of continuous improvement of the conditions of the laboring class. And the middle class, excepting the houseowners, felt vitally interested in the maintenance of tenants protection. "To the middle classes, impoverished by inflation, it [tenants protection] has afforded one of the few alleviations of their unfortunate situation."[161] It had given them the opportunity to avoid complete proletarization by subletting parts of their dwellings. It had enabled them to preserve their cultural habits, for example, to continue their old traditions of musical evenings in small circles of friends. It had enabled the small trader and producer to work with reduced costs and thus to withstand the competition of big firms. It would have been, therefore, the proper function of the conservative parties to defend the middle class by preserving tenants protection.[162] As it was, the conservative parties saw themselves compelled to leave this task to Social Democracy.

To paraphrase the language of a Socialist writer, the fight for the favor of the middle class was first and foremost a fight for tenants protection.[163] Extensive organizational work was carried on. The workers' party actively supported the huge tenants' union which in 1928 had 229,183 member households. This organization supplied lawyers without fee in all cases of conflict between tenants and landlords and gave legal advice to its members.[164] But it also had political

[160] Otto Bauer, *Der Kampf um die Macht* (Wien, 1924), p. 25.

[161] Layton and Rist, *op. cit.*, p. 42.

[162] G. Stolper, "Mieterschutz," *Der österreichische Volkswirt*, vol. 17 (Jan. 24, 1925), 452.

[163] Pertinax [Otto Leichter], *Oesterreich, 1934* (Zurich, 1935), p. 20.

[164] *Jahrbuch der österreichischen Arbeiterbewegung, 1928*, pp. 312–313.

tasks which were frankly disclosed by its representative to the 1925 party congress: "We consider the tenants' association as a means of bringing people into the party organization who stand apart from our party, and we can register big successes in this respect. To date we have won thousands of former opponents or indifferent individuals for the party."[165]

It is probably not an exaggeration to say that the stand taken on tenants protection induced the party to further extension of its middle-class policy. A part of this policy was the stimulation given to the Social Democratic Association of Small Businessmen and Handicraftsmen, but, as was shown in Chapter XII, it proved somewhat difficult to bring this stimulation into agreement with the traditional attitude toward the Socialist coöperatives. The Linz program of the party (1926) mentioned tenants protection only briefly and incidentally,[166] but it laid strong emphasis on the preference for a democratic development, and rejected everything which might destroy that quiet and order so dear to the hearts of the middle class. It is apparent from these points and from the general tenor of the program that in the minds of the party leaders the problem of tenants protection was the most important basis of their middle-class policy, and, consequently, of their general policy in state and society.[167]

Thus tenants protection assumed an importance far greater even than would have been warranted by its connection with the building policy of the city council of Vienna; and so it is understandable that adamant resistance, a stern "no," had to be the answer of the party to all efforts of the majority parties to abolish it. These efforts began some time after the elections of 1923. On July 29, 1924, two Christian Social members of parliament, Reiner and Fink, submitted a motion according to which the basic rent was to be combined with the maintenance rent and fixed at 10 groschen per peace crown of prewar rent beginning with November, 1924, and then raised 10 groschen on February 1 and August 1 of the following years until it reached 60 groschen on February 1, 1927. Because of much lower taxation and changes in the mortgage burden on houses

[165] *Parteitag, 1925,* p. 198.
[166] *Ibid., 1926,* p. 181.
[167] For comments on a very different interpretation of the Linz program which developed later, particularly in conservative quarters, cf. below, Vol. II, pp. 1048–1050.

this last figure would have brought the landlords' income very close to its prewar level. The right of the tenants to secure an audit of the maintenance rent was to be abolished, but the restrictions concerning the right of the landlord to give notice were to be only slightly changed.[168] The last point and the fact that the government refrained from submitting its own bill show that after the events of 1923 greater cautiousness was considered wise. The bill was duly submitted to the justice committee of the Nationalrat. It remained there for several months and seemed destined to share the fate of the previous motion of the Agrarian League, but, suddenly, on January 9, 1925, the chairman of the committee put it on the agenda for that day. The Social Democrats immediately began obstructive speeches on the question of the agenda and when the Christian Social chairman attempted to restrict the speakers' time, whistles and automobile horns went into action so that, as the *Reichspost* suggested, the Socialists succeeded in faithfully reproducing a scene characteristic of the imperial parliament.[169]

During the ensuing negotiations the majority agreed that according to the rules of order the attempt to impose time limits on speakers was illegal. Members of the workers' party went on with their filibustering. Since the clericals feared that, if pressed, the Socialists would not only extend the obstruction to other committees but even carry it to meetings of parliament, a compromise solution was found. On January 16, 1925, a new Christian Social motion, this time called Fink-Reiner, was introduced. It repeated essentially the stipulations of the Reiner-Fink motion, but shifted forward the dates of the schedule of rent increases so that the rent of 60 groschen per crown of peace rent was to be reached on November 1 rather than February 1, 1927. Furthermore, even the minor changes in the right to give notice provided by the former motion were withdrawn. In order to restrict the field of obstruction as much as possible a special subcommittee was created. The Socialists discovered that the order of business did not stipulate who was entitled to open the proceedings of the new group prior to the election of its chairman. In the subsequent amendment to the rules the president of the Nationalrat was given this function. The majority wanted Kien-

[168] Danneberg, *Die Geschichte des Mieterschutzes in Oesterreich* (Wien, 1928), pp. 4–5.
[169] *Reichspost*, January 10, 1925, p. 1.

böck, the minister of finance in the "reconstruction," to become chairman. Every Socialist on the committee declared his intention of speaking to the point. Some of these speeches lasted fifteen, seventeen, and twenty-one hours. The record was reached by Witternigg, who spoke for forty-two hours; during this marathon performance he proposed himself as chairman of the committee and considered it necessary to support the motion with a detailed autobiographical account which should prove that he had proper qualities for the post. Altogether one hundred fifty-four hours were spent in the election of the chairman. Finally, on July 29, 1925, exactly six months after the first meeting of the subcommittee, Kienböck was elected. But the majority dropped further proceedings. A partial compromise was reached: on July 30, 1925, the parliament passed a bill which exempted from tenants protection, first, dwellings and business places which on July 31, 1925, were neither rented nor allocated under the requisitioning law; and, second, dwelling rooms which were sublet after July 31 and had not been sublet on that date. In the second case the chief tenant had to retain at least one living room.[170] The Socialists declared they would vote against the bill but not filibuster against it because "nobody who today enjoys the benefits of tenants protection will be affected by it."[171] Thus their obstruction had succeeded in beating off the attack on tenants protection.

Undoubtedly, however, obstruction itself was a serious problem. Historically, it had proved the gravest threat to the victorious rise of parliamentarism.[172] It had discredited to some extent the dignity and moral influence even of the mother of parliaments, the House of Commons.[173] During the months of obstruction in the rent subcommittee of the Nationalrat the Christian Socials spoke repeatedly of an "assault against democracy," of "parliament tiredness," of an attack against the "rights of the parliament."[174]

There is little doubt that to the extent that the parliament proved unsatisfactory as an instrument for realizing the wishes of the majority parties, these parties felt prompted to seek other ways and means to achieve their purposes. This danger was certainly acute

[170] *Tätigkeits-Bericht,* Heft 19 (Wien, 1925), pp. 64–66; *BGBl.,* 1925, Nr. 303.
[171] Nationalrat, *Protokoll,* July 30, 1925, p. 2671.
[172] Cf. E. V. Zenker, *Der Parlamentarismus* (Wien and Leipzig, 1914).
[173] James Bryce, *Modern Democracies* (New York, 1921), vol. 2, pp. 345–346.
[174] Cf. *Reichspost,* February 2, 1925, p. 3; February 27, 1925, p. 1; March 4, 1925, p. 2.

in countries with a young and only weakly rooted democratic tradition. In such countries, however, democratic victories of the Socialist parties also worked in the same direction. And from a democratic point of view the core of the problem lay deeper. All who agree with such constitutional authorities as Kelsen that democracy does not mean unrestricted domination of the majority will also agree that obstruction is not necessarily opposed to the majority principle.[175] In certain cases the minority may by obstruction prevent the majority from adopting undemocratic measures. It was with this in mind that the *Volkswirt* said after obstruction had started in the justice committee of parliament:

> Whether . . . the rents should be raised 3,000- or 5,000- or 6,000-fold [equivalent to 30, 50, and 60 groschen per crown of peace rent]—the idea is *too crazy to be opposed otherwise than by trumpets and auto horns.* However, there was perhaps another method of opposition: to let the majority adopt their motion and then, after it was put into effect, see how they hold the state together—even for eight days. *For the first time in the Austrian parliament physical obstruction was really an act of preservation of the state.* . . . If the building activity of the Social Democratic community of Vienna is not tied up by the Bolshevism of the bourgeois parties, the housing market, in four to five years, may be in a condition that permits the abolition of all restrictions on free price formation.[176]

The Socialists argued that at the elections the majority of urban voters had expressed their desire to preserve tenants protection, and that the peasants had no right to participate in deciding this question. In reply to the criticism that they were destroying democracy, they proposed new elections; naturally nothing would have suited them better than a polling on the sole issue of tenants protection. If the majority parties shrank from elections, it would prove, they argued, that the people did not want the reform and that the majority knew this. Then the conclusion would be clear that the Socialists were defending a law approved by the Austrian people and thereby defending the spirit of democracy.[177] The argument was not without dangers, particularly since it claimed that a large part of the population lacked the right of decision on a fundamental problem. This questioned the unity and entity of the Austrian state.

[175] Hans Kelsen, *Allgemeine Staatslehre* (Berlin, 1925), pp. 354–355.
[176] *Der österreichische Volkswirt,* vol. 17 (Jan. 17, 1925), 418. Italics mine.
[177] Cf. *Arbeiter Zeitung,* February 28, 1925, p. 1, and March 5, 1925, pp. 1–2.

There is, however, another and more important consideration related to the clerical charge that the workers' party was destroying democracy by obstruction. Article 17 of the order of business of the Nationalrat provided that the majority of that house had the right to set a time limit to the discussions of a committee, and that if the committee did not submit its report before the limit expired, the house could proceed without it. In the Nationalrat itself obstruction in the sense of a systematic effort to delay the progress of business by speaking against time and the like could always be defeated by closure. Physical obstruction, by its very character, can hardly be more than a demonstrative measure, and cannot be used permanently. This seems to be the decisive point. With comparative ease the majority could have broken the Socialist obstruction. Since they did not proceed in this way, it may be argued that they had been brought to the realization that tenants protection affected vital interests of broad masses of the population. At any rate, after more complete examination of the circumstances, it seems that the obstruction by the workers' party loses much, if not all, of its allegedly undemocratic character.

Toward the end of 1925 the majority parties apparently believed again that a radical reform of tenants protection would be possible. As the reader will recall, the law concerning the requisitioning of dwellings was to expire on December 31, 1925. The Socialists moved its prolongation. On December 1 the government introduced a bill[178] providing that rents should be raised on February 1, 1926, to 20 groschen per prewar crown and then, by three steps, reach 60 groschen on May 1, 1927. After December 31, 1928, every restriction was to be removed and the free market restored. For higher grade business premises the time intervals were even shorter. It was suggested that a compromise could be found on the basis of votes from the majority parties for prolongation of the requisitioning law in return for Socialist abandonment of "appreciable parts of tenants protection."[179] The workers' party rejected this "blackmail," to use the *Volkswirt*'s term,[180] and the requisitioning law was not prolonged. The mayor of Vienna introduced immediately a system under which landlords were required to report to municipal au-

[178] Nationalrat, *Protokoll, Beilagen,* Nr. 467, p. 1.
[179] Cf. speech of Danneberg, *Parteitag, 1926,* p. 374.
[180] *Der österreichische Volkswirt,* vol. 19 (May 28, 1927), 927.

thorities all dwellings that became vacant, but this was in no wise a substitute for the law. Although the immediate effects were insignificant, the elimination of the statute proved in the long run the most effective stroke against the system of tenants protection. If the Socialists had foreseen the later development they probably would have preferred a compromise. As it was, they hoped that by clinging to tenants protection they would gain a parliamentary majority in the 1927 elections and be in a position to restore the requisitioning law. Attempts to discuss the government's bill in the subcommittee in the spring of 1926 led to another short outbreak of obstruction. The *rapporteur* then modified the bill so as to allow an increase of rents only to 40 groschen per peace crown, but the Socialist members, who had been empowered by a meeting of their party associates in parliament "to apply all purposeful means," demanded general elections and "blew up" the meeting of the subcommittee.

Since the majority parties had no desire to fight the elections of 1927 with tenants protection as the chief issue again, they were anxious to solve the troublesome question before the campaign became active. On June 1, 1926, it was decided at a meeting of state governors (with the exception of Seitz of Vienna) "that the struggle for the reform of tenants protection must be continued with all energy."[181] It became known a short time later that at least one of the Christian Social banks, which were in great difficulties just then, had indulged in extensive land speculations in the hope of an early reform of tenants protection. This provided fresh fuel in the struggle.[182]

Since the parliamentary efforts to solve the problem had utterly failed, another way had to be found. Toward the end of 1926 the landlords, who up to then had boycotted the state rent commissions, demanded their convocation. In these meetings they moved immediate raising of the maintenance rents—in some states up to 40 groschen per peace crown as contrasted with the basic 1.5 groschen of the law. In Vienna the demand was rejected; in Lower Austria the Socialists set in with obstruction. In Burgenland an increase to 10 groschen was accepted. In Styria, despite the absence of the representatives of the tenants and of the chamber of labor, the com-

[181] *Tätigkeits-Bericht,* Heft 21 (Wien, 1927), p. 41.

[182] Cf. "Report on Parliamentary Investigation of the Central Bank Affair," Nationalrat, *Protokoll, Beilagen,* Nr. 675, p. 84; and *Der österreichische Volkswirt,* vol. 19 (Oct. 9, 1926), 42.

mission adopted on December 15, 1926, an increase to 40 groschen per peace crown. Article 12 of the rent law had envisaged general advances of maintenance rent past the 1.5 groschen only to the extent of actual increases in wages and material costs in the construction industry after November 1, 1922. "The resolution in Styria was in contradiction with the clear meaning of Article 12 and represented an open breach of the law."[183] The basis for this categorical denunciation was the fact that building costs had risen since 1922 by about 50 per cent, which would have justified a general increase of the maintenance rent only to 2.25 groschen per peace crown. The result of the Styrian action was an energetic movement of resistance among tenants of all political parties, and not in Styria alone.[184] The Graz city council adopted unanimously a resolution of protest. Impressed by the general opposition the Christian Social governor of Styria hesitated to publish the resolution of the commission.[185] On December 22, 1926, a meeting of the Socialist party, the trade unions, and the representatives of the states took place. The Styrians served notice that a tenants' strike would be the consequence of the resolution; the party entrusted them with preparations for a defensive action.[186]

During the session of parliament on the day preceding the meeting just mentioned the government adopted a rather ambiguous attitude. Minister of Justice Dinghofer claimed that the text of the law was not clear, that the Styrian resolution was not "unconditionally illegal," and that the government had no right to intervene.[187] Although Dinghofer expressly declared that he was giving an exhaustive presentation of the case, the *Arbeiter Zeitung* was able, a few days later, to quote directions issued by the ministry of justice in 1923 in which the legal status was clearly interpreted in such a way as to leave no doubt of the illegality of the resolution.[188]

The threatened chaos was finally avoided by a ruling of the president of the Styrian commission on January 14, 1927, that the resolu-

[183] *Der österreichische Volkswirt,* vol. 19 (Jan. 15, 1927), 409.

[184] Cf. the unanimous decision of the Union of Christian German Tenants of January 20, 1927, rejecting the interpretation of the law attempted in Styria. *Reichspost,* January 23, 1927, p. 5.

[185] *Der österreichische Volkswirt,* vol. 19 (Jan. 1, 1927), 352; *Tätigkeits-Bericht,* Heft 21 (Wien, 1927), p. 42.

[186] *Parteitag, 1927,* pp. 7–8.

[187] Nationalrat, *Protokoll,* December 21, 1926, pp. 4205, 4206.

[188] *Der österreichische Volkswirt,* vol. 19 (Jan. 15, 1927), 409.

tion passed in the absence of representatives of the tenants and of the chamber of labor was invalid since the rules of procedure in conciliation boards had to be applied in state rent commissions.[189] The bitterness aroused by the episode is further demonstrated by the facts that when the intention of the president to declare the resolution invalid became known he received a flood of anonymous threatening letters, and that when the actual nullifying meeting took place it was consequently thought necessary to station large numbers of policemen at the building in which the meeting took place.[190]

It is interesting to note that some Catholic politicians must have conceived the plan to make use of Article 12 to dispense with tenants protection even at the time when the law was passed in 1922. With reference to this article Ramek wrote in 1923:

> Thereby the further development of rent formation has been removed once and for all from the struggle of the parties in parliament, certainly a tremendous forward step in the interest of the recovery of our housing conditions which cannot be overestimated. The last period of the parliamentary struggles over the tenants protection law was filled with stubborn negotiations just on these stipulations. [And he added meaningfully]: The minor concessions to the minority [appear] . . . to be mere beauty blemishes of the law. . . . It is to be regretted that it was just the landlords who have not yet fully grasped this fundamental stipulation of the law.[191]

The failure of this attack on tenants protection not only defeated the plan to solve the problem before the next elections, but on the contrary once more put the issue in the center of general attention. It enabled the Social Democrats again to make widest use of the question in their electoral propaganda—and this time they were effectively supported by the results of four years of building in Vienna and the new building program for the next five years. The Socialist electoral proclamation of March 18, 1927, dwelt with due length on the history of the struggle and admonished the electorate: "For four years the Socialists have defended tenants protection; now it is the task of the voters to secure it permanently. On April 24 the decision on tenants protection will be taken."[192] Simultaneously,

---

[189] *Arbeiter Zeitung,* January 15, 1927, p. 2.

[190] *Reichspost,* January 15, 1927, p. 2; *Arbeiter Zeitung,* January 18, 1927, p. 3.

[191] Rudolf Ramek, "Das neue Mietengesetz," *Das Volkswohl,* vol. 14 (Heft 1–2, 1923), 26–27.

[192] *Parteitag, 1927,* p. 13.

high over the Viennese streets appeared huge illuminated signs—a political innovation in Austria—in which the workers' party urged: "Secure tenants protection! Vote for Social Democrats!"

The majority parties, which with the exception of the Agrarian League formed a "unity list," found themselves in a difficult position. The history of the last four years spoke against them. They were bound by promises to landlords. But the pressure of Socialist propaganda had to be met. A few days after the workers' party started its "light campaign," Austrians walking in the evening through the streets of their towns or traveling by train through the country could read the reply of the Unity List glowing from millions of electric bulbs: "Tenants Protection Secured! Vote for the Unity List!" This, however, implied a certain mental reservation. As the Christian Social Spectator Noricus explained, to the Christian Socials "tenants protection" meant restriction of the landlord's right to give notice. To the Socialists, and, as Spectator Noricus admits, to the Austrian people also, "tenants protection" meant low legal rents.[193] In other words, the counterslogan was a quibble of dubious moral quality.

In spite of the advantage of the Unity List the majority parties lost additional votes and seats to the workers' party. The latter did not secure the majority, but once again it had won an electoral victory with the help of tenants protection and could deem itself on the right road. Only 8 per cent separated it now from a majority in the Nationalrat.

At the first meeting of the new parliament Seipel announced the government's intention to create a "modern rent law."[194] The opposition answered with indignant interruptions. Kunschak explained that the words "modern rent law" implied protection against the termination of the contract by the landlord; in this sense, he said, tenants protection was secured against any danger.[195] This concluded the second phase of the struggle. Two months later came the fateful events of July 15, 1927; their aftermath brought an intensification of Fascist pressure into the struggles against tenants protection, and finally made it impossible for Social Democracy to maintain a defense line which it had held so successfully for five years.

[193] Spectator Noricus, *loc. cit.*
[194] Nationalrat, *Protokoll*, May 19, 1927, p. 11.
[195] *Ibid.*, p. 24.

PRO AND CONTRA OF TENANTS PROTECTION AND CITY BUILDING

It is necessary to consider tenants protection and the housing policy of Vienna as reflected in the violent clash of opinions before discussing the final phase of the struggle. A detailed presentation would fill volumes. Only the main points will be reviewed here.

As is true with most issues which deeply agitate public opinion, problems of justice played an outstanding part in the controversy. Time and again it was stressed by the opponents of tenants protection that with the confiscation of the net income of the landlords many people who had worked and saved in order to secure for themselves a comfortable old age were deprived of the fruits of their labor.[196] Against this contention the friends of tenants protection had several answers. It is possible to abstract from broad hints that the fate of the landlords in postwar Austria was, as it were, the fulfillment of Aristotle's equalizing justice, although this point undoubtedly played its part in the opinions of the masses of tenants. It was a fact, however, that the landlords had emerged from the storms of inflation in a better position than any other group of the middle class. The rentiers who had placed their money in the hands of the state and in saving banks were completely deprived of their property. The landlords had still preserved the substance, and they could sell it—even though at a loss. Furthermore, this loss was greatly diminished by the fact that the houseowners "stood in the first rank of those favored by the inflation."[197] Before the war the aggregate value of Vienna houses was estimated at figures ranging from 4 to a little less than 5 billion gold crowns and the mortgages on them at from 2⅔ to 2½ billions. In other words, from 53 to 66 per cent of the value of the houses was owed by the "owners" to mortgage institutions;[198] that is, actually to masses of small savers in Austria. These sums were repaid by the landlords during the years of inflation in depreciated currency. An example is the mortgage loans on Vienna houses granted by the First Austrian Savings Bank which amounted in 1920 to 300 million crowns, wherefrom, by the end of

[196] Cf., for example, *Reichspost,* December 8, 1922, p. 3; Bundesrat, *Protokoll,* December 13, 1922, p. 760.

[197] Brauer, *loc. cit.,* p. 398.

[198] Danneberg, *Was wird aus dem Mieterschutz?* pp. 9–10; Bunzel, *loc. cit.,* pp. 122–123.

1922, only an infinitesimal amount was left.[199] Finally, the inflation had caused a great shake-up on the housing market. Foreigners and profiteers were buying houses. In the period between 1919 and 1923 some 11,000 houses, about 25 per cent, had changed hands.[200] In 1924 the ownership of the 42,321 houses in Vienna was distributed as follows:[201]

1. Federation and states	693
2. City of Vienna	3,206
3. Foundations	342
4. Churches	384
5. Joint stock companies	2,325
6. Small traders and producers	19,196
7. Foreigners	12,170
8. Widows and orphans	5,005

Thus only about 55 per cent (groups 6 and 8) belonged to people about whom there would be rather complete agreement that considerations of social justice should be applied.[202]

In the same field of ethical justification was the problem of rich people occupying dwellings in the house of an impoverished house-owner. This question assumed a much wider social aspect because of the fact that the more substantially built houses, in which lived the well to do, required much less maintenance cost than did the dwellings of the workers and "little people." Although there were no statistics available on the average amount of maintenance rent paid by the various groups of dwellings, an investigation made by the ministry of justice among its officials established the fact that the four highest paid 10.61 groschen per peace crown, whereas the four youngest *Amtsdiener* paid 38.1 groschen per crown of peace rent.[203]

To cope with this situation parliament adopted a resolution in 1922 requiring the government to present a bill by which people

[199] Paul Schwarz [general secretary of this savings bank], "Die städtischen Liegenschaften," *SVfS.*, vol. 169 (1925), 23.

[200] *Arbeiter Zeitung*, September 19, 1923, p. 7; Bunzel, *loc. cit.*, pp. 166–167.

[201] Eugen Amelung, "Die Entwicklung der Mieterschutz-Frage in Oesterreich," *Das Neue Reich*, vol. 7 (Jan. 10, 1925), 337. According to Breitner, Amelung was incorrect in assigning 1,460 buildings to the city and 1,746 to the state of Vienna; all belonged to the municipality as such. Letter from Breitner to Gulick, November 8, 1945.

[202] The inclusion of foundations and churches, which large groups would demand, would add less than 2 per cent.

[203] Schneider, *Der Tod von Wien*, pp. 11–12. The *Amtsdiener* was a petty clerk whose duties included those of an American office boy and some janitorial work.

with large incomes would be compelled to erect dwellings for people in need of apartments.[204] This bill never was presented.

More important by far was the government's failure to do anything about the creation of an equalization fund that would have distributed maintenance costs more equitably. This failure is particularly censurable because Article 11 of the 1922 rent law had specifically provided for such a fund in any community that desired it and had stipulated that the details were to be incorporated in a separate statute. As houses continued to deteriorate and the inadequacy and unfairness of the maintenance rent provisions became more evident, the pressure for the establishment of the equalization fund became more urgent. In May, 1924, the Socialists introduced a bill[205] for the purpose of effectuating Article 11. Nothing came of it. In October, 1925, the editor of the *Volkswirt* made a specific proposal to the same purpose. The vice-chancellor replied in the Nationalrat that the administration of such a fund would require a huge bureaucracy, that this bureaucracy would expend tremendous sums in investigating the conditions of houses, and that it would act arbitrarily. The editor pointed out that the housing office already knew the state of repair of a great part of the buildings and that [under the terms of Article 11] investigations would have to be made only when major repairs and reconstruction were under consideration. He asked, furthermore, whether the existing injustice frequently stressed by the enemies of tenants protection warranted an increase in rents for everybody. Again, in January, 1927, the *Volkswirt* criticized the government parties for their failure to institute the equalization fund.[206]

Possibly of more importance than the ethical questions discussed were the divergent opinions on the economic effects of tenants protection. Much space was given, especially by economists, to the threatening "petrification" of the economy in that the mobility of

[204] Nationalrat, *Protokoll,* December 7, 1922, p. 5013. Text of resolution: *Beilagen,* Nr. 1309, p. 34.

[205] Text reproduced in Danneberg, *Geschichte des Mieterschutzes in Oesterreich,* p. 5.

[206] *Der österreichische Volkswirt,* vol. 18 (Oct. 31 and Dec. 19, 1925), 128, 315; *ibid.,* vol. 19 (Jan. 1, 1927), 352. This last criticism was coupled with another of the Socialists for not offering sufficient resistance to the lapse of the dwelling requisitioning act. Previously the journal had also criticized the Socialists for not pressing more energetically their demands for an equalization fund; it noted, however, their conviction that without new elections parliament was not in a position to reflect public opinion on the whole complex of rent, housing, and tenants protection issues. *Ibid.,* vol. 18 (May 22, 1926), 943.

labor appeared seriously impaired by the system. It was argued further that this immobility implied losses in time and money for the workers and that it increased unemployment.[207] No one would contend that these arguments are without merit,[208] but it must be remembered that a fair comparison is not that with an ideal competitive economic order existing only in the abstract analysis of the liberal economist, but with prewar conditions in Vienna which did not make it easy to "follow the job" as the Viennese workers called moving to the vicinity of the factory where they were employed. Furthermore, as long as there was a requisitioning law, exchanges of dwellings could be effected. After 1925 the city council lost the possibility of influencing or compelling landlords to acquiesce in such exchanges. It is to be regretted that Hayek found it possible to deal with the problem without even mentioning this law, necessary supplement to the system though it was. The effects of the expiration of the statute may be seen from the table of the movement on the dwellings' market in Vienna, page 481.

The promises of landlords that they would rent dwellings becoming vacant after the expiration of the law to those registered as urgently in need were soon forgotten. From the apartments listed as "rented" in the following table during 1926, 1927, and 1928 only 600, 39, and 8, respectively, were let to persons registered with the housing office of the city of Vienna.[209] This made possible a large black market on which the old tenant and the landlord shared the booty in the form of a compensation they demanded from the new tenant. The receipt of such compensation was illegal and the payer was entitled to claim the amount within one year. Usually, the old tenant

---

[207] Cf., esp., Hayek, *loc. cit.*, pp. 260–261; Türr, *op. cit.*, p. 146. On the basis of the larger number of passengers on Vienna streetcars P. Vas computed that the population of the city paid about 63 millions of schillings a year for fares as a price for tenants protection. This obviously leaves out of account the facts: (1) that after the war the employment of women increased tremendously and that they were much less likely to walk; (2) that the policy of low fares adopted by the Socialists in the city council naturally increased the demand; (3) that after the war Sunday outings in the countryside became a characteristic habit of the Viennese. Scarcely more significant is another computation by Vas showing that from 70,000 workers in four districts only 50 per cent were employed in the same district. Here a basis of comparison is lacking since it is not known whether in prewar times this percentage was different. Moreover, distances to work places in a neighboring district may be shorter than to many of those in the same district. Vas is quoted in Bunzel, *loc. cit.* p. 161, and Hayek, *loc. cit.* p. 260.

[208] Cf. also similar complaints of industrial inspectors, e.g., Gewerbe-Inspektoren, *Bericht, 1926* (Wien, 1927), p. lxi.

[209] Kautsky, *loc. cit.*, p. 79; *Der österreichische Volkswirt,* vol. 18 (Jan. 16, 1926), 411.

received the payment and gave his part to the landlord since the new tenant did not wish to have controversies with the landlord. Once the new tenant moved in the former occupant frequently filed suit against his former landlord, obtained the money, and gave part of it to the new tenant. Occasionally, the old tenant waited until the year elapsed, filed suit on the very last day, was thus protected against a suit from the new tenant, and could avoid sharing the compensation with him.[210] These conditions certainly were unsound from economic and social points of view. But there is little doubt

MOVEMENT ON THE DWELLINGS' MARKET IN VIENNA*

	1925	1926	1927	1928	1929
Rented	9,313†	8,379	6,562	5,680	5,737
Exchanged	11,089	4,091	2,186	1,489	540
Another person living in same dwelling becoming main tenant	2,774	2,012	690	403	348
Totals	23,171	14,482	9,438	7,572	6,625

* City houses are not included in the table. *Wirtschaftsstatistisches Jahrbuch 1929/30*, p. 503.
† This figure included "allocated," as well as "rented" dwellings.

that they were not so much a consequence of tenants protection as of the wanton destruction of an essential part of the system.

Another shortcoming of the system was the high rents paid by the subtenants. They, as well as the compensations, could be regarded partly as a tribute paid by the young to the old generation. Hayek, moreover, made it seem plausible that these subrents were higher than they would have been on the free market, because tenants protection restricted the supply of sublet rooms.[211] Here also the requisitioning law would have prevented the evil to a large extent.

Hayek's claim in an earlier publication that tenants protection restricted building for the needs of the well-to-do classes and thus hampered technical developments in this sphere, which he contended would benefit all classes of the population in the course of time,[212] may be dismissed as unrealistic. It is too well known that in

[210] Cf. H. Klang, "Der gegenwärtige Zustand des österreichischen Mietengesetzes," *Deutsches Wohnungsarchiv*, vol. 3 (April, 1928), 178–182.

[211] Hayek, *loc. cit.*, p. 258.

[212] Hayek, *Das Mieterschutzproblem*, Bibliothek für Volkswirtschaft und Politik, Vortrag gehalten in der Nationalökonomischen Gesellschaft in Wien am 18. Dezember, 1928, p. 11.

prewar Vienna, despite all technical progress, mass dwellings had continued to present the appalling picture drawn by Philippovich in 1894.

A much more serious argument against tenants protection was the fact that under it houses had ceased to represent the basis for mortgage credit and thus restricted the volume of credit available in Austria. This argument was one of the most frequently used.[213] The Socialists were by no means unaware of the general problem; indeed, Otto Bauer once described the Austrian crisis as a "credit crisis" and was "rewarded" by the approving publication of his entire speech in the chief organ of the manufacturers' association.[214] No doubt every possibility of expanding the credit basis of the country had to be carefully examined, and per se a connection between reduced credit volume and tenants protection certainly existed. The question, however, was one of the quantitative significance of the influence. In this connection, it is valuable to note the statement of one of the best-known writers on Austrian economy, Gustav Stolper. He drew a distinction between the importance of capital invested in houses for the attraction of foreign and domestic credit, writing that, as far as foreign capital is concerned we "can only smile" about such contentions. The Austrian economy follows illusions. Against such illusions it is in vain to quote the fact that agricultural real estate is still not socialized but nevertheless suffers under a choking credit shortage. German industry was able to obtain credits "but we did not hear much about credits on the houses in Berlin. . . . If, therefore, some leading fighters against tenants protection go so far as to hold out a prospect of lower interest rates as a consequence of higher rents, this is ridiculous childishness that can be seriously discussed only in a country where the political leaders are almost without exception economic illiterates. . . ." As far as the domestic situation is concerned, he adds that some insolvency could be prevented, but that compared with the whole situation this is quite insignificant.[215]

---

[213] Cf., for example, *Reichspost,* January 1, 1925, p. 2; Layton and Rist, *op. cit.,* p. 42; Seipel in his speech to the meeting of the Styrian section of the Central Association of Manufacturers, *Die Industrie,* February 8, 1929, pp. 4–6, and almost every speech of the opponents of tenants protection in parliament.

[214] *Die Industrie,* August 9, 1924, pp. 4–9.

[215] G. Stolper, "Mieterschutz," *Der österreichische Volkswirt,* vol. 17 (Feb. 7, 1925), 509–510. Cf. Kautsky, *loc. cit.,* p. 84: "The interest rates would not become lower as

The most important problem, however, was whether or not a restoration of the free housing market would have rendered private building possible, that is to say, how much rents should be raised to make private building profitable. As long as tenants protection existed private building obviously was doomed to torpor. And this despite the fact that new houses were exempt from the stipulations of tenants protection. The first explanation of the situation was that prevailing wages took into account the low legal rents.[216] Second, if there were too wide a margin between the rents in the old and new houses, only a small part of the population could be induced to abandon the old and rent the new. Broadly speaking, both reasons were to a large extent questions of building costs and the rents necessary to justify those costs. The *Volkswirt* published in 1927–1928 two illuminating articles on the problem. After a careful computation of the building-cost index the author of the articles came to the conclusion that increases in wages, cost of building materials, and interest rates would make it necessary to secure rents of about 200 per cent of those of 1913 if private building were to begin again. That is to say, not a simple valorization, but a double valorization of rents would make building of new houses profitable.[217]

The real wages of Austrian workers were extremely low. An International Labor Office comparison of October, 1924, of 16 major cities of the world showed Vienna in next to the last place. Another comparison of October, 1928, including 18 cities showed Vienna in a tie with Rome and Warsaw for the last place but two. Vienna's position is brought into sharper relief by noting that in 1928 the index for Philadelphia was 180, whereas that for Vienna was 42.[218] But thanks to tenants protection money wages were still lower in comparison with other countries. This enabled Austrian industry to maintain a certain position as exporter on the world market, and

---

a consequence of restoration of peace rents, as the example of Germany reveals. However, that would be the only possible advantage because the Austrian economy, so far as it is sound, has obtained credit in sufficient amount—of course at very high rates of interest."

[216] Danneberg, *Was wird aus dem Mieterschutz?* p. 21.

[217] J. Jellinek, "Baukostenindex," *Der österreichische Volkswirt,* vol. 20 (Nov. 26, 1927), 236–239; *idem,* "Mietzins und Wohnbau," *ibid.* (Jan. 14, 1928), 433–436, esp. 436.

[218] See the documents arising out of conferences held at the International Labor Office in January, 1929, and March, 1930, convened by the Social Science Research Council of New York: *International Wage Comparisons* (Manchester University Press), p. 120; *Der österreichische Volkswirt,* vol. 17 (March 7, 1925), 616. In both years real wages in London were used as "100."

it is scarcely necessary to stress the vital importance of exports for the industry of a country which had lost its wide domestic market. At best, however, the export situation of Austrian industry was precarious enough. Separated by long distances from the sea, without sufficient raw materials, with its smaller factories and inadequate rationalization, Austrian industry could successfully compete on the world market, its goods could leap over the tariff walls of foreign countries, only because of the export premium industry received in the form of tenants protection.[219] Abolition of tenants protection would have made increases in wages unavoidable,[220] probably to a higher extent than the actual rent increases, because of workers' pressure. They would have had higher costs of living, not only in the rents they paid, but also in the higher prices of necessities that would have resulted from other higher rents. Furthermore, a rise in wages would involve, for some time at least, an appreciable increase in a large part of the social burdens such as social insurance contributions. These rises would not be confined to industry. Civil servants, a badly underpaid group, would put forward demands for increased salaries and the result would be increased taxation.

All these developments—social unrest, increased unemployment, a wave of strikes and decreased productivity, the disappearance of the export premium for industry—might possibly have been justified had they led to the revival of private building on a large scale.

[219] It could be expected therefore that Austrian industry would be a staunch partisan of tenants protection. This was not so. (Cf. Hauptverband der Industrie Oesterreichs, *Tätigkeitsbericht über die Zeit von Juli bis Ende September 1923*, pp. 3–4.) Though the report speaks in general terms of the advantages of private industry as against collectivism the real reason for this rather surprising circumstance must be sought partly in the fact that the Central Association of Manufacturers was dominated by the representatives of the big iron and steel industries in the states. For them the problem of tenants protection did not exist to the same degree, since most of their workers lived in "company houses" to which the law did not apply. Furthermore, they and other large groups of employers in industry believed that destruction of tenants protection would so weaken the Socialists that a reduction of social burdens would become possible and, on balance, would bring a gain to industrial firms.

[220] Hayek ("Wirkungen der Mietzinsbeschränkungen," *loc. cit.*, p. 262) maintained that since wage level has nothing to do with the living cost of the worker, the abolition of tenants protection would not necessarily lead to an all-round rise in wages. In fact, the increased cost of living might increase the supply of labor and lead to decreases in wages. Such considerations must, again, be dismissed as unrealistic in a country where high permanent unemployment continuously indicated an oversupply of labor and where wages were held by the trade unions at an artificial level. But even this level was so low, the "index" traditions in Austria so strong, and the indignation of the workers concerning suggestions to abolish tenants protection so great, that it is impossible to doubt that raising rents would lead, via a long series of intense social struggles, to increases in wages and thereby in some cases to increased unemployment.

But in view of the whole situation it was clear that this could not be expected. Hayek was correct in citing the fact that even the rents paid by subtenants in Vienna were below the level of rents which would permit profitable building. He used this point as a proof that the rents of the restored free market would be still farther below that level.[221] In another discussion of this topic, he concluded: "I am convinced that in the period immediately following the abolition of the controlled economy [tenants protection] we shall build less than we have built up to now."[222]

Whether or not the house-construction policy of the city council exercised a determining influence on the course of unemployment in Vienna as compared with the states was hotly debated. (Cf. above, Chap. XIII.) In this connection it must be remembered that workers in the building trades were and always had been, after agricultural workers, the largest labor category in Austria. The development of the building market was of decisive importance for unemployment in Vienna.[223] Throughout the whole period of municipal building activities Vienna's share in Austrian unemployment decreased conspicuously, and the Socialists made a reasonably good case in attributing the divergent development there and in the states to their policy.[224] At any rate the abolition of tenants protection and the discontinuance of city building, unless followed by a prompt revival of private building activities, would have had disastrous consequences for the employment situation in the country.

Then why abolish tenants protection? Only to restore "normal conditions"; that is, the income of some thousands of houseowners, many of them inflation speculators, at the cost of severe sacrifices and disturbances throughout the whole economic system? Only to destroy the housing policy of the city of Vienna? The latter reason weighed heavily with the political opponents of Social Democracy, as one of them testified.[225] The argument of economic theory, as usually offered, ran in terms of the scarcity of capital and of the necessity of allowing it to flow into those employments in which it would receive the highest return. The city buildings, which Stolper

[221] *Das Mieterschutzproblem,* p. 13.
[222] *SVfS.,* vol. 182 (1931), 319.
[223] *Wirtschaftsstatistisches Jahrbuch, 1932/33,* p. 430.
[224] Otto Bauer, "Wirtschaftliche und soziale Lage in Oesterreich," Gewerkschaftskongress, 1928, *Protokoll,* p. 406.
[225] Spectator Noricus, *loc. cit.*

called the "national economic counterasset against the depreciation of private houses,"[226] were regarded as impediments to capital formation in the optimum configuration. It is true that more than 700 million schillings were invested in the houses without interest and amortization on the invested capital because of the rent policy. The myopic sight of the theorists did not discern that interest on the invested capital was paid to the national economy in the forms of improved health and higher productivity of labor. And, moreover, the theorists forgot that the habits of inflationary times had left tendencies to excessive consumption so that the policy of the city council, far from preventing capital formation, actually rendered it compulsory in a great number of cases.

A great deal of the criticism launched against "city houses" does not deserve much attention. The problem "taxes or loans" was dealt with in the chapter on taxation. That continuous building, as planned by the city, was incompatible with financing by loans is self-evident.[227] Only as a curiosity it may be mentioned that when the Socialists planned in 1922 to use the proceeds of the rent tax for floating a loan for housing purposes the Christian Social press indignantly criticized the city because it was going to use "the groschen of poor people for transactions with capitalist banks."[228]

Complaints against the poor style of the "barracks cities"[229] were expressed with particular unction. So far as this criticism was genuine and not biased by political preconceptions, it may be said that the critics apparently were unable to understand the beauty of architectural constructions which were dominated by the principle *artis sola domina necessitas* and displayed a wonderful simplicity and purity of design.

The charge of the high cost of city building was likewise never forgotten by the opponents.[230] Frequent repetition did not alter the character of these statements. The reasons which enabled the city council to build at low prices have been mentioned. Even if the

---

226 Stolper, "Mieterschutz," *Der österreichische Volkswirt*, vol. 17 (Jan. 31, 1925), 481.

227 Cf. Hardy, *op. cit.*, pp. 112–113.

228 *Reichspost*, February 2, 1922, p. 6.

229 For example, among many others, Jehly, *Zehn Jahre Rotes Wien*, p. 40.

230 Cf. *ibid.*; Kunschak (quoted by *Arbeiter Zeitung*, February 9, 1927, p. 1): "I am a resolute opponent of dwelling-house building by the city . . . because the city builds poorly and dearly"; Kunschak's similar speech in parliament, Nationalrat, *Protokoll*, October 4, 1928, p. 1661; Rintelen's speech, *ibid.*, p. 1691.

abolition of tenants protection would at once raise land prices, the fact remains that city building could avail itself of all the advantages of a big and monopsonist undertaking.[231]

Closely connected with this kind of criticism was the ever-recurring charge of corruption in the city council. These allegations were proved libelous when the federal comptroller's office obtained the right to check the accounts and came to the conclusion that the city council building presented "a performance exact and correct even unto the smallest detail"—a performance that took into account the necessity of making the most of available resources "through a series of purposeful measures, particularly through centralized procurement of building materials and through the mass production of individual building units [doors, window frames] as a result of their standardization."[232]

The epithet "Bolshevism" was ever on the lips of the political opponents of Austrian Social Democracy. They were particularly fond of using it against the housing policy.[233] Not to controvert these meaningless charges, but to supply additional information on the ideological origins of that policy reference may be made to the direct line of thought which connects the works—not of Marx and Engels, but of Adolf Wagner, the great German economist and social reformer[234]—with the practical activities of postwar Vienna. Some connections with German land reform, particularly as advocated by Henry George's prophet, Adolf Damaschke, likewise existed,

[231] "It is beyond doubt that the city builds more cheaply than private individuals... dwelling construction by the city means rationalization and lowering of cost in building activity and thereby a profit for the national economy." Stolper, "Mieterschutz," *Der österreichische Volkswirt,* vol. 17 (Jan. 24, 1925), 453; but cf. Hardy, *op. cit.,* p. 115, for a view contrary to Stolper's. Hardy does not conclude that municipal construction was "dear"; only that judgments such as Stolper's were not proved. As is clear I am convinced that the evidence shows Hardy to be in error.

[232] Quoted by Winter, *loc. cit.,* p. 118. This author, a Catholic scholar, rejects the charge of "terror": "In spite of... the much criticized nonpublic allocation of contracts in the field of building and of dwellings in the city houses, the city offices today probably do not exercise a fraction of the terror which Lueger not only applied but also admitted in programmatic frankness." *Ibid.,* p. 123.

[233] To cite two instances from the hundreds that can easily be supplied: Pistor's speech in parliament, Nationalrat, *Protokoll,* October 4, 1928, p. 1681; *Reichspost,* January 31, 1922, p. 5. The *Volkswirt* made a special point of publishing from time to time little notes on tenants protection and municipal building policy in England, representing the Conservative British government as "housing Bolshevists." *Der österreichische Volkswirt,* vol. 17 (Feb. 21, 1925), 564; *ibid.* (March 7, 1925), p. 616; *ibid.* (April 25, 1925), p. 814.

[234] *Grundlegung der politischen Oekonomie,* Part 2 (Leipzig, 1894), esp. pp. 481–507 where the author severely criticizes the effects of private land and house property and, even though cautiously, advocates their municipalization.

although both sides probably would not admit it.[235] Finally, it is appropriate to refer again to the influence of the leaders of Revisionism and of Fabianism. All these men certainly had nothing to do with Bolshevism.

In a similar category of obfuscation belong the demands that the city administration should transfer its houses to the landlords' association of Vienna. The buildings were claimed to be the lawful property of the members of this group since they had been built with tax money which rightly should have gone as rent to the house-owners.[236]

The mutually annihilating allegations that the city houses were built as fortresses for the contingency of civil war and that they were flimsy and shoddy beyond belief are discussed at length in the chapter on the events of February, 1934, as is the charge that they were placed at points of strategic military importance. Another accusation may be disposed of here. Opponents of the housing program insist that it was in part a scheme to introduce proletarian voters into what had been strictly bourgeois districts. Some former Austrian Socialists grant that in one or two instances this might have been done to influence the results of the elections for district councils and district administrators. They, and others who deny the charge completely, point out that under the proportional electoral system in use such "electoral arithmetic" would have been to no avail in balloting for members of parliament or the city council. The evidence warrants the categorical statement of Dr. Hardy that, "The distribution [of the buildings], as shown on the map, does not support this charge."[237]

There remains for discussion the problem of tenement houses *versus* cottage settlements. As shown, the overwhelming majority of the new Vienna dwellings were in large buildings. This policy also was severely criticized by Christian Social opponents. They maintained verbally that sound family life can develop only in a garden

[235] A. Damaschke, *Marxismus und Bodenreform* (Jena, 1926), p. 29.

[236] E. Hoffmannsthal, "Das schutzlose Realeigentum in Oesterreich," *Deutsches Wohnungsarchiv*, vol. 4 (May, 1929), 195–199. Note also the demand of the Christian Social *Wiener Stimmen* that the city provide every Viennese with shares in the city houses because they had been built with tax money of the population of Vienna. The *Volkswirt* thereupon suggested a distribution of the contents of the art museums in Vienna among the taxpayers of the city. *Der österreichische Volkswirt*, vol. 18 (Feb. 6, 1926), 496.

[237] Hardy, *op cit.*, p. 59 n.

cottage[238] despite the fact that they were working hand in glove with the landlords of the slums and were solicitously avoiding any action that would, through competition, harm the interests of those landlords. In other words, since, in the seventeen years of their peacetime domination of Vienna, the Catholic politicians did nothing of importance to correct housing conditions and, after February, 1934, almost completely stopped city building activities, their complaints do not deserve any attention. But on this score the city received sharp criticism from much more serious sources. During the International Housing and Town Planning Congress in Vienna in 1926 it became evident that the majority of the delegates believed that the city houses were in every respect inferior to cottage settlements.[239] Representatives of the city council tried to justify its position. They explained that in order to provide cottage accommodations for the same number of people they had placed in tenement houses a garden city of 7.5 square kilometers would have been necessary. For this purpose appropriate land could be found only on the left bank of the Danube, 8 to 10 kilometers from the population center of the city. This would have involved construction of a subway connection at a cost of 260 million schillings, about one-third of the total investment in housing from 1923 to 1933. Furthermore, it would have been necessary to build a large sewage system; install gas, water, and electric current; and construct schools, official buildings, fire houses, and so on.[240] The tremendous costs of this plan had compelled the city to give preference to tenement houses. These considerations certainly deserve attention, for the house-building program started and continued under conditions of pressing housing scarcity so that the city had to build as cheaply and as quickly as possible.[241] It may he added, however, that the Social Democratic party did not regret too much that apartments had to be chosen. Its leaders scarcely feared, as was often suggested, that the population of cottage settlements would go over to the enemies of the party. In fact, the constituencies in such settlements as Laaerberg had estab-

[238] Cf., for example, *Wien im Aufbau: Wohnungswesen,* p. 5.

[239] International Housing and Town Planning Congress, *Report,* Part III (Vienna, 1926), pp. 70, 97, 115, 116.

[240] *Ibid., Papers,* I, 152, *Report,* Part III, 98–101.

[241] The International Congresses for New Building in 1929 and 1930 recognized that in the existing situation building of tenement houses with dwellings of small size was well justified. *Hochland,* vol. 28 (May, 1931), 119–120.

lished records in Socialist votes. This is not surprising in the conditions of a quasi village where the Socialist coöperative was the social center of the community. But it is entirely possible that it was some kind of *embourgeoisement* which the Socialists were hesitating to further;[242] they may have felt apprehensive that when next called to demonstrate on the Ringstrasse for school reform, or unemployment benefit, or even for tenants protection and building policy, the cottage settler would reply with the words of Candide: "Cela est bien dit ... mais il faut cultiver notre jardin."[243] Therefore, it is probable that for the time being the workers' party of Vienna was well satisfied with a solution which seemed to increase its striking power.

LAST PHASE: FASCIST PRESSURE AND THE REFORMS OF 1929

The foregoing presentation of the history of the struggles for and against tenants protection permits the exact formulation of certain conclusions already indicated. First, tenants protection and its corollary, the building policy of Vienna, enjoyed the support of a large part of the Austrian population and could, therefore, be successfully defended in parliament against an opposing majority. Second, the weak points in the case for tenants protection derived chiefly from inability to allocate continually the vacant dwellings to persons who needed them urgently. Third, as long as the Socialists advanced victoriously from election to election they could hope that in a not too remote future they would be able to obtain the majority and to reinstitute the requisitioning of dwellings. This hope, actually a conviction for some years, caused them to regard the shortcomings of the system of tenants protection as temporary, and aided them in pacifying a degree of discontent with the system which was becoming apparent in Socialist circles outside Vienna.

The expiration of the requisitioning law was felt much more severely in the states than in the capital. Some of the industrial cities had been carrying on building activities with borrowed money. As was to be expected, after a few years the service on these loans

---

[242] Cf. H. De Man, *The Psychology of Socialism* (New York, n.d.), p. 75: "Marxists have always been inclined to condemn the work of building societies, the provision of allotments, the encouragement of the back-to-the-land movement, and so on, as concessions to petty-bourgeois tendencies."

[243] Voltaire, *Candide ou l'optimisme* in *Oeuvres Choisies* (Paris, Édition du Centaire, 1878), p. 124.

had assumed a magnitude which rendered continuation of building prohibitive.[244]

The events of July, 1927, and their consequences made the situation far more critical; in fact, it has been stated by numerous commentators that the political power relationships in Austria had been radically altered by Seipel's staunch refusal to be moved out of office by the riots and by the subsequent collapse of the general strike. This is an oversimplification. Those relationships had been altered by the events and consequences of July per se; but perhaps more important was the complete revelation of an alteration that had been taking place over a period of years. The Social Democrats now realized that they had been mistaken in supposing that the police, gendarmery, and army would not fire upon demonstrators, strikers, and party members because many members of these executive organs were themselves carrying trade union and party cards.[245]

It is true that before calling off the strike the Socialists had obtained Seipel's promise not to avail himself of the situation in order to start immediately a general attack on social legislation. And Seipel kept this promise faithfully. But the whole outlook for the democratic development of the party until it attained the majority was changed. The by-elections after July, 1927, even brought some further increases in Socialist votes. But this was of less importance now. Up to 1927 the Heimwehr movement had been active only intermittently in political life. In July, 1927, it had been instrumental in breaking the railroad strike in Styria and Tirol. The government, that is to say, Seipel, determined to use the Heimwehr to introduce reforms which would have completely changed the political and social structure of the state and gravely reduced the power of the workers' party and the trade unions. Essentially this was nothing more than a revival of the plan formulated by the bankers and industrialists in 1921 and recorded by the Christian Social chancellor, Streeruwitz, but now the driving force of Seipel was behind

[244] Cf. the speech of Mehr, vice-mayor of Linz, to the 1928 party congress: "The municipalities are at the end of their strength. They are all so much in debt that they have no possibility whatsoever of securing credit for building dwellings. Linz, a city with more than 100,000 inhabitants, has up to now spent 11 million schillings for the construction of dwellings. These 11 millions, of course, came exclusively from credits. . . . We have completed and rented 700 dwellings, but 3,000 families were on the urgent waiting list. . . . At the same time, however, 300 dwellings in Linz stand vacant but cannot be occupied because of the lack of a requisitioning law." *Parteitag, 1928,* p. 34.

[245] For a more detailed presentation of this point, cf. Chap. XX, pp. 751–752.

it. The result was a substantial change in the policy of the labor party. The period of struggle for majority came to a close. Not to use democracy for final victory, but to preserve the democratic character of the republic became the objective of the working-class movement. The problem of tenants protection could not fail to be decisively affected by these developments.

In February, 1928, the government prepared a new rent bill which it did not submit to parliament; only the association of judges, chambers of labor, chambers of commerce, employers' associations, and similar bodies were asked to state their opinions. The bill introduced a new idea in attempting to fix the rents in accordance with the space in cubic meters. The artificiality of this method and the general lack of clarity in further stipulations concerning the raising of rents by state rent commissions led to an all-round rejection of the bill.[246] But this was only an interlude. In the summer of 1928 the government introduced another bill,[247] more cautiously formulated than its predecessors. It stipulated much more gradual increases in rents, so that not until 1940 would a rent of 60 groschen per peace crown in Vienna, and of 65 and 70 groschen, respectively, for state capitals and the rest of the country, be reached. In addition it provided that "free agreements" between tenants and landlords might fix rents at any level.

Meanwhile, Fascist pressure increased. Threats against parliamentarism and democracy were on the agenda of the day. Heimwehr leaders declared that if the parliament did not demonstrate its ability to solve the urgent problems and to solve them in a way approved by the Heimwehr movement, they would not shrink from destroying the parliamentary system by violence. A Heimwehr mass demonstration was planned for October 7, 1928, in Wiener-Neustadt, an industrial town near Vienna, long a citadel of Social Democracy and the originating point of the January, 1918, strikes against the continuation of the war. Thus the Heimwehr plan was a direct provocation to labor and caused wide excitement throughout the country. The Socialists decided on a counterdemonstration of their much more numerous adherents. Many people held that the seventh would lead to an outbreak of civil war.[248] The connec-

[246] Danneberg, *Die Geschichte des Mieterschutzes in Oesterreich,* pp. 6–12.
[247] Nationalrat, *Protokoll, Beilagen,* Nr. 192, pp. 1–2.
[248] For a detailed discussion of this episode, see Vol. II, Chap. XXI, pp. 790–802.

tion between these developments and tenants protection was not far to seek; tenants protection was one of the "urgent problems." And in September the *Arbeiter Zeitung* was able to publish a report on a secret Heimwehr meeting in which the forthcoming "conquest of Wiener-Neustadt" was explained as necessary because of the imminent discussions on tenants protection in parliament. If the Heimwehr demands were not complied with in parliament, civil war would start.[249] The landlords soon formed one of the most radical elements in the Heimwehr and supported its intensified activities, particularly in Vienna, with propaganda and large financial subventions.[250]

The Social Democratic party congress of September, 1928, found itself in a difficult position. On one hand, the Heimwehr was exerting severe pressure. On the other, the hopes of restoring the requisitioning law in a reasonably short time, if at all, had vanished, and as time went by the situation was becoming more and more critical and the voices of the Socialists in the states more and more urgent. These special reasons, in addition to the general situation which had developed, caused the party congress to give an extraordinary amount of attention to the problem of tenants protection. In his main speech Otto Bauer formulated a program along the following lines: The parliament elected in 1927 on the Christian Social promise, "tenants protection *is* secured," had no right to do away with tenants protection. Only the people had the right to decide by new general elections or by a plebiscite. But the Socialists recognized the necessity of solving the housing problem in Austria and of providing accommodations for the needs of the young generation. Bauer conceded that even in Vienna, in spite of building activity, it had been impossible to overcome the shortage. Since private building was ruled out by the unbearable rents in the new houses, only public building activities on the largest scale with participation of the federal state could alleviate the situation. The party, he said, was always ready to commence serious negotiations on this problem. The position he thought the party should take in such negotiations was made clear by his demands for an allocation law, as a milder substitute for the old requisitioning act, for the establishment of

[249] *Arbeiter Zeitung*, September 11, 1928, p. 3.

[250] *Jahrbuch der österreichischen Arbeiterbewegung, 1929*, pp. 53–56, citing numerous passages from landlord publications.

an equalization fund, and for an expropriation act. The last would facilitate public building activities. The pending rent bill of the government, the only objective of which was to increase the landlords' income without remedying the housing situation, was rejected by Bauer.[251]

The congress unanimously adopted Bauer's resolution.[252] Its objective was to secure tenants protection as a permanent institution. But it was recognized that the preferred road to that objective, the attainment of a parliamentary majority, was blocked for the indefinite future. The changed situation was emphasized not so much by the wording of the resolution as by the fact that the Social Democrats were now willing to negotiate on the tenants protection issue after they had, for years, rejected almost any contact with majority parties on it.

On October 3, 1928, the first reading of the rent bill began in parliament. Because of Socialist tactics this reading lasted, in daily meetings, until October 12. These tactics were less an outright obstruction than an indication that the party was still resolved to resist the abolition of tenants protection. The bill went to the housing committee where the first filibustering speech of a Socialist member filled the meetings from November 14 to November 27. On the thirtieth Seipel and Kienböck appeared in the committee and proposed a bill concerning federal promotion of private building. The funds were to be obtained from a general tax on tenants.[253]

The Socialists answered with elaborate counterproposals, based primarily on the principles laid down by the party congress. On December 20, 1928, two days after the Constitutional Court had rejected the appeal of two states to declare the tenants protection act unconstitutional, the following agreement was reached between the parties and announced in an official statement.

> The general debate in the housing committee will be interrupted. The registered speakers remain on the list. The housing committee will elect

[251] *Parteitag, 1928,* pp. 18–27.

[252] *Ibid.,* pp. 4–6. Very important was the admission: "Social Democracy does not fail to recognize that the expiration of the requisitioning act and the fact that municipalities outside of Vienna partly do not build at all and partly have been able to build only with borrowed money have created . . . unendurable conditions" (p. 6).

[253] As Spectator Noricus stated, this proposal was made in order to counteract the Social Democratic propaganda and to make the government's bill more popular. *Loc. cit.* It is enlightening that this excellently informed writer gives only political reasons for Seipel's action.

a subcommittee to which all bills and motions, present and future, are to be submitted. The subcommittee will attempt by serious work to reach, before the end of February, an agreement on the whole complex of the housing problem. If an agreement should prove impossible in the subcommittee, the chairmen of the parties will convene again and decide on the further treatment of the subject, which will take place either in the subcommittee, the committee, or in the meetings of parliament. There is an agreement among the parties that the housing committee will not be convoked before agreement among the chairmen of the parties has been reached on the procedure in the further treatment of the matter. The representatives of the Social Democratic Association [of deputies] declare that they will not object at any time to the convocation of the housing committee if they obtain the guarantee that the final decision on the rent bill remains with the people.[254]

Negotiations were resumed, but they proceeded in an atmosphere of Heimwehr threats of *coup d'état* and civil war. On February 14, 1929, the police occupied Socialist party headquarters in Vienna and searched for arms. In labor circles this was held to be an intolerable provocation. For some time during the search the leaders even considered summoning the workers to the party building. The result of the government's drastic action was immediate discontinuance of negotiations on the housing issue. The housing committee was resummoned for April 3, 1929. In this meeting, the Socialists were prepared to announce that negotiations had been fruitless and to resume obstruction. Then, half an hour before the committee was to meet, Seipel resigned. A new political situation had been created.

The Christian Socials announced that a radical change in the internal policy of the government was imminent, but demanded settlement of the pressing problems, first and foremost of tenants protection, before the new cabinet should be elected. After a month of intense negotiations, which several times were discontinued and resumed, a compromise was reached. Streeruwitz, a man of proconstitutional attitude, became chancellor.

On June 14, 1929, the Streeruwitz government attained its "first highly important success"[255]—the reform of tenants protection. The changes were embodied in three laws.[256] The first of them dealt pri-

[254] *Jahrbuch der österreichischen Arbeiterbewegung, 1928,* pp. 143–144.

[255] Kunschak, *op. cit.*, p. 108.

[256] *BGBl.*, 1929, Nr. 200, 201, 202. Since the section (*III Abschnitt*) of Nr. 200 which deals with rents is actually only a list of the changes in the law of 1922 as amended in 1925, the student will find Nr. 210 *ex* 1929 much more convenient; it presents the final form of the law on rents after June 14.

marily with changes in the rent law and with the promotion of building activities. Under the new stipulations there were three components of the rent instead of the four of the statute of 1922. A so-called main rent replaced the basic rent and maintenance rent, but the landlord was supposed to meet ordinary maintenance costs out of the main rent.[257] The other two were the tenant's share of the operating costs and of the taxes (with certain exceptions) as they had been since 1922. For the purposes of the main rent three groups were differentiated: Vienna, the larger cities in the states, and the rest of the country. Maximum permissible rents were to be raised on the dates and to the levels shown below:[258]

	Group I	Group II	Group III
	(in groschen per crown of peace rent)		
August 1, 1929	20	25	30
August 1, 1930	24	30	36
August 1, 1931	27	34	40

It was argued that higher increases were justified outside Vienna because the peace rents had been lower there, whereas the 1929 level of maintenance cost was equal throughout the country. For a dwelling let after the law had gone into effect, an additional increase in the main rent of 20 groschen per crown of peace rent was allowable. "Free agreements" were permissible after the rent contract had been in effect for six months, but only in the higher categories of dwellings. Vienna tenants again were treated more favorably in this respect.[259] If the rents were still insufficient for maintenance purposes they could be raised by the rent commissions. The tenants' auditing or checking rights on the use of maintenance funds were curtailed, but if the landlord claimed that major repair work was necessary, the tenants could demand that any excesses in "maintenance" or "main" rents over actual costs during the last three years should be used for this purpose.

One other feature of that part of the first law of June 14 dealing

[257] *BGBl.*, 1929, Nr. 210, § 6.

[258] For dwellings in Vienna with an annual peace rent from 1,000 crowns upward and business premises with a peace rent of 1,200 crowns upward, the respective figures were 23, 27, and 30 groschen.

[259] This was one of the most difficult points of the negotiations. For some time it seemed that "free agreements" would be allowed without restrictions. The unexpected result was an outburst of criticism in the major bourgeois press, which, in turn, induced the *Volkswirt* to make sarcastic remarks about the newly converted "housing Bolsheviks." *Der österreichische Volkswirt*, vol. 21 (May 4, 1929), 817.

with rents deserves particular mention because it resolved the old problem of the equalization fund. The method was the rather extraordinary one of repealing Article 11 of the law of 1922 that had authorized such funds and announcing, through the report of the housing committee of the Nationalrat, that the states already had the authority to create equalization funds without a federal enabling act and that even the communities had the authority if they did not raise the funds by creating some new source of income. The city council of Vienna took advantage of the new situation by a resolution of June 25, 1929.[260]

The building-promotion scheme included in the first law provided for indirect federal subventions to builders, who might be private individuals building for their own use, speculative contractors, coöperative building assocations, or communities. The inclusion of the latter two was a victory for the workers' party since the original plan had been to limit assistance to individuals. The prospective builder had to show that he or it owned the ground or had the right to build thereon. Second, he had to show that he could from his own means provide at least 10 per cent of the total necessary (20 per cent for a single family house). The value of the land or the building right was included in these percentages. Next, he had to demonstrate that he could secure a first mortgage which, together with his own means, would cover 40 per cent of the costs (50 per cent for a single family house). Finally, he had to show that, under the assumption that a federal subvention would be forthcoming, a mortgage institution was willing to lend him the remaining 60, or 50, per cent of the necessary sum. To raise the money for these second mortgage loans the financial institutions were authorized to issue bonds which bore a maximum interest of 7 per cent over a maximum period of forty years. The federal government guaranteed the interest and amortization of the bonds. The property owner, however, paid only 1 per cent interest on the second mortgage, and this to the federal state. The owner also paid the federation 60 per cent of the net returns on the building as a contribution to the amortization of the second mortgage.[261] To finance the obligations it had thus assumed the government introduced a

[260] *BGBl.*, 1929, Nr. 200, III Abschnitt, Artikel I, 23; Danneberg, *Das neue Mietengesetz* (Wien, 1929), p. 154.

[261] Certain categories of builders paid a fixed percentage amortization.

new tax on tenants of 1 groschen per crown of prewar rent which the executive committee of the Nationalrat was authorized to raise to 2 or 3 groschen. The tax and the subventions were to cease after December 31, 1932. Contemporary estimates were that about 450 million schillings would be put into some 30,000 new dwellings as a result of the plan. Since the purpose was to encourage the construction of small- and medium-sized dwellings subventions were to be granted only for those of 100 square meters or less floor space, or, in exceptional circumstances, up to 130 square meters. Dwellings built by or for communities or states, however, could not exceed 60 square meters.[262]

The second of the 1929 laws gave to Vienna the right to allocate certain dwellings. Since it was limited to those vacated because the tenant had obtained a new apartment in a house built in whole or in part from public funds, and since the allocation could take place only after the dwelling had been vacant for two months, the scheme was of little importance.

The last of the three statutes replaced the old expropriation act of February 4, 1919, and gave to all communities in the country a much more satisfactory basis on which to purchase land and carry out slum clearance projects.

It is appropriate now to turn to an appraisal of the reforms and their effects. In order to estimate the actual increases in rents brought by the new system it is necessary to remember that individual increases of maintenance rent had considerably raised its average level and consequently that of total rent. Unfortunately no exact statistics are available. It is known that from 1923 through 1927 a total of 34,868 cases of increases in maintenance rent were approved in one way or another by Vienna rent boards and that the sum involved was 140.6 millions of schillings.[263] In 1928 there were 7,607 increases totaling 35.2 millions. During the first half of 1929, that is, just before the new law was approved, the figures were 4,356

[262] An interesting by-product of the new legislation deserves mention. Vienna still had its antiquated building ordinance. Between 1919 and 1929 this was no practical disadvantage because the city was the only builder of mass dwellings. With the adoption of the laws of 1929 the situation was expected to change, and so the city council hastened to introduce a new code in conformity with modern requirements. Since the Socialists had frequently and bitterly denounced the old ordinance in the Lueger era, their procrastination, from the viewpoint of principle, was inexcusable.

[263] Danneberg, *Geschichte des Mieterschutzes in Oesterreich,* pp. 7, 8.

and 18.1 millions.[264] The distribution of increases during these six months appeared as follows:

Increases up to	5 groschen per 1 crown peace rent....	925
" " "	10 " " " " " "	831
" " "	12 " " " " " "	376
" " "	14 " " " " " "	358
" " "	16 " " " " " "	306
" " "	18 " " " " " "	321
" " "	20 " " " " " "	285
" " "	25 " " " " " "	393
" " "	30 " " " " " "	267
"	of more than 30 groschen per 1 crown peace rent	294
Total	....	4,356

The figures do not give a complete picture, of course; tenants developed an increasing willingness to agree to advances in maintenance rent without going to the rent boards. Contemporary estimates were that in 1928 and the spring of 1929 average total rents amounted to about 15 or 16 groschen per crown of peace rent in Vienna.[265] Therefore, the increases in rents under the new law were by no means so great as a comparison with the general initial stipulations of the act of 1922 would indicate. If the estimates just quoted are accepted, however, the main rent alone in August, 1929, was 25 per cent above total rent in Vienna a few months earlier and in August, 1931, was about 69 per cent above. If the movement of the index of housing expenditure in the general Austrian cost of living index is followed, the conclusion is reached that the reform increased housing costs in 1929–1931 by about 82 per cent—the index being 2,157 (1914 = 1) in July, 1929, 3,074 in August, 1929, 3,630 in August, 1930, and 3,926 in August, 1931.[266]

According to the investigations of the Vienna chamber of labor, housing costs represented, in 1928, 3.40 per cent of the total expenditure of a worker's family; in 1932, 5.41 per cent. This, however, gives only an imperfect picture because the studies were largely confined to workers' families with a relatively high standard of living.[267]

---

264 *Wirtschaftsstatistisches Jahrbuch, 1928,* p. 435; *ibid., 1929/30,* p. 505.

265 *Jahrbuch der österreichischen Arbeiterbewegung, 1929,* p. 119; *SVfS.,* vol. 177, pt. 3 (1930), 80.

266 *SHfRO.,* vol. 10, p. 141; vol. 11, p. 144; vol. 12, p. 146.

267 *Wirtschaftsstatistisches Jahrbuch, 1928,* p. 375; *1932/33,* p. 332.

After the increases of the reform had been carried out the annual rent for a worker's small apartment in Vienna (which had cost 360 gold crowns in 1914) amounted to about 130 schillings. In other words, the reformed rent amounted to about 25 per cent of the prewar rent in gold.

ANNUAL RENT FOR A WORKER'S APARTMENT*
(in schillings)

Main rent (360 times 27)	97.20
Housing tax	10.80
Rent groschen tax	10.80
Running costs	10.55
Total	129.35

* Türr, *op. cit.*, p. 224.

The burden of the tenants was appreciably increased. For the first time since the war the landlord received a net income. Its amount probably varied between 5 and 10 groschen, about 3.5 to 7 gold heller, per crown of peace rent. Since in prewar times he had received from 20 to 25 per cent of the rent as net income, the new law formally restored about 20 per cent of his prewar returns. Actually his net income was increased to a higher degree because his *obligation* to carry out maintenance work was not so precisely set forth as before. Otherwise stated, the stipulations of the law directly induced the landlord to postpone maintenance expenditures until after the expiration of the three-year period in which tenants could demand the use of part of the main rent for repair purposes and then to claim additional payments from the tenant. For some years the city of Vienna had been granting landlords special credits at low interest for maintenance expenditures. It is significant that after 1929 they made less and less use of this opportunity. The volume of credits amounted to 7.5 million schillings in 1928; 5.8 million in 1929; 3 million in 1930; and 2.2 million in 1931.[268] This distinctly reveals a tendency which became apparent as a consequence of the law; namely, for the landlords to consume a substantial part of the rent which prior to the reform had been given over to maintenance of the house. From the point of view of the national economy, therefore, it may be argued that the reform led to an undesirable result.

[268] *Wirtschaftsstatistisches Jahrbuch, 1931/32*, p. 407.

The increases in rents and the restoration of a small net income to the landlords could scarcely be expected to stimulate building activities. To that extent a contributor to the *Volkswirt* was certainly correct in maintaining that this restoration had no economic sense.[269] It is clear that there was no organic connection between the advances in rents and the building-promotion scheme. But, as was shown, the connection was established through a political compromise. Therefore, had the promotion plan led to an alleviation of the housing shortage, the reform of tenants protection might have been justified from a political point of view. Unfortunately, the way in which it was carried out gave many grounds for disappointment. It is impossible to record here the long and painful story of the struggles which took place from 1929 to 1931 in the special committee set up in the ministry of social administration to examine applications for credits. Suffice it to note the results of the federal building-promotion scheme.

As mentioned before, the expectation was that 30,000 dwellings would be built. On the day of the adoption of the laws in parliament the Christian Social member Kollmann, former minister of finance of the republic, even spoke of 40,000 dwellings.[270] The average cost of a dwelling was expected to be 15,000 schillings. As soon as the scheme went into effect, however, it became apparent that the tendency of the majority of the committee was to grant credits on dwellings the cost of which largely exceeded the original plans. Substantial sums were granted for villas and luxury apartments built in most expensive districts. The costs of some of these dwellings exceeded 100,000 schillings and the average cost of the 130 single family houses approved was 70,500.[271] Even the Christian Social *Weltblatt* found this impossible to stomach for it wrote on January 10, 1932: "The federation erects villas and houses for its wards [*Protektionskinder*]. Naturally, the people foot the bill. . . ."[272] On the other hand, the committee and the minister were very hesitant, particularly at the beginning, in granting credits to municipalities, especially to Vienna. Innitzer, then minister of social administration, justified this policy in parliament by saying that the city of

[269] Franz Klein, "Mietenfriede," *Der österreichische Volkswirt,* vol. 21 (June 15, 1929), 991.
[270] Nationalrat, *Protokoll,* June 13, 1929, p. 2657.
[271] Anon., *Antimarxistische Wohnbaupolitik* (Wien, 1932), p. 12.
[272] Quoted in *ibid.,* p. 18.

Vienna charged rents which were too low and that this presented "a grave danger to private building activities."[273] Christian Social undertakings as well as Catholic institutions were favored. The committee held that the social qualification of the builder was irrelevant and that the only intention of the law was to promote building and thus to decrease unemployment. But this was not correct, even from this narrow viewpoint, because in a number of cases credits were granted for luxurious dwellings which would have been built in any case. As a matter of fact, the first effect of the new system was actually to slow down private building activities; since subsidies could not be granted for houses already under construction, not a few individuals preferred to wait until the red tape could be unwound and assistance provided.[274]

Up to December 31, 1931, 15,812 dwellings were built at a total cost of 364.6 million schillings; that is, at an average cost of about 23,000.[275] This average, however, is held down by the cheap dwellings built by the municipalities with federal subventions. For Vienna alone it is possible to deduct these dwellings. The average cost there for the others then rises to more than 40,000 schillings.[276] Against this policy "it had been rightly said that the federal funds were raised by a groschen rent tax imposed on every tenant in Austria; and that, therefore, the proceeds should have been used for social purposes."[277] With the amount of 364.6 million schillings the building-promotion scheme was as good as exhausted. The remainder was insignificant. It may be added, in view of the foregoing, that the importance of the whole plan is not to be exaggerated. If the actual results of the scheme are compared with the program laid down by the Social Democratic party congress of 1928, in which continued building activities by public bodies were demanded in order to secure tenants protection permanently, the conclusion is that the Socialists did not get the better part of the compromise concluded in the spring of 1929.

But why did the Socialists strike what seemed even in 1929 a bargain of dubious value from their point of view? Seipel's resignation

---

[273] Nationalrat, *Protokoll*, July 2, 1930, p. 4039.

[274] Richard Kerschagl, "Wohnbauförderungsgesetzgebung nach der letzten Mietenreform in Oesterreich," *Deutsches Wohnungsarchiv*, vol. 4 (Dec., 1929), 571–572.

[275] *Wirtschaftsstatistisches Jahrbuch, 1931/32*, p. 403.

[276] *Antimarxistische Wohnbaupolitik*, p. 12.

[277] Bunzel, *loc. cit.*, p. 137.

in April, 1929, appears, in the light of subsequent history, not as an act of exasperation, as an admission of defeat, but as a link in an ingenious chain of political moves. After having exercised pressure on the workers' representatives for months through the medium of the Heimwehr movement, he considered them ripe for a compromise on tenants protection, withdrew into the background, and let Streeruwitz come to terms with them. They gladly seized the proffered hand of the new man. Their chief problem was to clear away the continuous threat of Fascism and civil war held warningly over their heads by Seipel and his Heimwehr. The latter continued to deride parliamentarism. They spoke scornfully of the "gossip joint" (*Quatschbude*) which was unable to perform the necessary legislative work. The Streeruwitz government made it possible for the Socialists to show that with the right man as head of the cabinet the parliament could work, and work quickly. This, they thought, would restore the reputation of the legislature. But they were badly mistaken. When the weapon of tenants protection—one of the most powerful in the arsenal of the Social Democrats—had been satisfactorily blunted, the "black man" behind the stage pulled his strings again, the marionette Streeruwitz disappeared,[278] and the big attack of the Heimwehr upon the constitution of the republic was launched. The great diplomat of the Austrian counterrevolution had completed his masterpiece.

Conclusion

The last dramatic chapter in the history of tenants protection in Austria is quickly told. Paradoxical as it is, the system survived the party which *in hoc signo* had fought some of its fiercest battles. The constitutional weakness of Austrian Fascism prevented the Dollfuss and Schuschnigg regimes from giving the *coup de grace* to an institution which their members had so often and so bitterly denounced as Bolshevism and Communism.

It was the housing policy of Social Democratic Vienna which was the victim. The building of healthy dwellings for the people of Vienna was discontinued when people's rule in Austria came to a temporary close. The cannons of Austrian Fascism brought death

[278] E. Streeruwitz, *Springflut über Osterreich* (Wien, 1937), pp. 419–420. Some Austrian Socialists believe that Seipel succeeded in wresting this weapon from their leaders completely.

and destruction into dwellings destined for life and happiness. But it was in vain. Probably more than anything else the "city houses" had made the Vienna worker realize that he was not a propertyless stranger in a society that was not his. In looking at their massive contours he experienced the same pride which the medieval baron felt when he looked at the walls of his castle. "The stones will speak!" In the days when a brutal dictatorship ordered and commanded, when liberty and peace were trodden under foot, the stone witnesses of a ten-year building policy reminded the men and women of Vienna of the peaceful forces of democracy which created through the people and for the people. They helped to keep aglow the longing for a freedom which has come again.

CHAPTER XV

Welfare Work

VARIOUS MEASURES designed to protect workers and salaried employees have been discussed in the chapter on social and labor legislation. Welfare work[1] partly supplements such legislation and partly extends its aims beyond the groups directly protected. Thus it contributes toward the attainment of the final goal of both types of activity; namely, the "uplift of the people, and thereby of the individual as a part of the whole, in economic, physical, intellectual, and moral respects."[2] With this objective in mind the Austrian Socialists tried to coördinate an extensive system of social work with their other activities in order to secure the welfare of all members of society. Most of the welfare work to be described in this chapter came under the jurisdiction of the cities and states. The political situation in Austria caused the Social Democrats to center their activities in Vienna which alone had the political will and the financial and legislative power to enact the welfare measures envisaged by the party. In the rest of Austria welfare activities in excess of the obligatory poor relief consisted chiefly of the work of youth offices and antituberculosis centers inaugurated by federal legislation. Outside of Vienna, cities under Socialist governments, such as St. Pölten, Wiener-Neustadt, Graz, and Eisenstadt, had not the means to provide for a well-rounded program of social work; they tried to follow Vienna's leadership but no comprehensive data are available on their achievements. Therefore, by and large, the discussion will be restricted to activities in the capital.

Welfare work everywhere started with some kind of aid to paupers and cripples. In Austria the grant of autonomy to the cities in 1848 shifted care of the poor to them. Thus the state freed itself from a burden which it had administered systematically, with the help of

[1] Grateful acknowledgment for assistance in the preparation of this chapter is hereby made to the late Dr. Alfred Goetzl, for many years a resident of Vienna and associate of Dr. Julius Tandler in that city's welfare program. Dr. Goetzl not only provided me with documentary material, but also permitted an examination of his own work on Tandler while it was in manuscript.

[2] Heinrich Weber, *Das Lebensrecht der Wohlfahrtspflege* (Essen, 1920). Quoted in *Grundriss der Sozialökonomik,* vol. 9, pt. 2 (1927), 487.

the Church, since 1783. A law of 1863 gave the victims of poverty a legal claim to aid from their home communities. In 1873 the existing Church institutions for the care of the poor were replaced in Vienna by 10 poor-relief offices which subsequently—with the growth of the city—were increased to 21, corresponding to the number of the urban districts. Until 1879 the citizens who carried on the work of these offices were appointed by the city government; later they were elected by the district councils. The basic welfare activities of the capital city were regulated by an ordinance of 1901 which was frequently amended in later years. But for a long time welfare work consisted chiefly in poor relief as prescribed by the imperial law of 1863. In 1928 this law was embodied, with modifications, in the Vienna statutes. It obliged the home community of the indigent to support him so far as he could not procure his livelihood himself and no other persons were legally bound to do so.[3]

The rise to power of the Christian Social party, which began primarily as a reform movement against the Austrian expression of Manchester Liberalism, gave some impulse to the development of the city's welfare work, particularly with respect to institutional welfare (*Anstaltsfürsorge*). The home for the indigent in Lainz was built to replace the old and dingy poorhouses, a big city hospital was erected, the insane asylum Am Steinhof was founded, and homes for orphans and neglected children opened. Protection for children and youths received increased consideration from the city administration; on the basis of an amendment to the civil code (1914), the city's legal guardianship of illegitimate children was organized. This reform period covered approximately the years between 1900 and the outbreak of the First World War.[4] Since the public institutions provided only for the most indispensable wants of a limited number of people there had developed a host of private charitable agencies which in a more or less haphazard way cared for various needs arising from the shortcomings of human nature and of our social system.

As it has been necessary to emphasize in several chapters, the misery of the population and its need for aid increased steadily during the war. The lack of foodstuffs, of fuel, and of many other

[3] Cf. *Das Neue Wien*, vol. 2 (Wien, 1927), pp. 342, 347–348; *RGBl.*, 1863, Nr. 105, Chap. IV, §§ 24, 26; *LGBl. für Wien*, 1928, Nr. 32.

[4] *Wien im Aufbau: Wohlfahrtswesen* (Wien, 1937), p. 6; *Das Neue Wien*, vol. 2, p. 374.

necessities of life, as well as the rising costs of living, brought increased hardships to the poor. Venereal diseases, heart trouble, pulmonary diseases, kidney diseases, rheumatism, mental afflictions, and various kinds of deficiencies of the sense organs spread rapidly as consequences of the war. Further deleterious results of the lower standard of living were the increased consumption of alcohol and drugs. The general mortality rate as compared with prewar times increased 60 per cent; that of children, 100 per cent.[5] In the period immediately following the war, misery did not decrease; it became even worse. Food shipments from foreign countries did not arrive immediately and even when they did proved insufficient to eliminate all hardships. The growing inflation increased enormously the number of the totally impoverished. In addition to wide groups of workers, important sections of the middle class fell into or close to the pauper class. A comprehensive system of social welfare to overcome the direst needs of an unprecedented number of persons was imperative. The private social-work agencies, not adequate in times of prosperity, tried their best; but were powerless to cope with the tremendous demands upon them. Besides, inflation and war fatalities had robbed them of funds and of most of their former sponsors. Necessarily everybody looked to the state and the city for help.

At this time Social Democrats dominated the governments of state and city and, in spite of possible misgivings on the part of a few staunch representatives of a more radical wing, they acted not only as the hour but also as their party tradition warranted. "At all times the spreading of our ideas was furthered best by the energetic promotion of the practical interests of the workers' groups."[6] But though they built up their system realistically on the basis of the existing institutions they drastically changed the spirit behind them. As traditional denouncers of charity they tried to replace it by the idea of the right of the needy to social service given by the community. This conception was expressed bluntly by Professor Tandler, the creator of the new Viennese welfare system: ". . . everybody living in a commonwealth has the right to social service; the commu-

[5] Julius Tandler, "Krieg und Bevölkerung," Address to the Viennese Medical Association, *Wiener Klinische Wochenschrift,* vol. 29 (April 13, 1916), 445; R. Danneberg, *Das Neue Wien* (Wien, 1930), p. 39.

[6] *Victor Adlers Aufsätze, Reden und Briefe,* Heft 4 (Wien, 1925), p. 91. (From a speech to the party congress, June, 1892.)

nity, the obligation of social service."[7] But still another viewpoint was important in the considerations of the Austrian workers' party and led to the extensive development of the Viennese system of social work well over and above the arrangements prevailing in most countries. This viewpoint, perhaps more precisely described as a firm conviction, was that the working class must be "physically and mentally able to fight" in order to achieve its goal, that is, a better human society.[8] Many measures put into effect by the welfare department of Vienna—even if they seem of little significance in terms of the number of persons benefited by them in their initial stage—should be considered with this conviction in mind.

Preliminary to a more detailed description of the welfare system elaborated by the municipality, a warning may be in order: the system was not conceived as the complete recipe for a better world. As previously indicated, it was to a great degree only a supplement to social and labor legislation, supporting those who were not eligible for social insurance, or who had been hit by some particular mishap. It was not to replace the fight of organized labor for a better standard of living through trade unions and coöperatives, and its effectiveness depended greatly on the simultaneous efforts of educational and cultural institutions and youth organizations to improve the mental and physical health of the youth.[9]

On the other hand, as also noted above, welfare work was not conceived by Tandler and his associates as restricted to the task of aiding individual indigents or particular groups of them. In order to succeed it always must keep in mind the general welfare of the community.[10] A collaborator of Professor Tandler quotes him as frequently summarizing his ideas on social welfare as follows:

the health of the people as a whole is dependent on the health of each individual as determined both by his constitution and by his environment. Therefore, the first step must be to improve the heredity of each person. Next, the environment must be improved to the extent that it

[7] Tandler, *Wohltätigkeit oder Fürsorge?* (Wien, 1925), p. 4.

[8] Adler, *op. cit.*, p. 5.

[9] All these subjects have been treated in previous chapters or will be in subsequent ones. Cf. esp. Chapters X–XII, XIV, XVI–XVIII.

[10] It is interesting to note that a famous American, Charles A. Beard, has expressed ideas on the tasks of public welfare similar to those held by the Vienna city government. He writes: "In many great cities departments of charity have become departments of public welfare. Why this change? It is due in part to the magnitude of the problems raised by the changing economic conditions which have subjected city dwellers to new hazards and deprived them of sunlight, air, outdoor exercise, and

affects favorably the growing generation from both the physical and mental standpoints. Such effort must include not only the prevention of disease, but the eradication of conditions that might lead to other physical handicaps. Any rational, all-embracing policy will, therefore, need to be governed chiefly by the concept of preventive medicine. In this task the family as a unit must be preserved insofar as it is possible to preserve it. Ethical, social and economic reasons all have equal importance. From the administrative standpoint the effort must be to attain in each individual case the optimum benefit with the least possible expenditure. This will require a concentric structure of the welfare organization.[11]

Care of Children and Youth

Since a fundamental idea of the Vienna welfare system was social service from birth to death for all in need of it, it seems logical to begin the discussion with those sections of the program which were concerned with children; as indicated above, care of youth is the basis of all welfare work.

> For the more we take care of the youth, the less we shall have to do it for the aged; the healthier, the more fit for life, the more efficient in the struggle for existence this youth will be. What we lay out for youth shelters [*Jugendhorte*] we save on prisons. What we spend for the care of pregnant women and of babies, we save on asylums for lunatics. Large-scale and exhaustive welfare work for the youth is the most thrifty method in the administration of organic capital, that is, of the human beings of a community.[12]

In accordance with this idea of comprehensive social service, care of the child began before it was born, even before it was conceived. A counseling service for couples contemplating matrimony was founded as early as 1922. It was given the task of preventing the misfortunes resulting from an imprudent marriage of persons physically or mentally not likely to have healthy children or not able to take care of them. The activity of the physician in charge was chiefly advisory; examinations that could not easily be made during his office hours, such as for venereal diseases, tuberculosis, and mental

---

certainty of employment. With the progress of democracy, moreover, there has come a demand for a higher standard of individual enlightenment, comfort, and welfare, even at the sacrifice of that exaggerated notion of private rights which would allow every person to do as he pleases as long as he does not positively deprive his neighbors of life and limb." *American Government and Politics* (New York, 1939), p. 756.

[11] Alfred Goetzl and Ralph Arthur Reynolds, *Julius Tandler* (San Francisco, 1944), p. 23.

[12] Tandler, *Wohltätigkeit oder Fürsorge?*, p. 5.

disorders, were referred to the special services of the city and the social insurances, or—if the patient could afford it—to private practitioners.

Though the idea of such a counseling service was certainly commendable, it may be doubted that it was adequate to replace other means of protection; for instance, an obligatory physical examination prior to issuance of a marriage license, which did not exist in Austria. Since, as explained in the preceding chapter, it was fairly common practice to enter into alliances without religious or civil formality, even the license and examination system was considered ineffectual in preventing the spread of diseases; therefore, the voluntary counseling service certainly could not hope to do much unless it drew a large voluntary clientele. And that apparently was not the case. Though the service was utilized not only by those planning to be married but also by others having matrimonial and sexual difficulties, it was frequented by an average of less than 900 persons annually throughout its existence. Of course, office hours twice a week for one hour in the evening do not indicate that the service had the full-hearted support of all circles concerned.[13]

Chiefly as a means of combating hereditary syphilis the Viennese welfare department urged prospective mothers to visit one of the many counseling offices for mothers (*Mutterberatungsstellen*) within the first four months of pregnancy. If they did so they were examined; and, if found syphilitic, treated free of charge. As a special inducement to pregnant women to make use of this free service all who were not covered by the compulsory health insurance system were promised a cash bonus during the first four weeks after the birth of the child. Subsequent to the spring of 1924 this bonus was given to about 800 women annually. Naturally they also received advice intended to protect them before and during childbirth.[14]

As soon as a child was born the city youth department (*Jugendamt*) was notified either by the clinic, the attending physician, or the midwife. By putting social workers in all maternity wards, where in 1932, for instance, 83 per cent of all children were born, the majority could be taken care of immediately. With respect to the rest,

[13] *Das Neue Wien,* vol. 2, pp. 569–570; *Statistisches Taschenbuch . . . Wien,* 1928, p. 14; 1929, p. 14; 1930, p. 14; 1931, p. 14; 1932, p. 15; 1933, p. 14.

[14] Cf. S. Rosenblum, *Die sozialpolitischen Massnahmen der Gemeinde Wien* (Bern, 1935), p. 30; *Das Neue Wien,* vol. 2, p. 381.

the department immediately informed the district office concerned and it in turn sent out a social worker to the home of the new baby. The social worker had to determine whether or not help from the city was needed. If not, the worker simply conveyed congratulations to the parents in the name of the city government and no further steps were taken. In cases of need the welfare department helped with linens, food, or money, but as a matter of principle subsidies in kind were preferred by the youth department. If the home conditions were such that adequate care for the baby could not be expected, it could proceed to transfer the child to the children's reception center (*Kinderübernahmsstelle*).

In 1927 the city added a new service to its child-care activities. Every woman—irrespective of wealth or income—who made application at the district youth office during the eighth or ninth month of her pregnancy had the right to receive free a complete layette, valued at approximately 55 schillings, as soon as the child was born. The rather amazing fact that every mother who had applied, regardless of need, was given such a present by the city was justified with the argument that otherwise many of the poor would be ashamed to make the request. In addition, the layette served educational purposes. Its composition, quality, and suitability were expected to bring about a more hygienic and more satisfactory care of the baby and to induce mothers to make regular use of the counseling offices the addresses of which were printed on the box containing the outfit. Since the action was widely publicized, 8,000 to 12,000 such outfits were given away annually between 1928 and 1933, an average equaling about 60 per cent of the number of babies born.[15] However, it must be noted that the plan originated during the election campaign of 1927 in which the Social Democrats hoped to make considerable inroads into those groups which did not necessarily tend in their direction; there can be little doubt that the generous offer must be partly attributed to its propaganda value with the impoverished middle class.

A very important part of municipal welfare work was legal aid to the mothers of illegitimate children. Stemming from the public guardianship (*Amtsvormundschaft*) of children who received poor

[15] Cf. Rosenblum, *op. cit.*, pp. 30–31; Tandler, *Wohltätigkeit oder Fürsorge?*, pp. 8–9; *Statistisches Jahrbuch der Stadt Wien*, 1929 (2. Jahrg.), p. 72; *ibid.*, 1930–1935, pp. 17, 20, 64.

relief from the city—established in 1910—it was put on a broader basis after the 1914 amendment of the Austrian civil code which authorized a general guardianship of orphans and illegitimate children. Further authority was granted by the foster-children decree of 1919, but only in 1922 did Vienna take full advantage of its legal authority and make its protection available to every illegitimate child born there after 1922 and subject to the jurisdiction of a Viennese juvenile guardianship court (*Vormundschaftsgericht*). The responsibility of the city ended only when the child became self-supporting.

The general guardianship was comprehensive. Legal advice was given to pregnant, unmarried women. If necessary, court procedure was instituted against the father for recognition, for deposit of funds adequate to cover the expenses of delivery, to support the mother for six weeks and the child for three months. Also provided for were legal representation of the child in court, collection of maintenance funds through execution, and administration of modest estates. If the father did not make the maintenance payments regularly and punctually, he was required to give them directly to the district youth office for immediate transmission to the mother. This procedure permitted close control of the payments and prompt prosecution of delays, as well as avoidance of disagreeable discussions for the mother. Meanwhile, the youth office gave advances to her. In those cases in which the support of the child could not be secured the city provided foster homes or shelter in its own institutions. As the courts traditionally had been quite lenient toward the fathers of illegitimate children, thus burdening the economically weaker mother with the greatest share of the support of the child, the guardianship office exerted great effort to bring about a change in this practice; it claimed that through the numerous cases brought before the courts support up to 15 to 20 per cent of the father's income was collected.

The extent of this legal guardianship by the city can be illustrated by a few figures. In 1914, after the legal provisions had been in force one year, Vienna was taking care of 737 wards; in 1918 this number had increased to 1,171. Then it rose steadily to 6,855 in 1922 and jumped to 10,890 after the reorganization of the system in that year. By 1928 there were 24,541 wards of the city, a figure that was approximately maintained in the years to come. The necessary work was carried out by the chiefs of the district youth offices, the public guardians (*Berufsvormünder*), that is, administrative city officials, and social workers. On an average one guardian had to take care of 450 wards.[16]

A decree of the (federal) secretary of social administration (*Ziehkinderordnung*) increased the responsibility of the city by authorizing it to supervise all legitimate or illegitimate children under fourteen years of age "who are cared for, with or without compensation, by other persons than father or mother." No private person was permitted to rear the child of another without explicit permission from the youth department. This decree, based on the federal law of February 4, 1919, went into effect September 1, 1919. By 1933 the city was supervising the care of 27,689 youngsters under the decree.[17]

In all district youth offices, as well as in many of the large municipal housing projects, the city maintained counseling offices for mothers, best to be compared with the "well baby clinics" in the United States. There the mothers could get detailed advice regarding nutrition and care of children by a specially trained pediatrician. If the child was found ill the physician gave only the absolutely necessary instructions, or some simple preventive medicine, such as cod liver oil, and referred the mother to the appropriate private doctor, clinic, or hospital. At the weighing, measuring, and physical examination of the child a social worker of the district was present in order to follow up the case and to find out by home visits whether or not the mother had followed the doctor's advice.

The municipal well baby clinics came into existence as a consequence of the public guardianship and developed rapidly in republican Austria. The original 6 Viennese clinics in 1917 were increased to 35 by 1932. They handled a steadily increasing number of cases; for instance 26,658 in 1919, 186,343 in 1929, and a peak of 267,342 in 1932.

Except for wards of the city and children in the care of foster parents, who had to report to the offices regularly every month, the visits were purely voluntary. However, the mothers became so accus-

[16] Cf. *Das Neue Wien,* vol. 2, pp. 372–378; Tandler, *Wohltätigkeit oder Fürsorge?,* p. 9; *Statistisches Taschenbuch . . . Wien,* 1928, p. 11, 1933, p. 11; *Statistisches Jahrbuch der Stadt Wien,* 1930–1935, p. 64.

[17] *RGBl.,* 1914, Nr. 276, § 54; *StGBl.,* 1919, Nr. 76, 202; *Statistisches Jahrbuch der Stadt Wien,* 1930–1935, p. 64.

tomed to making use of this service—originally restricted to babies—that it had to be extended gradually to school children and youths; for them separate office hours were held.

In order to unify infant care in Vienna the well baby clinics took over this service from the social insurance institutions for a nominal fee. Thus many of the 50 privately run child welfare clinics disappeared. Unquestionably this development conformed to the wishes of the welfare authorities who considered the counseling service to be in the first place an "educational influence on the mother and indirectly on her whole neighborhood with the goal of achieving a hygienic and at the same time simple practical nutrition and child care."[18] The success of this welfare work, though credit is due to other contributing factors, can be demonstrated by reference to the steadily decreasing infant mortality rate. Per 1,000 live births it was 158 in 1918; 137 in 1923; 87.5 in 1928; and 60 in 1933.[19]

Infant and baby care was followed by that for children of preschool age. For them nursery schools and kindergartens (between which the Vienna system did not differentiate) had to be provided. Since care for children under six years came under the jurisdiction of the welfare department the treatment of kindergartens belongs in this section. They were primarly designed to alleviate the burdens of working mothers. Furthermore, they looked after children whose mothers were, because of mental instability or physical incapacities, found unsuited to care for them during the day. In such cases the children were usually assigned to a kindergarten by the district youth offices; the kindergartens were also permitted to accept children independently, but only up to one-quarter of their capacity. If space allowed, children of well-to-do families could be taken into the municipal kindergartens. For pedagogical reasons preference was given to an "only" child from such families. With the confirmation of the juvenile court parents could be forced to send their children to a kindergarten. Frequently the welfare department placed children there instead of paying cash relief to the parents. As a matter of principle everyone was expected to pay a small tuition fee (about 7 cents a week in 1931); however, the fee was lowered or waived completely if the parents could not afford even this sum.

[18] Cf. *Das Neue Wien*, vol. 2, pp. 387–388; Rosenblum, *op. cit.*, pp. 32–33; *Statistisches Taschenbuch . . . Wien*, 1932, p. 11.

[19] Rosenblum, *op. cit.*, p. 33; *Statistisches Taschenbuch . . . Wien*, 1933, p. 7.

In order to fulfill their main purpose the kindergartens had to be kept open during the working hours of the parents. Therefore most of them were kept open from 7 A.M. to 6 P.M. In order to help working mothers the established minimum age of three years could be lowered to two years and the children could remain in the kindergartens until they reached their sixth year. The cheerful playrooms were furnished with little tables and chairs, and every new kindergarten was equipped with shower baths. Every unit had outdoor playgrounds. The authoritarian system employed formerly was replaced by modern methods permitting children great freedom in the choice of their activities. In other words, the methods of child development taught by Dr. Montessori and modern psychology were increasingly utilized. Aside from shelter, play, and education kindergarten children received breakfast, lunch, and afternoon tea at very low costs; these costs too could be waived partly or wholly if it were deemed necessary. Doctors and social workers supervised the physical and mental well-being of the children. Their regular care was provided by trained nursery schoolteachers and nurse helpers (*Kinderwärterinnen*). In order to familiarize the teachers with the new principles of education a municipal kindergarten-training institute was founded in 1924.

Though municipal kindergartens existed in prerepublican times the Social Democratic city government not only incorporated them in the social welfare system, but also increased their number. Thus in 1931 the city maintained 111 kindergartens whereas it had taken over only 51 from the Christian Social administration. Before 1918 a nursery schoolteacher had to take care of 50 children; the new administration reduced this number to 25 or 30. In 1931 the 111 municipal kindergartens had a daily average attendance of 6,738. According to a statement of the head of the kindergarten division, Frankowski, they could then accommodate all children in need and even a few more. After 1931 a slight decrease in the number of kindergartens, as well as in the attendance, took place. After 1926 all new kindergartens were placed in municipal housing projects.[20]

Important services were rendered by the city in maintaining and

[20] *Das Neue Wien,* vol. 2, pp. 403–405; Rosenblum, *op. cit.,* pp. 37–38; Philipp Frankowski, "Die Aufgaben des Kindergartens im Wandel der Zeiten," *Blätter für das Wohlfahrtswesen,* 1929 (Tandler issue), pp. 79–80; *Statistisches Jahrbuch der Stadt Wien,* 1930–1935, p. 65.

improving the welfare of school children, that is, of those between six and fourteen years of age. They can be divided into services provided in the school, care after school, and arrangements for rest and recreation during the vacation period (*Erholungsfürsorge*).

As in the kindergartens, the city provided medical supervision for all school children. It consisted in a thorough examination of every child in the first, fourth, and last grade of any public school, and in weekly office hours during which the school physician examined those children whom he had found in need of regular supervision, as well as those who, in the opinion of teacher or social worker, showed signs of illness. In the school year 1930–1931, for example, this medical service was given by 50 physicians, who spent an average of twelve hours weekly in schools and kindergartens, and by 234 school social workers. Approximately 3,000 children were cared for by one doctor. After the physical examination the social worker informed the parents of what measures or precautions were to be taken and instructed them accordingly. No treatment was given by the school physician. In addition to carrying on the examinations, he supervised the hygienic conditions of the school and made recommendations concerning referral of handicapped children to special schools, school meals, and vacations in recreation homes for needy children. For special examinations an otologist, an orthopedist, and a specialist in speech difficulties of children were provided. In preparation for antituberculosis work a tuberculin test was administered to every child in the first grade. This test could not be given without the consent of the parents, but 80 to 90 per cent of them gave it. If necessary, an X-ray examination was made. If a child reacted positively to the tuberculin test, the parents were induced to undergo a medical examination and were given information on the dangers of tuberculosis. If necessary, a child could be referred to a recovery center or to a hospital. In May of each year all needy children were vaccinated or revaccinated against smallpox.

In addition, every child belonged to a school dental clinic, established in 1922, and had his teeth examined twice a year. With the permission of the parents the children received free treatment in these clinics; the only charge was an annual registration fee of 20 groschen, approximately 3 cents. In the clinic the children were also instructed in the regular care of the teeth, particularly in the correct use of the tooth brush. It was rightly assumed that such instruction would also have a wholesome effect on the child's parents and relatives. In 1930–1931 there were 37 dentists as well as numerous technical assistants engaged in the work. Another special medical service was the central eye clinic for school children established in 1929. Under the supervision of the teachers the children went in groups to the clinic for examinations. Prescriptions for glasses were given only to poor children.

In order to provide every child with a warm lunch (the chief meal in Austria), it was served in all municipal schools in Vienna. This system stemmed from the American child relief, discontinued in 1922, and was badly needed because of the poor economic conditions of postwar Vienna. In 1924–1925 a total of 141,777 school children and 36,296 kindergarteners were served 3,378,417 meals, of which only 61,426 were completely paid for by parents. Even in 1929 these meals were provided for nearly 13,000 children daily—for approximately 80 per cent, free of charge. The rest paid a quarter, a half, or the full price. To assure fresh milk for all school-age youngsters municipal and parent organizations arranged for the issuance of half-pint bottles of milk as a "second breakfast" to each of them. Before the war a private agency had provided a few hundred lunches daily to the neediest.[21]

Obligatory instruction in gymnastics and swimming, in addition to school hikes, supplemented the care for the physical well-being of Viennese school children.[22]

After school hours, day care centers for children of school age

[21] The various examples given may have raised some questions in the reader's mind concerning the financial aspects of Vienna welfare work. For examples, layettes were given to all mothers who applied for them regardless of their economic status, whereas prescriptions for glasses were given only to poor children. In the first case, there was the avowed purpose of avoiding embarrassment to less well-to-do families; in the second, this purpose seems to have been forgotten. Concerning Tandler's position there can be no doubt; he strongly opposed wasteful or unwarranted disbursement of public funds. To him an expenditure was unwarranted when the recipient was not in real need (cf., for example, *Wohltätigkeit oder Fürsorge?*, p. 4); but he and his critics defined "wasteful" and "unwarranted" in different ways, as the discussion of "welfare inflation" in Chapter XIII brought out. The actual practice is illustrated by the two examples just given; that is, it was a mixture and, at times, political considerations were involved.

[22] *Das Neue Wien*, vol. 2, pp. 579–591, 408–409; Hans Redtenbacher, "Schulärztliche Tätigkeit an den öffentlichen Pflichtschulen und Kindergärten der Gemeinde Wien," *Blätter für das Wohlfahrtswesen*, 1929 (Tandler issue), pp. 28–31; Erna Greiner, "Schulzahnpflege in Wien," *ibid.*, pp. 31–33; Rosenblum, *op. cit.*, pp. 40–44; *Wiener Wahlhandbuch*, 1932, Heft C, pp. 11–13.

(*Horte*) were provided for those whose parents were not able or willing to supervise them properly and who therefore would have been exposed to the dangers of the street. The main emphasis in these institutions was put on physical training and workshops, but they provided also libraries and facilities to do homework under supervision. In 1930, 34 such *Horte* were maintained by the city and attended by more than 3,000 youngsters daily. After 1932 two-thirds of the *Horte* were combined with kindergartens into "youth homes." The children were accepted under the same provisions as in the kindergartens. Lunches and afternoon tea were also served in them. They formed an important part of the city's organization for the care of its wards, supplemented by similar private undertakings which offered additional facilities to the municipal authorities. Special sections cared for handicapped children.[23]

Rest and vacations were offered to school children through a joint venture created by the city and voluntary (private and semiprivate) welfare institutions: the *Wiener Jugendhilfswerk* or *Wijug*. Founded as a substitute for the relief organizations which brought undernourished Austrian children to foreign countries after the First World War, it provided vacations, in 1929 for instance, for 28,426 children in the 219 institutions (8 of them in foreign countries) which were at its disposition. In addition, the *Wijug* promoted the hiking movement by aiding youth hostels and by obtaining reduced fares on railroads and streetcar lines. The youth office of Vienna directed the organization but provided only one-eighth of the necessary funds. The remainder was collected through a lottery, donations, and contributions of the parents of participating children so far as their means permitted. The social insurance institutions provided additional sums for the children of their members. For those children who stayed in the city, day hostels (*Tageserholungsstätten*) were instituted or supported by the *Wijug*. In short, its task was "to coördinate all the public and semipublic funds which are at the disposal of Viennese children, and to use them for its purposes according to a uniform plan." In addition, the city provided a great number of playgrounds and bathing pools distributed all over Vienna. The latter were used as skating rinks during the winter.[24]

---

[23] *Das Neue Wien*, vol. 2, pp. 405–408; Rosenblum, *op. cit.*, p. 38; *Statistisches Jahrbuch der Stadt Wien*, 1930–1935, p. 65.

[24] *Das Neue Wien*, vol. 2, pp. 410–412; Rosenblum, *op. cit.*, pp. 39–40.

As an aid to youths, and their parents, in choosing the right occupation a municipal office for vocational guidance was founded in 1922; beginning in 1925 it was directed jointly with the chamber of labor. It gave advice after testing the applicants by consultations, written examinations, and psychotechnical methods. At the same time it acted as an employment agency for young people who had just completed their schooling, primarily, however, for wards of the city's youth department. Through extensive propaganda and informative campaigns over the radio, in schools, parents' meetings, voluntary welfare agencies, and the professional groups, wide circles of the population were made aware of the benefits of vocational guidance. A special publication distributed to the children leaving school urged them to think clearly about their vocations and to get advice from the bureau. This propaganda led to an increased case load; in 1932 it reached 31,736 visits, and 2,036 qualification tests. Though guidance service was also occasionally given to older unemployed people, the number was insignificant. In addition, it may be mentioned that, as far as possible, youths found in poor health were referred to apprentice homes, youth hostels, or similar institutions in order to make them physically fit.[25]

The discussion of the "general guardianship" of illegitimate children has given some evidence of the great responsibility assumed by the city of Vienna in their behalf. For another group, youngsters whose parents had died or were entirely unable or unsuitable to rear them (*Pflegekinder*), the municipality provided complete care. The first step was the transference of the child to the Children's Reception Center (*Kinderübernahmsstelle*), the pride of the city's welfare organization. It was completed in 1925 at a cost of more than 3,000,000 schillings. Professor Tandler claimed that the Center was the largest in the world; and, in reply to critics, added that, "We are of the opinion that for the children the best and most beautiful is just sufficiently good and beautiful."[26] Constructed according to the newest techniques it combined the requirements of modern hygiene with high architectural and artistic qualities. Its three main sections could accommodate 204 children. One section was intended for newborn babies, another for small children, and a third for young-

---

[25] Rosenblum, *op. cit.*, pp. 48–50; *Statistisches Taschenbuch ... Wien*, 1932, p. 13; *Statistisches Jahrbuch der Stadt Wien*, 1930–1935, p. 87.

[26] Tandler, *Wohltätigkeit oder Fürsorge?*, p. 11.

sters of school age. The adjacent children's hospital provided a clinic and a ward for contagious diseases in addition to its general services. Each section of the Center had its own kitchens, service rooms, and stairways so that it could be isolated from the others in the event of an epidemic. The single floors were subdivided into compartments, most of them for 5 to 6 children; the partitions were made of glass in order to allow easy supervision. In this reception center the children stayed only temporarily; for sixteen to twenty-one days they were carefully observed and their physical, mental, and social status investigated. Finally, their definite placement was decided upon.[27]

If the children were found not fit for definite placement they were temporarily transferred to the Central Children's Home (*Zentralkinderheim*), or to one of the reception homes, the largest of which was Schloss Wilhelminenberg. The Central Children's Home had been erected in 1910 by the Christian Social administration, but was reorganized after the war. Whereas it served formerly only as a foundling home, now every child within the fixed age limits entitled to city care was accepted, irrespective of legitimacy. It provided room for 520 children and 280 mothers. The latter were accepted only if they were still nursing their children. In 1924 a special division for youngsters afflicted with venereal diseases was opened. In addition the Central Home served pedagogical purposes; its staff arranged lectures and practical exercises for high school girls and young women and was a training center for students in the municipal school for nurses. Wilhelminenberg was a remodeled Habsburg castle which had been purchased by the city in 1927; situated on one of the wooded hills near the city limits, it was surrounded by a large park with ideal play and sport grounds. The huge complex contained six departments with day rooms, dormitories, bathrooms, auditorium, theater, gymnasium, and dental clinic. The former gardener's house became a clinic; the laundry an emergency hospital. After its adaptation the Central Home could shelter several thousand children per year for a longer or shorter period of time.[28]

For definite placement various institutions were at the disposal of the youth office: foster homes, orphanages, apprentice homes,

---

[27] *Das Neue Wien,* vol. 2, pp. 457–467.

[28] Friedrich Wilhelm, "Die Jugendfürsorgeanstalten der Stadt Wien in den letzten zehn Jahren," *Blätter für das Wohlfahrtswesen,* 1929 (Tandler issue), p. 57.

educational homes, or a reform school. "Wherever possible the foster family is preferred."[29] Such a family was accepted only after a thorough investigation, including among other things the size and the hygienic conditions of the dwelling and the reputation of the family; alcoholics were explicitly excluded. Furthermore, every attempt was made to be certain that children were not being taken by foster parents for selfish reasons, that is, only to secure relief money. They remained under constant supervision. Only absolutely healthy children could be put into a foster family. By 1933 the city had so placed 5,000 of its wards.[30]

If a child was considered unacceptable for care in a foster home but acceptable in a public school, he was placed in an orphanage which, in contrast to the past, accepted not only children who had lost their parents, but also those whose parents were found unqualified to rear them. In addition, poor children in need of institutional care could be placed there, whether or not they were poor in the strict sense of the poor law. In accordance with the preference for foster homes, three of the original five municipal orphanages had been discontinued between 1928 and 1932 and one had been transformed into a reform school. In its last years, then, the Socialist municipal administration was maintaining only one, though considerably enlarged, orphanage (Hohe Warte) which became a modern educational institution for children presenting problems. The financial strain also may have played a role in the decision to discontinue all city orphanages but one. In addition to it, however, several recognized private homes were available for the placement of needy children.[31]

For children with more serious family and educational difficulties and for those who had come into actual conflict with the law, separate institutions existed. Though there had once been five such educational homes only two remained in 1932. One was situated in Klosterneuburg near Vienna and accommodated 150 girls who had grave educational deficiencies; the other was the reform school for boys and girls in Eggenburg, also situated not far from the cap-

[29] *Das Neue Wien,* vol. 2, p. 395.
[30] Tandler, *Wohltätigkeit oder Fürsorge?,* p. 10; *Statistisches Taschenbuch . . . Wien,* 1933, p. 12.
[31] *Das Neue Wien,* vol. 2, pp. 437–438, 440–442; *Statistisches Taschenbuch . . . Wien,* 1929, p. 10; 1930, p. 10; 1932, p. 11; Wilhelm, *loc. cit.,* p. 52.

ital city in Lower Austria. The latter institution ran its own elementary school in eight grades, a continuation school, workshops for several handicrafts, and a farm. The educational program was carried out according to the modern principles elaborately described in *Das Neue Wien*. Although it is impossible to detail the methods employed, it may be indicated that in contrast to the prisonlike system of the past, work education was stressed and great freedom given to the youngsters. To fulfill the new tasks the former wardens were replaced by well-trained educators. Modern psychological methods were employed for solving individual problems. But, as happens frequently with pedagogical experiments, Eggenburg and its various directors were blamed from one side for too much leniency toward the inmates and from the other for continuing antiquated educational methods under the guise of modern pedagogic; according to information given by persons familiar with the institution there can be little doubt that after Vienna took it over from Lower Austria in 1922 progress was achieved. Eggenburg accommodated 534 children and youths. Approximately 500 endangered youths were cared for by private institutions.[32]

In former times apprentices had customarily lived with their masters. After the First World War this practice became obsolete and the city had to provide shelter for its wards. In 1920 the first emergency apprentice homes were erected. In order to unify the welfare work for apprentices, the administration of the two municipal homes was later transferred to the apprentice relief project, a joint program of federal government, states, municipalities, and social insurances, founded in 1921. In the institutions of this project the city could accommodate additional wards by paying a sustenance fee.

For 130 "work students" the city provided two homes which were intended to enable sons of workers to attend the University; they accommodated particularly students whose parents lived outside Vienna. Their administration was turned over by the city to the association of working students.

The city of Vienna also owned and operated three children's hospitals. They were taken over in 1924 and 1925 from private

[32] Rosenblum, *op. cit.*, pp. 47–48; *Das Neue Wien*, vol. 2, pp. 442–455; *Statistisches Taschenbuch . . . Wien*, 1932, p. 11; 1933, p. 10; *Statistisches Jahrbuch der Stadt Wien*, 1929 (2. Jahrg.), p. 82.

foundations which were unable to carry the financial burden any longer.[33]

The youth protection work of the city of Vienna described above is certainly impressive in its wide ramifications. Together with the educational reforms described in the next chapter it drew from the Swiss pedagogical reformer, Adolphe Ferrière the comment that Vienna was the "capital city of the child." In this connection it may be noted that Tandler always worked closely with the chief figure in the Viennese school reforms, Otto Glöckel.[34]

Particular attention, however, should be paid to the closely knit structure and the coördination of the youth protection work; this was possible because it was administered by one agency and backed not only by the full authority and financial strength of the city government, but also by the full support of the masses. Professor Tandler had fought for this popular support since he had taken over the welfare department of Vienna in 1920. In his own words, Tandler's first task was "to make the people responsive to well-regulated social care." How he went about this and how he succeeded is recorded by his biographers.

> With tremendous energy, Tandler, aided by a staff of trained medical and lay workers, accomplished this preliminary task within a short time.
>
> The Social Democratic Party of Austria consisted of two main branches, the economic, which was composed of the trade unions, and the political. This type of organization offered him ample opportunity to contact closely every economic and social stratum of the population by means of innumerable meetings. During this period the people had the opportunity of hearing him speak nearly every evening; indeed, one might call his activities during this period missionary work.[35]

And after the program was well under way Tandler continued to emphasize the tremendous importance of popular support for effective welfare work. At a conference on public hospital work in October, 1926, he stated: "Everything requires psychological influence. . . . In spite of all the misery of the time" the pauperized population of Vienna was "mentally captured." The people "were prepared to

[33] *Das Neue Wien,* vol. 2, pp. 455–457, 484–491; Wilhelm, *loc. cit.,* pp. 56–57; *Jahrbuch der österreichischen Arbeiterbewegung, 1928,* p. 340; *ibid., 1929,* p. 402.

[34] *Otto Glöckel,* pp. 105, 106. This volume is partly an autobiography and partly the work of Dr. Hans Fischl and others.

[35] Goetzl and Reynolds, *op. cit.,* pp. 20–21.

go along . . . because each had learned from personal experience that only the collective viewpoint of mutual obligation, freed from so-called benevolent activity, that is, an obligation based on rights and duties, is the basis of any welfare work." This could not be done "by decree, by square yards of pages covered with writings," but solely by "concrete and direct contact with the people."[36]

Care of Indigent Adults

As mentioned early in this chapter, the care of indigents in the capital city was based on the poor law of 1863 which rigidly limited social service to the absolutely necessary wants of life, the provision of shelter and sustenance and care in sickness. This aid was limited to persons who could demonstrate citizenship in Vienna. The reforms of 1921 also influenced the care of adults, but the changes were by no means so significant and manifest as in children's welfare work. In a resolution of the city council of June 20, 1921, the principles of the new policy were outlined. "At present the task is no longer simply to provide the necessary maintenance of life, plain economic support, but to enable the economically weak, the uneconomic man, to find again a suitable place in economic life through systematic advice and guidance and by pedagogically influencing his behavior as a whole."[37] In order to make this theory workable emphasis was placed on so-called open welfare work (*offene Fürsorge*) rather than on care in poorhouses or similar institutions. It was felt that through adequate contributions, preservation of the natural family environment, and expert advice it would be possible to make relief recipients again self-supporting. Many kinds of material aid, which frequently surpassed the minimum prescribed by the law, were given to the poor, but the goal of making a significant number of them self-supporting was not attained because of the economic crisis which never ceased to harass the Austrian republic. Thus the new spirit will be found more in the attitude in which help was given, in the efforts to relieve the recipients of a feeling of inferiority, and in similar intangibles, than in the actual work done.

The backbone of the open welfare work was simply poor relief in

[36] *Blätter für das Wohlfahrtswesen,* 1929 (Tandler issue), p. 3.
[37] *Das Neue Wien,* vol. 2, pp. 342, 350–351.

cash, called *Erhaltungsbeiträge*. It was granted "to all qualified persons in Vienna who because of age, sickness, physical or mental deficiencies are unable to provide the most elementary livelihood for themselves and their dependents, do not have property, but with the relief allotted can maintain themselves outside an institution."[38] This regular poor relief was given as long as the conditions persisted. The sums thus spent were considerable and rose steadily; they amounted to 11,929,921 schillings in 1929, distributed among a monthly average of 40,604 persons, and to 15,318,979 schillings for a monthly average of 44,466 persons in 1933.[39] These amounts were appreciably larger than the legal situation (explained in the note) required because the city refused to be bound by a rigid interpretation of the law. On the other hand, it attempted to recover the relief granted from the community in which the recipient was *heimatzuständig* if that community was not Vienna.

Temporary relief was given to those who left the poorhouse voluntarily in the hope of gaining economic independence. Though such a move agreed perfectly with the aims of the welfare system, only very few people made use of the opportunity, again because of the hopeless economic prospect. Unemployed, ineligible for federal relief, received support in cash, wearing apparel, fuel, and so on.

In individual emergencies the city was prepared to give assistance in money or provide food, garments, tools, or fuel. The poor who were not covered by compulsory health insurance received medical aid from a city doctor, medicines and medicinal baths, glasses, artificial limbs, and teeth. If needy persons were to be released from an insane asylum the welfare department of the city was notified before they left. They received temporary or steady support and garments; they were provided with shelter in the city or railway tickets to enable them to travel to relatives or friends.

A roof for the night could be found in the "home for the shelterless." Distressed people could also get breakfast, dinner, clothes, and shoes, or money to return to their communities if they were not

[38] Rosenblum, *op. cit.*, p. 51. "Qualified persons" is an unsatisfactory translation for "*heimatberechtigte Personen.*" *Heimatberechtigt,* or *heimatzuständig,* was a legal status upon which depended such rights as voting and receiving support in the event of need; it was acquired automatically by birth in a community and could be acquired under stipulated conditions by petition.

[39] *Statistisches Jahrbuch der Stadt Wien,* 1929 (2. Jahrg.), p. 92; *ibid.,* 1930–1935, p. 71.

heimatzuständig in Vienna. The home for the shelterless provided 2,340 beds in 1933, for example. Unfortunately, they were all too well used. During the period 1926 to 1933 an annual average of 700,000 overnight accommodations were provided by this institution. A second home, giving shelter for a longer period, had 470 beds. Two separate houses were provided for girls who had lost domestic jobs and with them their shelter. They accommodated 208 persons. In addition, they offered cheerful day and dining rooms and an employment office. The houses were administered by the union of the domestics. During the day the homeless and those who could not afford fuel for themselves found a haven in "warm rooms" which were maintained in some of the poorest districts of the city during the winter. In these "warm rooms" soup and bread were served. According to Rosenblum, the number of people seeking refuge depended not only upon the severity of the weather, but also upon the housing situation. In the extremely cold winter of 1929/1930, 109,325 persons came to stay in the "warm rooms," but a comparison of the winters of 1926/1927 and 1930/1931 shows a drop from 95,839 to 56,274. Between 1931/1932 and 1934/1935 the figure fluctuated between 56,742 and 77,809; in 1935/1936 it soared to 122,675.[40]

Some other welfare institutions maintained by the city were concerned with helping to readjust people in economic life. Thus the welfare agency for unemployed workers, in addition to distributing federal relief and city contributions,[41] conducted an employment agency and suggested training classes. Separate counseling services, combined with employment agencies, existed for the blind, and for the deaf and dumb. They were founded in 1926 and 1927, respectively. An extremely valuable aid to many poor people was the Legal Aid Bureau (*Rechtshilfestelle*). As the successor of a similar institution founded during the war, it came into existence by resolution of the city council of February 27, 1919. Its members

[40] Rosenblum, *op. cit.*, pp. 55, 59–60; *Blätter für das Wohlfahrtswesen*, 1929 (Tandler issue), p. 88; *Statistisches Jahrbuch der Stadt Wien*, 1930–1935, pp. 70, 71. No satisfactory explanation could be found for the figure for 1935/1936. As is probably clear, the data do not support Rosenblum's suggestion concerning the relation of the housing situation.

[41] The city not only supplemented the federal unemployment benefits, but also provided a pint to a quart of fresh milk daily for children of the unemployed up to the age of one year. Karl Wortner, "Einige Reformen der offenen Fürsorge," *Blätter für das Wohlfahrtswesen*, 1929 (Tandler issue), p. 66.

were appointed partly by the mayor, partly by the chamber of lawyers; they served without compensation. Office space and clerical help was contributed by the city. Some 10,000 to 12,000 persons annually made use of the services, consisting of legal advice, drafting of applications, and representation before the courts. Through public lectures and the distribution of pamphlets and handbills, various legal subjects were treated in a popular manner in order to spread knowledge of the law among the poor.[42]

To carry on its open welfare the department relied chiefly on the well-knit organization of 21 welfare offices (*Fürsorgeinstitute*), one for each Vienna district. It was stated that through this organization "there was achieved not only that direction and administration of the open welfare work of the metropolis by which unified tendencies and working methods are realized, but also the avoidance of those incongruencies—which nowhere have a more disturbing effect than in social work—arising between the single great branches centrally coördinated in the welfare department."[43]

In order to bring the still-existing private welfare agencies into the whole system every district set up a welfare committee (*Bezirkswohlfahrtsausschuss*) combining representatives of the city with those of the private agencies.[44] The latter were appointed by the mayor of Vienna after hearing the private associations. These committees had their offices in the city's welfare institutes and enjoyed the privilege of using all their facilities.

Each district welfare institute comprised a director, two deputies, a secretary, and the "welfare councilors" (*Fürsorgeräte*). The office of welfare councilor was an honorary one; the councilors were elected by popular vote and numbered more than 6,000 men and women. On their shoulders lay the main responsibility for the functioning of the open welfare activities of the city. It is noteworthy

---

[42] Rosenblum, *op. cit.*, pp. 57–58, 54; *Das Neue Wien*. vol. 2, p. 367.

[43] *Das Neue Wien*, vol. 2, p. 348.

[44] Private welfare agencies were considered valuable in some Socialist circles, though not by Tandler, as supplementing the activities of the public agencies, particularly in performing pioneer work. The oldest private groups were Catholic organizations combined in the *Caritas* association. It provided nursery homes for babies, day nurseries for preschool children, homes for wayward girls, hospitals, homes for the old and for domestics. The welfare agencies of the working class were united in the central organization, *Societas*. It maintained homes for preschool as well as for school children and recreation homes, offered counseling services, and gave support in money and kind. In 1928 its agencies were called upon by 50,000 persons. Many independent agencies centered their activities on special groups. Cf., Marie Bock, *Die Fürsorge in Oesterreich* (Wien, 1929), pp. 16–18.

that in the years after the war of 1914–1918 an increasing number of workers and salaried employees took over the strenuous and thankless tasks of welfare councilors. In 1927, for instance, 56.4 per cent of them belonged to the working class, whereas previously the councilors had been more or less exclusively businessmen. In preparation for their activities the welfare councilors were required to take courses extending over a period of three months. In them the legal foundations of welfare work, social legislation, and the tasks of the various branches of social services were taught.[45]

Persons who were unable to subsist outside an institution, particularly incurables and those needing special care, found refuge in one of the poorhouses maintained by the city of Vienna. In general, recipients of aid had to be *heimatzuständig* in Vienna, but for incurables this requirement was waived. Friends or home communities were assessed for the maintenance cost of non-Viennese incurables; if it was medically certified that they could be safely moved, they were sent to those communities. All the existing poorhouses were an inheritance from prewar times; they were, however, reorganized by the new city administration in order to make life more enjoyable to the unfortunates who had to resort to them. One reform was to centralize the reception and placement of the applicants. That was accomplished by the creation of a special reception department in the poor home in Lainz where everyone had to undergo a thorough medical examination and an observation period of eight days after which he was placed in a suitable institution. All sick applicants remained in Lainz and were referred to one of the special wards newly created for the care of surgical cases or of certain afflictions such as tuberculosis and nervous disorders. The others were either placed in the ordinary pavilions in Lainz or sent to one of the other poorhouses. The efforts of the municipal welfare department were directed toward a complete separation of the infirm and the other poor unemployables. Generally males and females were placed in separate institutions; only Lainz had a pavilion for married couples. In the interest of greater hygiene special day rooms were set up in all poor homes, whereas previously the old people had to stay all day in bedrooms if the weather was inclement. The residents of the institutions elected representatives whose task it

[45] *Das Neue Wien,* vol. 2, pp. 348–350.

was to bring grievances before the director of the house. The 9 poor homes, which were mostly surrounded by parks and partly situated outside the city, had 8,892 beds, of which Lainz alone had 5,658.[46]

Care of Sick

Closely connected with general welfare work is aid to the needy sick, of which certain instances have been cited above. The following section considers the hospital care provided by the city and the fight to prevent the spread of common diseases and to improve public health.

To accommodate the sick who needed institutional care the city of Vienna owned the large hospital in Lainz with 1,077 beds. For this hospital the city hired the best specialists available to take care of the poor, which, incidentally, led to the charge that Professor Tandler intended to build up a competitor of the medical school of the University of Vienna.[47] Among the most important departments were those for the treatment of tuberculosis and cancer, discussed below. Every ward of the Lainz Hospital had a clinic for those patients who did not need hospital care. Connected with the hospital was a municipal school for nurses.

Persons with mental diseases were treated in the asylum Am Steinhof in Vienna or in the sanitarium Ybbs an der Donau in Lower Austria. These two institutions accommodated 5,200. They employed work therapy; that is, they furnished workshops as well as facilities for gardening and farming. A new feature, the ward for alcoholics at Am Steinhof, will be discussed separately. Another genuine achievement of the Social Democratic era was the modern maternity hospital with 125 beds constructed in the Twentieth district, one of the poorest sections of Vienna.[48] Three hospitals for children were mentioned in the foregoing discussion of child welfare.

Of primary importance for the welfare of a city are measures to prevent and suppress easily spread contagious diseases. To these ends general hygiene must be furthered and adequate institutions to fight the diseases created. To secure the former the supervision

[46] *Ibid.*, vol. 2, pp. 497–512; Rosenblum, *op. cit.*, pp. 58–60.

[47] *Reichspost,* December 20, 1930 (quoted in *Wiener Wahlhandbuch,* Heft C [1932], 32).

[48] Rosenblum, *op. cit.*, pp. 78, 77.

of drinking water was made stricter by rigid control at the sources and the reservoirs, disinfections were given free of charge in city-owned institutions, travelers coming from infected areas were closely supervised and could be put into the city-owned quarantine station. Vaccination against small pox was propagandized and dispensed free in an effort to overcome the facts that there was no law to enforce vaccination directly, nor even a city ordinance that children could not be admitted to a school unless vaccinated. Parental approval of vaccination of school children had to be secured. The general success of this propaganda is evidenced by the fact that by 1925 only 2.4 per cent of the 137,636 youngsters in kindergartens and in the first eight years of public and private schools had never been vaccinated. The collection of garbage was completely reorganized and the open wagons replaced by special closed trucks into which the refuse could be put from tightly covered containers which were provided for every household. The mechanical arrangements by which the containers were emptied into the trucks were such that no dust or garbage could be dropped to litter passageways or streets—a pleasant contrast with the all too frequently sloppy, not to say nauseating, methods used in most American cities. As further betterments in municipal hygiene, the cleaning and sprinkling of the streets were improved and the public market system reformed by the creation of a quarantine market and considerable renovations of the existing market places.[49]

The greatest task faced by the health authorities of Vienna after the First World War was the fight against tuberculosis, significantly called "the Vienna sickness." Even toward the close of the imperial era the death rate from this disease was higher than that of other comparable large cities for which data are available. That rate, per 10,000 civilians, is shown in the table on page 531.[50]

Though the death rate was already scandalous in 1913 only the private agencies conducted a hopeless struggle against the disease. The appalling increase during the war finally induced the government to move. In 1917 a decree of the imperial ministry of the interior promised subsidies to private and prospective public agencies fighting this plague by establishing and managing antituber-

[49] Rosenblum, *op. cit.*, pp. 64–65; *Wiener Wahlhandbuch*, Heft C (1932), 46, 52, 60; *Das Neue Wien*, vol. 2, pp. 543 ff.

[50] *Das Neue Wien*, vol. 2, p. 554.

culosis clinics. These clinics were to be coördinated by district and state councils under the supervision of the ministry. Their main tasks were the examination, sometimes the treatment, of patients, the institution of measures to isolate the sick, the promotion of hygiene in living quarters and of correct nutrition, the supervision of released patients, disinfection, and educational propaganda.[51]

Though Vienna, in expectation of the decree, had created a Central Municipal Office for Tuberculosis Welfare in 1916, it did not

City	1913	1918
New York	20.0	18.6
London	16.5	21.4
Chicago	16.6	14.6
Paris (only tuberculosis of the lungs)	32.8	24.8
Berlin	18.4	32.7
Vienna	30.1	60.7
Moscow	26.7	20.2
Leningrad		37.0

begin active participation in the campaign until 1919. In that year the city council voted appropriations for 5 antituberculosis clinics and opened 2 of them. But to meet the tasks noted above the whole city had to be covered by clinics; therefore, between 1919 and 1929, the municipal council erected 12 such institutions. They were aided by 7 owned by private welfare associations and 6 constructed by the compulsory health insurance institutes.[52] These 25 clinics acted under a coördinated program of which the directing agency was the State Central Organization of Vienna for Combating Tuberculosis (*Landeszentrale Wien zur Bekämpfung der Tuberkulose*). Its chairman was the mayor of Vienna; the current business was carried on by the health director of the city (*Oberphysikus als Landessanitätsreferent*) assisted by an executive committee of physicians.[53] The case load of the tuberculosis clinics steadily increased up to 1930. In 1919 they examined 36,864 persons; in 1925, 73,661, and in 1930, 126,316. Of the last total 74,623 examinations were carried out by the municipal clinics, 28,033 by the private clinics, and 23,605 by

[51] Decree of the Ministry of the Interior, Nr. 7461/S-1916, of January 2, 1917; reprinted in *Das österreichische Sanitätswesen*, vol. 29 (1917), Nr. 1–8, pp. 3–8.

[52] In the rest of Austria there were 76 tuberculosis clinics. A. Goetzl, "Die wirtschaftliche Not und ihre Wirkungen," *Volksgesundheit*, vol. 7 (Nov., 1933), 157.

[53] *Das Neue Wien*, vol. 2, p. 556.

those of the health insurance institutes. Special examinations were carried out by a city-owned sputum laboratory, opened in 1927, a blood-examination center, and four X-ray laboratories. In the 25 clinics no treatment was given; patients were referred to doctors, recuperation homes, or other institutions as circumstances required. In addition, some of the 60 social workers specially trained for anti-tubercular work visited the homes of the patients to instruct the family, help to improve living conditions, and discuss the possibilities of isolating the patient or removing children temporarily. These social workers were also instrumental in securing assistance in cash and clothing for needy families.

An incidental task of the clinics was to carry out scientific research, as for instance, on the relations between tuberculosis and alcoholism or the connection between the former and certain professions. In 1933 they were instrumental in the selection of cases for the investigation of the League of Nations on "The Effects of the Economic Depression on the Population of Vienna."[54]

Most visitors to the tubercular clinics came voluntarily; they were referrals from health insurance institutions, schools, public agencies, hospitals, and—comparatively few—from private practitioners. A federal decree required that all cases of contagious tuberculosis and deaths from tuberculosis be reported to a city physician of the district who in turn informed the appropriate clinic. Information on tuberculosis of the skin was obtained by voluntary agreements. Another decree of the ministry of social administration obliged all public hospitals to report all releases of patients to the proper clinic. The clinics also arranged for reports from the health insurance agencies. Thus, together with the tuberculosis tests made in the well baby clinics and the regular examination of school children mentioned previously, a great number of cases of tuberculosis were under control. In 1929 it was estimated that 40 per cent of the persons afflicted with pulmonary tuberculosis in its infectious stage were known to the clinics; by 1937 the estimate was 73 per cent.[55]

Several recuperation homes and sanitariums were maintained for curable patients. They were situated partly in the outer districts of

[54] The Health Organization of the League of Nations, *Quarterly Bulletin*, Vol. III, 461 ff. (Extract No. 17).

[55] *Das Neue Wien*, vol. 2, pp. 556–557; Rosenblum, *op. cit.*, pp. 65–70; A. Goetzl, "Die Tuberkulosebekämpfung in Wien," *Blätter für das Wohlfahrtswesen*, 1929 (Tandler issue), p. 17; conversations with Dr. Goetzl.

the city, partly in other suitable places in Austria; two homes for tubercular children were established in Italy. In 1929 the city could accommodate 1,151 patients in its own homes and additional persons in beds rented from other institutions. Acceptance in these institutions was effected only through the central admission office after the patient had been examined by the local tuberculosis clinic. As a matter of principle, he was required to contribute to the costs of his treatment as much as his means permitted. Ordinarily he stayed four to six weeks in the recuperation home or sanitarium, but upon recommendation of the directors of these institutions, the central office could prolong these periods to three months or longer.[56] For the most serious cases the city erected a new building with 320 beds on the grounds of the Lainz Hospital. It was completed in 1930 at a cost of 5,000,000 schillings, or just above $714,000.[57] In addition, 250 incurable persons could be accommodated in the tuberculosis ward of the poorhouse in Lainz and 1,500 otherwise than in city hospitals.[58] Incidentally, it should be mentioned that in spite of considerable cuts in the 1932 municipal budget no reductions were made in the expenditures for the campaign against tuberculosis. They were maintained with 2,670,440 schillings.[59]

The systematic war against the white plague proved successful. The mortality rate per 10,000 persons dropped spectacularly:[60]

Year	Rate	Year	Rate
1913	30	1920	39
1918	61	1925	20
1919	53	1930	16

It seems scarcely necessary to emphasize that this success depended, in addition to the special measures described, upon concerted action with other measures such as rehousing a great part of the population, reorganization of garbage disposal, school meals, maintenance of recreational facilities, and sport activities.

The first comprehensive measure against the great increase of venereal diseases resulting from the war was a decree of the republi-

[56] Cf. Rosenblum, *op. cit.*, pp. 67, 69; *Statistisches Jahrbuch der Stadt Wien*, 1929 (2. Jahrg.), p. 56.

[57] Alfred Baldass, *Wien*, p. 84.

[58] A. Goetzl, "Zur Geschichte der Tuberkulose," *Blätter für das Wohlfahrtswesen*, 1930, p. 270, as cited in Rosenblum, *op. cit.*, p. 67.

[59] *Wiener Wahlhandbuch*, Heft C (1932), 28, 29.

[60] Goetzl, *Blätter für das Wohlfahrtswesen*, 1931, pp. 44, 217, as cited in Rosenblum, *op. cit.*, p. 70; *Das Neue Wien*, vol. 2, p. 554. The figures for 1919 through 1930 are computed on the basis of the 1923 census.

can ministry of public health of November 21, 1918.[61] It obliged everybody afflicted with a communicable venereal disease to undergo medical treatment, gave the public health authorities the right to examine those who there was reason to believe were infected, and required physicians to report patients if spread of the disease was to be feared.[62] If the appropriate city physician received such a report he invited the patient to his office, acquainted him with the government order, referred him to a clinic, and supervised him until the treatment was completed. Federal and municipal evening clinics provided for the free treatment of needy working persons. In Vienna they were all administered by the city since Vienna had become a self-governing state. Because of the return to more normal conditions and the systematic fight against social diseases the original 22 evening clinics were reduced to 4, of which 3 belonged to the federal state; all continued to be administered by the city. The number of clients decreased from 9,321 in 1921 to 4,320 in 1932. During the day patients were cared for by the clinics of several hospitals which were equipped for such work. To advise persons who were fearful of having contracted a venereal disease a free counseling service was opened by the city in December, 1923. Though it operated independently of the clinics it apparently had great difficulty in overcoming the shyness of most people, so that only approximately 400 persons annually made use of it. The work was carried out by a physician on two evenings a week. In addition to this counseling service, the city maintained 2 Wassermann centers (1 for men, 1 for women) in which anyone could get a free test without giving name or address. During the first year of their existence (1929) they were utilized by 620 persons. Other means to fight venereal diseases were the mothers' aid, the well baby clinics, and the special ward in the Central Children's Home. Every applicant for a city job had to take a Wassermann test and, if the reaction was positive, had to prove that he was being treated before going to work.[63]

[61] *StGBl.*, 1918, Nr. 49.

[62] It may be mentioned that Professor Tandler complained in a speech to the Constituent Assembly that the last provision mentioned above did not become satisfactorily effective because the necessary orders to the doctors were never issued. At the same time he announced the preparation of a bill for effectively enforcing the treatment of all persons afflicted with a venereal disease. Evidently this bill was never enacted. Konstituierende Nationalversammlung, *Protokoll,* May 18, 1920, p. 2796.

[63] Cf. *Das Neue Wien*, vol. 2, pp. 561–563; Rosenblum, *op. cit.*, pp. 71–73; *Statistisches Jahrbuch der Stadt Wien,* 1929 (2. Jahrg.), p. 59; *Statistisches Taschenbuch . . . Wien,* 1932, p. 15.

Alcoholism was viewed as a common disease and for several years private associations had endeavored to combat it by education and propaganda. In 1922 the Vienna state government founded a bureau for furthering this fight which, like the State Central Organization for Combating Tuberculosis, coördinated the interested groups. It served in an advisory capacity to the government. As a public body, the city could not openly attack the problem by directly fighting drinking habits, the primary roots of alcoholism, but it did subsidize the abstinence movement. It also initiated a comprehensive program for the care of alcoholics, the number of which had increased considerably during the postwar period. Although the sanitarium for inebriates founded in 1922 was connected with the Am Steinhof insane asylum, the inmates of the two institutions were completely separated. Some alcoholics came to the sanitarium voluntarily; others were sent there by police headquarters. From the moment the patient entered he received no alcohol and no medicines. The treatment was mainly individual educational work with every inmate; in addition, everybody worked, either in the garden or in a workshop, under expert supervision. The individual treatment made it necessary to limit the number of patients to 50 at one time, and since it averaged six months, only cases which offered some hope of improvement were accepted. On this principle no women were admitted because experience had taught that alcoholism among them was almost always incurable. In order to avoid relapses after discharge from the institution the authorities fostered a club for former inmates with which they kept in touch constantly. On Sundays parties and lectures were given and the directors of the club investigated members who had not appeared for some length of time. Joint parties of former and current inmates of the sanitarium were found helpful for both groups. No statistics of definite cures were available, but sanitarium officials estimated that 25 per cent of those released became definitely abstinent. In addition to the sanitarium, the city opened a counseling service for alcoholics in 1925; it served mainly relatives of alcoholics seeking protection or advice. By personal interviews with members of the family, possibly with the alcoholics also, as well as by investigation of home conditions and family relations, the physician or the social worker in charge of the service could often give advice and aid that contributed to the solution of existing problems. Several hundred persons made use of the institution each year—for example, 689 in 1933.[64]

In March, 1926, a counseling service for those afflicted with nervous and mental ailments (*Beratungsstelle für Nerven- und Gemütskranke*) was instituted. Its task was to advise and aid persons who had apparently regained sanity, those with mental disorders, and their families. Its officials also kept in touch with released inmates of insane asylums in order to aid them or their families should it be necessary. Their connections with the other welfare agencies facilitated the reference of their clients to those organizations where they could find other services than medical advice. The supervision of such persons who were not in absolute need of institutional treatment had also the additional advantage of relieving the overcrowded insane asylums. In 1933 the counseling service was used by 1,032 persons.[65]

An orthopedic clinic was opened in May, 1928, to advise and care for cases of physical abnormalities. Though its main work was with small children, it also assisted adults. Altogether 2,177 persons were aided in 1930, 1,637 in 1933. A special institute for the care of cripples gave advice to those in need of artificial limbs and orthopedic apparatus and to those who could not afford them. These appliances were produced directly by the institute for distribution to the poor under city care and to municipal employees. In 1930, for instance, it carried out 6,873 orders, for orthopedic appliances valued at 188,622 schillings.[66]

The last remarkable action of the Social Democratic welfare administration of Vienna was the purchase of 5 grams of radium for the treatment of cancer. The frequency of this disease had shown a dangerous increase. As part of the countermeasures a ward with 100 beds was opened in the city hospital in Lainz. By resolution of the city council of January 30, 1931, 1,900,000 schillings or $267,600 were allotted for the purchase of the radium and the adaptation of the former tuberculosis ward. Since no other Viennese institution possessed the necessary quantities of radium or adequate facilities

[64] *Das Neue Wien,* vol. 2, pp. 563–568; *Statistisches Taschenbuch . . . Wien,* 1933, p. 14.

[65] Cf. *Das Neue Wien,* vol. 2, pp. 578–579; Alfons Huber, "Die offene Fürsorge für Geisteskranke im Jahre 1928," *Blätter für das Wohlfahrtswesen,* 1929 (Tandler issue), pp. 26–27; *Statistisches Taschenbuch . . . Wien,* 1933, p. 14.

[66] Rosenblum, *op. cit.,* p. 76; *Statistisches Taschenbuch . . . Wien,* 1930, p. 14; 1933, p. 14.

for its use, every resident of Vienna without respect to means had access to this special ward; however, those who could afford to pay for treatment were charged the customary fees. Recognizing that the early treatment of cancer afforded the best chance of curing it, the city established 2 clinics, mainly to advise cancer-suspect persons, in the spring of 1932. They were also charged with the supervision of persons who had once been treated for cancer.[67]

In closing this section it may be noted that a voluntary blood-donor service was organized in Vienna as early as 1928. It was based on the idea of the "blood relationship of the Viennese workers." The blood donors were divided into factory and district groups and contributed their blood free of charge. The city of Vienna maintained a central register of all blood donors, as well as a blood-testing station.[68]

Recreational Program

The Viennese newspapers on July 1, 1931, reported "150,000 customers in the municipal summer swimming pools" on the two preceding days.[69] There can be no doubt that the city's bathing establishments were of the greatest importance for the health and well-being of large groups of its population. To be sure, a number of establishments had existed in the times of the monarchy, but bathing and swimming as mass sport developed only after the First World War. To accommodate the demand the number of public bathing institutions was increased from 36 in 1913 to 79 in 1933. They were intended to meet two distinct needs: to provide warm baths for many Viennese who did not have their own bathrooms, and to serve bathing and swimming fans at low rates. The full importance of these bathing establishments can be demonstrated by a few figures. For instance, in 1932 the municipal baths (including the children's pools mentioned above) were visited by 10,851,438 persons. Of these 6,997,645 used the warm, Turkish, or medical baths (*Kurbad*); 3,853,793 the swimming, wading, or sunbathing establishments provided in the swimming halls and along the Danube or in other open

[67] *Wiener Wahlhandbuch,* Heft C (1932), 29–31. To explain the full significance of the radium purchase it may be mentioned that at the time of its acquisition the world's total stock of pure radium was approximately 400 grams and that of all European cities only Paris and Stockholm possessed more than 5 grams, that is, 7.2 and 6 grams, respectively.

[68] *Blätter für das Wohlfahrtswesen,* 1929 (Tandler issue), pp. 21–22.

[69] *Wiener Wahlhandbuch,* Heft C (1932), 41.

areas in and around Vienna. In 1913 the municipal baths were frequented by only 4,049,000 persons. In 1926 the city erected the Amalienbad in one of the largest workers' districts which was particularly poorly provided with bathing facilities. This bath cost approximately 10,000,000 schillings and was certainly one of the largest and most modern establishments in Europe. It included a large swimming pool, warm, Turkish, and medical baths. To enable as many persons as possible to make use of these bathing facilities the fees were fixed so low that they did not even cover the operating expenses; the deficit, as well as the total investment, was charged to the city.[70]

The other great health resorts of the Viennese population were the many public parks spread all over the city. By planting gardens in the courts and surroundings of the municipal housing projects, laying out new, and enlarging old, parks, and converting old cemeteries[71] the new city government greatly enlarged the air reservoir of Vienna. The former 351 municipal parks were increased by 79 to 430; their territory, without considering the garden courts in the municipal houses, from 1,900,000 square meters in 1913 to more than 2,600,000 square meters in 1933. In addition, a number of private and public parks were declared unavailable for building purposes, and thus preserved for the public. In order to provide the poor districts with more adequate open areas the city not only placed the new parks chiefly in the poorer districts, but developed also a completely new idea: the "people's small-garden parks" (*Kleingarten-Volksparks*). To aid the "Schreber" garden movement, Vienna had set aside areas in the suburbs of the city to be used exclusively for this healthful and culturally valuable purpose. To make these places useful to still wider groups of the population the authorities began to build tree-shaded promenades, squares, and playgrounds along them and between the single blocks, and opened them to the general public for recreational purposes. The first experiment in this direction was made in the Twenty-first district over an area of approximately 140,000 square meters.[72]

---

[70] Cf. Danneberg, *Das Neue Wien*, p. 71; Rosenblum, *op. cit.*, pp. 79–81; *Statistisches Jahrbuch der Stadt Wien*, 1930–1935, p. 61.

[71] The overwhelming area of Viennese cemeteries was city property (3,738,000 square meters in 1935, for example); the rest belonged to religious groups (652,000 square meters). *Statistisches Jahrbuch der Stadt Wien*, 1930–1935, p. 63.

[72] Cf. Danneberg, *op. cit.*, pp. 71–72; Baldass, *op. cit.*, pp. 67–69.

In recognition of its value for public health the city health department, through its Division for Sport and Physical Culture, regulated the construction and distribution of sport and playgrounds. Sport clubs and similar institutions were promoted by cash subsidies and by making available to them the gymnasiums of the public schools. In addition, many new sport facilities were created, for instance, the swimming pools mentioned above. But certainly the largest gift of the city to the sport community was the stadium in the largest public park of Vienna, the Prater, completed in 1931. Built at a cost of 6,600,000 schillings, it was one of the most modern sport establishments in the world. The main section included a football field, two running tracks, and general facilities for so-called field sports; it accommodated 60,000 spectators. A special swimming pavilion and a bicycle racing track supplemented the main structure.[73]

Evaluation of the Welfare Program

The foregoing pages have covered, in varying degrees of detail, the widespread activities of the Vienna city government in the fields of social welfare and public health. Though hampered by the impoverishment following the war and the continuing crisis of the Austrian economy, a coördinated and, basically, nearly complete system of social welfare was created of which the whole Austrian working class was justly proud. It remains to list some areas in which little or nothing had been done. Thus, for example, no provisions were made by public welfare agencies for the reinstatement of released criminals in normal life or for adequate support of their families; provisions for helping cripples to secure gainful employment were nonexistent. Likewise, only the very first steps had been taken for the care of alcoholics.[74]

As was to be expected, the social welfare program of the Social Democrats did not remain unchallenged. In the discussion of Vienna tax reforms it was seen that the Christian Socials generally opposed the amount of the welfare expenditures, coining the term "welfare inflation." They attacked particularly the "luxury" with which the new institutions were equipped. Other charges were that the administrative costs were excessive and that the welfare institutions

[73] *Wiener Wahlhandbuch,* Heft C (1932), 39–40.
[74] Bock, *op. cit.,* pp. 18–21.

were abused for political purposes. To deal with these accusations in detail would necessitate an analysis of the accounts of every single branch of the welfare work described, and for this the data are not available. Moreover, such an attempt would give undue honor to most of the accusations since they were made in very general terms that hamper any precise discussion from the outset.

"Luxury," of course, is a relative notion. Certainly, many of the new institutions represented tremendous progress as compared to the former poor relief; on the other hand, they hardly seem excessive to an observer familiar with modern welfare institutions in the United States. The new kindergartens and the municipal bathing establishment, Amalienbad, were the most frequently denounced by the opposition; therefore, the reaction of the far-from-revolutionary London *Spectator* is of some interest. Its reporter stated that the kindergartens, destined for the very poor children of the city, recall the "nurseries in the homes of prosperous parents in large English country houses," and that "one of the largest public baths in the world" was placed in a workers' district; but he did not charge the Socialist administration with spendthrift extravagance as its Viennese critics did. His reaction was: "If poor, impoverished Vienna can have a princely bathing establishment like this in a poor district, why can not rich London . . . do the same?"[75]

In amplification of the charge that administrative costs were excessive it was claimed that half or more of the expenditures for kindergartens and children's homes went for personnel and other administrative charges, and that the private Catholic welfare agencies were able to take care of children much more cheaply than the city. Thus, for instance, Jehly claims that the average cost for one child in a municipal children's home (Central Children's Home, orphanages, educational homes, etc.) was 3,200 schillings annually, whereas in the institution of the Catholic Charity Organization Society this average amounted to only 720. Similar charges were made by the *Reichspost*.[76] Although the data given by the critics do not allow an analysis of this alleged discrepancy, the reply of the Social Democrats to some of these accusations may be noted. First, they said, it was not permissible to mix together all kinds of different

[75] *The Spectator*, October 5, 1929, pp. 431, 432.

[76] Cf. Eduard Jehly, *10 Jahre Rotes Wien*, pp. 33–34; *Reichspost*, March 21, 1933, p. 7.

institutions. It was self-evident that the personnel in an educational home like Eggenburg cost much more than that of an ordinary orphanage. On the other hand, the expenditures for temporary homes where the inmates change ten to twenty times in a year will be for many reasons larger than those of a home which houses the same children throughout the year. Such an institution not only spent much more for linen, laundry, and clothing, but also for the treatment of contagious diseases, separation of wards, and so on. Care of babies (often with their mothers), as in the Central Children's Home, caused additional expenses. In fact, in the orphanages and educational homes the average expenditure per child was 1,285 schillings, not 3,200, and even in Eggenburg annual costs for a child were only 2,737.50 schillings. Second, the statement concerning the 720 schillings spent in Catholic institutions was lacking in clarity. If the sum comprised only the costs of food, which might be concluded from the expression *"vollständige Verpflegung,"*[77] 720 schillings would not be so little, for the city provided, in addition, room, clothing, supervision, education, and care for sick children; if, on the other hand, all these services were given for the above figure "the poor youngsters [in the Catholic institutions] . . . are not to be envied." That the children in the Catholic agencies really were "not to be envied" was also indicated by the statement of the *Caritas* that it spent for its 4,000 *Hort* children 168,000 schillings annually, or 14 groschen (less than 2 cents), per child and day! Though this Socialist criticism obviously disregards the possibilities, for example, that if afternoon tea were provided much of the materials therefor might have been donated, and that the supervisory staff might have been largely voluntary, the sum remains almost incredibly small so that the benefits to the children were scarcely comparable. Finally, and probably most significantly, the Social Democratic reply pointed out that Catholic welfare organizations refused to join, and thereby to submit financial statements to, the General Association for Voluntary Youth Welfare despite the fact that membership brought a subvention from the city. Thus the Catholic organizations avoided financial audit by the General Association. Such audit was possible at any time with respect to the city welfare.[78]

[77] In Austrian usage the term can mean either complete board or complete maintenance.

[78] *Wiener Wahlhandbuch*, Heft C (1932), 20–22.

The charge of extravagant expenditures for political reasons was directed particularly against the issuance of free layettes to every prospective mother who applied for them, irrespective of her financial status. But city funds were allegedly misused in the interest of the Socialist party for propagandizing not only among mothers but also among children. As Jehly put it, the number of costly kindergartens was steadily increased *only* because they were really "elementary schools for Socialism."[79] In spite of the alleged preparedness of the Social Democrats to "poison the souls of children," extraordinary efforts spent on propaganda just among the three- to six-year-olds seem—to say the least—strange. The workers believed that the charge came with particularly poor grace from spokesmen for a religious group whose priests had consistently opposed the marriage of Catholics and non-Catholics, agreeing to it only when the promise was given that offspring of the union would be reared as Catholics, who were trying to establish a "confessional" school in Austria, and who had frequently stated that if they could control the training of a child until he was seven years of age they were willing to take their chances thereafter. But this was not the only inconsistency pointed out by the Socialists. Whereas for years the papers of the opponents of the municipal program had been full of complaints about "welfare inflation" which ruined the taxpayer, all of a sudden, in 1927, the Christian Socials discovered that the city was spending only a "paltry" amount for social welfare, though the total expenditures were estimated at 73,300,000 schillings, or nearly 15 per cent of the total budget of 481,500,000.[80] The peak of budget expenditures for social welfare purposes was reached in 1931 with 113,205,068 schillings; they had to be reduced in 1932 to 98,136,886 and to 91,129,697 in 1933. It may be noted that the expenditures of the Clerico-Fascist city administration in 1935 were 95,338,727 schillings.[81]

The simple fact is that certain needs must be filled. The Socialist administration of Vienna had drawn the blueprints for an imposing edifice of social welfare and had constructed a good part of it, but when the welfare expenditures had to be cut in 1932, as a result of

[79] *Op. cit.*, p. 35.

[80] Benedikt Kautsky, "Das Breitner-Budget," *Arbeit und Wirtschaft,* vol. 5 (April 15, 1927), 321; *ibid.* (April 1, 1927), 261. The amount definitely spent was 82,093,388 schillings (62,652,724 net). *Statistisches Jahrbuch der Stadt Wien,* 1929 (1. Jahrg.), p. 274.

[81] *Statistisches Jahrbuch der Stadt Wien,* 1930–1935, pp. 227, 228.

the economic crisis and decreased revenues, an appreciable part of the building remained for completion. After the Clerico-Fascist regime came into power in February, 1934, it was unable to justify any important change in the plans prepared by its reviled opponents even had it dared to attempt them in the light of the economic situation. As already indicated, the spirit and methods of the Clerico-Fascist welfare policy were something else again. The details, however, belong in Volume II, Chapter XXIX.

CHAPTER XVI

Education for Democracy

"DRILL SCHOOLS!" "Beating schools!" Such were the epithets flung at the schools of imperial Austria by working-class parents and middle-class educational reformers in protest against the mechanical instruction and severe discipline of which the children were the victims. Even more bitter were the comments on the discrimination against poorer pupils which made it difficult if not impossible for them to enter the secondary schools[1] and the universities. Other grievances were the restrictions on the freedom of teachers and the domination of the schools by the Roman Catholic Church. With the collapse of the empire the protesting groups planned to reform the schools in a manner similar to that advocated about a hundred years earlier in the United States. In both countries there was a determination to secure what the American workers had specifically termed "republican education." Although fewer persons were seriously concerned over the religious issue, it engendered greater intensity of conflict than any other. Just because Austria has always been so overwhelmingly Catholic, those who desired a nonsectarian public school system such as Americans take for granted found their task all the more arduous. And because Americans may have some difficulty in understanding a system of *public* education against which the charge could be brought that it embodied a doctrine of occupational and social predestination, it seems expedient to examine the background of the complaints.

A third of the eighteenth century had passed before the imperial government made any attempt to control or limit the authority of the religious orders in matters educational. The complaints had by this time become so vigorous, however, that in 1735 Emperor Karl VI issued the *Patent* of November 16 altering the teaching methods of the Jesuits and establishing some supervision to guarantee that the changes were carried out. This imperial action and a similar one in 1747 were of no practical significance, and the central govern-

[1] The Austrian term for secondary schools was "middle schools." There were two chief types, the *Gymnasium* and the *Realschule,* but, as will be brought out, varieties and combinations of them developed.

ment continued to enforce certain Church regulations on religious instruction and to settle disputes among the priests, the manorial lords, and the communities involving the selection and dismissal of teachers.

One of these controversies, in which the clergy of Carinthia attempted to assume complete control of the appointment of instructors, acquired importance because during it Maria Theresia decreed that the management of schools would continue to be a state affair. Her active interest as well as the steadily growing opinion that the government should exercise more authority in the field of education were the chief factors that brought the first major reforms.

As an initial step in these reforms a Central School Commission (*Studienhofkommission*) with wide powers and independent status was created in 1760. It functioned to some degree as a ministry of education, but little positive action resulted until after the expulsion of the Jesuits in 1773. Immediately the scope of state authority was greatly expanded and on December 6, 1774, the first general school law was promulgated by the empress. Under it three general categories of institutions were established. Each province was required to maintain a normal or "model" school. In each small city or borough and in each village where there was a parish church there had to be a primary or "trivial" school. Finally, in the capital of each canton there had to be a higher primary or "principal" school. Attendance was compulsory from the sixth year of age until the children were "sufficiently instructed to choose a trade or profession." The law proceeds with the quaint expression: "we shall see with satisfaction, if parents send them to school during six or seven years, and permit them to attend even longer."[2] It seems that the enforcement of this ideal was indirect because of the requirement that no child could be taken into service or enter a trade without a certificate of attendance. In 1775 the Central School Commission was reorganized and an important advance made with the introduction of an entirely new set of textbooks. The Toleration Charter of 1781 permitting Protestants, Greek Catholics, and Jews to erect

[2] Henry Barnard, *Systems, Institutions and Statistics of Public Instruction, Part I—Europe—German States* (New York, 1872), pp. 28, 879, 881; and Peter Mosser and Theodor Reitterer, *Die Mittelschulen in Oesterreich*, vol. 1 (Wien, 1929), pp. 1, 2. The English translation of the law of 1774 printed by Barnard, pp. 879–884, is probably not complete (his translation of the law of 1868 is not) but I was unable to secure the German text.

their own schools was soon deprived of much of its significance by the ruling that in localities where Catholic schools already existed the establishment of other schools was "unnecessary." Somewhat later, however, Jews were required to have their own school wherever there was a synagogue.

Other reforms instituted by Joseph II included strengthening the financial support for schools, punishing nonattendance by fine, abolishing the additional charge for instruction in arithmetic, and exempting poor children from all tuition fees. Generally speaking, however, the schools were open to the same criticisms which were stressed more than a century later: instruction was uniform and mechanical, supervision was largely in the hands of the Roman Catholic Church, and discipline was severe.

Conscious of the persistence of popular complaints, Emperor Franz II took up with Chancellor Count Rottenhan the possibilities of improvement. The attitude of this advisor is clearly enough indicated by his opposition to any degree of self-government for teachers, despite steps already made in that direction, and by his belief that the true purpose of the lower schools was "to make thoroughly pious, good, tractable, and industrious men of the laboring classes of the people." With this object in view he advocated a restriction of the scope of the schools, the use of simple laboring men as teachers, the abolition of tuition fees, and emphasis on instruction in industrial employments.[3] Finally, after it had been discussed for ten years by a Board of Educational Reform (*Studienrevisionskommission*), the constitution of the German common schools was issued by the emperor in 1805. According to its terms supervision of the "trivial" and country "higher" elementary schools was primarily the duty of the respective pastors, but Jewish schools remained solely under Catholic superintendence.

> The method of instruction must endeavor first and foremost to train the memory; then, however, according to the pressure of circumstances, the intellect and the heart. The trivial schools [i.e., the teachers] will strictly refrain from any explanations other than those exactly prescribed in the "school and method book" and strive to make certain that what has been learned by heart is retained so that it can be applied in individual instances.[4]

[3] Karl Strack, *Geschichte des deutschen Volksschulwesens* (Gütersloh, 1872), p. 327.
[4] *Ibid.*, pp. 329–330.

No charges were exacted from poor children or from those whose fathers were in the army and each pair of such children was provided with one textbook. The number of pupils per teacher was "limited" to 80 to 100, but this ratio could be doubled in half-day schools. Consequently, despite the recognition by Emperor Franz of the need for improvement the net results during his reign were a retrogression from the level maintained under Maria Theresia and Joseph.

The Revolution of 1848 brought a stimulus to educational reform and an even more widespread recognition in all strata of the population of the necessity for such reform. Among the things actually accomplished were the creation of a ministry of education; a revision of financial arrangements to guarantee more adequate support; abolition of most of the half-day schools; improvements in the status of teachers, particularly of assistant teachers; advances in teacher-training programs; and the introduction of new and better textbooks.[5]

To those favoring secular education, however, the concordat of 1855 was sufficient reason for believing that all progress had been reversed. According to the fifth article "The entire instruction of Catholic youth in all public, as well as nonpublic, schools will be in accordance with the teachings of the Catholic religion; the bishops, however, by virtue of their pastoral offices, shall direct religious instruction in all public and nonpublic institutions of learning, and watch over them carefully so that there may be nothing in any branch of instruction that shall run counter to Catholic faith and moral purity." This language did not mean that Catholic bishops were authorized to see to it that nothing contrary to their faith was taught in Protestant or Jewish schools. The real point is that the efforts of the "forty-eighters" to eliminate, or greatly decrease, the supervisory power of the Church had been defeated. This power was not restricted to religious training but was extended over the "entire instruction" of Catholic youth; moreover, it had been guaranteed in what amounted to an international treaty signed by the pope and the emperor. In this connection the first sentences of Article 8 are also significant. "All teachers in elementary schools designed for Catholics are placed under the supervision of the

[5] *Ibid.*, pp. 334–336.

Church. The chief school superintendent of the diocese is to be appointed by His Majesty from those proposed by the bishop." For the secondary schools the prescriptions of Article 7 were even more decisive: "In the *Gymnasien* and secondary schools in general that are designed for Catholic youths, only Catholics will be appointed as professors or teachers."[6] Small wonder that a writer of the Schuschnigg era wrote of this concordat, "It was a treaty the like of which the Church had not been able to carry through for a long time."[7]

Meanwhile, the Toleration Charter of the preceding century had apparently not been completely observed; some Austrians say it had been "forgotten." At any rate Franz Joseph issued in 1861 the Protestant *Patent* reaffirming the rights of Protestants. Section 11 guaranteed that these groups might set up their own schools in any place, nominate teachers in accordance with the general laws, and determine the extent and method of religious instruction.[8]

Serious breaches were made in the concordat of 1855 by legislation of May, 1868, concerning civil marriages, the relations of State, Church and school, and interconfessional relations. The statute of 1868 of most interest to this discussion provided that the "supreme direction and supervision of all instruction belongs to the state," that without impairment of this general power the respective religious faiths retained supervision of religious instruction, but that "instruction in the other subjects is independent of the influence of any church or religious society." Schools founded or supported in whole or in part by public funds, a provision that covered many Roman Catholic institutions, were open to adherents of any faith. Teaching positions in publicly founded or supported schools were open to all citizens who had demonstrated their qualifications. Attendance in a school or educational institution for members of a particular faith was not prohibited by law to those of another confession, but another statute adopted the same day did prohibit the compulsory enrollment of a member of one church in the school of another.[9]

The secularization of the school system was continued in the

[6] *RGBl.*, 1855, Nr. 195.

[7] Taras von Borodajkewycz, "Die Kirche in Oesterreich," in Josef Nadler and Heinrich von Srbik, *Oesterreich, Erbe und Sendung im deutschen Raum* (Salzburg-Leipzig), 1936, p. 311.

[8] *RGBl.*, 1861, Nr. 41.

[9] *RGBl.*, 1868, Nr. 48 and 49, Art. 10.

famous common school law of 1869. For example, the minister of education could establish the curriculum on the basis of proposals from the provincial school authorities or on his own responsibility after listening to them. Improvements in the system included the requirement of eight years' attendance for pupils and of four years' training for teachers. In the cities there was a five-year elementary school (*Volksschule*) and a three-year higher elementary or grammar school (*Bürgerschule*); in rural districts an eight-year *Volksschule*. The minimum number of subjects in which instruction had to be given was increased. Pupils per teacher were limited to 80, but no distinctions were made between full- and half-day sessions.[10] In general, it may be said that this statute represented distinct progress along lines favored by leading educators of the time throughout Europe and America.

As might have been expected, the Catholic hierarchy was by no means pleased with the changes from the concordat. A contemporary French writer, in discussing the new provisions for state inspection of the schools, reported that "the Church authorities have refused to submit themselves to it," and added that "In Tirol, instigated by sermons from the pulpit, the populace chased out the lay inspectors by throwing stones at them."[11] This might be considered the exaggeration of some rabid anticlerical were it not for the background. On June 22, 1868, Pope Pius IX delivered an allocution against the constitution of December, 1867, and the laws of May, 1868. He characterized the constitution as "truly accursed" and went on: "Through this law is established an unconditional freedom of all opinions and publications, of faith, of conscience and of teaching; citizens of every religion are granted permission to establish training and educational institutions; all religious communities of whatever sort are put on the same footing and recognized by the state." With reference to the school law he asserted that it "eliminates all influence of the Church" and pointed out that under it "every religious community without distinction can establish its own schools for the children of its faith." Concerning all the laws, including the constitution, His Holiness said in one phrase that they were "abominable" and in another that they were "detest-

[10] *Ibid.*, 1869, Nr. 62.
[11] Émile de Laveleye, *L'Instruction du peuple* (Paris, 1872), p. 171.

able and damnable." Then, on his "apostolic authority," he "repudiated and damned" the constitution and all the laws and declared them and all their implications "as completely null and forever void." Bishop after bishop in Austria issued similar condemnations.[12]

It is scarcely necessary to labor the fact that the Tirolese peasant has a centuries-long tradition of being a man of vigorous, not to say violent, action; in other words, he is not content with mere verbal condemnation. More important is the faithful reproduction of the attitudes of Pius IX by opponents of the Vienna school reformers in later years, particularly in 1934.

The reader has probably taken for granted that the school reforms of the late 1860's were a part of the general liberal movement. They represented concessions forced from the reactionary elements in control of Austria as the result of the military defeats in 1859 and 1866 in the same way as were the workingmen's rights of organization described in Chapter II. But when the liberal era came to an end with the accession of Taaffe as prime minister in 1879, the opponents of school reforms began to make headway and in 1883 managed to secure a law which definitely worsened the system. Among the changes was one which increased the maximum number of pupils allowed per teacher to 100 in cases where only half-day sessions were held and another which exempted country children and children of the poorer classes in towns from regular attendance after completion of the sixth year. Such exemptions might be for a part of the year, a part of the week or a part of the day, and might cover whole rural school districts when the communities therein so requested. Although these new regulations did not formally reduce the required attendance from eight to six years, the practice approached this rather closely in many rural districts. As a step back toward the concordat school it was also provided that no person might be appointed as a school principal (*Schulleiter*) who could not prove that he was qualified to give religious instruction in the faith of the majority of the pupils.[13] The practical result was to exclude Protestants from positions as principals in the overwhelming majority of schools. And, since the principal was often

[12] *Neue Freie Presse*, June 26, 1868 (A.M.), pp. 2, 3–4. The *Presse* reprinted a German translation of the allocution which had appeared in the Catholic publication *Volksfreund* the day before.

[13] *RGBl.*, 1883, Nr. 53, esp. §§ 11, 21, 48.

the only teacher in small communities, Protestants were excluded from teaching at all in such localities. These two laws of 1869 and 1883 remained the basis for the common public elementary school throughout the remaining years of the empire. Even the curricula remained practically unchanged after some revisions carried through between 1884 and 1890.

To this point the secondary or "middle" schools have received no consideration. They developed from the medieval Church grammar schools and the Jesuit, Benedictine, and Piarist *Gymnasia* of the seventeenth and eighteenth centuries. When the Jesuits were suppressed in 1773 the government appropriated their property and utilized the greater part of it for educational purposes so that their *Gymnasia* became state-endowed institutions. Three years earlier the *Real-Handlungs-Akademie* had been created for the purpose of training merchants and technical experts. The new institution crystallized the distinction between the training for the sons of the "better classes" and for those of the lower middle class. At this date workers' children were considered well served by the common schools. In 1808 the regulations concerning secondary schools were brought together in a gymnasial code comparable to the constitution of 1805 for the common schools. During the next year the business and technical academy in Vienna was reorganized to conform with general proposals concerning *Realschulen,* and in 1819 the curriculum of the *Gymnasien* was altered to put more emphasis on Latin and Greek, to reduce the time spent on history and geography, and to eliminate natural history, geometry, and physics altogether. The next proposals for essential changes in organization appeared in 1849 in the form of the "Plan For the Organization of the *Gymnasien* and *Realschulen* of Austria" drafted by Franz Exner and Hermann Bonitz. Their ideas concerning the *Gymnasien* received provisional imperial approval in the same year, became final law in 1854, and remained, at least until 1938, the basic principles of this type of secondary school. The *Gymnasium* was after 1849 an eight-year school receiving pupils of ten or eleven years of age, emphasizing ancient languages, and embodying the idea that the culture of the ancients is a model for all time. It remained the training ground for the upper classes and its completion was the most common preparation for entrance to the universities. Although the

Exner-Bonitz plans for the organization of the *Realschulen* could not be carried through, a law of 1851 altered the *Realschule* proper into a six-year institution which continued to emphasize mathematics, mechanics and mechanical engineering, architecture and technical chemistry, and included a modern language as an optional course. Under the constitution of December, 1867, legislation concerning these schools was reserved to the individual provinces, but as a matter of fact the laws actually passed conformed in all essential respects to a bill drafted by the central government. The results were the addition of a seventh year, the dropping of many practical courses from the curriculum and substituting therefor two modern languages, and the alteration of the aim of the *Realschule* in the direction of offering not only a preparation for work in technical colleges but also a general higher education emphasizing mathematics and natural science. New vocational schools took over much of the former task of the *Realschule* in preparing students for industrial and commercial occupations. Meanwhile, in 1864, a four-year *Realgymnasium* had been introduced. Its purpose was to provide training past the first four years of *Volksschule* that would enable the pupil to proceed into either the last four years of a *Gymnasium* or of a *Realschule*. Although received favorably at first it became less popular and important. Nevertheless, continued and sharp criticism of the strict separation of "classical" and "practical" secondary schooling led in 1908 to the creation of an eight-year *Realgymnasium* and a *Reformrealgymnasium* which were, as the names indicate, different degrees of compromise between the conflicting ideals.[14] During the remaining years before the collapse of the empire the organization and curricula of the secondary schools underwent no alteration worth mentioning in a nontechnical discussion.

From the account thus far given it is evident that Austria had developed the typical European dualistic school system. This system provided only eight years of free compulsory common schools for poorer, chiefly working-class, children; but for the progeny of the better classes it provided seven or eight years of secondary or middle schools, in addition to four or five years of primary training. (It must

[14] Cf. Barnard, *op. cit.*, pp. 67 ff.; and Mosser and Reitterer, *op. cit.*, esp. pp. 1–12, and *passim*. The latter is particularly valuable because it reprints the texts of state laws and of other documents.

not be forgotten, of course, that the middle schools required entrance examinations and charged fees.) For reasons already stated, workers and their leaders were thoroughly dissatisfied with the whole school system—elementary and secondary. The changes effected attracted world-wide attention. Before discussing them, however, reference must be made to the official position on education taken by the workers' political organization.

It will be recalled that Viktor Adler achieved the unification of the Social Democratic groups as a party at Hainfeld in 1889. The program adopted there included an unequivocal demand for the democratization of educational opportunities: "In the interest of the future of the working class, compulsory, free, and nondenominational instruction in elementary and continuation schools, as well as gratuitous accessibility to all higher educational institutions, is absolutely required; the necessary prerequisite to this is the separation of Church and State and the declaration that religion is a private matter."[15] As already pointed out, the Austrian workers were here requesting only what practically every American now takes for granted, except the point concerning gratuitous accessibility to *all* institutions of higher learning. A revised program, approved in 1901, amplified the section on education with demands for free food, textbooks, pencils, copybooks, and similar materials for all children in the elementary schools, and the same demands for those pupils in higher institutions who had the capacity for further training.[16]

The man to whom most individual credit for the postwar reform of the Austrian, and particularly the Viennese, schools belongs is Otto Glöckel. Born in 1874, the son of a public schoolteacher in a small village in the Wiener-Neustadt industrial district, Glöckel secured, shortly before he was nineteen, a position as probationary "under teacher" in a school in one of the most poverty-stricken districts of Vienna. Along with Karl Seitz and other kindred spirits, who revolted against the persistence of unequal educational opportunities and held that Socialism was the remedy, the future administrative president of the Vienna school council took an active part in the movement of The Young Ones who vigorously attacked

[15] *Parteitag, 1889*, p. 4.

[16] *Ibid., 1901*, p. 4. The reference to "food" is not entirely clear; it probably referred to lunch and, in the light of developments during the republican era, possibly even to breakfast or "second breakfast."

existing defects. This group attained some successes in the elections of teachers' representatives in a district school council in 1897. On September 14 of that year Glöckel read in a newspaper that he and four other under teachers had been summarily dismissed by order of Lueger, Christian Social mayor of Vienna. Thus forced out of his chosen life's work the young man first found employment in social insurance organizations and then entered politics, serving for many years in the imperial and republican parliaments. As early as 1898 appeared the School Program of The Young Ones in which the indissoluble connection between pedagogical and social problems was emphasized and in which the reforms of the 'twenties were foreshadowed. Again in 1916 a committee in which Glöckel, Seitz, Hartmann, and Ofner played the leading roles worked out a reform program; in it even clearer outlines are seen of the principles later adopted. On March 15, 1919, Glöckel was placed in charge of the ministry of education, though his title was only "under secretary."[17]

At this time there was fairly general agreement that the imperial school system was outmoded—that the new Austria needed "republican" schools. Naturally there remained differences on details, various political and religious groups wishing to make the new design conform to their ideals. As late as November 28, 1919, the extremely conservative Pan-German deputy Dr. Angerer declared to the Constituent National Assembly that, "In the first place one thing is to be set down as established from which the necessity of a thoroughgoing reform can be seen forthwith, namely, that the school of earlier times did not serve the people, although it was called people's school (*Volksschule*) and in its continuation 'middle school' and university for the people; but the people's school, indeed our whole school system, served particular privileged circles, the dynastic and aristocratic interests, and everything was arranged to educate our youth from this point of view."[18]

Years later an independent American investigator described the

---

[17] Ferdinand Heger, "Am Grabe Otto Glöckels," *Der Kampf*, vol. 2 (Sept., 1935), 404 ff. For an extended treatment of Glöckel's life and work, see *Otto Glöckel, Selbstbiographie* (Zurich, 1939). Actually, less than one-quarter of this work was written by Glöckel, and it breaks off just before November, 1918. The next section, written by Glöckel's close friend and collaborator in the school reforms, Dr. Hans Fischl, completes the story. The remainder includes reprints of speeches and documents and a discussion of Glöckel's relations with Swiss school reformers by F. Briner of Zurich.

[18] Konstituierende Nationalversammlung, *Protokoll*, November 28, 1919, pp. 1197–1198.

imperial schools in slightly less forceful language but with the inclusion of certain illuminating details.

The educational system of the time before the reform forced the young Austrian to follow one of three educational paths. In making a decision, consideration had to be given to the period of compulsory military service which would begin at the latest when the young man had reached his twenty-first year.

He could attend Volksschule and Buergerschule (Elementary and Higher Elementary School), and on graduation from the latter could take a course at a Lower Vocational School. In this case his army training extended over a period of three years and he could not attain to the rank of officer.

Or he could, at the age of fifteen, enter a Higher Vocational School. In this case, his entire general and vocational training came to an end when he was about eighteen or nineteen years old. He had to have but one year of army training and could become an officer.

Finally, he could, at the age of eleven, enter a regular secondary school and from there he could go on to a university or a school of equal standing. In this case too, his military training was only one year and he could become an officer.

Thus, a decision as to the child's future career had to be reached at the end of the elementary school period when the child was eleven years old. It had to be decided, not only if he was to be a manual worker or was to enter a profession, but also what type of profession, for the division of secondary schools into those with classical and with realistic courses of study made a later transfer difficult.

The whole system tended to emphasize the traditional division into social classes. Handworkers and brain workers were separated from each other at an early age. When the young people were twenty-two years old, the division into rulers and ruled was complete. The gulf between the two groups which had steadily widened during the period of schooling became even more obvious in the officer-men relationship of army days.[19]

Another result of the situation thus outlined is revealed most clearly by the prereform proportion of middle school to common school pupils. In the predominantly middle and upper class central districts of Vienna there was 1 secondary school child to each 2.7 children in the compulsory schools; in the proletarian districts the ratios were 1 to 15 or 20 or 22. When the comparison was made with reference to occupations it was found that for 1 manual worker's child in the secondary schools in Favoriten there were 100 in the

[19] May Hollis Siegl, *Reform of Elementary Education in Austria* (New York, 1933), p. 21.

compulsory schools; in Floridsdorf the ratio was 1 to 138. The two districts named were, and are, overwhelmingly proletarian.[20]

The dominating ideas of Glöckel and his associates ran along three lines: political, economic, and pedagogical. The new republic needed citizens trained in a democratic way to exercise their rights in self-government. It needed skilled workmen, independent and self-confident, as far removed from wage slaves as might be. It needed to make the best use of the results of research in the field of education for the common good. These ideas involved the democratization of the schools and their administration in the most complete sense, the delegation of their supervision to trained educators, the improvement of the training of teachers, and the improvement of the methods of instruction. As the first steps, the ministry of education was reorganized and a "reform division" created within it. This was done without the clean sweep that characterizes so many reorganizations, in fact, Glöckel removed only one former official; but, for example, the lawyers who had previously performed so much of the work of the ministry were now limited to strictly legal activities and educational experts took over the tasks for which they were more competent. They were, however, not to become bureaucrats but sooner or later were to return to the classroom duties from which they had been called.[21] As evidence of the realization of the democratic aim in school administration, it should be noted that a number of active teachers were members of the reform division, that the Vienna city school council had 18 teachers in a membership of 109, and that all city school councils became more representative as a result of the extension of the franchise after November, 1918.

But much more important was the first major move toward the democratization of the schools themselves—first, only because of the pressure of circumstances. The empire had maintained a number of military academies, several of them at points within the new frontiers. In the early weeks of the republic wide approval was secured for the idea of transforming these institutions into state boarding schools for exceptionally capable youngsters, particularly those from homes so poor or so remote from secondary schools that they had no hopes of attending them. Three of the academies began

[20] Hans Fischl, *Sieben Jahre Schulreform in Oesterreich* (Wien, 1926), p. 14.
[21] *Otto Glöckel,* pp. 72–73, 192.

to operate as *Realschulen* on January 1, 1919, but for months the situation remained chaotic with both military and educational authorities exercising a degree of control. The law of November 28, 1919, finally put a legal foundation under the "federal educational institutes," as they were called, and established six.[22] Their official name was first *Staatserziehungsanstalt* and later *Bundeserziehungsanstalt.*

Shortly after assuming office in the ministry of education Glöckel undertook a reorganization of these educational institutes. They became to some extent laboratories which carried on experiments in reforming methods and curricula. Nevertheless, the original purpose of providing secondary education in a boarding school where many scholarships were available was maintained; at least as long as Austria remained democratic in form, the majority of the students always came from extremely poor homes. Second, more and more children came from outlying provincial towns so that another objective was reached. Moreover, the institutes remained "conspicuously free from creeds" and their existence and success provided "a support and argument in favor of all forward tendencies in the Austrian Middle Schools."[23] This judgment of an American scholar is echoed in the generous praise accorded to them from educators throughout the world. Further, this praise is ample vindication, if any be needed, for those who created the institutes in those places "where once the young people were taught how one can best and quickest kill men." All the more is it to be regretted, then, that the Schuschnigg dictatorship returned some of the institutes to their original purposes and discontinued others.[24]

Naturally the reformers were not devoting their entire time to the institutes just described. Glöckel issued ordinances, for example, abolishing compulsory attendance at religious exercises in elementary and secondary schools; abolishing the secret reports made by school inspectors on teachers in the elementary schools; and permitting women to study law, engineering, and agriculture

[22] *StGBl.*, 1919, Nr. 542. For other details on the early history of the institutes, see Glöckel's remarks in the Constituent Assembly, *Protokoll,* November 28, 1919, pp. 1193 ff.

[23] Beryl Parker, *The Austrian Educational Institutes* (Vienna, 1931), pp. 36, 37, 164–173. This is a beautifully illustrated and detailed account.

[24] The quotation is from a speech of the Christian Social deputy, Dr. Georg Gimpl in Konstituierende Nationalversammlung, *Protokoll,* November 28, 1919, p. 1202. The Schuschnigg decrees appear in *BGBl.,* 1934 I, Nr. 145; 1935, Nr. 232, 448, 487.

in institutions of university grade. Vienna abolished the old regulation which prohibited married women from holding positions as teachers. In the provinces the prescriptions concerning compulsory school attendance had been materially relaxed during the war; this situation was now corrected in most of the new states.

On April 22, 1919, Glöckel made an extensive report to the committee on education of the Constituent Assembly concerning past actions and plans for the future. Coöperation of parents was to be solicited and parents' associations formed; chambers of teachers were to be organized in all branches and stages of education; reforms in the terms of appointment of *Dozenten,* in the salaries of assistants, and in similar matters in the universities were to be furthered; committees of university students to represent their own interests were to be constituted. But the most important part of Glöckel's report lies in another aspect of it: for the first time, apparently, he formally stated to legislative representatives the basic principles of the reformed schools. These principles were: (1) learning through self-activity, and (2) a single type of school for the first eight years of schooling. These will be discussed later. Significant in this meeting, moreover, were the demands of the German Nationalists that all confessional and private schools, including teacher-training institutions, should be transformed into state schools, and the vigorous opposition to these demands made by the Christian Socials.[25]

From this time on Glöckel made reports to the educational committee at intervals of about three months; from these it is learned that experimental classes and experimental schools were begun with the school year 1919–1920, that the size of such classes was limited to thirty, and that the teacher was freed from the duty of observing the customary curriculum. In the same school year, girls were permitted to enter what had formerly been termed "boys' middle schools." A new set of readers for elementary pupils was prepared and introduced generally on November 12, 1919, the first anniversary of the republic. Incidentally, as a part of the democratization process, it may be observed that in 1921 a new textbook commission began to function. Half of the group was composed of active teachers; it was to make its decisions "in full view of the public."[26] In

[25] *Tätigkeits-Bericht,* Heft 12 (Wien, 1919), pp. 41–44.

[26] *Ibid.,* pp. 44–46; Fischl, *op. cit.,* p. 34. A great reduction in the number of pupils in a class was one result of the reforms; to this result the decrease in the birth rate contributed of course.

February, 1920, Glöckel was able to state to the committee the basic ideas of what soon became famous in Austria as the Guiding Principles (*Leitsätze*) of the reform. In July he reported the adoption of a provisional teaching plan.[27]

The Guiding Principles were the result of the general dissatisfaction already discussed, but specifically they grew out of the work of the reform division of the ministry of education, the experiences in the experimental classes, and the innumerable discussions in teachers' associations and voluntary study groups (*Arbeitsgemeinschaften*) of the teachers. As a fundamental consideration, the Principles pointed out the necessity of the schools making more of an effort than they had previously to bring out a consciousness of social and national solidarity and of the duties arising therefrom for every member of the community. To this end it was insisted that the schools must be so organized that children and their parents and advisers would not have to make a decision at too early an age about what type of school the child should enter. As already stated, the practical result of the prereform arrangements was, in almost all cases, to force a decision concerning occupation or profession at the age of ten or eleven. The obvious solutions suggested were a unified school going further than was then true, specifically, for the first eight years rather than for the first four, and the facilitation of transfers from one type of school to another. From these proposals it is clear that the reformers did not intend to disregard individual differences. On the contrary, it was a second fundamental consideration that the schools offer various possibilities so that the individual—for his own benefit and that of the community--might secure that training which corresponded best to his particular gifts and to the requirements of his future vocation. For this purpose classes in the second four years of the proposed unified school were to be separated into a first division comprising the children of middle and exceptional capacity and a second division made up of those of lower ability. The separation was to be based upon the previous record, not upon examinations; but those children assigned to the second division could undertake examinations for admission to the first, and great flexibility in transferring from one division to the other was provided. Moreover, the curriculum of the second four years

[27] *Tätigkeits-Bericht,* Heft 13 (Wien, 1920), p. 52.

was also to be flexible, especially for children in division one. Unity of both divisions was maintained in the common school life and in common instruction in such subjects as singing, handwork, drawing, penmanship, and gardening. Finally, the Guiding Principles proposed lower and higher trade schools, as well as general "upper schools," which corresponded to the last four years of the *Gymnasien* and *Realschulen*.[28]

Curiously enough the postulates just summarized make no reference to the trio of ideas which most educators think of first in connection with Austrian school reforms. Perhaps the explanation is found in Fischl's statement that the matter of the renovation of teaching methods was "a ripe fruit that had only to be plucked."[29] The innovations were self-activity, use of the accustomed environment, and integrated instruction. Such ideas were far from new among educators throughout western civilization, but the important point here is the objective which these Socialist school reformers were attempting to attain through their utilization. Certainly they were convinced that a child is not simply a miniature adult; certainly they believed that a child does best what he can do with pleasure. But they also were convinced that middle-class children would acquire more respect for hand labor by trying it and thus discovering that it was not so simple as it frequently appeared. Partly on these social grounds, but also for economic reasons, they provided all students in the compulsory schools with books, paper, pencils; in fact, supplies in general, at no cost. The reformers were seeking to break down some of the class distinctions which the old schools had fostered. Most important of all they were desirous of training citizens of a democratic republic, not subjects of an empire.

Self-activity meant something more in the reformed school than is suggested in the phrase above concerning hand labor. Before 1919 rules of spelling, for instance, were simply handed out as rules, a few examples written on the blackboard, and then by dictation an attempt made to enforce the rules on the minds of the children. After the new methods were adopted the youngsters were required to get the material together for themselves; for example, to build a list of words with "tz," to examine them, and to work out the rule

[28] For the text of the principles, see Fischl, *op. cit.*, pp. 59–62.
[29] *Ibid.*, p. 17.

for themselves. The teacher confined herself to direction and gave as little help as possible.

The idea of accustomed environment was partly that the break between home and school should be as gradual as possible, and partly that every advantage should be taken of immediate surroundings in the classroom, the town, and the surrounding countryside. The unceasing torrent of "why's" and "how's" which flow from the tongues of all children concerning everything they see and hear and feel and smell was to be the starting point. From immediate surroundings the boundaries of interest naturally expanded to include broader geographical and intellectual areas. Since almost all the youngsters entered school speaking a dialect, it was utilized as the basis of instruction in language and grammar. To obviate the formality of the usual schoolroom with its rows of benches or desks, it was frequently the practice to place the teacher's table in the middle of the room and group the children's chairs around it.

Closely tied to both of the preceding principles was that of integrated instruction (*Gesamtunterricht*). Certain goals of knowledge and technique were set up which had to be attained within set periods of each year of instruction, but considerable latitude was left to the individual teacher to determine precisely how and when they were to be introduced and mastered. Particularly in the earlier grades the subjects were not taught separately so that no program of class subjects was formulated; in other words, there was no such thing as a "reading period" or a "spelling period." The work of the pupils was organized around observation of the environment and human life (*Heimat- und Lebenskunde*). Beginning with some simple theme such as "the clock tells the time," or "Mother goes to market" the teacher encouraged the children to contribute their observations. Sometimes the topic was utilized for a day or so, sometimes for two weeks or more. The basis of the longer discussions was most likely to be an excursion to the famous St. Stephen's Cathedral, to the Vienna woods, to a museum, or to a factory. A minimum of four such excursions was required during the year for each class and, as a matter of fact, the average was something like ten. An example of the utilization of these trips will illustrate the whole method. For the one which follows I am indebted to a friend who was for several years a teacher in the elementary schools of Vienna.

Her pupils were in the fourth grade at the time they made an excursion to the Danube.

In preparation for the trip the youngsters were divided into two groups: the members of one were to make certain general observations; those of the second to secure specific bits of information. During the discussions that followed some of the children commented on the various types of boats they had seen, ranging from the collapsible pleasure craft so common in Europe to the fine passenger ships that carried excursionists to Budapest or beyond; other children talked about the docks and warehouses, the cranes used in unloading cargo, the freight railroad along the banks, or the broad basin designed to meet the emergencies of floods; still others, on the types and quantities of goods being handled in the warehouses that day and the freight charges thereon. During the following days this pooled information provided material for instruction of various kinds. The children wrote short compositions on some aspect of the excursion after a brief explanation of what was wanted and of the spelling of the most difficult words they were likely to need. Certain propositions referring to the excursion formed the basis of a lesson in grammar; for instance, the pupils learned the formulation of present participles from phrases like, "the water flows—flowing water," or "the boat drifts—the drifting boat." The connection here was actually only superficial, but it was argued that there remained a pedagogical value in maintaining even this formal unity. Instead of something entirely unrelated the reading or literature study at this time was the well-known children's folk tale, "The Danube Nixie," from a collection of Viennese legends. The facts collected were further utilized for problems in arithmetic. On the day of the excursion one vessel had brought in 15,342 kilograms of apples from the Wachau district and another 258,000 kilos of grain from Hungary. How much larger, by weight, was one cargo than the other? If the crane transferred 4,320 kilos in each load and shifted 12 loads in an hour, how much cargo could be put on the docks in an eight-hour day? How long would it take to transfer 77,760 kilos from hold to dock? Given the dimensions of the schoolroom and of a box of apples how many boxes could be stacked in the room? Naturally, the child understood relative sizes much better when one measure was something with which he was entirely familiar. The old fortifications on the left bank of the river, the so-called Napoleon Bastion, gave the teacher occasion to discuss the battle of Aspern and the French invasion of Vienna in 1809. Analogously, observation of the crane was used for some instruction in physics, at least to the extent that the children became acquainted with the properties of the pulley. Connected therewith was a little handwork in the construction of a model crane. A discussion of the typical trees growing along the Danube lead into the field of botany. During the excursion each child had made a drawing of anything on or near the river that suited his fancy—a fisherman, a bridge, a boat. Later he tried to improve his sketch, or perhaps make another from memory. In the week or more following the excursion the pupils learned the mermaids' song, "The Waves Murmur," from Karl Maria von Weber's *Oberon.* As an exercise in penmanship each youngster wrote the text of the song, following particular instructions concerning neat spacing and the drawing of a border of conventionalized waves.[30]

Not the least interesting aspect of this emphasis upon and elaborate use of *Heimat- und Lebenskunde* is that Socialists were responsible; Socialists who were forever being damned as unpatriotic internationalists were following methods that certainly should have contributed greatly to the establishment of a deep-seated love for the fatherland.

As already indicated, it was basic to the whole reform that each child should express himself freely on whatever was going on in the schoolroom. With smaller children, particularly, this freedom meant a student discussion (*Schülergespräch*) that raised problems of discipline. A reversion to the old idea that the child spoke only when spoken to by the teacher would have been destructive of the purposes sought. And so it was left to the youngsters to find out for themselves that everyone understood better when only one person spoke at a time. In the same way they were allowed to learn that tardiness interfered with the discussions. Sooner or later they came to an understanding on these and other matters and established some regulations. Naturally the rules were often violated. In such cases it was in some schools also left to the pupils themselves to decide what punishment there should be—a far cry indeed from the "beating schools" of an earlier period!

Unfortunately, no brief description of these methods can do them justice. Perhaps it is not out of place to say that my observations of them, particularly in the case of my daughter who attended a Vienna school in which they were applied in somewhat modified form, convinced me of their outstanding excellence. Certainly, earnest efforts were made to avoid compartmentalization of knowledge, to encourage individual work, and to stimulate the instinct of workmanship.

[30] For numerous other examples, cf. Robert Dottrens, *The New Education in Austria,* edited and supplemented by Dr. Paul L. Dengler (New York, 1930), pp. 72–87; Siegl, *op. cit.*, pp. 57–112; *Das Neue Wien,* vol. 2, pp. 229–230.

And, in the opinion of the much more competent Swiss and American investigators previously cited, Dottrens and Siegl, these efforts were largely successful. Almost needless to say the major credit for the success of the new methods goes to the teachers. There were, of course, exceptions. Some instructors did not approve of the innovations; some were not able to proceed along the new lines until after a retraining period in the Vienna Pedagogical Institute. A decisive majority, however, were appreciative of the greater latitude given them and worked enthusiastically in the spirit of the reforms.

Toward the close of the first year of the experimental classes, that is, in April, 1920, the first draft of the new curriculum was published; and at the beginning of the school year 1920–1921 it was introduced in all schools throughout the country. The intention was to test the plan for one year and then make final decision concerning its adoption. But on June 16, 1921, Vice-Chancellor Breisky, who was also in charge of educational matters within the ministry of the interior and education, issued a decree extending the probationary period for four years and laying down seven conditions which had to be met before the reforms could proceed further. Had the decree remained in full force it would have greatly impeded, almost stopped, the progress made thus far; but the Social Democrats raised such vigorous protests that on June 25, Breisky issued a "commentary" that for all practical purposes did away with the conditions. The four-year additional test period remained, however.[31] During this time a special curriculum was worked out by the reform division and rather generally adopted.

In 1925 appeared a report prepared by secondary schoolteachers on their observations of the group of children who had been with them one year after four years in the reformed elementary school. The chief advantages found were: an awakening interest in schoolwork; increased ability in observation; naturalness and vividness in oral and written expression; appreciable progress in drawing and handwork; better understanding of applied problems in arithmetic. The chief defects noted were: less accuracy in spelling, grammar, and formal arithmetic; incorrect speech; insufficient drill in spelling, grammar, and arithmetic; insufficient memory training;

[31] Fischl, *op. cit.*, pp. 75–76; Otto Glöckel, *Die österreichische Schulreform* (Wien, 1923), p. 26; *Reichspost*, June 21, 1921, p. 5 and June 26, 1921, p. 2; *Arbeiter Zeitung*, June 22, 1921, p. 2 and June 26, 1921, pp. 2, 3.

insufficient power of concentration; lack of discipline. To these observations the author of the most comprehensive American study of Austrian elementary school reform makes the following comment:

> Such criticism from the secondary school teachers is robbed of any sting by the obvious fact that they are considering the achievement of the elementary school child from the viewpoint of the Lernschule. The defects are unachieved Lernschule aims, which emphasize knowledge and skills more than traits and attitudes. On the other hand, the advantages are real Arbeitsschule achievements. If these considerations are admitted, then it is fair to say that the "advantages" far outweigh the "defects."[32]

In the summer of 1925, however, the parties to the controversy were in no frame of mind to balance nicely and academically the opposing arguments. Most of the final decisions had to be embodied in legislation; that is, they had to be thrashed out in a parliament in which party antagonism was great and bitter. In order to understand better the decisions reached in 1926 and 1927 it is necessary to retrace a few steps and to outline the basis of this political fight.

First, it is important to restate the fact that the reforms had not been the achievement of Socialists alone; individual pedagogues belonging to conservative parties had certainly had a share in the work. On the other hand, there can be no doubt that the Christian Social party was distrustful of the school-reform movement. This was shown in the first election program issued after the formation of the republic; in it the party insisted that youth be educated in a "moral-religious" fashion and rejected the nonconfessional school. The program contained no reference to school reform whatsoever.[33] In sharp contrast the Social Democratic program declared that the basis of a free state is a free school in which the instruction shall be "freed from priestly intolerance and monarchical legends," and demanded equality of educational opportunities for all.[34] On the day before the election for the National Constituent Assembly the Catholic workers' paper carried a statement that the school reforms were instigated by Jews, that they involved Jewish domination of

---

[32] Siegl, *op. cit.*, p. 113.

[33] *Christlichsoziale Arbeiter-Zeitung,* December 28, 1918, pp. 1, 2, prints the complete text of the program.

[34] *Parteitag, 1919,* p. 39. The complete text of the proclamation of December 29, 1918, is reprinted here.

the middle schools, and that the only way to avoid the dire consequences was to vote Christian Social. It was also pointed out that during the war pupils were conscripted to serve soldiers at the railroad stations and to perform auxiliary work in offices, both of which were more purposeful than some of the reformers' proposals.[35] These comments are all the more interesting because they represent the point of view of the most liberal wing of the Catholic party. What that party feared most, of course, was that in the development of the school reforms a complete separation of Church and State would be accomplished in the field of education; that is, that compulsory religious instruction would be banished from the schools. Chiefly for this reason it had not been possible to settle the school issue in the constitution of 1920.[36] The matter had to be postponed for years. During this period every school law had to be passed by parliament and by the diet of each state, so that no general law was possible without the enactment of ten identical statutes.[37]

Under these circumstances it is easy to understand why the Christian Socials violently attacked Glöckel's decree which prohibited all attempts to make attendance at religious exercises compulsory. Glöckel had based his ruling upon the still valid Article 14 of the constitutional law of 1867, the third paragraph of which read: "No one can be compelled to [attend] an ecclesiastical ritual or to participation in a church ceremony, so far as he is not subordinate to the statutorily established authority of another."[38] According to one of the best works on Austrian public law, published years before the controversy under consideration, the primary "authority" meant in the law was that of the parent or guardian of a child under fourteen. Said parent or guardian might transfer his "authority" to the school.[39] The Christian Socials argued that Glöckel's decree was a violation of Article 1 of the elementary school law of 1869 which stipulated that education must be of a "moral-religious" character, and that the "authority" included that of the school.[40]

[35] *Christlichsoziale Arbeiter-Zeitung,* February 15, 1919, p. 2.

[36] Konstituierende Nationalversammlung, *Protokoll,* September 29, 1920, p. 3397.

[37] Cf. Hans Kelsen, *Die Verfassungsgesetze der Republik Oesterreich,* Pt. V, *Bundesverfassung* (Wien, 1922), pp. 304 ff., 324.

[38] *RGBl.,* 1867, Nr. 142.

[39] J. Ulbrich, *Das österreichische Staatsrecht* (Tübingen, 1909), p. 199. This volume was the tenth in *Das öffentliche Recht der Gegenwart,* edited by G. Jellinek, P. Laband, and R. Piloty.

[40] Cf., for example, *Das Volkswohl,* vol. 13, Heft 3 (1922), 85–86.

After the Catholic party acquired a firm hold on the ministry of education it went on the offensive. In many localities children of parents who had left the Church and declared themselves without any religious faith (*konfessionslos*) were nevertheless compelled to attend lessons in religion. If they persisted in refusing, they were not advanced to the next grade because they had no mark in religion. The Vienna school council freed such children from this obligation, but in the rest of Austria the practice was generally the reverse. Parents were fined and numerous cases were litigated. The Constitutional Court and the Administrative Court handed down several judgments condemning the practice described as unconstitutional, but since only individual cases could be handled the ministry of education and local authorities continued to exert pressure.[41] What the Christian Socials wanted, of course, was a return to the concordat school of 1855. Of the innumerable pronouncements to this effect from high-ranking Catholics and in responsible Catholic publications one from Seipel is among the most illuminating. Speaking to the Christian Social party council of Vienna on October 18, 1924, he referred to the principles and objectives of Roman Catholics in school matters as laid down in the *Codex Juris Canonici* and stated that in his judgment it would be "completely in *contradiction* to these principles and to the entire spirit of the rights of the Church *to construe the concept 'Catholic children' so that the right would be given to parents to determine* whether their children were to be considered Catholics or not and *whether they should attend Catholic or so-called free schools.* It is not permissible to give such a right to the parents for, by so doing, we make ourselves equally guilty of the fact that, because it suits their parents, innumerable Catholic children grow up without hearing anything of God and of Divine matters. . . ." According to the report in the *Presse,* obviously a reproduction of a release from the Catholic party, Seipel's speech was rewarded with "tumultuous applause lasting for minutes."

Although the *Presse* was generally a warm supporter of Seipel, it editorially characterized his statement as a "political mistake" and an "attack against the modern educational system." It asked: "Was it really necessary precisely at this moment to discuss the educational

[41] Cf. *Neue Freie Presse,* March 30, 1927 (A.M.), p. 5; *Die Sozialistische Erziehung,* vol. 8 (Oct., 1928), 277–278. This periodical is cited hereafter as *SE.*

program and to present the concordat school and the determining influence of the bishops on the educational system as the desirable ideal?"[42]

Another significant pronouncement appeared in the Catholic paper *Schulwacht* just as the controversy concerning the elementary school curriculum was coming to a head. After criticizing severely the liberal state of the nineteenth century for "its most brutal step," the seizure of the schools, the statement continues: ". . . there remains no other solution than to permit the churches to take over education and instruction so that they can develop and thoroughly and generally impart, a *Weltanschauung* wherever there is a possibility of doing it."[43] Even clearer is the language of Monsignor Karl Umlauf, president of the Association of Religious Teachers of Vienna: "The crucifix still hangs on the walls of the classrooms of the public schools of Austria, and the Catholic population will also take care that it continues to hang there." And in another passage Umlauf bluntly stated the real fear behind this determination to dominate the schools—a fear that Seipel had shown only slightly less plainly. After noting that persons who do not understand Austrian conditions sometimes say that because of the interconfessional character of the Austrian schools it would be better to give the religious instruction in the churches, he writes: "If that should happen, then a great part of our youth would be lost for the Catholic Church."[44]

In continuation of the struggle, and of the ideas of Pius IX and Seipel, the minister of education, Rintelen, issued on August 27, 1926, an order that children who had not been promoted because they lacked a mark in religion might be admitted to the next class on condition that some time during the first semester they successfully passed an examination on the course in religion of the preceding year.[45]

[42] *Neue Freie Presse*, October 19, 1924, p. 8; October 20, pp. 1–2. Italics in original.

[43] Quoted from *Schulwacht*, No. 1 (1926–1927), by Siegl, *op. cit.*, p. 13.

[44] Alois Hudal, ed., *Der Katholizismus in Oesterreich* (Innsbruck, 1931), pp. 98, 99. This volume is the equivalent of the American *Catholic Yearbook*. In it Umlauf had an article on "Religious School Problems in Austria," pp. 95–109. Incidentally, in the light of the objections by spokesmen for the Church to "interference" in educational matters by the state and their violent denunciations of the "atheists" and "Bolsheviks" who administered the capital city, another quotation from this article is pertinent. "In Vienna all children in the primary and grammar schools receive all schoolbooks, *including religious booklets, Bible history, catechism and Church history*, from the city administration free of charge; only the gratis provision of the diocesan prayer books and hymnbooks could not be arranged for up to this time" [1931], p. 101. Italics mine.

[45] *SE.*, vol. 6 (Oct., 1926), 231. Text of decree reprinted here.

On the other hand, the Social Democrats were unyielding in their determination to destroy what they termed "priestly domination" and to secure completely secular public schools. In the program of 1926 their party gave considerable space to the school question, connecting it closely with the issue of separation of Church and State.[46] The Christian Social party program of the same year stated that the confessional school was its objective. ". . . where this aim cannot be attained [the party] insists emphatically upon the recognition of religious instruction, including religious exercises, as an obligatory subject in all middle and lower schools, as well as upon freedom for private confessional schools; for the latter it demands support out of public means." Furthermore, the program demanded a school system "graduated in accordance with the educational needs of the different occupational estates (*Berufsstände*)."[47] In other words, the party demanded a "class" school controlled by the Roman Catholic Church. And the state, from which no interference was to be tolerated, was to pay the bills.

Thus the school question had become even more what the Austrians designate as an "avowed *politicum*." So strained was the situation in the summer of 1925 that, as noted above, the decision on the elementary curriculum was postponed for another year. During that time Glöckel, in his capacity as "administrative president" of the Vienna school council, was negotiating with the Christian Social minister of education, Dr. Emil Schneider, concerning both elementary and secondary school reforms. An agreement was reached toward the end of May, 1926, that would have brought about important changes in all the Vienna secondary schools except the classical *Gymnasien*. Briefly stated these changes involved making the first four years of the secondary schools into very close equivalents of the common middle school, here used to mean the second four years of compulsory schooling, which had been one of the objectives of the Guiding Principles. No conclusions were reached on the elementary schools. Glöckel left for France on a

[46] *Parteitag, 1926*, pp. 185–188.

[47] *Christlichsoziale Arbeiter-Zeitung*, January 8, 1927, p. 3. Text of program reprinted here. Exactly what is meant by a "confessional school" is explained in a pastoral letter issued by the bishops of Austria on February 26, 1922: "It would be entirely incompatible with the religio-moral character of the confessional school if, in any textbook or through any teacher, principles and theories were represented that do not agree with the principles of Catholic faith and morals." Text of letter in *Reichspost*, February 26, 1922, pp. 5–6. Quoted in *Educational Yearbook*, 1926, p. 10.

long-planned trip. Almost immediately the ministry issued a denial of the existence of the agreement, and Schneider proclaimed a "definitive" curriculum for the elementary schools which the Social Democrats charged would have undone much of Glöckel's work and put all instruction in the service of the Catholic Church. Glöckel hastened back to Vienna. This time he insisted that the agreement be signed by responsible members of the Christian Social party, including its acting chief, Kunschak. (Seipel was in the United States.) The agreement, reached on June 11, practically reaffirmed the former one concerning secondary schools and supplemented Schneider's "definitive" curriculum for elementary schools in a way that "safeguarded" the reforms "for industrial towns."

Immediately a storm of protest broke out from Catholic quarters. Richard Schmitz, subsequently minister of education and still later mayor of Vienna, denounced the agreement before large mass meetings; the Roman Catholic daily, the *Reichspost,* demanded Schneider's resignation. Thereupon the Christian Social chancellor, Ramek, declared he could not approve the settlement. Schneider resigned on June 16. To his credit Kunschak resigned his position as party head. He considered himself bound by his signature to the agreement.

On June 25, Dr. Anton Rintelen became minister of education and, on July 7, requested Seitz to begin negotiations; the Socialists refused. Rintelen was therefore more or less compelled to suspend Schneider's "clerical curriculum" on July 18. The immediately following negotiations resulted in the issuance of an elementary curriculum that, in the words of Dr. Siegl, "confirmed in the main points, the principles which had formed the basis for the experimental curriculum."[48] Social Democrats claimed that the original agreement of two months earlier was largely preserved.

Although Dr. Siegl's statement just quoted is accurate, it is incomplete. Actually the compromise was clothed in ambiguous language (apparently deliberately), so that each side claimed victory; actually the compromise meant that as long as the Social Democrats

[48] Siegl, *op. cit.,* p. 48. For details, cf. the *Reichspost* and the *Arbeiter Zeitung* during these weeks; for summaries differing slightly, *Tätigkeits-Bericht,* Heft 20 (Wien, 1926), pp. 77–81; and Siegl, *op. cit.*, pp. 8–12. A Christian Social point of view opposed to that of the *Reichspost* appears in the *Christlichsoziale Arbeiter-Zeitung,* June 19 and 26, 1926 (editorials). Fischl states that Schneider read of his "resignation" in a newspaper while returning to Vienna from Cologne. *Otto Glöckel,* p. 118.

remained politically dominant in Vienna and certain industrial localities they would maintain Glöckel's principles, whereas in the country the Christian Socials would direct the schools more in accordance with their ideas. In fact, a curriculum especially adapted to their wishes was tried out in rural elementary schools during 1926–1927.[49]

There remains, however, another political aspect of the school controversy suggested by *Der österreichische Volkswirt.* The Christian Socials were desirous of amending the rent laws for the benefit of the landlords who had for years supported them, but the preceding parliamentary election campaign fought partly under this slogan had been unsuccessful. New elections were coming up in the spring of 1927. If something could be done to arouse religious feelings prospects would be improved; consequently, there was a flood of editorials and articles in Christian Social publications concerning the decay of the school system, the depravation of the youth under the pernicious plans of the Socialists, and the need for religio-moral education.[50]

The suggestion of the *Volkswirt* is apparently supported by the actions of Richard Schmitz who succeeded Rintelen as minister of education on October 20, 1926. Indeed, the selection of Schmitz indicated that a more energetic policy in the school question had been decided upon by the government. The new minister, fervently Catholic, personal friend of Seipel, and chief representative of the intransigent wing of his party, had actually been the leader of the *fronde* against Schneider in June, 1926. As already indicated, the negotiations carried through by Rintelen had resulted in a settlement of an ambiguous character, but at any rate that settlement was more definite about the curriculum of the elementary school than about the education of children between the ages of ten and fourteen. It will be recalled that the Guiding Principles of 1920 had developed a comprehensive plan for the reorganization of the middle years of schooling. Actual achievements in this direction up to 1926, apart from the federal educational institutes already described, were chiefly confined to two new types of schools, the com-

[49] Cf. *Der österreichische Volkswirt,* vol. 18 (Aug. 7, 1926), 1241; and *Educationa Yearbook,* 1926, p. 18.

[50] Cf. *Der österreichische Volkswirt,* vol. 18 (June 19, 1926), 1045; *Christlichsoziale Arbeiter-Zeitung,* June 26, 1926, p. 1, quoting the *Reichspost,* but with some disapproval.

mon middle school and the German middle school, and they, primarily to Vienna. These additions might conceivably be viewed as further complications of a system which was already intricate enough, but before considering the proposals of Schmitz for a legislative adjustment it is again necessary to review certain developments.

The curriculum of the common middle school drawn up in 1922 sought to realize the aims of the Guiding Principles to create a common compulsory school for all Austrian children between ten and fourteen and to make allowances for differences in ability. Radical "leveler" circles within the Social Democratic party objected to the separation of classes into the first and second divisions on the ground that working-class youngsters were most likely to be assigned to the latter. The reformers replied that the common school with such divisions was the closest approximation to "democratic" education possible within the framework of the existing capitalistic society, particularly in a country with a tradition of a dualistic system of education;[51] and, perhaps more important, that said divisions were thoroughly approved by most progressive educators throughout the world. Although designed to form part of the compulsory system, the common middle school was introduced on an experimental basis. Its successful appeal to parents and children is amply demonstrated by the fact that in 1926–1927 there were 144 classes with 4,540 pupils.[52] What was happening, then, for those who attended these schools, was that they were completing four years of *Volksschule* (instead of the former five), and four years of common middle school (instead of the fifth year of *Volksschule* and three of *Bürgerschule*).

The second new type, the German middle school, represented a somewhat different approach toward the same objective: identical schooling from the tenth to the fourteenth year. In the words of one of the reformers this type was organized, "In order to adapt the lower sections [first four years] of the *Gymnasium, Realgymnasium,* and *Realschule* to the principles of the general secondary school. . . ."[53] Moreover, the curricula in the two new types were practically the same except in language instruction. The chief dif-

[51] Fischl, *op. cit.*, p. 65.
[52] *Die Wirksamkeit des Stadtschulrates für Wien, 1926–1927*, p. 56.
[53] Viktor Fadrus in *Educational Yearbook*, 1926, p. 31.

ferences lay in the fact that the common middle school was part of the compulsory system and free, whereas the German variety was optional, charged small fees, and required extrance examinations. The second type also proved successful: in 1926–1927 in Vienna there were 156 classes with 5,745 pupils.[54] Though the common middle school was confined to Vienna the German middle school spread elsewhere—in Graz with some modifications. Through both of them the reformers were making definite progress toward another goal, the postponement of the selection of a profession or occupation until the fourteenth year.

As was to be expected, these innovations and their growing popularity were viewed with alarm in certain quarters. University authorities feared that their students would come inadequately prepared; many teachers in the *Gymnasien* and *Realschulen* preferred to retain traditional methods, chiefly because they were traditional; bureaucrats in the ministry of education shared in greater or less degree these fears and prejudices. But the unfortunate truth is that numerous opponents of the reforms preferred the old types of secondary schools just because they helped to preserve class distinctions.

Schmitz was no democrat—as subsequent events were to prove only too well. As minister of education he was in an excellent position to attempt to check the reforms which he had so bitterly attacked. Just at Christmas, 1926, he issued the Directive Lines for the Legal Regulation of the Austrian Middle School System and for the Reorganization of the *Bürgerschule* (*Richtlinien für die gesetzliche Regelung des österreichischen Mittelschulwesens und für die Ausgestaltung der Bürgerschule*). As the Swiss scholar Dottrens points out, the directives were "in many regards in opposition to the *Leitsätze*" (Glöckel's Guiding Principles). Curiously enough Schmitz had not mentioned these directives in an extended speech before parliament on the educational budget the day before he gave them to the press. Their main points were:

1. The *Bürgerschule* was to be changed from a three- to a four-year institution and was to be lifted to the rank of a selective school by the requirement of entrance examinations. It was not, however, to attain the level of the first four years of the secondary schools such as the *Gymnasien;* in fact, children wishing to transfer from it to the secondary schools had to pass further examinations and could be sent back during

[54] *Die Wirksamkeit des Stadtschulrates für Wien, 1926–1927,* p. 54.

a probationary period. Nevertheless, if a child could get into it, his way to the secondary schools was easier because, practically speaking, it had been almost impossible to move from the old *Bürgerschule* to the secondary institutions.

2. Children who were not able to secure admittance to the *Bürgerschule* were to continue for another four years in the *Volksschule*. In other words, not used in the Directive Lines, the common compulsory school was to have an *Obervolksschule* for less gifted pupils.

3. The secondary schools were to be reduced to two main types, the classical *Gymnasium* and the *Realschule,* but the second was to be divided into *Realschule* proper and Latin *Realschule*. In the classical secondary school and in the Latin variety of the *Realschule* that ancient language was still begun in the second semester of the pupil's fifth year in school and in the former Greek was begun in the eighth year.

4. A new school, the *Aufbauschule,* was to be a five-year institution having one transitional year and four others. It was designed primarily to meet the needs of pupils who were capable but who for some reason had not been able to attend a *Bürgerschule* or one of the secondary types; that is, mostly youngsters in rural areas. A modern language was compulsory in the transitional year and thereafter; Latin began in the first regular year. In this way the pupil could acquire the two foreign languages necessary for admission to institutions of higher learning. Generally speaking the *Aufbauschule* was equivalent to the upper half of a secondary school with a curriculum closely resembling that of the *Reform-Realgymnasium.*[55]

The Directive Lines aroused a storm of indignation among the school reformers. It was claimed, for example, that Schmitz's scheme was a retrogression in the secondary schools as compared with the reforms of 1908 and in the elementary as compared with the law of 1869. Glöckel went so far as to say that the proposal, instead of opening the way to the secondary schools to the children of the proletariat, had as its purpose the closing of the *Bürgerschule* to them.[56] On the face of it these criticisms may seem too harsh, particularly because of the possibilities offered by the *Aufbauschule,* but the fact is that it never amounted to anything. Ten years later, just before Hitler seized Austria, only one *Aufbauschule* had been established and it had only 113 pupils.[57] The reformers could not have

[55] The text of the proposals of Schmitz appeared in *Volkserziehung* (Pädagogischer Teil), Jan. 1, 1927, pp. 1–13. Cf. also Dottrens, *op. cit.*, pp. 120 ff., 210; *Die Wirksamkeit des Stadtschulrates für Wien, 1926–1927,* pp. 19–23; Hans Fischl, "Auf dem Wege zur Einheitsschule," *Der Kampf,* vol. 20 (Oct., 1927), 449–454.

[56] *Otto Glöckel,* p. 120.

[57] Max Lederer, *Secondary Education in Austria, 1918–'38* (Bulletin No. 9, 1941, U. S. Office of Education), p. 19.

foreseen this failure but they did see correctly that nothing constructive was offered by Schmitz in the way of unifying the second four years of schooling and that the changes in the *Bürgerschule* involved, on the contrary, another "selective" school and more of the distinctions they wished to avoid. Consequently, the Socialist press criticized the plans most vigorously; associations of teachers and others passed resolutions of protest; the school council of Vienna published a severe comment. From the Christian Socials came retorts of the same kind: resolutions favorable to the proposals from associations of conservative teachers; other resolutions from mass meetings; attacks on the "school-Bolshevism" of Vienna. Passions reached the boiling point when Schmitz issued a decree prohibiting officials of his ministry from taking part in public discussion of the Directive Lines. The Social Democrats shrieked gag rule, and Schmitz replied by quoting Glöckel's order against "malevolent opposition" as incompatible "with the duties of the teachers." There was a good deal of hairsplitting, but the Socialists later had the satisfaction of seeing Schmitz's decree held unconstitutional by the Constitutional Court. One thing is clear: the whole discussion was becoming more and more influenced by the impending parliamentary election.[58]

But the fact just stated must not be permitted to cloud the real, and much larger, issue. According to the ideas of the reformers, the unification of the schools and the abolition of selective schools for the first eight years of training would aid in bringing about a thoroughgoing democratization of the country. For this purpose children of different social groups and different economic positions should be kept together as long as possible. There can be no doubt of the fact—it was fully confirmed by subsequent events—that precisely what the young republic lacked was a sound democratic tradition. And there can also be no doubt that democratic school reform—given sufficient time—could have been an essential factor in fostering and stabilizing this tradition. The struggle between Schmitz and Glöckel, between Directive Lines and Guiding Principles, was but a part of the fundamental struggle between autocracy and democracy in Austria.

[58] The issues of the *Reichspost, Neue Freie Presse,* and *Arbeiter Zeitung* during January, February, and March, 1927, gave an almost incredible amount of space to this controversy. The summary in the text has been drawn from these issues, the sources cited in note 55, conversations with Austrian friends, and *SE.,* vol. 7 (March, 1927), 50–55.

The educational and political phases of the issue were so closely interwoven that it is not surprising that the resolution of the secondary school problem was largely dependent upon the political development of the country. The elections of April, 1927, considerably strengthened the position of the Socialists in the Nationalrat. On May 19 the reëlected chancellor, Seipel, made the usual government declaration. The Socialists chose as their speaker, not, as was customary, one of the Big Four—Bauer, Renner, Seitz, Danneberg—but Glöckel; they wanted to emphasize the importance they ascribed to the school problem.[59] Obviously impressed by the results of the election, as well as by the strong opposition to the Directive Lines, Schmitz introduced bills concerning the *Bürgerschule* and the secondary schools that represented material retrocessions from the position of December. Though the Social Democrats recognized these improvements they still held the bills unacceptable. But the events of July 15 shifted the balance of political power against the Socialists, negotiations were resumed, and on August 2 the Nationalrat passed still further modified forms of the Schmitz bills.

The essential features of the laws follow:

1. The common middle school and the German middle school disappeared—under those names at least. The traditional *Gymnasium, Realschule,* and *Realgymnasium* were retained; but the study of foreign languages was to begin in the second year, not the first. In the *Realschule* and *Realgymnasium* the second foreign language was to begin in the fifth year, that is, after the child had passed the upper limit of the compulsory school age. Apart from foreign languages, the curriculum for the first three years was identical in all three types of schools; and remained identical, again except for languages, in the fourth year of the *Realschule* and *Realgymnasium.* This comparatively far-reaching unification of the curriculum of the lower half of the secondary schools was the most important inheritance of the new system from the German middle school.

2. The old three-year *Bürgerschule* was transformed into a four-year *Hauptschule* beginning with the fifth year of training; it was a compulsory free school, with no entrance examinations, for those who did not go to a secondary school. The new institution adopted the rule of separation of classes into two divisions as advocated in the Guiding Principles and demonstrated in the common middle schools, but dropped coeducation. Furthermore, the *Hauptschule* offered optional foreign language courses. Pupils in the first division who had made a "good" (equivalent

[59] *Christlichsoziale Arbeiter-Zeitung,* May 28, 1927, p. 2; Nationalrat, *Protokoll,* May 19, 1927, pp. 12–23.

of "B" in our usage) record in all required subjects and at least a "satisfactory" in such language courses could transfer to the next higher class of a secondary school without examination.

3. Workers' middle schools were to be established to give employed adults an opportunity to prepare for the matriculation examinations required for admission to institutions of university grade.

4. The *Aufbauschule* previously described was to be instituted. Both of the last two schools were to be experimental for a time.

In order to avoid the previously mentioned difficulty of securing the passage by all the states of identical statutes, the two just summarized were adopted as constitutional laws.[60]

As usual, partisans of both sides claimed that the new laws represented a victory for them. Some Christian Socials even asserted that they were a realization of the Directive Lines. The Socialists retorted that Schmitz had won only so far as "names" were concerned whereas they had won on the "facts." The *Volkswirt* commented that "The majority availed itself of the helplessness of the opposition in consequence of July 15 to put through a school reform that leaves unfilled all progressive wishes." In support of this judgment the journal asserted that so far as the selection of an occupation was connected with the selection of a school type, the situation was now worse. Instead of making the choice at the end of the fifth elementary school year, the pupil must make it at the end of a four-year *Volksschule* or, at best, at the end of the first class in a secondary school. The close identification of the curricula in lower sections of secondary institutions did not eliminate differences resulting from the introduction of instruction in foreign languages at too early a time—differences that forced an early choice. In this connection it may be noted that in its rejection of the Directive Lines the school council of Vienna had stated that the early introduction of foreign languages was the "chief impediment" to the urgently necessary postponement of the selection of a school type.[61] Schmitz had proposed beginning the foreign language in the second half of the child's fifth year in school; the new law provided for it in the first half of the sixth.

Now it is undeniable that measured against the ideal of a common nonselective school for all children between the ages of ten and fourteen the legislation of 1927 was unsatisfactory—the secondary

[60] *BGBl.*, 1927, Nr. 244, 245, 246.

[61] *Der österreichische Volkswirt*, vol. 19 (Aug. 6, 1927), 1197; *Die Wirksamkeit des Stadtschulrates für Wien, 1926–1927*, p. 21.

schools with entrance examinations and tuition fees were maintained. But the *Hauptschule* represented a material improvement over the old *Bürgerschule*. The comparatively easy transfer from the *Hauptschule* to the secondary schools greatly expanded educational opportunities for working-class children, and could thus be regarded as a further extension of the basis for continued democratization of the country. To the objection that the possibility of such transfer was exceptional, an official of the ministry of education replied: "It was, on the contrary, regularly possible under prescribed conditions frequently fulfilled, and use was made of the opportunity in numerous instances with remarkable success."[62] As already stated, the *Aufbauschule* proved insignificant. The same is true of the workers' middle schools. Although 3 were provided for, there were after ten years only 2 with a total enrollment of 270.[63] On the other hand, there had been some heretofore unmentioned innovations in the secondary schools which represented improvements from the point of view of the reformers. These included the introduction of a limited amount of instruction in manual trades, more "self-activity" by the students in their natural science work, a degree of student self-government, and emphasis on physical education. The last found its chief expression in an afternoon of outdoor sports each week and a day of hiking or some other excursion each month. In summary it may be said that the changes were a partial success for the reformers, unequally spread over the *Hauptschule* and the secondary schools; the moderate achievements in the latter field were more than balanced by the gains in the former. And, since the elementary school question had been regulated in the preceding year, it would seem that the whole educational system had now been brought to as satisfactory a situation as the political circumstances would permit.[64]

Unfortunately, the political situation continued to deteriorate. These developments are presented in detail in Volume II, Chapter XXI. Here the significant point is that when the Heimwehr and its

[62] Lederer, *op. cit.*, p. 14.

[63] *Ibid.*, p. 19.

[64] It must be added that reforms in teacher training were actually postponed *ad calendas Graecas*, a substantial part of the institutions for this purpose being in private hands; that is, operated by the Catholic Church. The problem had been partially solved for Vienna by its Pedagogical Institute in which prospective teachers had received training on the university level since 1925.

quasi-Fascist allies among the Christian Socials decided in 1929 that the time was ripe for a change in the federal constitution their plans involved another attack on the school reforms. Vienna was to become a federal city (*bundesunmittelbare Stadt*); that is, it was not only to lose its status as one of the states but also was not to be a part of any state. This alone would have greatly reduced the scope of the activities of its school council, since state councils had greater powers than those of a community or a district, but the proposed constitutional alterations went further. The whole field of secondary schools, trade schools, and teacher-training institutions was to be withdrawn from the jurisdiction of the Vienna school council, leaving it only the elementary schools. The former groups were placed directly under the federal ministry of education. As if to emphasize the crudeness of the attack, such institutions in all other states were to be left under the supervision of their respective state school councils. In passing, it may be noted that over half the secondary school pupils of Austria were in Vienna so that for them elected representatives were no longer to have any voice in administration.

Long parliamentary negotiations finally preserved the status of Vienna as a state and thereby the position of its school council except that legislation for secondary schools became a purely federal affair. This eliminated the direct influence of the city government on such legislation and involved some dangers to the reforms, but these dangers were lessened by the previously noted fact that the laws of August 2, 1927, were constitutional laws and could be altered only by a two-thirds majority in parliament.[65] By and large, therefore, Glöckel and his supporters had maintained their position.

The Burgenland elementary schools still remained, however, a dark island in the stream of Austrian school reform. It will be recalled that Burgenland was not incorporated in the republic of Austria until late 1921. Since it had formerly been a part of Hungary, its schools had not been controlled by the *Reichsvolksschulgesetz* of 1869; but, according to Hungarian law, had followed the principle of confessional schools, that is to say, Burgenland had a

[65] Nationalrat, *Protokoll* (III Gesetzgebungsperiode), *Beilagen,* Nr. 382, pp. 1, 10, 20; Nr. 383, pp. 1, 4; *Otto Glöckel,* pp. 126–128; *SE.,* vol. 9 (Nov. 1929), 235; H. Kelsen, "Die österreichische Verfassungsreform," *Der österreichische Volkswirt,* vol. 22 (Oct. 26, 1929), 99–102 esp. p. 101.

system differing only slightly from that of the Austrian elementary schools in the time of the Concordat, 1855–1868. After 1921 it would seem a matter of course that the *Reichsvolksschulgesetz* would be effective in the new state; but the Christian Socials always opposed its application, so that Burgenland common schools remained under the supervision of the Catholic Church. In the first instance this supervision was exercised by the so-called school chair (*Schulstuhl*) under the chairmanship of the priest. No one could be elected to this school chair, or supervisory committee, unless he was beyond reproach from the religious point of view, and on this matter the priest made final decision. In addition to this control over the committee, the priest acted as director of the school in pedagogical and administrative matters; the teacher was directly subordinated to him and upon appointment had to take an oath to obey the orders of the Church authorities. As a matter of course subjects and methods of instruction were determined by the Church. Other conditions under which the teachers worked were far from ideal, since their salaries, on a starvation level, consisted largely of payments in kind and since they were usually required to perform the duties of a sexton. Even in the early 'thirties most of the school buildings were thoroughly dilapidated and classrooms dark and damp.

Soon after Burgenland became part of the federation the Social Democratic majority of the state diet, in open and deliberate violation of the still valid Hungarian law, attempted to establish at least a few interconfessional schools and secured the abolition, by state governor's decree, of teachers' salary payments in kind. Then, in 1924, the diet of Burgenland voted for the extension of the *Reichsvolksschulgesetz* to that state; and, beginning in 1925, the Social Democrats in parliament offered every year during the budget debate a resolution requiring the government to carry out the wishes of the Burgenland diet. In 1926 and several subsequent years these resolutions secured a majority, but the government never complied with them. The conclusion seems justified that in this respect the attitude of the Roman Catholic Church had more weight with the government than did the will of the majority of the elected representatives of the people.

How keenly apprehensive the Church was of the danger of secularization of Burgenland schools may be perceived from the pastoral letter written by Cardinal Piffl and read in all Burgenland Catholic Churches on January 23, 1927. In it the cardinal vigorously demanded of all Catholics in the state that they oppose the execution of the parliamentary resolution mentioned above. "Hold . . . fast to the good old inheritance of your Catholic schools; never let them be torn away from you; cry out to all those who would disturb their existence a loud, not to be misunderstood, 'Hands off.'. . ." Then the cardinal pointed out that it was proposed to introduce interconfessional schools in which "the teachers do not have to be Catholics; they can just as well be Protestant or Jew or without any confession. . . . Therefore, the Austrian Catholics for a long time have wanted to know nothing more about these interconfessional schools. . . . The Catholic folk of Burgenland has a historic right to its Catholic schools . . . and this parental right, confirmed by law and custom, may be violated by no one, least of all in a democratic state in which the will of the people is praised so often and so loudly as the foundation of all political freedom."[66] In view of the resolutions passed by the freely elected diet of Burgenland and the likewise freely elected parliament of Austria, this appeal to democracy was ill-chosen, to say the least.

This anomalous situation was partly rectified by the constitutional law of August 2, 1927, concerning the *Hauptschule* since it applied to the entire federal territory. During the remaining years of democratic Austria, however, the lower elementary schools of Burgenland remained under an exceptional law.

For the rest of the country 1926 and 1927 brought the codification of a large measure of the reforms which Glöckel and his associates had sought. On the basis of the changes described the remnants of the dual undemocratic school system of the empire might well have given place to a system really corresponding to the needs of a democratic republic. But 1927 also marked the beginning of the decline of democracy in Austria. The effects upon the schools of the first authoritarian regime are discussed in a later chapter. Meanwhile, this section of the discussion may best be terminated by a quotation from one of my colleagues who is internationally known as an authority in the field of education. After noting that Austria was determined to "turn misfortune to advantage" after the war of

[66] *Neue Freie Presse,* January 18, 1927 (P.M.), p. 3.

1914–1918, he points out that because of the great decrease in the number of children of compulsory school age Vienna might have discharged 2,000 elementary teachers. Instead, the city "retained these teachers and decreased the size of classes by half, thus permitting greater care for individual differences and the inauguration of a system of creative education unsurpassed in any other country."[67]

[67] F. H. Swift, *The Financing of Institutions of Public Instruction in Austria* [European Policies of Financing Educational Institutions, III] (Berkeley, 1934), p. viii.

CHAPTER XVII

Children and Youth in the Labor Movement

ORGANIZATIONS FOR children and youths found full recognition in the Austrian labor movement only after a long time. The reasons are simple. In its first decades the labor movement was striving to strengthen its political, trade union, and coöperative branches in order to win general suffrage and to improve working and economic conditions for its members; for none of these tasks could youth be of much help. Furthermore, in those days only a few people were conscious of the particular needs of youth in a world of adults. Otherwise stated, an important obstacle preventing the recognition of youth's rights was the psychological situation in which a worker, particularly in Central Europe, found himself before he had obtained at least his political rights.

> It is a matter of experience that the more man is oppressed the more he looks for a compensation for this oppression. The modern proletarian is everywhere most rigidly enslaved; at his work place; within the social and political order by laws, authorities; as a soldier, taxpayer, party sheep. . . . All conditions have a depressing effect upon him, degrade him, make him small and unimportant. His desire for authority cries for emergence, higher esteem, recognition. Other fields being eliminated, there remains only the family. Here he draws himself up; here his master ideology, his prestige, grows. . . .[1]

Even after the revolution, which had brought complete political democracy to the working class, the desire for authority in the family was quite common in proletarian circles; fathers remained distrustful of the youngsters who tried to take the future into their own hands. Thus, long after organizations for children and youths had been firmly established and generally recognized as important assets in the fight of labor for a better world, party as well as trade unions kept a watchful eye on them in order to prevent unsupervised steps. But in the early stages of organization even the more farsighted workers had neither time nor means to alleviate the distress-

[1] Otto Rühle, *Die Seele des proletarischen Kindes* (Dresden, 1925), p. 69.

ing economic and moral plight of their children or to organize "fighters for the future"; unwillingly, they had to rely upon the inadequate provisions of the state and upon private, chiefly Catholic, charity.

ORIGINS IN THE WORKING-CLASS MOVEMENT

Partly in spite of, partly because of, these difficulties the first youth groups sprang up independently of the labor movement as early as 1893.[2] The membership was mainly fourteen- to eighteen-year-old boys who worked as apprentices in various crafts or as helpers in factories. The purpose of the groups was twofold: first, to supplement training in those subjects which were insufficiently taught in public and apprentice schools and to secure the addition of other subjects; second, to improve economic conditions by organized effort.

Although it was politically neutral and had originated among German middle-class youth, the *Wandervogel* or Free German Youth Movement must be mentioned as a strong ideological force influencing the later development of the Socialist youth movement. In short, the German organization was a revolt against authoritarian school and parental education. It sought the creation of a sounder and cleaner life among young people as contrasted with what it considered customary modes of living among adults. Shortly before the First World War the *Wandervogel* movement had swept over all Germany and had gained some influence in Austria. It gathered youngsters in small groups; uncontrolled by parents or teachers they went on hiking and camping trips in areas most distant from civilization. They dressed unconventionally in shorts and sport shirts even in the city. In 1913 they formulated their goals at a meeting on the Hohe Meissner as follows: "The free German youth wants to shape its life according to its own design, under its own responsibility, and with inner sincerity."[3] However, this nonpolitical youth movement, not clearly aware of its economic limitations, did not develop positive aims. Its only merit was in having created uncertainty among parents and teachers who had been too firmly convinced of their own authority and of the righteousness of the existing

---

[2] R. Danneberg, "Die österreichische Jugendorganisation," *Der Kampf*, vol. 1 (Aug., 1908), 511.

[3] Rühle, *op. cit.*, pp. 168–169.

order. Thus the free German group, by shattering the cocksureness of adults, became pathfinders for labor youths who, in addition to carrying on the fight against antiquated forms of living, were also able to provide a more positive content for this fight: a better social and economic order for all mankind.[4]

The most famous unit in the Austrian workers' children's movement, the *Kinderfreunde* (Friends of Children), had an unpretentious start. To the writings of its founder Anton Afritsch, and to numberless conversations with his son, who was connected with it throughout its existence, I am indebted for many details otherwise unavailable. The elder Afritsch was a journeyman carpenter and later the editor of a provincial Social Democratic newspaper. According to his account, as supplemented by his son, everything started by his playing with his four children on a vacant lot near his home or taking them for long hikes during his spare time. Soon many other children from the neighborhood joined the family group. From their stories Afritsch learned how much the children of workers, whose parents rarely found time or leisure to play with them, were in need of a little fun. "... the conditions in the house of the parents, those in the school, the boundless ignorance of the parents, the hopeless neglect of the children ... in addition, the scanty beginnings of public social welfare and the ruinous activity of the clericals in this field—all these things soon made the idea tangible."[5] With a few other Social Democrats, and in spite of "a pitying smile and a mocking shrug of the shoulders" from those party comrades who considered "every activity only from the viewpoint: how many more party stamps can we sell through it, how many party members do we gain by it?"[6] Afritsch went ahead, succeeded in obtaining the approval and support of the city authorities of Graz in 1908, and founded the *Kinderfreunde* as a parents' association. Though created and guided by Socialists, the *Kinderfreunde* was not originally a party organization. It showed, however, that the workers themselves were able to provide for a sound development of their children in a Socialist spirit and to create for them a better and more enjoyable life. But the organization had educational

[4] *Ibid.*, pp. 165–170; Walter Fischer, "Jugend und Autorität," *Der Kampf*, vol. 23 (Oct., 1930), 431–433.

[5] Anton Afritsch, "Vor vierzehn Jahren," *SE.*, vol. 1 (May 15, 1921), 14.

[6] *Ibid.*, p. 15.

as well as recreational aims, and these received additional emphasis after its fusion with the Free School Association. Moreover, these educational aims permeated the whole movement of and for children and young persons—which leads now to further considerations.

As shown, particularly in the preceding chapter, the need for reforming the public school system was always stressed by the Austrian workers' party. But regardless of possible achievements it was felt that this system had to be supplemented by a specific Socialist education through party organizations. Originally the idea prevailed that the educational work was to supplement the unsatisfactory and biased formal training which the schools of imperial Austria offered to children of the working class; consequently, various makeshifts were tried, such as the provision of additional lectures and classes for young workers within the party organizations. However, after the proclamation of the republic it soon became evident that school reforms could not replace Socialist education. Even in Vienna, where the Social Democratic administration could usually prevent abuses of the schools by reactionism and by clericalism, it was recognized that a public school system, as a part of a capitalistic world, was unsuitable for teaching Socialism. As Professor Max Adler has pointed out, social development becomes possible only through the conscious activity of the individuals who compose society. Thus it may easily happen that "the insight won becomes opposed to the subjective stand of the student in the actual process of development proper. Instantly it becomes clear that those espousing causes and forces which coincide with recognized trends will see themselves furthered by science, the others, however, see themselves hampered thereby. And these last will retaliate—it does not have to be consciously and usually it does not happen that way—but rather by sacrificing science instead of their social future and their already self-assured present."[7]

On the basis of the teachings of Adler and other Socialist educators a Socialistic pedagogical system developed after the First World War. It made the workers skeptical of the possible achievements of "neutral" (and more inclined to favor a specific Socialist) education as a preparation for the new order which seemed on the horizon.

[7] Max Adler, "Die Unmöglichkeit der neutralen Erziehung," *Der Kampf*, vol. 16 (Nov., 1923), 374.

Also favorable to the recognition of Socialist pedagogic was the tendency of workers to turn away from the strictest form of orthodox Marxism (sometimes denounced by opponents as "vulgar" Marxism) which taught that economic circumstances are the sole determinants of psychological and intellectual development, thus asserting an absolute determinism unchangeable by personal efforts. It is evident that such a concept limits the function of education to perfecting the knowledge of our surroundings, that is, to supplementing the incomplete school training, because the greater our knowledge of reality is the more likely we are to attain our goal.[8] Among Austrian Socialists it was again chiefly the teachings of Max Adler that changed the belief in this kind of determinism. He argued that economic conditions help to determine the ego, but also that, vice versa, the "active ego" produces and changes economic conditions—that the ego itself is a part of the production process.[9] According to him, Marxian sociology has clearly shown that human society develops necessarily in the direction of Socialism, but economic forces always must be realized "through the human spirit and the human will."[10] Thus Socialist education acquired a new significance. To improve the training of workers' children, thus enabling them to obtain a better job or to adjust themselves more satisfactorily to the demands of existing society, was a task of the public schools; it was a responsibility of the party organizations only to the extent that the struggle for better schools had not been won. Socialist education, on the other hand, had the task of preparing fighters for a Socialist society; it was "a link in the social process of evolution as demanded by the development of social life."[11]

In contrast to the leaders of the Communist youth groups, who advocated active participation by the younger elements in the political struggles of the party, the Austrian Socialists clung essentially to education preparatory for such struggles as the main task of their youth organizations even though the scope of the educational work underwent gradual changes. By and large this attitude was accepted

[8] Karl Kautsky, *Die Materialistische Geschichtsauffassung* (Berlin, 1929), vol. 2, p. 716.

[9] Desiderius Breitenstein, *Die sozialistische Erziehungsbewegung* (Freiburg im Breisgau, 1930), p. 99, citing Adler's *Der Marxismus als proletarische Lebenslehre,* pp. 17 ff. Breitenstein was a Franciscan critic of the Socialist education movement, generally recognized by leaders of the *Kinderfreunde* as sharp but honest and fair.

[10] Max Adler, "Sozialistische Erziehung und Politik," *SE.,* vol. 2 (May, 1922), 109.

[11] Breitenstein, *op. cit.,* p. 101, paraphrasing Adler.

by the members of the youth groups despite controversies which flared up from time to time between the leadership and certain factions in the organizations. Thus the party policy concerning "youth and politics" for a long time adhered strictly to the program that had been adopted by the annual meeting of the youth organization in 1909 and unanimously confirmed in 1912. According to this program, it was the chief task of the Austrian youth organization

> systematically to educate the proletarian youth who had graduated from school to become class-conscious workers; to provide for their training particularly in those fields of knowledge that were either neglected in the elementary and vocational schools or abused for patriotic or clerical purposes. Primarily, attention must be directed to the aim that the mother tongue be mastered with the utmost skill in speaking and writing. Then, also of first importance, the members shall receive an insight into the development and the essence of the capitalistic economic order as well as of the class state with all its institutions; therefore, economics, history, political science, and sociology, as well as law studies, should be stressed. The study of the revolutionary epochs of history and the history of Socialism, the description of political rights and of social legislation, particularly so far as they concern the young workers and apprentices, and the thorough discussion of militarism are of special importance.[12]

After the First World War some leaders became more and more convinced of the need for greater political activity by youth organizations. They realized that the active fight against the first manifestations of Fascism demanded more than educational work among young workers. As early as 1923 the program adopted at the meeting of the Socialist Youth International in Hamburg reiterated the old principles, but emphasized the necessity for participation of youth in the struggle of adult workers. In spite of this realization and the Hamburg program, there was a period of several years in which cultural activities largely superseded all others; thus sports, folk dancing, group recitations (*Sprechchöre*), hiking, and camping became integral parts of Socialist youth programs. By guiding young workers into these fields Socialists were able to protect numbers of them, who had won leisure by the general adoption of the eight-hour day, from the dangers of alcohol and nicotine, as well as from the cheap pleasures of the amusement industry. The increased emphasis

[12] Karl Honay, "Proletarische Jugendorganisation und—Politik," *Der Kampf*, vol. 11 (April, 1918), 260–261.

on cultural activities also reflected a measure of concession to the great influx of new and less intellectually minded members who were only gradually to become Socialists.[13] This partial turning away from a purely rationalistic attitude aided in the acceptance of *Wandervogel* ideas by Socialist youth organizations, first, by the *Kinderfreunde*. The increasing threat of counterrevolution, however, did not permit indefinite absorption in dance and play; particularly older youths demanded an active role in the fight against Fascism. Practically speaking, the threat to youth organizations as such came primarily from the Nazis; their members, nevertheless, were also interested in fighting the Heimwehr brand of Fascism on general principles. Finally, in the fall of 1931, the Young Front was founded; it was to encourage greater political activity by the young generation within the Socialist party. Thus, under pressure of developments, the aims of youth, as expressed in the program of 1909, shifted from emphasis on education preparatory for political struggles to cultural activities and back to politics in a more active sense.

Before leaving the analysis of the various roots of the youth organizations in the working-class movement it is necessary to emphasize one more point; namely, the ability of Austrian Socialists to maintain a firm hold on great numbers of young people—chiefly, of course, in industrial communities. This achievement, in contrast to the situation of Socialists in other countries, is to be explained by the combination of close party control with allowance for sufficient initiative on the part of the youth groups.[14] It may well be attributed to successful youth work that 60 per cent of the Socialist party in Vienna were persons under forty.[15] Even during the most fateful years of the party the young Socialist workers remained "the cadets

[13] Cf. K. Heinz, *Kampf und Aufstieg* (Wien, 1932), pp. 157–158; *idem*, "Der Aufstieg unserer Jugend," *Der Kampf*, vol. 22 (July, 1929), 314–320.

[14] Party and trade unions, particularly after the party convention of 1907, subsidized the youth organization. It had its own representatives in the party and trade-union congresses, and its branch organizations formed a part of the local adult groups. The foundation of a local youth group could take place only with the consent of the local political organization or of a local trade union. As soon as a member of the youth organization became a journeyman he was obliged to enter a trade union or leave the youth group. Libraries and meeting places often were common to youth organization, party, and trade unions. R. Danneberg, "Die österreichische Jugendorganisation," *Der Kampf*, vol. 1 (Aug., 1908), 515.

[15] Käthe Leichter, "Die Struktur der Wiener Sozialdemokratie," *Der Kampf*, vol. 25 (June, 1932), 265–266. Her comparisons of the age composition of the Vienna party with that of the whole population of the city are statistically invalid.

of Social Democracy," a designation they had applied to themselves during the struggles for general manhood suffrage in 1905.[16]

As is clear from the foregoing discussion of their origins, youth organizations in the Austrian labor movement were made up of many different elements and objectives: education, betterment of economic and social conditions, political activity, entertainment, and outdoor sports. Gradually these were welded together into a movement of a specific character that embodied conservative and revolutionary elements; that was independent but devoted to the mother party; that emphasized fun and play, but that was prepared to defend democracy against Fascism.

HISTORY AND ANALYSIS OF INDIVIDUAL ORGANIZATIONS

The Kinderfreunde

As mentioned above, the *Kinderfreunde* was founded in Graz by a few Social Democratic parents in the year 1908. The goal, according to the first constitution, was "to further the intellectual and physical welfare of children."[17] Soon afterward several units were formed in various parts of Styria, and, after the vacation trip of a children's group to Carinthia, workers in that province went ahead with their *Kinderfreunde* organizations. The Styrian and Carinthian groups then founded the Alpine branch of the *Kinderfreunde*. The second vacation trip of the new association was to Vienna and led to the decision of the workers of that city to form a branch for Lower Austria in 1911. Within a short time most of the Viennese districts had local groups and more sprang up in other towns of Lower Austria. By 1914 all Viennese districts had units of the association. In these first years the *Kinderfreunde* did not have a well-rounded program of children's education; however, all branches had in common the impelling desire to offer to youngsters some enjoyment away from the dangers of the street and the influence of the strong Catholic institutions. To achieve the goal parents and voluntary helpers organized plays and hiking trips and collected

[16] Heinz, *Kampf und Aufstieg*, pp. 145–146.

[17] Max Winter, *10 Jahre* (Wien, 1927), p. 5; *idem.*, "Vom Verein Kinderfreunde zur sozialistischen Schul- und Kinderfreundeorganisation," *SE.*, vol. 11 (May, 1931), 102–105.

good books for children's libraries. With the aid of recitations of fairy tales and other juvenile stories the youngsters were stimulated to read. Ottakring, one of the large workers' districts of Vienna, was the first to start a *Hort;* that is, a day-care center in which children could spend some hours after school. In this *Hort,* which was open twice a week, the children busied themselves chiefly with drawing, carpentry, and pottery work. Other districts, which followed the example of Ottakring, emphasized various different children's activities. By continuous exchange of ideas the helpers, mostly inexperienced, grasped the principles of modern pedagogics and acquired the knowledge necessary to keep the children occupied.[18]

Then the war came. Large numbers of the best collaborators of the *Kinderfreunde* movement were drafted, wounded, or killed. Many groups encountered difficulties. Undernourishment, lack of shoes, transfer of children to other schools because of war emergencies, and the tendency of youngsters to become more and more wayward as the war progressed made the work increasingly hard. In order to cope with the rising difficulties a closer union between the existing organizations was brought about through the foundation of the National Association of the Friends of Children (*Reichsverein der Kinderfreunde*) in February, 1917. It comprised 8,000 members in 32 local groups spread over Lower Austria (including Vienna), Styria, and Carinthia.[19] But the war also brought about other developments which were decisive for the future of the organization. The new members were primarily interested in a place where children could find protection as well as shelter and food; consequently, educational work frequently had to yield to welfare service. From the viewpoint of the leaders the favorable aspect of this development was not only that many more persons joined the *Kinderfreunde,* but also that it was an incentive toward the creation of youth hostels which, designed to provide health and recreation centers for workers' children, became finally "the birthplace of Socialist education."[20] Strangely enough the imperial ministry of war provided the barrack used for the first day hostel owned by the *Kinderfreunde* and supplied the military personnel which built it.

[18] Winter, *10 Jahre,* pp. 5 ff.
[19] *SE.,* vol. 11 (May, 1931), 102, 103.
[20] *Ibid.,* p. 103.

That happened in 1916; from then on all other groups clamored for hostels, and it was not long before several others were opened. The maintenance costs of the hostels, however, exceeded the funds derived from the small membership fees and the voluntary contributions which worker members could afford; therefore, a special fund for the creation of hostels was proposed. The workers' daily appealed for contributions from labor at large. The response of individuals and organizations was excellent, so that by 1918 each of the 6 *Gaue* into which the 21 Vienna districts were divided possessed either a regular hostel or at least a meadow with a rain shed. Building costs were kept down by workers who volunteered their labor. These contributions were called "robot for the children."[21] The groups outside of Vienna followed its example.

Another development of the war was the "children's penny" (*Kinderheller*). The goal was that every worker should obligate himself to give 1 per cent of his total wage income to the *Kinderfreunde*. Although this ambitious objective was not attained, many individuals, and even whole crews, pledged the "children's penny" or at least some regular contribution. Thus large sums were collected and used to further recreational welfare work and to purchase buildings for *Kinderfreunde* activities. Particularly helpful were the workers of Lower Austria.[22]

The expanded work with a greater number of children in the youth hostels necessarily intensified existing pedagogical problems and created new ones. The question arose: Shall we apply the old methods of a more or less authoritarian education or shall we attempt to take a new course? A combination of circumstances showed the way. The first hostel occupied by the *Kinderfreunde* was surrounded by prune trees on which the fruit was just beginning to ripen. The poor city children, some of whom had never seen prunes on trees, bolted them greedily. The result was a case of dysentery on the first day; the next day there was another. The health department consequently issued a stern warning to the director of the hostel asking adequate pedagogical measures to prevent new incidents. Should another case of dysentery occur the hostel faced an order to close. In this predicament Hermine Weinreb, who

[21] Winter, *10 Jahre,* pp. 13–15.
[22] *Ibid.,* pp. 16–17.

was in charge of the new undertaking, found "the finest expedient in Socialist spirit. . . . She adopted the American method of appealing to the endangered themselves to help the endangered."[23] At first she explained the situation to the 10 children whom she considered the most intelligent. Then she asked them whether they could guard the trees. Assured of their coöperation, she brought all the others into the scheme. The trees were counted and the youngsters divided into an equal number of groups, each in charge of one tree. Every group selected a responsible leader. In order to give an appropriate incentive to the children, the group whose tree bore the most fruit was promised a *Gugelhupf* (a famous Viennese coffee-cake, particularly appealing in wartime). In addition, all children were to celebrate the harvesting of the ripe prunes with a substantial prune-dumpling feast. The plan worked satisfactorily; during the whole vacation only one child climbed a tree and, in consequence, was excluded from the hostel for two days. Although there was a great drought during the summer the children watered the trees so faithfully that the harvest from the *Kinderfreunde* grounds was much greater than that on all neighboring properties. Instead of one prune-dumpling spread there were four, and still the children could take home an appreciable quantity of fruit. This experience led to the first pedagogical report at a convention of the association (1917). "It culminated in the sentence: 'Our goal must be: the free children's community in the framework of a free parents' community.' "[24]

The idea of children's self-government thus began to take root at this time; it was realized on a large scale during the first year of the republic in the children's camp at Gmünd. Throughout one summer 700 children under the leadership of young Felix Kanitz, assisted by a few still younger helpers and the representatives of the children, lived under their own laws and according to the rulings issued by a camp council. The first section of their constitution read as follows: "The children of Camp Gmünd integrate themselves voluntarily into the community, obey self-made laws, and obligate themselves to live together in good comradeship." Under the constitution each of 10 bedrooms housing children ten years of age and

[23] *Ibid.*, p. 21.
[24] *Ibid.*, pp. 22–23.

over elected a room steward. All stewards together formed the camp council: 6 boys and 4 girls. The council was the legislative body of the camp. Under the chairmanship of the camp leader it made the laws and regulated the life of the child state. It could inflict punishments; the defendant child had the right to appeal to the general camp meeting. Neither the camp director nor his aides had the right to punish a child or a living group; they could only notify the council of an offense. Then the council, which met each week, acted upon the matter. The heaviest possible punishment for a group was the temporary abrogation of its constitutional rights. Though the council had complete authority among the children they made full use of their right to bring grievances before the general camp assembly. From the experience with the behavior of children in Camp Gmünd the magazine *Kinderfreund* drew the conclusion that "these people will never give up either their rights as citizens or their merely human rights; they will, however, always fulfill their obligations toward the community, by participating and coöperating for the general welfare."[25]

It is evident from the foregoing examples that the term "education toward Socialism" was used by *Kinderfreunde* writers in a very broad sense. In fact, it would have been more appropriate to write "education for democracy"; and it may even safely be added that very similar ideas also underlay the more radical phraseology of later years.

In addition to the idea of self-government, other principles were developed which were to control subsequent *Kinderfreunde* activities. One of them was the replacement of Church festivals by nonsectarian celebrations. The goal was to exclude clerical influence but at the same time to make children "familiar with the inestimable values of human culture. Truth, love of humanity, labor, beauty and art, the inner voice and the mysteries were discussed with the children, and they themselves entertained the group with music, songs, dance, and play."[26] The fight against the power of the Church, a fundamental concept of the *Kinderfreunde* which resulted in the boundless hate of most clericals, is evident.

---

[25] Viktor Fadrus, "Die Kinderfreundebewegung in Oesterreich und Deutschland," *Die Erziehung*, vol. 5 (Jan., 1930), 242; Winter, *10 Jahre*, pp. 39–40.

[26] Winter, *10 Jahre*, p. 40.

Another important step stressing the educational ideal of the organization was the foundation in the children's home in Schönbrunn of a school to train Socialist educators. This home, housed in part of the former imperial summer residence, had been established in the fall of 1919 to shelter 100 workers' children. In 1920 it was decided to utilize it also for the training of young people from the ranks of the *Kinderfreunde* children as teachers and assistants for the *Horte* and hostels. One reason for the decision was the conviction that the "teachers' colleges provide us with bad material"; another, the fact that "the Catholic School Association [*Katholischer Schulverein*] has not less than two teachers' colleges."[27]

The goal of Socialist education, as formulated by Kanitz in 1920, was mutual assistance as the basis for the development of humanity in contrast to the bourgeois concept of the struggle for subsistence.[28] Another *Kinderfreunde* leader, Alois Jalkotzy, justly remarked that by this formula Kanitz had not circumscribed a specific Socialist goal but "a general human ideal."[29] The children's home at Schönbrunn, however, quickly became a laboratory for the practical testing of new theories by means of systematic observations of proletarian children.

In conformity with the original plan to select future educators of *Kinderfreunde* children from their own ranks, 25 youngsters who had reached their fourteenth year were chosen for the first course. It was hoped that those who had experienced the mistakes of their adult teachers would correct them after they had become educators themselves. The financial burden for the education of the 25 trainees was borne by the *Kinderfreunde* of Lower Austria. Felix Kanitz became principal of the school; Anton Tesarek, subsequently founder of the Red Falcon movement, assumed responsibility for the home. At first a curriculum of two years was planned for the new school; later it was extended to three. The subjects taught were psychology,

[27] F. Kanitz, *Die Erziehungsaufgaben des Arbeitervereines "Kinderfreunde"* (Wien, 1920), pp. 14–15. The first quotation may startle the American reader familiar with the general praise given to the Vienna school reform. It must be remembered, however, that in 1920 instructors still came from federal and Catholic teachers' colleges little influenced by political changes. Five years later Kanitz declared that the *Kinderfreunde* was naturally for the school reform but that it was not sufficient. Cf. "Was ist sozialistische Erziehung?" *SE.*, vol. 5 (Aug.–Sept., 1925), 209.

[28] Kanitz, *Die Erziehungsaufgaben des Arbeitervereines "Kinderfreunde,"* pp. 3–4.

[29] A. Jalkotzy, "Entwicklung der sozialistischen Erziehung," *SE.*, vol. 5 (Nov., 1925), 279.

introduction to Socialism (sociology), hygiene, physics, chemistry, history of art, theory of education, general and Socialist doctrines of education, world history, geography, literature, natural history, mathematics, *Hort* economics, English, rhythmical gymnastics, and handicrafts. Among others, professors of the University of Vienna, such as Max Adler, Wilhelm Jerusalem, and the internationally known psychologist Alfred Adler, joined the staff of this young Socialist teachers' college. By the spring of 1922 the first graduates could be appointed to various state organizations of the *Kinderfreunde*. In fact, this was the only occasion on which it could provide its groups with personnel trained in Schönbrunn. Shortly thereafter the economic crisis forced most of the groups to rely again on voluntary helpers, and the students who graduated later had to look for employment in public welfare and *Hort* work. Finally, in the summer of 1924, the school, as well as the children's home, had to be closed because of inadequate funds. The living symbol which Schönbrunn left was the salutation *Freundschaft* (friendship); it became a generally accepted form of greeting among Austrian workers. As a partial substitute for the closed school, individual courses of shorter or longer duration were offered by former teachers in it and other enthusiasts.[30]

Several other actions give further proof that the *Kinderfreunde* had definitely embarked on a great working-class educational venture and had avoided the temptation to become a charitable association. At the annual meeting in 1920 an Advisory Council for Education (*Erziehungsbeirat*) was created. It was to convene at least twice a year to discuss thoroughly all questions of education—a forum "where we can talk about everything that is harassing us and find the road which we have to take." Another reason for the creation of the council was the desire to induce the Social Democratic party to take the *Kinderfreunde* "more seriously than it has done up to now."[31] More bluntly put, it was still necessary at this time to "educate" the political branch of the working-class movement to the point where it would abandon the notion that the *Kinderfreunde* was just another charitable institution. On May 15, 1921, the first issue of the magazine *Die Sozialistische Erziehung* was pub-

[30] Cf. Winter, *10 Jahre,* pp. 42–43; *Parteitag, 1925,* pp. 89–90.
[31] Kanitz, *Die Erziehungsaufgaben des Arbeitervereines "Kinderfreunde,"* p. 15.

lished in spite of great financial difficulties. Its aim was the scientific discussion of pedagogical questions.

But the decisive step in the direction of a new education was taken at the first meeting of the International Federation for Socialistic Education (*Internationale Arbeitsgemeinschaft für sozialistische Erziehung*) which was held in Castle Klessheim, near Salzburg, in August, 1922. There Kanitz amplified his former statements on education. Socialist education, he stated, does not mean "to educate people for a Socialist style of life" because we do not know how it will be constituted. "What we can do today is to educate children for the fight for Socialism, that is, for the class struggle." To achieve this, children should be trained "to think in terms of cause and effect in the field of society"; and that, in turn, could be achieved by making children familiar with life itself and by showing them the basic principles of Socialist methods of production. As a second principle, Kanitz returned to his concept of mutual collaboration and emphasized the need for an education that would develop a strong feeling of solidarity. This, together with an equally strong feeling for social right and wrong and knowledge of the economic conditions of the proletariat, would result in a sturdy class consciousness. As a practical means of education, Kanitz recommended for the schoolroom a "class community" joining children and teachers. Only the correct sort of education could "prepare the new, Socialist society." Therefore, the tasks of the *Kinderfreunde* were: (1) To create independent educational organizations in which Socialist educators—teachers or parents—help the children of the proletariat to become mentally and physically fit for the fight for a Socialist society. This was to be achieved by working with children outside of school hours, on hiking trips, special play days, in Sunday schools, libraries, children's homes, *Horte,* camps, and kindergartens. By the publication of magazines for children and parents the *Kinderfreunde* could fight the opponents of the workers. Since these activities supported the Socialist movement in the struggle for its final goals, the *Kinderfreunde* asked for moral and financial aid from the party, the trade unions, and the consumer coöperatives. (2) To create a "Socialist cultural forum" to liberate the proletariat from the fatal influences of existing society in family, school, and daily life. (3) To reform existing public educational institutions so that their indoctrination of pupils with an antiproletarian ideology (imperialism, clericalism, capitalism) will be reduced to a minimum.[32]

It is interesting to note that the other main speaker, Dr. Kurt Kerloew-Loewenstein, leader of the German *Kinderfreunde* movement, opposed Kanitz's viewpoint regarding the preparation of children for the class struggle because that struggle is carried on in the field of economics and children are not economic factors; because it is a political fight and children are not political forces; finally, because it is a spiritual fight and children are not spiritual factors.[33]

There is no evidence, however, that Kanitz was seriously challenged in Austria; at most his opposition claimed that the fight he and his friends made for their educational principles was "perhaps a little too passionate, perhaps a little too hot tempered."[34] Practically without debate the *Kinderfreunde* was recognized as a Social Democratic organization by the party convention in October, 1922, and from then on had the right to two delegates to the annual meetings. A year earlier it had secured official recognition from the trade-union *Kommission.*[35]

In his systematic description of Socialist educational principles some years later, Kanitz modified his views concerning preparation for the class struggle, recommending the restriction of specific preparation to those children who had reached mental maturity. The younger ones were to be given "class sentiment" on an emotional basis.[36]

The decision of the workers' party to recognize the *Kinderfreunde* was interpreted as the last move of the party to integrate all branches of society because a Socialist order can be erected only if "we finally imbue to the greatest extent our future generation with the spirit of Socialism."[37] Closer relations to party and trade unions naturally brought advantages to the *Kinderfreunde.* The *Kinderheller,* which had lost its importance through the mounting inflation, was replaced

[32] "Protokoll der Klessheimer Tagung am 22. und 23. August 1922," *Mitteilungen der Internationalen Arbeitsgemeinschaft sozialistischer Erziehungsorganisationen* (Oct., 1922), 1–4. Published as a supplement to the September–October, 1922, issue of *SE.*

[33] *Ibid.,* p. 6.

[34] Winter, *10 Jahre,* p. 52.

[35] Cf. *Parteitag, 1922,* pp. 194, 196; *SE.,* vol. 1 (July 15, 1921), 25, 26; and vol. 1 (Dec., 1921), 2.

[36] F. Kanitz, *Kämpfer der Zukunft* (Wien, 1929), pp. 46, 55.

[37] Jalkotzy, "Kinderfreunde und Partei," *SE.,* vol. 2 (July, 1922), 164.

by the *Kindergroschen* after the stabilization of the currency. To be quite correct, not a full groschen was turned over to the *Kinderfreunde* from wages; however, the trade unions gave one-third of a groschen out of every schilling of union dues to the organization. Thus it received a secure income of approximately 100,000 schillings a year. This sum enabled it to employ four traveling teachers who instructed local leaders and parent groups; to lower the price of books for children; to found circulating libraries; and to create a hostel fund (*Heimfond*). An additional contribution of 3 groschen monthly made by each member of the railway workers' unions brought in about 25,000 schillings annually.[38]

It may well be assumed that the Roman Catholic Church indirectly helped to increase appreciation of the *Kinderfreunde* within the workers' party and that it was partly responsible for some of the radical phraseology used by Kanitz at the Klessheim meeting. Confirmation of these assumptions appears in the pastoral letter against the *Kinderfreunde* issued by the Austrian episcopate on February 26, 1922. It labeled the association a "revolutionary socialistic-communistic youth organization" which was "not only totally incompatible with Christianity but directed in fact toward dissolution of the whole present social order." Demanding that the legislators break the "terrorism" of the workers' organizations, the bishops threatened that otherwise "the Christian people" would have "to resort to justified self-help"; furthermore, they warned parents that the *Kinderfreunde* wanted to deprive them of the right to educate their children, and exhorted them to take up the fight for the schools. In this connection the bishops set forth at length the "rights of parents."[39] A Socialist commentator construed this passage as an admonition to parents: "Do not spare the rod because rod and punishment give wisdom."[40] Significantly enough, though he was

[38] Max Winter, "Vom Verein Kinderfreunde zur sozialistischen Schul- und Kinderfreundeorganisation," *SE.*, vol. 11 (May, 1931), 104.

[39] The complete text of this letter could not be found in available sources. Excerpts in Roman Catholic, Socialist, and other publications are in substantial agreement. Cf. *Reichspost,* February 26, 1922, pp. 5–6; Z. Fischer, *Sozialistische Erziehung* (Wien, 1926), pp. 174–176; *idem, Kinderfreunde und Rote Falken* (Wien, 1929), pp. 96–99; *SE.*, vol. 2 (Feb., 1922), 40; *Neue Freie Presse,* February 27, 1927 (P.M.), p. 4. Incidentally, it seems in order to remind the reader that the Roman Catholic prelate Seipel inconsistently denied the "right of parents" to decide whether or not their children were Catholics for the purpose of religious instruction. Cf. above, p. 567.

[40] Winter, *10 Jahre,* p. 52; *SE.*, vol. 3 (Jan., 1923), 30.

caustically critical of Socialist observations on the pastoral letter, Father Fischer registered no protest against this construction—nor, so far as could be ascertained, did any other spokesman for the Church. At any rate, during the remaining history of the independent working-class movement, the letter was effectively used by the Socialists in their long-standing fight against "beatings" as an educational instrument. Even more specifically it was used for propaganda for the *Kinderfreunde*. "Quite frankly," its journal stated, "we must say that the Austrian bishops have recognized the revolutionary significance of the *Kinderfreunde* better than many a party comrade of ours. . . . We thank the Austrian bishops for their great attention; it has proved to us that we are on the right track in our work." In fact, this first pastoral letter against the *Kinderfreunde* was used for a new membership drive that brought a 25 per cent increase within the year in which the letter was released. The 14,356 new adherents raised the total to 71,875.[41] The struggle between the *Kinderfreunde* and the Catholic Church became increasingly violent in subsequent years, but before elaborating on this matter it is necessary to note other important events in the development of the organization; first its fusion in January, 1923, with the Social Democratic School Association Free School.

THE FREE SCHOOL

The Free School had been founded by a group of liberals and Social Democrats in March, 1905, with the announced purposes of fighting for a reform of the reactionary school laws and of resisting effectively the strongly organized clericalism. No wonder that it immediately encountered the hatred of the Roman Catholic Church. And, because of the strength of that Church in Austria, it is again no wonder that it was a long time before the new educational group was able to realize its project to open schools in which more modern methods of instruction would be used. Finally, with the help of a representative membership assembled from all progressive camps, the Free School succeeded; however, it had to comply with a decision of the Supreme Court (*Oberster Gerichtshof*) by which the schools were compelled to appoint teachers for religious instruction. On the basis of its experience, and after long and thorough studies, the Free

[41] *SE.*, vol. 2 (Feb., 1922), 41; Winter, *10 Jahre*, p. 53.

School formulated a new educational program which became one basis of the Viennese reform. This program was submitted to the public at a mass meeting in one of the largest halls of Vienna on January 7, 1917; the reporter was Otto Glöckel. After the revolution it became increasingly clear that the practical work of the association was being carried out by Social Democrats only. Many non-Socialist members drifted more and more into the camps of the bourgeois parties and sought protection for their material goods from the Catholic party. Thus after the war the Free School became a Social Democratic association. In this capacity it assumed a new function, the organization of the parents' councils in the public schools. Probably as a result of its efforts 93.6 per cent of the 400,000 mothers and fathers voted for Social Democratic candidates in the elections to those councils in 1922. This success is the more remarkable because it was won against the most vigorous opposition of the Catholic organizations which through the Church could still exert considerable influence, particularly on women. The transformation of the Free School into a purely Social Democratic association and the increasing emphasis put on educational aspects by the *Kinderfreunde* suggested the merger of the two. This was accomplished by the votes of both groups and in January, 1923, the Social Democratic Educational and School Association Free School-Friends of Children came into being. Before the merger the Free School had a membership of 34,420; after it, the new organization numbered 88,314 members; that is, 16,439 or 23 per cent more than the *Kinderfreunde* alone. Probably many individuals had held membership in both organizations; an assumption partly supported by the fact that the membership of the Free School had increased during the last year before the merger from 12,839 to 34,420. It should be noted that Max Winter, chairman of the *Reichsverein der Kinderfreunde* and a member of the old guard, expressed the opinion that the union of the two organizations meant that "the workers . . . above all expect for their children an education toward Socialism."[42]

THE HORT AND SOCIALIST EDUCATION

The *Hort* was long considered the cornerstone of Socialist education. It has been shown that the *Hort* owed its general accept-

[42] Cf. *SE.*, vol. 3 (Jan., 1923), 1–4, 29–31; *ibid.*, vol. 10 (April, 1930), 73–75; Winter, *10 Jahre*, pp. 53–54.

ance chiefly to the economic strains of the war; it developed with the influx of those members who expected from the *Kinderfreunde* primarily shelter and protection for their children. The numerous *Horte* erected for this purpose gradually acquired political significance; they "snatched many children from the clerical gang."[43] Soon their domain was widened. The slogans after 1920 were: "Our *Horte* shall become workshops of Socialist education" and "every local group shall have a *Hort*."[44] Thus the *Hort* came to be considered the primary goal of a *Kinderfreunde* group, the place in which children would live in a Socialist atmosphere for some hours every day. After a few years, however, an increasing number of persons voiced their disappointment in the benefits of the *Hort*. They asserted that it was not likely to attract the voluntary attendance of children, particularly not of older boys; that its costs were too high relative to the number of children it could accommodate; and that many groups had to spend all their means and energies just to keep the *Hort* going, thereby neglecting all other activities. Other criticisms were that the coercion to attend which existed in some *Horte* prevented a Socialist education, and that even where no coercion was exerted the necessary mass training prevented the free occupation of the children in accordance with modern pedagogical principles. Frequently the opinion was expressed that the maintenance of *Horte* was the task of public agencies, particularly in localities with a Socialist majority. Kanitz himself joined the critics, emphasizing that many things could be done by the *Kinderfreunde* without a *Hort* and pointing out how much had been accomplished during the first years of the organization. He frankly admitted that he and his collaborators had overestimated their strength with respect to Schönbrunn by giving all their energy and money to this venture, and warned that many groups were making a similar mistake by investing everything in the maintenance of a *Hort*. Therefore he recommended greater concentration on hiking trips, revolutionary festivals, and library work with the aid of voluntary helpers, particularly from the ranks of young party members. By intensive effort within such a program of mass education he hoped

[43] Kanitz, *Die Erziehungsaufgaben des Arbeitervereines "Kinderfreunde,"* p. 14.

[44] *SE.*, vol. 4 (Dec., 1924), 443; and Paragraph 2c of the 1923 constitution (quoted in Fischer, *Sozialistische Erziehung*, p. 62).

to influence quickly an increasing number of children, their parents, and, finally, the whole working class. But further proof that he was no doctrinaire is offered in his confession that "We have many theories of Socialist education but still little practice."[45]

In spite of all criticism there was no intention of dissolving the existing *Horte* wholesale; their maintenance was demanded by too many parents. Some of them, however, were converted into so-called workers' children's homes, permitting more flexibility of administration, as well as greater independence for the children. By a new policy of free admission of children to various activities cultivated in the homes, irrespective of parents' membership, these homes secured contact with an increased number of children. The larger size of the homes made it possible to set up small groups, each engaged in a particular activity such as gymnastics, singing, crafts, or reading. Thus, the workers' children's homes were "nothing but a system, but another possibility of getting hold of a mass of children—all kinds of methods of bringing in children must be united in it. Workers' children's home is the name for a new work technique which will really make possible the activities of youth."[46] Obviously the creation of such homes was dependent upon the financial strength of the organization and therefore unfeasible in many communities. Vienna, however, was able to erect 8 units by 1931.[47]

Of the festive days which the Social Democrats wished to emphasize the most important were November 12 and May 1, both republican legal holidays. On these holidays children's groups gathered and celebrated by songs, plays, and sports events. With more or less success an attempt was made to center the festival around a talk by one of the youth or party leaders. A particularly solemn celebration called "youth dedication" (*Jugendweihe*) took place for those children who were leaving school. Another inspiring ceremonial was the "spring festival," admittedly competing with the Corpus Christi celebration which had always served to demonstrate the might of the Catholic Church. The pompous processions, with

[45] Kanitz, "Der Weg nach Vorwärts," *SE.*, vol. 4 (Aug., 1924), 297; cf., also: *ibid.* (Aug. 1924), 293 ff.; *ibid.* (Jan., 1924), 2 ff.; *ibid.* (Dec., 1924), 442 ff.; *ibid.* (Oct., 1924), 350 ff.

[46] *SE.*, vol. 8 (April, 1928), 97 ff. This article also contains a comprehensive criticism of the *Horte*. See also *ibid.*, vol. 11 (Nov., 1931), 251.

[47] *Ibid.*, vol. 11 (Nov., 1931), 250.

their banners, bands, priests, and soldiers in colorful costumes, were a great attraction for children. They were accustomed to participate, dressed in white, the girls with flowers in their hair, and often carrying candles or other religious symbols. The spring festival was carefully designed to prevent children from joining the Church celebration and at the same time to offer them adequate compensation. Similar considerations led to the arrangement of Christmas festivities by the *Kinderfreunde*.[48] Such political considerations, however, were by no means solely determinant for the cultivation of festivals. As indicated above, they were designed to bind the children sentimentally to Socialistic ideas and to the organization. It was hoped that they would produce in children a feeling similar to that experienced by most people while celebrating the Christmas and Easter holidays in traditional fashion. "Socialist festivals, Socialist songs, participation in Socialist parades, all that can attach children emotionally to the Socialist movement."[49] This emotional attachment was an important factor contributing to the success of the Red Falcon movement which became decisive for the future development of the *Kinderfreunde*.

THE RED FALCON MOVEMENT

That the Red Falcons were a genuine children's movement may be doubted,[50] but certainly they were a new phenomenon within the workers' party in general and among the *Kinderfreunde* in particular. In spite of the preceding experiments with children's self-government they presented for the first time an effective challenge to the notion still prevailing among many adult members "that primarily the parents . . . have to provide for the well-being and for the education of the children."[51] As has been shown, the parents' organization had grown in the course of the years and "quiet and self-confidence established in the organizational leadership of the central bodies." However, Kanitz remarked, "Sometimes I had the feeling of an internal stagnation of our movement."[52] Into this peace burst the Red Falcons. They were greeted with cheers by children,

[48] Fadrus, *op. cit.*, p. 248.

[49] Kanitz, *Kämpfer der Zukunft*, p. 52.

[50] Anton Tesarek, "Rote Falken," *SE.*, vol. 6 (April, 1926), 89.

[51] F. Kanitz, "Für und wider die 'Roten Falken' " (I), *SE.*, vol. 6 (May, 1926), 113 ff., esp. p. 119.

[52] *Ibid.*, p. 114.

as well as by adults—a unanimity between youths and grownups that was still only too rare an occurrence. In this case it was probably partly explained by the fact that the latter had not yet grasped the full meaning of the new movement. At any rate the Red Falcons were recognized by the national association of the *Kinderfreunde* in 1926, hardly a year after they had first been mentioned. The older group, however, deemed it necessary "to warn against an overestimation of this institution." Vienna and Wiener-Neustadt, nevertheless, rendered full support to the Red Falcons from the start. For reasons not clear in the literature, other parts of the country followed more slowly.[53]

The concept of the Red Falcons originated with Anton Tesarek. He wanted to utilize the "gang ideology," found particularly among older boys in the *Kinderfreunde,* for educational purposes. Looked at in another way his aim was to offer something to those who were found unsuitable for *Hort* education. Closely following Boy Scout traditions, he tried to utilize the boys' desire for independence, their longing for activity, yearning for adventure, revolt against authority, desire for close companionship with boys of the same age, and their readiness for voluntary subordination to a beloved leader. At the same time he had to take into account their lack of consideration for, almost cruelty toward, smaller and weaker youngsters.[54] As Tesarek points out, these tendencies, as well as the romanticism inherent in the minds of young boys, were correctly used by the Boy Scout movement to make out of a "small, persecuted savage" a boy who was orderly and always prepared.[55] But the Boy Scout tradition was by no means taken over as a whole; on the contrary, some of the Boy Scout precepts, such as the hierarchy of leadership, were rejected. Rejected also were the red Indian and trapper plays because they were opposed to the idea of the equality of races and to the fight for liberation from oppression. Most important, however, was the conviction—correct or incorrect—that Boy Scouts and their leaders everywhere marched on the side of the foes of organized labor, whereas the Red Falcons were proud to belong to the workers. Thus they accepted most of the outward appearance of the Boy

[53] *Rote Saat,* 1926 [6th Report of the *Kinderfreunde*] (Wien, 1927), p. 58.
[54] Kanitz, "Für und wider die 'Roten Falken' " (II), *SE.,* vol. 6 (June, 1926), 142–143.
[55] Tesarek, "Wege zur Kinderbewegung," *SE.,* vol. 5 (Aug.–Sept., 1925), 223.

Scout movement but borrowed the content of their own "from 'modern surroundings,' from the world of the proletariat."[56]

According to Tesarek, the new movement started with a short account published in the July, 1925, issue of *Kinderland* (Children's World), the magazine for workers' and peasants' children issued by the *Kinderfreunde*. The heroes of this story were four boys who used to meet in a park. They founded a League of Red Falcons[57] and gave it rules and regulations. The report fired the imaginations of the young readers of the magazine. From many localities in Austria, but also from Germany and Czechoslovakia, came letters and postal cards with questions and requests for more details. Quick to seize the opportunity, youth leaders carefully answered all inquiries with the result that many groups were formed. After a short while a few Falcon leaders met in Vienna; from their discussions originated many of the rules which regulated the movement.[58]

Boys as well as girls between the ages of twelve to sixteen could become Falcons.[59] They were organized into hordes (*Horden*) consisting of not more than 10 or 12 children. Some hordes were composed of boys or girls only; others were mixed. The members of the horde worked, played, hiked together, and elected a leader. Although the horde was the smallest, it was the most important unit of the movement. Five or six hordes formed a group with a maximum membership of 60. These 60 elected a group leader. If there were several groups in one community they formed a local group (*Ortsgruppe*) under the direction of a leader elected by the leaders of the smaller groups. The latter made up the "leader circle" which trained the horde and group leaders. By further organizational steps district, state, and national federations were formed. All groups together were called the *Reich*. Under certain circumstances the ten- to twelve-year-old children could be united in Young Falcon

[56] *Ibid.*, p. 224; cf. also A. Tesarek, *Das Buch der Roten Falken* (Wien, 1926), pp. 10–12, 27.

[57] The name "Red Falcons" originated when the boys in the midst of their play saw two falcons soaring in the air and, impressed by their strength and their freedom to fly wherever and as high as they wished, decided to call themselves "Red Falcons." "Since that time we call ourselves that and we like the name more and more. We want to be brave and free like the falcons and red like our grown-up comrades." Tesarek, *Das Buch der Roten Falken*, pp. 6–7.

[58] *Ibid.*, pp. 6–8.

[59] Originally Tesarek had planned to accept only boys. Cf. *SE.*, vol. 5 (Aug.–Sept., 1925), 221–222.

groups the activities of which consisted mainly of play and recreational gatherings.

The Red Falcons were uniformly dressed in green hiking shirts and shorts or short skirts. Only in formal assembly did they also wear the red neckcloth, the symbol of the organization, which was never to be dishonored. The Young Falcons were not permitted to wear this symbol. The common sign for a horde or a group was a red triangular pennant with figures indicating the identity of the particular subdivision. Every Falcon was obliged to obey the orders of his leader and to maintain discipline. Once a week, however, in the so-called *Zausestunde* (free-for-all discussion period), members could tell a leader frankly that they were not satisfied with him. If his explanation was unacceptable to the group it might elect a new leader. The highest law for all Falcons was their twelve commandments, namely: (1) to adhere to the working class; (2) always to be loyal to comrades; (3) to consider every working man as a friend and brother; (4) to be always ready to help; (5) to respect everyone's sincere convictions, even though opposed to them; (6) to comply always with the orders of the elected leader; (7) to be brave and never to lose courage; (8) to be truthful, responsible and punctual; (9) always to be pure in thought, word, and deed; (10) to be abstinent and to fight narcotics; (11) to protect the body and to keep it fit; (12) to be a friend and protector of nature.[60]

The high ethical standard of these commandments is self-evident. Some of them, however, merit a few words of discussion. For instance, the bitter controversy between the *Kinderfreunde*[61] and the Church is reflected in the comment to the fifth commandment: "Mockery and scorn about religious customs is not only stupid but it also damages our cause."[62] With respect to the tenth it was stated that it was not sufficient to abstain from drinking and smoking, but that a Falcon had to help the abstinence associations in their propa-

[60] Tesarek, *Das Buch der Roten Falken,* pp. 13, 14, 16, 18, 19, 26, 82–86. Tesarek explains that he selected the term *Horde* because of its anthropological meaning of a small group of humans of the Ice Age, for example, who managed through joint effort to maintain existence despite all physical handicaps.

[61] The Red Falcons always remained a *Kinderfreunde* organization.

[62] Tesarek, *Das Buch der Roten Falken,* p. 29. Apparently the children adhered to this rule. As the Catholic weekly *Das Neue Reich* reported, the teacher of religion in an unnamed community had had great trouble with the *Kinderfreunde;* but after the Red Falcons appeared the lesson hours were quiet, the children studied, and they even greeted one another with "Praise to Jesus Christ." Zyrill Fischer, "Gerechtigkeit auch für den Feind," *Das Neue Reich,* vol. 10 (June 2, 1928), 756.

ganda work.[63] The significance of the abstinence education was early recognized by opponents; for instance, the Franciscan Father Zyrill Fischer, a stanch foe of the Socialist youth organizations, wrote: "Just this education without alcohol and nicotine merits particular attention because it provides the Socialists with sober members who steadily pursue their aims and who make us more trouble than a thousand beer-drinking squabblers."[64]

Half a year after joining, a Red Falcon had to pass an examination on the twelve commandments, the organization of the Falcons, its relation to the labor movement, some labor history, orientation by stars and sun, reading of maps and time tables, swimming, first aid, sewing, tent erection, as well as a general demonstration of mental and physical alertness.[65] Former members told me that these examinations were not mere formalities.

The new organization did not take in all the youngsters who belonged to the *Kinderfreunde*. To prevent the Falcons from developing a feeling of superiority they were asked to aid their younger comrades and to participate in at least one of their play afternoons each month. Another task assigned to them was the organization of regular children's meetings in those localities where they were not already in existence. The various children's groups cultivating sports, singing, or hiking were to be invited, and in this way an all-inclusive children's movement developed.

The Red Falcons were also expected to help in other ways. On their hiking trips they were advised to aid poor tenant farmers or to play with their children. The party organization gave them handbills for distribution in the city and in the country. In addition to such "voluntary work" the leader circle assigned to the groups "obligatory work" such as the distribution of invitations to party meetings to members living in those districts of the city which were hard to reach and regular companionship service for old or ill persons. All members were expected to keep alert at all times and to become familiar with the social and economic conditions under

---

[63] *Ibid.*, p. 31.

[64] Z. Fischer, *Sozialistische Erziehung* (Wien, 1926), p. 107. Father Fischer complained, however (*ibid.*, p. 13), that the *Arbeiter Zeitung* had falsified his praise of the abstinence work of the *Kinderfreunde* in a previous booklet into the exact opposite. On the other hand, as he did not note, the official organ of the *Kinderfreunde* quoted him correctly on the first page of its issue for December, 1924.

[65] Tesarek, *Das Buch der Roten Falken*, pp. 36–37.

which workers and farmers lived.[66] Naturally the Red Falcons participated in all workers' festivals and added color to the various celebrations discussed above. They did not attend the *Hort* but met for play, work, and discussion in the *Horst* (eyrie).

One of their rules was to maintain close contact with parents. The children were expected to explain their activities and obligations to them, as well as to demonstrate that they were meant seriously. The leaders were requested to hold parents' meetings every month and on these occasions to advise them on the next projects. At such meetings various types of entertainments, staged by children, were offered. The leaders were obliged to notify the parents if a child had not appeared at group meetings for some time.[67] Thus the close contact among *Kinderfreunde,* Social Democratic party, and Red Falcons was maintained. "Unorganized" children were accepted, but after a while their parents were asked to become members of the *Kinderfreunde.* The latter also financed the Falcons since they were not permitted to collect fees independently except for funds for particular purposes such as hiking expeditions.[68]

The development of the Red Falcon movement was rapid. By the spring of 1927 there were 181 groups with 5,100 members; in 1928, 210 with 5,210, of whom about two-fifths were girls. The report for 1929 showed 312 groups with 8,300 youngsters. During the next year the number of groups dropped to 300 but the members increased to 8,500. The figures for 1931 were 335 and 10,198; for 1932, 446 and 15,117.[69]

This growth took place in spite of—as already noted, the Socialists claimed because of—the relentless hostility of the Catholic Church and its Christian Social allies. Not disheartened by the evident failure of the pastoral letter of 1922 they continued their attacks, one of the sharpest being another pastoral letter read from all pulpits in December, 1925. Again the bishops declared Socialism to be the herald of hatred of God and decried the *Kinderfreunde*

[66] For the effectiveness of their work, testimony from the Catholic press can again be cited: "If thunderstorms are threatening they help the small farmers, farm hands and girls, thus overcoming the 'short circuit' between city and country. [It is] apostle work of enthusiasm." Fischer, in *Das Neue Reich,* vol. 10 (June 2, 1928), 75.

[67] Tesarek, *Das Buch der Roten Falken,* pp. 37, 83–84, 95–98, 107–108; *SE.,* vol. 11 (Sept., 1931), 203, 204.

[68] *SE.,* vol. 6 (March, 1926), 57.

[69] *Jahrbuch der österreichischen Arbeiterbewegung, 1927,* p. 261; *1928,* p. 344; *1929,* p. 406; *1930,* p. 415; *1931,* p. 385; *1932,* p. 350.

movement as designed to ruin youth. Then they continued: "And Christ would add with all the terrible sincerity that he was accustomed to incorporate in his words: 'Whoever destroys the faith of one of the little ones and blights his eternal salvation deserves that a millstone be hanged about his neck and that he be drowned in the depth of the sea.' (Matthew 18:6)."[70] Except for some other statements from the same or similar sources, reproduced elsewhere in this volume, spokesmen for a Christian denomination have rarely expressed themselves so bluntly.

The reply from the Socialists was equally blunt, and, if possible, more vigorous. They asserted that whereas the letter of 1922 had given proletarian parents the counsel "Don't spare the rod!" the one of 1925 meant: "If you have sons, bend them in good time"; that Cardinal Piffl favored "brutal methods of education"; and that those subordinate to him applied them. They emphasized the idea that they did not want men who had been bent, but rather those who were upright. They charged that the bishops, in offering such counsel, were actually serving the Mammonism they decried in other parts of the letter. But more significant than these polemics was the practical reply. The *Kinderfreunde* announced a drive for the foundation of more circulating libraries for their local groups; the new name was "millstone libraries." The goal was to supply every group with at least one millstone library worth 100 schillings. Each book bore the following inscription: "The Austrian bishops in their pastoral letter of Christmas, 1925, have wished for a millstone around the neck of the *Kinderfreunde*. We have collected money in the form of 'millstones' and have transformed this money into millstone libraries for our children. This book belongs to such a library." The first year of the drive resulted in 150 children's libraries; by 1932 a total of 467 had been established.[71]

Evidently the attacks from the pulpits were not considered suffi-

---

[70] Cardinal Fr. G. Piffl and the Austrian episcopate, *Zu sozialen und kulturellen Fragen* (Wien-Leipzig, 1932), pp. 102–103. The entire pastoral letter is reproduced in this collection of documents edited by August M. Knoll and authorized for publication by the archbishopric of Vienna on July 2, 1932 (pp. 77–127). The King James version of the passage reads: "But whoso shall offend one of these little ones which believe in me, it were better for him that a millstone were hanged about his neck, and *that* he were drowned in the depth of the sea." As is clear, an almost literal translation of the German text of the Catholic Testament conveys more precisely the meaning of the Austrian bishops.

[71] *SE.*, vol. 6 (April, 1926), 84, 85, 87; Fadrus, *op. cit.*, p. 247; *Jahrbuch der österreichischen Arbeiterbewegung, 1932*, p. 350.

ciently effective. At any rate, it was with Cardinal Piffl's blessing that Father Zyrill Fischer published his book, *Sozialistische Erziehung*, carefully reproducing in it any utterances of Socialists or their foes which the author could construe as proof that the *Kinderfreunde* was instructing children to fight *against* Church and family, and *for* a Socialist society. He cited "facts" in order to prove the damage done to the physical and moral well-being of children by this education; other quotations were intended to demonstrate insubordination and political radicalism. At the risk of some repetition, the reader should be reminded that the *Kinderfreunde* did at times arrange excursions, hikes, and celebrations on Sundays and Church holidays with the deliberate purpose of combating what it considered the pernicious "clerical" influence on children. At other times, according to Father Fischer's own testimony, such excursions and celebrations were planned so that children could attend Mass. And he added: "The German Nationalist gymnastic association was not so considerate. . . ."[72] But, as has been said more than once, many Social Democrats believed the Roman Catholic Church in Austria was much more a political than a religious organization. Since the *Kinderfreunde* was an educational institution with Socialist aims it was to be taken for granted that it sought to train children to fight for Socialism, and since the Catholic Church had been denouncing Socialism for decades it was also to be taken for granted that it would fight back. In other words, a good part of Father Fischer's indictment is an elaboration of the obvious. With reference to his charges concerning the family, insubordination, and immorality it must be said that he did not overexert himself to prove that they were the result of *Kinderfreunde* influence. Frequently he made the organization responsible for nuisances which could be attributed to children's behavior irrespective of any such affiliation. And despite his claim of intention to do justice "even to the enemy" and the isolated cases already cited in which he did so, his treatment of the problem of sexual morality is more typical of his methods—officially endorsed though his writings were by the highest dignitary of the Church in Austria.

Father Fischer begins with a quotation from the Free Mason, Weishaupt: "Only change morals and the revolution is inevitable."

[72] *Das Neue Reich,* vol. 10 (June 2, 1928), 756.

Then he attacks coeducation, nudism, and education in sexual matters, utilizing several quotations from the official organ of the *Kinderfreunde,* and concludes that it is no wonder that among the children who had been "freed of moral hypocrisy" syphilis had spread to such an extent that "Vienna had to make available a special ward for 250 syphilitic children. In spite of that it was still not possible to accept all the children afflicted with syphilis."[73] There is not the slightest attempt to prove that the sick children were in any way connected with the *Kinderfreunde.* On the other hand, there can be no denial of the fact that juvenile sexual immorality increased during and immediately after the First World War just as it has in other war periods. The priest's argument is a perfect *non sequitur.* As has been shown, Vienna's action in opening a ward for syphilitic children was only one of its many efforts to stamp out this curse which had been spread so terribly during and after the war and had been transferred to children chiefly on a hereditary basis or as a consequence of living in crowded quarters. (Cf. Chap. XV, pp. 510, 520.)

Needless to say the *Kinderfreunde* reacted strongly to Fischer's attack. Since he had seen fit to cite individual acts of immorality, it retorted in kind.[74] But, of course, the real issue is the validity of the priest's allegation that "Godless" education resulted in sexual immorality. Now there are various ways of attempting to measure such immorality. One is the percentage of illegitimate births to legitimate births. And if Father Fischer's argument is followed to its logical conclusion that percentage should be highest among freethinkers and atheists and lowest among Roman Catholics. The previously cited Austrian equivalent of the American *Catholic Yearbook* records the fact that almost the opposite was true. Bishop Hudal and his associates report that during 1928 there were 328 illegitimate and 1,701 legitimate children born to parents who registered themselves as "without religion" (*konfessionslos*), whereas there were 29,832 illegitimate and 82,072 legitimate babies born to Roman Catholic parents. The respective percentages are 19 and 36. The only religious groups with a better record than the *konfessionslos* were the Jews with 7 per cent and the Calvinist Protestants

[73] Fischer, *Sozialistische Erziehung,* pp. 96 ff., esp. p. 100.
[74] *SE.,* vol. 6 (May, 1926), 121–124.

with 13. The only group with a worse record than the Roman Catholics was the Greek Catholics—and that by only 1 per cent. Moreover, since the recorded births to Greek Catholics were only 7 illegitimate and 19 legitimate, the percentage has little if any significance.[75]

Not the least interesting facts of this whole controversy are that the *Kinderfreunde* publicly denounced Father Fischer as a liar and a slanderer, challenged him to sue the organization for libel, and that he chose not to accept the challenge.[76]

After attempting to frighten parents by a lurid account of the dangers of the *Kinderfreunde,* our author exhorts "Christian" parents to join the Catholic school association and to send their children to the Christian Social organization Happy Childhood (*Frohe Kindheit*) founded in 1919 by several Catholic groups to compete with the *Kinderfreunde.* In 1929 Happy Childhood comprised, according to Fischer, more than 180 local groups with 18,000 children, 50,000 members, 10 hostels, and 200 *Horte* and playgrounds.[77]

In the spring of 1928 another pastoral letter was published; it repeated the former arguments and singled out the *Kinderfreunde* by linking it, according to the now well-known recipes, to Bolshevism. It warned that "ruin originates from Bolshevism and from the Austrian Social Democracy through its *Kinderfreunde* movement." The new letter also appropriated the idea of the children's penny and asked everybody to donate the Catholic *Kindergroschen* for Catholic welfare work.[78] Since the Church had long realized that mere opposition to the *Kinderfreunde* was not sufficient, it fairly

[75] Hudal, *Der Katholizismus in Oesterreich,* p. 58. Data segregated by confessional groups were not reported for years other than 1928.

It may be objected that the comparison in the text disregards the possibility that parents "without religion" would be more likely to resort to abortion than would Roman Catholics. I presume to doubt that were the figures available they would alter the percentages of 36 and 19 sufficiently to provide much support to Father Fischer. This doubt is buttressed by the statement in the Catholic source just cited that the ratio of illegitimate births had remained practically unchanged since the middle of the preceding century; that is, since a time when the Socialists were insignificant and the *Kinderfreunde* undreamed of.

[76] *SE.,* vol. 11 (Feb., 1931), 28. The American reader should be reminded that such suits were much more commonly brought in Austria than in the United States. The *Kinderfreunde* did not sue Father Fischer for libel, according to Austrian attorneys, because it would have had to prove that no single case of venereal disease had ever resulted from reformed educational methods—an obvious impossibility.

[77] Cf. Fischer, *Sozialistische Erziehung,* pp. 187, 189; *idem, Kinderfreunde und Rote Falken* (Wien, 1929), pp. 109–110.

[78] The complete text of this letter could not be found in available sources. Brief extracts or summaries appear in Piffl *et al., op. cit.,* pp. 150–153; *Das Neue Reich,* vol.

promptly set up a counterpart of the Red Falcons under the name Blue Falcons. Youth dedications were instituted and young priests led children into the country after an early Mass. Even a children's swimming pool for both sexes was opened on the banks of the Danube. Large amounts of money were spent for new children's hostels. Young nuns and priests volunteered in increasing numbers to help the Happy Childhood movement which was trying to get a foothold in the industrial communities. The Catholic children's groschen was made obligatory by the bishops. Educational methods in the Catholic schools were modernized. Throughout 1927 and 1928 *Das Neue Reich* gave considerable space to the work of the *Kinderfreunde*. Thus the struggle for supremacy became increasingly more serious so that the Austrian workers had "to employ great efforts in order to make these important armaments ineffective."[79] But again the *Kinderfreunde* won; evidently the poor reputation in certain respects of the Catholic Church among large groups of Austrian workers could not be so quickly wiped out by the hasty application of new methods. The last great gains of the *Kinderfreunde* had taken place in 1923 when it had reached a membership of 88,314. This number was approximately maintained until 1926; then a new rise began and in 1927 the organization reported 95,308 adherents in 359 local groups. In 1929 it reached its peak with 100,540. Thereafter, as a consequence of unemployment and reduced incomes, the number of members gradually declined, but in 1932 there were still 91,385 in 434 localities. The greatest concentration, of course, was in Vienna: 46,550 members.[80]

The economic crisis brought welfare activities to the fore again. In 1929, 7,789 children were sent to 8 camps and 38 hostels at a cost to the *Kinderfreunde* of more than 650,000 schillings. Shrinking funds forced strict limitations on the recreational work, but intensified efforts in 1932 enabled the organization to take care of 7,386 children in 8 camps and 29 hostels, appreciably more than in the two preceding years.[81] Closely connected with aid for the children

---

10 (March 3, 1928), 465–466; Fischer, *Kinderfreunde und Rote Falken*, p. 101; *SE.*, vol. 8 (April, 1928), 89–92; *Neue Freie Presse*, February 22, 1928 (P.M), p. 2. The *Reichspost* for this period was not available.

[79] Jalkotzy, "Kampf um die Erziehung der Arbeiterkinder," *Der Kampf*, vol. 21 (Oct., 1928), 479–484; *Jahrbuch der österreichischen Arbeiterbewegung, 1929*, p. 407.

[80] Cf. *Jahrbuch der österreichischen Arbeiterbewegung, 1927*, p. 258; *1929*, pp. 404, 407; *1932*, p. 349.

[81] *Ibid., 1929*, p. 405; *1932*, p. 350.

of members was support for proletarian children from areas particularly hard hit by unemployment. As early as 1926 the *Kinderfreunde* had organized assistance for the children of striking workers in Steyr (the Austrian automobile manufacturing center) by collecting money and by extending invitations to approximately 800 of them to spend some weeks in the homes of Social Democrats living in other communities.[82] In 1931, in coöperation with the Socialist party, it staged a drive to place children of unemployed workers from the *Alpine* "empire" in the homes of more fortunate workers for six weeks. During the first year of the campaign 1,692 children were accommodated. The rising tide of unemployment prevented the maintenance of so large a number the next year, but even then the *Kinderfreunde* managed to take care of 921 children. The Red Falcons also participated in this work of brightening the lives of children by making toys and distributing them throughout the country; in 1932 it was reported that they had given out 32,000 toys.[83]

In concluding this survey of the development and activities of the Austrian *Kinderfreunde* movement it seems appropriate to emphasize a fact that is already clear; namely, that it was marked by the same intrinsic trait that was characteristic of the political party organization: a strong will to fight for a better world order combined with a realistic attitude toward everyday problems. Naturally enough, the relatively greater occupation with ideological issues and the youth of its active leaders and members made the *Kinderfreunde* appear more radical than most of the party organizations. Loewenstein has characterized the aims of the *Kinderfreunde* movement very clearly. "This education does not have a *Weltanschauung* in the sense of the old churches; it is scientifically based on social facts. But it is also not neutral in the sense that it does not pass a judgement [*Werturteil*] and does not lay down a principle; rather it affirms most strongly the social and democratic tendencies of our time."[84]

It may be noted further that, following the Austrian model, the first *Kinderfreunde* units were founded in Germany shortly after

[82] *Parteitag, 1926,* pp. 111–112.

[83] Cf. *SE.,* vol. 11 (Sept., 1931), 201; *Jahrbuch der österreichischen Arbeiterbewegung, 1931,* p. 385; *1932,* p. 350.

[84] K. Kerloew-Loewenstein, *Sozialistische Erziehung* (Berlin, 1929), p. 3; quoted in Fadrus, *op. cit.,* p. 301.

the First World War. Other *Kinderfreunde* and Falcon groups were then formed in Czechoslovakia, Poland, Switzerland, Hungary, Rumania, Argentina, and even in the United States. In other countries, such as Denmark, Belgium, and Latvia, Red Boy Scout groups with principles similar to those of the Austrian Red Falcons came into being. These national groups were united in the Socialist International for Education which held its first international conference in Brussels in 1928.[85]

Workers' Youth Organizations

The Association of Socialist Workers' Youth

Although, as noted at the beginning of this chapter, the first Socialist youth organization actually originated outside the labor movement, it soon came under the influence of adult Socialists, and in the literature is frequently referred to as "the youth organization." The immediate impetus to joint action was the hardships to which young apprentices were subjected in the shops of small craftsmen—hardships that became intolerable with the growing competition between craftsmen and rapidly expanding mechanized industry. Working hours from 5 A.M. until 8 P.M. with additional toil in cleaning the premises were not unusual. The apprenticeship customarily lasted three years; during it the apprentice generally worked for room and board only. Usually parents had to compensate the master for his efforts to teach the apprentice the secrets of the trade, an instruction which for a considerable length of time consisted mainly in ordering the youngster to do the housework for the master's wife or to handle heavy pushcarts in which materials and tools were transported. Frequently the food was bad, the living quarters dirty and situated in humid basements. Under the terms of the "training contract" (*Lehrvertrag*), concluded between the master and the parents of the apprentice, the latter became completely dependent upon the master for the duration of the fixed learning period. Because of the long working hours the compulsory continuation school for apprentices between fourteen and sixteen could hold classes only on weekday evenings and on Sundays. Need-

[85] Cf. Fadrus, *op. cit.*, pp. 294, 298; *SE.*, vol. 11 (Sept., 1931), 204; *Jahrbuch der österreichischen Arbeiterbewegung, 1932*, p. 351.

less to say most of the pupils did not profit greatly from such an education. In revolt against these circumstances a few apprentices in Vienna organized independently two workers' youth groups, and from these beginnings in the early 'nineties developed a general workers' youth organization. The founders were a little better off than the great majority of their fellow apprentices. Their primary purpose was to supplement their poor education by studying together on Sunday afternoons, an aim characterized by the fact that one of the two original groups called itself Book Scorpion. In addition to the joint reading of books of social and scientific content, the members of this small circle busied themselves with the study of shorthand and with formal recitations. The last foreshadowed the subsequent emphasis on public speaking in workers' education. The second group, the Youth Union (*Jugendbund*), had approximately the same program. Soon the two groups met and decided to form an association of young workers which, according to Austrian law, had to obtain official authorization. Guided by the counsel of adult Socialist party members, the apprentices held meetings in many Viennese districts during 1894 and in spite of the opposition of the masters, who tried to intimidate the boys as well as their parents, proceeded to form their association. Its first formal meeting took place on November 4, 1894.[86]

The purposes of the new organization, as subsequently summarized by *Der Kampf* from a contemporary leaflet, included the statement: "We want to put an end to the inhuman treatment and exploitation of apprentices; we want to do for ourselves what the Association for the Prevention of Cruelty to Animals does for dogs and horses." The Young Workers then demanded day instead of evening classes in the continuation schools and abolition of Sunday instruction. Other aims were the foundation of a library, improvement of the education of the members, and the replacement of the customary "spirit-killing" Sunday entertainments by choral singing, dramatic performances, joint hikes, swimming, and so on. Further, they announced their intention of helping apprentices who had been dismissed by their masters. Significantly, they added:

[86] Karl Heinz, *Kampf und Aufstieg* (Wien, 1932), pp. 5–12. It may be noted that Catholic as well as nationalist youth organizations existed prior to the Socialist organization, originally called the Association of Young Workers (*Verein jugendlicher Arbeiter*). In November, 1919, the organization adopted the name Association of Socialist Workers' Youth (*Verband der sozialistischen Arbeiterjugend*).

"With political questions we shall not occupy ourselves, although we do not conceal [the fact] that we see our support and representation among the Social Democratic workers." The leaflet concluded with the words which remained the motto of the association: "Education makes [men] free" (*Bildung macht frei*).[87]

The Association of Young Workers met instant and fierce opposition from the non-Socialist press; school authorities forbade attendance at its meetings; local groups as well as district assemblies were dissolved by the police. In spite of these hardships and the fact that "only very few [of the adult party and trade union] comrades recognized at this time the importance and significance of the youth organization for the party and the unions," the association made steady progress and was able to form many local units.[88] As early as October, 1902, the Vienna organization published the first issue of its monthly magazine in an edition of 5,000 copies. The distribution resulted in the formation of numerous new groups all over Austria. On February 11, 1903, these locals received approval from the authorities for the constitution of a national association. In the same year the Young Workers were officially recognized by the Social Democratic party in a resolution which obligated all party members to give the youth organization their most vigorous support.[89] A more rapid growth took place after 1907 when party and trade unions decided not only to support the association but also to promote the formation of new groups "wherever conditions permit." This was explicitly stated in an amendment to the bylaws of the party which likewise provided that every local organization should take care "that the youth of the working class is educated in the spirit of Socialism and filled with class consciousness." The regular participation of the members of the youth organization in all demonstrations of their adult comrades for the general suffrage and the rule obligating all members to join a union as soon as their apprenticeship was over had found their reward.[90]

Thus the Association of Young Workers had become for youth

---

[87] Anton Jenschik, "Die österreichische Jugendorganisation," *Der Kampf*, vol. 6 (July 1, 1913), 450–451.

[88] *Ibid.*, p. 451.

[89] Heinz, *Kampf und Aufstieg*, pp. 25, 26, 29. Discussions concerning the youth organization and its demands for better economic conditions had taken place in the congresses of 1898, 1900, 1901, and 1902. Cf. *ibid.*, pp. 28–29; *Parteitag, 1907*, pp. 155–156.

[90] *Parteitag, 1907*, pp. 100, 209; Jenschik, *op. cit.*, p. 453; R. Danneberg, "Die österreichische Jugendorganisation," *Der Kampf*, vol. 1 (Aug., 1908), 515.

the organizational medium of the Socialist party as well as of the trade unions. Its task was to prepare the young generation for activity and leadership in the political and economic branches of the working-class movement. The youthful workers were to become conscious fighters for the cause of labor, and this purpose could best be achieved by systematic education. In addition, the youth association was designed to prevent them from joining various clerical or nationalist groups the influence of which might block their future adherence to workers' organizations. Though secondary to the educational task, other duties similar to those carried on for the adult workers by their trade unions had to be met by the Young Workers. The reason was that the established unions were neither spiritually prepared to do the job nor practically able to intervene successfully in small shops or plants which employed few or no journeymen. However, the trade unions were quick to recognize that "The apprentice who joins a local group of the youth organization learns quite early to wage struggles, to appreciate the value of an organization, and to move in it as a disciplined member."[91]

The youth organization administered its affairs independently but in close contact with the workers' party; for example, a new local group could be formed only if it were approved by the local party organization. It is characteristic of the attitude of the adults that again and again assurances were given that the work of the association would not interfere "with the jurisdiction of the party and the unions."[92]

The age composition of the Austrian youth movement, mainly the youngest workers,[93] the legal restrictions on the political activity of minors, and, last but not least, the philosophy of the Austrian labor movement make it clear why "the primary task of proletarian youth organizations has to be the training of the workers' youth to class consciousness by *educational* work and fights of an economic nature."[94] It should be understood that the "fights of an economic nature" consisted primarily in pointing out the hardships which

---

[91] *Der österreichische Metallarbeiter,* 1907, (Nr. 51), quoted in *Der Kampf,* vol. 1 (Aug., 1908), 514.

[92] Cf., for instance, Danneberg, *Der Kampf,* vol. 1 (Aug., 1908), 514.

[93] The first age statistic available (1906) showed that 61 per cent of the members were under eighteen; by 1911 this group had increased to 82 per cent; in 1918 it was down to 68 per cent. K. Heinz, "Revolutionsaufgaben der Jugendbewegung," *Der Kampf,* vol. 12 (August 30, 1919), 572.

[94] *Ibid.,* pp. 570–571. Italics mine.

young workers suffered, in suggesting programs for improvement, and, through meetings and leaflets, in demanding relief. Aid had to come from parliament and from the government; to obtain it the organization had to rely upon the few representatives of the workers' party in the legislative bodies of imperial Austria. In spite of discouragements these men led an unceasing fight for the goals of the association and for the legal protection of apprentices. Stanch resistance was offered by the non-Socialist parties, particularly by the Christian Socials as the chief representatives of the interests of the master organizations.[95]

The Association of Young Workers steadily pressed its efforts to increase its membership and to extend its educational program. From only 3,556 members in 1906, it grew to 7,764 in 1911 and to 16,196 on the first of June, 1914, that is, just before the outbreak of the war. These gains were registered in spite of numerous difficulties encountered by the organization in its propaganda as well as by the individuals who dared to join. Interestingly enough it was not until March and April of 1914 that the first girls' groups were founded; by the end of 1915 they had been merged with the boys' groups.[96] Another interesting aspect of the composition of the membership is the fact that the apprentices who had founded the association soon became a minority therein. In 1912, for instance, they accounted for only 35.8 per cent of the total; except for a few home workers the balance were journeymen and unskilled factory laborers. Although expanding industrialism played a part, the intimidation of apprentices by masters and school authorities was held responsible for this development.[97]

The emphasis on the educational program is reflected in various accounts and reports. For example, in the period between January, 1903, and September, 1904, the 14 Viennese groups held 138 lectures on Socialism, 123 on history, 94 on literature, 87 on hygiene,

[95] Heinz, *Kampf und Aufstieg*, pp. 45–81. A first success was the Lower Austrian law of November 30, 1907, providing that classes in the continuation schools might not close later than 7 P.M. on weekdays and might be held only between 9 and 11 A.M. on Sundays. The Christian Socials refused to eliminate Sunday classes as proposed by the Social Democrats; the trade representatives continued their fight against the modest law adopted, contending that it was ruinous for the trades. In fact, the statute was by no means generally enforced. *Ibid.*, pp. 54, 56.

[96] *Der Kampf*, vol. 12 (Aug. 30, 1919), 572; Heinz, *Kampf und Aufstieg*, pp. 109–110, 113.

[97] Jenschik, *op. cit.*, pp. 453–454; Gewerkschaftskommission, *Bericht*, 1928, p. 154.

and 95 on industrial questions. In addition, they engaged in 199 discussions on the lectures and organized 105 open meetings and 51 excursions. According to the report of the library of one of the strongest Vienna groups the authors most intensively read were Schiller and Lassalle.[98] In 1909 the organization decided upon a detailed educational program directed toward the goals referred to above. To effectuate this program a great many talks and lectures were given, hiking trips and theatrical performances organized, and circulating libraries exchanged among the local groups. At the annual convention in 1909 a National Educational Committee (*Reichsbildungsausschuss*) was founded to coördinate the work. It was recognized from the outset that the program could not be carried out in full. The hindrances were not only the lack of suitable teachers and of adequate funds, but also the long working hours, the late school classes, and the natural desire of youngsters to spend their few leisure hours in some other way than attending lectures or poring over books. Nevertheless, by the end of 1912 the association owned 50 circulating libraries and had held lecture courses for its officers in numerous towns and cities in the empire. A course given in Vienna in 1912 had 148 participants. The topics of these courses included party and union organization, the party program, the Austrian constitution, legal doctrine, youth protection, scientific Socialism, anarchism and Socialism, Christianity and Socialism, militarism, and even correct behavior in society. In 1913 the National Educational Committee organized a course for the leaders of excursions and of recreational activities; it drew 90 participants. Individual talks and lectures, in addition to the courses, were frequent. In Vienna during 1910, 1911, and 1912 there were 1,207 with audiences aggregating 46,988. Correspondence courses in shorthand were given to members free of charge. A book division selected and procured at reduced prices small books and pamphlets. In return for an additional 10 heller remitted with his monthly dues a member received one of these pamphlets or books each quarter. After one year of existence this division had enlisted 2,000 members. Some of the publications contained poetry and fiction of social significance, but generally they were concerned with Socialism, youth problems, alcoholism, and so on—all presented in a popular fashion.

---

[98] Danneberg, *Der Kampf,* vol. 1 (Aug., 1908), 512.

During the two years prior to the outbreak of the First World War the various sections of the Young Workers held 12,840 open meetings with an attendance of a little more than 300,000.[99]

Two features of the educational program of the Austrian youth movement merit particular attention: its position toward alcohol and toward pacifism. The fight against alcohol was initiated at the second national convention in April, 1906, when it was decided that meetings should not be held in places where alcohol was sold; if no other places could be found then soft drinks should also be available to members. It was agreed further that lectures on abstinence should be given at regular intervals and that propaganda material should be distributed in all local groups. The 1912 convention voted for the formation of separate abstinent sections within the youth organization. In 1913 the sale of 99,971 pamphlets against alcoholism was reported. After the war voluntary abstinence by members was nearly complete; however, officers were obliged to be abstinent. In 1922 the executive committee of the organization requested the Socialist representatives in parliament to obtain a legal proscription of alcohol for young people, and on May 12 of that year a statute was enacted prohibiting the sale of alcoholic beverages to youths under sixteen years of age.[100]

The fight against militarism and for the maintenance of peace did not play so important a role in the Austrian youth movement as in other countries. One reason for this difference was the lower age of the majority of the Austrian members. Another, given at the international youth conference in Stuttgart in 1907, was the "nearly unpolitical and limitedly antimilitaristic character" of the Austrian youth movement caused by the retarded economic development of the country. Furthermore, it was contended that "If class consciousness has been aroused among the apprentices, specific antimilitaristic propaganda among the workers of draft age would be superfluous. . . ."[101] Nevertheless, the Association of Young Workers joined the International Union of Socialist Youth Organizations immediately after its formation at the Stuttgart conference and thereby declared its intention to fight against militarism which, aside from

---

[99] Jenschik, *op. cit.*, pp. 455–456; Heinz, *Kampf und Aufstieg*, pp. 63, 93–94.

[100] Cf. Heinz, *Kampf und Aufstieg*, pp. 47, 88, 94, 158; F. Kanitz, *Unsere Arbeit* (Wien, 1928), p. 162.

[101] Heinz, *Der Kampf*, vol. 12 (Aug. 30, 1919), 572; Danneberg, *ibid.*, vol. 1 (Aug., 1908), 511–512.

Germany and czarist Russia, had its main stronghold in imperial Austria. Under the system of obligatory service the military clique was the most powerful group in the monarchy so that, naturally enough, antimilitaristic propaganda brought about great dangers for the organization. In spite of this situation the approaching war and the increasing age range of the membership led to a steady intensification of pacifist propaganda until the outbreak of hostilities. The countermeasures included intensified persecution of the organization, prohibition of meetings for draftees, and confiscations of *Der Jugendliche Arbeiter*—which had begun to publish separate antimilitaristic issues in 1911.[102] Once the conflict had been initiated, however, pacifist sentiment in the youth organization and in the party proved too weak to offer any effective resistance. The first article in the first issue of *Der Jugendliche Arbeiter* published after war had been declared showed that the youth association was following closely the policy of the party majority. It will be recalled that the gist of this policy was quick endorsement of the Austrian and German governments in the hope that they would smash Russian absolutism promptly and thus prevent the loss of the rights which the Austrian working class had gained in its long struggles during previous decades. In the early stages of the war, therefore, the work of the organization consisted mainly in holding itself together and in continuing the educational program as far as possible.

But the longer the war lasted the clearer it became to the workers that a victory of the Habsburgs and the Hohenzollerns would mean the erection of a military dictatorship over Europe and the suppression of the Socialist labor movement; hence, the left wing of the party, which had denounced the war from its outset as an imperialistic venture, became increasingly influential and won adherents, particularly among the young generation. The result was, of course, that the youth organization again participated in the fight against the war policy. This changed attitude was clearly shown in the resolution adopted by the district conference of the Vienna organization on March 5, 1916, demanding the early termination of the war and the destruction of the military dictatorship. In accordance with the policy of the middle way, however, the conference rejected the Zimmerwald principles and expressed its sympathy with the inter-

[102] Heinz, *Kampf und Aufstieg*, pp. 95–98.

national Socialist youth office in Zurich. During subsequent months the influence of the "left" grew. Many voices openly criticized the official policy of the party and demanded an independent and active antiwar policy in the youth association. At the conference of the Viennese organization on April 22, 1917, the left wing commanded a majority. The meeting adopted a resolution which stated: "We cannot follow those comrades who support the war morally and who have concluded an armistice with the foes of the proletariat. Neither [can we follow] those who see the essence of the proletarian class struggle not in a revolutionary mass movement but solely in the formation of the most extensive organizations, the gain of many seats in parliament, in order that the leaders may obtain parsimonious advantages for the workers by compromises, by alliances with sections of the opponents, by clever diplomatic moves, and so on within the capitalist order." This resolution was to be sent to the other groups; but the board of directors of the national association refused to forward it, asserting that it was a purely political enunciation and in contrast to the statutory educational purposes of the organization. At the convention of the national body on August 12, 1917, the viewpoint of the board was upheld. The discussion in this meeting emphasized the necessity of avoiding a party split and of stressing the educational tasks of the youth organization. Differences of political opinion should be discussed within the party and not within the youth group. This decision brought accusations from left wingers that the board of directors had used highhanded methods to squelch the opposition. In further protest a number of members of two Viennese district groups (Favoriten and Leopoldstadt) left the association and formed a new organization, Free Youth, to advance the idea that the youth institutions should be "the storm troops of the proletarian revolutionary army."[103] After this showdown the bulk of the Association of Young Workers maintained the principles upon which it had been founded: education, struggle for better working conditions, and social welfare. As a result of war and postwar conditions the second and third principles received increased attention in the bills of demands.

The Revolution of 1918 was hailed by young workers with an

[103] Cf. Heinz, *Kampf und Aufstieg*, pp. 103, 105–106, 113, 115–121, 127–128; and *Der Kampf*, vol. 11 (Aug., 1918), 586–588. In the article cited in *Der Kampf* an anonymous "leftist" presented the viewpoint of the opposition.

enthusiasm equaling that of adult party comrades. The restrictions on the right of youth to freedom of assembly and to membership in political associations fell. Since the masters' organizations had not given up hope of continuing their exploitation of the apprentices, the youth organization fought on for such demands as the forty-four-hour week, thirty-six hours uninterrupted Sunday rest, annual vacations of four weeks, and the erection of recuperation homes for young workers. Further demands were the general introduction of day classes, excluding Sunday, at the continuation schools and the creation of state workshops to replace apprenticeship with masters by systematic vocational education. An extensive program for a reform of the apprenticeship regulations of the industrial code (*Gewerbeordnung*) was introduced by Danneberg in the Constituent Assembly in April, 1919.[104]

The first issue which came up again was day classes in continuation schools. One prompt success was the unanimous vote of the Vienna city council on December 30, 1918, to subsidize exclusively those schools which held classes only on weekdays and terminated instruction not later than 6 P.M. But since the resolution had fixed the starting date of the new schedule in September, 1919, and since the masters' associations had immediately begun a campaign of delay and obstruction, the young workers' association carried through a strike of the students of the continuation schools on Sunday, March 2, 1919, and requested the Socialist Sever to aid them in securing the abolition of evening and Sunday classes. On March 7, he introduced an "urgent motion" in the Provisional Assembly of Lower Austria demanding that the "cabinet" of that state proceed to immediate abolition. The motion was passed unanimously. On April 9, the Provisional Assembly adopted an amendment to the continuation school law requiring that instruction be given only on weekdays and between the hours of 7 A.M. and 6 P.M. There remained, however, substantial areas in Austria in which evening and Sunday classes persisted; consequently, Danneberg introduced at a meeting of a subcommittee of the budget committee of the Constituent Assembly of the republic a resolution requesting the ministry of trade to exert its influence in securing the abolition of such

[104] Heinz, *Kampf und Aufstieg*, pp. 132–133, 135–137; Konstituierende Nationalversammlung, *Protokoll*, 1919, *Beilagen*, Nr. 137.

classes. This resolution was reported as approved in a report of the subcommittee dated February 12, 1920; it was approved by the Constituent Assembly on May 18. Despite this clear-cut action it seems that the practice was actually abandoned only in those communities where sufficient pressure could be brought by the Socialists and the youth organization. In 1923, after the bourgeois parties had acquired a majority in the diet of Lower Austria, they amended the continuation school law to permit instruction until 6:30 P.M. instead of 6 P.M. Meanwhile, on February 11, 1920, Lower Austria had passed a statute requiring that an equal number of representatives of labor, including two young workers, and of employers be appointed to the boards of continuation schools.[105]

The next action, particularly important because of the terrible health conditions and the undernourishment of most of the young workers, centered on the demand for four weeks of summer vacation. To achieve this the Association of Young Workers organized a great number of meetings (*Versammlungssturm*), and by means of the pressure thus created achieved at least a partial success. The Social Democratic secretary of social welfare decreed on May 9, 1919,[106] that all young workers who came under the social security law should be given an uninterrupted vacation of four weeks between the months of May and October if a medical examination demonstrated the urgent need for such a vacation and if the beneficiary proved that he could spend the vacation in the country. By the workers' vacation law of July 30, 1919, all young workers obtained the right to a vacation of two weeks irrespective of physical condition.[107] In order to provide rural recuperation institutions the ministry, aided by the city of Vienna and the obligatory health insurance system, began at the same time the erection of youth homes, two of which were opened in the summer of 1919. A general limitation of the work week was secured by the law of December 17, 1919, extending the eight-hour day to small shops.[108] This was of special importance for young workers because these shops employed great numbers of apprentices.

---

[105] Heinz, *Kampf und Aufstieg*, pp. 133–137, 149, 159; Konstituierende Nationalversammlung, *Protokoll*, 1920, Beilagen, Nr. 667 (section dealing with "group XII" of budget, pp. 8, 11); *ibid.*, *Protokoll*, May 18, 1920, p. 2750.

[106] *StGBl.*, 1919, Nr. 262.

[107] *Ibid.*, Nr. 395.

[108] *Ibid.*, Nr. 581.

Another demand of the organization, legal minimum compensation for apprentices, was partly satisfied by the law of July 11, 1922. Those apprentices who had completed at least one-third of their term received a gradually rising compensation expressed as a percentage of journeymen's pay.[109] The demand for unemployment compensation for all young workers, however, could not be obtained; such benefits were restricted to those who had completed their apprenticeship, or who had not reached their sixteenth birthday and had no relatives, or who had to support a family. In order to protect the legal rights of the apprentices the Vienna chamber of labor inaugurated "apprentice protection centers" in October, 1921. The Vienna center was put under the direction of Anton Kimml, until then executive secretary of the youth association. Other centers were soon established in the states.[110]

It has been noted that after the war of 1914–1918 the trade unions seriously undertook the task of organizing apprentices and young workers. Several factors contributed to this changed attitude. By 1920 and 1921 a very high percentage of all adult workers had been organized into one union or another so that the might of organized labor had increased tremendously. Because of the altered political situation there was more time for organizing the young generation. The position of young workers had been greatly improved by the new social legislation. Under these circumstances the unions could see better opportunities of organizing the youthful group and could appreciate more correctly the value of educating it adequately for the broader labor struggles to come. Well-trained union members would also be able to represent more effectively the economic and political demands of labor in conferences with employers and government officials. Some of the unions emphasized their interest in improved training of apprentices for the craft as a means of safeguarding the job security of future journeymen. Early in the republican era, therefore, it had become the unanimous opinion of the unions that early entry into the apprentice sections resulted in a higher-grade membership.

The first apprentice division after the First World War was created

[109] *BGBl.*, 1922, Nr. 451.

[110] Heinz, *Kampf und Aufstieg*, pp. 139–141, 148, 151, 156, 159. As may be recalled, several of the statutes cited in the preceding pages were mentioned in Chapter X. Despite the repetition involved it seemed more useful to collect them here than to refer to a number of pages scattered through that chapter.

by the organization of bank employees; it functioned successfully until the bank crisis broke out in 1924. Other unions followed quickly. The largest apprentice groups developed among the metal-workers (whose activity in this field actually began in a different form in the 1890's), the commercial employees, the building-trade workers, and the printers. Their growth made it necessary to define clearly the jurisdiction of the apprentice sections of the unions, on the one hand, and of the Socialist Workers' Youth, on the other. This was accomplished in 1925 by an agreement which transferred union and occupational questions, as well as educational matters related to them, to the apprentice sections of the unions, whereas political education was to be the responsibility of the workers' youth association. Cultural activities were carried on by both groups but were to be organized jointly as far as possible. The coöperation of the organizations was to be secured by declaring *Der Jugendliche Arbeiter* to be their common journal, by reciprocal delegation of representatives to the executive bodies, joint educational committees, and joint work in the continuation schools. In short, the intention of the agreement was to establish a division of functions similar to that which was traditional between the workers' party and the unions. In furtherance of the plan the trade-union *Kommission* created its own apprentice section which federated the sections of the various trade unions. By 1928 the apprentice sections numbered 13,785 members, of whom approximately one-third were metal-workers. Most successful were the printers; they had enlisted 95 per cent of all young workers in the trade.[111]

In an earlier section of this chapter the conflict within the youth association precipitated by its "left opposition" during the last years of the war was discussed. Communist youth groups, who tried to gain influence, were responsible for certain frictions for some time. The final showdown came at the annual convention in Bruck on May 15 and 16, 1921. There it was decided to join the International Association of Socialist Youth Organizations (*Internationale Arbeitsgemeinschaft sozialistischer Jugendorganisationen*). This group had been founded by youth associations that had refused to join the Communist Youth International, but also did not wish to enter the Workers' Youth International which had been formed by the

[111] Gewerkschaftskommission, *Bericht,* 1928, pp. 157–159, 161–163, 165, 166, 169, 177–178.

Social Democratic youth organizations of Denmark, Germany, Holland, and Sweden. The last-named international emphasized chiefly the cultural tasks of youth. In his program speech at the Bruck convention the executive secretary of the Austrian organization pointed out that the purely welfare viewpoint, as well as the *avant-guard* policy, should be rejected.[112]

This development had been foreshadowed by a conference of the Viennese organization on April 10, 1919, which had voted 74 to 31 for a resolution combining the purely educational goals with political demands. The gist of the resolution was that the chief task of the organization was to educate young workers to become class fighters. Independent action by youth organizations could be taken only in questions pertaining to the protection of youth and to the improvement of its standard of living. Political action required the closest coöperation with those adult organizations which endorsed the class-struggle theory. Finally, however, the resolution emphasized the intention of youth to take an independent stand if the Socialist party should abandon the class struggle or the principles of internationalism. The national convention of November, 1919, endorsed this point of view, by and large, stressed again the educational function of the association, but indicated its political consciousness by changing the name of the organization to Association of Socialist Workers' Youth.[113]

Its task remained the same: to prepare young workers to enter the Social Democratic party as well-disciplined and well-trained class fighters. This viewpoint was never seriously challenged prior to the 'thirties, but the methods of training had to undergo some changes the more the youth organization developed into a mass movement in contrast to the "intellectual elite of young workers"[114] which it had been in earlier years. The former emphasis on lectures and discussions shifted gradually toward lighter entertainment. The character of the new members, more leisure, less economic strain, and the influence exerted by the *Kinderfreunde,* as well as by the German *Wandervogel* spirit,[115] combined to create a new temper.

[112] Heinz, *Kampf und Aufstieg,* pp. 152–154.

[113] *Ibid.,* pp. 142–143, 145.

[114] Otto Bauer, *Die Arbeiterjugend und die Weltlage des Sozialismus* (Wien, 1924), p. 23.

[115] The influence of Germany became greater when, in connection with the revival of the Socialist Workers International (Second International), a merger of the Inter-

During the convention at Linz in September, 1923, Kanitz pleaded for the adoption of gaiety and sociability as propaganda and educational methods of the organization, contending that they were more appropriate to the psychological qualities of young people. The practical result of the new attitude was the cultivation of song, square dance, and recitation in chorus. At the same conference Julius Deutsch emphasized the importance of physical training and military sport (*Wehrsport*), as well as of discipline, among the youth as means of combating Fascism. As a consequence of his appeal it was decided to form a Youth Guard (*Jugend Ordner*) within the association, open to all physically fit members over sixteen years of age.[116]

In 1923 the Association of Socialist Workers' Youth reached the highest membership of its history: 37,868. Of these 30,145 were male, 7,723 female. The Viennese organization numbered 14,220. The local groups totaled 269. The great majority of the members were between fourteen and eighteen years of age; that is, 46.5 per cent between fourteen and sixteen and 30.4 per cent seventeen or eighteen. Another 14.7 per cent were between nineteen and twenty-one; the small remainder were either older or of unreported age. The total number of members in 1919 had been 16,146.[117] After 1923 the membership dropped and vacillated between 28,000 and 32,000. Lest these figures seem rather small it should be noted that they do not tell the whole story. Whereas in the first years after the war the Association of Socialist Workers' Youth enjoyed practically a monopoly, there sprang up in the following period new youth groups which attracted considerable numbers of potential members of the original organization. Already mentioned were the youth sections of the trade unions; many between the ages of fourteen and sixteen stayed with the Red Falcons. The increasing interest in sports and cultural activities caused other youngsters to flock into the workers' gymnastic and swimming societies, into their singing and folk-dancing clubs, and into the Friends of Nature, the large hiking association. All of these were quick to set up special youth sections

---

national Association of Socialist Youth Organizations with the Workers' Youth International took place at the international youth congress in Hamburg, May 24–26, 1923. Heinz, *Kampf und Aufstieg*, pp. 157, 160.

[116] Heinz, *Kampf und Aufstieg*, pp. 160–161; *Die Praxis*, vol. 8 (Jan., 1929), 22–23.

[117] *Parteitag, 1924*, pp. 71–72; Heinz, *Kampf und Aufstieg*, p. 145.

which, in addition to their chief purpose, carried on at least some Socialist education. Exact figures for these and other groups which competed with one another for the Socialist workers' youth are not available, but there is no doubt that in the aggregate they constituted a specific mass activity which no other group outside the general labor movement could even approximate. Although it proved impossible to realize the unified mass movement that had been envisaged, close coöperation of all groups, at least at major events, was obtained. The high point of this coöperation was the international youth gathering in Vienna in 1929 when 50,000 young Socialists from many parts of the world were greeted. The farthest step toward organizational unification was the creation of a "youth division" within each Social Democratic state organization in 1931.[118] But there is another good reason why a youth association cannot grow above certain limits; it is necessarily a transition organization which trains its members for a few years and then releases them to other bodies. The effect of this structural quality is that many more persons are influenced by its spirit than may appear on casual consideration. In 1928, for instance, the youth organization reported almost 22,000 new members, whereas the net increase from 1927 to 1928 was only 3,951; approximately 16,000 transferred to the Socialist party. It was claimed that every fourth young person in Austria had been a member of the Socialist Workers' Youth for a longer or shorter period and had thus been brought into contact with the labor movement.[119]

The years between 1921 and 1929 were characterized chiefly by the gradual adaptation of the youth association to changes in the character of its membership and to the requirements of the political conditions. Primary emphasis was put on strengthening the organization. No differences of any consequence within the association or in its relation to the party developed; the ninth convention in 1928 was of "rare unanimity and closed ranks." At this meeting great emphasis was laid upon the need for much more intensive work in the organization of farm youth. The program outlined for the drive demanded the improvement of the economic, political, and cultural

[118] *Jahrbuch der österreichischen Arbeiterbewegung, 1929,* p. 399; *Parteitag, 1931,* pp. 3, 83.

[119] *Jahrbuch der österreichischen Arbeiterbewegung, 1927,* pp. 248, 249; *ibid., 1928,* p. 333; *Die Praxis,* vol. 7 (April, 1928), 115.

conditions of young workers on farms and large estates.[120] This formidable task was one of the most discussed topics of the next years. The first visible success of the campaign was presented to the delegates to the 1930 national convention in Eisenstadt, the capital of Burgenland. Before them paraded more than 1,000 boys and girls as representatives of the farm workers' youth of that state. The following years brought a steady increase in the number of local groups in the farm youth organization.[121]

The unanimity praised at the Graz convention of 1928 was not to last. It became more and more difficult to make increasingly large numbers of young people who had grown up after the revolution and lacked the enthusiasm which was so characteristic of those who remembered this "heroic time" of Social Democracy into conscious Socialist fighters. And this was true despite the exciting events of July, 1927, the rising power of the counterrevolutionary Fascist groups, and the constitutional struggle of 1929. There was a strong undercurrent of feeling among the workers, particularly the younger ones, that they could not expect to participate in these events and struggles, that the top leadership was always admonishing caution, always putting on the brakes. The result, as already indicated, was that part of the adolescents visualized the youth movement solely in that section of it represented by the workers' sport organizations or by the (often paternalistic) union youth divisions.[122] Another group turned against the policy of the Social Democratic leadership, demanding more action against political opponents and greater influence for youth within the party. In 1929, in fact, the never-perishing conflict between young and old dominated the scene. At the party convention in October of that year Julius Deutsch brought up the problem and supported the right of youth to greater influence in the party organizations. A step in this direction was made immediately by granting, for the first time, to the sport and cultural organizations, in which youth held a prominent position, a total of 14 delegates to party conventions.[123] Otherwise, it seems that not much was done at this time to satisfy the wishes of the young group.

---

[120] Cf. *Die Praxis*, vol. 7 (May, 1928), 139; *Jahrbuch der österreichischen Arbeiterbewegung, 1928*, pp. 334–335.

[121] *Die Praxis*, vol. 9 (May, 1930), 111; *Jahrbuch der österreichischen Arbeiterbewegung, 1932*, p. 343.

[122] *Die Praxis*, vol. 8 (March, 1929), 69.

[123] *Parteitag, 1929*, pp. 3, 4, 16–17, 55.

Nevertheless, as a well-disciplined organization, the Socialist Workers' Youth maintained its efforts to increase its membership by new means of propaganda such as phonograph records, film, and radio. Pamphlets were distributed all over the country and a national network of youth schools was planned.[124] Sport organizations *within* the Socialist Workers' Youth were furthered and used more systematically to imbue their members with the spirit of Socialism. The idea behind this activity was that "We cannot carry on our fight solely with resolutions; today we can fulfill our political tasks only by untiring, devoted, day-to-day toil in all fields."[125]

The program of mass propaganda was designed chiefly to counteract the growing activity of the Nazis, the Heimwehr, and the Catholic organizations. Fear that the general spiritual interest of the young proletariat was steadily decreasing was expressed quite openly within the Socialist Workers' Youth. From these friendly critics, as well as from others in the movement who thought their fears were a bit exaggerated, came various suggestions such as more political activity, the creation of opportunities to do something of immediate practical value, and the formation of special training groups. Underlying these proposals was the idea of reëstablishing (or refurbishing, or maintaining—depending upon the point of view) the high intellectual standards of the youth organization. Some of the critics were decidedly pessimistic over the prospects. They claimed that the majority of adolescents preferred sports and political slogans to serious educational work, and that many children born during the war were backward, not only physically but also mentally. Political apathy among the mentally alert youths was explained by "the repressions which the defensive attitude of democratic Socialism imposes upon the young generation. The seeming unsuccessfulness of the spiritual fight, becoming apparent in the growing bourgeois and Fascist counterrevolution, strengthens this spontaneous anti-intellectual attitude of the youth."[126]

The demand for better political training was partly fulfilled in Vienna by the inauguration in 1931 of a "leader school" which held classes and courses on week ends. Outstanding Austrian and German

---

[124] Heretofore most of the schools had been in Vienna.

[125] *Die Praxis,* vol. 9 (May, 1930), 112.

[126] Karl Czernetz, "Das geistige Leben der Arbeiterjugend," *Die Praxis,* vol. 10 (April, 1931), 90; cf. also: *Ibid.* (Feb., 1931), 43–44; *ibid.,* vol. 9 (Dec., 1930), 271–274.

party leaders discussed intensively problems of youth, democracy, the International, war and the League of Nations, and Socialist policy during the crisis. Similar courses, with steadily increasing audiences, were given twice in 1932.[127] The desire for greater political activity and the wish "to do something" found outlet in the reorganization of the *Wehrsport* groups. New emphasis was laid on the task of youth to fight actively against Fascism. The fourteen- to eighteen-year-old group worked along lines similar to those of the Red Falcons; members over eighteen were trained in accordance with the methods of the Republican Defense Corps.[128] For children who had just left school a new organization, the Young Guards, was founded. Its task was "to activate the politically indifferent fourteen-year-olds by participation in work appropriate to their age"; that is, its job approximated that of the Red Falcons. Jurisdictionally, however, the Young Guards were placed under the Socialist Workers' Youth—a fact emphasized by their use of the blue hiking shirts of that organization. It was stipulated that they should never become independent bodies in competition with either the Red Falcons or the *Wehrsport* groups. They served only to prepare youngsters for entrance into the Association of Socialist Workers' Youth.[129]

From the foregoing it should be clear that many of the new activities of the young workers were definitely influenced by the pattern set by the *Kinderfreunde* and Red Falcon movements; in fact, after much initial friction the collaboration of the two organizations, furthered by several officers who served in both, was so close that it "has become a pleasant matter of course."[130]

So far as total membership data are conclusive the Socialist Workers' Youth seems to have demonstrated a remarkable resistance against the crisis that set in in 1929, as well as against the efforts of competing groups from both right and left. The figure was 30,011 in 1929 and 28,036 in 1932. But in this same period the number of local groups had increased from 313 to 528. Actually what had happened was that there had been serious losses in Vienna and Burgenland and a less significant one in Styria. These had been partly compensated for by gains in the other states and by the

[127] *Die Praxis,* vol. 10 (June, 1931), 168; *Jahrbuch der österreichischen Arbeiterbewegung, 1932,* p. 341.
[128] *Die Praxis,* vol. 10 (Sept., 1931), 217.
[129] *Ibid.,* p. 219.
[130] *Ibid.* (May, 1931), 135.

establishment of new local groups. Moreover, subsequent to the parliamentary elections of 1930, concern was expressed over the indications that the Heimwehr and the Nazis had had an unpleasant degree of success with young voters despite the further indications that this success had been almost exclusively at the expense of the Christian Socials and the Pan-Germans.[131]

The severe depression following 1929 naturally brought welfare measures and the struggle to preserve hard-won social legislation into the foreground again. The Socialist youth association therefore decided to coöperate with the interparty organization Youth in Need which had been initiated by the Vienna chamber of labor in December, 1930. This new body established "day homes" for unemployed youth which, in the winter of 1932–1933, were partly transformed into workshops by the Youth at Work movement. In these workshops unemployed youth not only learned different trades but also produced various things which could be used by the participating organizations.[132]

At the same time the still unsatisfied appeal of the young generation for more political action received further attention from the adults. The debate at the 1931 party congress[133] resulted in the creation of organizations of young party members who formed themselves into "young voters' committees" early in 1932. This led to the establishment of the Young Front which was formally recognized at the party convention in November, 1932. Though formally a part of the adult organization, that is, of the party, it actually was more of a link between the Socialist Workers' Youth and the political wing; in fact, it became one of the most active factors in the whole Social Democratic organization. It remains then to discuss the Young Front in connection with the Socialist youth movement.

The problem of these young people had been clearly pointed out by Julius Deutsch in introducing a proposed amendment to the party bylaws.[134] His argument ran as follows: The situation of youth-

[131] *Jahrbuch der österreichischen Arbeiterbewegung, 1929,* p. 399; *1932,* p. 341; *Die Praxis,* vol. 9 (Dec., 1930), 271.

[132] Anton Kimml, *5 Jahre 'Jugend in Not'* (Wien, 1935), pp. 9, 13, 43 ff.; *Jahrbuch der österreichischen Arbeiterbewegung, 1932,* pp. 340, 341.

[133] *Parteitag, 1931,* pp. 13–14, 16–17, 18–19.

[134] The main sentence of the amendment read: "For the work with young voters, as well as for the recruiting and training of young party members, some officers (Young Front reporters) shall be elected by the local (section) and district conferences." *Parteitag, 1932,* pp. 3, 12, 17.

ful workers never has been so desperate as at present. Innumerable youths become unemployed as soon as they finish their apprentice training. The mental depression, the hopelessness, the despair caused by such a situation make them responsive to any slogan, whether it come from the right or from the left (Nazis or Communists). This makes it extremely difficult to appeal to them with cool reason. Previously the young people came to us from a job, from a trade union. They had learned to fight for a shorter day, for higher wages; they had acquired an insight into economic conditions; they had learned to identify their economic opponents by personal contacts. The youth of today lacks this experience; it frequently comes to us from sport organizations and consequently brings with it some unfortunate inferences from athletic contests. Whereas the young men schooled in the unions had learned the necessarily slow and long-drawn-out character of a struggle for shorter hours or better pay, the youngsters from the sport clubs are more likely to reason in terms of a football game that is over in two hours and that ends with one team the winner. These young people want to get the most out of themselves and of the whole class. Therefore we must use other methods today to win them and to fit them into the proletarian movement. Combining the youth in the Young Front has proved a good method. ". . . the Young Front has stood the test splendidly in all the fights we have led, in the election campaign, as well as in the struggle against the National Socialists, and in all other actions. The activity of the Young Front, its burning enthusiasm, its devotion, and its party loyalty are beyond any doubt."[135] Another speaker stressed the importance of keeping close contact with the younger groups, with the Socialist Workers' Youth as well as with the Young Front. By such coöperation and in spite of tremendous unemployment, he declared, the Socialists had been able to increase their votes in the city of Wiener-Neustadt, whereas neither the Communists nor the Nazis had been able to make any gains.[136]

In a proclamation of September 30, 1932, the Young Front appealed to all youthful workers to fight for the minimum demands of the day. These included a just distribution of work, guarantees against further cuts in wages and unemployment benefits, and an extension of the upper age limit for compulsory school attendance

[135] *Ibid.*, p. 17.
[136] *Ibid.*, p. 26.

from fourteen to fifteen. At the same time it called for a relentless struggle to establish a Socialist order of society which would give every young person an education adequate to his ability; a job the performance of which would not only serve the whole people but also bring personal happiness to the worker; conditions of employment which would guarantee the protection of health and satisfaction in working; compensation high enough to cover cultural as well as physical needs; and the right to beauty, culture, pleasures of life, and coöperation in the advancement of humanity.[137]

Students' Youth Organizations

THE ASSOCIATION OF SOCIALIST STUDENTS OF AUSTRIA

On the fringe of the workers' youth movement were the organizations of Socialist students. They warrant discussion though it will have to be brief because of the scarcity of material. In 1895 a Free Association of Socialist Students and Academicians (*Freie Vereinigung sozialistischer Studenten und Akademiker*) was founded. Prior to the First World War it acquired neither size nor prominence. The rise to control of a Communist element in the group brought about the withdrawal of a number of members. They organized under the slightly different name, Association of Social Democratic Students and Academicians. During and after 1918 it grew considerably in spite of the incessant fight waged against its members, particularly at the universities and other institutions of higher learning where the radical Pan-German (the later Nazi) students, assisted by Catholic comrades and reactionary professors, dominated the scene. Manifestations of Socialist sentiment, as well as expression of opinions not agreeable to the majority, were likely to result in wild riots. By 1924, nevertheless, there were organized groups of Socialist students in all the universities and colleges except the School of Mines in Leoben, Styria.[138] They disseminated Socialist ideas by means of meetings and literature, pointed out time and again the illegal practices of the so-called Chambers of German Students as well as of the academic authorities, and protested against increases of tuition fees. Because of the autonomy of the universities and the other schools of the same rank, in principle a desirable situation, it

[137] *Jahrbuch der österreichischen Arbeiterbewegung, 1932,* pp. 21–24.
[138] *Parteitag, 1924,* p. 75.

would seem, the recognition of the Socialist students' organization as equal in rights with the Chambers of German Students by the ministry of education was of little avail.[139] But it should be kept in mind that there was a physical "autonomy" which traditionally barred the police from trespassing on "academic ground." Of course the Socialists favored and fought for autonomy in the sense of freedom of research and teaching; they opposed, however, the physical autonomy which in practice meant that reactionary students could "beat up" Socialist classmates with little or no interference from university authorities.

The growth of the association and the affiliation to it of the organization of students in secondary schools led to a reorganization and the adoption of the new name Association of Socialist Students of Austria (*Verband der sozialistischen Studenten Oesterreichs*) in 1925. At this time it comprised 2,600 members at universities, colleges, and secondary schools and claimed to be the largest organization of Socialist students in Europe. The university and college students were grouped in several divisions according to their special field of study. These divisions (*Fachvereine*) dealt with specific educational, academic, and trade-union problems. Interest in the last was by no means only "academic," for some groups actually joined unions while students. The official publication was *Der Sozialistische Student,* replaced after September, 1928, by the *Sozialistisch-Akademische Rundschau* which also served the Socialist students of Germany. In order to cope with more personal economic questions the association founded the Economic Aid for Working Students (*Wirtschaftshilfe der Arbeiterstudenten*) which operated student homes (in 1932 there were 3 of them accommodating 151 students), compiled lists of suitable vacant rooms, provided lunches and dinners at reduced rates, and made health insurance available to its members. Other activities were the procurement of coaching jobs and part-time employment, sale of lecture notes, advancement of small loans, and maintenance of a students' hostel for the vacations. A great portion of the financial means was contributed by trade unions, consumers' coöperatives, chambers of labor, and public bodies, particularly the city of Vienna.[140]

---

[139] *Ibid.,* p. 76; *ibid., 1926,* pp. 103–104.

[140] *Parteitag, 1924,* pp. 77–78; *1925,* pp. 86–88; *1926,* pp. 105–107; *Jahrbuch der österreichischen Arbeiterbewegung, 1928,* pp. 339–340; *1929,* pp. 400 ff.; *1932,* p. 346.

As indicated above, The Federation of Socialist Students of Secondary Schools (*Bund sozialistischer Mittelschueler*) was affiliated to the Association of Socialist Students of Austria, but apparently operated as an almost completely autonomous body. It was organized in local and district groups as well as in divisions resting upon differences in the course of study. The students in lower grades (*Untermittelschueler*) were united in the Hiking Federation (*Wanderbund*) which worked with the Red Falcons. The Federation did systematic educational work and cultivated group recitations and extempore theatrical performances. Beginning in 1926 it published the magazine *Schulkampf*.[141]

The year 1927 brought a significant incident. The rector of the University of Vienna, Professor Molisch, granted permission to the leader of the so-called German Student Body, who was actually a Nazi and not registered as a student, to make a speech in a small hall ordinarily reserved for official University affairs. The purpose of the address was to advocate the introduction of the *numerus clausus;* that is, a limitation on the number of Jewish students. Thereupon the Socialist students requested that the same hall be made available for a talk on the "social *numerus clausus.*" This was also granted; and so, for the first time in their history, the Socialists scheduled a meeting on "academic ground." But the Nazi students did not intend to give up any of their privileges. First, a small number of them got into the meeting and forced the speaker to abandon his efforts. Then, reinforced by a larger group, which had come in by a back door armed with sticks and iron rods, they attacked those of differing political belief. The official report of the Academic Senate, published June 22, stated that the instigators and participants had managed to conceal their identities; but exactly one week before it had announced the suspension for one semester of the president of the Socialist Student Body. The alleged reason for this action was the distribution at the University of circulars containing "violent invectives" against University authorities—*in the preceding February*.

At the beginning of the fall term of 1927, according to the report in the *Jahrbuch* of the workers' movement, the Socialist student organizations in all the institutions of university grade in Vienna

141 *Parteitag, 1925,* p. 88; *1926,* pp. 107–108.

were asked to submit their membership lists to the authorities of those institutions. This action was contrary to preceding practice. After considerable debate the representatives of the groups decided in December to comply with the request despite their conviction that its purpose was to secure additional control over the membership. No details appear for other institutions, but the list for the University carried 1,721 names. The total membership of the association at the time was 2,797.[142]

About two and a half years later the then rector of the University, Professor Gleispach, presided and spoke briefly at another meeting of students at which the *numerus clausus* was demanded. This meeting was also attended by the "Academic Senate and many other University professors." In a sharp editorial the *Presse* commented that Gleispach "had no ground for announcing through his presence that he was in agreement with the *numerus clausus*."[143]

The regime of domination and riot by the "German" students, which had existed long before the First World War and had been directed against other national groups and against the Roman Catholics, continued practically unabated until 1932 when their group was finally disbanded in preparation for an organization more appropriate to the coming Clerical Fascist government. Meanwhile, in 1929, the Nazis had tried to break up a lecture by Professor Tandler but had been thrown out by the Socialists.[144] The next year the academic authorities announced regulations for the elections of students' representatives which restricted the suffrage to those who proved their "affiliation to the German people." This typical Nazi formula was intended to exclude Socialists as well as Jews; after all, as internationalists, Socialists were not "Germans." These regulations, however, were declared unconstitutional by the highest court of Austria. Another apex in the discrimination against Social-

[142] *Neue Freie Presse,* June 11–22, 1927, particularly June 22 (A.M.), p. 7, and June 15 (A.M.), p. 6; *Jahrbuch der österreichischen Arbeiterbewegung, 1927,* pp. 254–255. Nothing could be ascertained about whether or not similar lists were requested from other student groups. Nor is it clear from the record whether the Socialist list was turned over with or without the permission of individual members. The recollection of former members now in the United States is that all of the 1,721 signed a new list for this purpose.

[143] *Neue Freie Presse,* November 27, 1929 (A.M.), p. 7; November 27 (P.M.), p. 1.

[144] In March, 1923, Socialist students had formed an Academic Legion in commemoration of the seventy-fifth anniversary of the revolutionary days of 1848. In the course of the years the Legion had been strengthened and was ready to repulse attacks against Socialists. It was affiliated with the workers' Republican Defense Corps. *Parteitag, 1924,* p. 77.

ist students was reached in 1931. In order to check riots which had developed after an attack by Nazis against Socialist students participating in the traditional parade on November 12, the academic authorities appointed Nazi and Heimwehr students as monitors to preserve "order" in the University. Similar occurrences took place at the colleges of engineering, agriculture, and commerce in Vienna, as well as in the academic institutions in the provinces.[145] Throughout the years the Socialist students fought against such acts of discrimination and tried unsuccessfully to bring about a revision of the attitude of the authorities and a cessation of the rowdyism of the students.

In spite of its difficulties the association grew until 1931 when it reported a membership of 3,342. Of these 2,068 were enrolled at universities or colleges; the rest were alumni who had maintained their affiliation. In 1930 the organization had claimed to represent 10 per cent of all Viennese university and college students. The severe economic crisis, which hit the working students before the others, was probably the chief reason for the sharp fall of the student membership to 1,576 in 1932. As might be expected, the great majority of members of the affiliated secondary school organization was recruited from Vienna as were university members. Possibly because of the control of the schools in the capital by the workers' party the younger group was not subjected to political terror. Its membership increased until 1930 when it numbered 3,497. The 2,700 from Vienna also represented around 10 per cent of all secondary school pupils there. In 1932 the total membership of this group had dropped to 2,526.[146]

The relation between Socialist students and workers' organizations was generally satisfactory. It is necessary to point out, however, that the different background of most of the students as compared to that of the great majority of the workers and the different way of life—even though the student had come from a worker's family, as was increasingly true in the course of years—prevented at times a complete understanding. Particularly the conservative older officers of the organizations who were engrossed in their everyday party

[145] *Jahrbuch der österreichischen Arbeiterbewegung, 1929,* p. 401; *1930,* p. 411; *1931,* p. 380; *1932,* p. 344.

[146] *Ibid., 1930,* pp. 411, 413; *1931,* p. 381; *1932,* pp. 345, 346; *Statistisches Jahrbuch der Stadt Wien,* 1930–1935, p. 177.

duties often resented the attitudes of Socialist students who, inspired by their idealism, had little patience and understanding for the daily routine work and for what they considered the slow progress of an overcautious policy in improving the economic standards of the laboring class.[147]

In the workers' youth groups the Socialist students were active chiefly as speakers and instructors; they also directed groups interested in choral, orchestral, and dramatic work, and helped with the arrangement of festivals. Only rarely did they become members of the youth organizations—primarily because the latter felt that they would sooner or later dominate the groups. Many of the Socialist students became employees of the city of Vienna and of other Social Democratic communities, thus gradually replacing the officials of the old regime. Their work there, as well as in the various Socialist organizations, was certainly an asset to Austrian labor.

In spite of the fact that full development of the forces embodied in the workers' youth movement was often hampered, it succeeded for a long time in checking the rising Nazi tide. Until 1932 at least, and more probably until 1934, the Hitlerites were able to make scarcely any gains within the young working generation.[148] This was particularly remarkable because the deepening depression and the primarily defensive policy of the Social Democrats after 1927 were not conducive to bringing young persons who had been reared in political freedom into Socialist youth associations; consequently, it was much more difficult for them to gain new members than it was for the adult organizations which could rely on the unswerving allegiance of the many members who had participated in the long years of struggle under the Habsburgs.

It would be a great mistake, however, to consider the youth movement only an advance guard against Fascism or a source of party officers. Above all its achievement lay in helping to give its members a fuller life than any generation of young workers in Europe had ever enjoyed. It fostered a spirit of good companionship among the

[147] An outspoken opposition from some students was expressed during the years immediately prior to the destruction of the Austrian republic by the Marxist Study Group (*Marxistische Studiengemeinschaft*); most of its members attacked the hesitant policy of the party leadership.

[148] An apparent partial exception to this success, the University student body, was not actually one. It had always been a center of the rabid Pan-Germanism that was simply transformed into Nazism. Indeed, the Socialists scored no small achievement in securing, at times, the adherence of 10 per cent of the students.

youth and taught them to seek pleasure in the beauties of nature and in the treasures of culture. The excitements inherent in the fight for a better world replaced the passing pleasures of commercialized entertainments and the stupor of alcohol. Without the help of charitable benefactors labor had created a movement which was preparing a young generation of workers to become the leaders into what they believed would be a better future. As has been said before and will be necessary to say again, the fact that that future was visualized as a Socialist society should not deter those of us who do not agree with the goal from recognizing and giving credit to the idealism and the achievements of the Austrian labor movement. It was my good fortune to become intimately acquainted over a period of fifteen years, first in Vienna and later in the United States, with many individuals, leaders and rank and file, in the children and youth organizations of republican Austria and thus to form definite impressions of the influence of those organizations. I doubt that anyone who had a similar opportunity could deny to them in particular the recognition and credit suggested above.

CHAPTER XVIII

Workers' Cultural Activities

THE GERMAN language is extremely generous in its idiomatic usage of the term "culture." It comprises not only science, the humanities and arts, but also wide aspects of everyday life. It may embrace the various aspects of the *dopo lavoro,* in which instance it assumes the specific character of a value judgment. This becomes apparent when—as here—certain traditional habits of workers are rejected as *Unkultur* (lack of culture). The elasticity of the term allows the German to say that it is "culture" not to get drunk; it is culture to develop through sport and gymnastics a sound body—the seat of a sound mind; it is culture to go hiking and to enjoy the beauty of lakes and mountains; it is culture to have modern space- and work-saving furniture in our houses. The fashion in which women wear their hair and the way people bury their dead fall under the same broad concept of culture. The range of what was called in Austria the Educational and Cultural Movement of Social Democracy[1] was, if possible, still wider than the idiomatic scope of the term. It covered workers' universities and proletarian wrestlers' clubs, Socialist string orchestras and Marxist rabbit breeders' associations. It was, however, the genuine educational activities which, genetically, formed the basis of the tremendous superstructure erected in the course of the development, and, most notably, after the First World War.

As Professor Tönnies justly remarked, the struggle for moral and spiritual preëminence in society forms a part of every class conflict.[2] It is hard to find a better example of the truth of this statement than the history of the European, and, most notably, of the Austrian labor movement which carried the slogan Education is Power (*Bildung ist Macht*) from its infancy throughout all the stages of its development. The origins, theory, and practice of the movement

[1] Cf. any year of the *Jahrbuch der österreichischen Arbeiterbewegung.* Some of the activities regularly treated under the rubric quoted in the text have been presented in the preceding chapter. Since there is no possibility of confusion with the yearbook of the trade unions, the source just referred to will be cited *in this chapter only* as *Jahrbuch.*

[2] Ferdinand Tönnies, *Geist der Neuzeit* (Leipzig, 1935), p. 166.

combined to bring about this situation. The education of the workers to a knowledge and understanding of the world they had to live in was implied in the fundamental idea that they must be made class conscious before they would be able to concentrate upon the transformation of capitalist society. In the Hegelian terminology of Marx the class *"an sich"* had to become the class *"für sich."* The "scientific" Socialism of Marx and Engels was to become a power when accepted and understood by the masses. Since Lassalle had proclaimed the "alliance between science and the worker" as the aim to which he promised to devote his life,[3] the task of "enlightenment of the workers" always kept its honored place within the scope of activities of the Socialist parties. In fact, for decades to come, Socialism—first and foremost in German-speaking countries—was to draw a great part of its moral force from this connection between its political program and science. What could more strongly reinforce the ethical impetus of the rising movement than the belief that in its propaganda it had to do nothing but disclose the truth—and, to boot, the scientific truth? "To state what is . . . this is the most powerful political instrument," said Lassalle.[4] Every seed of knowledge planted in the minds of the workers promised to bear some day a rich harvest on the tree of the revolution. The "Workers' Marseillaise," one of the most popular songs of German and Austrian workers in the last quarter of the nineteenth century, contained the significant words:

> Der Feind, den wir am tiefsten hassen,
> Der uns umlagert schwarz und dicht,
> Das ist der Unverstand der Massen,
> Den nur des Geistes Schwert durchbricht.[5]

The "sword of the spirit"; it was brandished in hundreds, and, later, in thousands of lectures and courses, in daily papers and monthly magazines. In this struggle against the "ignorance of the masses" the Socialists had what could be called an almost universal educational program. It is not certain that in the beginning the social sciences formed even the center of gravity. Any elementary

[3] Ferdinand Lassalle, "Die Wissenschaft und die Arbeiter," *Reden und Schriften* (Berlin, 1893), vol. 2, p. 83.

[4] *Idem.*, "Was nun? Zweiter Vortrag über Verfassungswesen," *op. cit.*, vol 1, pp. 527, 531.

[5] "The enemy we hate most deeply, that hems us in black and close, is the ignorance of the masses, which only the sword of the spirit cuts through."

knowledge was useful to the functionaries of the local trade unions. Natural science—the sovereign of the nineteenth century—was the destined ally in the struggles against the political power of the Church. Nor were belles-lettres excluded. The then modern trend of realism and naturalism was congenial to the general ideas of Socialist education. Hauptmann's *Die Weber* was in its effects very much akin to Friedrich Engels' *Die Lage der Arbeitenden Klasse in England* (1844). As far as poets, playwrights, and novelists were willing to describe "truth," particularly "social truth," they were considered by the rising movement as strong promoters of its cause. Thus from the very outset the educational activities of Social Democracy were placed on a broad and comprehensive basis.

If Socialist theory vigorously pushed the movement in the direction indicated, the incidental and accidental circumstances of practice had similar effects. In Germany and Austria alike the general reaction after the defeat of the Revolution of 1848 rendered political activities by workers well nigh impossible. Substitution, or evasion, or both, was found in workers' educational associations. Historically they became—in both countries—the predecessors of the Social Democratic parties. The political life of young Bebel began with membership in such an educational club.[6] Thus also as a problem of organization the origins of workers' educational and political activities were intricately interlocked.

The belief in Socialist revolution dominated the educational propaganda among the workers in the beginnings of the movement. At least as a training toward class consciousness the educational policy of Austrian Social Democracy remained true to these origins throughout the lifetime of the party. But this should not cause us to overlook either the multiple real effects of its educational activities or certain changes in their character. The interaction between the general trend of economic development and the educational activities of the professedly anticapitalist party was one factor worthy of consideration. The progressive mechanization of production naturally required a higher standard of knowledge on the part of men who were to operate the equipment of modern factories. This development led to the general and compulsory elementary school. To a large degree the educational work of the party had the func-

[6] August Bebel, *My Life* (London, 1912), pp. 44 ff.

tional value of a *Gymnasium*. Increasing the general education of the workers was bound to increase their professional skill and to enhance the productivity of the economy. It is evident that these effects were not to be attributed to elementary knowledge only. If, to quote an example, Socialist education persisted, as it did, in combating Luddite instincts, this was instrumental in changing the attitude of workers toward modern methods of production. Thus in its very origins the educational work which avowedly was bent upon final destruction of the capitalist system had effects, or by-effects, which were by no means diametrically opposed to the ends and interests of that system.

Another important aspect of the same matter was the relation of educational activities to the general problem of democracy. "Giving a ballot to a man who cannot read it is a travesty on free government."[7] But the truth inherent in this statement lies in the fact that nowadays inability to read precludes *political* literacy, and no one who sincerely believes in people's government can deny that the higher the cultural standard of the electorate the closer democracy will approach its ideal form and the more meaningful will become the phrase: "government by the consent of the governed."

Supplementing these general considerations, and, in fact, more momentous, were certain internal developments in the nature of cultural activities. To the degree that the revolutionary character of the movement increasingly gave way to a more reformist attitude, those activities had to be brought into line. The effects concerned not only what was being taught but also, to no smaller extent, the general spirit of the activities. Gradually the idea gained strength that education is not only "power" but also a source of joy and happiness for the individual and, consequently, an aim in itself. It would not be consonant with the actual state of affairs to contend that in later years educational activities became fully divorced from their original aims. The reasons why this could not happen are probably clear to the reader who has grasped the essential character of the policy of the Austrian Socialists; namely, that singular combination of revolutionary or revolutionary-sounding words with reformist actions. Thus the history of revolutions and the sociology of revolution still played a part in Socialist education which was not

[7] William Bennet Munro, *The Government of the United States* (New York, 1925), p. 111.

to be underestimated. But there was a feeling that these teachings had become less and less a preparation for practical action and had assumed more and more an academic character. Even quantitatively; that is, in comparison with the growing number of problems relating to the daily life of the movement, their importance waned to the verge of eclipse. And although some observers might contend that this generalization goes too far, most of them would agree that between 1923 and 1927—during the period which will be described as the Struggle for Majority—its validity is greater than at any other time. In this period falls the most striking expansion of cultural activities in the more proper and genuine sense of the term. The workers' libraries developed at an amazing rate. The Art Office opened the doors of the theaters to the masses of the workers. Trips abroad as far as Turkey and Scandinavia were organized. The membership of the Friends of Nature experienced a mushroom growth. Obviously, it was the purpose of these organizations and activities to increase the pleasures and happiness of living—and to do so not in the promised lands of a distant future, but for the current generation for which life within existing society was to be made less dull, less monotonous, and more beautiful. The gloomy aspects of a theory of increasing misery as *primum mobile* of the revolution were hardly compatible with this concept. And the old antinomy between the ascetic and hedonistic elements in the Socialist movement seemed to approach an "undialectical" solution in favor of the latter.

One further point deserves attention. Whatever the contents of all these activities, it is fair to say that they had one important political side. It was the tendency of Austrian Social Democracy to tighten as much as possible the bonds between the individual and the party; the fact of his adherence to the party should be always present in his mind; whether he played chess or tried to revive the old traditions of folk dances and costumes, his party consciousness should be preserved. This implied a policy of trying to boycott the so-called neutral clubs in which the workers were exposed to the influence of opponents of the party and in which they usually, so the Socialists alleged, had to be content with paying their dues. In other words, they were customarily excluded from the administration of those associations. Thus organizations were called to life and fostered which had not and could not have anything specifically Socialistic about them; but their existence assuredly increased the sphere of control of the party and also the degree of coherence among the membership.

Lest it be thought that there was something peculiarly Socialistic about boycotting the organizations of an opposing group, the reader is again reminded that the Roman Catholic hierarchy had preached such boycotting against all the institutions of Social Democracy for decades. One of the most important instances was the previously mentioned papal encyclical, *Rerum Novarum* of 1891, which gave the most decisive impetus to dual Catholic workingmen's organizations in Austria. Other examples were cited in the preceding chapter. That of the pastoral letter of Advent 1925 is particularly specific. In it the bishops of Austria listed the Socialist institutions, associations, newspapers, and so on with which the faithful dare not contaminate themselves. They were warned that adherence to Social Democracy would one day have to be answered for "before the court of God." With use of a long quotation from II Corinthians the bishops characterized Social Democracy as godlessness, darkness, Belial, heathenism, and an unclean thing.[8] This, of course, was really more than the recommendation of a boycott; it was a threat of eternal damnation.

The following pages offer a brief survey of the cultural activities of the Austrian working-class movement. Lack of statistical material from the provinces, however, will usually compel limitation of the presentation to Vienna.

Science for the People

Nonselective Activities

It goes without saying that not all the mental food dished up by the Socialists for their adherents would stand the test of even lenient scholarship. But it is necessary to remember—because it is essential for an understanding of the nature of the movement—that Socialist educators were sincerely convinced that the theory of scientific Socialism enabled them to present even political problems of the day in a thoroughly scientific fashion.

[8] Cardinal F. G. Piffl *et al., Zu sozialen und kulturellen Fragen* (Wien, 1932), pp. 103–107.

Looking through the last pages of the daily issues of the Vienna *Arbeiter Zeitung* in one of the years when the party was on the crest is an illuminating occupation, for it gives an impressive picture of the amplitude and regularity of those educational activities in the city of two millions which were organized or sponsored by the Social Democracy. Printed in the smallest type, there are four, five, six, and sometimes more columns crammed with announcements of lectures, courses, educational films, exhibitions, and evening schools of various sorts. A very large part of these announcements refer to meetings of the party sections and youth sections in Vienna. In normal times—electoral campaigns used to interfere with these activities—every one of the several hundreds of party sections had weekly lecture meetings on some general subject. These meetings were usually held in the back premises of small restaurants. About 30 to 50 party members attended on an average. After the lecture, which as a rule lasted for about one hour, there were a few short "discussion speeches"—asking questions after the Anglo-Saxon fashion being uncommon in Austria. The lecturer's reply to his critics closed the evening.

The heterogeneous character of the audience implied that the level of these lectures had to be rather popular. Ordinarily the lecturer adjusted his presentation to that degree of knowledge which could be assumed as acquired from regular reading of the political daily. Much, of course, depended on his skill and experience. For example, an academic friend told me that he once attended an excellent lecture on tariffs in which the pros and cons of the case were presented in a clear, simple, and thoroughly scientific way to an exclusively proletarian audience in one of the gloomiest and poorest parts of Favoriten. On the whole, however, political questions of the day presented in a more general fashion formed the preferred themes. Significantly, they were by no means confined to Austria; especially from 1924 on the problems of English politics received much attention. After the beginning of the depression the problems of the trade cycle shifted to the center of interest; on these occasions the question: "A capitalistic crisis or a crisis of capitalism?" was discussed and usually answered in favor of the former part of the alternative. From 1931 on the experiment of the Five-Year Plan formed the subject of a large number of lectures.

The choice of the theme was ordinarily made democratically; that is, the section committee decided that it was desirable to have a lecture on a certain question and then applied to the central organization to provide the speaker. This arrangement had the great advantage that the subject treated was likely to meet with the interest of the audience; but since the task of working out an extensive program of lectures with a certain educational view in mind generally exceeded the competence of the section committee, it had the drawback of being somewhat haphazard in character. On the other hand, it could be argued that it fitted best the purpose of broadening the outlook of the more or less amorphous mass of people who formed the audiences at the meetings.

In order to remedy to a degree the lack of coherence in the lecture programs of the sections, the central educational organization had resorted even before the First World War to the device of "courses." These were usually comprised of five or six lectures given at consecutive weekly meetings by the same speaker. Through this method a more detailed treatment of the subject was possible and the lecturer had the opportunity of becoming better acquainted with the audience and thus of adjusting himself to its needs and interests. Frequently used themes for such courses were: "the theory of the state," "the history of the labor movement," "the problem of democracy and parliamentarism," and "world economy." In 1926, for instance, the preliminary draft of the Linz program of the party was explained and discussed in such courses in the majority of the sections of Vienna. As may have been taken for granted, the general selection of the subjects for courses was left with the central organization; it submitted to the sections a list of three or four themes from which the committees had to select the one best fitted to their groups. Many committees adopted the practice of referring the subjects to a meeting of the section, with or without recommendation. The proposal of the committee, if offered, was usually accepted; but frequently a member suggested that some other subject should be offered later as a course.

It is impossible to give anything like a complete statistical survey on the magnitude of these activities: first, as previously mentioned, because of the absence of figures for the whole country; second, even for Vienna the available data do not cover the whole field. The

Central Educational Organization—or Educational Center as it was usually called—collected statistical material only on its own work. But, aside from the Center activities, in the years after 1918 so-called Teaching Organizations were established in most of the 21 districts of Vienna; under the general supervision of the Center they carried on educational work of their own. Even with these qualifications in mind the statistical record of lectures arranged by the Educational Center in a year unaffected by a political campaign is still impressive. According to the report in the *Jahrbuch der österreichischen Arbeiterbewegung* in 1928, 4,547 lectures and readings were presented by the speakers of the Center. From this total about 71 per cent were delivered to party and youth sections and 27 per cent to trade-union groups; the rest represent lectures in factories and to other organizations.[9]

The subjects offered and the number of lectures follow.

Subject	Lectures	Subject	Lectures
Socialism	421	Cultural questions	451
Economics and sociology	482	Religion and Church	140
History	503	Natural science	141
Current politics	335	Hygiene	286
Trade unionism and social legislation	200	Municipal policy	39
Labor movement	385	Literature and readings	1,176

On the whole the above list corresponds to what would be expected from a Social Democratic educational organization; however, certain points are worth noting. First is the fact that natural science obviously played the role of Cinderella with about 3 per cent of the total number of lectures. The generation of the time of the Hainfeld congress had experienced the strong influence of Darwinism; endless discussions on Darwin versus Marx were the order of the day. But since the close of the nineteenth century the social disciplines had come to be regarded as independent branches of science. After 1918 this development was considerably accelerated so that only through the books of a few veterans of the movement, Karl Kautsky for example, did natural science still find some consideration in Socialist literature. But long before the First World War the tendency to minimize the attention to natural science had

[9] *Jahrbuch, 1928,* p. 318. The total of the list in the text, taken from the same source, is 4,559. There was no way of determining the cause of the discrepancy.

been heightened by the organization of the People's University (*Volksheim*) in 1900. Founded by Ludo Hartmann, the Socialist professor of history at the University of Vienna, the People's University had its central seat in Ottakring, a pronounced proletarian district of the city, and the Socialists had contrived to maintain their influence over it. Although social subjects had an important place, the records indicate that the teaching of natural science was predominant. The facilities offered in the form of chemical and physical laboratories, collections of scientific specimens, and so on were excellent. The great interest of workers in problems of natural science remained unabated. This interest was understandable with respect to the functional position of workers in the process of production; moreover, the awakening mind is first puzzled usually by the riddles of nature; it tackles the conundrums of society later. In any case, the presence of the People's University had enabled the party to concentrate Socialist educational activities proper on social sciences to a much larger degree. The situation outside Vienna, where there were no institutions directly comparable to People's Universities, differed a great deal.

The second point, which is rather striking, is the almost complete lack of discussions of "municipal policy." To be sure, many a lecture listed under "current politics" of necessity contained references to what was being done by the city council of Vienna. Yet it might have been expected that more serious attempts would have been undertaken to deal with the various problems of municipal Socialism. As it was, the 39 lectures delivered on this subject during 1928 must be taken as an indication that the adjustment of the educational activities to the practice of the movement was a rather slow process.

Finally, the great number of meetings devoted to literature and readings is worth attention. Almost a quarter of the total of 4,547 evenings was spent in this way. Although the majority of these literary evenings are explained by the custom of having an assembly of each of the sections on the anniversary of the establishment of the republic, at which time revolutionary lyrics of Freiligrath, Herwegh, Heine, and others were recited, genuine interest in literature was very keen among the members of the party. Lecturers in that field naturally gave preference to authors who treated social subjects, to Russian novelists especially. But there was a strong group which tried to continue the traditions established by Franz Mehring in Germany and thus to arouse an understanding of the whole treasury of national literature. The endeavors of the Educational Center in this respect were marked. This is important because it reveals the tendency to combat the narrow "class struggle" point of view of those in the labor movement who found a large part of German literature "unsuitable for the workers" because of its "bourgeois" character. Some discussions in the *Arbeiter Zeitung* on the occasion of the hundredth anniversary of Goethe's death are significant in this respect.[10]

LECTURES IN VIENNA*

1903/04	865	1924/25	3,430
1908/09	1,091	1925/26	3,889
1910/11	1,452	1927	3,269
1911/12	1,499	1928	4,547
1912/13	1,746	1929	4,864
1917/18	*ca.* 150	1930	4,556
1921/22	613	1931	6,006
1922/23	883	1932	6,650
1923/24	1,442		

* *Parteitag, 1912*, p. 32; *1913*, p. 33; *1919*, p. 87; *1924*, p. 64; *1925*, p. 71; *1926*, p. 75; *Jahrbuch, 1927*, p. 233; *1928*, p. 318; *1929*, p. 370; *1930*, p. 376; *1931*, p. 348; *1932*, p. 318. Prior to 1927 the year ran from July 1 to June 30; after 1928 it was the calendar year. The figures are not 100 per cent accurate; in fact, those for a given year, when repeated in a later report, rarely check. But they undoubtedly show the general trend.

The preceding discussion has cited figures indicating the importance of lectures during one postwar year; the tabulation above shows the impressive development of lectures from the beginning of the century to 1932.

Among other things these data show that the number of lectures in the last years before the war was by no means inconsiderable. Then, as was to be expected, it dropped tremendously: in 1917/18 to less than one-tenth of that in 1912/13. The first postrevolutionary years brought only a slow recovery of the educational apparatus. Not until the year following the elections of 1923 was the average immediate prewar level approximately reached. But then the concentration of the party on educational activities as a part of its general propaganda campaign for the majority began to show results. In the next year the number of lectures was almost doubled as com-

[10] *Arbeiter Zeitung*, March 20, 1932, pp. 1–2, 15–17; March 22, p. 7.

pared with 1912/13. In the last year on record, 1932, it had risen to about four times the prewar figure.

The numerical development of the general courses arranged for Vienna by the Center showed strong fluctuations. In 1928, for example, there were 131 courses spread over 681 evenings; this figure is appreciably higher than the immediate prewar years in which the number of evenings varied between 300 and 450. The years after 1928 have the same fluctuations: 302 evenings in 1929; 151 in 1930; 572 in 1931; and 106 in 1932.[11]

The activities just described have been dwelt upon at some length because they must be regarded as the main body of the party's "mass education" proper. Before the higher rungs of the Austrian Social Democratic educational ladder are reached it is well to pause a moment on one of the lower rungs.

Small local libraries for the use of the members of workers' educational clubs were organized in the earlier days of the movement. By the late prewar years a process of concentration had taken place in Vienna as well as in some of the provincial capitals, particularly Graz. The Vienna libraries were put under the supervision of the party. The sloppy type of novels, which the Germans call *Kitsch*[12] or "backstairs literature," was ruthlessly eliminated.[13] At the same time began the first attempts at centralized purchasing of books. In 1912/13 the Vienna workers' libraries had a stock of 52,000 books. The number of loans was 151,091 in 1910 and rose well over 300,000 in the last years before the war, to judge from a remark made in the official report in 1922.[14] During the war the workers' libraries naturally were no exception to the general doldrums of the movement. In 1918 the number of loans in Vienna had fallen to 100,000.[15] The recovery was rapid, as may be seen from the following figures:[16]

1918/19	108,368	1920/21	236,885
1919/20	208,935	1921/22	302,359

[11] *Jahrbuch, 1928,* p. 318; *1929,* p. 372; *1930,* p. 377; *1931,* p. 349; *1932,* p. 319; *Parteitag, 1912,* p. 32; *1913,* p. 33.

[12] It may elucidate the connotations of this widely used German word to note that although etymologically it comes from the English "sketch," even educated Germans are frequently of the opinion that it is a derivative of the English "kitchen."

[13] *Parteitag, 1913,* p. 34.

[14] *Ibid., 1922,* p. 81; *Jahrbuch, 1928,* p. 322. The 1919 report, however, gives the number of loans in 1914 as "over 200,000." *Parteitag, 1919,* p. 88.

[15] *Parteitag, 1919,* p. 88.

[16] *Ibid., 1921,* p. 71; *1922,* p. 81.

From this time on the increase in loans proceeded at a really phenomenal rate: 442,719 in 1922/23; 497,808 in 1923/24; 578,221 in 1924/25; and 740,846 in 1925/26.[17] During this same period continuous efforts were under way to improve the organization of the libraries; the number was increased; district libraries frequently established a number of distributing points, which likewise increased circulation. Moreover, more attention was paid to the training of librarians, whose positions, incidentally, were always merely honorary ones. In some instances the librarians supplemented the customary general advice by holding special office hours in which they drew up reading programs for individual readers. Of great help to librarians were the monthly issues of *Bildungsarbeit* (Educational Work), a magazine founded in 1914. After the war, it carried short reviews, seldom more than 20 to 30 lines of a narrow column, in which a great number of new books were briefly announced and rated according to a system indicating the quality of the book. From this magazine, which also contained valuable information for party lecturers, many librarians compiled reference memoranda which they used when advising readers. Very often Socialist university students or schoolteachers were in charge of the libraries. Since they were generally well-read, they fulfilled their tasks to the entire satisfaction of the readers and the Educational Center. The building program of the city of Vienna was also propitious to the workers' library movement in that premises for the libraries were often reserved in the larger municipal houses.

During the calendar year 1926 the number of loans reached 887,250. This encouraged the Center to set the goal at one million loans for 1927. It was exceeded by almost 90,000. The Center, raising its sights, announced that the circulation must reach three million within a few years and that every trade-union member must read at least five books a year.[18] In 1928 three million seemed a fantastic figure, but apparently it too would have been surpassed.

1928	1,377,528
1929	1,710,595
1930	2,024,670
1931	2,316,749
1932	2,784,639

[17] *Ibid., 1923,* p. 84; *1924,* p. 69; *1925,* p. 75; *1926,* p. 79.
[18] Sources cited in preceding note and *Jahrbuch, 1927,* p. 237; *1928,* p. 322.

In passing, it may be observed that the advent of Fascism interrupted this promising development. Under the pretense of establishing a "Christian" state, Dollfuss and his helpers closed the libraries. An indeterminable number of them were reopened after having been purged of every volume, scientific or popular, that was "undesirable."[19] As the reader has seen and will see in numerous instances later, the rulers of Austria during 1934–1938 who have been given so much credit for fighting Hitler were actually slavishly imitating his methods. In this case the reply of large groups of workers was to refuse to patronize the libraries. It is possible that in the total sum of values which perished with Austrian democracy the fate of those libraries is negligible. They were only one of the many small fields where peaceful cultural work was being done. But it is easy to imagine how deeply the approximately 1,500 educational functionaries in Vienna felt the discontinuation of a work to which so much untiring and materially distinterested effort had been devoted.

By the end of 1931 the workers' libraries of Vienna contained 293,800 volumes. Of these 216,210 were fiction or poetry; 47,103 were in the field of social science and 30,487 in that of natural science. It is plain from these figures that the actual function of the libraries was not to spread political propaganda among the workers, but to raise their cultural level and to educate their literary taste in a direction which would make them detest the 20-groschen accounts of the adventures of Nick Carter or of the sorrows and final matrimonial happiness of a poor-but-virtuous governess. The percentage of scientific books in the workers' libraries of Vienna was 26. No complete figures are available for all postwar years, but for 1928–1932 the percentage of scientific books borrowed in Vienna mounted steadily to about 12. In 1930, 4.7 per cent of the circulation was in social science; that is, only a little better than one-quarter of the proportion of social science literature in the libraries; furthermore, it is interesting that with 7.1 per cent of the circulation, books on natural science were absolutely and relatively far ahead of those on social science.[20]

An important branch of the activities of the Educational Center

[19] *Reichspost,* April 29, 1934, p. 5.
[20] *Jahrbuch, 1928,* p. 322; *1929,* p. 377; *1930,* p. 386; *1931,* p. 356; *1932,* p. 325.

was the organization of excursions or tours for party members. They usually led to the art museums of Vienna, or to big factories, or, in later years, purported to provide a general view of the achievements of "The New Vienna"; that is to say, of the houses and the welfare institutions of the city. Party members from the states frequently came to the capital in order to take part in excursions, especially of the last kind. The success of the tours is evidenced by their increasing number.[21]

1927	728	1930	2,221
1928	907	1931	2,652
1929	1,742	1932	2,108

Most of what has been said about educational work in Vienna applies also to the states, but only as far as basic principles are concerned. The quantity was incomparably smaller; it lacked the clock-like regularity of the Vienna organization. In earlier postwar years there were no special central educational organizations in the states. They developed slowly so that in the meantime the overworked central and local political bodies carried the burden of educational activity; consequently, it fell into a position of secondary or tertiary importance. The lack of educational personnel was also severely felt outside Vienna, since the Socialist intelligentsia was concentrated there. The institution of "traveling teachers" by the Educational Center remedied this situation, within rather narrow limits.

SELECTIVE ACTIVITIES

The opponents of Social Democracy in Austria used to regard the formidable party machine with frankly admitted envy. But it is essential to state here that the strength of this machine was largely derived from the formation of a large group of men[22] who enjoyed the confidence of the workers and upon whom the party could rely in having the policy of its executive committee explained to, and defended before, the masses of the membership. In many respects the influence of such a local leader upon the rank and file, from whom he had sprung and with whom he remained in daily contact, was larger than that of the gods and demigods of the central leader-

[21] *Jahrbuch, 1927,* p. 235; *1928,* p. 320; *1929,* p. 374; *1930,* p. 381; *1931,* p. 352; *1932,* p. 322.

[22] The previously explained *Vertrauensmänner.*

ship. In this respect the development was closely similar in Austria and in Germany, and it is highly significant that men of such widely differing character and outlook as Otto Bauer and Philipp Scheidemann described the outstanding role played by these workers' representatives in preventing the bolshevization of the Social Democratic bodies in both countries in almost identical words.[23] The number of these "small functionaries" of the Austrian party was extraordinarily large. In Vienna alone there were about 15,000 of them performing various services for the party. The education of these men to a deeper understanding of economic and political questions was regarded as one of the most important tasks of the party, but the first reference that could be found in party literature to schools specifically designed for them appears in 1922. They were called Political Representatives Schools (*politische Vertrauensmännerschulen*) and apparently developed out of the more general Workers Schools (*Arbeiterschulen*) of the imperial era. Except for 1922 and 1923 the statistics for both types of schools are, unfortunately, lumped together. The peak year of their activities was 1929 with 120 schools meeting for 1,021 evenings.[24] Closely connected with them were the Works Councils and Trade-Unionists Schools. For the members of the trade unions such work had been carried on previously on a narrower basis by the unions themselves. After the war the Educational Center largely took over these activities, with the result that a higher level of teaching was offered. From what has been said above (Chap. VIII) the vital importance of educational work among members of works councils will be easily understood. The top year in this field was 1931 when 85 such schools held 1,178 evening meetings in Vienna.[25]

Special importance was likewise attached to the training of the functionaries of the youth movement, who were regarded as the natural successors to similar positions in the adult organizations of the party. For a number of reasons this ideal succession did not work with the desired smoothness. But the efforts directed to the education of young officials were sincere and serious; moreover, because of the special conditions of the postwar generation and in spite of

[23] Philipp Scheidemann, *Memoiren eines Sozialdemokraten* (Dresden, 1928), vol. 2, p. 292; Otto Bauer, *Die Oesterreichische Revolution* (Wien, 1923), pp. 185–186.

[24] *Parteitag, 1919,* p. 87; *1920,* pp. 64, 65; *1921,* pp. 69, 70; *1922,* p. 77; *1923,* p. 80; *1924,* p. 65; *Jahrbuch, 1929,* p. 372.

[25] *Jahrbuch, 1931,* p. 349.

the age of the students, the teaching level frequently compared favorably with that in some of the evening schools for the adult functionaries.

Another selective educational activity was embodied in the so-called Women's Schools. Arranged by the Center with the coöperation of the *Frauenorganisation* (Women's Organization) of the party, these schools closely resembled the general schools for the workers which were attended by both sexes. The only difference was that in the Women's Schools special attention was given to the problem of woman in society.

Still another aspect of the educational work of the Austrian party, one that merits the designation specialty, was the courses for members of juries and of Juror Courts.[26] The Socialists claimed that under both arrangements, but particularly under the second, the professional judges exercised undue and unfair influence on their lay associates. Since political trials were frequently brought before Juror Courts and juries, the party undertook to advise the prospective jurors on their rights and duties. Well-trained lawyers were in charge of this instruction. Although these courses were given at least as early as 1925/26,[27] they became more important after the events of July, 1927, described in Chapter XX. They were severely criticized by political opponents and distinterested observers alike on the grounds that they were an undemocratic institution and that they perverted the jury system. With these judgments no person trained in the Anglo-Saxon tradition is likely to disagree. Whatever the merit of the Socialist claims indicated above, the juror courses were certain to discredit further the jury system. They represent a thoroughly reprehensible deviation from the party's usually consistent adherence to democratic principles.

If the last type of course is disregarded, the schools briefly described in this subsection formed the lowest level of the selective education of the party. The next stage was accessible only to those men and women with a certain general background who had dis-

[26] Under the law of the republic juries of 12 persons had to pronounce a verdict on those accused of any of a long list of political or particularly grave crimes. In other relatively milder criminal cases the court was usually composed of two jurors or "lay judges" and two professional judges. The second arrangement was called a Juror Court (*Schöffengericht*). Cf., Ernst Lohsing, *Oesterreichisches Strafprozessrecht* (Wien, 1932), pp. 80, 81, 89–90.

[27] *Parteitag, 1926,* p. 74.

played more than average capability in their work in various fields of the labor movement. There were two schools on this level: the Party School and the Trade-Union School.

The Party School was first established in 1910, but the outbreak of the war forced its suspension. Curiously enough it was not resumed until early 1924. It was planned for the exclusive use of those living in Vienna or the immediate vicinity. The duration of the course was about five months in the first year of revival and eight to nine thereafter. In the first years, classes met twice weekly; later, thrice. Of the persons who registered, anywhere from a fifth to a third failed to complete their work, the most common reason being pressure of party duties. The number who finished varied from 60 to 100 a year. All of them had been carefully selected with two chief purposes in mind: to secure individuals of the highest abilities, but also to maintain a fair distribution of the students among the districts of Vienna. For some time after 1924 university students, whatever their position within the movement, were usually precluded from attending the school, and endeavors were made to ensure a high percentage of manual workers. Younger persons were given preference so that the age of most of the students ranged between 20 and 30. From graduates of the University of Vienna who had been admitted to the school in later years I gathered certain reactions to the subjects offered and to the instructors. Economic theory on a strictly Marxist basis was taught by Dr. Benedikt Kautsky, son of the famous Karl Kautsky and director of one of the departments of the chamber of labor. These acquaintances felt that whether or not one was prepared to share, for instance, Mr. Keynes' view of *Das Kapital* as an "obsolete economic textbook" which has no bearing on economic reality,[28] Kautsky's lectures left the impression that he tried very hard, while preserving the approach and terminology of Marx, to lead his students to an understanding of the problems of a modern economy. Lectures on modern state and society in Europe were usually delivered by Siegmund Kunfi, brilliant Hungarian Socialist and member of the staff of the *Arbeiter Zeitung* whose articles revealed both a deep knowledge of history and sociology and a striking mastery of the German language. Adolf Schärf, distinguished statistician and expert on coöperatives, offered courses on

[28] M. Keynes, *Essays in Persuasion* (New York, 1932), p. 300.

the social, economic, and population statistics of Austria. Oskar Trebitsch, a well-known lawyer and writer, taught constitution and government in Austria. Among other courses the speech training of Otto Koenig should be mentioned because of the extraordinary results achieved. Incidentally, his knowledge of the German language and its literature was generally recognized in Austria.

Effective in 1929/30 the program was expanded so that the complete course comprised two years. In the second year more special problems were treated, for example: the materialistic conception of history, finance capital, and the international labor movement. Usually the students of the school remained in touch after their two years had elapsed by instituting discussion meetings which were frequently directed by one of the former teachers.

After the period of schooling the students as a rule were entrusted with some fairly responsible work within the movement. To say, however, as some party spokesmen did, that the purpose of the school was to prevent the functionaries from losing sight of the great goals of Socialism covers the facts only to some extent. The choice of subjects and their treatment indicated that the party was much more anxious to enlarge the horizon of the functionaries and thereby to increase the quality of their work for the party.[29]

The Trade-Union School, for which there was no precedent before the war of 1914–1918, was first opened in the fall of 1926. The students were selected from various branches of the free trade unions in Vienna. In many respects the school was similar to the Party School, but instruction was given only once a week and was designed to emphasize more strongly the special problems of trade unionism. The period of the course was three years. The purpose to train high functionaries who would live up to the difficult task of leadership and representation was probably even more distinct here than with the Party School.[30]

The apex of the educational structure of the Socialist party was the so-called Workers' University (*Arbeiterhochschule*). For it too there was no precedent in prewar times. When, in 1925, the party had to abandon its unfortunate experiment with its bakery, the *Hammerbrotwerke,* and compounded the error by precipitously

---

[29] Benedikt Kautsky, "Die Wiener Parteischule," *Sozialistische Bildung,* June, 1931, pp. 167 ff.; *Parteitag, 1923–1926,* esp. *1923,* p. 81, and *1924,* p. 66; *Jahrbuch, 1927–1932.*

[30] Gewerkschaftskongress, 1928, *Protokoll,* p. 221.

selling it to the profiteer Bosel, the conviction developed that in order to combat criticism within the working-class movement something had to be done to demonstrate to the rank and file that the party was still anticapitalistic; therefore, a large part of the proceeds from the sale were used for the establishment of a university of Socialism. Contrary to usual practice it was not under the supervision of the Educational Center; its director was immediately responsible to the party executive. A small building on the edge of the Vienna woods, once allegedly a castle of Maria Theresia's, was acquired. After it had been rebuilt to adapt it to its new purpose, the first school year began in January, 1926. This institution differed from the Party School. First, students in the Workers' University were not restricted to persons living in Vienna and vicinity. Second, it was not simply a higher type of evening school. For six months, usually from October to March, the students had to live at the university; they received full room and board and even pocket money for visits to theaters and the like. Their number varied between 20 and 30. The majority fell within the age limits of twenty to twenty-five; almost 90 per cent were between twenty and thirty. Ordinarily, four or five women were included in the group. Although there was considerable variation from year to year, it remains generally true that about two-thirds of the students were selected by the party, that is to say, by the party executives in the states, including Vienna; that one or two individuals were named by the central party executive; that approximately one-quarter to one-third were delegated by the trade-union *Kommission;* and that the remainder came from the youth organizations. Vienna, the Socialist citadel, was the home of a little less than half of them; the rest of the student places were allotted to the individual states according to the relative importance of the party memberships therein. On one occasion a man delegated by the German Social Democracy of Czechoslovakia was allowed to take part in the courses. The teaching staff was partly the same as in the Party School, but was reinforced by the best brains of the party. For example, Friedrich Adler, Otto Bauer, and Karl Renner taught at the Workers' University. To have as teachers men who were surrounded by all the *charisma* of great leaders tremendously stimulated the ambitions and energies of the students; indeed, it was claimed that what was accomplished in the short period of six months equaled two years of regular study by an average student at the University of Vienna. Among the teachers who did not hold a place in the party leadership probably the most outstanding was Otto Neurath, director of the Vienna Economic Museum and author of the so-called Vienna (pictorial) method of statistical presentation. The curriculum was quite similar to that of the faculty *rerum politicarum* at the University, as may be seen from the following schedule of subjects and hours in the school year 1926/27.

Subjects*	Hours
Economics	82
Political science and government	62
History	176
Trade unionism, coöperatives, organization	88
Labor and industrial legislation	72
Seminar work in industrial law, statistics, journalism, and public speaking	126

* *Parteitag, 1925*, p. 50; *1926*, pp. 82-84; *Jahrbuch, 1927*, p. 241.

Contrary to some generalizations above, it must be pointed out that the presence of the highest party leaders on the teaching staff proved at times to be a drawback; for example, in 1929, when the political situation required the full attention of the leadership, the institution did not function. After 1931 the crisis made it impossible to continue it. But so long as an independent labor movement continued to exist in Austria a "party university man"—the designation within the movement for one who had successfully completed the curriculum at the Workers' University—was regarded with a certain respect and was frequently entrusted with the very responsible position of local party secretary.

As is probably taken for granted, the building was not allowed to stand idle during all the months the university was not in session but was utilized for various schools. Not the least interesting was that for leaders of workers' choral clubs. At other times special short courses were offered for agricultural laborers, for members of the soldiers' trade union, for coöperators, and for various other groups.[31]

[31] *Jahrbuch, 1927*, pp. 241–242; *1928*, pp. 329–330; *1929*, p. 391.

OTHER EDUCATIONAL ACTIVITIES

Not in line with the educational activities of the party described above but loosely pertinent to the same field were the evening courses for workers arranged to help them to pass the much dreaded *Matura*[32] and thus to enter the sacred halls of the university. In 1922 a small group of workers in Vienna decided to prepare for the final examinations at a *Gymnasium*. Out of these modest beginnings grew a larger organization sponsored by the party in which 25 Socialist *Gymnasium* professors worked for a salary which actually was not much more than a contribution to their expenditures. Every student paid 7 schillings a month. Instruction was offered daily from 6 to 9 P.M. except on Saturdays when the hours were 5 to 9. The period of preparation was four years; the curriculum conformed to that of the *Reformrealgymnasium* and included English and Latin. The number of students rose from 126 in 1923/24 to 404 in 1928/29.[33] Subsequently the crisis brought about a decrease in attendance. Obviously enough the task of the students who had to attend the courses after a day of work in a factory or an office was an arduous one that required great energy and devotion to the self-imposed goal. But it may be doubted if anyone who has not learned at firsthand the degree of interest of Vienna workers in skiing and hiking can fully comprehend the sacrifices involved. And it should be observed further that the study of languages involved extreme difficulties for young people of whom the majority had not mastered High German and spoke a variety of the Middle Bavarian dialect. Under these conditions it is not surprising that the total number who completed the course and took the comprehensive examination was small and the number who passed it even smaller. In 1927/28, from a class that had started 180 strong, only 30 remained to take the test and only 20 scored a complete success. From 14 candidates In October, 1928, only 4 were successful. By 1932 a total of 101 students had qualified for admission to an institution of university

---

[32] This was a comprehensive examination in the main subjects at the end of secondary schoolwork. Its successful completion is generally recognized in the United States as proof that the student has achieved the status of a graduate of a junior college or of a third-year student in a university. As was indicated in the chapter on school reforms, the sociological importance of the *Matura,* which drew a line between the classes of the population almost more rigid than that of differences in income, can scarcely be appreciated in a country with widespread, free high school and college education.

[33] *Jahrbuch, 1927,* p. 243; *1928,* p. 330.

grade. The available data do not show how many had four years of study but do show that a little more than 1,500 had registered during the ten years of the program.[34] Judged in terms of its objective the program can scarcely be said to have been successful. Taken absolutely, even the number of registrants is not impressive.

The Workers' Shorthand Association should also be mentioned in this connection. Founded in 1895, this organization had the chief purpose of spreading knowledge of stenography among the workers and thus enabling members to go from manual to white-collar jobs or improve their prospects in a clerical post. A subordinate purpose of some importance was the training of stenographers for the needs of the movement. The scope of activities was subsequently enlarged by instruction in foreign languages, particularly French and English. In 1927, for example, it had just under 3,000 members.[35] It published a monthly magazine, *Der Arbeiterstenograph,* partly in shorthand.

As was said before, the Workers' University was not under the supervision of the Educational Center. The two last-mentioned organizations were independent and registered only as affiliated Social Democratic associations. But there were a few special activities of the Center which should be mentioned.

Cheap holiday journeys in Austria and to foreign countries were organized by the Center. In 1928, for instance, it arranged trips for 881 persons to various places, some as far as Turkey, France, and Scandinavia.[36] By continuous purchases the Center acquired a number of series of instructive lantern slides which it lent to local organizations for particular lectures. In 1930, 1,668 such series were lent.[37] Other successes were scored with loans of phonograph records of workers' songs, recitals of poetry, and so on, and with loans of short educational films. Also in 1930 a total of 2,371 loans of films were made.[38] At electoral times special propaganda films were produced under the supervision of the Center. After 1930 loans of so-called narrow films became more frequent. They were easier to carry, simpler to use, and less restricted by fire-prevention regulations. By 1932 there were 2,781 such films available.[39]

---

[34] Cf. *ibid., 1927–1932,* esp. *1927,* pp. 244–245; *1928,* p. 331; *1932,* p. 336.
[35] *Ibid., 1927,* p. 245.
[36] *Ibid., 1928,* p. 323.
[37] *Ibid., 1930,* p. 383.
[38] *Ibid.,* p. 384.
[39] *Ibid., 1932,* p. 325.

Art for the People

Long before Adolf Hitler's paintings became known to mankind Munich had been the capital of painters in German-speaking lands. Vienna had much the same position in the fields of music, opera, and drama. It was consonant with the basic principles of a democratic movement that Socialists were keenly alive to the fact that those pure and inspiring delights were the privilege of a relatively small group in the huge city. Theaters were expensive; the masses of the workers had neither time, nor money, nor, last but not least, interest for genuine art. The Socialists felt deeply that the social criticism of Hauptmann and Ibsen, the main pillars of the prewar repertoire, did not reach those who, in their opinion, should have been most intensely concerned with them. They felt that the life of millions remained plunged in eternal gloom because one of the greatest emanations of humanity, the light of art, did not penetrate into the crowded misery of workers' slums. The great task was to democratize art, to make it accessible and understandable to the masses of the population. How well did the Socialists succeed in these efforts?

Before the war the achievements, with one possible exception, were moderate. An association called People's Stage (*Volksbühne*) tried to organize performances of good plays with the help of second-rate artists and occasionally contrived to make arrangements for cheap tickets in major theaters for a very limited part of its membership. The war virtually finished the organization, but it was only a *coup de grace* because financial breakdown had been imminent.[40] Although the *Volksbühne* claimed to be a politically neutral organization, this was at best a half-truth. After the war a new organization, the so-called Social Democratic Art Office (*Sozialdemokratische Kunststelle*), was founded and took over about 1,000 members still on the lists of the *Volksbühne*. A quick upswing followed so that in 1922 the Art Office numbered about 40,000 members.[41] Its chief task was to make the theaters of Vienna, especially the famous Opera and Burgtheater, accessible to its members. To accomplish the aim it undertook to sell to members a given number of tickets for a certain

[40] David J. Bach, "Warum haben wir keine sozialdemokratische Kunstpolitik," *Der Kampf*, vol. 22 (March, 1929), 139.
[41] *Parteitag, 1922*, p. 99.

play or opera. The price was greatly reduced, and in the early years of postrevolutionary enthusiasm the local organizations of the party easily sold the tickets, especially when announcements of the Art Office recommending the performances were brought to the attention of party members. During this period the city council of Vienna generously supported the Art Office, thus enabling it to fix prices even below the favorable ones granted to it by the theaters. Unfortunately, after the stabilization of the currency, considerations of economy impelled the so-called State Theaters to curtail not only the number of evenings on which seats were reserved for the Art Office but also the number of seats available. As long as the stock exchange boom continued this was bad policy from the point of view of people's education, but good policy from that of the finances of the theaters. After 1924 parlous times came to these theaters; nevertheless, they did not revert to a more favorable attitude to the Art Office. Indeed, the Socialists claimed that they were discriminated against as compared with the various similar institutions run by non-Socialists. Partly because of difficulties of this kind the membership of the Socialist organization declined appreciably in subsequent years, fluctuating between 15,000 and 20,000. On the other hand, it became increasingly apparent that it was not enough to provide access to good theaters to the workers; in the long run it was also necessary to stimulate their interest in such theaters. As early as 1923 the report of the Art Office had cautiously observed that it was necessary "to pay attention to the needs of each group [among the membership] and to lead them slowly to higher and higher levels."[42]

The quantitative achievements of the Art Office were rather impressive. In 1919–1928 it sold "more than two million tickets."[43] In 1929–1932 the annual average of about 200,000 tickets was maintained. But an analysis of the distribution of these tickets among the various theaters shows what might have been expected from the foregoing remarks: the share of the State Theaters was extremely low. In 1927, for instance, from 193,639 tickets sold through the Art Office only 11,407 were for the Burgtheater and 6,180 for the Opera.[44] Among the rest, in first place and far ahead of the field was

[42] *Ibid., 1923,* p. 105.
[43] Bach, *op. cit.,* p. 140.
[44] *Jahrbuch, 1927,* p. 239.

the *Deutsches Volkstheater.* This was a good theater with an excellent ensemble, but it was increasingly devoted to light plays of little educational value. Furthermore, a growing number of tickets was sold for the so-called operetta stages; in 1928–1932 such tickets amounted to almost 123,000.[45] This development aroused strong criticism, especially among the younger groups in the movement. They were vigorously supported by Karl Kraus, the famous Austrian writer.[46] These critics had no objections to operettas as such; in fact, Kraus contributed a great deal to the popularity of Offenbach in Austria. But they violently rejected the policy of the Art Office on the ground that it led the workers to the worst variety of the "traditional and senseless amusements of the bourgeoisie."

In 1928 the Art Office undertook to run a theater of its own. It began by staging *Lenin,* a play by a Viennese Socialist writer named Ernst Fischer, and continued with a half-forgotten piece of Grabbe's, *Scherz, Satire, Ironie und tiefere Bedeutung,* which was not devoid of literary merit. Then, unfortunately, came financial difficulties involving the Berlin director who, as it turned out, had borrowed substantial sums of money from his own ensemble. Thereupon a sharp attack against the Art Office was launched by a younger member of the staff, and subsequent editor in chief, of the *Arbeiter Zeitung.*[47] He maintained that its policy was not Social Democratic and demanded a reorientation because he was convinced that in some respects that policy paid more attention to the tastes of the literary gourmands in the *cafés* of the Inner City than to the needs of the workers in the alehouses of Favoriten. The director of the Office replied with a long statement[48] of its achievements in which he seemed to have the better of the argument. He admitted that by no means all the plays and other performances to which tickets were sold by the Office were productions of high cultural value, but he stressed the fact that it had only the right of refusing to partici-

---

[45] *Ibid., 1928,* p. 327; *1929,* p. 388; *1930,* p. 398; *1931,* p. 366; *1932,* p. 333.

[46] Kraus is probably best known for his magazine, *Die Fackel,* and his play, *Die letzten Tage der Menschheit.* His vivid personality was reflected in his writings and it is not too much to say that he acted as a catalyzer in the political as well as the literary life of Austria. Though he was something of a muckraker, he is generally given credit for driving out of Austria one of the most corrupt publishers who ever disgraced that country.

[47] Oskar Pollak, "Warum haben wir keine sozialdemokratische Kunstpolitik?" *Der Kampf,* vol. 22 (Feb., 1929), 83 ff.

[48] Bach, *op. cit.,* pp. 139–148.

pate in the distribution of tickets to a particular attraction and thus only a very indirect possibility of influencing the programs of the theaters. He also emphasized the point that even insignificant plays when performed by a genius like Bassermann acquired great educational value. Furthermore, he mentioned the number of classical and Socialist playwrights whose works had been produced.

But probably the most convincing part of Bach's defense was that concerning the Workers' Symphony Concerts. They were a prewar institution, the first of them having taken place as early as 1904. After the war the generally enhanced position and importance of Austrian Social Democracy contributed to a considerable improvement of them. Their popularity increased tremendously so that by 1926 the five hundredth concert had been performed. Presented in one of the best and largest concert halls of the music capital, they were always completely sold out. The fact that the Art Office was offering high-class performances was generally recognized. During 1927, the Beethoven Year, for instance, its presentation of his Ninth Symphony, together with the 130 members of the Choral Club of the Art Office, was enthusiastically reviewed by the press of political opponents. This might be regarded as a matter of course had it happened in London, but certainly took on a different significance in Vienna. As Bach and others pointed out, it was the policy of the Art Office not only to present Beethoven, Bach, and Tchaikovsky to the workers, but also to encourage young and still unknown composers. For example, it may be of some particular interest to the American reader to know that in 1930 a symphony called Lindbergh Flight composed by Weill was successfully performed.[49]

At the time the articles of Pollak and Bach were published there was a tendency within the party to regard them as a part of the struggle between young and old; that is, as caused by the efforts of youth to obtain control of the Art Office. This interpretation is not without foundation in fact; but the real issue at stake, in spite of Pollak's careful qualifications, was whether art for the workers was to be conceived primarily as a way of furthering the development toward a future Socialist society or as a means of increasing the joy in living of the current generation.

Apart from the symphony concerts and the provision of cheap

[49] *Jahrbuch, 1930,* p. 398.

theater tickets there were various other activities of the Art Office. It organized recitation groups which gave short performances at the meetings of various organizations and participated in electoral campaigns. A special attraction was provided through the regular expositions, Art to the People, which were visited by large numbers. The Office published a magazine, *Kunst und Volk* (Art and Folk), that carried explanatory articles on plays, operas, concerts, and so on with which the Office was connected in some way or other. It also arranged for the presentation of plays, either with amateur actors or with professionals who were willing to give their free time to such purposes. Usually the productions were one-act pieces like *Der Grüne Kakadu* by Schnitzler or *Le Commissaire est bon enfant* by Courteline. The first was utilized because it made the audience feel the hot breath of the French Revolution; the second because it made fun of the police and thus appealed to the instincts of the Austrian workers. Still another activity of the Office developed in connection with what the Austrians called Festival Culture. The arrangement of festive meetings on certain memorial days, such as the anniversary of the death of Karl Marx, or of the Hainfeld party congress, or of the outbreak of the Revolution of 1848, had long been a tradition of the Austrian labor movement. Now the Art Office began to manage the artistic program of those festivals.

In this task the Office was effectively supported by the old Workers' Choral Clubs which had been founded long before the war but had experienced a strong increase in membership as well as an improvement in technical quality thereafter. This was connected with the fact that before the revolution many teachers in elementary schools—the predestined preceptors of the clubs—did not feel at liberty to join Social Democratic groups because of fear of possible discrimination in their vocation. The choral clubs had about 15,000 members in 1927.[50] In the same category were the activities of the Federation of Workers' Musicians Associations of Austria, an organization with about 2,000 members and a monthly magazine, *Die Volksmusik*.[51] The two last-named organizations performed particularly valuable work in the provinces where in many respects they may be regarded as a substitute for the Art Office in Vienna.

Related to the matters under discussion in this section but not

[50] *Ibid., 1927,* p. 271.
[51] *Ibid., 1929,* p. 414.

under the supervision of the Art Office was the previously noted (above, Chap. XII, p. 347) venture of the Labor Bank into the motion-picture business through the *Kiba*. Until about the middle 'twenties the attitude of Austrian Social Democracy toward most films, with their inevitable osculatory happy ending, had been one of contemptuous rejection. The positive policy of the *Kiba* to attempt to influence the choice of productions brought to Austria was hampered by the natural desire of the Labor Bank to secure a fair return on the considerable amount of capital it had invested. Had the *Kiba* limited itself to the small number of really outstanding and valuable pictures it would only have made a capacity use of the theaters impossible; therefore, its influence was reflected in bringing as many such pictures as possible and, more important, seeing to it that they were shown not only in a few "exclusive" houses but also in the small, not to say tiny, establishments in the proletarian districts of Vienna and in industrial towns and villages in the provinces. Another part of the policy was to secure a large number of copies of new films and thus induce more and more of the small theater owners to come to some form of agreement with the *Kiba*. Within the party there was a certain amount of criticism against this policy on the ground that it interfered with the most efficient prosecution of the struggle against *Kitsch* pictures. On the other hand, it was generally recognized among the party membership that the *Kiba* was a political asset in that through it party propaganda (notably, electoral films during the campaigns of 1930 and 1932) could be brought to people outside the reach of the electoral machine.

In general evaluation of Socialist activities in the field of art for the people during the republican era it is not too much to say that in the light of the size of the task and of the comparatively short span of years the achievements were remarkable. But in many respects they were only a modest beginning. From time to time there were complaints that the party did not pay enough attention to the field of art. This was natural. Political struggles, housing, educational reforms, and welfare activities, for example, were more significant from the point of view of a political organization. But what was done showed the sincere efforts of the Austrian labor movement to make the workers understand and enjoy the beauty of art which, in the words of Schiller, is the guardian of the dignity of humanity.

Sport for the People

To no less degree than the education of the mind the education of the body was prominent among the cultural activities of the party. In a tremendous central organization, The Workers' Federation for Sport and Physical Culture in Austria (*Arbeiterbund für Sport und Körperkultur in Oesterreich* or *ASKO*) which had been founded in 1925, there were united some 16 organizations of varying age with about 200,000 members.[52] These organizations represented not only a wide variety of sports as ordinarily so termed, but also, at times, such a group as the Workers' Radio Federation. Hiking and skiing in the mountains, rowing and swimming in the Danube, playing football and handball, hunting and fishing, gymnastics, boxing, wrestling, jujitsu, track and field athletics, cycling and motorcycling, tennis, ice sports, gliding—every one of these sports had a separate organization. Several of them had been founded before the war of 1914–1918 but the great and rapid development of workers' sports in Austria falls in the years after the revolution. One reason was the generally greater strength, power, and importance of the labor movement and another the financial aid with which the city council of Vienna generously furthered the development; but the actual prerequisites were such parts of the social legislation of the republic as the eight-hour day, paid vacations for manual workers, special regulations for youthful laborers, and absolute rest on Sundays, or, at any rate, one day in the week. It is difficult to exaggerate the importance assumed by sport in the life of the average worker during the period 1918–1934. The movement was by no means confined to youth. Middle-aged Viennese women used to attend regularly the weekly evenings of the *Turnverein*. Every Sunday tens of thousands of people, many of whom (some former active Socialists say "most" of whom) prior to the war had been accustomed to spend the afternoon in the beer halls or liquor shops, moved out to the hills of the Vienna woods or the banks of the Danube. There could be seen hundreds of tents, most of them flying a small red flag, in which a good number of persons stayed from Saturday noon until early Monday morning. Specially skilled members of the swimming club kept watch on the river and earned much credit for their ex-

[52] Cf. *Parteitag, 1925,* p. 116; *Jahrbuch, 1927,* p. 280.

ploits in lifesaving. On warm Sundays the vast premises of the Workers' Swimming Bath were crowded, and in the afternoons little rowboats came down the Danube carrying members of the club who had gone upstream by rail on Saturday night and spent Sunday in being driven back to the city by the strong current. In the winter the Danube was deserted, but thousands—young and old—were skiing in the hills which surrounded the city in a huge amphitheater. Everywhere the little badge of the Socialist Friends of Nature was seen. A Sunday walk in the environs would persuade the most skeptical observer of the popularity of sport among Socialist workers.

Although it is impossible to give details on the history and activities of each of the associations united in the *ASKO,* the Friends of Nature merits particular attention. It was founded in October, 1895, in Austria and spread to many countries of Europe, including Germany, Switzerland, Czechoslovakia, Hungary, Yugoslavia, Bulgaria, Poland, Holland, Norway. Even in Australia and the United States local groups were formed.[53] In 1927 there were 1,401 such local units with 150,000 members, 69,000 of whom were in Austria and 51,000 in Vienna. By 1930 the Austrian membership had reached 95,958; then, under the influence of the depression, it began to sink.[54] The accomplishments of the organization for its members were substantial. By special contracts with the federal railways it provided tickets for trips into the mountains at greatly reduced rates, so low, in fact, that the annual membership dues of 5 schillings were more than met by the savings on one round trip to the Rax, the "Home Mountain" of the Viennese as it was frequently called. Thanks to these arrangements many Viennese workers were enabled for the first time in their lives to leave the city for a railway trip of some length. The Friends of Nature were also busily occupied with the construction of Alpine huts and hostels in which members were able to get sleeping accommodations, and sometimes food, at prices which did not include any profit. Consumption of alcohol was strictly forbidden in these places. Another important step in the development of the association was the acquisition of a huge tract of land high on the north side of the majestic Sonnblick; it was reserved for the training of ski enthusiasts among the members, and special trains

[53] The first branch in the United States was established in 1910; the strong San Francisco group in 1912. *San Francisco Chronicle,* July 13, 1942, p. 10.

[54] *Jahrbuch, 1927,* p. 282; *1930,* p. 438; *1932,* p. 367.

took thousands of them into this lofty realm of firs, granite, and snow. Instruction in climbing, skiing, hiking, and map reading, supplemented by lectures on geography and geology, was carried out on a large scale. A special photographic section supplied the magazines of the labor movement, as well as the monthly journal of the Friends of Nature, with artistic Alpine views. In later years it undertook the production of short Alpine films. Out of these activities arose in the summer of 1931 the Federation of Socialist Workers' Photographers; it produced a social film, "Our World," which met with appreciable success. Skiing and climbing equipment was sold to members at prices substantially below those current commercially and on long installment-payment terms. Membership in the party was not a prerequisite to joining the Friends of Nature, but the number of nonparty members was very small. During electoral campaigns members of the association were accustomed to take along on their hikes propaganda material for distribution in the villages and hamlets.

With reference to workers' sport in general, three principles were clearly discernible. One was the strong aversion to "recordism." The leaders of the Austrian workers' sport organizations held that the goal was not championship achievements by individuals but physical education for the masses. When 50,000 persons went to watch a game of soccer played by 22 boys the Socialists contemptuously compared it to a circus and maintained that it had nothing in common with true people's athletics. Extension and not intensification of sport was their aim;[55] therefore, "buying" great players was almost completely unknown in Austrian workers' sport. A second principle, and from the viewpoint of some of the leaders the most important one because of its political implications, was the isolation of workers' sport from so-called neutral associations; that is, the boycott policy previously discussed. The greatest difficulties in this respect were experienced with the soccer clubs. Finally, in 1926, the separation was accomplished. From then on no workers' soccer club in Austria played a match against a club which was not a member of the Workers' Football Union. The third principle, indicated more than once heretofore, was preparedness for physical resistance to a Fascist counterrevolution.

[55] Cf. J. Deutsch, *Unter roten Fahnen! Vom Rekord- zum Massensport* (Wien, 1931).

It seems fair to say that, more than the attempts to educate to a knowledge and appreciation of science and art, the sport movement changed the living conditions of the Austrian working class. In a way this was a revolution, a revolution of habits and as such a necessary supplement to the improvement in working conditions brought about by the republican legislation. It is perhaps superfluous to add that from the point of view of people's hygiene, as well as from that of the productivity of labor, the spectacular development of workers' sport was highly beneficial after the devastations of the years of war and inflation.

For and Against Religion

The basic attitude of the workers' party on questions of religion will be dealt with at some length in the chapter on Austro-Marxism. Here it suffices to survey briefly the activities of Socialist organizations concerned with these problems.

The Federation of Freethinkers, like many of the organizations discussed herein, had its roots in imperial days. As far back as February 20, 1887, the authorities had approved the creation of an Association of Agnostics. This was not a workers' group, but its fourth president, elected in 1891, was a Socialist. The passage of years brought greater Socialist influence, changes in the name of the organization, and a predominantly working-class membership. The avowed aim of the Freethinkers was to combat the widespread tendency among the ruling classes to keep the proletariat under the influence of a religion of resignation and submission to economic and social inequalities—in the famous phrase of Marx, a religion that was an "opiate for the people." The special position of the Roman Catholic Church in Austria with its far-reaching influence over ruling circles of the Habsburg state and over the strong Christian Social party naturally directed the chief activities of the Freethinkers against Austrian Catholicism. Before the First World War these activities were largely of an educational, or, if the term be preferred, propaganda, character. The chief media were lectures, usually on questions of natural science and philosophy, in which the flat mechanical materialism of Büchner, Vogt, and Moleschott was rather uncritically treated. The *Welträtsel* (World Riddles) of Haeckel represented the Bible of the movement. These manifestations, undeniably crude as they were, aroused the Catholic charges of *Halbbildung* (half knowledge, or half education), so frequently leveled against their opponents. After the war the Freethinkers, like almost all Socialist organizations, greatly increased their membership. The conflict had left a bitter feeling against the Church. In the regularly recurring phrases of the speeches and publications of the Freethinkers the priests had "blessed the arms"; they had "approved the slaughter." Up to 1927 the exact membership is difficult to ascertain because of the lumping together of "ordinary" and "extraordinary" members, but in that year it was reported as 41,705 in 254 groups. The monthly magazine *Der Freidenker* (The Freethinker) had a circulation of about 40,000.[56] In addition to continuing and improving the quality of their educational activities the Freethinkers began to take a more active part in practical matters. One of the most important of these was to assist their members in carrying out the formalities required for leaving the Church. Another was what they called "the struggle for the child"—namely, the fight against attempts to compel children without religion to take part in religious instruction and religious exercises. The association provided the parents of such children with lawyers at no cost to the parents. As was noted in an earlier chapter, several cases were fought through the Administrative and Constitutional Courts. After the events of July 15, 1927, the Freethinkers greatly intensified their continuing propaganda drive to induce all and sundry to leave the Church; they claimed that prelate Seipel was really responsible for the fatalities in Vienna of that day.

Among Socialist organizations the Freethinkers' federation was obviously the one most bitterly hated and despised by the Christian Social party and the Roman Catholic Church. Although that party had regularly used its power to bring about the confiscation of leaflets and posters published by the federation, such cases became even more the order of the day after 1927. It is, therefore, not surprising that the Dollfuss government disbanded the Freethinkers in June, 1933,[57] three months after the elimination of parliament and long before the final destruction of the independent labor movement. But it should not be overlooked that the Social Democratic party also had experienced considerable trouble with the organization. For one thing its membership was probably more radical than that

[56] *Jahrbuch, 1927,* p. 272.
[57] *Arbeiter Zeitung,* June 21, 1933, p. 3.

of any other cultural organization of the party. The Communists attempted to utilize this circumstance and the fact that membership in the party was not obligatory for admission to the Freethinkers; that is, exasperated by their complete failure to build up a mass party of their own, they tried to get a foothold in the Freethinkers' groups in the form of a "revolutionary opposition." As usual, however, the Socialists repulsed these efforts.

In general, it should be remarked further that the observer who read the articles published in *Der Freidenker* and attended the meetings of the association was frequently struck by the tendencies to undue simplifications and appalling one-sidedness. From the point of view of a sincere Freethinker, of course, these tendencies were only the inevitable reaction to the uncompromising attitude of the Church, to its perennial efforts to enforce the rule of its dogma upon the thinking of men.

Closely connected with the Freethinkers was the Workers' Crematory Society, The Flame. As is generally known, the Roman Catholic Church vigorously opposes the cremation of the dead; nevertheless, the crematory built by the city of Vienna, in spite of strong attacks from the Church and the Christian Social party, firmly established the practice of cremation there. Membership in The Flame rose from 28,000 in 1924 to 167,315 in 1932.[58]

For a number of reasons the workers' party did not commit itself unconditionally to the Freethinkers. Not the least important of these, as expressed by Otto Bauer, was the conviction that too many of its members were under the influence of one or the other of two misconceptions. The first was the idea of many bourgeois liberals of the nineteenth century that religious emancipation must precede political and economic emancipation. The second was the notion that the Russian example of including in the labor party only the advance guard of the proletariat should be followed in Austria. These concepts Bauer condemned as illusionary and undemocratic, respectively. Precisely because his party sought to encompass at least the whole working class, it readily found a place for religious associations of workers. For example, there was an Association for Biblical Socialism that guarded the traditions of Lamennais and Weitling. Its journal had the chief purposes of demonstrating

[58] *Parteitag, 1924,* p. 116; *Jahrbuch, 1932,* p. 363.

that the principles of Socialism had been pronounced in both Old and New Testaments, that a true Christian had to be a Socialist, and that formalized religion had perverted or falsified the teachings of the Scriptures.[59] More important was the Union of Religious Socialists, founded in 1927 with the professed aim of bringing together those who envisaged Socialism as a realization of the religious forces in the world.[60] The Union published a magazine *Menschheitskämpfer* (Fighter for Humanity). Though this organization developed satisfactorily it never approached the Freethinkers in importance or size.

Other Cultural Organizations

As indicated in the first paragraph of this chapter, a list of the cultural organizations of the Austrian working-class movement is long and comprehensive. Unfortunately, however, the record of them available in the two chief official sources, the reports of the party executive to the party congresses before 1927 and the yearbooks of the labor movement thereafter, was compiled in an unsatisfactory, not to say haphazard and arbitrary, fashion. For a number of the associations, federations, and so on consecutive accounts appear, but for others this is not true. On the other hand, it is highly significant that the total number of groups increased continuously almost to the day of the destruction of the independent labor movement. They sprang up in almost every conceivable field of interest and activity. In addition to those already mentioned there were Socialist philatelists and chess players. There was a Socialist union of adherents of Alfred Adler's individual psychology, another of Socialists interested in Alpine costumes and dances, and still others of Esperanto students and mandolin players. Socialist Friends of Animals had their own organization with its inevitable magazine. Even this supplement does not complete the list, and it is no exaggeration to state that a reasonably adequate account of their development and achievements would fill a fat volume. In such a presentation the Workers' Abstainers Union would merit such a prominent place that it is appropriate to close this discussion of specific organizations with it.

It was not easy to propagate antialcohol ideas in Austria and espe-

[59] Otto Bauer, *Sozialdemokratie, Religion und Kirche* (Wien, 1927), pp. 37 ff.; *Jahrbuch, 1929,* p. 418.

[60] *Jahrbuch, 1927,* p. 273.

cially in the city which since the days of the Romans had carried the Latin *Vinum* in its name—in the city of the *Heurigen* of Grinzing and Sievering. Though a magazine called *Abstinent* in which prominent Socialists published articles had begun to appear in 1902, the Union was not founded until 1905. Its propaganda, lectures, leaflets, booklets, in short, all its attempts to show the disastrous effects of the use of alcohol on the moral and material conditions of the workmen were of very limited effect for a discouragingly long time. Century-old traditions were hard to break. And the party was dependent upon the little beer and wine houses for rooms for meetings. Even when it began to acquire buildings and to establish Labor Temples the idea was dominant that the service of their mortgages compelled the sale of liquors in the restaurants which were generally established within them. As a physician the unifier of the party, Viktor Adler, was of course opposed to the intemperate consumption of alcohol, but it was only after some hesitation that he joined the ranks of the total abstainers. Once he had done so he gave himself wholeheartedly to the cause and some of his best speeches and articles were devoted to it. Always there was emphasis on the relation of the fight against alcohol to that for a Socialist society. "Alcohol is a part of the machinery of oppression." "Whoever wants emancipation from exploitation must want liberation from alcohol." One of the most effective of his appeals was delivered to the trade-union congress of 1907. The people before him were the elected representatives of the working class—individuals in whom the rank and file had placed their confidence. As such they were exhorted by Adler to observe as their highest duty the obligation to keep their weapons clean and ready for use—the weapons of brains and nervous system.[61] These remained the basic arguments of the Socialists in their propaganda against alcohol; Otto Bauer repeated them twenty years later when he emphasized the number of people who, but for it, would have been doing excellent service for the working class. In an oft-cited speech on the question Bauer also stressed the inevitable connection between bad housing conditions and the beer hall. But at the same time he also warned that the postwar improvement in housing conditions per se was inade-

[61] *Victor Adlers Aufsätze, Reden und Briefe,* Heft 3 (Wien, 1924), pp. 32, 40, 41.

quate to bring about a decrease in alcohol consumption, if not supplemented by educational propaganda.[62]

Despite handicaps and discouragements the movement attained a substantial success in the almost three decades of its existence. It was, however, less successful with the adult workers than with the young generation of the movement. As has been shown, the youth organizations were strong opponents of alcohol. In this fight they were, of course, greatly aided by the mushroom growth of proletarian sport in the postwar years. On the other hand, another political consideration hampered the party campaign against alcohol. Especially after 1925, when the "struggle for the soul of the peasants" had begun, the leaders felt that numerous "wine farmers" would be prevented from joining the party if that campaign were too strongly accentuated. And, more generally, the prospects of the Abstainers' Union were never good among peasants and workers in the villages of the provinces. As a delegate to the party congress of 1926 expressed it: "Now just picture to yourselves life in a little village! On the one side the inn, opposed by the teetotalers; on the other side the Church, opposed by the freethinkers. But they are the only distractions of the rural folk."[63] Thus the idea of antialcoholism could strike deep roots only in large places like Vienna and Graz; and even in them, as said before, chiefly among the young generation. There were, of course, numerous individuals everywhere within the labor movement who were strong partisans of temperance or total abstinence.

To summarize and repeat, it was the policy of Austrian Social Democracy to stimulate and support a multiplicity of cultural organizations. And no one can deny that the idea of promoting class solidarity and thus increasing the power of the party was one of the guiding principles of this policy. But this does not exhaust the case. Equally strong was the sincere desire and the strong will to create a new generation of men and women with healthy, sport-trained bodies, with eyes open to the eternal beauties of nature and art, as well as to the significance of science. The Socialist leaders fought the dull monotony of a laborer's life and with Ferdinand Lassalle they told the workers: "Neither the vices of the oppressed, nor the

[62] Otto Bauer, *Mieterschutz, Volkskultur und Alkoholismus* (Wien, 1929).
[63] *Parteitag, 1926,* p. 344.

idle distractions of the thoughtless, nor even the harmless frivolity of the insignificant are becoming to you."[64] They wanted, within the narrow borders of their small country, to make the culture of humanity the culture of the people. It is from this point of view that the mutilation or destruction of so much of their work by the Clerical Fascists is particularly deplorable.

[64] Lassalle, *Reden und Schriften*, vol. 2, p. 48.

CHAPTER XIX

Struggle for Majority, 1923-1927

THROUGHOUT THE preceding chapters it has been observed repeatedly that in republican Austria all issues tended to assume a political character, and in certain chapters the politics were brought out in some detail. A treatment of this nature, though necessary, has the drawback of blurring the outlines of political developments. Since those developments have been traced through 1922 in Parts One and Two, it is the purpose of this chapter, the last in Part Three, to pick up the thread and follow it through the elections of 1927. The reason for the second date has also been indicated several times above: the shift in the balance of political power that took place, or at least became clearly evident, in the summer of 1927. For a better understanding of the political evolution in this period, however, it is necessary to keep in mind certain economic factors which influenced that evolution, and, more particularly, the policies and tactics of the workers' party. Among these factors were the aftermath of the currency stabilization, the collapse of the stock exchange boom, and the increase in unemployment; underlying them was the structural dislocation pervading the entire Austrian economy.

The full effects of stabilization did not become visible at once. To be sure, the export industries felt the shock immediately and the decline of the German mark further aggravated their situation by rendering competition with German industry practically impossible. The policy of strict economy in certain parts of the federal budget, most notably the wholesale dismissals of civil servants, was bound to reduce domestic purchasing power. Nevertheless, for more than a year, the true economic situation was concealed by the boom on the stock exchange. Under the benevolent eyes of the Commissioner General of the League of Nations the shares of Austrian industrial undertakings experienced a sharp upswing. Wide publicity was given to computations according to which the stabilization had left stock prices badly undervalued.[1] Since Austrian

[1] League of Nations, Austria, *Fourth Report by the Commissioner General of the League of Nations at Vienna, March 15–April 15, 1923*, p. 10; O. S. Phillpotts, *Report*

exchange had ceased to fall, further speculation in the crown had been rendered impossible; but the stock market provided a substitute much welcomed by large strata of the population. Inflation had revolutionized the habits of the people. The saving instinct had been almost destroyed. The wish to consume as much of income as possible; in fact, to live beyond income, was everywhere apparent. Above all a gold-rush atmosphere was created in the impoverished country, so that computations like those cited found ready credence. Only rarely did anyone stop to think of the havoc war and inflation had played with the capital of business undertakings—to wonder whether higher prices for shares were really justified. As the *Volkswirt* pointed out even many experienced and distinguished bankers fell into this form of economic insanity. The boom on the market continued unchecked throughout 1923, and thus maintained, amidst increasing economic difficulties, the illusion of growing prosperity. Finally, however, the upward movement of stock prices began to slow down; the first signs of a reversal became visible. But the Austrian public refused to believe that the period of easy profits was over. At that time, early in 1924, the downward tendency of the French franc began to accelerate. The Austrians, considering themselves experts in matters of inflation, firmly believed that Austrian and German history would faithfully repeat itself in France. A new rush ensued; huge commitments had been made in bear speculations on the French franc by April of 1924 when Morgan's intervention proved successful and the sudden recovery of the franc began. The effects of this unexpected turn were disastrous for Austria. The curtain of the artificial boom was rudely lifted and very soon the distressful conditions of the Austrian economy became apparent in all their gloomy nakedness. Stock exchange activities dwindled to a trickle of their former volume. Bank failures followed in great numbers. Throughout the inflation and the year 1923 these institutions had experienced a mushroom growth so that when the crisis began there were "over 70 joint stock banks, and over 300 private banking houses" in the country. By the end of the summer of 1925 about 100 banks, including 23 joint stock institutions, had

on the Financial, Commercial and Industrial Situation of Austria, Revised to July, 1924 (London, 1924), p. 13; *Neue Freie Presse,* January 1, 1924 (A.M.), p. 19. Cf. also the warnings of *Der österreichische Volkswirt,* vol. 15 (June 2 and 9, Aug. 11, 1923), 944, 983, 1261.

disappeared or were *in statu liquidationis.*[2] Industry was badly hit. Toward the end of 1924 unemployment figures began to rise with appalling rapidity; details appear in the table below.

The figures reveal the immediate effects of the stabilization in the fall of 1922 and in the following winter. It is worth noting that the number of unemployed in the last two months of 1923 was lower than in the foregoing year as a result of the effects of the stock

PERSONS ON UNEMPLOYMENT RELIEF IN AUSTRIA, 1921–1928*

End of the month	1921	1922	1923	1924	1925	1926	1927	1928
Jan.	16,217	33,554	161,227	119,766	187,099	231,361	235,464	230,754
Feb.	14,520	42,933	167,417	125,783	188,917	228,763	244,257	223,964
March	9,790	42,231	152,830	106,908	175,580	202,294	208,345	193,449
April	9,518	44,281	132,226	82,524	148,434	173,115	181,176	154,817
May	10,103	38,567	107,965	68,969	130,778	154,821	158,332	130,393
June	11,035	33,355	92,789	63,556	118,366	150,981	145,136	118,737
July	11,702	30,967	87,155	66,457	117,183	152,495	136,909	115,211
Aug.	11,349	31,247	83,891	74,191	116,365	151,050	135,938	113,851
Sept.	10,594	38,000	78,787	77,550	119,103	148,111	129,948	112,595
Oct.	8,709	58,008	75,810	89,016	130,905	151,183	127,352	122,557
Nov.	9,822	82,923	79,289	113,484	159,244	168,820	159,783	155,235
Dec.	16,713	117,144	98,050	154,492	207,834	205,260	207,100	202,659

* *Wirtschaftsstatistisches Jahrbuch, 1925,* pp. 105–106; *1926,* pp. 450–451; *1929/30,* p. 549.

exchange boom and, most notably, of the stabilization of the German mark in November, 1923. The latter influenced the development of Austrian industrial activities in 1924 and largely accounts for the fact that contrary to what might have been expected after the collapse on the stock exchange they showed for some months an astonishing power of resistance. The speedy recovery in Germany and the heightening of tariff walls in the succession states quickly destroyed the few illusions which might still have been cherished concerning the economic future of Austrian industry. Beginning in November, 1924, when all the blast furnaces in the iron and steel center in Donawitz were extinguished, unemployment climbed to unprecedented levels. Now the inheritance from inflation—the shortage of capital—became apparent; exorbitant interest rates rendered industrial investments almost impossible, though such invest-

[2] O. S. Phillpotts, *Report on Commercial and Financial Conditions in Austria, Revised to August, 1925* (London, 1925), p. 14.

ments were all the more necessary after the maladjustments of the inflationary era. But apprehensions about the safety of the currency and pressure from the Commissioner General of the League prevented a timely reduction of the interest rates and thus a credit crisis was added to the constitutional market difficulties of Austrian industry. From 1924 onwards it never experienced a real upswing. In 1927, when conditions in Austria began to improve under the influence of favorable world trade conditions, the betterment was so slow, came so belatedly, and passed so quickly, indeed, almost unnoticed, that it could not destroy the pervading popular impression of a permanent crisis which held the Austrian economy in its throes. The cyclical upswing was unable to offset the structural dislocation brought about by the dissolution of the economic unity of the Habsburg empire. The unemployment situation was only aggravated by the modest rationalization measures actually adopted. Even in the "good" year 1928 the number of unemployed on relief held roughly to the level of 1925—a year of grave depression. The permanent existence of this large army of unemployed influenced to a very large extent the policy of Austrian labor in the period under consideration and altered the relative weight of the main factors within the movement.

In addition to the economic background just outlined it is also necessary to keep in mind certain political factors that directly influenced the development of the republican Austrian variety of the two-party system. But at the outset it must be noted that though it was really a two-party system it would be incorrect to assume that it bore much resemblance to the traditional political forms in the old democracies of England and the United States. A major difference is that in those countries that system was and is a democratic one, whereas in Austria it represented rather an arrangement within which the struggle for and against democracy was being fought out. Certain technical peculiarities of the Austrian arrangements rather aided in increasing this divergence.

The two-party system in the western democracies involves periodic changes in the government party. The vote of the people there can exercise prompt and tremendous effects; it can produce a certain rhythmic rotation of a party between government and opposition. This was not so in Austria, chiefly because of the electoral system adopted after the revolution. The creators of the Austrian constitution had chosen to make the parliament a microcosmic reproduction of the electorate through the device of proportional representation. D'Hondt's method, adopted for the first elections of the republic, was a close approach to the principle that every vote should find equal representation in the parliament.[3] For the elections of 1920 this system was even improved in that provisions were made for central distribution of the "surplus votes" among the parties.[4] Prior to the elections of 1923 a further change was introduced. For the allocation of seats to the parties in the electoral districts the so-called Hagenbach-Bischoff system was adopted; surplus votes had to be pooled in one of the four combined electoral units (*Wahlkreisverbände*) into which the country was divided and then distributed according to the method of D'Hondt. It is generally assumed that the Hagenbach-Bischoff method is more favorable to small parties than that of D'Hondt.[5] This, however, is true only for D'Hondt's "unreformed" system in which the surplus votes receive no special treatment. Therefore, the reform of 1923 could not be said to have created a more advantageous position for the small parties. On the contrary, it lessened their chances; not only because of the—probably unconstitutional—decentralized allocation of the surplus votes, but also, most notably, because it required that a party gain at least one seat in one of the electoral districts before it became entitled to further allocations by virtue of its remaining votes.[6] Thus these deviations, which impaired the purity of the principle, furthered the general tendency toward the two-party system.

The proportional system accounted to a very large degree for the continuous presence of a strong minority in the Austrian parliament. Furthermore, as was generally recognized, it exercised a certain influence on the rate at which the relative strength of the parties in parliament changed. "Electoral revolutions" of the British type—in which a party with an overwhelming majority sometimes found itself reduced by one blow to a hopeless minority, only to rise again at the next elections—were ruled out in Austria. An additional element of significance was the fact that the "party of nonvoters"—the

[3] *StGBl.*, 1918, Nr. 115.
[4] *Ibid.*, 1920, Nr. 316, 351.
[5] Cf., for example, Georg Fleischer, *Oesterreichische Wahlreform* (Wien, 1929), p. 31.
[6] *BGBl.*, 1923, Nr. 367, esp. Art. 76.

old source of electoral surprises—was small at the outset and after some increase in 1920 became smaller and smaller from election to election. The percentage of nonvoters in national elections in 1920 was 19.73; in 1923, 13.05; and in 1927, 11.00.[7] Added to the proportional system as a deterrent to electoral revolutions was the fact that at least until 1927 the group of independent voters was quite small. In that year Seipel apparently forced many people out of the Pan-German group by his device of the Unity List so that the votes for it were 157,000 less than the combined Christian Social and Pan-German votes in 1923. This represented a drop from 58 to 49 per cent of the total valid ballots. Moreover, to move somewhat ahead of the story, the elections of 1930 showed that a number of voters had been attracted to the rising Fascist groups, chiefly the Heimwehr which for the first time offered candidates for parliament. Even these voters were in large part young persons casting their first or second ballot, so that it remains true that according to Anglo-Saxon ideas a disproportionately large number of people regarded themselves as convinced adherents of a once chosen party and considered voting for another an act of dubious moral quality. Still another among the more or less distinctive features of the Austrian political scene was the introduction, with the republican era, of the system of rigid lists (*gebundene Liste*) of candidates which virtually compelled a voter to give his ballot to a party rather than to an individual. Proponents of the scheme preferred to say that it required voting for a program rather than for a personality or an effective speaker. They also insisted that it had the advantage of bringing into the legislative bodies men and women who had been selected by their party organizations because of their experience, special abilities, and demonstrated willingness to work hard and conscientiously but who were not able to appeal successfully to the general public. Opponents attacked the plan precisely because the respective party executive committees actually chose the candidates and thus, in their opinion, hampered the free working of democracy. They claimed, moreover, that party hacks were too likely to worm their way into places on the lists so that the results were exactly the opposite of those stated by proponents.

As a result of the combined operation of the factors just described,

[7] *SHfRO.*, vol. 4, p. 140; vol. 8, p. 190.

it was the habit of Austrian political leaders, at least during approximately the first decade of the republic, to think more in terms of trends than fluctuations as significant for developments in the electorate; consequently, minor alterations which Britons or Americans would have considered quite likely to be reversed at the next elections gave rise in Austria to conjectures about long-run tendencies. A gain of two seats, which left the parliamentary situation exactly as it had been, was regarded as a great victory. But such thinking, particularly in an immature democracy containing strong elements that despised it, bore the germs that might easily prove fatal for democracy itself. Since behind the changes in the electorate observers believed they perceived underlying trends; since every change was supposed to be lasting, in the sense that it was unlikely to be reversed in the next elections, then what was more natural than that those groups which saw the—real or imagined—trend working against them should begin to moot plans for escaping the apparently inevitable eclipse. The idea of destroying the system, of jettisoning democracy, rooted itself in minds which were only too willing to receive it. Thus I come back to what was said above: the "two-party system"—for several decisive years the specific form of Austrian democracy—was bound to put the problem of democracy itself on the agenda of Austrian politics.

The foregoing generalizations are important to the discussion of the elections of 1923. As was brought out in Chapter XIV, they were fought largely under the slogan: "Reconstruction *versus* Tenants Protection." Their results changed the political situation to a degree which can only partly be accounted for by the numerical alterations in the votes and parliamentary seats secured by the individual parties. (See the table, p. 690.)

According to these data the Socialists succeeded in 1923 in wiping out most of the losses they had suffered in 1920. In absolute figures they obtained 100,000 votes more than at the "revolution election" of 1919; in percentages their share was only 1.16 per cent below the results of 1919. With reference to seats in the legislative body they did not do so well, since in 1923 they were still 2.1 percentage points below their position in 1919. Nevertheless, they could, and did, argue that the "trend" which had gone against them in 1920 had been reversed. Obviously, on the face of the figures, the Catholic party had a much more solid foundation for satisfaction. It had increased its percentage of votes by 9 and of seats by 10 between 1919 and 1923; moreover, it had done this without a slump in 1920. Thus its leaders could have claimed that the trend was steadily in its favor. The Socialists maintained that the proper way to measure the development was to compare their votes with those of the

CHANGES IN VOTES AND PARLIAMENTARY SEATS SECURED BY INDIVIDUAL PARTIES*

Party	1919		1920		1923	
	Absolute	Percentage	Absolute	Percentage	Absolute	Percentage
POPULAR VOTES AT GENERAL ELECTIONS						
Christian Socials....	1,068,382	35.93	1,245,531	41.79	1,490,870	45.00
Social Democrats...	1,211,814	40.76	1,072,709	35.99	1,311,870	39.60
Pan-Germans......	545,938	18.36	514,127	17.25	422,600	12.76
Other parties.......	147,920	4.95	147,961	4.97	87,266	2.64
Total..........	2,974,054	100.0	2,980,328	100.0	3,312,606	100.0
SEATS IN THE CONSTITUTENT ASSEMBLY (1919) OR IN PARLIAMENT (1920 AND 1923)						
Christian Socials....	63	39.6	85	46.5	82	49.6
Social Democrats...	69	43.4	69	37.7	68	41.3
Pan-Germans......	24	15.1	28	15.3	10	6.1
Other parties.......	3	1.9	1	0.5	5	3.0
Total..........	159	100.0	183	100.0	165	100.0

* *SHfRO*, vol. 1, pp. 3–4; vol. 3, p. 130; vol. 4, pp. 141–142.

combined non-Socialist parties. To some this may seem to be self-deception, but the historical willingness of bourgeois parties in all countries to join forces whenever a Socialist political organization developed threatening strength is too well established to permit the summary dismissal of the point. Actually, a correct appraisal of the psychological effects of the elections of 1923 hinges upon appreciation of the fact that the Christian Socials had been operating on the principle that the Socialist measuring rod was the proper one. They had entered the electoral campaign with hopes running high. They had presented themselves as the saviors of the country who had carried out the stabilization of the crown. They had cherished the thought that if only a few per cent of the total electorate could be taken from the Socialists, a non-Socialist majority of two-thirds would appear in the new parliament. The road would thus be open to radical changes in the constitution. A decisive victory won under the auspices of stabilization might have made the elections of 1923 the last occasion on which the Christian Socials had to expose themselves to a real decision of the people—a loathsome task for at least some elements in the party,[8] and elements that were destined to become stronger. Moreover, there were schemes against the bourgeois allies as well. It will be recalled that the Pan-Germans had played a miserable role in connection with the Treaty of Geneva in 1922. Their party had been compelled to lend active support to an international agreement which was in plain contrast with the avowed and almost sole important aim of its program—union with Germany. The Pan-Germans had a long quasi-liberal tradition in problems of education and marriage laws. For many years the regularly recurring riots between Catholic and nationalist university students had been fought by the latter under the slogan of a "school free from Rome." But in the republican parliament, at least since 1920, the Pan-Germans had to support a party which regarded the preservation of the indissolubility of Catholic marriage and the increase of Catholic influence in education as cornerstones of its policy. Was it unrealistic under these circumstances for the Christian Socials to hope that union with them would become disastrous for their ally?

The results of the elections of 1923 revealed that though this hope was exaggerated it was by no means devoid of foundation. The percentage share of the votes received by the Pan-Germans was reduced by about one-third; that of "other parties" dwindled down to almost one-half of what it had been. Aside from the recovery of the Socialists this shrinking of the so-called middle parties, that is, between the clericals and the Socialists, seemed to be the major outcome of the balloting. As will be shown, this tendency reached its climax in 1927; and though the elections of 1930 brought substantial increases in strength to parties other than the two major ones, there was, of course, no way of foreseeing that in 1923. Thus it may be

[8] Cf. Joseph Eberle, "Demokratie als Weg zum Bankrott," *Das Neue Reich,* vol. 3 (Nov. 14, 1920), 126: "The general franchise is in contradiction with the Christian sociology."

said that the Austrian variety of the two-party system appeared clearly by 1923 and that the struggle between the Christian Socials and the Socialists became the characteristic feature of the political life of the country for several years. To be sure, the middle parties were still there, and since the Christian Socials had not succeeded in obtaining even an absolute majority in parliament, the votes of the Pan-Germans were still needed for its current work; but the latter lacked by a great deal having a free hand in shaping a policy of their own. As has been brought out, the struggle against the Socialists was the center and most of the periphery of Seipel's policy. If the Pan-Germans refused to coöperate with the Christian Socials in parliament they had to reckon with sharp criticism from large and influential sections of non-Socialist public opinion for having betrayed the idea of a "bourgeois front" against the party of Bauer and Renner. And their refusal might easily have forced the Christian Socials to abandon Seipel's concepts and to revert to some sort of collaboration with the Socialists, either in an outright coalition cabinet, or in a Christian Social minority government supported by the Socialists. It may seem to some readers that the Pan-Germans might better have returned to opposition and, after four years of consistent criticism of the government, attempted to make good at the next elections the smashing losses they had suffered in 1923. But even had the Austrian electoral system been more favorable to such a course a policy of withdrawal into opposition would have been advisable only for a party with a distinct character and program. The Pan-Germans, however, had already surrendered their program. Moreover, they represented sociologically much the same group with the same tendencies, leanings, opinions, and interests as the "town wing" of the Christian Socials. Under these circumstances mere opposition against the government, not buttressed with an alternative constructive program, seemed of little promise. Finally, the Pan-German fraction in parliament obviously preferred a bird in the hand in the form of the various immediate advantages of participation in the government to a bird in the bush in the form of dubious future gains. Thus the Pan-Germans felt impelled to renew their coalition with the Catholic party. They did so as a powerless and little respected partner so that from the point of view of the basic constellation of the "two-party system" the fact that there were two parties on the government side was almost irrelevant. In Otto Bauer's whimsical phrase: "What difference did it make that a part of the Christian Socials called themselves Pan-Germans?"

After the elections of 1923 a fundamental problem of parliamentarism began to assume a sinister aspect. Can the system work efficiently and smoothly when there is an abyss between the governing and the opposing party? It can be imagined what would become of the "mother of parliaments" if, say, the Tories and the Communists were the two major parties in the House of Commons. What separated the majority and the minority in the Austrian Nationalrat in the period under consideration was certainly nothing like so far-reaching as this drastic comparison might indicate, but the abyss was there. On the one side was Seipel with his dominating idea that the restoration of the prerevolutionary status in some form should be the long-run objective of the non-Socialist parties of the country. Behind Seipel stood the mighty organization of the Roman Catholic Church in Austria, full of hatred—or righteous wrath—against the "godless ways" of Social Democracy. In their previously quoted pastoral letter of Advent, 1925, the Austrian bishops wrote: "The Savior gravely addresses these words to the workers: what do you gain when you obtain better working conditions, seize power in the state, establish a dictatorship over other strata of the population, and satisfy your craving for power—but at the same time forfeit your eternal salvation?! . . . Social Democracy is your destruction and the destruction of society."[9] Behind the prelate-chancellor also stood Austrian industry. Earlier chapters have described industry's formal resolution to solve the problem of inadequate influence in parliament "by instruments of force created particularly therefor," its struggle against the "social burden," its outbursts of fury against Vienna taxes and "welfare inflation," and its storms against the housing program. Under the impact of economic developments sketched at the beginning of this chapter, that is, the more remote the days of the inflationary fata morgana and the greater the pressure of the crisis, industry became increasingly convinced that its burdens were unbearable. But it also became increasingly convinced that under existing political arrangements its efforts to sabotage social legislation in the country and social policy in general in

[9] Cardinal Fr. G. Piffl *et al., Zu sozialen und kulturellen Fragen* (Wien-Leipzig, 1932), pp. 102–103, 107.

Vienna were unavailing. All this fitted to a nicety Seipel's idea of restoring the prerevolutionary status. And whatever he may have thought at this time, industry felt more and more that the change was not too dearly bought at the price of the inevitable disturbances of social peace.

On the other side stood Otto Bauer, Seipel's antagonist. The leader of Austrian Social Democracy had found warm and almost enthusiastic words for the postrevolutionary period of "equilibrium between the classes"; the idea of coöperation between the classes strongly appealed to him. But he wanted real coöperation. His sociologically disciplined mind was wont to search for social reality behind the screens of appearance. With his acute sense for power politics he refused in 1920 to lead the Socialist party back into a coalition in which it would have to play—*toutes proportions gardées*—the pitiable role of the Pan-Germans. What could have been the result of such a coalition? Further disappointment among the workers, rising discontent, expansion of the Communist party, transplantation of the internecine struggles in the working class to Austrian soil. Bauer felt deeply the implications of the fact that he had inherited the party leadership from Viktor Adler. With Adler, who had released the party from suicidal internal struggles and thus opened the road to a successful development, the unity of the organization was always a value in itself, a *conditio sine qua non* of the very existence of a political labor movement.[10] In his address to the 1927 party congress Otto Bauer found a drastic formula for expressing the same sentiment: "It is a hundred times better to go the wrong way united—for errors can be corrected—than to split in search of the right way!"[11] This meant that the preservation of the unity of the party was in itself the right policy. The labor movement in the sister country, Germany, was torn asunder beyond repair. In Czechoslovakia, the former comrades of Viktor Adler had to give a large part of their political energy to fights with Communists. Among the majority of European countries Austria seemed a happy island in this respect.

The collapse of the coalition in 1920 materially reinforced the

[10] Cf., for example, Adler's speech to the party congress of 1917, in *Victor Adlers Aufsätze, Reden und Briefe,* Heft 9 (Wien, 1929), p. 200; and *ibid.*, Heft 7, p. 50: "There is a principle which forms the basis of every proletarian policy: the principle of the unity of the organization."

[11] *Parteitag, 1927,* p. 128.

position of the party among the workers. But could this situation last? Could the party hope to grow and prosper in the role of continuous opposition? The revolution had aroused the will to power of the Austrian workers. They wanted a continuation of the reform work. They saw that the Austrian economy, prostrate in its doldrums, was able to solve neither the problem of wages, nor that of unemployment. They expected salvation from a "new deal" to be set in motion by the state under the energetic leadership of their party. A mere opposition, therefore, militant as it might be, would have had in the long run much the same disappointing effect as participation in a coalition government. The expectations of a large party with a membership five or more times greater than in prewar days were a social category of an altogether different character from the earlier expectations. Long inactive waiting periods are not devoid of danger even for a relatively small group. They are unendurable for a party of half a million, composed to a large extent of men discontented with existing conditions and desirous of new arrangements. The kinetic energy of the Communist party was negligible; its potential energies were never to be underrated. It had to be realized that "even though only 3 per cent of the Austrian workers are members of the Communist party, this does not mean that there are only so few people with a Bolshevist orientation in Austria."[12]

To be sure, thanks largely to the policy of the Vienna city council, even the period of opposition was not devoid of constructive work. But the psychological effects were complex. "Vienna" revealed that the Socialists were able administrators, that there were large possibilities for a creative social policy. What was being done in Vienna may have made the period of opposition more palatable to the workers. On the other hand, it was precisely the successful work of the city council which stirred up the masses and increased their impatience to see the rehearsal in Vienna repeated on the national stage.

The policy of Otto Bauer after the elections of 1923 was a composite of all these considerations. It implied the continuation of opposition. But the period must be short. In view of the remarkable recovery of the Socialists in the 1923 elections, as compared with

[12] Oskar Trebitsch, *In Moskau sass der Feind* (Wien, 1933), p. 75.

those of 1920, it could be argued with considerable plausibility that the "trend" was turning favorably for them. Tenants protection had proved a formidable weapon. There might have been much surprise in the success of 1923, but it appealed more to the minds of the political leaders to envisage it as an expression of the irresistibility of the Austrian working class. A period of four years lay before the party. In these four years the great effort was to be carried out. Three or four hundred thousand voters diverted from the bourgeois parties to Social Democracy would swing the decision. The peaceful conquest of power by the workers' party—not in a faraway future, but perhaps at the very next elections—was an objective worth striving for and likely to inflame the imagination of the people. With this aim in mind the otherwise so dangerous opposition could become politically endurable. Schism could be avoided and the unity of the movement preserved.

And, indeed, preserved it was. The ideological unity of Austrian labor was never greater than from 1923 to 1927. It was one of the most significant events of this period that during it the divergencies of opinion between the Social Democratic party and the free trade unions which had made themselves apparent after the revolution were reduced, practically speaking, to the vanishing point. Although, as indicated at the close of Chapter XI, there were isolated instances in which differences reappeared, the cementing job had been well done. Earlier difficulties have been discussed in previous sections. For the purposes of this chapter, however, it is necessary to review one issue on which the two organizations did not at all times see eye to eye: the problem of further participation in the government. The collapse of the coalition in 1920 did not meet with the full approval of the trade unions. When Bauer, in his main speech to the 1921 party congress, declared that the party was not willing to be forced into the coalition "by certain groups of the workers"[13] he meant precisely the opposition of the trade unions. This divergence persisted to a varying degree for almost three years after the final withdrawal of the Socialists from the government. Even as late as June, 1923, an outstanding trade-union leader, Frühwirth of the textile workers, sharply criticized Hueber for refraining from discussing the problem in his address to the

[13] *Parteitag, 1921,* p. 152.

trade-union congress: Hueber "did not explain which position the trade unions had taken toward the disruption of the compulsory coalition marriage with the Christian Socials. We trade-union men feel it on our own hides that it is not a matter of indifference for the proletariat whether it is our highly respected comrade Hanusch who sits in the ministry of social administration, or a Pauer or even a Schmitz (Very true!)."[14]

Hanusch replied: "Let us be glad that the coalition disintegrated. If this had not happened, considering the mood of the workers at that time, unpleasant consequences for the party and the trade unions could have resulted; at least splits might have taken place. I must frankly say that the whole governing business, in my eyes, is not worth the unity of the party and of the trade unions."[15]

Episodes such as this became practically impossible after the elections of 1923. The ideas that the opposition was to be considered as a transitory stage only, that after the acquisition of a clear majority in parliament far wider fields of reform work would be thrown open, and, most notably, the fact that Bauer's concept implied faithful adherence to democracy—all met with absolute approval in the unionists' camp so that they subordinated themselves willingly to the leadership of the party. The development was aided by the general economic situation in the country sketched in the first pages of this chapter. In this connection the table on page 698 reveals interesting divergencies in the numerical evolution of the membership of the party and of the trade unions.

The revolution's effect upon the membership of both groups was tremendous; for the sources (note to table, p. 698) indicate, without establishing, the fact that toward the end of 1918 both had about regained their 1913 levels so that the differences between the 1913 and 1919 figures in the table probably represent gains registered chiefly in 1919. In 1920 the party membership remained stable, but the trade unions increased their membership by more than 16 per cent. In 1921 both organizations registered a notable expansion. For the trade unions this expansion resulted from the continuation of the inflation boom; for the party the spectacular increase of more than 37 per cent was, beyond doubt, caused by the disruption of the coalition government. At that time the trade unions were numeri-

[14] Gewerkschaftskongress, 1923, *Protokoll*, p. 240.
[15] *Ibid.*, p. 265.

cally more than twice as strong as the party. As long as the government proved unable to check the inflation, the influx to the party continued and 1922 again marked an increase of about 20 per cent; in this year began, slowly, the downward movement in trade-union membership, indicating that the economic downswing of the later stages of the inflation had begun. From then on the membership of the trade unions kept continually decreasing except in 1927 when

MEMBERSHIP OF PARTY AND TRADE UNIONS*

Year	Party	Trade unions	Year	Party	Trade unions
1913	89,628	253,137	1926	595,417	756,392
1919	332,391	772,146	1927	669,586	772,762
1920	335,863	900,820	1928	713,834	766,168
1921	461,150	1,079,777	1929	718,026	737,277
1922	553,022	1,049,949	1930	698,181	655,204
1923	414,273	896,763	1931	653,605	582,687
1924	566,124	828,088	1932	648,497	520,160
1925	576,107	807,515			

* Pertinax [Otto Leichter], *Oesterreich 1934* (Zurich, 1935), p. 28; *Jahrbuch der österreichischen Arbeiterbewegung, 1932*, p. 79; Gewerkschaftsbund, *Jahrbuch, 1932*, p. 37; Gewerkschaftskongress, 1919, *Protokoll*, p. 17; *Parteitag, 1917*, pp. 38–39. The figures for 1913 were adjusted by Pertinax to include only the area of republican Austria. Data for 1914–1918, though reported in various sources, are more or less incomplete and inaccurate because of war conditions. So far as they are of value they indicate that the membership of the unions fell through 1916 and of the party through 1917. All union figures are as of December 31. Party figures are as of June 30 from 1913 through 1925; thereafter, as of December 31. Since they were unimportant for present purposes, the trade-union members unaffiliated to the central body were not included in the table. Cf. above, the table on page 271.

a slight improvement took place. This trend probably would have continued in 1928 had not it been interrupted by the rise of Heimwehr trade unions fostered by the employers, first and foremost by the big *Alpine Montan Gesellschaft*. By this time the free trade unions had lost more than one-quarter of their record membership in 1921.

The further development of the party membership was quite different. Here, too, 1923 marked a setback. The fact that Seipel and not Otto Bauer had stopped the inflation cost the party almost 139,000 members. But the elections of 1923 were a turning point. By the middle of 1924 the losses of the previous year were more than recouped and for five years there was a steady increase, all the more remarkable in that it was not interrupted in 1927. At the end of 1929 party adherents were not quite 20,000 less than trade-union members. This tendency helps to explain how, under the pressure of accumulating economic difficulties, the center of gravity in the labor movement shifted more and more toward the party and away from the unions. In the period under consideration the idea of the supremacy of the party within the movement became common among Austrian workers. The unions were increasingly regarded as the economic arm of an essentially political movement. On the whole they ungrudgingly acquiesced in this situation and concerned themselves, apart from their current work, chiefly with the difficult task of reorganization on the basis of industrial as distinguished from craft lines. From 1923 on for a good number of years Bauer could rely on their unconditional coöperation and, in matters of general policy, virtual subordination. This was obviously a great success from Bauer's point of view. Also within the party no significant voice of opposition was heard. Bauer's old opponent, Karl Renner, devoted his time and energies to the coöperatives and the newly founded Labor Bank so that the former's control over the party was practically unrestricted. Not only his influence but also his popularity among the workers grew from year to year. With great persistence he worked on his great objective. Tenants protection seemed to secure growing adherence within the urban middle class. The agricultural program of 1925 initiated a campaign intended to break the influence of the Christian Social party in the villages and to win the small peasantry over to Social Democracy. One year later the Linz party program was adopted: the struggle for the majority found its programmatic expression in the solemn declaration of the faithfulness of the party to the political system of democracy. The dictatorship of the proletariat was rejected except in the case of an attempt on the part of non-Socialist groups to overthrow democracy and establish a dictatorship of their own.[16] The debates in the famous party congress at Linz assuredly revealed differing shades of political conceptions, but they also showed that from Renner, outstanding right-wing leader, to Max Adler, chief representative of the left, the party was unanimous in approving the program drawn up by Otto Bauer and explained by him in two impressive three-hour speeches. Viktor Adler's heritage was apparently in good hands.

It seems clear, when looking over the general political development between 1923 and 1927, that had the policies of the non-

[16] The ideological significance of both programs is presented in some detail in Volume II, Chapter XXVII.

Socialist governments been more successful the hopes of the Social Democratic party might easily have been nipped in the bud. But the basic economic conditions of the country and the disastrous ineffectiveness of those governments combined to improve the chances of the Socialists. The stabilization of the currency had been popular. But what followed was likely to arouse the indignation of the populace. Mr. Zimmermann, the Commissioner General of the League Council, sat in Vienna. With Argus-eyed conscientiousness he watched over the financial policy of the republic. The virtue of Austrian *Gemütlichkeit* was foreign to the nature of the cool Dutchman. In his monthly reports he untiringly criticized the government, emphasized its shortcomings, demanded more and more economies, more and more sacrifices from all classes of the population. Kienböck had succeeded in an astonishingly short time not only in eliminating the deficit, but also in creating a large positive margin between expenditures and revenues. But Commissioner General Zimmerman pressed the government to stabilize the budget on a much lower level, insisted that the budget limits to which Seipel had agreed in Geneva be strictly observed, and took the position that until this was brought about the control had to continue. Almost every report snubbed the national pride of the Austrians so that gradually the Socialist press found itself less alone in voicing indignant protests against the treatment of the country. The government had hoped—and the government parties had made the people believe—that League control would be of short duration. From 1924 the Austrian ministers had to make pilgrimages to Geneva. And every time they had to come back, after having listened to sulky admonitions from the financial committee, and announce that not even a relaxation of the control could be obtained. The Socialist propaganda was not slow in giving the maximum of publicity to these fiascos.

Now whatever the merits of the Social Democratic criticisms may be, the position of the government was not exactly enviable. The attempts of the Commissioner General to obtain influence over the financial policies of the states led to some alignment of the Socialists with the Christian Socials there. As if to complete the difficulties a wave of social conflicts rolled over the country in 1924. Seipel was too clever a politician to let things develop to a situation which would greatly impair his personal position and prestige. On June 1, 1924, an unemployed man seriously wounded him; his recovery required weeks. Shortly after his reappearance in the chancellery the railroad men struck. Seipel declared that their demands endangered the work of reconstruction and resigned on November 8, 1924. It is probable that Chancellor Seipel hoped that this drastic action would provoke a storm of support all over the country, stifle the opposition in his own camp, and render a second Seipel government possible. The Vienna Christian Socials certainly pressed in this direction. Kunschak declared: "Behind Seipel stands the strong Christian Social party and for the party the problem is not, Seipel or another Christian Social chancellor, but, Seipel or no Christian Social at all! . . . We, Christian Socials, declare: For us there is no other chancellor but again our Doctor Seipel!"[17] But there is little doubt that the strike was only a pretext—all the more so because on November 13, 1924, it was settled by a peaceful compromise and the railroad men returned to work. Seipel conferred with the Christian Social state governors on the question of the participation of the states in national revenues, but the negotiations failed. On November 18, 1924, Ramek, a member of parliament from Salzburg, became chancellor of Austria. Thus Seipel was actually overthrown by a wing of his own party. The official declarations from him and his party obscured this fact only partly.[18] Kunschak's paper, with its bitter complaints against "the egotism of the states" which aided Breitner in his antigovernment policy, admitted the truth with an unusual amount of frankness.[19] Whether, in this situation, Seipel himself did not feel content to leave the burden of the government with his opponents in the party is another question. It was a promising plan to let them try to steer the ship through a sea of trouble and then in the right moment appear again as the savior of the country.

The return of the "states Christian Socials" into key positions in the ministry rendered more complex the political configuration in Austria. It has been shown that the states were the centers in which anti-Socialist private armies were being organized and equipped. Graz, Innsbruck, Salzburg were the strongholds of reactionary forces in Austria. The Styrian vice-governor Ahrer, who became minister

[17] *Reichspost,* November 10, 1924, p. 1.
[18] Cf., for example, *Reichspost,* November 21, 1924, p. 3.
[19] *Christlichsoziale Arbeiter-Zeitung,* November 22, 1924, p. 1.

of finance in the Ramek cabinet, was one of the chief organizers of the Heimwehr in his state. To a smaller extent the same was true of the Tirolese Thaller, the new minister of agriculture. Therefore, it would have been expected that once in the government the representatives from the states would have pursued with intensified vigor Seipel's anti-Socialist policy. This, however, was not so. The provincial Christian Socials were not only politicians; they were, to no less degree, businessmen. During the inflation and the succeeding stock exchange boom a situation developed, most notably in Styria under the aegis of Rintelen, the state governor, in which the connections between politics and profits became perniciously close. The dilemma of the state politicians was more or less as follows: they certainly wanted to get rid of democracy with its unpleasant and painful controls. But as long as democracy existed a prudent policy which did not harass the opposition too much was obviously advisable. Therefore, the "wild men" from the states chose a more conciliatory policy toward the Socialists; it is even possible that they would have welcomed a coalition with them.

By this time, however, the Socialists had already firmly embarked upon their campaign for the majority. The weakness and lack of competency displayed by the new government suited them perfectly well. To be sure they did not refuse to supply the government with constructive schemes. The interesting attempt to introduce a sliding tariff on corn sprang from a plan of Otto Bauer's. And there was, as a rule, much contact between the opposition and the government behind the scenes. But at the same time the sharp struggles over the tenants-protection issue provided much material for the Socialist attacks. Subsequently, the school problem (cf. Chap. XVI) led to grave conflicts and even temporarily to the severance of all personal relations between the leaders of the workers' party and members of the government. Nevertheless, it may be said that it was neither the economic crisis, nor the humiliating delays in the abolition of League control, not lifted until June, 1926, nor the ill-starred attempts of the government to destroy tenants protection which provided the propaganda quivers of the Socialists with their sharpest arrows.

Beginning in April, 1924, a great number of banks founded or managed by Christian Socials or Pan-Germans collapsed. In itself this would not have been so noteworthy; investigation revealed, however, that in the large majority of these cases there had been serious mismanagement, sometimes fraud, and almost always political corruption in widely varying forms. Most of these institutions had been founded in order to free the peasants from the domination of Jewish finance capital; that is, of the big banks.[20] The idea came very close to the "breaking-up of interest slavery" subsequently propagated by the Nazis with so much success before they came to power in Germany. This "practical anti-Semitism," as the Christian Socials had proudly styled the policy, assumed "in practice" rather strange aspects. When the banks got into difficulties it became known that in several cases Jewish capitalists had obtained great influence in them and sometimes even owned them. In numerous other instances in which the situation of such a "Christian" bank had become grave, the government put the big Jewish banks under severe pressure in order to induce them to lend their help to institutions which had been destined to fight them.[21] One of the first of such instances was that of the Agrarian Bank in Tirol.[22]

The crucial point is naturally not simply the political inconsistency involved, but the fact that political slogans had been used to induce the peasants' Raiffeisen institutions and other coöperatives to invest their funds in Christian Social banks. It is inappropriate in a volume of this character to essay a comprehensive survey of the sinister story of their life and death. Such a survey would deserve a long chapter in a history of morals during the inflation in Central Europe. Suffice it to recall the affair of the Central Bank of the German Savings Institutions because here the parliamentary investigations succeeded in disclosing facts, relations, and connections which render possible a deep insight into the moral corruption among large and influential sections of the ruling party in Austria.

---

[20] Cf. the speech of the Christian Social Gürtler in the Constituent Assembly: Konstituierende Nationalversammlung, *Protokoll*, April 28, 1920, pp. 2311–2312.

[21] It is worth noting that although the political representatives of the Roman Catholic Church in Austria applied to the large banks for help in the salvation of the clerical institutions, its ordained representatives continued to thunder against them: "The banking and credit organization, with stock exchange gambling, has become a poisoned tree. It serves the financial powers in order to exploit and rob the peoples, to take away almost all savings from the industrious and to drive wider and wider circles through poverty into complete dependence, and into a virtual slavery." From the previously quoted pastoral letter of the Austrian bishops, Advent, 1925, *Reichspost*, December 28, 1925, p. 2; Cardinal Fr. G. Piffl *et al., op. cit.*, p. 86.

[22] *Der österreichische Volkswirt,* vol. 18 (Oct. 31, 1925), 119.

Toward the end of June, 1926, it became known to the government that the Central Bank would not be able to survive the month. The government put the amount of 62.5 million schillings—a large sum for Austrian budgetary conditions—at the disposal of the institution in order to meet the prospective run. The Socialists moved the impeachment of the government for having ignored the budget rights of parliament, but merited the criticism they got from the *Volkswirt* for not having proceeded more energetically at an earlier date. Although the majority rejected the motion, a special parliamentary investigating committee was set up. Its records present a depressing contribution to the problem of the degeneration of democracy. Throughout the year and a quarter of his finance ministry Ahrer had propagated what he euphemistically called the bank-merger policy. This meant that political banks the mismanagement of which had brought them into difficulties were to be taken over by other banks in order to prevent the scandals from becoming public. Thus the Central Bank had been urged by the government to take over several banks, among them the Peasants' Bank of Lower Austria and the Styrian Bank of Ahrer and Rintelen. In order to make the unprofitable transactions more palatable the National Bank and the Postal Savings Institution supplied funds to the Central Bank which were deliberately given irrecoverably in order to cover the prospective losses. This was done despite the fact disclosed by the investigation that as early as 1924 Kienböck had warned his political friends against any connection with the Central Bank; in his judgment it stood at that time on the brink of ruin. The committee report shows that the Peasants' Bank, founded and managed by the most prominent Christian Social politicians of Lower Austria, such as Buresch, Stöckler, and Zwetzbacher, had attracted the funds of 554 Raiffeisen coöperatives and about 100 other agricultural coöperatives. The peasants had confidence in their political leaders. The overabundance of money thus assembled was used for bear speculations against the French franc and for purchases of real estate in the hope that tenants protection would soon be abolished. "Now we know why the representatives of the peasants took so much interest in the abolition of tenants protection!"[23]

---

[23] *Der österreichische Volkswirt,* vol. 19 (Oct. 9, 1926), 42. Cf. also the resolution of the Peasants' Federation of Lower Austria which demanded that the government begin

All the political leaders mentioned above had personally engaged in French franc speculations. They did it, interestingly enough, on a common account with a Polish Jew named Aberbach who subsequently left the country without paying his losses to the bank. Almost 6 million schillings were lost by the institution on such accounts and in a great number of cases the owners of the accounts were not even known to it. All this took place notwithstanding express prohibitions in the charter of the bank against transactions for the purpose of obtaining differential gains. That this type of management received sharp criticism before the committee probably goes without saying, but it is worth noting that one of the severest verbal castigations came from Reisch, president of the National Bank.

The case of the Styrian Bank was, if possible, still worse. Here again the connections between politics and personal profits for the politicians were the regular business of the day; here again the responsible leaders had thought it permissible to engage in French franc speculations. The politicians found a simple device for covering the debts to the bank. First the state government of Styria decided to buy the shares of a Styrian water-power company. The politicians and high officials of the state government acting as individuals purchased the shares. Next, in their capacity as owners and managers of the bank, they arranged for the bank to drive up the price of the water company's stocks. Finally, as members of the state government, they purchased the shares. The huge gains more than covered the old losses. Needless to say the whole operation was transacted at the expense of the state; that is, of the public. Even after the collapse of the Central Bank Rintelen's interventions succeeded in securing 400,000 schillings of federal government money for the Styrian Bank which, although owned by the Central Bank, was still formally independent. Streeruwitz, the representative of the government in the salvage operations on the Central Bank, mentions the cunning devices by which Rintelen tried to obtain even more government funds for the Styrian Bank.[24]

The investigation revealed, furthermore, the appalling careless-

"immediately" the abolition "by stages" of tenants protection. *Reichspost,* December 9, 1925, p. 4.

[24] Cf. Ernst Streeruwitz, *Springflut über Oesterreich* (Wien, 1937), p. 263.

ness and incompetency of Minister of Finance Kollmann, who succeeded Ahrer in the second Ramek government of January, 1926. Ahrer himself could not be questioned by the committee; he had gone to Cuba.[25] Evidence before the committee had disclosed the fact that the government had lent 21 million schillings to the members of the Federation of Banks at a low rate of interest on condition that they provide 500,000 schillings for the Styrian agricultural coöperatives—again *a fonds perdu*. The whole transaction was obviously an illicit favoring of organizations politically connected with the government party at the expense of public funds. The Central Bank got a fair share of the 21 million schillings and the money was subsequently lost when the bank collapsed. On cross-examination by the committee Kollmann stated definitely that all the banks were jointly responsible for the 21 million schillings. Half an hour later the committee established that each bank was responsible only for the amount it had received.[26]

The results of the investigation, only a small part of which have been summarized in the foregoing pages, were distressful for the government parties. A year earlier a similar committee had had to concern itself with the private business affairs of Mataja, then Christian Social minister of foreign affairs. Parallel with the investigation of the Central Bank ran the affairs of the Postal Savings Institution which had likewise participated in speculations of all kinds with the bank of Bosel (*Unionbank*), the notorious war profiteer. The result of these transactions was losses which at the time were estimated by the *Volkswirt* at 84 million schillings,[27] but which in all probability finally proved to be considerably higher. Attempts to settle the Bosel affairs of the Postal Savings Institution had materially increased the losses of the federal state and led to the common belief that the minister's connivance with Bosel's proposals was based on personal interests. In the previously cited memoirs

[25] In his memoirs published several years later Ahrer emphatically denied that he "fled." The *Volkswirt* wrote at the time that when his party "bethought itself of 'straightforwardness and purity' [*Zielsicherheit und Reinheit*], it sent him to America"; but subsequently apparently accepted his explanation that he had left Austria for family reasons. Jacob Ahrer, *Erlebte Zeitgeschichte* (Wien-Leipzig), 1930, pp. 261, 266, 279 *passim; Der österreichische Volkswirt,* vol. 19 (Oct. 9, 1926) 34; *ibid.,* vol. 23 (Jan. 3, 1931), 349.

[26] Cf. on the whole affair: Nationalrat, *Protokoll, Beilagen,* Nr. 675, II Gesetzgebungsperiode; *Der österreichische Volkswirt,* vol. 18 (Sept. 25, 1926), 1437, 1445–1450; *ibid.,* vol. 19 (Oct. 2, 9, 16, 23, 1926), 6–7, 13–17, 41–43, 69, 102.

[27] *Der österreichische Volkswirt,* vol. 19 (Nov. 13, 1926), 183.

Ahrer denied the charges and claimed to have concluded his disastrous agreements with Bosel with the full knowledge of Chancellor Ramek. With reference to the insinuations of bribery the *Volkswirt* expressed the judgment that Ahrer's indignation gave the impression of genuineness.[28] As is clear, it is scarcely possible to unravel completely the intricate skein of these affairs which ten years later led to the suicide of Buresch, meantime minister of finance and then governor of the Postal Savings Bank in Dollfuss Austria.

It was the general feeling of the public that the government parties had plunged the country into a sea of corruption. The Social Democratic party, however, had not remained absolutely aloof. There was an unpleasant business of faked invoices in the Tirolese Socialist coöperatives; there was the mysterious connection of the Social Democrats with Bosel, to whom they had sold the *Hammerbrotwerke*. There was, above all, the case of Eisler, member of parliament from Styria, who did not refuse to act as a lawyer for his state government and to accept a large fee for his services. As if this were not bad enough the national executive committee of the workers' party ruled that his actions had been compatible with his official position. This they most certainly were not. In the words of the *Volkswirt:* "If the Eisler case is not to become the beginning of the end of the hitherto unimpeachable moral integrity of Austrian Social Democracy, the decision of the party executive of September 30 must not remain the last word of the party in this matter."[29] Actually, it was not; the party later compelled Eisler to return the fee. More important, as indicated above, compared with what had been done by the other side, the difference in quantity and quality was so overwhelming, and most notably, the administration in Vienna was so nearly above all suspicion, that the general public rightly distinguished between individual cases of corruption and a corruptionist system.[30]

[28] Ahrer, *op. cit.*, pp. 150, 153; *Der österreichische Volkswirt*, vol. 23 (Jan. 3, 1931), 349.

[29] *Der österreichische Volkswirt*, vol. 19 (Oct. 2, 1926), 5.

[30] The personal composition of the Central Bank investigating committee is worth recording. Concerning the Pan-German Angerer and the Christian Social Buchinger nothing need be said here except that Angerer was an ordinary run-of-the-mine politician, and that Buchinger had done good work as minister of agriculture. The other two representatives of the Catholic party were Gürtler and Odehnal. During his ministry the former had been involved in an affair concerning speculation against the Austrian crown; Odehnal had been characterized by the *Volkswirt* as the man who had caused the federal state to lose more money than anyone else. The Socialist president

An outburst of indignation in the camp of the government parties was only partly prevented by political considerations. In October, 1926, Aemilian Schoepfer, an old-guard Christian Social member of parliament, published an article under the significant title: "State Policy and Private Policy."[31] In it he stressed the general duty of the Christian politician always to be aware of the common good and recalled the traditions of the former mayor of Vienna, Lueger, who refused to tolerate any corruption in the Catholic party. But most significant is Schoepfer's statement that these old traditions have gradually faded away. He admitted that the connection of banking with Christian Social politicians was then a "general subject of conversation" and concluded with the words: "If ever the old slogan of Lueger's, 'the purity of the party from any and every corruption and ruthless fight against it, whenever it occurs,' is realized—then and only then will the Christian people establish again the confidence which has been so badly shattered." Half a decade later his admissions were even clearer: "Mistakes committed in the purely political field by Catholic deputies or even by the whole party provide the most effective agitation material for the Social Democrats at the elections. With what vigor and with what success at earlier elections were the questions of tenants protection and of workers' insurance, as well as the participation of Christian Social leaders in bankrupt banks and similar affairs, played up!"[32]

On October 15, 1926, the Ramek cabinet resigned, to be replaced four days later by the second Seipel government. The plans of this ambitious man had ripened. Once again he could be hailed as the savior of the country, this time from corruption within his own party. He condemned what he called the "last effects of the inflation" and emphasized the necessity of forgetting the past and beginning a new life.[33] Prisching, the compromised governor of Styria

of the committee, Eldersch, was contaminated by close connections with Bosel. A second Social Democratic member, Eisler, was certainly not the most appropriate person to judge the activities of the Styrian Christian Socials. That the committee in spite of this dubious composition succeeded in unraveling as much of what had been going on as it did was a personal triumph for the third Socialist, Danneberg; in his case the sharpness of his eyes was not clouded by a bad conscience, and to his deep-probing questioning must go most of the credit for cleaning up these particular stalls in the Augean stables of corruption.

[31] Aemilian Schoepfer, "Staatspolitik und Privatpolitik," *Das Neue Reich,* vol. 9 (Oct. 9, 1926), 27–29.

[32] In A. Hudal, *Der Katholizismus in Oesterreich,* p. 454.

[33] Nationalrat, *Protokoll,* October 20, 1926, p. 3891.

had to go, but the Rintelen system was left unmolested. Instead, Seipel promised to make public in parliament the names of its members who had intervened with the government authorities on behalf of some person or institution. Faithful to this promise he read on November 20, 1926, a long list of interventions carried out by Christian Social and Pan-German representatives, including himself. This method of fighting corruption was generally derided as an attempt to secure publicity for the services of members of parliament and was never repeated by Seipel. But the adverse reaction did not disturb the artful politician. He was not at a loss to find other means to make people forget the unpleasant happenings. The Socialist press was crammed with caustic articles on bourgeois corruption in Austria. The investigation of the Postal Savings Institution promised to furnish even more dangerous material. Then Seipel proposed to the Socialists the bargain which has been discussed in the chapter on social legislation. Its gist was silence among the Social Democrats concerning the Postal Savings affair in return for prompt adoption of old-age insurance. The Socialists finally decided that they could not reject this tempting opportunity to secure in a few months a long-standing wish of the Austrian workers. It has been shown that, in fine, they were badly deceived. Nevertheless, time seemed to be working for them. Seipel felt that every month was precious and determined to hold as soon as possible the elections due some time in 1927. Moreover, the government could now use the old-age insurance proposals in its electoral propaganda.

Early in March, 1927, parliament dissolved itself and set the elections for April 24. Even before the elections were decided upon, Seipel had brought off another clever stroke against the workers' party. It was known to the government that in the days after the revolution the Socialists had hidden quantities of arms and ammunitions from the old army depots in the towers of the Vienna Arsenal. The Socialists claimed that an agreement concerning these stores existed between the parties.[34] Through an informer the government obtained exact knowledge of their location. On March 2, 1927, Vaugoin, minister of the army, who had held this post without interruption since 1922, ordered certain detachments of troops, all of them carefully selected Christian Socials, to occupy the Arsenal

[34] Cf. Pertinax, *op. cit.*, p. 42.

and to carry away the arms. It was an exciting evening in Vienna. Masses of workers gathered in front of the Arsenal. The lights went out. In the near-by barracks groups of soldiers still faithful to the Socialists tried to get into the streets and join the workers. And two miles away in the party house on the bank of the Vienna River the leaders sat discussing the situation. Shall we tolerate it or not? Shall we mobilize the Schutzbund, call a strike, prompt a decision by violence? Or, shall we wait quietly and take our democratic revenge at the elections? The latter opinion, which was much more consonant with the nature and character of the party, prevailed;[35] and, on the following morning, scornful articles in the Socialist press told the workers that only old rusty arms had been taken away. The connections between the coming elections and the action of the government were obvious. It was also fairly plain that the raid on the Arsenal was intended to counteract the effects of the anti-corruptionist propaganda which the Socialists had started again. The *Volkswirt* clearly understood the connections when it wrote: "Let us hope that at the next disclosure of a case of corruption which hits his party Herr Vaugoin will not give the command: Fire!"[36]

In spite of all efforts to exploit it, however, the Arsenal episode could not seriously affect the position of the Socialists. The government parties had accumulated too many sins; their policy had been too inefficient, incompetent, absolutely lacking in vitality. The unemployment situation was desperate. And against this the Socialists could emphasize the excellent work of the administration of the city of Vienna, which in spite of some irresponsible charges had maintained a reputation as outstandingly honest and efficient; the period from 1923 to 1927 had been filled with constructive work. The Vienna city council had dissolved itself on the same day as did parliament and had set the election for the new council on the same day as the general elections. Weeks before, as noted in the chapter on Viennese taxes, the Christian Socials had started a violent campaign against the Breitner system, including vigorous obstruction in the council during the debates on the budget. Now their electoral

[35] Cf., for example, the comment of the *Volkswirt:* "But at the same time he [Seipel] also proved, contrary to his intention, that the Social Democratic opposition, whose sense of responsibility alone prevented an open clash, is much more faithful to democracy and the constitution than the Christian Socials would like it to appear." *Der österreichische Volkswirt,* vol. 19 (March 12, 1927), 629.

[36] *Ibid.*

placards depicted Breitner as an enraged devil towering over the subjugated city and waving a terrible scourge each tail of which represented one of the city taxes. But Seipel himself felt that in view of the general situation this was far from being an adequate basis for an electoral campaign. The government was in want of a broader program. This was found in the idea of anti-Marxism. To mobilize against the forward-driving Socialists all non-Socialist forces of the country, to stir up the last reserves of the bourgeois electorate, to lead them in the great battle against the *Austrobolschewiki*—this was Seipel's electoral program. Ideologically it was not essentially new. The concept of anti-Marxism had played a major role in 1922 and 1923 and had never disappeared completely from the political stage. But the technical execution was new. With great persistence and patience Seipel bent every energy to pushing his program of uniting everything and everybody non-Socialist in a Unity List. A long bargaining about the places on the election lists ensued. Finally Seipel succeeded. He had brought together on his Unity List not only the Christian Socials and the Pan-Germans, but also small groups like the Middle Class People's party, the Monarchists, a part of the Nazi party, and another nationalist group. The Agrarian League had refused to join Seipel and expected to make gains by basing its propaganda among peasants on the corruption charges against the Christian Socials. A Catholic professor of theology at the University of Graz, Ude, had founded a party which proposed to fight against corruption and for the reëstablishment of cleanliness in political life. Ude's name headed his party list. But at this juncture the Church intervened on Seipel's behalf. Early in March, 1927, the bishop of Seckau (Graz) prohibited Ude from attacking the Christian Social government and from propagandizing for his party on the ground that a professor of theology had to devote all his time to his teaching. Quotations from a papal encyclical reinforced the order. Incidentally, Seipel also was a professor of theology. The prohibitions were lifted on March 28, but a fortnight later Ude was forced to withdraw his candidature—allegedly because he had not applied for the permission of the Church as prescribed by canon law. At any rate, Ude's party was decapitated.[37]

[37] Cf. *Arbeiter Zeitung*, March 3, 1927, p. 4; *Neue Freie Presse*, March 28, 1927 (P.M.), p. 2, April 13 (A.M.), p. 4, April 14 (A.M.), p. 5. The last-cited issue of the *Presse* reports the public statement by Ude that he had been offered money to join the Unity List.

The electoral campaign was the fiercest ever fought in Austria. The whole population seemed to be divided into two camps: Socialists and non-Socialists. Techniques of modern propaganda unheard of before in Austria were used. Finally the big day came. It brought the results set out in the table below. For ease of comparison, data on the distribution of parliamentary seats in 1923 are also included.

RESULTS OF THE ELECTORAL CAMPAIGN OF 1927*

Party	Popular votes, 1927		Seats in Parliament	
	Absolute	Percentage	1927	1923
Unity List	1,756,761	49	85†	..
Christian Socials	....	..	73	82
Pan-Germans	....	..	12	10
Social Democrats	1,539,635	42	71	68
Agrarian League	230,157	6	9	5
Other parties	114,973	3	..	..

* *SHfRO.*, vol. 8, p. 192. These official figures were rounded off to the advantage of the Unity List; actually, it received only 48.2 per cent of the votes. The Socialists polled 42.3 per cent.

† This figure 85 is, of course, the sum of the seats of the Christian Social and Pan-German groups.

The Christian Socials lost 9 seats; the Pan-Germans, who otherwise would probably have been annihilated, gained 2 seats because of favorable places Seipel had granted them on the electoral lists. The Agrarian League was able to harvest 4 additional representatives out of the peasants' indignation with the Christian Social methods of dealing with their money. The Socialist group was augmented by 2 representatives from Styria, the center of Christian Social corruption, and 1 from Vienna. In terms of votes, as mentioned earlier, the Unity List fell 157,000 below the combined results for the Catholics and the Pan-Germans in 1923. And this, in spite of Seipel's efforts to drag in every non-Socialist, including—a fact which merits particular emphasis—the Nazis. The workers' party gained 228,000 votes in these four years. Otherwise expressed the figures show that the Unity List attracted only 48.2 per cent of the voters as contrasted with 57.8 for the Christian Socials and Pan-Germans in 1923, and that the Socialists received 42.3 per cent as against 39.6. By 1930, to get ahead of the discussion again, the clerical party had dropped to 35.7 per cent of the vote, or two-tenths of 1 per cent less than it received in 1919. Though there were no more parliamentary elections, local balloting in 1932 revealed that the clerical party had again lost heavily. Whether or not Seipel correctly foresaw this development is, of course, speculation; but it is indisputable that his actions after 1927 were consistent with a realization that the "trend" was against his party.[38]

For a short time it looked as if the Catholic party and the Pan-Germans would be unable to carry on the government as in the old coalition; five votes were scarcely enough for a safe majority. Within the largest bourgeois party the disappointment was great and Seipel's Unity List was severely attacked as a bad mistake which had cost the party valuable seats in parliament.[39] But the great tactician very soon took his revenge by persuading the Agrarian League, despite its ruthless attacks on his party during the campaign, to join the government. Again the Socialists were a strong, but isolated, minority in parliament. So nothing was changed? Not quite. To be sure the Socialists' hopes of obtaining a parliamentary majority had been frustrated. But despite the utmost efforts of their enemies they had been able to win three seats; they represented now a little more than 42 per cent of the population. The non-Socialist storm against "Red Vienna" had been beaten off. The party had even increased its majority in Vienna. The elections of 1927 were not the great victory it longed for—but they were a victory. They showed that the party was on the march; its self-confidence had been strengthened. To intensify the propaganda, to improve the organizations, to persuade more people, to fight the government, to disclose mercilessly its shortcomings, to continue and expand the practical work in Vienna—this remained the program of the Socialists. A little more patience, a great deal more work, and the final victory would be theirs. Unfortunately for them Seipel also saw that Social Democracy was on the march.

---

[38] *SHfRO.*, vol. 1, p. 4; vol. 12, p. 210; *Jahrbuch der österreichischen Arbeiterbewegung, 1930*, p. 174. The *SHfRO* again rounded off the figure for the Christian Socials to 36 in 1930, though it had not given them such advantage in 1919.

[39] Cf. Leopold Kunschak, *Oesterreich 1918–1934* (Wien, 1935), p. 87.

PART FOUR:
THE TURNING POINT?

CHAPTER XX

July 15, 1927

Pressure produces counterpressure. The applicability to social life of this law of Le Châtelier has become a truism. But the nature of counterpressure, the forms it assumes, the speed at which it develops present such a multiplicity of varieties that an exhaustive sociology of countermovements remains to be written. An accident of history willed it that the events of the summer of 1927 in Austria should become a focus for the rays of a countermovement. By looking through the lens of "July 15" there is hope of obtaining a deeper insight into the development of hostile spirits raised by Austrian Social Democracy and also into the nature of the crisis of democracy in Austria.

In any democracy the existence of antidemocratic groups presents an intriguing problem. This is particularly true in a young democracy where the revolutionary act of the breach of the old constitution is still vividly present in the memory of men. Earlier in this study references were made to the plans of Monarchist groups in Vienna a relatively short time after the revolution, to the formal resolution of industrial and banking interests to create "instruments of force" the purpose of which was to destroy parliamentarism, to the shift of the center of gravity of these antidemocratic activities to the states. Nevertheless, a considerable number of small groups with partly varying interests remained in Vienna. For a while they did not make themselves conspicuous, but after Seipel's stabilization victory in the fall of 1922 they blossomed out. At that time the individual groups had little mutual contact. Some called themselves Front Fighters (*Front-Kämpfer*), the ex-service men; others, Swastika Men; still others flatly stressed their pro-Habsburg character. The most important group was the Heimwehr, itself containing divergent tendencies. But all of them had one common emotional bond: bitter hatred against democracy and the republic. A major tactic consisted in arranging meetings, with a special predilection for provocative gatherings in working-class districts housing an overwhelmingly Socialist population. Most of these groups also excelled in anti-Semitic demonstrations, such as lightning raids on *cafés,* beating pedestrians whom they believed to be Jews, and so on.[1]

The response of the workers to a meeting of people they considered reactionaries and Monarchists was, as a rule, quick and violent. They did not bother themselves about what went on in the inner districts of the city, but they resented any appearance of Front Fighters or Swastika Men in the vicinity of their homes. Crowds gathered before the building where the meeting was being held and, in many cases, the police urged its dissolution on grounds of public order and security. Then, the participants left under a hail of insults, sometimes of stones; occasionally a few of them got thrashed. The feelings of the small group retiring from the wrath of hundreds can easily be imagined: rage of the defeated, fear that the wild threats they heard might be carried out. The majority of the individuals belonging to Swastika groups or, strangely enough, even to the so-called veterans' organizations, were quite young, frequently boys under twenty. Their self-control was in itself not great. It had been further decreased by the general ideas of violence which were rife in these organizations. In Germany their brethren in spirit terrorized the democratic elements and one leader of the republic after the other fell victim to the bullets of assassins. In Austria, Hugo Bettauer, a left journalist and novelist was murdered in this way. When going out to meetings in workers' districts the youngsters were equipped with long-range pistols, "Just to give the men a feeling of safety" as an organizer of such a group explained once in court.[2] The results of these ever-recurring situations were not surprising. Time and again rage, or panicky fear, or both, pulled the trigger and the blood of workers stained the streets. Thus, in February, 1923, the works councillor, Birnecker, was killed and two other workers seriously wounded in a proletarian district in the west part of Vienna; in May, 1923, a railroad worker, Still, was killed in the Favoriten district of the capital; in September of the same year 30 Swastika Men from Vienna came to a little industrial village some fifteen miles out of the city: the death of a seventeen-year-old worker, Kowarik, was the spoil of the day. On May 22, 1925, Vienna

[1] Cf., for example, *Neue Freie Presse,* July 18, 1925 (A.M.), p. 7; (P.M.), p. 3.
[2] *Ibid.,* May 19, 1923 (A.M.), p. 10.

ex-service men assembled in the small near-by town of Mödling, stormed a workers' street there and, firing their guns, seized a Socialist city councillor, Müller, and mistreated him with knives and spades in such a manner that he died later in a hospital.

Then came the trials. In each case the court was confronted with that difficult situation common to all mob actions. There was no doubt that manslaughter, perhaps murder, had been committed. But how to ascertain that precisely those individuals sitting in the dock, who were only a part of the band of firing men, were responsible for the crime that had occurred? Then, how to learn who among the defendants had fired the fatal bullet? Moreover, the accused always claimed that the wounds had been inflicted by the misdirected shots of the party comrades of the victims. Probably needless to add they also invariably claimed that they had acted in self-defense. It was not easy to reconstruct what had happened in some ill-lighted street in the suburbs from the testimony of witnesses whose minds at the time of the event were naturally agitated by fear, hatred, and excitement. But it is also fair to note that all too often the men who had to pronounce judgment "in the name of the republic" felt undue sympathy with the youths in the dock. As old servants of imperial Austria they frequently lacked the conviction that the new democratic state stood on a firm legal basis; their rearing, their environment, their social position were likely to prejudice them in favor of the accused. Some of them were more or less definitely adherents of the Heimwehr or the Nazis. The more politicized the country became, the more difficult it was for them to preserve the impartiality of justice. The outcome of the trials was a composite of all these circumstances and considerations.

In the Birnecker case the chief accused received the light sentence of two years in prison; his comrades received a few weeks of detention.[3] Of the five men charged with the death of Kowarik, two were cleared and the other three convicted only of the illegal possession of firearms. They were assessed a fine of about $1.50 each but excused from paying it because they had been held for some time in "examination custody."[4] During the Still trial the chief defendant, one Herterich, declared himself to be a National Socialist. Before

[3] *Ibid.*, May 20, 1923 (A.M.), p. 18.

[4] *Ibid.*, December 12, 1923 (A.M.), p. 12.

his death the victim had identified Herterich as the man who had wounded him. But the Nazi was found guilty only of illegal possession of arms and of a "violation of bodily security." His punishment was again a fine of $1.50, but again it was excused for the same reason as in the Kowarik case. The second defendant, Nosko, was fined 75 cents for unlawful carrying of arms—excused for the same reason. "The guilt in the death of the unhappy Karl Still remains unatoned for," wrote the *Presse*.[5] The two chief defendants in the Mödling trial were sentenced to one year and eight months imprisonment, respectively; it was again the same paper which spoke editorially of the "remarkable clemency" of the punishment.[6]

When even non-Socialist papers deplored the mildness of sentences in trials for political murder, there can be little wonder that the Social Democratic newssheets foamed with indignation at these "emanations of class justice."[7] Naturally, they never forgot to stress that it was always the workers who lost their lives in such clashes.[8] These articles found a passionate echo amongst the Austrian and particularly the Viennese workers. "We have created this state and now it does not give satisfaction for the spilt blood of our comrades"—this was the phrase that could be heard in the factories and in workers' meetings.

Was this attitude justified from a democratic point of view? Did the clashes between workers' crowds and armed groups of their opponents originate in *prima facie* instances of highhanded interference by the workers with the exercise of their democratic rights by Monarchists, National Socialists, and other rightist bodies? Or, did the latter bear the ultimate responsibility because they deliberately and provocatively arranged their meetings in proletarian

[5] *Ibid.*, May 20, 1924 (A.M.), pp. 9, 10.

[6] *Ibid.*, December 19, 1925 (P.M.), p. 1.

[7] Cf., for example, *Arbeiter Zeitung*, December 12, 1923, p. 1, and December 20, 1925, p. 2.

[8] Against this contention opponents cited the case of Mohapl, a member of the Nationalist sport association. While watching the funeral procession of ex-Mayor Reumann on August 1, 1925, he had the misfortune to burst out laughing at the antics of a married couple who stood near by. The crowds misunderstood the meaning of his amusement and threatened him; the young man fled, but was overtaken and stabbed to death by one Seidl, a member of the underworld. The whole scene occurred in the vicinity of Prater Stern, the center of the Vienna "apaches." The *Presse* emphasized the fact that this was not a political crime and put the blame for the disturbance which had led to Mohapl's flight on the shoulders of the Hitlerites who at that time terrorized the streets of the city and were responsible for what the paper called "the atmosphere of irritation." Cf. *Neue Freie Presse*, August 2, 1925 (A.M.), p. 1, and August 3 (P.M.), p. 1.

districts? No simple answer to these queries is possible. In any democracy the moment may arrive when the denial of democratic rights to certain groups becomes vital to the maintenance of democracy. An old and well-established democracy may well announce through the mouth of one of its highest servants: ". . . we should be eternally vigilant against attempts to check the expression of opinions that we loathe." But even Justice Holmes, the author of these ringing words, found it necessary to qualify them immediately by adding: ". . . unless they so imminently threaten immediate interference with the lawful and pressing purposes of the law that an immediate check is required to save the country."[9]

In a young democracy the problem is far more complicated. A thoroughly democratic constitution per se does not transform a country into a ripe democracy. On the contrary there is a question of the wisdom of adopting a radically democratic constitution in a country that lacked democratic traditions. But clearly in such a country it is not always the rule that the democratic constitution will form under all circumstances the basis upon which conflicts between individual groups of the society are fought and solved. Moreover, the Austrian republic was a postrevolutionary state. Whether what happened in 1918 was a revolution or a collapse is immaterial in this connection. The workers were convinced, rightly or wrongly, that they had overthrown the monarchy and erected the republic in its stead. No revolution of any significance was ever milder in its treatment of the friends of the *ancien régime.* A *ci-devant,* a lamp post, and a rope had been closely associated notions in the great French Revolution; but no Monarchist was put in prison, let alone to death, in the course of Austria's transition to the republican form of government.[10] The imposing monuments of imperial history stood unmolested in the streets and squares of the capital. The example of the Russian Revolution, which had destroyed or removed so many of the symbols of Czarist Russia, found no imitation in Austria, for acts of revolutionary vandalism remained practically unknown there. But although the Socialist leaders succeeded through laborious processes of education in making the workers grasp the necessity for respecting the political rights

[9] *U. S. Supreme Court Reports,* vol. 250 (1919), 630.

[10] It is significant that the most frequent complaint, read or heard, against the republicans was that they tore the insignia from the coats of former imperial officers.

of representatives of those parties which like the Christian Socials and the Pan-Germans at least officially professed their recognition of the republic, the Viennese masses were never convinced that Monarchist opinion had the right to display itself freely. In this they were supported by the leadership of the party since it had founded its military organization, the *Republikanischer Schutzbund,* precisely for the purposes of fighting attempts at restoration and other forms of counterrevolution.[11]

Particularly since Hitler's accession to power it has become more and more common to argue that it is of questionable value to apply indiscriminately measurements borrowed from an ideal concept of a democratic state to definite historical situations; in other words, that it may well happen that the guardian of democracy has to resort to undemocratic methods in order to strengthen democracy. Even those who are not prepared to share this view have to recognize the fact that this was how the problem presented itself to the masses of the Socialist party membership.[12]

Still another point cannot be overlooked in appraising the psychological effects of the clashes with reactionary minorities and of the subsequent acquittals of those who had made such disastrous use of their arms.[13] Exertion of power by a social agent presupposes that he is conscious of his power. But very frequently there is a discrepancy between the amount of power in reality and in the imagination of a social group; both underestimation and overestimation may occur. The history of social movements and, most notably, of revolutions is crammed with examples of such psychical maladjustments and their momentous effects. The Austrian working class labored under an overestimation of its power in the years prior to 1927. This mental attitude was partly a holdover from the early years of the

[11] It is worth noting that this necessity was admitted by at least one leader of the Christian Social party. Cf. the speech of Drexel, Nationalrat, *Protokoll,* July 27, 1927, p. 233. After some remarks concerning his observation of the Schutzbund and the reasons for it, he continued, "I was told: because of the Monarchist danger. I made inquiries. There were people who wanted to restore the monarchy, one way or another! Sometimes in a fantastic way. As long as this was true I had to admit the right of the Schutzbund to exist...."

[12] In this connection it is perhaps also useful to remember the role which the original concept of democracy as the rule of the demos continued to play throughout the era of modern democracies. The old association of democracy with the rule of certain classes of the population still occupied the popular mind although disproved by the facts.

[13] It must be noted that, with some help from Socialist propaganda, the mild sentences also were usually transformed in the memory of workers into outright acquittals.

revolution and partly a discounting of the expected Socialist victory at the polls. The bequests of the revolution included the belief that the general strike was invincible; the belief that the armed might of the state could not be used against the workers because of the large Socialist majorities in the army, police, and gendarmery; the belief that there was a great qualitative difference between the well-organized and geographically concentrated proletariat and the non-Socialist population dispersed in the little provincial cities, in the Alpine villages and hamlets. From year to year on May 1 and on November 12 hundreds of thousands responded to the call of the party. The masses of the opponents were unseen. Only the electoral records revealed that they were still there. But crowds do not like to think in facts and figures. It is the language of images that they prefer. Such manifestations of the number and the discipline of the workers' party membership were naturally likely to inflame the imagination of the masses. They greatly aided in raising the hope for a coming electoral victory almost to a certainty[14]—perhaps even to a higher degree than did the whole economic and political development of the country between 1923 and 1927 sketched in Chapter XIX. It was a striking, but under the given circumstances almost natural, illusion that made the Austrian workers feel themselves to be, in anticipation, the masters of the republic. The stronger this feeling grew, the more bitterly the workers resented acts of violence directed against them, the more passionately they demanded revenge from the courts, the more suspiciously they watched the work of the machine of justice.

And this machine began to creak dangerously. Indeed, to change the figure, the blindfold on the eyes of the Austrian Themis was becoming strangely transparent when wishes and desires of the government were on the horizon. No state prosecutor could be found to indict the prominent members of government parties who had been responsible for the tremendous sums from private and public funds lost and wasted in dark transactions. The trial of the director of the Anker bakery has been mentioned (above, Chap. XII, p. 328).

[14] To be sure, the certainty of *final* victory is a feeling generally typical for the psychology of Socialist, and particularly of Marxist masses. Cf. Robert Michels, "Psychologie der antikapitalistischen Massenbewegungen," *Grundriss der Sozialökonomik*, vol. 9, pt. 1 (1926), 288–300. But what the historian of this period perceives in Austria was the belief in an *almost immediate* victory.

At that time the government hoped to draw political benefit from the unsavory affair by dragging the managers of the Socialist Hammer bread concern into the dock also. As recounted, the Socialists perceived the danger and sold the factory in a hurry. Meanwhile the accused director had been sentenced to a stupendous fine, which under the existing laws went to the city of Vienna. The natural result would have been a strengthening of the despised Breitner system, and so an attempt was made to change the law in parliament. When this failed the judgment was rescinded.[15] In 1926 the editor of a super-radical newssheet in Vienna, Alexander Weiss, was convicted of extensive extortions. The Christian Social press exulted in the sentence. But immediately after the trial the resourceful man changed over to the government camp and founded several papers in which he fought the left as viciously and unscrupulously as he had the right a short time before. His calculations proved correct. The execution of the sentence was postponed several times and then every facility was offered so that he could carry on his editing job from prison. The *Volkswirt* commented bitterly that the administration had "made the sacred office of justice a farce" and spoke of numerous criminals left at large if the prosecution was against the wishes of the ruling circles.[16] It was a dangerous path. *Justitia Regnorum Fundamentum* was the inscription Emperor Franz I of Austria (Franz II of H.R.E.) had ordered chiseled above the gates of his palace. With confidence in justice vanishing the foundations of the republic threatened to give way.

The year 1926 brought no major disturbance of peace. What the workers considered a series of deliberate murders seemed to have been discontinued. In Vienna the forces of reactionary violence had entrenched themselves only at the University. The situation in this microcosm appeared to be exactly the converse of that in the rest of the capital. The revolutionary traditions of 1848 in the student body had long since petered out. With the connivance of academic authorities Nationalist students had, as early as 1921, prevented Socialist leaders from delivering speeches in the University buildings. The organization of German students was given facilities for target practice on University premises. As was brought out in Chapter XVII, the autonomy of the University, once a liberal measure, for-

[15] Nationalrat, *Prokotoll,* July 26, 1927, p. 180.
[16] *Der österreichische Volkswirt,* vol. 19 (July 23, 1927), 1149.

bade the police to enter the buildings and at more or less regular intervals Socialist and Jewish students were dragged out of classrooms and severely beaten. This situation seemed so strange an anachronism in the Vienna of 1926 that time and again during these "beating periods" factory workers threatened to march to the University in order to "give a lecture in practical politics to the drinking, duelling, and rioting good-for-nothings."[17] But the representatives of the party and the unions always managed to dissuade their colleagues from taking such action. Thus the University remained in the heart of "Red Vienna" a "breeding place of reaction" and a source of irritation to the workers.

General election campaigns are a period when political passion runs high, and not only in countries plagued by the infantile diseases of democracy. The apprehension of those who had expected some revival of the unhappy clashes in the electoral year 1927 were only too soon to be justified. On the evening of January 30, 1927, even before the date of the elections had been definitely agreed upon, extras sold in the streets of Vienna told the story of a new disaster. A worker and a worker's child had been killed and several persons injured. The place of the tragedy this time was not Vienna, nor was it in the immediate vicinity of the capital. It was Schattendorf. The name of this tiny, obscure village in Burgenland, hard on the Hungarian border, will never be erased from the annals of the republic. For what happened there on a clear winter Sunday was but a prelude, or a proximate cause, to the catastrophe which was to shake the country to the roots a few months later.

The story of Schattendorf, as far as it can be reconstructed from conflicting reports and the contradictory evidence at the trial, may be summarized as follows. Burgenland, so belatedly incorporated in the Austrian republic, was still a center of unrest. Hungary never acquiesced in the loss of West Hungary, as the territory had been called as long as it was ruled by the crown of St. Stephen. Irredentist propaganda from across the boundary never ceased; in fact, it increased as years went by and reached an unprecedented intensity just about the time of the events in Schattendorf.[18] Burgenland was

[17] Even in 1937 I heard frequent references to these episodes from workers and former students.

[18] Cf. the speech of the deputy of the Agrarian League, Professor Schönbauer, Nationalrat, *Protokoll,* February 3, 1927, p. 4520.

administered by a coalition of Social Democrats and Christian Socials. In view of the precarious situation of the border state both parties agreed to abstain from building up any private military formations there in order to avoid occurrences which might be used as a pretext by Hungary. For several years the agreement was observed, but in 1926, so the Socialists charged, organizations of the Front Fighters pentrated Burgenland. Only then were formations of the Schutzbund established.[19] The policy of the Christian Socials with respect to Burgenland had always been ambiguous. The hopes of the preponderant majority of the party for a Habsburg restoration dictated a friendly policy toward Hungary. "We have to look where our waters flow"; in this cryptic language Seipel once expressed his preference for intensified coöperation with the neighbor to the east. The infamous affair of the French franc forgeries in Hungary in 1926 revealed the close connections between Hungarian reactionary circles and the Styrian Christian Socials. In Burgenland itself the majority of the Catholic party seemed to reject pro-Hungarian propaganda. They were not unconditionally convinced of the value of the Front Fighters despite the fact that the central organization of this "veterans' " group enjoyed the full support of their party and its press. But the owners of big estates, mostly Hungarians, and the intelligentsia in the little towns and villages were obviously dissatisfied with the Austrian administration. They saw that across the border people in their social position were still the Úrember, the "master men," infinitely superior to the masses of small peasants and laborers; members of their groups were just the persons who managed to obtain the leadership in the new Burgenland Front Fighters' organizations. On the other hand, many individuals in Burgenland suspected that the veterans' formations were in touch with Irredentist circles in Hungary, and consequently they considered the activities of the former a much more serious and immediate threat to the democracy of their state. This accounts for the particularly bitter feeling among the Socialists against the Front Fighters. Naturally, the tension was greatest in the immediate vicinity of the border. There passions ran high and weekly clashes

[19] Cf. Renner's remarks in parliament: Nationalrat, *Protokoll,* February 3, 1927, pp. 4505–4507. No attempt to rebut these contentions was made during the debate. Locally, that is, in Schattendorf, the fact that the foundation of the Front Fighters' group had preceded that of the Schutzbund was admitted by a member of the former organization. *Neue Freie Presse,* July 5, 1927 (P.M.), p. 3.

between the inimical groups were rapidly becoming a substitute for Sunday entertainment. On New Year's Eve, 1926, Front Fighters fell upon a peaceful social gathering of Social Democrats in a little village near Schattendorf. The inn was badly damaged and several persons wounded. Two of the attackers were arrested and brought to a small city, the seat of the district court. Thereupon Front Fighters besieged the court building for two days and finally forced the release of the culprits.[20]

It was this atmosphere of lawlessness and violence that foreshadowed the events of January 30 in Schattendorf, a typical "street village" of the Danube plains, situated so close to the border that the spires of the Hungarian town of Ödenburg were clearly visible from the church square. A Front Fighters' meeting was arranged by their Vienna headquarters for this date in Schattendorf so that local members expected visitors from adjoining villages and from the capital. On the morning of January 30, however, two meetings were announced by the local town crier; the Schutzbund had also decided to assemble. They likewise invited their comrades in the surrounding villages, and there is little doubt that they were determined to prevent their opponents from gathering. The respective headquarters of the parties were in inns situated but a few hundred yards apart. When the Front Fighters became aware of the intentions of the Schutzbund they placed several rifles and a supply of cartridges in a second-floor room of the dwelling of the proprietor of their inn; its barred windows commanded the village street. Then the frictions began. A number of Schutzbund men appeared in the hostile "fortress." Although they sat there peacefully enough drinking wine, their very entrance constituted a provocation. Only when additional members of the Front arrived did a dispute begin about the correct form of greeting,[21] but a gendarmery officer came in and induced the Schutzbund men to leave. Shortly thereafter about 200 members of the Socialist formation marched out to meet the opponents who were coming to Schattendorf. A short clash on the highway ensued and the Front Fighters retreated. Next, the Schutzbund surrounded

[20] These facts were essentially, although unwillingly, confirmed by Seipel in his reply to a Socialist interpellation in parliament. Nationalrat, *Protokoll,* February 3, 1927, p. 4499.

[21] Greeting formulas also had become a matter of politics in Austria. The reader will recall that the Socialists used the word "friendship" (*Freundschaft*), whereas their opponents retained the old German, *Heil!*

the near-by railroad station. When about a dozen Vienna leaders of the rightist corps arrived and attempted to walk to Schattendorf, leather belts went into action and they were forced to retire to the station. There an agreement between them and the leaders of the Schutzbund was concluded to the effect that the meetings of both groups were to be abandoned. The Front members returned to Vienna and the Schutzbund group to Schattendorf. When the last columns were passing the inn of the "enemies" a few Schutzbund men ran to the door and shouted the time-honored formula of Austrian peasant boys: "Come out, if you dare, and let's have it out!" The others, being a minority, were not too anxious to accept the invitation. Meanwhile, the two sons of the owner of the inn and some other Front Fighters had retired to the room where the rifles lay. Whether these men were prompted by fear that the Schutzbund would storm the house; whether their blood was stirred by the obviously highhanded actions of the Schutzbund; whether they were particularly incensed by the grossly exaggerated rumors about what had happened to their comrades on the highway; whether they were simply prompted by hatred and malice will never be established.[22] At any rate they suddenly began to fire indiscriminately into the crowds that filled the street. A World War veteran, Csmarits, who had lost an eye and had been crippled in the field, was killed, as was a child. A few persons received superficial wounds.[23]

In the following days the country, and particularly the capital, trembled with excitement and apprehension. In most of the big factories in Vienna and in the industrial towns the workers struck. Spontaneous protest meetings vociferously expressed the wrath of the workers. Of all the reactionary organizations the Front Fighters were probably the one most obnoxious to the workers at this time, and not only because of its legitimist tendencies; it glorified the

[22] The indictment apparently accepted the last view. The evidence of one of the Front Fighters that they continued playing cards during the trouble and were not overly excited points in the same direction, as does the testimony of the old mother of two of the accused men to the effect that she had not been frightened. Cf. *Neue Freie Presse,* July 5, 1927 (P.M.), p. 3; July 7 (A.M.), pp. 8, 9.

[23] For the "Schattendorf story," cf. the reports on the trial, *Neue Freie Presse,* July 5, 1927 (P.M.) to July 15 (A.M.); the *Reichspost* for the same period; the Socialist report and interpretation appear, of course, in the *Arbeiter Zeitung* and are supplemented by Julius Braunthal, *Die Wiener Julitage 1927, Ein Gedenkbuch* (Wien, 1927), pp. 5–9. Cf. also the laconic statement of a qualified observer on the question of guilt: "The shots were unprovoked, although in an earlier quarrel the same day the Socialists were to blame." G. E. R. Gedye, *Heirs to the Habsburgs* (Bristol, 1932), p. 89.

memories of a war in which the passionate pacifism of the workers saw nothing but horror and misery, and, to boot, the most infamous crime of the vanished dynasty. Voices became loud, most notably in Floridsdorf, urging the workers to march to the Inner City. Again, the functionaries of party and unions succeeded in persuading their colleagues to return to their jobs.[24] Late in the afternoon of January 31 a meeting in the city hall where Breitner had been scheduled to speak became an impressive demonstration of protest. The broad square before the building was filled by crowds who could not gain entrance to the hall. Unscheduled speakers shouted passionate words of condemnation and from all sides rose a wild outcry of demands for exemplary punishment and for dissolution of the Front Fighters.

Non-Socialists also joined the chorus of indignation. "In this case the guilt of the Front Fighters is particularly condemnable," wrote the *Presse;* although the paper noted that the Schutzbund too had committed mistakes, it declared them of little weight compared with the unimaginable brutality shown by the other side.[25] Speaking for the Christian Social party in the diet of Lower Austria, Governor Buresch solemnly "condemned the criminal outrages" and expressed his "vivid sympathy with the unhappy victims" of Schattendorf.[26] The Burgenland diet was even more outspoken; it passed a resolution moved by the Socialists which not only urged the people of the state to fight their political battles with mental arms, but also contained a vigorous declaration of unwillingness to bear again the Hungarian yoke.[27] The implications of this declaration are all the more interesting in the light of the fact that four days after the fatal shooting Seipel had stated in parliament that he had asked the governor of Burgenland "upon his honor" to tell what he knew about the pro-Hungarian movement and had reported the governor's reply that no such thing existed in his state.[28] To say the least this was unconvincing, and the unfavorable impression was increased by the sleek words of excuse found by the chancellor for what he called the indigenous (*bodenständig*) part of the Burgenland population who still preserved certain pious memories of their

[24] *Neue Freie Presse,* January 31, 1927 (P.M.), p. 4; *Arbeiter Zeitung,* January 31, 1927, p.2.
[25] *Neue Freie Presse,* February 1, 1927 (A.M.), p. 1.
[26] *Ibid.,* January 31, 1927 (P.M.), p. 4.
[27] *Arbeiter Zeitung,* February 9, 1927, p. 1.
[28] Nationalrat, *Protokoll,* February 3, 1927, p. 4496.

old fatherland. But even he could not abstain from promising that everything would be done so that "the crime will receive the punishment it deserves";[29] the resonance throughout the country had been too loud. Pro-Habsburg leanings, antipacifism, workers' blood, and high treason seemed to be boiling in the witches' caldron of Schattendorf.

On February 2 the dead were buried. The Socialist party had prepared an impressive funeral for the victims. A proclamation by it and the unions called for a fifteen-minute general strike on the day of the funeral as a sign of mourning and as a demonstration for the dissolution of the pro-Magyar organizations.[30] From all accounts the call was responded to without exception. The railway trains halted wherever they were. The streetcars in Vienna became immobile and the motormen managed to block some of the big thoroughfares of the city so that automobile traffic also was partly stopped. Telephone operators became deaf, salesgirls stood motionless behind their counters and even in the *cafés* the service of coffee with whipped cream was discontinued. The factory whistles sounded for a quarter of an hour and short meetings were held. Then the workers returned to their tasks. The Socialist organizations had succeeded in turning the mass protest into nonviolent and dignified channels.

The trial of the three men who had confessed to firing the fatal shots in Schattendorf began five months later, July 5, in an atmosphere of considerable political tension. The workers felt that the electoral victory of April, 1927, had been won in vain. The entrance of the Agrarian League into the cabinet had provided Seipel with a stronger majority than he had had before. To be sure, the cohesion of the new alliance was still not great and this peasant party was dissatisfied with the way in which Seipel treated its demands.[31] The Socialists obviously tried to throw sand into the parliamentary gears precisely where the interests of the Agrarians were concerned. They hoped that, at length, the latter would leave the coalition in disgust. The negotiations on the question of the new customs tariff dragged out and parliament seemed once again "paralyzed," to use another favorite word of Austrian political jargon. For ten weeks, in fact, there were no sessions. The language of the Heimwehr leaders in

[29] *Ibid.*, pp. 4496, 4497.
[30] *Arbeiter Zeitung*, February 1, 1927, p. 1.
[31] *Der österreichische Volkswirt*, vol. 19 (July 2, 1927), 1065.

the states became, if possible, more threatening. Richard Steidle told a meeting of this formation in Wels that, "We are prepared to clear the way for an energetic government which will work for the common weal, a strong government that will lead and reign and not stagger from one compromise and embarrassment into another. . . . Now it is up to men who are willing to secure the freedom of the fatherland not by words but, if necessary, by their fists."[32]

On the trial itself there is little to say. The court's contribution to the clarification of the events in Schattendorf was utilized in the preceding pages. The presiding judge conducted the proceedings with a wisdom and impartiality which were fully recognized, even by the Socialist press. The state prosecutor was in the unenviable position of a civil servant who has to act against the wishes of the government. His rejection of several of the prospective jurors as possibly biased led the counsel for defense, a noted National Socialist leader, to lodge a complaint against him with Chancellor Seipel—an action which the workers' organ was eager to interpret as an attempt to exert pressure on the prosecutor.[33] Nevertheless, his attitude was generally irreproachable. There is no reason to believe that he spoke against his better convictions when, in his closing speech, he urged the jury to pronounce the accused guilty before the law, but added that the moral responsibility for the events rested with the Schutzbund.[34] The effect, however, of such a remark upon the jurors should not be underestimated.

Meanwhile, outside the crowded courtroom, excitement and tension grew. The Socialist and the Christian Social press competed in publishing highly biased reports on the "truth about Schattendorf." Men castigated as most dangerous criminals by the *Arbeiter Zeitung* were presented as angels in distress by the *Reichspost*. Even members of the jury were attacked, a breach of all traditions of the Austrian press. Six days before the trial ended the funeral of a

[32] *Neue Freie Presse,* July 5, 1927 (P.M.), p. 2; July 6 (A.M.), p. 1. The comments in the editorial of July 6 are worth recording because they reflect the great impression left by the Socialist victory at the polls: "Can Herr Dr. Steidle change the voting relationships in the parliament? Can he undo the loss of nine seats by the Christian Socials and the one-quarter million new votes gained by the Social Democrats?" Mr. Benedikt, editor in chief of the *Presse,* would probably have had nothing but an indulgent smile had someone told him that only a few days later an affirmative answer to his queries would not sound so fantastic as he seemed to believe.

[33] *Arbeiter Zeitung,* July 8, 1927, p. 3.

[34] *Neue Freie Presse,* July 14, 1927, (A.M.), pp. 8–9.

member of the *Rainer,* a private military formation, in a working-class district (Favoriten) of Vienna led to a two-hour riot. The disturbance began partly because of the participation of a detachment of Front Fighters, but chiefly, it seems, because of rumors that the Schattendorf men had been acquitted. One day later a real battle took place in Klosterneuburg, a little town on the Danube a few miles from the capital. Front Fighters had provocatively approached a sport festival of the Socialists. Fortunately, no lives were lost, but thousands of peaceful hikers—it was a Sunday—fled in terror when the two warring groups clashed.[35]

The most significant aspect of the Favoriten incident is that the evidence indicates it was precipitated by rumors of an acquittal. After the events of July 15, both sides, that is to say, the police and the Social Democrats, took the position that it had been impossible to foresee that the fury of the people would burst out with such vehement force. Formulated in this way their claims cannot be challenged as devoid of merit; nevertheless, they took such inadequate precautions that it does not seem too much to say that they practically disregarded the warning of the Favoriten riot as reflected in the facts and in an editorial in the *Presse* on July 11.

Finally, late in the evening of July 14, the long and nerve-racking trial was brought to an end. After three hours of deliberation the jury found the accused men not guilty. Amidst a deathlike silence the president, pale and disconcerted, pronounced the acquittal.

> The audience remains dumb. Nobody moves—no suppressed exclamation is audible. There is an oppressive silence. Is there no one here who is horrified that two people, a poor child and an invalid, were put to death in Schattendorf and not even a slight punishment was inflicted upon those who fired the fatal shots? There is no one here. . . . Would that some breach of discipline take place. Is it really so clear that the defendants acted in blind fear or indeed in justified self-defense, when they killed a child and a cripple? At least a protest of a minority, an expression of doubt should be muttered.[36]

By the time the Viennese read these lines from the *Presse* the silence had been broken and more than a "breach of discipline" had taken place.

---

[35] *Ibid.*, July 10, 1927 (A.M.), p. 11; July 11 (P.M.), pp. 1, 4.
[36] *Ibid.*, July 15, 1927 (A.M.), p. 12.

The deplorable verdict of the jury calls for little explanation. The unrestrained propaganda of the government press had its share in it. The unfortunate phrase of the prosecutor might have been accountable, to some extent, for the result. But probably more important was the fact that at this time Viennese juries, as happens to juries anywhere, were in the midst of a streak of acquittals. To exonerate infanticides was an old tradition, but in the months preceding the Schattendorf trial a Vienna jury had acquitted a man who had slain and then cut to pieces his wife; a woman who had shot her husband, a renowned star of the Vienna opera; and another woman who had induced her husband to hack off his leg in order to receive a huge insurance payment.[37] On the whole, the verdict of July 14 was apparently an unfortunate accident, to be regretfully accepted by those who believe in the advantages of placing justice in the hands of twelve men of the people, and who consider that institution as inalienable from the concept of democracy.

This problem of the occasional failure of the jury system was the chief difficulty faced by the Socialist leaders in the hot summer night of July 14. They knew that the reform, indeed abolition, of jury courts was one of the greatest wishes of the reaction, a part of a wider program to curtail democracy. Was it possible under these circumstances to call a major demonstration of protest against the verdict of a jury, a demonstration against democracy? For the Austrian Socialists, to pose the question was to answer it. The leaders did not understand that slavish adherence to the ideology of democracy may in certain situations jeopardize democracy itself. In politics the straight line is not always the shortest connection between two points. Besides, they too labored under an overestimation of their power—their power over the masses of their adherents. In the nine years since the revolution they had rebuilt and reinforced the powerful party machine. Whenever they pressed the button the cogs moved smoothly into place and the huge wheels turned. Was it not easy to fall victim to a logical fallacy and to assume that the wheels never would move, unless the button was pressed? But still the excitement of the masses was undeniable and though the leaders decided to abstain from initiating any act of mass protest, they believed

[37] In 1938 this ingenious lady was executed in Vienna for having murdered several persons, among them her husband.

that they had to use strong language, to direct serious words of warning to the government, to speak out about the indignation of the workers and thus provide an outlet for it. Thus was written the editorial in the *Arbeiter Zeitung* of July 15 which later was so greatly and so frequently disparaged—even regarded as the provoking cause of the subsequent events:[38]

> This acquittal is as scoundrelly a trick . . . as was ever registered in the annals of justice . . . they play a frivolously dangerous game. For if the workers *should have to* recognize that there is no justice for them in this capitalist world . . . then belief in justice will be destroyed. . . . Refusal of justice is the worst thing that can be done to working men. . . . The bourgeois world always warns against civil war. But is not this unconditional, agitating acquittal of men who killed workers itself civil war? We warn them all! For from the seeds of injustice nothing can arise but grave disaster.[39]

There is little doubt that the editorial was intended to be not a call for action but a substitute for action. Construed in this manner it was at first accepted by many as a proof of Socialist moderation. Only later did this attitude change.

While the printing presses of the *Arbeiter Zeitung* were still turning out copies, the works councillors of the city electrical works appeared in the building which housed the offices of the paper and the party. They asked for instructions. There were none. At 3:00 A.M. Mayor Seitz was called by telephone and told of the electrical workers' intention to strike. He dispatched Julius Deutsch, leader of the Schutzbund, to pacify them. At dawn a meeting of both shifts decided upon a one-hour strike, between eight and nine o'clock. Meantime, the workers were arriving in the factories. Everywhere the excitement was boundless. These men were ill-prepared to give thought to academic considerations about the democratic character of the jury courts. To their minds the facts took a primitive, but all the more impressive and irritating form: again, members of their class had been killed in a cowardly fashion and again, the killers had been exculpated; men who wanted the partition of the state, whose

[38] Cf. *Ausschreitungen in Wien am 15. und 16. Juli 1927: Weissbuch* herausgegeben von der Polizeidirektion in Wien (Wien, 1927), p. 6 (cited hereafter as *Weissbuch*); Ernst Streeruwitz, *Springflut über Oesterreich* (Wien, 1937), p. 228. For a Socialist criticism of the editorial, see Renner's speech in *Parteitag, 1927*, p. 135.

[39] *Arbeiter Zeitung*, July 15, 1927, pp. 1, 2. Italics mine; note the conditional phrase. This editorial was reprinted in full in the *Weissbuch*, pp. 53–56.

very existence was a continuous threat to freedom and right had been turned loose! Was then the worker an outlaw, or game to be shot at discretion? Long accumulated wrath, hopes, illusions, disappointments had reached the explosion point. After short passionate meetings one crew after the other left the works and departed to the Inner City to protest against this "justice"—to remind the government of the power of the workers. At 8:00 A.M. the streetcars ceased to move, and in the city, where since the first of December, 1921, no major movement of the workers had taken place without the order of the Socialist party, a wild general strike broke out.

The "Breach of Discipline"

Thus began the memorable July 15. What happened after eight o'clock must be pieced together out of a maze of contradictions. Even if political passion had not, consciously or unconsciously, falsified the accounts of the events, the fact would remain that most of them were given by persons who could not detach themselves completely from that specific quasi-hypnotic state of mind well known to anyone who has concerned himself with the psychology of crowds.[40] Therefore, although various sources were used for the following account—official publications, reports of newspapers of different political colors, evidence in subsequent trials, comprehensive historical works and memoirs, and information furnished to me by eyewitnesses of the events—nevertheless I feel that absolute accuracy could not and probably never will be established.[41]

The first group to arrive on the Ringstrasse were the electrical workers who, despite Deutsch's remonstrances, refused to be dissuaded from going to the Inner City. They were highly excited and the streets resounded with their indignant shouts; but they marched

[40] Gustave Le Bon, *Psychologie des Foules* (Paris, 1913), p. 33: "... one is faced by the impossibility of establishing the truth of the most tangible and carefully observed events."

[41] Cf. particularly: *Neue Freie Presse, Reichspost, Arbeiter Zeitung,* especially for July, 1927; the *Weissbuch* of the Vienna Police; *Die Wahrheit über die "Polizeiaktion" am 15. Juli, Der Bericht der vom Wiener Gemeinderat zur Untersuchung der Ereignisse vom 15. Juli eingesetzten Kommission,* Erstattet von Robert Danneberg (Wien, 1927); Pertinax [Otto Leichter], *Oesterreich 1934* (Zurich, 1935), pp. 47–52; Leopold Kunschak, *Oesterreich 1918–1934* (Wien, 1935), pp. 89–94; G. E. R. Gedye, *Heirs to the Habsburgs* (Bristol, 1932), pp. 89–91; *idem, Fallen Bastions* (London, 1939), pp. 30–34; Julius Braunthal, *Die Wiener Julitage 1927* (Wien, 1927); Nationalrat, *Protokoll,* July 25–27, 1927, pp. 125–236; *Der österreichische Volkswirt,* vol. 19, esp. Nr. 43 (July 23, 1927); Kurt Schuschnigg, *My Austria* (New York, 1938), pp. 118–119.

in an orderly procession, led by their works councillors. The initial disturbance occurred in front of the University. At this hour, as usual, students of theology in their priestly soutanes were flocking through the big doors. Some of them lingered and looked down the steps on the men who tramped by with loud threats and curses against the "Fascist nest." Upstairs a student laughed derisively. In a trice a large group of the demonstrants stormed up the steps to take revenge for the scorn of the "black man." The students fled into the building. The doors were closed, but the panes behind the bars were immediately smashed. A police officer who intervened was disarmed. At this moment, however, several workers' representatives arrived on the scene and quickly induced the enraged group to join their marching comrades. The whole affair was over in a few minutes. Meanwhile, a column of municipal civil servants had appeared on the Ringstrasse; the City Hall being in the immediate vicinity of the parliament building, they wanted only to march around the latter and to return to their work. They found the broad street closed by a chain of policemen. The civil servants stopped, the shouts became thunderous, the ranks became confused; for a moment it looked as if they might attempt to force a passage, but then the leaders persuaded the police to let them through and the noisy but harmless demonstrants paraded around the parliament back to the City Hall. A gap of about one hundred yards was open between the rear of this column and the van of the electrical workers' column approaching from the University. The police hastened to bar the Ringstrasse again. Now for years workers' street demonstrations had not come into contact with the police because such occasions had been arranged by the party, the Schutzbund had always preserved order, and the police, although present, had remained concealed. This policy not only contributed to the successful solution of the problem of how to lead 200,000 men, sometimes keyed to a high emotional pitch, in an orderly and peaceful procession; it also aided in meeting the vital issue of the maintenance of good relations between workers and officers of the law.[42] On December 1, 1921, when wild crowds ransacked the Inner City, the policy were practically

[42] Needless to say this issue remained important despite the fact that the overwhelming majority of the officers belonged to a free trade union. The union elections on March 1, 1927, showed 4,310 votes for the Social Democratic and 1,392 for the Christian Social list. Kunschak, *op. cit.*, p. 89.

invisible. They dispersed a few small groups of Communists, but of that the masses of the workers knew little. When on July 15 the demonstrants saw the police standing there to bar their course, they conceived it as an unheard of provocation. The action was also technically ill-chosen. To bar a street to a procession, particularly in a place where no detour was possible and the masses had to turn around, was bound to create confusion under any circumstances. To do so without a sufficient force was, beyond doubt, criminal folly.

The truth is that the police were caught unawares. Under normal circumstances a force of 150 guarded the surroundings of the house during a meeting of parliament. This time, according to the Socialist report, only 67 men, some of them mounted, were concentrated around the building.[43] The Social Democratic party had always entertained excellent relations with the police administration, and the organization of demonstrations had always been carried out in perfect collaboration between the party secretariat and Johannes Schober, police president.[44] In the evening of July 14, the Socialists informed Schober that no demonstrations were planned. Confidence in the ability of the leadership to control the rank and file was so great in police quarters that they abstained from making any adequate preparations. Seitz also, when called in the small hours of the morning, was convinced that Deutsch would easily pacify the workers. At eight o'clock Deutsch telephoned the police to say that workers were marching toward the Inner City and to express his hope that the functionaries would succeed in leading them back after a short demonstration.[45] Only then did the police administration begin slowly to call its men together.

But to return to the events on the Ringstrasse. The masses pressed against the thin file of uniformed men. The latter gave way. At this moment, obeying an order from their commander, about 25 mounted police charged the crowds at full gallop, brandishing their sabers.[46] With shouts of amazement and indignation people ran

[43] Danneberg, *Die Wahrheit über die "Polizeiaktion" am 15. Juli*, p. 11. The police administration refused to answer questions concerning the exact number of its force at the building.

[44] This coöperation was a time-honored object of pointless scorn from the Communists. Cf. L. Trotsky, *Terrorism i Kommunism* (Moscow and Leningrad, 1925), p. 17 (Russian).

[45] *Weissbuch*, p. 7.

[46] Otto Bauer charged that this was the first time in "decades" that mounted men had been used for such purposes "on the Ringstrasse" (Nationalrat, *Protokoll*, July

across the park bordering the street, followed by the police. Several of the demonstrants, among them one woman, were hit by sabers and fell to the ground. The nerves of the policemen likewise proved ill-conditioned for such an attack. One of the mounted men galloped back and forth over the grass of the park already deserted by the demonstrants; with his saber high in the air he shouted unintelligible words at the top of his voice.[47] In a moment the dispersed marchers were flocking back from all sides. Five minutes before their demonstration had had no direct aim. They had only wanted to cry out their protests. But now they saw the blood of their comrades. Their feelings were similar to those of the men trodden down by the horseshoes of the yeomanry at Peterloo more than a century earlier—men whom the muse of Shelley has rendered immortal:[48]

> And at length when ye complain
> With a murmur weak and vain
> 'Tis to see the Tyrant's crew
> Ride over your wives and you—
> Blood is on the grass like dew. . . .

Now the wrath of the workers had an objective:

> Then it is to feel revenge
> Fiercely thirsting to exchange
> Blood for blood—and wrong for wrong. . . .

The demonstrants rallied. Stones prepared for street repairs had been piled in an alley off the Ringstrasse and when the police charged again they were met by a hail of heavy missiles. Workers' representatives stood in front of the heaps of stones and implored their comrades to be reasonable. But the people were roused to frenzy. A streetcar conductor jumped down from his car, tore off the jacket of his white summer uniform and made an incensed

---

26, 1927, p. 137). The report of the Vienna city council contains the statement that according to the memory of those best informed on the history of the Vienna labor movement there had been only two instances in the twentieth century of mounted police charging demonstrants: on November 2, 1905, and September 17, 1911 (*Die Wahrheit über die "Polizeiaktion" am 15. Juli,* pp. 12–13). Although there is room for some hairsplitting, turning on the expressions "on the Ringstrasse" and "charging," the contemporary accounts leave little room for doubt that mounted police were used against Communist demonstrants in the Hörlgasse on June 15, 1919, and that they "drew their sabers" (*Neue Freie Presse,* June 16, 1919 [P.M.], p. 3). At that time the police were under the Socialist minister of the interior, Eldersch.

[47] Personal account made to me by an eyewitness.

[48] Percy Bysshe Shelley, The "Mask of Anarchy," John Keats and Percy Bysshe Shelley, *Complete Poetical Works* (New York, 1932), p. 370.

speech—to which nobody listened. The demonstration against the verdict of a jury had become a fight against "Seipel's crew"—the Vienna police.

It was at about this juncture that Otto Bauer, who had just reached the parliament building, intervened and asked the commanding officer to withdraw his men.[49] Schabes, a member of the Bundesrat, also protested to the commandant. According to the police *Weissbuch*[50] the mounted officers were "held back for a short time," but the demonstrants continued to attack. Soon thereafter the police retired to the Palace of Justice, separated from the legislative house by a small park. The street in front of the latter building emptied. Then another column of workers from the Ottakring district arrived, passed the parliament with wild cries of protest, but otherwise inoffensively, and turned around the corner on the homeward journey. Only a few of the marching men remained on the scene to join the dispersed electrical workers who were standing in groups in the vicinity of the Palace of Justice.

This was the moment when relatively small forces of the Schutzbund could easily have restored full order. But this organization was conspicuous only by its absence. The party, and above all the Schutzbund leader, Deutsch, had been no less remiss than the police. The formation had not been mobilized. No instructions had been received by its group leaders so that its members had marched to the city as individuals along with their comrades in the factories. It was only after the first clashes that the party decided to mobilize the Schutzbund in ten districts. The best opportunity to avert the disaster had passed. Suddenly came another charge by the police. The people fled, but since the small force was insufficient to draw a cordon around the parliament district, they appeared again as soon as the charge was over. Another column of demonstrants approached; apparently following contradictory orders the police disappeared and then charged again. "Order, counterorder, disorder!" Young workers climbed on the scaffolding of a house which was being painted and began to tear it down. In a trice the crowd was armed with huge boards and proceeded against the police. This time they had to flee. Some of them, unfortunately precisely those who had showed greater reticence in attacking the crowd, were dragged from

[49] Nationalrat, *Protokoll,* July 26, 1927, p. 137.

[50] P. 13.

their horses and badly mistreated. On the big steps in front of the Palace of Justice a few dozen others tried to keep at bay the steadily growing multitude. It was then that the first shots were fired, whether by the attackers or by the hard-pressed police in legitimate self-defense will never be established.[51]

What followed can be regarded as one single chain of illustrations for Le Bon's psychology of crowds: suggestibility, impulsiveness, authoritarianism, sense of brotherhood, lack of tolerance, sudden changes from cruel ferocity to noble generosity, the tendency for every idea to be transformed into immediate action, heroic courage alternating with base cowardice, lack of intellectual inhibitions, and a feeling of omnipotence and invincibility—on this hot July day the streets of Vienna gave rich evidence of all the phenomena of mass psychology.[52]

The policemen in front of the Palace of Justice fought until their ammunition was almost exhausted. Shortly after they withdrew into the building the masses forced an entrance. Bundles of documents thrown from the windows began to pile up on the street. Then a huge picture of Franz Joseph appeared and was greeted with indignant cries: "That is what our republican justice looks like!" Young workers set fire to the pile. Whether fires had previously been started within the building is particularly a matter of dispute, but there seems no room for doubt that blazing bundles of papers were thrown back through broken windows. Within a short time the subterranean parts of the structure were in flames.

It was an unfortunate accident that it was precisely the Palace of Justice in which the police sought refuge. The crowds took, or rather mistook, the building for a symbol of that "justice" against which they had come to protest. As indicated, the Palace was completely devoid of any such symbolic character. It was the seat of the real-estate registry and of certain courts concerned with peaceful matters

[51] After the events each side charged the other with "firing the first shot." This question is not of decisive importance; at any rate the story of the authorities was surely not entirely controverted by the fact that the man who immediately after the fighting had been apodictically named by the police as the person whose gun had gone off first, was able subsequently to prove his innocence and had to be released. *Neue Freie Presse,* August 19, 1927 (A.M.), p. 5.

[52] Cf. Le Bon, *op. cit.,* esp. pp. 23–25. Le Bon's characteristics apply to what he calls heterogenous masses. But it should be noted that the workers' crowds in Vienna, with their particularly strong feeling of group solidarity and their uniformity in thinking and feeling, were to a large degree homogenous, which only meant that all the typical forms of the behavior of a man in a crowd appeared overemphasized in this case.

like guardianship; therefore, it had nothing whatever to do Schattendorf trial. But when excited crowds are on the pa it is of no avail to Cinna the Poet to protest that he is not Conspirator. "It is no matter, his name is Cinna!" It wa of *Justice* and so it had to fall.

Contemporaneously with the events just described, th spread in other directions. A number of officers had retre police station in a side street near the justice building. V station was stormed they withdrew again into private fla same building. The station was set on fire. During the Scha trial the *Reichspost* and the *Wiener Neueste Nachrichte* respectively of the Christian Social and Pan-German par made themselves conspicuous in their defense of the accu offices of both newspapers were invaded by the crowds. the Pan-German paper comparatively slight damage was the *Reichspost* paid a heavy toll. Here also the buildi on fire while the wild throng assembled in the street sh headline of the paper's editorial on the outcome of th clear judgment!"

At noon there was a pause. The masses were tempora ous over the inferior forces of the police. The latter appeared from the streets. Fury subsided after its so created objective had vanished. The crowds in the vicin parliament were larger than ever, but on the whole they w ful and contented themselves with watching the flames Palace of Justice. It was unendurably hot and volunteers h lished little stations on the corners where they offered the th a glass of cold water. The wildness of enraged demonstrants w replaced by the ordinary curiosity of onlookers.[53]

Again the Social Democratic party had its chance; this time, th last. During the lull a sufficient number of Schutzbund men could have dispersed the crowds with a minimum of effort. Had this been achieved the day would have ended undisputedly with a moral victory for the party. But the main force of its armed organization was still being rallied in the outlying districts. At the scene of the riots were only small detachments, many of them formed from those

[53] This confirms another observation of Le Bon (*op. cit.*, p. 40): "Abandoned to themselves they [the crowds] soon weary of disorder."

membe ...s who could be found amidst the crowds. There is little doubt th... ...t most of these men acted in a way which must be described as heroic. With great effort and after considerable time they cleared the stree...s in front of the burning police station and enabled the fire depa...rtment to get to work, whereupon the blaze was quickly extinguis...hed. According to some accounts the same was true at the *Reichsp...ost* building, but the evidence is convincing that this is false. The gre...atest difficulty, of course, was at the Palace of Justice; in it not o...nly policemen, but also judges, civil servants, and private persons in appreciable numbers had been trapped. Led by Körner, a genera...l of the old army and at that time the military adviser to ...tzbund, its men entered the building, gave plain clothes ...cemen in order to save them from injury by the crowd, ...d one by one most of those in the place, which by this ...ompletely wrapped in smoke and flames.[54]

...t problem was to clear the way to the Palace of Justice ... equipment. Together with the Schutzbund the highest ...e party bent to this task. Time and again the impressive ... mayor of Vienna appeared atop a fire department auto- ... spoke, he implored. A few people in the crowds replied ...s. The vast majority cheered Seitz wildly, but showed no ...ingness to let the firemen pass. Finally, after more than ...tempts, persistence brought success: the place was cleared; ...gines neared the building; in a moment the work could ...l at this moment the head of a Schutzbund column ap- ...nd halted in front of the parliament, the men armed, as

...few of the trapped policemen apparently escaped through the sewers. Though ... evidence is clear that some members of the Schutzbund were guilty of excesses as ...dividual atoms in the crowds, the statement in the text reflects the general attitude ... soon as they became again a part of an organized body. Even the *Weissbuch* of the ...olice had to admit reluctantly a number of cases in which rescued officers had been ...rotected by Schutzbund men with their own bodies against the attacks of the mob. (Cf., for example, *op. cit.*, pp. 113, 126, 127, 129, 152.) The *Reichspost* wrote: "We are fair enough to state that individual detachments of the Schutzbund courageously combatted the criminal elements." (July 18, 1927, p. 3.) From then on praise in the non-Socialist camp became faint or inaudible. During the two days of parliamentary debate over the catastrophe, except for a phrase from Kunschak and several clauses from Hartleb, only the very last non-Socialist speaker, Drexel, mentioned the merits of the Schutzbund. "The Schutzbund men ... actually undertook the attempt to beat off the crowds. I know of several superior judges who owe their lives to the assembled Schutzbund, who alone were still able to rescue them. To be sure, the superior judge was told: 'If you are questioned, then you are a witness'; he was not allowed to be a judge. But they helped them to get out; they also helped policemen to get out." (Nationalrat, *Protokoll,* July 26, 1927, pp. 153, 161, 170; *ibid.,* July 27, 1927, p. 234.)

usual, with their thin leather whips. The column was so long that its tail disappeared in the distance behind a curve of the Ringstrasse. At length, the workers' own formation was there in real force to cope with the crowds and to maintain order. Suddenly the sharp rattle of musketry rose above the cracking of the flames. The members of the crowd and of the Schutzbund fled. A few men dropped and remained lying on the ground. The police, armed with rifles and carbines, had fired their first volley.[55]

What had happened? For almost three hours the scene of the disorders outside the Justice building had been completely deserted by the police. In the interval the Socialist leaders had met Seipel and proposed that he should resign to make place for a coalition govern-

[55] The statements in the text concerning the Schutzbund column are based on an eyewitness account given to me.

The conclusion that the Schutzbund and Social Democratic functionaries succeeded in opening the way for the fire department has been, and probably will again be, attacked as unwarranted. The *Weissbuch*, for example, states categorically in one sentence that it "does not correspond to the facts." In the next sentence, however, its authors admit that the fire fighters did succeed in coming forward on one side of the Palace of Justice and attempting to begin their work, but add that they had to withdraw immediately. Naturally enough the police try to utilize the official reports of the fire department and the testimony of its officials. In the most charitable phraseology possible it may be said that they do this in a curious fashion. First, they give the exact times at which numerous reports of the fire were made, at which equipment left the stations, at which the central office was notified that the equipment could proceed no farther, and so on, claiming that these data support the correctness of their presentation. Next, they state that Fire Chief Anton Wagner "corroborates" the fact that extinguishing work could not begin until sometime between 2:54 and 3:25 P.M. To this they add that it was during this period that "the police cleared the Schmerling Place by rifle salvos so that the equipment could drive forward to the fire."

It will be noticed that the last quotation was not from Wagner. And although the *Weissbuch* contains no less than sixteen exhibits relating to this aspect of the tragedy of July 15, it does not include a word from, or even any reference to, a two-column interview given to the *Presse* by Wagner. The police might have used the following sentence from that interview: "Because of the salvos and the panic of those fleeing, the Place before the Palace of Justice was cleared for a moment and we utilized this to drive forward quickly and seize [*besetzen*] the hydrants." The reason they did not use it or refer to the interview seems to appear in another sentence a few lines above in the *Presse:* "Now, as *with the help of members of the city government* we had *already pushed forward far enough* and wanted to begin with the extinguishing work, rifle salvos suddenly roared from all sides." (Cf. *Weissbuch*, pp. 25–27, with *Neue Freie Presse*, July 18, 1927 [P.M.], pp. 6–7. Italics mine.)

The truth is that the *Weissbuch* account was carefully put together to leave an impression which "does not correspond to the facts." The two-thirds of a page giving the precise times at which certain events occurred prove only that there was a long delay—which no one could or did deny. They have no bearing on the bitterly debated question: did the Social Democrats (Schutzbund, functionaries, and members of the city government) clear the way for the fire department so that if the police had waited only a few minutes more there would have been no excuse for firing? Moreover, the *Weissbuch* conspicuously fails to explain why the fire department had to withdraw after it had admittedly reached "one side" of the building, as it fails to state which side this was. Though the evidence is conflicting, some of it supports the conclusion that the temporary withdrawal was forced by the rifle fire.

ment which would master the situation. If by that time a large force of the Schutzbund had been busy restoring order, Seipel might have been persuaded that his resignation was the only alternative to civil war and, consequently, might have complied with the request. In this case it is not only not impossible, it is probable that the whole political development of the country would have taken a very different course. On this day the political scales in Austria oscillated violently and no man could know where they would come to rest. But Seipel was informed that the Socialists were still gathering the Schutzbund together. He knew that they had no intention of providing it with arms other than the customary whips. Besides, its military strength had been weakened by the successful coup of Vaugoin in the Arsenal. He knew that the Socialists, true to their old traditions of revolutionary years, preferred to rely upon the force of persuasion. Although perhaps indistinctly as yet, Seipel's sharp eye perceived in this situation the possibility of improving and strengthening his own position by a shrewd blow. He dismissed the Socialists coolly and ordered Schober to suppress the riots at any cost. The latter asked Seitz as governor of the state of Vienna for permission to summon detachments of the army. Seitz refused. Thereupon Schober equipped 600 men with rifles and carbines and sent them against the crowds which filled the environs of the parliament. At the same time he applied over the head of Seitz for military assistance. A part of the 600 officers had participated in the events of the morning. All of them were roused to fury by atrocity stories about ghastly mutilated and brutally killed policemen. They likewise were subject to the psychology of crowds.[56] And, above all, they too were frightened because they knew that their mere appearance would provoke the crowds to new outbursts of anger and violence.

But even if full consideration is given to the psychological position of the police what followed can be described only as a series of acts of unspeakable horror and criminal cruelty. After the first volley the police proceeded with carbines in their hands to hunt the crowds. Their numbers were still insufficient to draw cordons and to block the thoroughfares. A few minutes after the shots the

[56] There seems little foundation for the Socialist charge that faked atrocity stories were deliberately spread among the policemen by their commanding officers. As brought out before, there were without doubt some instances of atrocities against policemen by demonstrants.

crowds assembled again a few blocks away. Many people were still coming in from the outskirts attracted by the huge fire. The latter, with a few possible exceptions, were unarmed. In the morning some of the demonstrants had carried their tools along, objects that might have been used as weapons, and others had provided themselves with such things as stones, pieces of scaffolding, and lengths of reinforcing steel. A few, chiefly of the criminal element that joined the marchers, had knives or pistols. In the afternoon the first volleys were fired against groups that to some extent and in some fashion were armed, but, as indicated, the crowds were being steadily swelled by curious onlookers who stood absolutely defenceless before the murderous fire of the police. The way in which the police went about their work may best be made clear by a quotation from an early story in the *Neue Freie Presse,* a paper not exactly partial to demonstrations, rioting and arson, and passionately anti-Socialist:

The shots and their echo provoked horror. Women and children shrieked. The crowds ran as if obsessed. They pushed their way into the houses and into the few shops which were still kept open. *The police went on shooting.* Since the shots were fired here, there, and yonder, people were seized by a ghastly panic. No one knew where he should flee. In the pauses between the salvos the victims were carried into the House of Parliament—many dead and numerous gravely wounded. Mostly head, chest, and abdominal wounds. Incessantly ambulances transported the severely wounded to the hospitals. Three hours long this shooting continued—between two and five o'clock. *Wherever people had crowded together and cried their "boos" against the police, irregular shots fell instantly.* The police *proceeded firing from street to street.*[57]

Even the ambulances of the Red Cross were damaged by bullets.

Was there method in this madness? Undoubtedly. Both the Socialists and the government were exerting every effort to restore order. Whoever succeeded in this task would be politically the victor of the day, and, indeed, the probable master of the future. Thus the brutal interruption of the Socialists' attempts at pacification by the

---

[57] *Neue Freie Presse,* July 18, 1927 (P.M.), p. 3. Italics mine. Cf. also the statement of the *Volkswirt:* The police "fired even where there was no attack against them, where there were only groups of excited men who stood or walked about and discussed the events. The police obviously had orders to spread terror. . . ." *Der österreichische Volkswirt,* vol. 19 (July 23, 1927), 1150.

The attempts, in the *Weissbuch* and elsewhere, to defend the actions of the police during the afternoon of July 15, except for a few instances, deserve no credence. This does not mean that their actions at other times were entirely justified—only that their methods during that afternoon were the most reprehensible.

sheer terror of the roving firing squads had good political sense. The government had utilized the wild instincts of the policemen, their lust for revenge, and their fear.

Little is to be added to the story. The Schutzbund, reduced to the position of a helpless target of the police, was withdrawn immediately.[58] The hundreds of men standing on the Ringstrasse were never used. Slowly the crowds retired to the workers' districts. From time to time a police car sped through the streets, firing without warning or discrimination into the groups of men and women who stood there. The working-class quarters of the city were seething with rage and the cry, "Give us arms!" was heard everywhere. In fact, arms were obtained by small individual groups and in the night and on the following day a police station was stormed. But then larger forces of police appeared, the carbines fired again, and more blood was spilt.

Altogether 89 persons were killed: 85 demonstrants or spectators and 4 policemen.[59] From the latter group only one man was killed during the fighting in the morning on July 15. Two lost their lives in the following night by shots fired from ambush as their car passed under a railroad bridge. One was killed on July 16 when the police station in the outskirts was besieged. Two of the four were members of the Social Democratic party. It is significant that there were no fatalities among the police on the afternoon of the fifteenth. During those two days 1,057 wounded persons were carried to the hospitals. Of them 328 private citizens and 163 policemen were retained for longer treatment, whereas the rest were dismissed after their wounds had been bandaged.[60] Since the days of the Revolution of 1848 Vienna had not seen such a catastrophe; for the first time since the foundation of the republic a demonstration of Social Democratic workers had been fired upon by government forces.

The Aftermath

In the evening of the fateful day the party directorate met with the trade-union chiefs to draw the balance of the events and to work out

[58] Julius Deutsch, "Der 15. Juli," *Der Schutzbund,* vol. 4 (Sept., 1927), 129.

[59] The relation 85:4 is, in the words of Gedye, "indisputable evidence of where the real guilt for the slaughter lay." *Fallen Bastions,* p. 37.

Toward the end of the year one of the injured demonstrants died.

[60] *Parteitag, 1927,* pp. 21–22. Of the policemen 111 were seriously wounded. Cf. *Weissbuch,* Appendix B (following p. 180).

the policy for the near future. Probably never since the outbreak of the war in 1914, when they had witnessed the miserable collapse of the International, had there been such an atmosphere of depression among the leaders of this powerful and successful movement. One thing was clear: apart from unfortunate accidents, apart from grievous failures of the apparatus, the events of the day were the result of a contradiction between the real power of the movement and the illusions of the masses. The party had firmly committed itself to a policy of democracy and legality. It feared nothing more than outbreaks of violence, although now and then it used to threaten its opponents with such contingencies. Was it not tragic that a democratic success at the polls had been to a large degree accountable for the growth of illusions which proved so pernicious? At any rate the fact of the defeat had to be faced. One day seemed to have shaken to the roots the achievements of decades.

But mere laments and mutual recriminations were of little avail. Something had to be done at once. The masses, deeply wounded in their pride, were crying for arms. Could the party comply with this ardent wish? In the meeting of workers' representatives on July 17, Otto Bauer explained why it was impossible: "Comrades, I have to justify our action in deciding not even to attempt a disorderly and irregular arming of the wildly excited proletarian masses. In this hour of extremely tense passions a wholesale distribution of arms would have meant to begin an open civil war. But it is our first duty, as long as we can, not to do anything that could bring about civil war." And then he described the dangers of foreign intervention, of economic catastrophe, and reminded his audience of the helplessness of the workers in the states.[61] Whatever the value of the argument, it is striking that Bauer did not even mention the possibility of arming the Schutzbund. This omission is significant because it shows that the party never seriously considered betraying its democratic traditions and trying to save the situation by force of arms.

But inactivity was likewise out of the question; it would have been misinterpreted by the government and by the workers. Weakness, would have said the former; treason, the latter. During the meeting of the party directorate in the night of July 15 it was de-

[61] Quoted in Braunthal, *op. cit.*, p. 51.

cided to proclaim a general strike. In the morning of July 16 the only paper was a party "information sheet" carrying a proclamation. It accused the police of having caused the disaster: first, by inadequate handling of the situation; second, by their demented actions. It admitted that a few hundred representatives of irresponsible elements mingled with the huge crowds had committed other actions not compatible with the dignity of the working class. "Enough blood had been spilt," the proclamation continued, "We do not want more blood to flow! . . . The power of the workers . . . consists in fighting with economic weapons." Four directives were issued: (1) A general strike of twenty-four hours; (2) A strike of railroad, telegraph, telephone, and postal employees without time limits; (3) Permanent alert of the Schutzbund; (4) Strict prohibition of street demonstration.[62] On July 17 these measures were supplemented by arrangements for the organization of a body of city council police (*Gemeindewache*) "for the days of danger." The plans were carried out by Seitz; the members were drawn from the ranks of the Schutzbund. The party hoped that if it were necessary the new officers could be placed between the demonstrants and the federal police and obviate fresh bloodshed.[63]

On the whole this was probably a wise policy. The workers saw that the party was prepared to use one of the strongest weapons in its arsenal. This permitted the political wing to regain the leadership it should never have lost; that is, to accomplish the main purpose of the general strike. On the other side the iron discipline with which the strike slogan was obeyed all over the country did not fail to produce an impression upon the government.[64] The Socialists wished to continue the transportation and communications strike until the government would agree to an amnesty of those who had been involved in the riots. They proposed a solemn declaration that both sides would regard the events as an elemental disaster and thus liquidate it as quickly as possible. In this case they would be willing to withdraw their demands for a searching investigation of the activities of the police. The situation began to look more promising.

At this juncture, however, another actor, the Heimwehr, stamped

[62] *Parteitag, 1927*, pp. 23–27.

[63] It is significant that the federal system provided arms (sabers) for the new organization.

[64] Cf. the statement of Pertinax who had all the advantages of "inside" information, *op. cit.*, p. 53.

in from the wings and disturbed the crystallizing plans of the Social Democrats so effectively that in Styria and in Tirol the continuation of the strike was suddenly jeopardized. In Innsbruck this Fascist formation, supported by the regular army, occupied the main railway station. The workers had to withdraw. Even the strike committee had to be transferred from Innsbruck to Salzburg. Thereupon members of Pan-German and Christian unions succeeded in resuming traffic, although to a limited extent only. The strike was not actually perforated in Styria but the situation was scarcely less precarious for the Socialists. The Heimwehr mobilized with impressive efficiency a force of 20,000 heavily armed men whose equipment included machine guns.[65] They presented an ultimatum to the state government in Graz, threatening an immediate march on that city if the strike were not called off. Governor Paul began negotiations with the Styrian Socialists. The leader of the Styrian Heimwehr, Pfrimer, came to Graz and showed a most uncompromising mood. The intimidation of the Styrian Socialists succeeded almost perfectly. Hysterical messages were dispatched to Vienna urging the party directorate to call off the strike in order to forestall its collapse or the outbreak of civil war. This executive group negotiated with Seipel. Strengthened by the Heimwehr offensive, he refused to commit himself to any official declaration. Meanwhile, there were reports that the Czech ambassador had called on Seitz to demand unhindered transport for goods from Czechoslovakia, that the Italians threatened to send trains to Germany through Tirol under the protection of their soldiers, and that Hungary had assembled troops along the Burgenland border. On July 26, Seipel emphatically denied in the Nationalrat that any *demarché* or threats had been made by a foreign government, but as has been and will be shown this by no means proves that they had not. Indeed, his party colleague, Kunschak, set them down as facts in a book published seven years later. Whether or not Otto Bauer believed the reports is not certain; at any rate, as shown, he acted and spoke as if he did. The impact of these developments shattered what remained of the Socialists' firmness so that they gave in after finally obtaining Seipel's unofficial promise not to avail himself of the outcome of the events for a general attack on the social gains. At midnight, July 18, work was

[65] *Reichspost,* July 21, 1927, p. 3.

resumed on the railroads and in the postal, telegraph, and telephone services.[66]

This was incontestably the second defeat within four days. Actually this time the failure was even more devastating. On July 15, that Black Friday for Vienna workers, it was, after all, only a minority that had been exposed to the fire of the police. Moreover, this minority had acted in violation of the wishes and intentions of the major political institutions of labor. A successful conclusion of the transportation and communications strikes would have preserved, or even enhanced, the prestige of those groups. But now the whole organization of labor, the party as well as the trade unions, had suffered a terrible blow.[67] All the self-comforting editorials of the labor daily could not undo the fact and the effect.[68] To be sure, as far as the numeric situation was concerned nothing was changed. The party had exactly the same number of seats in the parliament, the state diets, and the city councils. To a certain extent, and for a short time, the opinion prevailed in both camps that the government could make considerable gains by carrying out "khaki-elections" while the impression of the events was still fresh. But this opinion was far from general—witness the abstention of the government from any such attempt. The by-elections during 1928 brought new Socialist gains and revealed that "July 15" had not been followed by shifts in the electorate in favor of the government. But after that date it became plain to the most myopic sight that the constellation in the parliament is only one, and under certain conditions not even the most important, aspect and gauge of the power relations in a country. Ferdinand Lassalle used to call the army and the police, the financial interests and the big industrial entrepreneurs "a piece of the constitution." It is not intended to deny or even minimize the role played by vested interests in old democracies; *but it is safe to*

[66] Only in Innsbruck did the men refuse to return to work before the withdrawal of the armed forces which had occupied the station; the resulting delay amounted to eight hours.

[67] The significance of what had happened in Styria and in Tirol was fully understood in the camp of the opponents; a young member of parliament, Kurt Schuschnigg, said in his maiden speech: "It is of interest for us that for the first time we succeeded in breaking a railroad strike, at least partially." Nationalrat, *Protokoll,* July 27, 1927, p. 226.

[68] "A circular telegram signed by Tomschik [leader of the free railroad union] and all trains between Buchs [Swiss border] and Vienna stand still. A circular telegram of Tomschik's—and the trains roll again. So it was, so it is. And so long as it remains thus, nothing in the world can break us." *Arbeiter Zeitung,* July 19, 1927, p. 1 (ed.). This childish boast was not true.

assert that the more unstable or immature a democracy is, the more important become those elements of the "invisible government" which are not, like the political parties, essentially connected with the system of democracy. Although the street demonstrations so much favored by the workers' party were, for example, a part of this "invisible government," its general democratic attitude had veiled this fact to a certain extent. But when antidemocratic forces outside the parliament gained momentum the problem of the "meta-parliamentary government" was drastically brought home to democratic minds.

Beside the dead bodies of 89 persons lay fatally wounded the belief that army and police with their Socialist majorities could not be used against the workers. This was the other side of the anti-coalition policy. The Socialists had been gaining members and votes, but their opponents had had seven years in which to draw all possible benefits from the subordination of the individual policemen and soldiers to them. They could promote and bribe, they could punish and dismiss.[69] It was a well-known fact that in Vienna young policemen were not recruited from the population of the city but from the peasants of the Christian Social villages of Lower Austria. It was equally known that under the "system Vaugoin" a recommendation from the parish priest was necessary for admittance to the army. In 1920 the Socialists had left a military force which was, in fact, a Socialist organization since a non-Socialist soldier was an exception. Although, to a certain extent, this in itself called for a reaction, it is more than probable that given the situation of the period 1923–1927 the majority parties would have attempted to transform the military into an instrument of their policy.

From the democratic point of view the difference cannot be overlooked; under the specific Austrian conditions an army with a clear Socialist majority was a protection against attacks on a democratic constitution. As already indicated, it was not protection enough. Here again concepts of formal democracy fail to do justice to the intricacies of the problem. It should be remembered that in the variety of causes which led to the decay and overthrow of German

[69] A member of the soldiers' trade union complained to the trade-union congress as early as 1923: "There is almost no representative [of the union] who has not been punished for a period of three months at least with a 25 per cent reduction in his pay." Gewerkschaftskongress, 1923, *Protokoll*, p. 306.

democracy a momentous part was played by the fact that although the kaiser went his generals remained. Naturally the new Austrian army was also directed by imperial officers. To create a commanding staff of sincere republicans would have taken years, even if that policy had not been discontinued by the non-Socialist governments after 1920. It is necessary to remain aware of these facts but it is also necessary to realize the significance of the failure of the Socialists and the magnitude of their disillusionment. Their hope that leaving an army of Social Democratic soldiers in 1920 would per se render possible their long absence from the government, which they deemed essential for final victory, proved ungrounded.

This development reveals in a neat and clear-cut example the pathetic contradictions, in fact, the tragedy of labor's policy in Austria—and perhaps not only in Austria. The Social Democrats were sincerely determined to follow the road of democracy. But to obtain the majority in parliament implied abstention from the cabinet, implied surrender of key positions of power to their opponents. To have stayed in the government would have meant splitting up the forces of democracy and pushing a part of the working class into the antidemocratic camp. To leave the government, as they did, was bound to give the enemies of democracy a better chance to organize and to array forces ready to overthrow the system of parliamentarism. A Socialist majority at the April elections might have solved the dilemma. But instead came July, 1927, and caught Austrian democracy in the pincers of a fateful contradiction. Then it became clear that the purposeful daily influence that had been exerted by the government upon the policemen and soldiers weighed more than did the membership cards of the Social Democratic party in their pockets. After the events many of them hastened to leave the party and the free trade unions. The police authorities arranged new elections for the representation of the personnel in which the non-Socialist list obtained a large majority with 3,931 votes.[70] On October 16 the non-Socialist press could announce "the end of the red army in Austria" on the basis of the election results.[71]

---

[70] Pertinax, *op. cit.*, p. 60.

[71] *Neue Freie Presse*, October 16, 1927 (A.M.), p. 1 (ed.) and p. 10. The following figures reveal the progress of the Christian Socal union sponsored by the government and the army command in the period 1923–1925. (*Continued at bottom of p. 753.*)

Although the Socialists' losses (more than 16 per cent) were heavy enough, they still had the majority of votes even if those of officers, where the non-Socialists had a clear majority of 1,700 against 610, are added to the figures below recording the ballots of privates. But the decisive result was the redistribution of representation; it shows the amazing amount of gerrymandering Vaugoin felt himself powerful enough to carry through. With a vote of more than 56 per cent among the rank and file the Socialists obtained—in a proportional election!—only 45 per cent of the representatives. As already

Party	Votes		Representatives	
	Oct., 1927	Oct., 1926	Oct., 1927	Oct., 1926
Christian Socials	6,538	3,863	134	54
Social Democrats	9,243	11,170	118	202
Pan-Germans	659	290	7	1

indicated, however, with old soldiers finishing their enlistments and leaving the army it was only a matter of time until Vaugoin would obtain a genuine Christian Social majority. Whether the contingency of the use of troops against the workers would ever become actuality was another question, but everyone who knows the importance of Vaihinger's "as if" in social phenomena will understand the magnitude of the psychological shifts involved by these changes.[72]

Another result of "July 15," even more momentous in its effects, was the resurgence of the Fascist and antidemocratic Heimwehr. As with the army and police this resurgence had been prepared by the foregoing development. The Heimwehr had been active on the "domestic front" ever since 1920. It has been shown that from 1921 on it was supported financially by the Association of Manufacturers. There were years, however, in which it was relatively dormant—

[71] (*Continued*)

Party	1923	1924	1925
Christian Socials	1,225	2,787	3,498
Social Democrats	14,060	11,343	12,094

Cf. Franz Hemala, *Geschichte der Gewerkschaften* (Wien, 1930), p. 259. This author's figures for 1926 and 1927 show minor differences as compared with the data in the text from the *Presse,* but these discrepancies in no way affect the general picture.

[72] Cf. Hans Vaihinger, *Die Philosophie des Als Ob* (2d ed.; Berlin, 1913).

little more than a cadre in reserve.[73] But the progress of the Socialist party in the period 1923–1927 and the tangible successes of its administration of Vienna greatly enhanced the value of the formation in the eyes of many government supporters. The more threateningly the prospect of a Socialist majority loomed on the political horizon of the country, the stronger became the attractive power of the counter body, the more people there were who found themselves willing to conceive the necessity of using it against a future democratic government of the Social Democracy, or to nullify, or even to forestall, a Socialist victory at the polls. The reader has seen in this chapter how a few days before "July 15" the Heimwehr offered Seipel its help, even if in queer language, in solving parliamentary difficulties and breaking the restiveness of the Socialists. Immediately after Schattendorf an event occurred which passed almost unnoticed although full of significance. For the first time since the establishment of the republic the Socialists were compelled to call off a demonstration of protest because of the threats of the Heimwehr.[74] In much the same way as the anticoalition policy of the workers' party had its reverse side in giving the opponents time and opportunity to break the power of the Socialists in the armed forces of the state, the vigorous and progressing struggle for the majority had increased and strengthened the antidemocratic forces of the Heimwehr. These precisely were the things meant in the first paragraph of this chapter by the reference to the hostile spirits raised by the very policy of the Social Democracy.

Thus the role played by the Heimwehr in the days after "July 15" was by no means that of a *deus ex machina*. But, on the other hand, something new had happened. In those days both police and Heimwehr had been tested. The former had proved a usable tool in suppressing a demonstration that had got out of control. The latter had proved that it was able to wrest from the hands of labor a most efficient weapon which had, indeed, been thought invincible—the weapon of a transportation strike.

It is now possible to see more clearly in which sense it is true that

[73] Renner's statement that there were several years in the early 'twenties when the Heimwehr had no importance whatsoever (*Die Justiz*, vol. 7 [Jan. 1932], 146) goes too far. (See above, pp. 123–133 and the sources cited there, esp. Streeruwitz and Deutsch.) Renner's judgment in the article cited apparently reflects the general satisfaction of the Socialists over the collapse of the Pfrimer putsch in September, 1931.

[74] *Neue Freie Presse*, February 4, 1927 (A.M.), p. 5. The place was Innsbruck.

"July 15" should not be thought of as a turning point. The domination of the armed forces by the government and the strength of the Heimwehr were the results of a process—continuous in the first case, with interruptions in the second. The tremendous increase of both in the days of July was no more a turning point than reaching the boiling point is a turning point in the process of raising the temperature of water. This, however, should not convey the idea that the political development in Austria is regarded here from a fatalistic point of view. Water will not reach the boiling point if the fire under the pot is extinguished. "July 15" was not an inescapable necessity. A Socialist majority in the elections of April, 1927, might have reversed the development. Different and better tactics pursued on the fateful day in Vienna might have obviated the defeat. More courage in the face of threats might have diminished the magnitude of the failure. As it was, the fire had been allowed to burn, as the lesser evil, so that the natural effects took place.

But "July 15" *was* a turning point as far as the psychological situation in the country was concerned. Suddenly the workers' party found itself on the defensive, and not only because now a period began in which continuous and violent attacks upon democracy were launched. Perhaps even more important was the fact that the fifteenth of July had destroyed the general belief in the "trend," the conviction that the party was on the way to a safe and lasting majority in parliament. Although as suggested the conclusion was more psychological than logical, it is undeniable that the spell of Socialist invincibility in the struggle for majority was broken. It remains then to sketch briefly the political repercussions and the new problems raised within the Austrian labor movement by the catastrophe.

The dead of the July days were buried: the 4 policemen in the presence of the president of the republic and the members of the cabinet; 57 of the victims among the demonstrants in an impressive common funeral arranged by the city council of Vienna. On July 25 parliament met again, first to hear a short speech of mourning from its president and then on the two following days for a major political debate. Seipel spoke, coolly and unmoved. He attacked Seitz for having refused to call in the troops. With trenchant irony he offered to consider a reform of the jury courts. And he used two phrases which Socialist propaganda perpetuated in the memory of the Austrian people. He praised the behavior of the police: "Thank God, they have done their duty." He spoke of the men arrested because of their participation in the events and, turning to the opposition benches, added: "Do not ask anything from parliament and from the government that would seem merciful to the victims and to those who have made themselves guilty in the days of disaster, but [that] would be cruel toward the wounded republic."[75]

"The prelate without mercy!"—these words marked the inception of a great movement away from the Roman Catholic Church. *In the first ten days of August 2,734 persons left that Church!* The aggregate number in the second half of 1927 was 21,857, as against 7,227 in the same period of 1926.[76]

Bauer replied to Seipel. He began his speech with what he called "a moral examination of my own conscience." He confessed the terrific mistakes committed by the party in not organizing a demonstration of its own, in not having the Schutzbund ready, in not establishing the city council police earlier, which, as he said, might at least have saved the lives of those who died on Saturday (July 16).[77] Then he proceeded to an indictment of the police. He criticized the blunders committed at the beginning of the demonstration and concondemned as a crime the ruthless firing at its end. In the name of his party he demanded amnesty for those who had been or would be accused of offenses committed during the riots and urged the majority parties to acquiesce in a parliamentary investigation of the actions of the police.[78]

---

[75] Nationalrat, *Protokoll*, July 26, 1927, pp. 130, 131, 133.

[76] Kunschak, *op. cit.*, p. 93; *Jahrbuch der österreichischen Arbeiterbewegung, 1927*, p. 18.

[77] It is fair to note, however, that apart from programmatic considerations a demonstration, and, by consequence, a strike, because of the verdict of a jury would have exposed the party to bitter attacks. The fifteen-minute strike in February had induced the *Presse* and a Pan-German speaker in parliament to attempt a computation of the damage inflicted upon the Austrian economy by this brief interruption of work. Cf. *Neue Freie Presse*, February 1, 1927 (A.M.), p. 1 (ed.) and Nationalrat, *Protokoll*, February 3, 1927, p. 4515.

Bauer's reference to "Saturday" meant that the municipal police should have been organized on Friday evening rather than on Saturday. He claimed that this body prevented further shooting on Sunday and Monday in many dangerous situations. Nationalrat, *Protokoll*, July 26, 1927, pp. 133 ff.

[78] This demand for an amnesty was greeted with shouts of protest from members of the majority parties. With savage irony, induced by Seipel's speech, Bauer explained at some length that he had not hoped for an amnesty out of any feeling of compassion because "compassion is not the virtue of a statesman," nor out of humanity because "authority, not humanity, is your watchword," nor out of any sort of religious conviction because "the obligation is to be firm." He added, however, that he had hoped that

In the later course of the debate other significant speeches were made. Karl Renner, the man of mild and flexible tactics, addressed the chamber twice. Gürtler and Drexel, Christian Socials from the states, eagerly took up Renner's conciliatory tones. All three men obviously felt that the hostility separating the population into two camps had become unendurable. They longed for peace. For some time there were hopes that a compromise solution could be found, that both sides would be willing to try to salve the wounds made by the disaster. But Seipel and Kunschak, seconded by the Agrarian Leaguers and Pan-Germans, carried the day. The majority rejected the demands for an amnesty and a parliamentary investigation. Even in the non-Socialist camp this flat rejection met with cautiously expressed criticism and the *Neue Freie Presse,* although claiming that the spirit of hatred rendered a parliamentary investigation impossible, still deplored the circumstance that "the disaster of the bloody Friday will remain unavenged."[79]

In this connection a curious and very significant fact came to public knowledge. When Seipel formed the majority government in October, 1926, he had demanded and secured a formal undertaking from the parties to "put an end to the so-called Danneberg era; that is, never again to vote for setting up a parliamentary investigating committee if this were demanded by the present opposition."[80] This agreement to throttle one of the most vital rights of parliamentarism reveals as by a lightning flash the extent to which Seipel and his followers, long before the events of July, felt disgusted with a system which exposed them to the judgment of the people.

Thus the suggestions for appeasement and conciliation were

---

out of the most elementary reasons of state something would be done so that not too much bitterness would be left to rankle in the depths of the society, so that men could not feel that there was no justice in a system that freed the killers of Schattendorf but locked up those who had yelled "Boo!" at the police. (Nationalrat, *Protokoll,* July 26, 1927, pp. 147–150.) However oversimplified, perhaps inaccurate, this feeling might have been, every one of Bauer's hearers knew it was widespread. Probably needless to say, his plea was construed as a defense of plunderers, arsonists, and murderers (see below, p. 765).

[79] *Neue Freie Presse,* July 27, 1927 (P.M.), p. 1 (ed.).

[80] *Reichspost,* July 28, 1927, p. 2. Cf. also Seipel's admission in the budget committee of the parliament where he gave "certain experiences" as a reason for this decision. *Neue Freie Presse,* December 3, 1927 (A.M.), p. 5. These "experiences" undoubtedly were related to the investigation of the bank scandals, for the public discussion of the Christian Social financial affairs had been an unpleasant "experience" for Seipel and his party.

silenced by the bellicose chorus of Seipel's more numerous and more vociferous group. In this chorus the voice of the Heimwehr was distinctly heard. A few days before the meetings of parliament Steidle wired to Seipel: "In the name of all Heimwehr organizations in the Alpine provinces I request you to oppose unwaveringly all attempts to take into the government those responsible for the events of July 15. *Otherwise the Heimwehr would be obliged to undertake steps of gravest consequence.*"[81] This message was no longer on offer, as was that of a fortnight earlier; this was an open threat. By it the reader may gauge the development of Heimwehr strength during and after the days of riot and strike.

In spite of the collapse of conciliation, at least for the time being, parliament recovered its ability to carry on current work after a pause of almost three months; that is, immediately after the close of the debates on the mid-July events. The intimidated Socialists did not dare to continue their tactics of protracted negotiations. For example, the long-disputed school laws were now promptly passed. On the other hand, the outcome of those debates, namely the rejection of amnesty and investigation, led to a most violent and protracted campaign in the Socialist press against the police and particularly against its chief, Schober. It is impossible to record even a fraction of the charges voiced by the *Arbeiter Zeitung* in its impotent rage. Only one of them will be mentioned. It appeared from the terrible character of the wounds inflicted by the police fire that they had used at least some "target ammunition," which in its effects is similar to dumdum bullets. The police flatly denied the charge and made a similar countercharge.[82] It was conspicuous, nevertheless, that at the same time the police and Minister Vaugoin took pains to argue that in street fighting dumdum ammunition is even "more humane" than normal bullets because of the absence of ricochet wounds.[83] Under normal conditions such a charge would in itself have called for a parliamentary investigation. The city council of Vienna appointed an investigating committee of its own which, however, lacked the powers of a court. The police, after submitting a general report, refused by order of the government to

[81] *Neue Freie Presse,* July 23, 1927 (A.M.), p. 5. Italics mine.
[82] *Ibid.,* July 20, 1927 (A.M.), p. 4; *Weissbuch,* p. 47.
[83] Cf. *Weissbuch,* p. 47; *Neue Freie Presse,* July 23, 1927 (A.M.), p. 4.

give further explanations and to reply to the questions of the committee.[84] The issue of the dumdum bullets would have remained unsolved but for the admission to G. E. R. Gedye, by one of the highest officers of the police, that such ammunition had actually been used, albeit inadvertently, by their men.[85]

Criticism was not confined to the Socialists. So far as independent public opinion was still extant in the unhappy country it was deeply stirred by the brutality of Schober's men. The *Volkswirt,* although admitting the necessity of putting an end to the riots, severely castigated the authorities for having used their most murderous arms and repeatedly asked why neither tear gas, nor the high-pressure pumps of the fire department had been employed instead of the deadly carbines.[86] The famous Austrian writer Karl Kraus plastered the whole of Vienna with huge posters bearing the laconic behest: "Herr Polizeipräsident, I demand that you resign"; he followed up this peremptory request by the most violent personal attacks against Schober, whom he accused of having succumbed to the extortions of a journalist of evil repute. But, on the other side, the police had become in certain quarters the most popular authority in the country. Immediately after the events the cabinet tendered its thanks to Schober. A month later both Chancellor Seipel and Vice-Chancellor Hartleb, on the authority of a government resolution, reiterated in most emphatic language the expression of gratitude for the "rare prudence and the purposeful energy in each phase of the events," for the "exemplary handling" of the police apparatus. Schober was spoken of as the "firmest guardian of civil order."[87] Their letters were strangely reminiscent of the thanks which the Prince Regent addressed to the armed forces which had participated in the Manchester Massacre in 1819. The federal president decorated 130 policemen. But the thanks and the recognition did not remain platonic; large amounts of money were being collected for their wounded and for the dependents of their dead. By the beginning of December 793,534 schillings had been raised, including one gift of 100,000 which apparently came from the Association of Manu-

[84] Letter of the police to the city council committee, *Neue Freie Presse,* August 19, 1927 (A.M.), p. 4.

[85] Gedye, *Fallen Bastions,* p. 34.

[86] For example, *Der österreichische Volkswirt,* vol. 19 (July 23, 1927), 1150–1151.

[87] *Neue Freie Presse,* August 21, 1927 (A.M.), p. 7.

facturers.[88] The indignant criticism of the Socialists, who spoke of "bribery" and remunerations for killing, was of no avail.

Meanwhile a wave of denunciation swept over the city. The police arrested indiscriminately any and every person against whom the slightest suspicion rested. To cite one example: a student who spent the fatal day in the University taking his final examination for the doctorate remarked to his landlady in the evening that the Palace of Justice weighed little compared with human lives. Five weeks in police jail was the result. How lightheartedly, to say the least, the cases were treated may be judged by the fact that of 1,325 reported and then brought to the courts of justice no less than 758 had to be released.[89] Among them were hundreds whose only crime was imprudently discussing the occurrences over a glass of wine.

The trials began in September; first, for lighter offenses held in mixed courts composed of regular judges and laymen. People who had stopped private cars during the firing in order to transport wounded men—this was construed as a crime of extortion—and people who had cried "shame on you" to the police were sentenced to several months in jail.[90] Then a bombshell exploded. On September 22, Otto Bauer appeared in the justice committee of the Nationalrat and announced that the courts trying the July defendants had been packed. Workers had been arbitrarily eliminated from the lists of lay judges. Minister of Justice Dinghofer admitted the "tremendous importance" of the allegations and promised investigation. On the following day it was announced that the irregular composition was the fault of a subordinate clerk who had "misunderstood" the casually expressed wish of a professional justice for lay judges of higher intelligence.[91] The clerk had to bear the brunt. But the affair remained obscure, so that the *Volkswirt* was undoubtedly correct in saying that little was done to clarify it and in stressing the contradictions and the general incredibility of the official explanation.[92]

---

[88] *Ibid.*, December 2, 1927 (A.M.), p. 6. Figures given by Vice-Chancellor Hartleb. Cf. also the quasi-apologetic letter of the Association, in *ibid.* (P.M.), p. 2.

[89] Figures given by Minister of Justice Dinghofer in parliament. Nationalrat, *Protokoll*, November 3, 1927, p. 564.

[90] It is impossible to give a full account of a series of trials which lasted for more than four months. Only by way of illustration, cf. *Neue Freie Presse*, September 3, 1927 (P.M.), p. 3; September 19 (P.M.), p. 5.

[91] *Neue Freie Presse*, September 23, 1927 (A.M.), p. 6; September 24 (A.M.), p. 5.

[92] *Der österreichische Volkswirt*, vol. 20 (Oct. 1, 1927), 6.

Of the 140 persons brought before these mixed courts 101 were sentenced to an aggregate of one hundred eleven months and twenty-five weeks in jail unconditionally; twenty-five months, sixteen weeks and twelve days conditionally (i.e., the sentence would go into effect only in the event of a second conflict with the law); and ten months, twenty-three weeks and two days detention, this being a milder form of imprisonment under Austrian law.[93]

In the middle of November came the actual jury trials in which more serious offenses like arson and plundering were before the courts. The defendants were men who had confessed to setting fire to the police station near the Palace of Justice and others who had been accused and convicted in a lower court of participating in the storm on the police station in Hernals on July 16. Except for one man who was found guilty of petty theft, because of the appropriation of a policeman's pistol, all 31 of these defendants were acquitted by some one of 10 different juries. Inconsistently enough, the Socialist press this time spoke of the true voice of the people. It was nevertheless true that public opinion in general disapproved of the refusal to grant amnesty and felt uneasy at being continually haunted by the memories of the terrible days. The feeling had also become prevalent that in spite of the numerous arrests the police had not succeeded in finding the right men.[94] It may be added that the responsibility of individuals for actions committed by crowds is per se problematical enough. And it must be admitted that Le Bon is correct in saying that crowds may become criminal in the legal, but not in the psychological sense of the word.[95] The Austrian penal law placed heavy emphasis on psychological responsibility as prerequisite to legal accountability. But even if this were not so, it is clear that a jury always tends to ask for the former and cares little about the latter. At any rate, and paradoxically enough, the outcome of the jury trials greatly enhanced the position of the Social Democratic party. Far beyond the ranks of the Socialists that outcome was regarded as popular criticism of the government. In spite of all that had happened and was still going on, democratic ideas were still alive in Austria.

---

[93] *Jahrbuch der österreichischen Arbeiterbewegung, 1927,* p. 18.

[94] Cf. *Neue Freie Presse,* November 4, 1927 (A.M.), p. 4 (editorial written after the second rejection of the amnesty by the government parties).

[95] Le Bon, *op. cit.*, p. 139.

Before concluding this chapter it is necessary to turn to the effects of the July events upon the internal development of the Austrian workers' party. When this problem was last dealt with, toward the end of the preceding chapter, it was seen that the party was a political organization of exemplary unity in thought and action. Success is usually the best cement. It is equally true that defeat is usually the most likely cause of disintegration, working through the instruments of internal strife and discord. It was, moreover, only natural that after the experiences of July the party felt compelled to reconsider its tactics and methods. The general strike proclaimed subsequent to the demonstrations and the massacre, when passions had reached their highest point, represented actually a faithful pursuance of the old and oft-tested policy: "If the masses cannot be kept in check any longer, party executive and Trade-Union Commission place themselves in the van with a radical manifesto and a general strike order; the rest is negotiated behind closed doors."[96] But successful use of this method presupposed noninterference with such a radical measure as the general strike. As soon as it became possible, during the progress of negotiations in the privacy of the chancellery, to break a general strike by force in the open air of the provinces, then the old method became inapplicable unless the party was willing to push the struggle to its logical end—the open clash of civil war. But to push the development so far would have been in absolute contradiction to the spirit of the time-honored party policy. To a certain extent the same applied in general to the "radical phrase," an essential element of the policy of Austro-Marxism. It becomes difficult to "talk big" when somebody is prepared to challenge you to execute your threats.

If, immediately after July, 1927, the Gürtler-Drexel wing could have brought about a period of conciliation, if the parties could have agreed upon an amnesty and a parliamentary investigation, it would have been easier for the Socialist party to adapt itself gradually and inconspicuously to the new situation. As it was, Seipel's intransigent position induced Otto Bauer and the editorial board of the *Arbeiter Zeitung* to a violent campaign against a government whose doings were so generally despised and hated by the workers of Vienna. It may be admitted that it was difficult to pursue a dif-

[96] *Der deutsche Volkswirt,* vol. 1 (July 22, 1927), 1349.

ferent policy when hundreds of people were being arrested by the police, when not the slightest gesture was made to show the workers that the government was prompted by feelings other than those of hatred and revenge. But where would this policy lead, given the post-July situation? In the rage of the emotional fight against Seipel's "bourgeoisie block" people were little inclined to ask such questions. It provoked, therefore, almost a sensation in wide circles of the Austrian labor movement when Karl Renner published an article in Germany containing several general remarks about the danger of radicalism and the lack of discipline, as well as the sentence: "More distinctly than hitherto we have to separate ourselves from the suicidal tactics of the so-called Communists."[97] In Vienna indignation was particularly high. Did Renner mean to precipitate controversy at a moment when the party needed unity more than ever? Did he mean to criticize the old policy? Very soon it became clear that Renner had no intention of confining himself to casual remarks and veiled innuendoes. With greatest frankness he expounded in a number of speeches his opinion that the party should revise its anticoalition policy. The working class has a right to be represented in the government and Social Democracy is willing to show the road if the others are agreeable.[98] This was a plain and public offer of participation in the government. A follower of Renner's published a pamphlet in which he sharply criticized the policy of the radical phrase.[99] Otto Bauer's wing of the party was deeply perturbed. They considered Renner's action as a clear breach of discipline. The *Arbeiter Zeitung* tried with poor grace to ignore Renner's speeches, short reports appearing only after the whole non-Socialist press had discussed them. Renner retorted by going so far as to publish an article in the *Neues Wiener Tagblatt,* a non-Socialist paper. This was a new "crime." Ever since 1903, when the German Social Democrats had debated this issue at great length in the party congress, writing in non-Socialist papers had been proscribed. In an article in the monthly magazine of the party Bauer declared that "gossiping about the question whether a coalition government is

[97] Karl Renner, "Die Wiener Justiztragödie," *Sozialistische Monatshefte,* vol. 65 (Aug. 8, 1927), 607.

[98] From Renner's speech to a union of civil servants, *Neue Freie Presse,* October 7, 1927 (P.M.), p. 2.

[99] Oskar Trebitsch, *Der 15. Juli und seine rechte Lehre* (Wien, 1927).

desirable or not is entirely fruitless."[100] It seemed as if the situation of 1917 had been suddenly restored. The non-Socialist press was jubilant and forecast an early split. It is not impossible that had Renner's attempts met with helpful understanding from influential elements in the majority camp, they actually could have succeeded in driving Social Democracy to open cleavage. But by this time, the fall of 1927, the decisive government groups had already firmly embraced the idea that by pursuance of a radical policy against the Socialists they could succeed in eliminating the influence of the whole party. By this time also they had agreed to represent the events of July 15 in their propaganda as a well-prepared revolutionary attempt of the workers' party and, to a lesser extent, of their other organizations. During the parliamentary debates there had been several indications or direct charges to this effect from Vice-Chancellor Hartleb, and from Bichl, Aigner, and Pichler. Aigner said the whole thing was "open revolution" carried out "according to plan." Such was the beginning of the legend. Minister of War Vaugoin kept it rolling by declaring on September 30, 1927, that "July 15" was a well-prepared affair. In 1936–1937 I talked with scores of government supporters who believed the charge as implicitly as they believed some dogma of the Roman Catholic Church. In addition to the facts already presented it may not be superfluous to offer the evidence of Kurt Schuschnigg as a man of tested hostility to the Socialists. In his book published in his own country in late 1937 this Austrian chancellor wrote that "the Socialist leaders had by no means wished or encouraged the tumult" on July 15.[101]

The tactics described were completely understandable. As the French adage has it: *Quand on veut pendre un chien, on le dit enragé.* Nevertheless, the wisdom of the policy from a Christian Social point of view was open to doubt. At any rate it implied rejection of the coalition offer, a step which followed promptly. Again

---

[100] Otto Bauer, "Kritiker von links und rechts," *Der Kampf*, vol. 20 (Oct., 1927), 448.

[101] Nationalrat, *Protokoll*, July 27, 1927, pp. 204, 203, 207, 214; *Neue Freie Presse*, October 1, 1927 (A.M.), p. 5; Julius Patzelt, *Sozialdemokratie in Oesterreich* (Wien, 1934), an official government publication, where the idea of "July 15" is said to have been conceived in Linz (p. 24); Schuschnigg, *op. cit.*, p. 119; J. D. Gregory, *Dollfuss and his Times* (London, 1935). This last book as a whole is an example of the successful penetration of legends into the foreign literature on Austria. "On July 15, 1927 the Socialists considered the moment ripe for a definite trial of strength" (p. 129). It is hoped that the presentation in this chapter has convinced the reader that the official statements are only additional instances of the extent to which contempt for the truth can be carried.

Vaugoin was the mouthpiece: "Herr Doktor Renner, we don't make a coalition with the men of July and their protectors. . . . We do not want a coalition with people for whom amnesty of those guilty of arson and other crimes is more important than the weal of the peaceful citizens."[102] And a few days later came Seipel's famous Canisius Speech in which, although choosing his words with greater care, the chancellor went a good deal farther than his party friend. Seipel spoke of the coming "decisive battle," of a "peace which does not deserve this name," of "false compromises." And he concluded with a clear declaration of war: "When we see the enemies of Jesus Christ marching in better organized and *armed* groups, then we must do everything to eliminate the deficiencies of *our own armaments* and organization. The true love for the people must manifest itself in our not shirking the decisive battle within the people and for the people."[103] In taking this stand Seipel was naturally most enthusiastically supported by all those leaders of his party who had been involved in the various bank scandals. For them, a strong policy against the Social Democracy meant "the end of the Danneberg era," according to that precise formulation of the *Reichpost* which bears repeating; and it meant, therefore, the possibility of preserving their, not unprofitable, positions in public life.[104]

It is difficult to tell what effects the pursuance of a different policy by the Christian Social party might have had on the further destinies of Austrian democracy. On the other hand, it is reasonably clear that once the chance, immediately after the events, for a conciliation government had been missed, the attitude actually adopted preserved the unity of the labor movement, which otherwise would have been destroyed either by a split of the Socialist party in spite of all traditions or, more likely, by the rise of the Communist move-

[102] *Neue Freie Presse*, October 12, 1927 (A.M.), p. 4.

[103] *Ibid.*, October 18, 1927 (A.M.), p. 6. Italics mine.

[104] In October, Rintelen was again the chief of the Catholic party in Styria. "Under the impression of the Social Democratic election success [in April] the Christian Social party resolved to withdraw its all-to-compromised leaders from the forefront. After the defeat of the opponent it now seems willing to drop all reserve again. But the documents of the Steweag and Central Bank affair were not burned on July 15." *Der österreichische Volkswirt*, vol. 20 (Oct. 8, 1927), 30. It was exactly those "all-too-compromised" men who now were distinguished supporters of the Heimwehr. A meeting of the latter in Baden near Vienna was attended by Rintelen, Kollmann, and Mataja who listened to a speech made by Steidle. In commenting on a photograph of the gathering, Otto Bauer said: "Styrian Bank scandal, Central Bank scandal, and Biedermann Bank scandal on one picture." Cf. *Neue Freie Presse*, October 17, 1927 (P.M.), p. 3, and *Parteitag, 1927*, p. 110.

ment. The propaganda of the Communists tried to draw as much benefit as possible from the Socialist mishap. In these endeavors they exhibited their usual disregard for facts. Herman Remmele wrote that Seitz gave back to the workers at least as many "blue beans" (bullets) as they had given him ballots in the April election. This falsehood was repeated, with variations, some seven years later by Carl Radek in the statement that the demonstration "was crushed by the social-democratic mayor of Vienna, Seitz, with the troops of the Austrian bourgeoisie."[105] It was with the actual Christian Social policy in mind that Bauer wrote the paradoxical sentence: "Fortunately, the Austrian bourgeoisie is led by Seipel."[106]

It was indeed Seipel's attitude which permitted the Socialists to organize their annual party congress in the form of a debate between Bauer and Renner on the coalition issue. For the first time in the history of this assembly two members of the party directorate were scheduled to speak on the same point. This alone revealed the deep effects of the July events and presented a striking difference from the situation in Linz only one year before. Both speakers emphatically stressed the necessity of preserving unity; Renner, in fact, began his speech with the declaration that the party would not split.[107] This will to unity accounted to a great extent for "the impressively high level of the debates."[108] Except for Max Adler no one of those addressing the congress completely rejected coalition as a matter of principle. But undoubtedly Bauer and Renner differed considerably in their approach to, and evaluation of, a coalition government. The former viewed it as a necessity in certain political situations. He rejected one which was at variance with the feelings of the masses of the members of the party and emphasized the point that in the atmosphere of passionate hatred against the parties of the right which the happenings of July had left in those masses a coalition was less appropriate than ever. Seconded by Friedrich Adler, he vigorously opposed the suggestion of Trebitsch to drop the radicals even at the cost of their joining the Communist organization and transforming it from a "round table club" into a political

[105] *Kommunistische Internationale,* vol. 8 (Aug. 16, 1927), 1599; *International Press Correspondence,* vol. 14 (Feb. 23, 1934), 286.

[106] Otto Bauer, "Nach dem Parteitag," *Der Kampf,* vol. 20 (Dec. 1927), 549.

[107] *Parteitag, 1927,* p. 130.

[108] *Der deutsche Volkswirt,* vol. 2 (Nov. 4, 1927), 140.

party.[109] He condemned as illusory the notion that if they were dropped quiet reform work would then be possible and tried to show that only the unity of the party would allow the continuation of the reform program of "Red Vienna." Finally, along with some of his supporters, he stressed the fact that abandonment of the Breitner tax system would be the first price asked by the prospective partners if negotiations on a coalition were to start.[110]

Renner criticized an education of the masses which rendered breaches of dicipline possible. He argued that the "language" of the political organization had been misleading and dangerous. In his view the July occurrences were a consequence of the steady refusal to join a coalition government in past years. Only thus had it been possible for the opponents to transform police and army into willing tools of their policy and to arm the Heimwehr. Socialist participation in the government would have prevented this development, and still could check it. This was, in retrospect, after the party had lost the race between the attainment of a Socialist majority and the transformation of the armed forces of the state, undoubtedly the strongest point in his position—perhaps less as a historical evaluation than as a basis for the political reorientation of the party. Weaker was his exposition of a theory that the working class as a strong minority in the state has a right to be represented in the government. Against this demand for a proportional government of all parties[111] Bauer could easily show that such a solution would greatly jeopardize the work of a democratic system which consists in a division of labor between a governing majority and a controlling and criticizing opposition.[112] But in contradistinction with the congress in Linz the interest in theoretical considerations was in 1927 decidedly limited.

The debates on the political situation and the coalition consumed the better part of three days. Of the 25 speakers who followed Renner and Bauer, 14 were from Vienna; the overwhelming majority of them (11:3) opposed a coalition. Those from outside the metropolis, by the narrow margin of 6 to 5, also opposed it. There

[109] Trebitsch, *op. cit.*, p. 48; *Parteitag, 1927*, pp. 127, 151, 178.

[110] "A coalition is possible only if . . . the excesses of the Breitner system are removed." *Neue Freie Presse*, October 7, 1927 (P.M.), p. 2.

[111] As developed especially by Schneidmadl, *Parteitag, 1927*, pp. 154–155.

[112] *Ibid.*, p. 216. The same objection was raised by *Der österreichische Volkswirt*, vol. 20 (Nov. 5, 1927), 142; and by the *Neue Freie Presse*, October 17, 1927 (P.M.), p. 1.

were, however, 10 delegates who wished to speak on these points who never got the floor because of a vote to close the discussion. On the basis of an objection from Püchler of Wiener-Neustadt it seems clear that most, if not all, of these 10 were from the states. Those favoring, or conditionally favoring, a coalition included several of the most prominent and respected delegates. They emphasized the Heimwehr armaments, its attacks upon the workers, and its connections with the authorities outside the capital. In their judgment only a coalition government could attempt the necessary disarming of both sides and check the further progress of the Fascist organizations.[113]

Where the majority of the delegates stood was never established, for although the feeling grew as the debate proceeded that Renner was winning, a vote was not taken. The explanation for the more favorable attitude of the representatives of the states to a coalition, which as suggested almost surely did not secure full expression at the congress, was the reasonably successful operation of the so-called proportional governments in several of the states.[114] It was characteristic of the spirit of the Austrian party that a vote was not forced. Instead, a specially appointed committee, bipartisan, so to speak, in character, drafted a resolution which was then approved unanimously by the congress. In a difficult situation the political organization had contrived with Seipel's help to preserve the appearance of complete unity. And, in fact, though it was not complete it was more than mere appearance. As is already abundantly clear, the internal democracy of the party was in many respects far from being ideal. But it is certain that no other party in Austria would have dared to carry out a public debate in which the faults and deficiencies of its policy were exposed to such frank criticism. Just because the criticism was not throttled but allowed full expression the congress achieved considerable success in cementing anew the jeopardized unity of the party; nevertheless, the situation at the meeting in Linz the year before never was reached again.[115] On the

[113] *Parteitag, 1927,* pp. 103–222. For Püchler's comment, see p. 197.

[114] For a reflection of this attitude, see *Jahrbuch der österreichischen Arbeiterbewegung, 1927,* pp. 134–183, containing the annual reports for 1927 of the Socialist political organizations outside Vienna. The data from Upper Austria, pp. 140–143, are particularly illuminating.

[115] The cry for Bauer's head as a price for a coalition had been heard in some journalistic quarters not directly connected with Austrian party politics, but shortly after the congress the idea was recognized as unavailing and abandoned.

other hand, it was again a significant indication of the powerful cohesion of the labor movement that the leaders of the trade unions abstained from open participation in the debate, although most of them favored Renner's position and were undoubtedly responsible for some parts of the final resolution.

The resolution just mentioned contained two important practical points which clearly are to be construed as lessons drawn from "July 15." There were to be no demonstrations without the assent of the whole party, meaning actually its directorate, and no strikes in undertakings of vital importance, for example, food supply, without the assent of the Trade-Union Commission.[116]

Other sections of the resolution included sharp attacks against the Seipel government, which was charged with leading the country along the road to civil war, and reiterated the assurances that the party desired to reach its goals by means of democracy, detested civil war, and wanted internal disarmament. One passage bore on the crucial point of the coalition. After a reference to the general recognition of coalition by the Linz program it continued: "But so long as the bourgeois parties believe they can nullify the Social Democracy, which represents more than 90 per cent of the working class, the overwhelming majority of the urban and industrial population, 43 per cent of the whole Austrian people; so long as they believe they can exclude it from all that share in the *real* power of the state which corresponds to the interests and dignity of the working class, *no coalition is possible.*"[117]

Abstracting from the proviso that the share in power should be *real,* this part of the resolution contains little more than the platitude that a coalition was not feasible so long as the other side did not want to participate. That this was so had been known before the congress began its debates, and if the self-evident statement had been the chief result of a three-day dialectical tournament it is clear that time and energy had been largely wasted. Such, however, was not quite true. Behind the screens of theoretical and practical arguments and counterarguments there was something deeper and more

---

[116] It should be noted, however, that such undertakings had been put in a special category long before 1927. The "strike regulations" adopted in 1923 required that the *Kommission* be given sufficient time for attemps at a settlement of a dispute before it reached the strike stage. Gewerkschaftskongress, 1923, *Protokoll,* p. 193; *Parteitag, 1927,* p. 88.

[117] *Parteitag, 1927,* p. 87. Italics in original.

important in the proceedings. It was these three days which finally brought home to the whole political organization the importance of the events of "July 15." Specifically, and paradoxical as it may seem, only after these three days did it come into the consciousness of the party in general that in the peculiar geopolitical conditions of the Austrian republic even winning 51 per cent of the electorate would not warrant an unconditional and lasting possession of power. Even then they would have had to share power with other groups of the population and this would bear in itself all the germs of a repetition and the upshot of the development in 1918–1920. In the period of the struggle for majority, victory was conceived as the guarantee for a monopolistic and lasting domination of the republic.[118] Stated otherwise, the "51 per cent" had become a panacea in certain Socialist leadership circles. Although those circles had always stressed the importance of the power factor made up of their 40 or 43 per cent and had repeated that stress in the 1927 resolution, they had seemed to overlook the fact that the hypothetical 49 per cent remaining with their opponents, still entrenched in various offices and positions of authority even after the Socialist victory, would constitute a power factor of still more formidable force. Many Austrian Socialists believe to this day that the formula of the 51 per cent was an extremely harmful, if not a fateful, error. And for it they hold Bauer chiefly responsible. However this may be, it is worth repeating that the idea that victory at the polls would guarantee a monopolistic and permanent domination of the republic was shattered in the days of July, and that through the debates this fact was finally perceived and understood by the entire party. In this fundamental change in mental outlook the coalition was but a side issue. To be sure, the elastic policy necessary after "July 15" implied also a different attitude, not programmatic but mental, toward the question of coalition. But this was only a part of the more general idea to prepare the masses for coöperation with certain non-Socialist groups, whether in the form of a coalition or not.

It has been said that the conversion of the party to democracy was the real result of the debates. The whole preceding presentation has

[118] As has been noted earlier, this belief reflected the general idea common to all forms of Socialism that the establishment of a Socialist order would eliminate *once and forever* not only all kinds of exploitation but also the violence of men against men.

shown that Austrian Social Democracy did not need such a conversion. And if it is true, as Professor Rader contends, that "Democracy is an attempt to substitute persuasion in place of force,"[119] then precisely the methods applied by the Austrian Socialists in coping with the July riots bore out once more the democratic nature of their party. Therefore, the profound transvaluation of policy which characterized the memorable congress of 1927 had nothing to do with a "conversion to democracy." Quite the contrary: Austrian democracy had risen with the Austrian labor movement and was going to accompany it in its destruction.

In April, 1927, Austrian labor and with it Austrian democracy had reached the peak of power. In July, 1927, both crossed this peak. A new epoch of slow descent began. Only rarely a small elevation interrupted the sloping road. This road led over dangerous glaciers, along the edge of precipices, and ended in the abyss of a smashing defeat. But in this new period of struggle against a rising Fascism Austrian Social Democracy and the free trade unions were guided by a realistic conception of the novel and most difficult situation, a conception the basis of which had been laid at the party congress of 1927.

[119] Melvin Rader, *No Compromise* (New York, 1939), p. 43.